HISTORY OF THE DOGMA OF THE TRINITY

HISTORY OF THE DOGMA OF THE TRINITY

From its Origins to the Council of Nicæa

By

JULES LEBRETON, S.J.

Professor of the Study of Christian Origins at the Catholic Institute of Paris

VOLUME I

THE ORIGINS

Translated by

ALGAR THOROLD

from

THE EIGHTH EDITION

WIPF & STOCK · Eugene, Oregon

Wipf and Stock Publishers
199 W 8th Ave, Suite 3
Eugene, OR 97401

History of the Dogma of the Trinity, Volume 1
From its Origins to the Council of Nicaea
By Lebreton, Jules, S. J. and Thorold, Algar

Softcover ISBN-13: 979-8-3852-6610-4
Hardcover ISBN-13: 979-8-3852-6611-1
eBook ISBN-13: 979-8-3852-6612-8
Publication date 10/16/2025
Previously published by Burns Oates & Washbourne LTD, 1939

This edition is a scanned facsimile of the original edition published in 1939.

CONTENTS

FOREWORD

As indicated by its title, this volume deals only with the origins of the dogma of the Trinity; the dogma itself will be further studied in the writings of the ante-Nicene Fathers.

Whatever be the merit and interest of certain recent historical sketches, it is clear that no historian since Baur has treated the *ensemble* of this subject with the fulness it deserves; neither have general histories of Christian dogma or monographs devoted to different theologians filled the gap.

On the other hand, while scientific works have been rare, there has been in recent years an abundant crop of controversial writings, and it would be necessary to examine the origins of Unitarianism, two centuries ago, to find a similar intensity in the discussion of the dogma of the Trinity and its history.

The author hopes, in writing these pages, to be useful to science as well as to the Church. He thinks that this double aim will be attained by abstaining as far as possible from all polemics, and confining himself to an historical exposition of the origin and progress of the Trinitarian dogma.

His method has been controlled by his purpose: What he has looked for in the inspired books of both Testaments is not the rule of our faith, but the expression of the faith of their authors; the excerpts are not quoted as if they were juridical texts to decide a debate, but as historical documents to mark the development of a doctrine; they are quoted, not from the Latin of the Vulgate, but from the original texts transcribed, or directly translated.[1] For the same reason, care has been taken to point out the difference of aspect and the individual shades of meaning distinguishing the teaching of the various sacred writers, of St. Paul, for instance, or

[1] The Douay Version, however, has of necessity been used in this English translation, except in a few special passages.

of St. John. The theologian, anxious above all to get at the divine truth contained in the revelation, may justifiably ignore these variations; but in the eyes of the historian they are of the greatest importance, for they enable him to grasp, in all their diversity, the multiple echoes awakened by that revelation in human souls,—the faith and the life produced by that revelation in those souls. From the facts thus faithfully set forth the correct conclusions will follow of themselves. The primary duty of fidelity to facts has been the constant preoccupation of the author.

Not indeed that he has been systematically indifferent to the results of his enquiry, or that he has studied so great a subject without love; but that the more sacred the subject, the more scrupulous is the probity demanded of the historian; it would be a strange temerity to try to render the teaching of Christ more luminous, or writings inspired by God more explicit.

When an author undertakes the writing of a history of which several chapters have been so often related, he cannot be sure of knowing the whole bibliography of the subject; one man's life would not be long enough for the task; the present writer has at least endeavoured to profit to the fullest possible extent by the labours of his predecessors, not only of the Fathers and Catholic theologians, but also of critics of all shades of opinion. Only a small number of the references thus accumulated has been retained, for it appeared useless to draw up bibliographical catalogues which have already been carefully compiled by other historians. Apart from essential special works, the author's references indicate only those writers to whom he has been chiefly indebted, or those whose opinion on a particular point was specially authoritative. Controversy has been reduced to a minimum, in order to retain nothing from the works of contemporary scholars but that which helped the author better to understand the facts and the texts.

To attain this objective, the author has attached a supreme importance to the teaching of the Church, not merely in the sense of submission to her decisions which are imposed on all Catholics, but in accepting the inspiration of her guidance and her spirit; his view is that the living chain of our tradition binds us more closely and more surely to the past than the commentaries of exegetes and the dissertations of historians.

It was the author's wish to make that dear and holy past live again in these pages as nearly as possible as a contemporary would have seen it. His task ended, he feels how badly the book fulfils the hope of that dream. He begs the reader to excuse its imperfection, and our Master to forgive it.

In conclusion the author begs to thank his teachers and friends who have been kind enough to read it in manuscript and have suggested many a happy correction. A word of gratitude also to the students and audiences before whom he delivered, at the Catholic Institute, the first sketch of this history, and whose kind attention encouraged his efforts.

J. LEBRETON.

PARIS,
Christmas, 1909.

PUBLISHERS' NOTE

THE French original of this volume is a book of some 700 pages. A great part of this space is taken up by very numerous and lengthy footnotes. In order to bring the present work within a reasonable compass, these footnotes have been considerably reduced and abbreviated. The same remarks apply to the appendices at the end of the volume, called 'NOTES'.

Practically all the Author's references have been reproduced; but to relieve the footnotes somewhat, modern works, when fully described, have been placed in short Bibliographies at the end of the Section in which they are quoted.

INTRODUCTION

Of the three parts composing this study, the third alone, the longest, it is true, is directly devoted to the history of the dogma of the Trinity. The second part deals with the different doctrines preparing the Jews for this revelation; there is no need to justify its necessity or explain its significance. On the other hand, the first part may seem rather a digression; why should we, when discussing the Christian Trinity, talk about pagan mythologies or Hellenic speculations on the Logos and the Spirit?

Not assuredly to find therein the source of Christian dogma, but to show that its source would there be sought in vain. Many historians, anxious to explain Christianity without Christ, have thought that our theology had received the doctrine of the Trinity, or at least several of its essential elements, such as the enumeration of several divine persons, and the conception of the divine Word, from Hellenism or Alexandrinism. The best way to criticise these hypotheses is to consider the two doctrines intrinsically. It is easy to deceive oneself as to the significance of a philosophical or religious conception when detached from its parent system; when one seeks analogies between it and another fragmentary doctrine, it is only when each of the two religious syntheses has been studied as a whole, that these assimilations can be made without risk of error.

Apart from that, this preliminary study will serve not only to put aside erroneous hypotheses, but also to appreciate, by comparison, the transcendence of the Christian dogma. That dogma is so familiar to us to-day, it has for so long and so powerfully dominated our philosophy, that it is hard for us to see its superhuman element; in order to recover that impression we must, for an instant, tear ourselves from this Christian *milieu*, in which we live, and mingle with the Jewish and Pagan crowds that the first Apostles evangelised. There, without preoccupying ourselves with the new doctrines that are about to arise, we will listen to what is said around us and we will endeavour to find in humble legend and ambitious speculation the religious beliefs of our environment, as the disciples of Jesus saw them. When, in due course, the voices of the new preachers come to our ears, they will have something of that accent of novelty which took possession of their first hearers.

A knowledge of Pagan beliefs and Hellenic speculations will be still more necessary for us in the course of this history. To the generation of the apostles (who alone are studied in this volume), other disciples will succeed, whose teaching we shall hope to portray. The latter will have come from paganism and will sometimes be subject to its influence. When considering the religious psychology of converts, of those, for instance, who have passed over from Protestantism to Catholicism, we note that the beliefs they have abandoned almost always leave some trace in their minds, whether because their soul unconsciously yields to old habits, or that, contrariwise, they are carried by reaction to an excessive and *outré* defence of the very doctrines and practices most opposed to their previous devotions. So it will be no surprise to find analogous survivals of their old religion in the converts of the second century.

We must further remark that to the first theologians of Christianity, Pagan religion presented not only its popular mythology, but also several religious philosophies which had interpreted the ancient myths and resolved them into more or less profound symbols. Now these early theologians had been formed in this Pagan school, and, becoming apologists on their conversion to Christianity, had for the most part kept their philosopher's mantle when they undertook the task of making their new faith more accessible and venerable to their old friends. They were concordists by temperament and method, they underlined similar elements on both sides and clothed profoundly and radically opposed doctrines with a garment of at least similar terms.

So also when we read now the Pagan or Christian writers of the first two or three centuries, we are surprised to find so many similar expressions on both sides. The *Spiritus sacer* of Seneca has often seemed so Christian that an attempt has even been made to turn the philosopher into a disciple of St. Paul[1]; inversely, we find in the most uncompromising Christian writers, such as St. Irenæus, some formula in which the action of the Holy Spirit is expressed in terms of Stoicism.[2]

Sometimes similarity of expression deceived contemporaries: Origen observes that Celsus was thus taken in, and confused the Holy Spirit in whom Christians believed with the divine spirit believed by Stoic pantheism to be diffused throughout the world.[3]

In the case of the Logos, confusion was still easier, and more than one historian has thought he recognised in the Christian dogma of the Word the point of insertion of Hellenism in Christianity.

It appears very difficult to determine exactly the values of these influences, unless one has taken the trouble to study the pagan doctrines in and for themselves. When they are still isolated from Christian currents, it is easy enough to distinguish their intrinsic character and tendencies; to attempt such an analysis in the criss-cross of mid-stream, so to speak, is to condemn oneself to ignorance of their nature and action. This part will therefore be devoted to the study of the Hellenic conception of divinity and intermediary beings at the beginning of our era; the Christian doctrine of God and the Trinity will remain entirely outside our scope. Later on, when its origin on Jewish soil has been studied, we shall follow it in its first contacts and conflicts with Hellenic or Oriental Paganism.

The exposition of the Christian faith which will then be approached raises a very different problem of method from the one just discussed, but a more serious one. It must be explained and solved.

The reader who follows me to this point will no doubt observe that my narrative no longer follows the same methodical course; while Greek speculation and Jewish theology have been considered as doctrines, the coming of the Son of God is related as a fact. The result of this change of method is a discontinuity in the book as a whole, of which I am fully aware; and far from attempt-

[1] See below, p. 67. [2] *Advers. hæres.*, V, 2, 3. [3] *C. Cels.*, VI, 71.

ing to veil it, I propose to throw light on it and show that it is imposed by history itself.

In this first part, devoted to Hellenist religious philosophies, the exposition can flow smoothly on, following the homogeneous development of the doctrines; the appearance of many new conceptions has no doubt to be indicated, but all these legends and speculations, similar in their origin and significance, follow each other at the same level; they are more or less faithful and comprehensive representatives of a reality which remains transcendent, and is unattainable by history.

Jewish theology has another character, for it has another origin. Nevertheless, the divinely revealed truths proposed to the faith of Israel reach man through a human *magisterium,* the voices or writings of prophets. Looked at from this point of view, the condition of the Jew is the same as that of the Greek: neither attains immediately, in its concrete reality, the object of his belief; he apprehends it only in the doctrine taught him by his masters; an exposition of this doctrine is all that is required to narrate the history of his faith.

The development of dogma in the New Testament is altogether different; its point of departure is rather a Person than a teaching. Plato was the master of his disciples, Moses was the lawgiver of the Jews, for Christians Jesus is the very object of their faith.

This is a fact which every historian must recognise, whatever his interpretation of it. In the most ancient Christian writings, in the letters of St. Paul, appears not only a doctrine, but a new religion, based entirely on this Man who had died less than twenty-five years before. He was the goal towards which Jewish history tended, it was he whom the great men and the great events of the history of Israel prefigured, it was he whom the prophets predicted. The entire world can only be saved in him, only by him can it be reconciled with God; it is his death which slays sin, his resurrection which justifies the elect. Finally it is he who will judge all men, and it is his return, his glorious *Parousia* which the whole universe awaits.

An account cannot be given of this faith in terms suitable to an exposition of Stoic Pantheism, or the Alexandrine theory of the Logos: we have no longer before us a pure speculation, imagined by a philosopher, but a religion born of an actual person who lived, and finding its only meaning in him. Historians have sought analogies in the apotheoses so frequent at the beginning of our era; these pretended similarities will be discussed later, and it will then be easy to show that neither in its origin, nor in its object, has the cultus of Christ any resemblance to that of the Egyptian kings or of the Cæsars; born of the Jewish religion, the monotheism of which it has jealously preserved, it has nothing in common with these vulgar apotheoses; it does not offer to its God a lavish incense, but an exclusive adoration. Pausing for a moment at the point of view of the history of doctrine, I shall confine myself to pointing out the essential difference presented on this head by these two series of religious facts.

Neither the persons of the Ptolemies, nor those of Caligula or Domitian, transformed the religious conceptions of their contemporaries: they received the pompous title of Saviour, God, Lord, one after the other; it was but a commonplace purple that was thrown over their shoulders. The facile, often enthusiastic, welcome given to these apotheoses, at least in the East, shows how poor was the popular idea at that time of gods and worship; such was the idea of the apotheosis of the Emperors involving perhaps even further degradation if it was too exalted for them.

The person of Jesus exercised a very different influence on religious thought; it is impossible to find in the Christian faith a single concept that was not transformed and elevated by contact with him. We know what Jewish Messianism was in the time of Jesus Christ: the idea had lost much of its religious value, and too often was merely a form of nationalist illusion or apocalyptic dreaming. The title of Messias when applied to Jesus covers the purest signification ever given it by the prophets, and at the same time implies a divine filiation, which the Old Testament had never clearly indicated, and which no one in the times of Christ suspected.

Later this same Jesus will be called the Word of God: to explain the employment of this term we recall the theology of the Word roughly sketched out by the prophets and the Psalmists, the *Memra* of the Targumists, and above all the *Logos* of Philo. All these assimilations explain the term employed, but not the new significance with which it is laden. The Philonian Logos, the influence of which is specially invoked, was never conceived as a person; it was only very rarely called 'God,' and a secondary god at that, and as Philo himself says, 'by an abuse of the term'; it is only an idea of God, a support of the world, in a word no more than an intermediary being; through its means God can create a material world without losing his dignity; in it men, incapable of attaining the inaccessible God, may at least contemplate an image of him. The Word of St. John is no longer that: he *is* God, the entire gospel is written for no other purpose than to shew it; his power, his knowledge, his holiness, his action are identically those of God; he is the revelation of the Father. Whoever contemplates him need seek no higher vision, for in seeking him, he sees the Father.

If we ask why Christian theology has repudiated all these inferior categories, why its 'Word' as well as its Messias has been carried to equality with God, history has but one answer: faith in Jesus could not stop short of that. This reply is disconcerting: in the case of the Greeks and Alexandrines, all the more or less divine figures that pass under our eyes, demons, gods, Logos, spirit, powers, have to pay the price of their transcendence when they acquire even an imaginary personality, they only attain divinity by fading into abstractions. A too concrete reality betrays, by its vulgarity, the ambition of these dreams; in order to support them it has to degrade them. But in this case the dreams are too paltry to render the concrete and living reality; and the poor folk who were the first to follow Christ conceived of him so high an idea that the whole faculty of human conception fails in its interpretation.

If at last we turn to the title of 'Son of God,' which has become, as it were, the proper name of Jesus, further emphasis is given to all that has been said. The people of Israel were, as a whole, the Son of God, as were individual Israelites as such, and, more particularly, the righteous among them; by this term were marked out the privileged relations uniting God to his people and in particular to his faithful servants. But no human individual, not even the Messias, was called the Son of God.

Jesus claims this title and gives it a transcendent value: he teaches his disciples to regard God as their Father, he exhorts them to become the sons of God; but he never identifies their filiation with his own; he is the Son. The teaching of St. Paul and St. John echoes this witness borne by Jesus to himself: in their writings the Son appears as united to the Father by relations that are incommunicable and truly divine. Once more we have to ask the inevitable question—whence does this belief come?

Those who are unwilling to admit the incarnation of a God, or the divine revelation of a mystery, have multiplied vain attempts to solve the problem. Formerly it was thought that the source of the dogma would be found at Alexandria: the author of the fourth gospel, a pupil of Philo's, had introduced his master's speculations into Christian theology. Unfortunately this thesis broke down before three decisive objections: the doctrine of the Son of God is foreign to Philo; the author of the fourth gospel was not his pupil; the dogma, the insertion of which into Christian theology is to be thus explained, was not introduced by the fourth gospel, since it is certainly to be found in the writings of St. Paul.

Others pay St. Paul the compliment of this initiative; but what would have called it forth? Some reply: the influence of Hellenism and above all the necessity of interpreting the notion of the Messias in accordance with ideas familiar to Pagans; others insist on Jewish angelology and suggest that one can conceive easily enough a transition from the conception of Michael to the doctrine of the Son of God; others again, condemning these hypotheses, think that in certain Jewish *milieux* open to Oriental influence there existed a faith in a divine being, revealer and redeemer[1]; some of these, however, admit that 'there is practically no evidence of the existence of this Jewish Christology, but that we have to admit it if we wish to understand the New Testament.' (Gunkel.)[2]

These various hypotheses are self-refuting; the Jewish monotheism of St. Paul remained uncompromising, and rejected Hellenist polytheism as impiety; to suppose that

[1] Gunkel, *Zum religionsgeschichtlichen Verstandnis des N. T.*, pp. 89–96; Cheyne, *Bible Problems*, pp. 73, 213–232; Loisy, *Evangiles synoptiques*, I, pp. 193–4. [2] *Ibid.*, p. 94.

the Apostle yielded to its attraction or compromised with it, is to shut one's eyes to the evidence. As for the influence of angelology, it is sufficient to reread the epistle to the Colossians and see what an infinite distance separates the angels from Christ. Finally, it is superfluous to discuss the supposed Jewish Christology, as its very defenders have been unable to find a single trace of it. Enough will be said later about the doctrines of the period to show the unlikelihood of such a thing.

A few considerations must be added in condemnation of the various forms of this Pauline hypothesis. This doctrinal revolution attributed to St. Paul must have been accomplished in less than twenty years after the death of Christ; this interval is so short that Wernle, the ablest historical defender of the thesis, is obliged to say: 'It is absolutely prodigious that in so short a time the historic Jesus should have undergone so colossal a transformation.'[1] Moreover, in the ancient Christian community, St. Paul was neither isolated nor an innovator; the Judaisers attacked his attitude towards the Law, no one criticised or discussed his Christology for the reason that everyone recognised in it his own faith. We still find this common faith in the discourses of Acts, or in the narratives of the Synoptics; it may be that, in their present form, our gospels bear some traces of the influence of St. Paul, but we have to recognise that, taken as a whole, they represent an earlier catechesis than the Apostle's, and a less developed doctrine.

We are thus drawn to the very origins of Christianity, to Jesus. Here again certain critics try to find an Alexandrine influence; the doctrine of the divine filiation would have been introduced into Jerusalem in the Alexandrine Synagogue, and by that means have reached Jesus himself.[2] Really one might as well make Jesus a disciple of Plato. Celsus did so.

Thus, all these hypotheses fail to explain the Christian dogma of the Son of God, as well as those of the Word and of the Messias; to wish to interpret faith in Christ as one interprets human speculations, to claim to explain it by literary influences, by an interchange of ideas and doctrines, is to condemn oneself in advance to impotence.

[1] *Die Anfange unserer Religion*, p. 243.
[2] Ménégoz, *La théologie de l'épître aux Hébreux*, p. 202.

Even if the various elements of the new religion could receive in this way a plausible interpretation, it would still be necessary to explain the magic by which the personality of Jesus of Nazareth became the unique object of all these heterogeneous beliefs, and, by concentrating them in himself, could blend them in the unity of one and the same faith. The period we are studying saw the birth of many a syncretism, and many a compromise attempted between Judaism and Hellenism, simple associations for common worship like that of the clients of Zeus Hypsistos, or cenacles of theosophists and Gnostics; all these petty religions were never able to unify their disparate elements or protect themselves against the invasion of foreign ideas. Who will dare compare them with Christianity, whose doctrinal unity twenty centuries have failed to dissolve, or exhaust its power of resistance?

And yet, let me repeat it once more, it is not only the unity of doctrines that must be explained, it is their transcendence: not only did Jesus concentrate in himself all these beliefs, but he transformed them. This transformation has been briefly indicated in the three central conceptions of the Messias, of the Word, of the Son of God. We appreciate this fact still more when we note how the ancient faith in Jahve itself supplied more than one feature to the new faith in Christ: the Saviour, the Judge, the Lord, the King of Kings, the Living One, these are so many titles of the God of Israel now given to Jesus; from the first page of the gospels, more often in texts of St. Paul and St. John, the classical passages in which the prophets speak of Jahve are applied to Jesus; prayers, hymns, doxologies ascend to the Son as to the Father, and the new worship grows without shaking the foundations of the traditional religion, without relaxing the rigour or arousing the jealousy of its monotheism.

Here is the most disconcerting fact in the whole history of dogma, and a fact in which the personal action of Christ is most incontestable. What merely human master could thus have struck at the heart of the Jewish faith without wounding it to its death? What human doctrine could have transformed it so intimately without dissolving it?

Let us consider more closely the result of this transformation: this unity of Father and Son in one and the same action, in one and the same cultus, constitutes, from a purely rational and speculative point of view, a mystery disconcerting to the greatest minds, and remains, after centuries of Christian life, both imposed on their faith and impenetrable to their reason. It may be affirmed without fear, for it was no speculation that brought Christians to that affirmation, that had they been philosophers rather than disciples of Jesus, they would have elaborated their dogma in conformity with categories familiar to their contemporaries, they would have made their Christ one of those intermediary beings which Jewish or Greek Gnosticism multiplied between man and God: they would have placed him in one of those ever-open series of æons, demi-gods, or powers: and, without transforming their faith or doing violence to their philosophy, they would have paid satisfactory tribute to their own pious memories. They did not do so, because they were not philosophers, but believers, because they despised Gnosticism, but clung to their Master, and because this faith of theirs in Jesus carried them beyond the speculations and dreams of men, right up to the Divine Truth.

It should be well understood that in order to explain this action of Christ, it is not sufficient to suppose that by the holiness of his life and the tragic grandeur of his death he produced so profound an impression on his disciples, that their entire religion became transformed. No simple sentiment of fidelity and admiration can explain the origin of this doctrine ; if Jesus had been merely the initiator of a religious movement, and in no sense the revealer of a mystery, never would his disciples have translated their religious emotions into such novel and upsetting beliefs—beliefs, nevertheless, so coherent and lofty. No doubt the teaching of Christ, like all the teachings of God, had to be discreet and patient, slowly initiating prejudiced and carnal spirits into truths so contrary to their prejudices and so far above their feebleness ; and inasmuch as, in this case, the Master himself was the object of faith, since he was the Truth and the Light, he had above all to manifest himself, and by his daily companionship, his miracles, his conversation, reveal little by little to his disciples the thoughts, works, and life of God.

This is, in fact, the subject of the gospel narratives, and we should only have to follow their words to obtain a complete exposition of the origins of the Christian revelation. I think that even putting on one side all theological argument and omitting the other historical proofs, these considerations are sufficient to justify this method. No doubt we can delete from the gospels, as a theological insertion, all mention of a revelation or of an institution founded by Christ. We shall then have to explain how, in so short a time, in such various environments, under such unfavourable conditions, the Christian doctrines and institutions germinated with such vitality, such transcendence, and such cohesion. If we accept the testimony of the texts, all these natural impossibilities disappear, and the *ensemble* of the phenomena as well as the details are susceptible of an intelligible interpretation. But then we must recognise in Christ the supreme revealer of God or, rather, the self-revealing God. This means that we reach faith; I think it is better to do so than to grope about in a blind alley.

Having taken this decisive step, we must proceed to follow, in the writings of the Apostles, the progressive development of the Trinitarian dogma. The plenary revelation was not made at once, the apostles could not have borne it. It was necessary that after the Ascension and Pentecost, the Holy Spirit should remind them of the teachings of Jesus and interpret to them what they had only imperfectly understood, and already half forgotten. In this new period the Christian revelation will retain its original characteristic: the mystery of the Son of God remains the luminous centre of the whole faith and in particular of the Trinitarian dogma. The Heavenly Father is more intimately known because he has been manifested in his Son; Christians understand better than Jews the close union with him that they begin to enjoy here below, and that they will consummate in the other life, because they participate in the unique filiation of Jesus, because through him they have access to the Father, in him they are in the Father. If, conformably to the teaching of Our Lord, they believe in a divine Spirit, personally distinct from the Father and the Son, they have only been able to apprehend his personality by measuring it, so to speak, on the analogy of that other divine Person who appeared to them in Christ.

So Jesus was not only the Revealer, who, fully knowing his Father, was the first to tell us his secrets; he was also the Son, whose unique appearance manifests the Father and makes known 'the other Paraclete,' the Holy Spirit. The reader will therefore not be surprised that this study will concentrate above all on the doctrine of the Son of God; it is in and through that doctrine that the origins of the Trinitarian dogma will appear more clearly to us, because it was in the light of that doctrine that it was first perceived.

Perhaps this method of approach may enable us, following the example of the Fathers of the Church,[1] to catch a glimpse of the designs of Providence which determined the delayed promulgation and the progressive development of the dogma of the Trinity.

One single God in three Persons, a truth made familiar to us by faith, disconcerts human reason. Divine revelation may guarantee it to us in a certain fashion, which becomes for some of us self-evident, but the intelligence remains disturbed, chained by the will to a truth it cannot see, and its impatience threatens at every moment the sacrifice of one of the two terms, the harmony of which it cannot perceive: either the unity of the divine nature, or the Trinity of the divine Persons. And what a danger that belief would have been for the Jewish people in the days of Moses and the Judges if, barely converted from idolatry and surrounded by polytheistic neighbours, they had had to recognise in God the personal distinction of Father, Son, and Spirit. Inversely, too, after the Exile, how could Jewish monotheism, so rigid and jealous of its rights, have safeguarded the Trinity of Persons without reducing it to a question of purely modal distinctions? Lacking, as it did, the infallible *magisterium* which God was later to bestow upon his Church, could Judaism have maintained, in all its rectitude, a faith exposed to so many dangers?

The Incarnation was to be, in God's design, the certain manifestation of this mystery, and at the same time the source of richer and higher graces to sustain the Christian faith. The Person of Christ, detached against a background of clear light, fixed for ever these two truths which otherwise would have remained wavering. God is

[1] Cf. Greg. Naz., *Orat. theol.*, V, 26; Joan. Chrysost., *De incomprehens.*, V, 3.

one and unique, and yet there is in him a plurality of persons such as to found relations of love, of thought, of prayer. The Christian revelation goes still further, as we shall see, but this first feature suffices to characterise the God of Christians, to bring him forth from the penumbra of metaphysical speculations into the full clarity of concrete reality.

In vain does the Hellenic philosophy multiply in its dreams intermediary beings between God and the world. The Jewish faith itself is incapable of firmly apprehending the hypostases at which it dimly guesses. Henceforward these incertitudes will cease; he who believes in the Son of God as he manifested himself to us will be basing his Trinitarian faith on no human speculations, not even on an oracle of God, but on the central fact of Christianity. In the face of this decisive manifestation we can but repeat with St. Irenæus[1]: 'What new thing has the Lord brought us by his advent? Know that in himself he has brought us all things new.'

[1] *Hæres.*, IV, 34, 1.

Book I

THE HELLENIC ENVIRONMENT

CHAPTER I

God and the gods

1. *Popular Religion*

When Christianity, on leaving Palestine, began to expand in the Greco-Roman world, it found itself in contact and rivalry with religions, ancient indeed, but still alive. The Pagans converted by St. Paul are no sceptics and the *milieu* in which they live is both religious and superstitious: the people of Ephesus, for instance, so easily excited by the makers of statues of Artemis, who rush to the theatre, crying: 'Great is Diana of the Ephesians!'[1] It is necessary to remind the new converts that, while an idol is nothing in itself, the worship we pay it is, in fact, paid to the demons, puts us in communion with them and under their domination. They must be warned against this servitude which is likened to homicide, fornication, and witchcraft.

It is not long before persecutions attack the Church; and if magistrates are inspired by reasons of state, it is religion that excites the rabble against the Christians and makes them cry: 'Arrest the atheists!' The apologists of the time are familiar with this state of mind; their main efforts are not directed to the conversion of philosophers, but to that of sincere though deluded believers.

It is this religious belief, so generally diffused and long-lived, that must first be studied. A sketch of Greek, Roman, or Oriental mythology does not come into the plan of this history, nor an account of its legends or cultus. What we are concerned with is the disentanglement from these differing forms of religion of their animating idea, to the discovery of what, in the Hellenic world, in the first century, were the most widely diffused conceptions of the divinity, whether known as Zeus, Jupiter, or Serapis.

But it is not easy to describe the religion of these

[1] *Acts* xix, 23–40.

crowds: the Pagan world is at that moment in such strange confusion! For some two or three centuries the traditional frame of things has been destroyed: cities like Sparta, Athens, Thebes, Corinth, which for long defended their independent and enclosed lives, states like Persia, Carthage, Macedonia, which had snatched the neighbouring populations into the artificial and violent unity of their government, have returned to dust; the conquests of Alexander have first laid waste the Orient, then Rome has struck down all these ephemeral kingdoms, the Antigonides, the Lagides, the Seleucides, with Africa and the Spains and the Gauls, and has mixed them all up in the immensity of her Empire. And after each of these conquests myriads of prisoners have been sold in all the slave markets of the world, and, on attaining their liberty, have brought to Rome in return for the citizenship granted them, all their traditions, superstitions, and vices. A century and a half before the Empire, Scipio interrupted by the Roman crowd had answered them with contempt: 'If I have remained undismayed so often by the clamour of my armed enemies, why should I fear yours—the step-children of Italy?'[1] Since then these bastard sons of Rome have multiplied, freedmen from every quarter have not ceased to come there: all the overflow of the Orontes, the Nile, the Rhône, and the Danube.

How shall we define the religion of this Babel? It is as multiform as the origin of these pretended Romans. And the confusion reigning at Rome is to be found throughout the Empire, particularly in the great maritime cities: Alexandria, Smyrna, Corinth, Antioch, Carthage are no more homogeneous than Rome, but are aggregations of human flotsam.

Gods swarm there like men; the witticism of Petronius finds its application everywhere: 'Indeed, our land is so full of divine presences that it is easier to meet a god than a man.'[2]

These gods, for the most part, are newcomers in the Empire like their worshippers: the ancient Quirites are no longer at home in Rome and cannot endure this Greek city; thus are the old gods of the Capitol submerged by the flood of Oriental deities. These orgiastic cults did not obtain a footing in Rome without some opposition;

[1] VELLEIUS, *Hist. Rom.*, II, 4, 4.

[2] *Satir.*, 17, 5.

for a long time the worship of the Great Mother, introduced in 205, had been confined to the Palatine and her rites celebrated only by the Phrygians; under the Empire and particularly from the time of Claudius it invaded Rome with the blaze of its noisy and sensual ritual: for eight days, March 15-22, every corner echoed with the great Festival of Spring. Isis, at first after the death of Cæsar protected by the Triumvirs, then watched over by Augustus and even more closely by Tiberius, was definitely established by Caligula, who raised a temple in her honour on the Campus Martius in the year 38; the worship of Isis grew throughout the second century and reached its climax in the third. Towards the end of the first century, later than Isis, appeared Mithra in his turn, first, in the suite of the Great Mother, soon after, alone and powerful. In company of these Oriental deities, many others invaded Rome: Ma, goddess of vegetation, adored in the gorges of the Taurus with her cortège of fanatics, slashing their arms and sprinkling with their blood the statue of the goddess and her worshippers, was introduced by Sulla; Atargatis, the Syrian goddess, whose temple and worship is described at length by Lucian, was for some time the only deity venerated by Nero, soon to be cast out and outraged by him[1]; she was to have a temple in Rome under Alexander Severus.

Before these Oriental divinities with their enthusiastic and ardent religions, the ancient gods of the classic Pantheon grow pale and fade; the emperors at least make efforts to restore their worship: Augustus boasts of having restored eighty-two temples[2]: ancient historians and inscriptions praise Tiberius, Vespasian, Trajan, Hadrian, and Antoninus Pius for similar solicitude.[3]

By the last year of the Republic the old Roman beliefs, still living among the people, were seriously shaken in the higher classes of society. We know with what bitterness Lucretius attacked superstition as the source of all evils. Cicero is more reserved, more respectful towards ancient beliefs, but hardly more of a believer; this, for instance, is how he makes the academician Cotta speak:

> 'In this enquiry which we are undertaking on the nature of the gods, the first problem to solve is this: are

[1] SUETONIUS, *Ner.*, 56. [2] *Monument. Ancyr.*, 4, 17.

[3] Cf. WISSOWA, *Religion der Römer*, pp. 22–24.

there any gods, yes or no?—It is difficult to deny their existence, if the question be asked in a public discussion, but nothing is easier in a private conversation like this. Well, then. I am a priest, my view is that we should preserve with a jealous piety the ceremonies of public worship, yet I would be very glad to be able to prove to myself, not merely with probability, but with certainty, the existence of the gods. There are so many difficulties that trouble me on this head that I am sometimes inclined to think there are no gods.'[1]

This saying of a philosopher may be compared with the following confidence of the great orator unjustly banished : he writes to his wife:

'You have honoured the gods with a pure heart ; I have served men with my whole devotion ; neither gods nor men have shown us any gratitude.'[2]

But when he speaks to the people it is in a very different tone: an ardent faith in the gods of the Capitol and the protection with which they cover the city of Rome is then expressed.[3] The people would not have tolerated a light treatment of the forms of worship which guaranteed the security of the State.[4]

At the accession of Augustus these popular beliefs received the protection of an all-powerful administration determined to be obeyed. That old aristocracy, whose sweeping negatives, hesitations, and doubts and purely political faith, made known to us by the poem of Lucretius and the dialogues of Cicero, was decimated by the civil wars ; the Empire looked on it with suspicion, reduced it to impotence, often thinning its numbers by means of new proscriptions. The people of Rome, the point of confluence of myriads of freedmen from every quarter but mostly of Eastern origin, were ridden by every kind of superstition, to which they gave themselves up with a kind of restless passion. Raised above them, the Emperor, anxious to restore the ancient Roman traditions after so much disorder and destruction, made it his first task to impose the respect and practice of the

[1] *De Natura Deorum*, I, 22, 61. [2] *Ad famil.*, XIV, 4, 1.
[3] *Catilin.*, III, 8, 18 *sq.*
[4] See AUGUSTINE, *De civ. Dei*, VI, on Varro's views.

Roman religion. Dion Cassius puts in the mouth of Mæcenas a discourse expounding and recommending the whole policy of Augustus: 'Honour the gods according to the custom of your fathers and force others to honour them; for those who introduce novelty into divine worship reserve your hatred and punishments . . . permit no one to be an atheist or a charlatan.'[1] Is not the command which the crowds will soon be repeating: 'Away with the atheists!' plainly heard in this discourse of the counsellor of Augustus?

And whatever we may think of the speech of Mæcenas, it is only too certain that it is a faithful statement of the policy of Augustus and his successors. The princes, who, as statesmen, were most attached to the Roman tradition, were also the most vigilant and severe guardians of the religious institutions. The most dangerous persecutors for the Church were not monsters of cruelty like Nero or Domitian, whose very cruelty, falling not only on Christians, but on the best Roman citizens as well, condemned their tyranny and paved the way for more clement rulers; far more dangerous were strict and rigid statesmen like Decius and Diocletian; such as these hurled against Christianity in one supreme effort all the strength remaining to Pagan Rome. In this conflict they were supported by public opinion. Between the people and its gods a contract existed. If men acquitted themselves faithfully of the worship of the gods, they had a right to expect their efficacious protection; if they were negligent in their duty, they were at the mercy of every kind of misfortune. At the period we are studying calamities pour in upon the Empire from every quarter: invasions, epidemics, famines. Is not the cause of these troubles to be found in the guilty desertion of those who abandon for foreign faiths the religion of their ancestors? This prejudice was most formidable and tenacious: it was primarily in order to overthrow it that St. Augustine wrote his *City of God*. 'There is a vulgar proverb,' he says, 'among fools that if there is no rain, it is the fault of Christians.'

To disarm these attacks, a mere trifle was required: a grain of incense, and the greatest and least credulous Pagans made no difficulty. After having mercilessly

[1] DION, LII, 36.

criticised in his *De Superstitione* the extravagance of the worship of the Capitoline gods, the grave Seneca draws this conclusion: 'A wise man will preserve all these things as ordered by the laws, not as pleasing to the gods.' And a little further on, in the same book, he says: 'We will worship all this ignoble crowd of gods, congested through many ages in an ancient superstition, not forgetting that their worship belongs rather to public conduct than to fact.'[1]

This state religion which asks and exacts from everyone the observance of its rites, is imposed not only in Rome and on Romans, but on all the subjects of the Empire; Egyptians, Syrians, Celts, and Iberians preserved their national forms of worship, uniting with them the cultus of the Roman divinities, and no one objected.[2]

The deities adored all over the world were so badly defined that they were confused with each other: Cæsar attributes to the Gauls the worship of Jupiter, Mercury, Apollo, Mars, and Minerva.[3] It is needless to say that these Gallic gods had originally no relationship with the Latin divinities whose names they borrowed; but then the Latin divinities themselves in the old Roman mythology had nothing in common with the gods of Homer.[4]

The same procedure of identification is applied to other foreign religions: thus, in the Egyptian Thoth the Greeks recognise Hermes and the Romans Mercury. The great African divinities become in the same way Saturn and Juno, and examples of this may be found everywhere. The legends are pliable to a degree, and the traditional characteristics of the gods are susceptible of such modifications that no one would think of any difference in the originals which the statues represent. Lucian thus describes the statues he venerated at Hierapolis:

> 'In the enclosure were placed statues of Jupiter and Juno; although they give them different names. These two statues are of gold, and Juno is seated on lions, Jupiter on bulls. The statue of Jupiter is a perfect representation of this god; with his head,

[1] *Ap.* August., *De civit. Dei*, VI, 10.

[2] Toutain shows this clearly in the conclusion of his study of pagan cults in North Africa, Spain and Gaul, *Les cultes païens dans l'Empire romain*, III (1920), 466–7.

[3] *De bello gall.*, VI, 17.

[4] Cf. Wissowa, *op. cit.*, p. 60 *sqq.*

costume, and throne, it is impossible to mistake him. Juno presents a greater variety of details ; on the whole she is evidently Juno, but she has definite traits of Minerva, Venus, Luna, Rhea, Diana, Nemesis, and the Fates . . . . Then we come to a throne with a statue of Apollo, but not as he is usually represented. All other peoples regard Apollo as a young man, and represent him in the flower of his age. The Syrians alone give their statues of Apollo a beard, and are very vain of this custom.'[1]

We know that the Syrian goddess, worshipped at Hierapolis seated on lions, was neither the Juno of the Romans nor the Hera of the Greeks, but the goddess Atargatis ; and that it was not Apollo who was worshipped there, but Hadad. Plutarch gives a whole dissertation by way of proving that the god of the Jews is Dionysos, giving some strange reasons which it is superfluous to discuss ; they prove at least the tendency of Pagan syncretism to assimilate and bring to one level all forms of worship.

It was this complacent syncretism that gave the official religion its great power of penetration: Rome superimposed on all local cults the cults of the Capitol and enforced its observance on the peoples she conquered. For one who sees these facts from a distance and judges them in the light of Christianity, this seems a violation of conscience. But Pagan consciences were unaware of any such violation: it merely meant that Syrians or Celts associated with their national gods others exactly like them ; in neither case was there any act of faith demanded or any specifically religious adhesion, merely the exact accomplishment of certain rites.

And then in their turn these foreigners invaded the Empire and in the confused *mêlée* of religions it was these exotic and, as it were, heavily perfumed cults that went to the heads of the population, attracted and intoxicated them. We shall see, in the second volume of this History, when glancing at Pagan religion in its second-century development, how, under this Oriental invasion, Greco-Roman Paganism became transformed,

[1] *Of the Syrian Goddess*, 31, 32, 35.

grew more ardent and more mystical, though the ardour was blind and the mysticism sensuous. In the first century this conquest was not yet complete, the old religions are already growing pale and losing their grip on souls, but are not yet universally supplanted by the Oriental faiths and their mysteries.[1]

In the period with which we are dealing the question of idols and of the worship due to them was hotly discussed, even among the very Pagans, and still more among Jewish and Christian writers. For the latter, for St. Paul as also for the apologists of the second century,[2] idolatry is one of the most shameful defects of Paganism. Many critics of to-day see nothing in their charges but a misunderstanding, if not a calumny. Thus the late Dean of St. Paul's, Dr. Inge, thinks that if Jews and Christians condemned idolatry, it was through a defect of æsthetic sense:

> 'The early Christian horror of idolatry was a legacy from the Jews, who were, on the æsthetic side, too unimaginative to understand a mode of worship which, for other races, is natural and innocent.'[3]

It is certain that no Pagan theologian of this period made so gross a blunder. Those who defend the use and worship of idols, Dion of Prusa, for example, see in them images of the divinity, suggesting their characteristics and recalling them to our memory.[4] They also admit that the gods inhabit them by their spirit, that is to say, that the divine element properly so called, the πνεῦμα, dwells in these idols, thus rendering them venerable and beneficent.

It must, however, be admitted that these theological precautions are not very familiar to the crowd. Nor can we be surprised at this: experience teaches that the incline leading from the worship of images to idolatry is very slippery. The danger is a real one even among our-

[1] Cf. Wendland, art. Σοτήρ, in *Zeitschr. f. N.T.W.*, V (1904), 353.

[2] *Rom.* i, 23. Cf. the Rabbinical texts in Strack-Billerbeck, III, 53 *sq.* For the apologists, cf. J. Geffcken, *Zwei Griech. Apologeten*, p. xx *sqq.*, 77 *sqq.*

[3] *The Philosophy of Plotinus*, I, 67.

[4] Dion, *Or.*, 12, 60; Plotinus, IV, 3, 11. Cf. Zeller, *Philos. d. Griech.*, V, 625; also Photius, *Biblioth.*, *cod.* 215 (*P.G.*, CIII, 708).

selves, all of whom have been taught by our catechism that God is a pure Spirit and that, in consequence, no image can reproduce his likeness, still less be confused with him.

For the Pagan, on the other hand, how easy such a confusion! Before the time of Julian, no religious teaching was given in the temples. The only initiation into the religion of the City was through the reading of the poets, chiefly Homer and Hesiod, read by children under the direction of the grammarian, and through the popular traditions orally transmitted. All these legends are grossly anthropomorphic and strongly encourage idolatry, showing the gods, as it were, chained to their statues, transferred with them from one town or sanctuary to another and practically identified with them for the purposes of worship and piety.

In point of fact, we note that idolatry is widespread,[1] Pagans themselves see and deplore it. Seneca ridicules the inconsequent devotees who take the statues for gods and adore them, but nevertheless despise the workmen who made them.[2] Elsewhere he makes fun of the idols with faces of men or beasts or fishes, so hideous that if they really had any existence they would be taken for monsters; and yet it is out of such statues, formed of vile and inert matter, that holy, immortal, and inviolable gods are made.[3] Varro also notes that the worship of idols had taken from men the fear and respect of the gods and had increased their errors.[4]

It has been truly said that Jewish or Christian apologists writing against idols found all their arguments in Pagan controversialists. This proves that these aberrations stimulated a healthy and vigorous reaction among the philosophers, and also that these errors were very widespread, the Pagan world being indeed practically given up to them. Moreover, certain philosophers[5] seem to have accepted this and to have despaired of giving any higher religion to the people. After the second century, *literati* and philosophers let themselves be carried away

[1] Cf. FARNELL, *The Cults of the Greek States* (Oxford, 1896), I, 20; GRUPPE, *Griechische Mythologie* (Munich, 1903), 980 *sq.*

[2] LACTANTIUS, *Diu. instit.*, 2, 2 (14); cf. *ibid.*, 6, 25 (3).

[3] AUGUST., *De civit. D.*, 6, 10, 1.

[4] *Ib.*, 4, 31, 2.

[5] ARNOBIUS, VI, 24.

in large numbers in the wake of the populace, and lent the weight of their speculations to popular superstitions.[1]

Even those who could transcend idolatry and reach the gods themselves beyond their statues, had but a poor sort of religion. The anthropomorphism[2] which was the basis of Paganism continued to penetrate them with its spirit. The god was more powerful than us and knew more than we did. But he was subject to the same passions. He could inspire fear but not respect, familiarity but not love. Plutarch gives us a portrait of the superstitious man who approaches the gods as if they were savage beasts[3]; in this attitude he sees impiety, and rightly, but his own counsel in the matter is hardly more religious. He tells us with admiration[4] the following story of the philosopher Stilpo, who had a vision in his dreams of Poseidon angrily reproaching him for not having offered a bull in sacrifice, as was the custom of priests:

> 'What are you thinking about, Poseidon; do you mean to say that your are grumbling like a child because I did not borrow money in order to fill the whole town with smoke, but offered you a modest sacrifice out of the materials I had at home?'

Poseidon gave him his hand and smiled, and said that for love of him, he would bestow on the inhabitants of Megara a rich shoal of sardines.

This is a poor sort of religion and, while it is better no doubt to treat Poseidon as a comrade than as a wild beast, it seems unfortunate not to be able to treat him as a god. And such features as these are to be found in the works of Plutarch, who is one of the most distin-

[1] See Bouché-Leclercq, *Histoire de la divination*, II (1880), p. 129, n. 3; J. Geffcken, *Der Bilderstreit des heidnischen Altertums. Archiv fur Religionswissenschaft*, XIX, 2–3 (1919), 286–315.

[2] I say nothing about animal-worship; at the beginning of the Christian era, it only survived among the Egyptian cults, and for most Greeks and Romans was a source of wonderment if not of scandal (Cicero, *Tusc.*, V, 27, 78; *De Nat. Deor.*, III, 15, 39). Many traces of it, however, can be found, as well as of the worship of trees and stones; see O. Seeck, *Geschichte des Untergangs der antiken Welt*, III (Berlin, 1909), 170.

[3] *De superstitione*, 9.

[4] *De prof. in virt.*, 12.

guished as well as one of the most sincerely religious spirits of that age.

Piety may have been more ardent among the people, but it was still less respectful. Gross and immoral legends were always related about the gods, and such episodes were frequently recalled by their images and statues. The exegesis of the learned was able to explain these things, but the people accepted them literally and were influenced by them. As Dionysius of Halicarnassus says:

> 'I am aware that many philosophers explain most of the impurest fables by means of allegory; but such philosophy is confined to a small minority, the greater number, the public, always take these fables in their very basest sense, and either despises the gods for their depraved conduct, or reaches the point of not recoiling from the most guilty actions, because the gods do not abstain from them.'[1]

To sum up, what was chiefly lacking to Pagans of this period was the conception of the infinite grandeur of God, of his holiness and goodness: it was the absence of this that was responsible for an almost total lack of adoration and love in worship.[2]

The penetration of Oriental religions into the Roman Empire was on this point, as on others, greatly to enrich Hellenic Paganism, not indeed by bringing it more purity, more firmness or strictness, but at least a higher, more mysterious, less definitely anthropomorphic conception of divinity.

At the beginning of the Christian era, this action is only slightly perceptible; only the Phrygian goddess, the Great Mother, and the Alexandrian divinities Serapis and Isis, have already conquered numerous worshippers and have a considerable influence.[3] The myths of Isis, like the Hellenic myths, have already been interpreted

[1] *Ant. Rom.*, II, 69, quoted by GRÉARD, *La morale de Plutarque*, 325.

[2] It would be unjust to pass over the more elevated aspirations which do come to light here and there; e.g., VARRO, *vide* AUGUST., *De civit. D.*, VI, 9, 2. On the paternity of the gods, see HOEFER, art. *Pater* in the *Lexicon* of ROSCHER, and A. ZINZOW, *Der Vaterbegriff bei den röm. Göttheiten* (pr. Pyritz, 1887).

[3] Cf. G. LAFAYE, *Histoire du culte des divinités d'Alexandrie hors de l'Egypte* (Paris, 1884); AD. RUSCH, *De Serapide et Iside in Græcia cultis* (Berlin, 1907).

by philosophers and have received from them, as we shall soon see, a higher and more profound symbolic meaning than they present at first sight.

Soon the Syrian Baals will arrive in their turn, and, particularly from the second century onwards, will appear as sovereign, all-powerful, and eternal gods. These doctrines will grow purer by contact with Jewish belief, and the Jupiter Sabazius of the Phrygians will be adored by a small circle of initiates as the most high god, θεὸς ὕψιστος. But here we are leaving Pagan beliefs properly so called to enter, if not the actual domain of Jewish or Christian religion, at least its zone of influence.

In proportion as Christianity expands, that influence will be wider and more active; and two or three centuries after the period we are studying, in the days of Julian the Apostate or Symmachus, the Pagan conception of divinity will have grown much nearer what we call the spiritualist or theistic conception, if not the definitely Christian conception of one God in three Persons. But in the first century the Pagan conception is as far from anything of the kind as the Oriental cults or Greco-Roman Paganism. Cumont, a most competent judge and unlikely to be suspected of attenuating the affinities of the Oriental cults with Christianity, speaks thus of the differences separating them:

> 'I do not disguise from myself how very considerable these differences were; the fundamental divergence is that Christianity, by placing God beyond the limits of the world in an ideal sphere, was determined to free itself from any attachment to a frequently abject polytheism.'[1]

The preceding sketch will, I hope, have sufficiently established this conclusion. I will only add a word on the special subject with which we are dealing here, on the question of the Trinity. Fifty or a hundred years ago, when it was thought that the vestige of a primitive revelation which was already a complete Christianity could be found everywhere, investigators loved to recognise a belief in the Trinity in many a Pagan legend. Gladstone

[1] *Les Religions orientales*, p. xxiv.

believed he could find it in the Homeric mythology.[1] Denis,[2] starting from different premisses, reached the same conclusions, and saw in the legend of the birth of Athene from the head of Zeus the first form of the doctrine of the generation of the Word; V. Duruy saw a true Hellenic Trinity in Zeus, Poseidon, and Hades. But it is chiefly in the works of the traditionalists, Chateaubriand, Lamennais, and Bonnetty that the most unexpected assimilations are accumulated: the Trinity is discovered everywhere, in China, Thibet, and Egypt. I do not think it necessary to discuss all these fantasies; they indicate a curious phase of the history of religions, now completely superseded.[3] In reality, mythology, as such, has made no contribution to Trinitarian theology: the most interesting assimilation, noted by the Fathers, is that of Hermes and the Word; it does not arise, properly speaking, out of the Pagan legends, but out of the exegesis with which Stoic thinkers interpreted them. We shall have the opportunity of discussing this point rather more closely when we deal with the philosophic conception of the word and the spirit.[4]

Before proceeding to these literary speculations it is necessary, in order to complete this sketch of popular religion, to recall a cultus, perhaps the most popular of all in the period with which we are dealing, and to which, more than once, considerable influence on early Christian beliefs, and in particular on the dogma of the divinity of Jesus Christ, has been attributed; I mean the worship of sovereigns.

Bibliography.—In addition to the works cited in the text of the above Section 1: G. Boissier, *Étude sur la vie . . . de Varron* (Paris, 1861); *La religion romaine d'Auguste aux Antonins* (1878). Ed. Meyer, *Ursprung u. Anfänge des Christentums* (Stuttgart, 1923). G. Lafaye, *Hist. du culte des divinités d'Alexandrie hors de l'Égypte* (Paris, 1884). F. Cumont, *Les religions orientales dans le paganisme romain* (Paris, 1909).

---

[1] See his *Juventus mundi* (London, 1869), 250, 267.

[2] *Histoire des theories et des idées morales dans l'antiquité*, II (Paris, 1856), 229.

[3] On this subject, see H. Usener, *Dreiheit*, in *Rheinisches Museum fur Philologie*, Neue Folge, LVIII (1903), 1–47, 161–208, 321–362, especially pp. 36–37. Cf. N. Söderblom, *The place of the Christian Trinity and the Buddhist Triratna amongst holy Triads* in the *Transactions of Third International Congress for the History of Religions* (Oxford, 1908), II, 381–410. Cf. C. Clemen, *Religionsgeschichtl. Erklär. des N. T.*, 125–8; and Harnack, *Entstehung der Kirchenverfassung* (Leipzig, 1910), 187–198.

[4] And we will there discuss the real or pretended influence of the Egyptian doctrine of the Word on Christian theology.

2. *The Worship of Sovereigns*[1]

The worship of sovereigns was popular in the East, where its origins are to be found, long before the Roman conquest. We find it in the Egypt of the Pharaos: the most ancient Kings had been gods; their successors are the sons of gods, and from the Fifth Dynasty onwards. sons of Râ, who from that time is conceived as the sovereign god of Egypt.[2] The Greek sovereigns, Alexander and his successors, took advantage of this hold which Egyptian superstition gave a ruler over his people; but at first they accommodated these Oriental conceptions to the habits of Greek thought[3]; Greeks honoured the founders of cities as heroes. Alexander could claim that title at Alexandria. He aimed higher; he visited the great Oasis and there consulted the oracle of Ammon and got himself recognised by the god as his son.[4] Soon the Lagides succeeded Alexander and claimed the same divine honours; their subjects of Greek origin had some difficulty in accepting these pretensions; the first Ptolemies were only deified after death, but Ptolemy II Philadelphus took advantage of the death of his wife Arsinoë to associate himself with her in a common apotheosis, and inaugurate the cultus of the 'Brother-gods.'[5]

The worship of the Seleucides took root less easily: the Lagides could prefer their claim to the traditional cultus of the Pharaos, the Seleucides could find support in no similar tradition. They found, however, all the complaisance to which at this date the Greek cities were

[1] Cf. E. Beurlier, *Le culte impérial* (Paris, 1891), and his Latin thesis *De divinis honoribus quos acceperunt Alexander et successores ejus* (1890). J. Toutain, *Les cultes païens dans l'empire romain*, I (1907), 19–179. Boissier, *La religion romaine*, book 1, ch. ii, *l'apothéose impériale* (I, 109–186). E. Kornemann, *Zur Geschichte der antiken Herrscherkulte*, in the *Beiträge zur alten Geschichte* of C. F. Lehmann, 1 5–146 (Leipzig, 1901). P. Wendland, art. Σοτήρ, in *Zeitschr. f. N. T. Wissenschaft*, V (1904), 335–353, and *Die Hellenistisch-Römische Kultur* (Tübingen, 1912), 123–127, 147 *sq.*, 406 *sqq.* H. Lietzmann, *Der Weltheiland* (Bonn, 1909).

[2] Cf. Ed. Meyer, *L'Égypte jusqu'à l'époque des Hyksos* (trans. A. Moret, Paris, 1914), §§ 199, 219, 250; also Maspero, *Histoire ancienne des peuples de l'Orient* (Paris, 1895), 258.

[3] Cf. Bouché-Leclercq, *Histoire des Lagides*, I (1903), 231 *sq.*; III (1906), 1–30.

[4] Cf. E. Babelon, *Catal. des monnaies grecques de la biblioth. nat. Les rois de Syrie, d'Arménie et de Commagène* (Paris, 1890), p. xix.

[5] Bouché-Leclercq, *Hist. des Lagides*, I (Paris, 1903), 232–276.

accustomed[1]; and the third of the house, who took the name of Antiochus Theos, claimed divine honours.[2] The Attalides grant themselves in their kingdom of Pergamus similar apotheoses, and also the Kings of Commagene. Even in Greece, which had remained free, the Athenians in the year 307, delivered from Cassandra by Antigone and Demetrius of Phalerus, recognised them as 'Saviour-gods' and associated them with the worship of Athene.[3] In Africa, we also find among the Moors the cults of Juba and several other Kings, Masinissa, Gulussa, and Hiemsal.[4]

And philosophy, particularly after Posidonius, contributed to the same result. Men liked to repeat that statesmen, such at least as were devoted to their country and had defended and saved it, were thereby assured of immortality and divine honours. Cicero, in the *Tusculan Orations,* recalls the example of Hercules, raised to divine rank on account of his heroic labours. In the *Republic,* he affirms that great men who have deserved well of their country are truly of divine race; in heaven they have a special place and they will enjoy eternal happiness.[5] Not long after, Pliny writes:

> 'He is a god to mortals who renders them service; this is the road that leads to immortality . . . to place such men among the gods is the most ancient way of showing gratitude to the benefactors of the human race.'[6]

It will be noted in all these texts, particularly those of Cicero, that the border-line between immortality and apotheosis is vague: Hellenic thought does not distinguish clearly between these two ideas; great men live for ever with the gods and share their immortality. They also share their cultus. After the death of Plato, his disciples paid him worship; and Epicurus and Homer were objects of a similar homage. It is said that Aristotle put up an altar to Plato.

Thus on every side there is a movement towards these apotheoses. No one is surprised to see Cicero, on the

[1] Bouché-Leclercq, *Histoire des Séleucides* (1913–1914), 610; *ibid.*, 469.
[2] E. R. Bevan, *The House of Seleucus*, I (London, 1902), 177.
[3] Plutarch, *Demetr.*, x.
[4] Minucius Felix, *Octavius*, xxi, 9.
[5] *Tuscul.*, I, 32; *Rep.*, VI, 13, 26; cf. I, 12.
[6] *Hist. Nat.*, II, 7, 18, 19.

death of his daughter Tullia, put up in her honour not a tomb but a temple.[1] And yet Cicero himself the following year wrote with reference to the apotheosis of Cæsar:

> 'Is there anything more absurd than to place the dead among the gods and adore them, when the only worship due to them is a few tears?'[2]

If this is the case in Rome, the force of the movement in the provinces may be guessed; there, generals and pro-consuls are the object of divine worship. Plutarch relates that Flamininus, who had conquered the Macedonians and delivered Greece in the year 196, was associated by the Chalcidians with the cult of Herakles and Apollo.[3] After the Republic, this custom became widespread, and the more tyrannical the Governor the more he was adored. Cicero often recalls the games instituted in honour of Verres and the inscriptions carved in his memory.[4] A little later, when, in the year 50, Cicero is Pro-consul of Cilicia, he prides himself on having declined the divine honours that it was proposed to pay him.[5] When his brother Quintus was governor of Asia, the province wished to erect a temple in honour of the two brothers; they declined, and Cicero saw in their refusal an admirable example of modesty.[6]

The civil wars raised ambition still higher and made apotheoses bolder and more brilliant: 'Cæsar received from the Romans themselves all the honour accorded to Quinctius Flamininus by the Chalcidians, and by the Athenians to Sulla.'[7] His violent death by exasperating the people, rendered his cultus still more enthusiastic and passionate. In the year 44 the law of Rufrenus definitely attributing to Cæsar the title of 'Divus' was voted; and 'we come up against a new factor in the history of Rome: official apotheosis.'[8]

In the following years each rival leader laid claim to apotheosis, as well as to the Empire: Sextus Pompeius proclaimed himself son of Neptune, Antonius became Bacchus, and Cleopatra Aphrodite. Octavius was more cautious and more fortunate: as long as the success of his

[1] *Ad Atticum*, XII, 35.
[2] *De Nat. Deor.*, I, 15.
[3] Plut., *Flamin.*, XVI, 4.
[4] Cic., *In Verr.*, II, 2, 154.
[5] *Ad Attic.*, V, 21, 7.
[6] *Ad Quint. frat.*, I, 1, 9, 26.
[7] Toutain, *op. cit.*, I, 26.
[8] Beurlier, *Le Culte impérial*, p. 8.

arms remained uncertain, he did not intrigue for divine honours, but when victory had decided in his favour, it was easy for him to receive them. This apotheosis, so prudent and so progressive like all that prince's policy, nevertheless had a definite purpose: the very name of Augustus, decreed in his favour in the year 27, belonged to the language of religion and introduced the Emperor into the Divine world. Public games called *Augustalia* were instituted in his honour, the month *Sextilis* was named *Augustus,* as *Quintilis* had been changed to *Julius;* at the cross-roads and in private houses worship was paid to the Genius of Augustus. Outside Rome, in Italy, in the western provinces, and above all, in the East, things moved further and more quickly: there altars were erected to him. The Emperor was too good a statesman to discourage this enthusiasm: the provinces, accustomed to these forms of homage, presented him with their worship, which he accepted. He understood well enough, as every Roman did, that this cultus tightened the bonds of empire. In the text quoted above, Cicero told Quintus that the homage of Asiatics should honour not him alone, but the Roman people with him. Under the Empire this union became still closer: everywhere Rome the goddess was associated with Augustus the god: the same altars were dedicated to both, the same priesthood instituted in their honour. Rome demanded such homage. It was in those days that Livy wrote these words in the preface of his history: 'If any people has the right to consecrate its origins by attaching them to the gods, the Roman people has acquired such glory in war, that when it claims to descend from Mars, the conquered nations have to endure these claims as patiently as they support the Roman Empire.' Augustus shared this lofty pride with every Roman: it seemed to him just and useful that Rome should be worshipped by her subjects. His own association with this worship was not indifferent to him; he accepted this cultus which, given his position, was the same thing as to exact it.

Such homage was not inspired by adulation alone; an additional powerful motive was the happiness of peace recovered after so many civil wars. Had not Cicero himself said to Cæsar: 'The life of us all depends on yours?'[1]

[1] *Pro Marcello*, 22.

No doubt in the mouth of the great orator so attached to republican institutions, this protestation was but half sincere: it was much more so on the lips of a subject of Augustus, for whom the Republic was only a distant memory, the charm of which had vanished among civil wars, proscriptions, and fratricidal battles. For not only Rome but the whole world drew a breath of relief.

An inscription has been discovered at Priene in Asia Minor of the year 9 B.C. in which the assembly of the province of Asia request that the date of entry into office of magistrates should be fixed for the future on September 23, the birthday of Augustus, that date being a point of departure of a new era for the whole of humanity; the motives of the petition are expressed thus:

> 'Given that the providence which directs everything in our life has granted us the maximum of happiness, of glory in Augustus, whom it has filled with all virtues so that he should be the benefactor of men, and that he has been sent to us and future generations as a saviour to bring war to an end, and pacify all. Given that Cæsar by his appearance has fulfilled the hopes of all those who were looking forward to his coming, and that he has not only surpassed all the benefactors of other days, but that, in the future, none will ever surpass him. Given that the birth of the god has been for the world the origin of all the benefits that have proceeded from him . . .'[1]

In another inscription of the same period discovered at Halicarnassus, we read:

> 'Given that the eternal and imperishable nature of the universe has crowned all its benefits by giving the supreme good to men; it has given us for our happiness Cæsar Augustus, who is the father of his country, Rome the Divine, and the paternal Zeus and Saviour of the whole human race, whose providence has not only fulfilled but surpassed the prayers of all. For both earth and sea rejoice in peace, cities are flourishing with prosperity, concord, and riches, all benefits abound and superabound . . .'[2]

[1] DITTENBERGER, *Orientis Græci Inscript.*, II, 458.
[2] British Museum Inscription 894; WENDLAND, *Hellenist. Röm. Kultur*, 410.

In the course of the civil wars, 48 B.C., Cæsar had been celebrated in similar terms by the Ephesians as: 'the god who has appeared to us, born of Ares and Aphrodite and universal Saviour of the human race.'[1] Pompey at the end of his Eastern campaign, in 62, had received from the people of Mitylene an honorific inscription which saluted him as 'Saviour and founder of the city.'[2] At the accession of Caligula, the inhabitants of Cyzicus celebrated him as 'the new sun Caius Cæsar Augustus Germanicus, who has deigned to illuminate us with his rays'; he re-established on the throne the sons of King Cotys, 'who, receiving the abundance of this immortal grace, surpass all their predecessors, for those succeeded their fathers, whereas these became kings by the grace of Cæsar Augustus, and associates of his divinity, and the graces of the gods are of as much greater value than human inheritance as the sun is greater than the night, and incorruptible nature than mortal nature.'[3]

The collections of inscriptions are full of these apotheoses, and no doubt at this date, these formulæ have become well-worn after having been laid at the feet of so many sovereigns. But in the opening years of the Roman Empire, there existed everywhere a feeling of deliverance from the ghastly nightmare of civil war, and it seemed that the accession of Augustus marked the beginning of a new era.

This impression of relief did not last long, but the attachment to the Roman Patria, powerful and pacific, remained; and this sentiment found expression in the worship of the Emperors. At Rome the majority of them during the first two centuries were only deified after death, by a decree of the Senate, and received the title of *Divus*, not *Deus*[4]; but these delays were unknown in Hellenic countries; they, apart from rare exceptions, adored the Emperors during their lives, as gods, not as heroes.

In order to disengage their religious significance from these facts we must note, first, the extraordinary popularity of these cults. In the whole Roman Empire, and more particularly in the East, no divinity was celebrated with greater enthusiasm than the Emperor's, no priesthood

[1] DITTENBERGER, *Sylloge*, 347.
[2] *Ibid.*, 337.
[3] *Ibid.*, 365.
[4] TACITUS, *Annal.*, XV, 74.

was more sought after than his, just as no privilege was more eagerly desired by cities than the title of 'Temple-sweeper.' It follows that this religion was not mere flattery or falsehood. No doubt adulation and servility played an obvious and deplorable rôle ; but they do not explain everything. If this cultus had not been an expression of something profound and sincere, it could not have lasted longer than the folly of Caligula or the exigency of Domitian. What it expressed was the veneration in which was held the majesty of Rome, frequently a beneficent, always an imposing, power, and which appeared to the Pagans of those days as truly divine. According to Duris of Samos, the Athenians had, in the year 307, sung these words to Demetrius of Phalerus: 'The other gods are far off ; thou art quite close to us, no god of wood or stone, but a true god.'[1] Compared with the Roman Emperor, his divinity was a trifling affair. By a pernicious but explicable confusion this worship became the mark of loyalty to the Empire, and because Christians refused their homage, they passed as disloyal subjects.

Euhemerism, then very widely diffused, facilitated this abuse ; if the gods of the Pantheon were but great men deified, could not the Emperor be compared with them without impiety? During the period of Imperial Rome the sovereign was no longer an incarnation of the divinity, he was a new god associated with the rest and sometimes substituted for them.[2]

It is easy to appreciate the moral and religious consequences of this worship: servile adulation wearing itself out to satisfy a pride that had grown insatiable, the more lavish in its homage in proportion to the unworthiness of the master ; then, more dangerous still, slavish subjection to a deified power, to a human will erected into a sacred law ; finally and above all, the degradation of the idea of a god ; if the proceedings of the Olympians, idealised as they were by the poets, had already seriously compromised it, what can be said of the example of these new gods displayed before the eyes of all in their unveiled turpitude?

Much has been said on the influence which these apotheoses are supposed to have had on early Christian

[1] Athen., *Deipnos.*, VI, 62.

[2] Chapot, 428 ; see bibliography at end of this Section.

theology; the rapid development of the adoration of Christ is thus partly due to the religious habits of Hellenism, multiplying with such facility its gods, its lords, its saviours. The study, made further on,[1] of the origin of the faith in the Lord Jesus will permit us to appreciate this hypothesis at its true value, but even now we can recognise the essential characteristics of this cultus of sovereigns which will enable us to discern its real or pretended influence.

In so far as the sentiment expressed was sincere—and only at that price could it have had any influence—the worship of sovereigns was a *political* cultus.[2] By honouring in days of old the hero-founder of the community, the Greek expressed his attachment to his city; by now adoring the Emperor, he made a profession of loyalty to the Empire, he venerated its power, he proclaimed its benefits. The study of the title of 'Saviour,' so often granted to sovereigns, throws a special light on this feature of the royal and imperial religion: the σωτὴρ is not the saviour of the soul who delivers it from sin, from evil, from the devil; he is the saviour or protector of the city, the kingdom, the empire. From this point of view, one of the essential differences distinguishing the cultus of the Emperor from the worship of Christ, is perceptible: the two religions are incompatible, as much so as the two cities to which they belong, the kingdom of men and the Kingdom of God.

Furthermore—and this distinction is still more profound—the worship of the sovereign could only develop in environments in which religion was very adaptable and the idea of God greatly lowered; the reaction provoked by it among faithful Jews in the days of the Machabees is well known, that opposition never relaxed even in the worst days of the Empire: Caligula himself could not impose his worship on the Jews.[3] Christianity always retained the strictness of the *milieu* in which it was born, and the worship of Christ developing within it made its monotheism more rigorous and its condemnation of all other cults more decisive[4]; and the reason of

[1] *Infra*, Book III, chap. ii.

[2] The worship of sovereigns is studied here principally as it appeared after its introduction into Hellenism as it was under this form that it made contact with Christianity.

[3] *Infra*, p. 76.

[4] *Infra*, Book III, chap. ii.

this was that, instead of degrading divinity to the level of Tiberius or Nero, it manifested its fulness in Jesus Christ.

BIBLIOGRAPHY, Section 2 :—G. Cardinali, *Il regno di Pergamo* (Rome, 1906). Humann and P. Puchstein, *Reisen in Kleinasien u. Nordsyrien* (Berlin, 1890). P. Wendland, *Hellen.-Römische Kultur* (1912). G. Boissier, *La religion romaine*, I. Wendland, *Zeitschrift f. N.T.W.*, V, 344. Cumont, *Revue d'hist. et de littérat. relig.*, I, 449. Dittenberger, *Orientis Græci Inscript.*, II, 458. Deissmann, *Licht vom Osten*, 316–17. J. Lietzmann, *Der Weltheiland*, 45. Harnack, *Als die Zeit erfullt war ; Der Heiland*, I (Giessen, 1906). Norden, *Die Geburt des Kindes* (Leipzig, 1924). S. Gsell, *Essai sur le règne de l'empereur Domitien* (Paris, 1893). D. Magie, *De Romanorum juris publici sacrique vocabulis sollemnibus in Græcum sermonem conversis* (Leipzig, 1905). V. Chapot, *La province romaine proconsulaire d'Asie* (Paris, 1904). B. Allo, *L'Apocalypse*. M. Goguel, *L'apôtre Paul et Jésus-Christ*. C. Clemen, *Religions-geschichtl. Erklarung des N. T.* Soltau, *Die Geburtsgeschichte Jesus Christi.*

3. *Philosophical Interpretations*

Poets and historians had, long before philosophers, worked over the old ground of Greek mythology ; in his lectures on the 'Evolution of Religion'[1] Edward Caird distinguished in the religion of Hellenism two tendencies developing one after the other without, however, one being entirely substituted for the other:

> 'First is developed the consciousness of the divine unity, conceived in very abstract fashion as a destiny or necessary law; then this abstract and pantheistic unity is surpassed and an advance is made towards the notion of the spiritual principle implied in monotheism.'

These lines indicate very exactly the direction of the movement. In old Homer the two conceptions jostle each other, and although, in his pages, Zeus is above even destiny, we must recognise in him, at least, some germs of later doctrines.

From the fifth century onwards, above all, it is apparent to any careful reader of the historians and poets, that many of them are carried on towards a fatalistic Pantheism. The concept of ἀνάγκη dominates the tragedy of Æschylus as well as the history of Herodotus, and a considerable part of the popular beliefs ; the Stoics have indeed some justification for basing their doctrine of destiny on universal consent.

[1] Glasgow, 1893, I, 278.

In this naturalist monism they had also been anticipated by the poets; I mean in their tendency to identify the gods of mythology with the forces of nature, and then unify them. Pindar already betrays this tendency in the well-known line: 'What is God? what is he not? He is all.'[1] Æschylus affirms it even more clearly; Prometheus sings: 'My mother is not only Themis and Gaia; she is the one form bearing many names';[2] and in a fragment of Æschylus, quoted by Clement of Alexandria and Eusebius, we read: 'Zeus is the air, Zeus is the earth, Zeus is the heaven, Zeus is all, and that which is above all.'[3]

Euripides himself, in his less sceptical moments, willingly interprets traditional mythology in this sense: 'Zeus, whether he be the necessity of nature or the thought of men . . .'[4]

Moreover, the naturalism which was the origin of Greek religion was still sufficiently perceptible in it to make it possible, at least in certain cases, to bring it without difficulty to the light. Thus, although Plutarch protests in one passage against the identification of Apollo with the sun,[5] he elsewhere recognises that this identification is almost universally admitted by the Greeks.[6]

These interpretations were, however, less easily admitted for most of the gods, outside a small circle of *literati* and thinkers. Cicero protests several times against the exegesis of the Stoics, which, he says, upsets all the conceptions usually made of the gods.[7]

Whatever, indeed, the naturalist character of Greek mythology may have been in its origins, it had become for some time more and more anthropomorphic: the development of the legends, rich in individual details, had attributed to different gods very individual personalities. The localisation of cults had helped still further, and more than all else, the use of paintings and statues, which gave a personal and distinct form to each divinity. These influences had acted too long and powerfully on the religious habits of the people for it to be possible to efface from their mind all these distinctions and make them worship, in the different gods, the forces of nature emanating from a single spirit.

[1] *Fr.* 117. [2] *Prom.*, 209–10. [3] *Fr.* 345.
[4] *Troyen.*, 886. [5] *De Pyth. orac.*, 12. [6] *De E.*, 4.
[7] *De Nat. Deor.*, I, 14, 63 *sqq.*

This, however, was the task on which the Stoics employed all their exegetical resources, interpreting the names of the gods by etymology, and their legends as allegories, effacing by their pitiless symbolism the most definite personalities. This method was already familiar to Plato, who had made fun of it;[1] Zeno resumed and developed it, and, after him, his successors, Cleanthes, Chrysippus, and the rest practised it with their tenacious and rather brutal energy.[2]

Here are some specimens which Cicero places in the mouth of the Stoic Balbus[3]: 'Cronos is time (χρόνος)': he owes his Latin name of Saturn to being saturated with years, *quod saturaretur annis;* when he is said to be chained by Jupiter, what is meant is that time is determined by the revolutions of the sky, for Jupiter is the sky; this is why he thunders and strikes with lightning, and this is the meaning given in the line of Ennius: '*Aspice hoc sublimen candens quem invocant omnes Jovem.*' The air is Juno, sister and wife of Jupiter, because it resembles the sky and is united to it.

It is useless to pursue further this rather tedious enumeration; Balbus gives a résumé of the doctrine of his school, and rediscovers in mythology the whole of the physical universe.

The only interesting point here is the religious value of his efforts, which is not hard to appreciate: all the disedifying and immoral details of the old legends vanished in symbols; scenes of obscenity receive a decent interpretation; by this means the work of the poets, which had so shocked Plato, becomes inoffensive and unattackable: and more than this, the great forces of nature have a more mysterious character and a more powerful activity than the futile personalities of the classical Olympus, and religious sentiment derives a richer nourishment.

The Stoics did not stop there: they conceived the entire world as penetrated and animated by a divine spirit. This spirit, this one god, received a thousand names in accordance with the various parts of the world inhabited and supported by him, Apollo, Poseidon,

[1] *Phædr.*, 229 c.

[2] *Stoicorum veterum fragmenta*, I (Zenonis), *Fr.* 152–177; II (Chrysippi), *Fr.* 1061–1100.

[3] *De Nat. Deor.*, II, 24, 63 *sqq.*

Artemis, Athene. These deities are distinguished from each other as are the different elements animated by them, but they are all emanations of the same divine spirit, who is coterminous with the world in which he has developed, who produces and sustains its multifold fecundity, who will in the end consume it and re-absorb it into himself.[1] And at the moment of that universal conflagration all the gods will vanish in the unique god from whom they have proceeded,[2] until the day when Zeus, re-commencing his fatefully-determined evolution, once more, and in accordance with the same laws, produces all gods and men.[3]

Hellenic mythology did not, it has been said, lend itself without resistance to this pantheistic interpretation; Egyptian religion, less anthropomorphic and more naturalistic, was more easily harmonised with it. It was at Saïs, on the statue of Isis, that the following inscription could be read: 'I am all the past, all the present, and all the future, and no mortal has raised my veil.'[4] Ammon, as Plutarch tells us, is held by the Egyptians to be identical with the universe: Apuleius puts these words in the mouth of Isis: 'I am the mother of nature, mistress of all the elements, the principle of the ages, the supreme divinity, queen of the Manes, first among heaven's inhabitants, the uniform type of gods and goddesses. . . . Unique in my power, I am adored by the whole universe under different forms, with different rites under a thousand names.'[5]

The Isis myths themselves are preferably interpreted by Apuleius and Plutarch in the sense of a dualist philosophy which does not identify the gods with the immanent activity of nature, but organises them into a hierarchy ruled by one supreme god. Thus, in this same eleventh book of the *Metamorphoses,* where Isis reveals herself as *Rerum naturæ parens, deorum deorumque facies uniformis,* Osiris is subsequently called 'the great God, the sovereign father of the gods, invincible Osiris,' or elsewhere 'the chief god.'[6]

We find here an echo of the religious speculations developed by Apuleius in his treatise on the demon of

[1] Plutarch, *De Stoic. repugn.*, 39.
[2] Plutarch, *De comm. not.*, 36.
[3] Lactantius, *Div. instit.*, VII, 23.
[4] Plutarch, *De Is.*, 9.
[5] *Metamorph.*, XI, 5.
[6] *Ibid.*, 27.

Socrates: following Plato, he sees the various gods as incorporeal, living, eternal, happy beings, and, above them, a sovereign deity transcending all action and passion, ineffable and incomprehensible.

Plutarch also represents Osiris as the first intelligible principle to whom the purified soul attains by ecstasy: if, he says, Osiris is the god of the dead, it is not that any defilement can touch him, but that he is the king and the chief of the purified souls who at length attain the invisible.[1]

Such an interpretation can only have meaning for an adept of Platonic philosophy, but the same tendencies are often more discreetly manifested and with a wider sphere of influence. The supreme god conceived by the dualist philosophy of neo-Platonists and neo-Pythagoreans is identified with the Zeus of mythology; from that moment the other gods become his subordinates and intermediaries in his relations with men.

This conception of the kingship of Zeus could plead the authority of the ancient Homeric mythology. Was not Zeus shown there as the father of gods and men? Men recalled the naïve image which expressed his supremacy; the one golden chain which all the gods on one side and Zeus on the other might pull in opposite directions, without the combined effort of all the gods availing anything against the power of Zeus. From those days the pre-eminence of Zeus over the other gods had remained the accepted belief of Pagans. Local divinities were always more popular and their festivals more devoutly observed, but they were themselves conceived as inferior to the supreme god. In those numerous syncretising identifications, by means of which the Oriental deities were assimilated to the gods of Greece and Rome, it was amongst the highest gods that Zeus or Jupiter was discovered: thus Serapis was commemorated by an invocation engraved on quantities of medals: *εἶ Ζεὺς Σέραπις*[2]; the Baal Chamim of the Syrians became *Jupiter summus, exsuperantissimus*[3]; the God of the Jews also became confused with the *Ζεὺς ὕψιστος*; and Celsus, wishing to prove that the Jewish religion had nothing more in it than

[1] *Is. et Osir.*, 77–8.

[2] E. Peterson, ΕΙΣ ΘΕΟΣ (Gottingen, 1926), 227–40.

[3] Cumont, *Les religions orientales*, 154.

the faiths of other people, wrote: 'I do not think there is any difference, whether Zeus is called Zeus or Hypsistos or Adonai or Sabaoth, or Ammon as the Egyptians do, or Papæus as the Scythians.'[1] Christian apologists themselves love to recognise in these popular invocations the cry of the 'naturally Christian soul'; Minucius Felix, after quoting them, adds: '*et qui Jovem principem volunt, falluntur in nomine, sed de una potestate consentiunt,*'[2] and Tertullian, when speaking of the efficacy of Christian prayers to obtain rain in time of drought, also mentions the prayers of Pagans, which he interprets in the same way: '*tunc et populus acclamans, deo deorum, qui solus potens, in Jovis nomine Deo nostro testimonium reddidit.*'[3]

It would be a complete misunderstanding of Minucius Felix and Tertullian to attribute to them the religious syncretism of Celsus: they are anxious to recognise in certain phrases familiar to Pagans the soul's instinct, which spontaneously turns towards the true God and forgets the paltry gods of mythology, but they are far from admitting the equivalence of Christian and Pagan religious conceptions. In point of fact, the difference between them remains irreducible, and, in spite of the meritorious efforts of philosophers and *literati* to elevate the popular religion, it remains, both in their case and in that of the people, genuine polytheism.

Those who, like Plutarch and Apuleius, are most conscious of their purpose, continue to address their adoration and offer their sacrifices to all the gods of the Hellenic Pantheon. These gods may be for them the subjects of the supreme god, or, as they say, satraps of the great king; they are nevertheless gods, with a nature similar to that of Jupiter, receiving the same homage and the same worship.

The other worshippers of the gods, in whom the same religious and philosophic culture has not developed a monotheistic instinct, are in the same case and even more so. In Jupiter they recognise no doubt a special excellence, but they are very far from putting the infinite distance between him and the other gods of his family, that separates the true God from all that is not himself.

I would not therefore venture to say with Boissier: 'that in the second century it was a general opinion, both

[1] *Ap.* ORIG., *C. Cels.*, V, 41. [2] *Octav.*, 18. [3] *Ad Scapul.*, 4.

among the ignorant and the educated, that, in some way, this world of deities had to be reduced to a single god.'[1] If one can distinguish at that time a powerful and partially successful effort to organise the city of the gods, to reduce it to a hierarchy under a single chief, one sees no attempt made to bring it back to the unity of one god only, a single person. This conclusion is also that of L. R. Farnell; if he notes in literature a monotheistic or at least a henotheistic tendency at work, he finds nothing of the kind in popular cultus and religion. He writes: 'Ideas become more indistinct, but no single idea of divinity clearly emerges. This theocrasia destroyed the life of religious sculpture and did nothing for monotheism, but a great deal for scepticism and the darkest superstition.'[2]

There is more. The philosophers who defend Paganism against the Christians, interpret it in a definitely polytheistic sense. They endeavour to prove, not that all these gods return to unity, but that their very plurality implies a higher religious conception. 'Among men,' writes Porphyry, 'one does not consider one who only reigns over beasts a monarch; in the same way, if Zeus has not other gods beneath him, he is not truly a king.'[3]

BIBLIOGRAPHY, Section 3:—Naegelsbach-Autenreith, *Homerische Theologie* (Nuremberg, 1884). G. Gruppe, *Griech. Mythologie*, 1041–58. A. Bremond, *Notes sur la religion de Pindare:* III, *le Panthéisme* (*Recherches de science religieuse*; Oct. 1918). Cornutus, ed. C. Lang, *Theologiae graecae compendium* (Leipzig, 1881). F. Wipprecht, *Zur Entwicklung der rationalistichen Mythendeutung* (Tübingen, 1902, 1908). Decharme, *La critique des traditions religieuses chez les Grecs* (Paris, 1904). R. Heinze, *Xenokrates* (Leipzig, 1892).

4. *The Religious Philosophies*

In the exegetical systems which have just been cursorily described, the two religious conceptions then reigning in the Hellenic world would already appear distinctly. It is nevertheless necessary that they should be studied independently, freed from the constraint of a mythological system which they did not create, and which they had difficulty in transforming into their own image. Such a study is rendered even more necessary by the fact that philosophical speculation is not alone involved in these

[1] *La religion romaine*, II, p. 372.
[2] *The Cults of the Greek States*, I, p. 83.
[3] *Apud* MACAR. MAGN., IV, 20.

conceptions; the religious life derived support from them. During these sombre and troubled periods many a soul found in them a little light and strength, and those who passed beyond these very imperfect philosophies to attain Christianity have, often enough, in their Christianity borne more or less recognisable traces of their earlier ideas.

For the Stoic the world is a closed system, issuing entire and complete from a single principle and developing according to its own laws.[1] More exactly it is a living being, a ζῷον, penetrated and animated by a soul.[2] At the beginning of our period, as of all others, this soul existed alone.[3] Let us not imagine it under the form of a pure spirit, for everything in action is material[4]; but this primitive matter is of all the purest and the most subtle, it is air on fire.[5] From thence have issued by successive degradations all the beings whom we see here below, but all of them, however insignificant they may be, contain something of that initial matter which is for ever the soul of the world. All that lives, lives through the heat which it contains, and even inanimate beings have something of this divine fire in them, like the stone from which friction causes a spark to leap forth.[6]

This primordial fire is intelligent; according to the classic definition, repeated by all the Stoics: 'it is a creative fire, following a route fixed at the birth of the world, containing all the seminal reasons by means of which everything is produced according to its destiny.'[7]

Its evolution is in fact inevitable, not as imposed from without, by an external constraint, but as necessarily determined by its own nature. All comes from, and all returns to, the primeval fire. 'The universal Logos grows ceaselessly until at length it has dried up everything and converted it into its own substance.' Then the body of the world is entirely consumed, and the soul alone survives; it is the end of one cosmic period, and the beginning of another; after this final conflagration, everything is re-established in its primitive condition, in order to recommence once more.[8] Not only are the physical elements disintegrated by the operation of the same laws,

[1] Chrysip. *ap.* Plut., *De Stoic. repugn.*, 39.
[2] Diog. Laert. VII, 142–3.
[3] *De Stoic. repugn.*, 41.
[4] Cicero, *Acad.*, I, 11, 19.
[5] Aetius, *Plac.*, I, 6, 1.
[6] Cicero, *De Nat. Deor.*, II, 9, 23–25.
[7] Aëtius, *Plac.*, I, 7, 33.
[8] Arius Didymus, *ap.* Euseb., *Præp. ev.*, XV, 19, 1–3.

fire once more becoming air and water, and the body of the world once more separating from its soul,[1] but the same events are reproduced, the same men are reborn to recommence the same life, maintain the same struggle and fall by the same death; for another Athens, another Socrates will be born, who will marry another Xantippe, who will be accused by another Anytos and another Meletos.[2] Such will be the destiny of all men and, indeed, of all gods but Zeus himself, identical with the Logos and equally imperishable; many a Helios, a Selene, an Apollo, an Artemis, a Poseidon have already passed away.[3]

Thus all is determined down to the last detail by the immanent law of the world, by its nature, by its soul. One may obstruct the action of a particular cause, one may avoid its action on oneself, but one cannot bring the world to a stop, nor escape its jurisdiction.[4] Man, said the Stoics, is like a dog tied behind a cart, he follows whether he will or no[5]; Cleanthes expressed more nobly the same thought in his beautiful hymn to Zeus: 'Lead me, Zeus, lead me, destiny; wherever you have indicated my place, I will follow with hesitation; if I am unwilling I shall follow badly, but nevertheless I will follow.'[6]

In these words of Cleanthes, one does not feel any accent of revolt, or of disappointment, or impotence; no doubt all is determined in the life of each of us, but this determination is not imposed on us by an external will, it rises from the very depths of our nature; we carry within us the law that rules us, our soul is a spark of the divine fire which animates the world. If this be so, what is there to complain of? Sure of his autonomy, the Stoic does not bother much about liberty.

We must above all notice the counter-effect on religion of these doctrines: man from the first finds himself the equal of the gods. 'The gods,' says Balbus in the words of Cicero, 'have only one advantage over men, they are immortal, and that fact adds nothing to their virtue.'[7] 'When virtue has been consummated,' says Seneca, 'a man is no longer the suppliant of the gods, but their equal.'[8] Elsewhere he represents the sage as being:

[1] CLEANTH. *ap.* STOB., I, 153.
[2] ORIG., *C. Cels.*, IV, 68.
[3] PLUTARCH, *De def. orac.*, 29.
[4] CHRYSIP. *ap.* PLUT., *De Stoic. repugn.*, 47.
[5] HIPPOLYT., *Philos.*, I, 21, 2.
[6] *Fr. st.*, I, 527.
[7] *De Nat. Deor.*, II, 61, 153.
[8] *Epist.*, 31, 8.

'Without fear of danger, out of reach of passions, happy in tribulation, peaceful in the storm, looking down on men from a position of equality with the gods,'[1] and again, 'the sage lives on equal terms with the gods.'[2]

He must not see in these expressions mere reminiscences of the school; they express a sincere conviction, we find them in the words of the least artificial and the least conventional of philosophers, Marcus Aurelius: 'Think,' he says, 'of what a world you are a part, of what a god you are an emanation.'[3] Chrysippus, that pillar of the Stoic philosophy, had said of old: 'Sages are nothing inferior to Zeus.'[4]

And, as a matter of fact, that equality is an immediate consequence of the doctrine which we are studying; one and the same soul animates the whole universe and its highest function is reason; from which it follows that, in man, or at least in the virtuous man, this divine force is to be found the same, as lofty and as pure as in the gods.

Each individual is thus constituted as the centre of the world; not only does he carry in himself the most sovereign and august element of the world; he is more, he *is* that quality by identity of his deepest and most intimate nature, he is the very god from whom everything comes, and to whom everything will return; and all the indefectible power and infallible wisdom, which he attributes to that god, all that is in himself, and by his own effort he may develop himself little by little and arrive at the full consciousness of his divine being.[5]

Considered under this aspect, Stoicism is the deification of the individual soul. No ancient doctrine had placed so high a value on the human personality, but equally none had so insanely exalted the pride of man.

Moreover, this very doctrine may present another aspect, in point of fact, more apparent at the imperial epoch; the soul is carried up to God, but at the same time absorbed in him. Her future beyond the grave does not belong to her; whatever doubts there may be about the Stoic doctrine on the fate of souls immediately after death, it is at least certain that the conflagration which closes each period of the world will also terminate all

[1] *Epist.*, 41, 4. [2] *Ibid.*, 59, 14. [3] *Commentar.*, 2, 4.
[4] *Ap.* Plut., *De Stoic. repugn.*, 13. [5] Seneca, *ep.* 92, 27–30.

individual lives. Already here below, certain humbler and more sincere souls feel their insignificance, in spite of all the assurances of the school; consequently, what they chiefly see in the Stoic doctrine is its fatalistic determinism: God is not for them a Father with whom they can have contact, a Providence in whom they can trust, he is an irresistible force which carries them with the whole universe in his advance, which nothing can cause to change or deviate. No doubt the end to which everything is moving is excellent, but that excellence can only be conceived in relation to the world as a whole, it is identical with the absorption of all beings in the divine fire from which they have issued, and meanwhile can be perfectly reconciled with the complete sacrifice of individual good and happiness. And this strange consequence follows; the philosophic doctrine, which has insisted most strongly on the existence of Providence, has justified the accusation of the denial of Providence.[1]

From this another consequence follows, namely, that God, who is the whole of reality, including ourselves, is nevertheless unknowable to us. No doubt, historically, such an agnosticism was developed by contact with neo-Platonism: but it also forms part of the most authentic Stoic doctrine; it is already to be found in Aristo of Chios, the disciple of Zeno.[2] He went indeed further and condemned all enquiry into the nature of the gods as only resulting in contradictions.

This helps us to understand what St. Justin tells us at the beginning of his Dialogue: he had entered the school of a Stoic philosopher and after remaining there a certain time, he left it on discovering that his master knew nothing about God and did not judge that the study of the divine nature was necessary. The words of Theophilus, accusing certain Stoics of atheism and placing Chrysippus side by side with Epicurus, should be understood in the same sense.[3]

To sum up, Stoicism has all the religious value of a materialist monism. Certain souls—and they were particularly numerous among the Stoics—are thrilled by this thought of the unity of the world and of their identity with God; they think that they and all here below re-

[1] TERTULLIAN, *De praescript.*, 7. [2] CICERO, *De Nat. Deor.*, I, 14, 37.
[3] *Ad. Autol.*, II, 4.

ceive an infinite value from the immanent god who dwells in the world and animates it, who is at once its principle, its law, and the term of its evolution. Others, on the contrary, feel crushed under this force which can neither be touched by prayer nor conquered by effort, nor escaped by flight. Both must have heard willingly the first words of St. Paul's discourse at Athens on the God in whom we have life and movement and being; but a personal God was for them an entirely new revelation, and only the Spirit could, from the depth of their souls, cause them to cry out: Father, Father!

Side by side with the current Stoicism and often, at the period we are studying, mingled with it, was outlined another current, already more powerful than the former, and which was soon to carry off religious souls outside Christianity; the Platonist and Pythagorean current.

Here, to the materialist monism of the Stoics, which knows no other reality but matter, and conceives of God not only as immanent in the world, but also as identical with it, is opposed a dualism which distinguishes and tends to separate spirit from matter, which isolates God, and places him outside the world, outside the reach of our knowledge, in a mystery accessible only to ecstasy. This mystical doctrine of the divine transcendence has seemed to certain historians a purely Oriental doctrine, imported into the Hellenic world with the religions of Egypt or of Syria.[1] Others, and among them the master of the history of Greek philosophy in the last century, Eduard Zeller, and one of its most profound historians, Edward Caird, have recognised in it an authentically Hellenic doctrine born and developed on Greek soil[2]: immediately after the death of Plato we find the Platonist dualism accentuated and taking a less metaphysical but more religious and moral character in the teaching of Xenocrates; a little later the dogmatism of Plato, and also that of the Stoics, are shaken by the attacks of the sceptics, and the soul, renouncing the attempt to embrace God by the intelligence, endeavours to rise towards him by ecstasy.

This second opinion seems more exact, provided it is

[1] See ZELLER, *Philos. d. Griech.*, V, 70.

[2] ZELLER, *op. cit.*, V, 70 *sqq.*; CAIRD, *Evolution of theology*, II, 182 *sq.*

not taken in too exclusive a sense; it is impossible to maintain that Platonism was in no way influenced by Oriental speculation, and merely represented a parallel current; the exchange of ideas between the two worlds was, at the beginning of the Christian era, too frequent and too considerable for us to be able to affirm so complete an independence between them. We must also remember that for a long time, i.e., from the sixth century, the religions and mysteries of the East had penetrated into Greece, and had cast germs into Hellenic thought that had slowly developed there. At least it is impossible to represent the action of the Oriental religions within the Roman Empire as a sudden irruption into a world, up to that moment closed to them, which they entirely transformed. A closer study of Greek thought before our era makes it evident on the one hand that ever since the fifth and fourth centuries Eastern influences were affecting Greek philosophy, and on the other hand, that the dualism and mysticism of Plutarch, of Maximus of Tyre, and of Apuleius, originated with Greek thinkers; first with Xenocrates, then with the sceptics, then with Stoic philosophers, or with the thinkers of the New Academy who were subject to their influence.

As has been said above, this movement was, at the beginning of our era, at the same time Pythagorean and Platonist. For at least three centuries the two schools had reacted to each other, and in spite of the persistent divergencies between their formal doctrines they agree in the period we are studying in several essential theses of their metaphysic and their theodicy.

To-day the Pythagorean school has disappeared with nearly the whole of its literary production. This loss should not make us fail to recognise an activity which was, in those days, intense. The sect being very much attached to its traditions, it became the custom to attribute almost all the treatises of this period to the revered names of the first Pythagoreans: Pythagoras himself, Timæus, Ocellus, Archytas, etc. We possess, for this period only, the titles of a hundred apocryphal treatises attributed to more than fifty different authors. Others bear the names of their real authors, for instance, Apollonius of Tyana, and Moderatus, while others again have assuredly disappeared without leaving any traces. We may judge by this of the vitality of the sect and the fecundity of its writers.

The venerable *noms de guerre* under which these writers loved to conceal themselves should not deceive us: these apocryphal treatises did not contain, it would appear, a very authentic Pythagorean doctrine. Photius relates, in his *Bibliotheca*,[1] his disappointment in reading the volume of Nicomachus of Gerasa entitled *Arithmetical Theologumena*; the title was very promising, but the work contained only the dualist doctrine so widely spread in the first century.[2] In point of fact, of all their arithmetical speculations, the Pythagoreans of this period seemed mainly to have retained the theory of the monad and dyad: the monad or unity, the principle of the good, the ordered, the simple; the dyad or duality, the principle of evil and of disorder. This doctrine is of Platonist origin; from the same source comes also the conception of the transcendence of God: most of the Pythagoreans conceived of God as distinct from matter and from the world, as inaccessible to the senses and knowable only by the intelligence. Apollonius of Tyana in a passage quoted by Eusebius[3] mentions this supreme god isolated and separated from all. The pseudo-Archytas describes him as being not a spirit, but something higher than a spirit. All recognise secondary gods below him, and place his glory in his reign over such noble beings.[4]

This theodicy, which, however, is not universally accepted in the school,[5] has nothing specifically Pythagorean about it. It may be found without any appreciable difference in the Platonists of this period.

The initiator of the movement, or the man whose contribution gave it most of its mystical character, was Xenocrates, the nephew and immediate successor of Plato. He interpreted the philosophy of his master in a definitely dualist sense, distinguished two first principles, one good, the other evil, and identified them with the monad and dyad. It appears to have been his influence which led Plutarch in the direction of dualism, both in his treatise on Isis and Osiris,[6] and his interpretation of Plato's *Timæus*. Guinet thought that he recognised here

[1] *Cod.* 187.
[2] See Delatte, *op. cit. infra*, 137–65.
[3] *Præp. evang.*, IV, 13, 1.
[4] Onatas, *ap.* Stob., *Ecl.*, I, 39 (ed. Wachsmuth, p. 48).
[5] On monism and dualism, see Schmekel, 403.
[6] *Is. et Os.*, 45.

Mazdean doctrines,[1] Gréard speaks even less exactly of Manichean sources[2]; R. Heinze, in the study of Xenocrates, has recognised without difficulty the source of Plutarch,[3] and has shown once more that the motive attributing so large a share to Oriental origin is often the result of imperfect knowledge of Greek thought. This dualist philosophy over-accentuates the transcendence of God: Plutarch indignantly rejects the concept of a god forming or destroying the world: it would be, he says, to compare him to a child building or upsetting his sand-castle.[4]

We also see in Plutarch the appearance of the thesis which will become so dear to neo-Platonists, that God cannot be reached intellectually by a distinct knowledge, but that he is only attainable through ecstasy or a sudden illumination: 'Objects of the senses,' he says, 'are within our reach and at our disposal; they change into each other, they appear and replace each other. The intelligible, the pure, the simple, on the other hand, shine out like a flash and, in a moment, permit the soul to touch and perceive them.'[5]

He willingly employs the language of the mysteries, and compares this illumination of the soul to the dazzling shock produced on the initiated by the revelation of holy things:

> 'Just as,' he says, 'the initiates, at first excited, crying out, surging to and fro, after the accomplishment and manifestation of the mysteries, become attentive, fearful, and silent, so when the pupil is on the threshold of his philosophical training he manifests nothing but agitation and chattering assurance, some indeed brutally struggling for the glory of the first place; when he has reached the interior of the doctrine and has seen the great light, as if the gates of the temple had been opened, he puts on a new dress, he is silent and timorous, he follows humbly and modestly the Logos as a god.'[6]

We must recognise that, in addition to the details here mentioned, we find in Plutarch, as in the Platonists of

[1] *Plutarque et l'Égypte* (from *Nouvelle Revue*), 18.
[2] *La morale de Plutarque*, 297. [3] *Xenokrates*, 30–37. [4] *De E.*, 21.
[5] *Is. et Osir.*, 77. [6] *De profect. in virtut.*, 10.

the second century, affirmations of a more intellectualist nature.[1] This juxtaposition of diverse elements should not surprise us in the case of philosophers whose spirit was very accommodating and slightly vague. It remains true that their conception of the divine transcendence, and their theory of ecstasy, are characteristic of their epoch and their school, which in the future will more and more absorb neo-Platonist philosophy.

At the moment, indeed, that conception leads to a consequence of the highest importance for our subject; it favours and develops the theory of intermediate beings.[2] God, completely separated from the world, not acting directly on it or being directly known by it, must be connected with it through beings of divine but subordinate nature; the Logos, spirits, powers, demons.[3] We must now study the transformation in the dualist philosophy of the Platonists of these various conceptions, nearly all originating in Stoicism.

BIBLIOGRAPHY, Section 4:—H. Schmidt, *Veteres philosophi quomodo judicaverint de precibus* (Giessen, 1907). A. Delatte, *Études sur la littérature pythagoricienne* (Paris, 1915). B. Latzarus, *Les idées religieuses de Plutarque* (Paris, 1920). J. A. Hild, *Étude sur les démons dans la littérature et la religion des Grecs* (Paris, 1881). M. Heinze, *Der Eudämonismus in der griechischen Philosophie* (Leipzig, 1907). J. Geffken, *Zwei Apologeten* (Leipzig, 1907).

[1] LATZARUS, *op. cit. infra*, 90 *sq.*
[2] PINARD DE LA BOULLAYE, *op. cit. infra*, I, 49.
[3] See Bibliography, *infra*.

CHAPTER II

THE LOGOS[1]

1. The Origins

THE theory of the Logos is anterior to the Stoics; it appears for the first time in the works of Heraclitus. This is no doubt the reason why that first of Greek philosophers was considered by St. Justin as a Christian before Christ.[2]

The Ionians who had preceded him, had not seen further than a rather naïve materialism, referring all things to water, or to the air, or to the infinite. The Eleatics had affirmed the exclusive existence of *Being* or the *One,* and had denied all plurality and all movement. Contrariwise, Heraclitus sees nothing anywhere but movement: one cannot cross the same stream twice, and everything here below is a stream; everything is in flux, in constant transformation, each being is the synthesis of two contrary principles of which one is perpetually chasing the other; this conflict is the father and the king of everything. Fire is at once the subject and the principle of all these transformations[3]; it is living and eternal, periodically kindling and extinguishing itself.[4] It is intelligent, the governor of the universe and its judge; and it will consume it in the final conflagration.[5] According to Clement of Alexandria this fire is the god of Heraclitus[6]; according to Stobæus it is destiny[7]; according to Sextus Empiricus it is the universal mind and the divine Logos; individual minds owe their intelligence and

[1] I am conforming to custom in keeping in its Greek form the word *logos*. 'Word,' apart from its application to the Word of God, has the precise meaning of 'spoken word,' whereas, as we shall see, *logos* is much less precise, much richer in diversity of meanings.

[2] *Apol.*, I, 46.

[3] *Fr.* 90 (ed. Diels), *ap.* PLUT., *De E.*, 8.

[4] *Fr.* 30, *ap.* CLEM. AL., *Strom.*, V, 14, 104, 2 (*GCS*, 396).

[5] *Fr.* 63–6; HIPPOL., *Philos.*

[6] CLEM. AL., *Protr.*, 5, 64; cf. DIELS, *Doxographi græci*, 129.

[7] STOB., *Eclog.*, ed. Wachsmuth, 78, 7.

rationality to their union with it.[1] As Logos, it is the law of the world, the criterion of truth, the rule of justice; to depart from it in favour of one's individual reason is a folly and a crime.[2]

These few points sum up nearly all we know of the theory of Heraclitus on the Logos[3]; they suffice us at least to recognise, in these lines almost effaced by the hand of time, a first sketch of the Stoic conception: the Logos who is the god immanent in the world, the reason that guides it, the law that governs it, the fire which feeds it and will one day devour it.

But before reconquering, in the Stoic system, the place that it had once occupied in the philosophy of Heraclitus, the concept of the Logos was to disappear for two centuries: this theory of an immanent God could only find a place in a pantheism; the philosophers of the fifth and fourth centuries B.C., were dualists and conceived of God as transcendent.

We have heard so often of the 'Logos of Plato,' and of the influence which this idea exercised on Christian theology, that it may seem paradoxical to deny that the theory of the Logos is to be found in his authentic philosophy. The fact is, however, certain; you may read through all the dialogues of Plato, but you will seek it in vain; if such an investigation is too tedious, glance through the article λόγος in Ast's *Lexicon Platonicum;* the result will be the same. Moreover, this fact is now recognised by all historians of philosophy: only a few controversialists still repeat the assertions of Vacherot and of Ernest Havet on the λόγος θεῖος of Plato.

This discovery, certain as it is, nevertheless surprises us: historians, philosophers, and theologians of all shades have discussed for so long the Logos of Plato that one has a certain difficulty in admitting that a false supposition has led to so much discussion. The fact is explicable in great measure by the too frequent confusion between Plato and Platonists, and also between the apocryphal and the authentic Plato. In the first centuries of our era the Pagan or Christian philosophers who speculated most on the Logos, were largely Platonists; on this point, as

[1] See SEXTUS, *Advers. Mathem.*, 7, 129; ed. BEKKER, 219.
[2] *Fr.* 2, *ap.* SEXT. EMPIR., 7, 133.
[3] See DIELS, *Nachtrag. Fragm. d. Vorsokrat.*, III, p. vii.

E

on so many others, they liked to claim the authority of their master, and discover their own ideas in him.

The apocryphal works of Plato also contributed to the same result. From St. Justin to Proclus all philosophers appealed to the supposed second letter of Plato with its famous theory of the three principles (312e), and everyone found there what he was looking for: some, the Christian Trinity, others the neo-Platonist triad. The *Epinomis*, which is no more authentic than the second letter, was at least a more ancient document, and the theory of the Logos was already to be found in it.[1]

Furthermore, such formal testimony was not necessary. The ancients, particularly at the period of Hellenism, took their exegesis fairly easily; just as they did not trouble to discuss the authenticity of the works they were studying, so also they were not greatly preoccupied with the literal meaning of their texts and the thought of their author. In the treatise of *Destiny*, the author, Plutarch, or one of his contemporaries, is giving a definition of destiny. He quotes two mythical stories from the *Phædrus* and the *Timæus* on the law of Adrastos and the 'laws given by God for the whole universe to immortal souls,' and in order to express them in simpler terms, he transposes them into Stoic formulæ; 'According to the *Phædrus*,' he says, 'destiny is the inevitable divine Logos acting through irresistible causes; according to the *Timæus* it is the law in conformity with the nature of the universe which regulates the sequence of all that happens.'[2] Such examples could easily be multiplied,[3] but it is unnecessary to do so since no one dreams of contesting the lack of the critical faculty in writers of this epoch; it is enough to have mentioned it in order to explain how the theory of the Logos, always foreign to Plato's thought, could for so long a time be attributed to him.

Nevertheless, if this conception is not in itself to be found in Plato, many theses are to be found in his works which, when later combined with the Stoic idea of the Logos, fertilised and transformed it; the principal of these is unquestionably the affirmation of the world of ideas, at once the model and principle of the world of actual experience. In time to come this will come to be identified with

[1] *Epin.*, 986 c. [2] *De Fato*, I.

[3] Cf. Plut., *De Is. et Osir.*, 57, 60, 77; *De Animæ procr. in Tim.*, 23.

the Logos,[1] and, as at that time,[2] subsisting ideas were considered as the thoughts of God, the Logos became an intermediary being, produced and sustained by the divine thought.[3]

Aristotle, like Plato, remained a stranger to speculations on the Logos,[4] yet he exercised a more immediate influence over them. The concept of nature as he developed it in his treatise on Physics rapidly invaded the whole Stoic philosophy and the theory of the Logos found there a new origin.[5]

BIBLIOGRAPHY, Section 1 :—M. Heinze, *Die Lehre vom Logos in der griechischen Philosophie* (Oldenburg, 1872). A. Aall, *Gesch. der Logosidee* (Leipzig, 1896). J. Lebreton, *Les théories du Logos au début de l'ère chrétienne*, in *Études* (5 Jan., 5 Feb., 20 Mar., 1906). E. Krebs, *Der Logos als Heiland im ersten Jahrhundert* (Freiburg im Breisgau, 1910). M. Lagrange, *Revue biblique* (1923). C. Ritter, *Neue Untersuchungen uber Platon* (Munich, 1910). J. Souilhé, *Lettres de Platon* (Paris, 1926). G. Rodier, *Evolution de la dialectique de Platon* in *Année philosophique* (1905).

2. *Ancient Stoicism*

What has already been said of the Stoic conception of God will make our exposition of the theory of the Logos shorter and easier. The Logos, like destiny, providence, law, nature, is but one of the many aspects under which the Stoics loved to represent the active and divine principle of the universe. As Zeno demonstrated that the world was alive, he also proved, and by the same argument, that it is rational, because 'the rational is better than the irrational, and nothing is better than the world'[6]; he added that the whole being better than the part, it is impossible that there should be rational beings in the world if the world as a whole is irrational[7]; and, finally, since the world engenders rational beings, it is necessary that the world itself should be rational.[8] These general arguments were confirmed by detailed

[1] See below, page 170. [2] See ZELLER, II^4, 664, n. 5 ; V^3, 120.

[3] The theory of the world-soul (*Tim.*, 30a *sq.*) and that of secondary deities (*ib.*, 41a *sq.*), has also had an influence on the concept of the Logos, and of the powers.

[4] In the same manner as Plato, he was later misrepresented as one who had speculated on the Logos. Cf. CICERO, *De Nat. Deor.*, I, 13, 33.

[5] See ARISTOTLE : *Phys.*, 2, 1, 192b, 21 ; *De cælo*, 1, 4, 271a, 33 ; *Pol.*, 7, 4, 1326a, 32 ; *De part. an.*, 5, 645a, 9. Also BONITZ, *Index Aristotelicus*, 835b, 836.

[6] CICERO, *De Nat. Deor.*, II, 7, 8, 20, 21. SEXTUS EMPIR., *Adv. Math.*, IX, 104.

[7] CICERO, *ib.*, 22 ; cf. *ib.*, 12, 32 ; SEXTUS, *ib.*, 85.

[8] CICERO, *ib.*, 22 ; SEXTUS, *ib.*, 77.

observation; since Socrates it was a commonplace of Greek philosophy to point out that nature is not blind, but that she works to a plan and in view of an end. Aristotle, in his treatises of natural history, had greatly developed these observations and confirmed this argument; the Stoics adopted it in their turn and, with sympathetic admiration, collected in nature all the traces of rational design: the whole of the second book of the *De Natura Deorum* of Cicero ought to be quoted here, with its descriptions of the heavenly phenomena, of the life of plants, of the instinct of animals, and such frequent exclamations as the following: 'Come, let us descend from heavenly to earthly things! What is there in them in which the proportion of intelligent things is not apparent?'[1] And further on: 'What shall I say? How much rationality is evident in animals?'[2]

What the Stoic Balbus is careful to show clearly is the presence and action of reason, of the Logos, in the world: 'If the works of nature,' says he, 'are more perfect than the works of art, and if art does nothing irrational, it follows that nature also is rational.'[3]

As has been remarked[4] in this abundant, sometimes prolix, argumentation, the Stoics overlook nothing that can establish the action of reason in the world; they are never anxious to prove that this reason does not transcend the world, but is its soul. The cause of this was no doubt partly that their principal enemies, the Epicureans and the Sceptics, attacked them less on this point, but principally because they were so accustomed to conceive the world as containing the totality of being, that they never bothered to demonstrate that fundamental principle.

The Logos then is the immanent reason of the world, penetrating it from end to end, 'as the honey fills the cells of the honeycomb,' in Tertullian's words.[5] The Logos thus assures the unity of the world, giving to the different bodies it contains their cohesion, and enclosing them all within one boundary.[6] It fastens the past to the present and the future; it is, as it were, the cable unrolling throughout the centuries, the destined series of

[1] 47, 120. [2] 51, 128. [3] 34, 87. [4] HEINZE, 81.

[5] *Advers. Hermog.*, 44. Cf. ZENO, *ap.* STOB., *Ecl.*, II, 11; CHALCID., *In Tim.*, 291.

[6] CICERO, *De Nat. Deor.*, II, 45, 115.

events[1]: or again, as Cicero says: 'The eternal truth which flows from all eternity.'[2] It was in order to imitate this chain of events by the very form of their thought that the Stoics preferred conditional syllogisms and dilemmas, which seemed to them to express better the necessary linkage of things.[3]

Thus the whole world is intelligible, rational, coherent; it is not a mere series or collection of independent beings, it is a living organism; and if the Logos is the law which governs and the boundary which encloses it, it is also, as *λόγος σπερματικός*, the germ from which it issues and the vital force which animates it[4]: 'as in the process of generation, the germ is enclosed in matter, so the god who is the seminal reason of the world, dwells in the humid element, making use of matter for his successive productions.'[5]

In the period of conflagration, the *λόγοι*, or particular potencies giving rise to particular worlds, are reabsorbed into the universal Logos; when the world is reborn they disengage themselves one after another and develop the particular features of the world. 'In the same way,' says Cleanthes, 'as all the members of a being develop from the germ at the right time, so also the parts of the world, and among them animals and plants.'[6] Once produced, each being continues to live by the Logos which brought it to the birth: Plotinus, stating Stoic doctrine on this point, compares the world to a plant: the life which mounts from the root puts forth branches as it will, nourishes them, intertwines them or lets them die; thus acts the soul of the world.[7]

In individual beings, as in the world in its entirety, the Logos is before all a principle of determination, a form; in inanimate beings it is the essential property which specifies them (*ἕξις*); in plants it is nature (*φύσις*); in men and gods it is reason (*λόγος*).[8] The Logos is also

[1] CIC., *De divin.*, I, 56, 127.
[2] *Ib.*, 55, 125; cf. CHRYSIP. *ap.* PLUT., *De Stoic. repugn.*, 47.
[3] PLUT., *De E.*, 6. Cf. BROCHARD, *Sur la logique des stoïciens* in *Archiv fur Gesch. d. Philos.*, V, 449–68.
[4] ZENO, *ap.* STOB., ed. Wachsmuth, I, 133, 3.
[5] DIOGENES LAERTIUS, VII, 136.
[6] *Ap.* STOB., I, p. 153, 15.
[7] PLOT., *Enn.*, 3, 1, 4 (ed. Volkmann, 219, 9).
[8] AETII, placita, *ap.* DIELS, *Doxogr.*, 306, 6.

a force ; in matter it is the principle of cohesion, which maintains the different parts in place[1] ; in plants it is the vital urge which causes roots to swell and to move rocks[2] ; in animals it is the principle of their movement, the impulse (ὁρμή) which carries them hither and thither under the action of external causes[3] ; in man, it becomes thought and speech, the interior Logos (ἐνδιάθετος) and the manifested Logos (προφορικός) ; through the former man participates in the soul of the world, the universal Logos ; through the latter he is united with the gods and with other men.[4]

Thus, if the Logos infallibly moves all beings, it is not as a law foreign to their nature, or as a restraint externally imposed on them ; it is as the most intimate force of their own nature. Everything moves towards the fatally imposed goal of its destiny, but it moves spontaneously and naturally. 'Inasmuch,' say the Stoics, 'as the action of each being is in conformity with its own nature, none of such natural actions can be different from what it is, but each is produced necessarily by its subject, not through a necessity of constraint, but through a necessity of nature, it being impossible that the circumstances of an action should be different from what they are, or that they should produce a different impulse.'[5]

It would, moreover, be criminal to wish to oppose the action of the Logos ; that supreme reason proceeds to its excellent end by the best of means: 'Providence,' say Chrysippus and Cleanthes, 'has omitted nothing necessary for the surest and most useful disposal of everything ; had another economy of the world been better, Providence would have chosen it.'[6]

This conviction that everything in the world is rational, that it can contain no disorder, no accident, no disturbance of any kind was a firm basis for the life of the soul, and it is well known how obstinately Stoics were attached to it, more particularly during the troubled times of the empire ; the hardest lessons of experience did not always succeed in shaking this tenacious optim-

[1] PLUT., *De Stoic. repugn.*, 43 ; ALEX. APHROD., *De Mixtione*, ed. BRUNS, 223, 25. [2] SEN., *Nat. quæst.*, 2, 6, 5.

[3] Cf. BONHÖFFER, *Epictet u. die Stoa*, 252 ; PLUT., *De Stoic. repugn.*, 11.

[4] Cf. ZELLER, *op. cit.*, IV, 67, n. 1 ; SEXT. EMPIR., *Hyp.*, 1, 65 *sq.*, *Math.*, 8, 225 *sq.* [5] ALEX. APHROD., *De Fato*, 13.

[6] PHILO, *De Provid.*, 2, 74.

ism. The reply to all objections was in one word: what matter the sufferings and faults of individuals, if, as a result, the world is happier and more perfect! Cleanthes had already in his hymn to Zeus proclaimed this great principle, and had, by means of it, solved the problem of evil and pain: all disorder disappears in the great harmony of the world as a whole; all things conspire towards its perfection. He said to Zeus: 'Thou knowest how to bring order out of disorder, how to conciliate contraries, how to reduce all good and evil to one and the same harmony, so that all depend on the same eternal Logos.'[1]

Chrysippus translated the same thought into more popular terms: 'In a comedy there are ludicrous speeches; in themselves they are ridiculous, but they give charm to the whole.'[2] And in later days Marcus Aurelius, applying these maxims to his own conduct, wrote in his memoirs:

> 'We all co-operate in the same labour, some knowingly, and others in ignorance . . . each of us works after his own fashion; even those who murmur and who try to upset and destroy their work. For the world has need of them also. Consider therefore which class of beings thou shouldst enter: in any case the Director of the universe will know how to make use of thee, and will enrol thee in one of his battalions of workmen and labourers. But do not thou for thy part choose for thine own in the comedy the foolish and ludicrous verses of which Chrysippus speaks.'[3]

We all, whether we are good or evil, follow the Logos; it is our duty to follow it spontaneously, that is the first principle of Stoic morals, and, indeed, the end and aim of the entire system; the physical theories of the system have no other *raison d'être* than to lead the mind to it[4]; inversely, it can only be reached through the study of nature: 'No other principle or origin of justice can be found than Zeus and the daily round of nature, it is from there that we must set forth to speak of good and evil.'[5]

[1] CLEANTH., *Hymn.*, V, 19 *sqq.* (*ap.* STOB., 27, 7).
[2] *Ap.* PLUT., *De Comm. not.*, 14. [3] M. ANTON., VI, 42.
[4] CHRYS. *ap.* PLUT., *De Stoic. repugn.*, 9, 5. [5] *Ib.*, 9, 4.

That study forms the reason in us,[1] and forms it aright, is a rule as infallible as the universal Logos from which it emanates; and since in man, as in the universe, the Logos is the one and only force,[2] as every impulse, every desire, every action, proceeds from it, the sage can never act except in accordance with the eternal law which he bears within him,[3] while the common man can never rise except by accident to that perfect rectitude.

Thus humanity is separated into two groups of very unequal numbers; on one side the common herd, on the other the *élite* of the wise; and the whole world is definitively divided into categories of beings according to their more or less perfect participation in the Logos: at the bottom, inanimate matter, where the Logos is only specification; higher up, the vegetable kingdom, where it is nature; the animal world, where it is soul; humanity in general, where it is mind; the wise, where it is righteousness.[4] Above the wise there is nothing: the gods and Zeus himself are their equals, not their superiors.[5] How indeed could we wish for a principle of higher perfection than right reason, identical with the very law of the world?[6]

It is evident how this theory of the Logos enriched the Stoic conception of God and made it more precise. Zeus is no longer merely the active principle of the universe, the soul of the world, the fire whch animates and will consume it; he is the λόγος σπερματικός, the living germ from which everything is developed and which diffuses itself in everything; he is the sovereign law determining all things, physical being, logical truth, and moral goodness; he is the all-wise and all-powerful reason which draws the world and each one of us towards the excellent end which he will infallibly attain.

This proud and rigid conception was soon to undergo adaptation to popular mythology.

How the Stoics took pains to interpret the ancient Hellenic legends in terms of their philosophy, and to

[1] Cf. CAIRD, *Evolution of Theology*, I, 310; BONHÖFFER, *Die Ethik des Stoikers Epictet*, 224.

[2] BONHOFFER, *Epictet u. die Stoa*, 253.

[3] STOB., II, 65, 12; 99, 3; PLUT., *De Stoic. repugn.*, 27.

[4] *Fr. st.*, II, 459. *ap.* PHIL. *De ætern. mundi*, 15. Cf. CIC., *De leg.*, 1, 7, 22.

[5] CHRYS. *ap.* PLUT., *De Stoic. repugn.*, 13.

[6] Cf. LEBRETON in *Études*, 5 Jan., 1906.

cover their metaphysical conceptions with the prestige of the gods of Olympus, is well known. The Logos received the honour of apotheosis: from the first it had been identified with the supreme god Zeus,[1] and the Stoic philosophers retained this interpretation.[2] It is, however, not to be found in the *Allegories* of Heraclitus, nor even in the *Theology* of Cornutus, although the latter author multiplies the personifications of the Logos, whom he discovers in Cronos,[3] in the Titans,[4] in Eros and Atlas,[5] in Pan,[6] in Agathodemon,[7] in Herakles.[8]

This exegesis has nothing popular about it; it rests solely on the theory of Stoicism, but it is vague and uncertain. Pan, Eros, Atlas, Agathodemon are vague figures in whom one barely recognises the features of the Logos. Cronos personifies the Logos, but he also personifies time, and the separation and mingling of the elements. The type of Herakles is the only one whose outline is definite, and who bears a clearly Stoic stamp; and he represents rather a moral ideal than a metaphysical conception, he is the god of effort, not the reason of the world.

This learned exegesis was supplanted by a very different popular interpretation which Stoicism had not created,[9] but was willing to utilise. For a long time the people were accustomed to see in Hermes the god of reason and language; he became the personification of the Logos.

We can readily understand what help and also what danger Stoic philosophy found in such an adaptation of mythology. By that means it reached the children on the school-benches of the grammarian, and made its conception of the world and of divinity penetrate their minds with the text of Homer. By the same means it was able to propagate itself among the less cultivated classes who had never heard of the physics of Chrysippus and who learned to recognise and salute the divine Logos in the statue of Hermes, so familiar an object in the street and in the shop. Contrariwise, to what distortions was the philosophic idea subjected by these archaic legends, and in the intercourse of these unrefined people!

[1] PLUTO, *De Stoic. repugn.*, 34.
[2] SENECA, *De benef.*, IV, 7.
[3] CORNUTUS, 17 (p. 31).
[4] *Ib.*, (p. 30).
[5] *Ib.*, 25–26 (p. 48).
[6] *Ib.*, 27 (p. 49).
[7] *Ib.* (p. 51).
[8] *Ib.*, 31 (p. 62).
[9] Cf. PLATO, *Crat.*, 408a.

We may note at once that the Logos which, according to Cornutus, was personified in Hermes, is rather speech than reason: the very name of Hermes is derived from the verb ἐρεῖν, to speak[1]; the tongue, as organ of speech, is consecrated to Hermes; he is called the son of Zeus and Maïa, because speech is the daughter of study and research; stones are heaped at the foot of his statues to indicate that his discourse is composed of small parts; he is said to be a thief because language sometimes robs us of our opinions and substitutes plausibility for truth; his feet are decked with wings because speech is winged.[2]

By a few features only does Hermes represent reason, and, even so, it is always human reason understood in the psychological sense, not the divine and universal reason, the soul of the world: Hermes is called ἀγοραῖος, because everything must be done with reason; νόμιος, because reason ordains what should be done and forbids what should be avoided; he is honoured along with Herakles in the *palæstra* because reason and force must be combined; he is said to be common to all, because reason is common to gods and men.[3]

All these similitudes, we may note, are of a very different character from those which we discovered in the interpretation of the myths of Zeus: in this case mythology no longer veils Stoic speculations, but only the concepts of the people. Before Zeno and Chrysippus no one dreamed of making Zeus the soul of the world, but for a long time previously Hermes had been worshipped as the god of speech and eloquence. In all that, then, there is nothing, properly speaking, Stoical; the most that can be found in it is a superficial adaptation of popular beliefs to the psychology and ethics of the school.

In this popular exegesis the Stoic concept of the Logos was greatly compromised and partially distorted: Zeus, king and ruler of the world, could alone represent the universal reason which determines everything by its law and animates everything with its own life; Hermes was a very inferior god to personify this sovereign force. He was only the messenger of the high gods; he filled, in mythology, the secondary rôle of intermediary and

[1] CORNUTUS, *loc. cit.*, ch. 61, p. 20, 22.
[2] Cf. VARRO, *ap.* AUG., *De civ. Dei*, 7, 14.
[3] CORNUTUS, *loc. cit.*, p. 25 *sq.*

messenger, which the Logos was soon to adopt in the Alexandrine philosophy, and we may well think that the myth of Hermes showed its influence in this direction on philosophical thought.

It is interesting to see how Cornutus defends, on this point, the purity of the Stoic conception. According to him the true meaning of Hermes being sent to us from the gods is merely that they have given speech to man,[1] and if he is called the messenger of the gods it is only because reason teaches us the divine wills.[2]

Such an exegesis was forced, and failed to impose itself on Pagan opinion; moreover, there was a still stronger contrast between the Stoic theory and popular mythology: Hermes was the god of speech; but the Stoic Logos, at least the universal Logos, was reason and not speech, and it was indeed one of the most marked differences between the Stoic and the Alexandrine philosophies, that the former conceived of the Logos as the reason of the world, and the latter as the speech of God. In order to remain even here faithful to the theory of his school, Cornutus only identifies Hermes with the human Logos which, for a long time, had been analysed by the Stoics into the interior Logos and the manifested Logos; the universal Logos always remains for him the reason of the world, and personified, as we have seen above, in Herakles, Atlas, Cronos, and other secondary divinities. But even here his efforts were in vain; this distinction of the two Logoi and the attribution to them of different divine rôles never became popular, and Hermes remained the one and only personification of the Logos.

About the same time as the *Outline* of Cornutus, was composed, under the name of Heraclitus, the *Treatise of the Homeric Allegories*.[3] The author is a Stoic, but he only puts forward the least technical part of his system. For him Hermes is the only god who represents the Logos, that is to say, human language and reason. The combat of Hermes and Leto symbolises the combat of speech and forgetfulness. Hermes is called Ἀργειφόντης not because he killed Argus—that impious fable may be left to Hesiod—but because speech manifests thought.[4] A

[1] Cornutus, *loc. cit.*, p. 20. [2] *Ibid.*, p. 21.

[3] Heraclitus, *Allegoriæ homericæ*, ed. Mehler, Leyden, 1851.

[4] *Ibid.*, ch. lxxii.

distinction is drawn between the subterranean and the heavenly Hermes ; they each receive a separate cult in order to honour in the former the subterranean Hermes who is concealed in the heart, and in the second, the heavenly Hermes who manifests himself at a distance.[1] On retiring to rest the worshipper pours out a final libation to Hermes to signify that sleep stops his voice.[2]

These characteristics, among many others, closely resemble such as can be found in Cornutus or in Varro[3] ; one nevertheless detects already in Heraclitus a tendency to apply to the divine Logos the different attributes reserved by Stoics for human speech and reason. Such an identification was inevitable, and it necessarily resulted in the discovery in Hermes of the intermediary between God and man, the divine word which governs and reveals.

This interpretation was very successful ; it is found not only in such mythographers as Varro, Cornutus, and Heraclitus, but also in Plutarch,[4] Seneca,[5] Aelianus,[6] Plotinus,[7] Porphyry[8] ; and St. Justin in his *Apologia* presents it as universally accepted by Pagans.

The concept of the Logos became, as we have seen, notably distorted ; but, inversely, the mythological character of Hermes was now and then modified by it, thereby acquiring here and there a new importance. A magical papyrus in London sings his praises as master of the world, sovereign eye of the world, guide of the sun.[9] One inscription greets him as all-powerful (παντοκράτωρ)[10] and this epithet of Jewish origin is nowhere else applied to any other Pagan god.[11]

3. *Alexandrinism and Platonism*

It was chiefly in Egypt that the rôle of Hermes developed ; he became identified with Thôt, the ibis or baboon god of Hermopolis, who, according to legend,

[1] Heraclitus, *Allegoriæ homericæ*, ed. Mehler, Leyden, 1851, ch. lxxii.
[2] *Ibid.*
[3] See above, page 50, note 2.
[4] *De Is. et Osir.*, 41, 54, 55.
[5] *De benef.*, IV, 8.
[6] *De natur. animal.*, X, 29.
[7] *Enn.*, III, 6, 19.
[8] *Ap.* Euseb., *Præp. evang.*, III, 11 (*P.G.*, XXI, 205).
[9] *Papyrus magique de Londres*, 46, 414, quoted by Gruppe in *Mythologie grecque*, p. 1339, n. 4.
[10] *Anthol. Pal.*, app. 282.
[11] See Gruppe, *op. cit.*, p. 1324.

produces the world by the sole virtue of his word: 'Creation was not for him the muscular effort to which the other gods owed their birth; he had accomplished that task by formula, or by his voice alone, at the first moment of his awaking in the Nou.'[1]

Seven or eight centuries before the Christian era an unknown scribe of Memphis was already celebrating in Horus and Thôt the omnipotence of the divine thought and word.[2]

These myths soon penetrated into Greece; Plato speaks twice of Theuth[3]; Hecatæus already identifies him with Hermes[4]; Cicero mentions two Egyptian Hermes'—'the first born of the Nile, whose name the Egyptians are forbidden to pronounce; the second who is said to have killed Argus, and on that account to have fled into Egypt and to have taught the Egyptians law and literature; the Egyptians call him Theuth and give his name to the first month of the year.'[5]

Under the Ptolemies this Thôt became very popular with the Alexandrines as the great Hermes Trismegistos, the revealing god, who of old had invented the alphabet and taught men letters, and had in mysterious books revealed to some hero or priest the secret of the birth of the world and the formula of magic evocations.[6]

For philosophers Thôt was, like Hermes, a personification of the Logos. There were indeed many others in Egyptian as in Greek mythology. The Logos was worshipped as Osiris, the father of Horus,[7] in the weasel[8] and in the crocodile.[9] We may imagine the strange legends which these bestial divinities added to the concept of the Logos. Of the countless treatises on religion and philosophy which appeared at this epoch, hardly any have survived, and with them have disappeared these bastard and transient conceptions. A few traces only of them can be found in the Hermetic books.

But beyond this popular mythology certain higher ideas were forming themselves in Alexandrine circles and

[1] G. Maspero, *Histoire ancienne des peuples de l'Orient*, I, 146.
[2] See Bibliography at end of this Section.
[3] *Phædr.*, 274c; *Phil.*, 18b.
[4] *Ap.* Diodor., 1, 16, ed. Vogel, p. 27.
[5] *De Natura Deorum*, III, 22, 56.
[6] See Scott, *Hermetica*, in Bibliography below.
[7] See Reitzenstein, *Poimandres*, 27.
[8] *De Is. et Osir.*, 74.
[9] *Ibid.*, 75.

have left more permanent traces in the writings of Plutarch and Philo.

These two writers present so many common features both in their vocabulary[1] and their philosophy, and more particularly in their conception of the Logos, that, if we exclude the hypothesis of direct borrowing, we must suppose that they made use of common sources.[2] These sources are often impossible to identify with precision[3]; but we should hardly be mistaken in looking for them, at least partly, in the Alexandrine religious philosophy. This influence is clearly to be recognised in Philo, and it cannot be denied in Plutarch; his 'Treatise on Isis and Osiris' plainly shows it, and it is here that the theory of the Logos is most fully developed. M. Bréhier, in his book on *The Philosophical and Religious Ideas of Philo of Alexandria,* has recalled the syncretism which brought together, at the beginning of the imperial epoch, Stoicism and the religious theories of Egypt. Of the philosophers whom he mentions, Chæremon, Hecatæus of Abdera, Apion, we know very little, but, considering the scarcity of our sources, this little is by no means negligible. These writers, contemporaries of Philo, or of a slightly later date, were no doubt not the authors who inspired him; but they witness to the existence of a philosophic and religious movement, the influence of which he also underwent.

Still more decisive was the influence of moderate Stoicism, represented chiefly by Posidonius. It is hard to-day to discover the almost effaced traces of his system, but a careful study of M. Schmekel[4] shows us its outlines; Posidonius introduced into Stoic physics Platonist exemplarism and Pythagorean arithmetic; he combined with the theory of the Logos the theories of ideas and numbers; this is the dualist and Platonising Stoicism that we find in Philo, Plutarch, and especially in Marcus Aurelius.

Besides Hellenic theories, Jewish ideas had so much influence on Philo that it is impossible to study his philosophy without a description of the Palestinian or Alexandrine Judaism on which it depends. On the other

[1] See Siegfried, *Philo von Alexandria*, 38–45.
[2] Cf. *Rech. de Sc. Relig.*, 1926, 321–4.
[3] Cf. Gruppe, *op. cit. infra*, I, 442.
[4] *Die Philosophie der mittleren Stoa*, 238–90.

hand, Plutarch is, above all, a Greek, and we do better not to separate him from the moralists and the philosophers whose tradition he continues.

The eclecticism of Plutarch is governed by the great Platonist theses: his god is transcendent to the world, and the conception of the Logos follows from this idea. For Plutarch, as for the Stoics, the Logos is a principle of energy and determination; but instead of being the immanent force and law of the world, he is the agent by whom God constructed it, and the model on which it was made.

In the *Treatise on the Cessation of Oracles,* Cleombrotus relates an Egyptian myth which he declares he heard from a savage whom he met near the Red Sea. There exist, says he, one hundred and eighty-three worlds arranged in the shape of a triangle, sixty worlds forming each of the three sides, and one occupying each angle; in the centre of the triangle is the plain of truth where dwell motionless the Logoi, the forms and exemplars of what has been and what will be; all around is the *æon,* from which time flows forth over the world. Once in ten thousand years the souls of the just are permitted to contemplate these eternal truths, to which the most beautiful mysteries we can conceive here below are but a dream.[1]

All this closely recalls the myth of *Phædrus,*[2] penetrated and transformed by Alexandrine mythology: the æon is an Egyptian god with a Greek name who has become the patron of Alexandria[3]; his cult is reserved to initiates, and in this mystagogy the Logoi have taken the place of ideas, and we surely recognise a Gnostic imagination in those one hundred and eighty-three worlds!

In his *Treatise on Isis and Osiris,* Plutarch relates: Horus, accused by Typho of bastardy, is judged and absolved by Hermes. He interprets this myth as follows: Horus is the visible world; he is bastardised by the corporeal element which is involved in it, and is not pure and unmixed like his father the Logos; Hermes, i.e., the Logos, intervenes and pronounces the visible world to be truly the image of the world of ideas. The later victory of Horus and Hermes shows that the Logos has organised

[1] *De Def. orac.*, 21, 22. [2] *Phædr.*, 247c *sq.*
[3] Cf. NORDEN, *Die Geburt des Kindes*, 30, n. 1.

everything, and that he has, if not destroyed, at least wounded evil. Plutarch concludes by summing up all this myth in a Platonist formula: nature is composed of three elements: the world of ideas, matter, and a composition of both.[1]

We find in this passage the characteristic traits of the Platonist Logos: at once the idea and the instrument of God; the exemplar and the demiurge of the world. This represents the transposition into a dualist system of the two characteristics of the Stoic Logos, law and force.

A little further on, having to interpret the myth of Zeus set free by Isis, and escaping from the desert, Plutarch gives the following explanation: the spirit and the Logos of God was at first solitary, withdrawn into the invisible and impenetrable; he began to move and manifest himself in order to produce the world.[2] Here we already see a theory of the double state of the Logos, 'innate' (ἐνδιάθετος) and 'uttered' (προφορικός), analogous to what will be developed later by the Apologists.

The transcendence of the Logos is, however, affirmed more explicitly by Plutarch in a curious discussion on the plurality of worlds. Chrysippus had said that it was impossible that there should be more than one Zeus. And why so? retorts Plutarch: the different worlds and their respective masters might be governed by the providence of Zeus, and, just as various army corps obey one commander, so several worlds might be ruled by one Logos. The Stoics, he adds, shut up their gods in the world like bees in a hive; it is more worthy of their dignity to hold them to be independent and separate from the world.[3] This last remark gives very exactly the reason of the two opposed opinions: it is absurd for the Stoics to suppose the existence of several worlds without, at the same time, attributing to them several souls, i.e., several Logoi and several Zeus'; this consequence does not follow in the system of Plutarch; the same Logos can reach and govern a whole army of worlds.

We may also remark in this passage the new sense in which Plutarch identifies the Logos and providence. For Chrysippus the providence of Zeus was the law of nature, necessity, and destiny. For Plutarch, providence is the direction given to the world by the personal God who is

[1] *De Is. et Osir.*, 54–6. [2] *Ibid.*, 62. [3] *De Def. orac.*, 29.

external to it and guides it.[1] Plutarch indeed recognises a certain necessity; but it is in the sense in which Plato understood it in the *Timæus,* or Philo in the *Treatise of Dreams.*[2] This necessity is material nature with its inherent defects, and the obstacles it opposes to divine action. Far from being confused with the Logos, it is opposed to him as matter to spirit, or evil to good; it is one of the two principles recognised by Plutarch in the world.

This dualism is very clearly expressed in the *Treatise on Isis and Osiris:*

> 'The principle of the universe must not be placed in soulless bodies, as in the doctrine of Democritus and Epicurus, nor should we imagine, like the Stoics, a unique Logos and providence, organising the formless matter, which surrounds and rules everything. For it is impossible that anything should be evil where God is the cause of everything, or that anything should be good where he is the cause of nothing . . . It is an ancient belief of poets and philosophers, of gods and legislators, that the world is not given over to chance, without a Logos or guide, and that, on the other hand, there is not a single Logos, governing and directing everything . . . but that there is a great number of things partly good and partly evil; or, rather, to speak clearly, that nature here below produces nothing unmixed. . . . Everything then comes from two contrary principles, and two opposed powers, one leading us straight along a straight road, the other turning us aside, causing us to deviate; and thus life is mingled, and at least our earthly and sublunary world, if not the entire world, is unequal and varied, undergoing every sort of change. Since, too, nothing happens without a cause, and that good cannot be the cause of evil, we must suppose in nature a source and a principle of evil as well as of good.'[3]

As a result of this new metaphysics the theory of the Logos became seriously changed. The Logos is no longer the one and only principle of being, or even of life. The

[1] *De E.*, 9; *De Is. et Osir.*, 67. [2] *De Somniis*, II, 253.
[3] *De Isis et Osiris*, 45.

world has been made by God; but the substance and matter from which it has been drawn existed eternally; before receiving the Logos, they were not without movement and soul, but they were irrational. Just as God has not made the matter of the world, so he has not made its soul, but he has given it reason, intelligence, harmony, and what at first was nothing but necessity has become the rational soul of the world.[1] To-day, then, the world still undergoes this double influence of blind destiny and of reason; Euripides was wrong in saying: 'Zeus, necessity of nature *or* human intelligence'; he should have affirmed both at once, for the force which penetrates all beings is at once necessity and intelligence.[2] It follows that the Logos is not all-determining, and that many details escape his influence.[3]

Everywhere, then, a double principle must be distinguished: the Logos coming from God, and necessity coming from matter. A further very important consequence follows that the physical or moral law which directs all beings is not identical with their nature, but is communicated to and imposed upon them by a superior being. This theory is developed in a curious passage in which the Platonist concept of providence is clearly set out:

> 'If no part of the world behaves in a contrary manner to its own nature, but if each remains in its normal state without needing, even in its fundamental principle, any transference or change, I do not see what the task of providence can be, nor what the supreme artist, Zeus, can make or produce. For in an army tactics would be useless if every soldier knew for himself the rank, the place, the post which he has to occupy or defend.'[4]

It would be difficult, I think, to contradict more radically the theses of the Stoics; for them the only rôle of providence is to imprint on each being a natural tendency to the good of the whole; for Plutarch, on the other hand, providence supposes nature and its individual inclination to exist already; it subsequently intervenes to

[1] *De Animæ procr. in Tim.*, 6.
[2] *Ibid.*, 27.
[3] *De Stoic. repugn.*, 37.
[4] *De Fac. in orbe lun.*, 13.

correct deviations and rectify the direction. A little further on, he states without ambiguity:

> 'To say frankly what I think, no part of the universe taken in isolation has a place, a position, a movement of its own which can be called natural as such; but when anything accommodates itself and makes itself useful for the purpose for which it has been made, when it suffers, acts, or is found useful for the conservation, strength, and beauty of that other being with which it is connected, then, indeed, its position, movement, and the manner of its being, may be called natural.'[1]

To sum up, everything is subject to a double law: the law of individual nature, which can only bring disorder into the world; the supreme and more powerful law of the Logos or reason, which places different beings in a system, and makes them serve a higher end.[2] The Stoics had affirmed the identity of nature and the Logos; Plutarch. on the other hand, sees the opposition and the warfare between them; left to itself, nature is evil, it is the kingdom of Typho; when the Logos intervenes, he can dominate it, but not bring it into entire subjection. The same dualism is to be found in the soul of man, which is but a part of the soul of the world. It is a profound error to confuse reason and passion, and to see in the soul merely the Logos under different forms.[3] Even Chrysippus is forced to agree with this position, since he speaks of the submission of the virtues to the direction of the Logos, which obviously implies that the two terms are distinct.[4]

Material beings also obey two opposed principles. God, when organising them at their birth, has placed within them a Logos which maintains their internal harmony.[5] His providence has placed in everything principles of action, germs, λόγοι.[6] But these sparks are, as it were, buried in matter; in the heavens and the stars they are pure and immutable, but in material creatures they are dissolved, destroyed, and buried until they reappear and shine again in new productions. These are the limbs of Osiris, scattered and buried all over the land of Egypt and sought for by Isis.[7]

[1] *De Fac. in orbe lun.*, 14. [2] *Ibid.*, 13. [3] *De Virt. mor.*, 3. [4] *Ibid.*, 9. [5] *De Def. orac.*, 37. [6] *Ibid.*, 29. [7] *De Is. et Osir.*, 59.

Evidently the thesis of dualism does not occur casually in an isolated and doubtful page of Plutarch's treatise on *Isis and Osiris*[1]; it penetrates all his writings and determines the direction of his thoughts in morals, in psychology, as in physics. We find in him, much more than in Philo, the belief in the perpetual and universal conflict between good and evil, between spirit and matter; and we can foresee the point to which Greek logic and Alexandrine ascetism will soon bring it; neo-Platonism is already there in germ. It was necessary to insist at this point on this tendency, which will in time exercise a decisive influence on the Gnostic theology of the Trinity.

BIBLIOGRAPHY, Section 3:—J. H. Breasted, *Philosophy of a Memphite Priest*, in *Zeitschrift fur agyptische Sprache und Altertumskunde*, XXXIX (1901). G. Maspero, *Sur la toute-puissance de la parole*, in *Receuil des travaux relatifs à la philologie et à l'archéologie égyptiennes et assyriennes*, XXIV, 168–75 (1902). A. Moret, *Le Verbe créateur et révélateur en Égypte* (*Rev. de l'hist. des relig.*, LIX (1909). R. Reitzenstein, *Poimandres* (Leipzig, 1904). Walter Scott, *Hermetica* (2 vols., Oxford, 1924–5). O. Gruppe, *Die griechischen Culte u. Mythen in ihren Beziehungen zu den orientalischen Religionen* (Leipzig, 1887).

[1] See E. GUIMET, *Plutarque et l'Egypte*, p. 18.

CHAPTER III

The Spirit

The conception of the Spirit is much less fruitful and complex than that of the Logos. In Hellenic philosophy it never became disengaged from its materialist origins or got beyond the system of Stoicism; in that system, however, the part played by it is by no means negligible whether we consider the universal spirit, God, or the individual spirit, the human soul, or some of the relations uniting them, such as inspiration and divination. All these notions have their intrinsic importance and, as we shall see later, they were by no means without influence on the Christian theology of the Trinity.

Long before the Stoics the word spirit (πνεῦμα) was employed by the Greeks, both in the psychological sense to signify the human soul,[1] and in the physical to signify air or wind. In the physiological treatises of Aristotle it frequently indicates the air which animals breathe in or absorb by nutrition[2] and which becomes in them the principle of movement and sound, etc.[3] In a sense not far removed from this, doctors call πνεῦμα or πνεύματα the spirit to whose modifications they attribute the temperament and disposition of the body.[4]

The Stoics re-state and develop these different meanings.[5] For them the soul is a spirit composed of the flaming air[6] which is diffused throughout the whole body[7]; it is transmitted to children by their parents[8]; but, in the embryo, it is imperfect and can only communicate a vegetative life.[9] When the child is born and breathes, the outside air, uniting with the spirit within him, cools it, purifies it, and turns it into a soul.[10]

1 Cf. Epicharm., *ap.* Plut., *Consol. ad Apoll.*, 15. 2 *De spir.*, 1, 481 a 6.
3 *Hist. nat.*, IV, 535 b 23. 4 Erasistrat., *ap. Doxogr. gr.*, 441.
5 See L. Stein, *Die Psychologie der Stoa*, I, 23–39, 87–125.
6 Nemes., *De nat. hom.*, 2.
7 Chrys., *ap.* Galen., *De Hipp. et Plat. plac.*, 3, 1.
8 Ar. Did., *ap.* Euseb., *Pr. evang.*, XV, 20.
9 Galen., *Defin. med.*, 445. 10 Plut., *De Stoic. repugn.*, 41.

This soul, this πνεῦμα ἔμφυτον,[1] is divided into eight parts, the principal part (τὸ ἡγεμονικόν), the five senses, the powers of speech and of generation[2]; these diverse faculties are represented by the Stoics as prolongations of the soul which, extending from the heart, where it resides, to all the members, animates the different parts of the body and perceives exterior objects.[3] 'Just as,' says Chrysippus, 'the spider, sitting in the middle of its web, holds the ends of all the threads, and is thus warned of a fly falling into its net, so the chief part of the soul, placed in the centre of the body, i.e., the heart, is in touch with the extremities of all its senses and thus perceives all they transmit.'[4] We see how completely materialist are these conceptions; and, in point of fact, the Stoics spared no effort to force the acceptance of the materiality of the soul[5]; for we must not be deceived by the employment of the word 'spirit': in their language a 'spirit' (πνεῦμα, *spiritus*) is essentially a material being, and the precise proof of the materiality of the soul is the fact that it is a 'spirit.'[6]

These general notions of Stoic psychology and physiology are a necessary introduction to the study of the universal spirit. As a matter of fact, Stoic philosophers considered man as a microcosm, and they conceived the organism of the universe on the model of the human organism: God, who for them was the soul of the world, was consequently a spirit extended throughout the entire world, as our spirit is in our members, as the principle of cohesion, life, feeling, and reason.

This conception of the universal spirit was a creation of the Stoics: the works of Plato and Aristotle in which we find it are apocryphal,[7] as are also the treatises of Pythagoras and Empedocles, from which Sextus Empiricus quotes it.[8]

It is, moreover, intimately connected with the conceptions of God and of the Logos that have been explained above; it merely throws light on another aspect of the active principle of the universe which, as well as

[1] This expression, which is a technical one among the Stoics, is of Aristotelean origin; see Bonitz, *Index Aristotel.*, 606 a 46 *sq.*

[2] Chalcid., *In Tim.*, 220.

[3] Aetius, *Plac.*, IV, 8, 1 (Doxog., 394). Phil., *De fuga*, 182

[4] *Ap.* Chalcid., *loc. cit.* (*Fr. st.*, II, 879).

[5] Stein, *loc. cit.*, 110, 112.

[6] Sext. Empir., *Pyrrh. Hyp.*, 2, 81.

[7] Ps. Plat., *Axioch.*, 10 (370 c).

[8] *Math.*, 9, 127.

being divine and reasonable, is also, when considered in its physical and material being, spirit, i.e., air on fire.[1]

The Stoics confirmed this thesis by physical arguments: the world as it exists actually is made up of two principles, one active, the other passive; of the four elements two, air and fire, are active; the other two, earth and water, are passive;[2] the soul of the world, then, is made of air and fire, but air and fire combined are spirit.[3]

We thus get a physical explanation of the rôle attributed to the active principle of the universe, whether it be called God or Logos. Cicero told us, as we have seen, that rational nature is, as it were, a chain which maintains the cohesion of every body and binds them together. The conception of the spirit throws light upon this property of the Logos frequently affirmed by Philo. The proper rôle of this divine element is to maintain (συνέχειν) all those beings who, having no spontaneous consistency, would without it become scattered and disintegrated.[4] If the question is asked, how spirit comes to possess this energy and force of cohesion, the Stoics reply that it results from its tension (τόνος, tonicity)[5]:

> 'Consider,' says Seneca, 'what a powerful and hidden force is concealed in those tiny grains of sand, so small that they find room in the crevices of stones; eventually they succeed in splitting great rocks apart and destroying monuments; the tiniest and most attenuated roots split rocks and blocks of stone. How does this happen if not from the tension of the spirit, without which nothing is strong and against which nothing can prevail? That there is unity in the air is sufficiently evident from the very cohesion of our bodies. For what maintains this cohesion if not the spirit? What puts our soul in movement? What is this movement, if not tension? Whence comes this tension if not from the unity of the whole, and this unity, if not from the air? What makes the crops shoot forth, and the slender ear of wheat emerge from its

[1] Sext. Empir., *Pyrrh. Hyp.*, 3, 218.
[2] Nemes., *De nat. hom.*, 5.
[3] See Alex. Aphrodis., *De mixt.*, 224, 14.
[4] Alex. Aphrod., *De mixt.*, ed. Bruns, p. 224.
[5] Plut., *De comm. not.*, 49.

> sheaf, what clothes the trees in their greenery, spreads their branches or points them to the sky, but the tension and the unity of the spirit?'[1]

Just as matter, being inert, is only kept in existence by the spirit, similarly, being without form, it receives from the spirit all its qualities. Its specification comes from the greater or less degree of tension: as has been said above of the Logos, whether the spirit is simply form (ἕξις) or nature (φύσις) or force (ὁρμή) or reason (λόγος) or virtue (ἀρετή), the being sustained by it is an inanimate body, or a plant, or an animal, or a man, or a sage,[2] Accidental qualities, such as resistance, colour, heat,[3] and likewise goodness, virtue, wisdom,[4] are also spirits diffused through matter and diversifying it.

Conformably to their habits of exegesis, the Stoics personify these spirits in the different gods of mythology:

> 'The spirit who engenders and feeds is Dionysos, the spirit who strikes and breaks is Herakles, the spirit who receives is Ammon, the spirits pervading the earth and vegetation are Demeter and Core, and the spirit who pervades the sea is Poseidon.'[5]

We should not see here an animist conception, transforming the forces of nature into personal and immaterial beings; none of these spirits has any more individual and independent existence than our faculties and senses have in us. All of them are but extensions of the principal spirit, its ramifications throughout the whole universe, in order to maintain and animate it.

The result of this extension of spirit is to assure the unity of consciousness and direction in the universe, as in man; all these perceptions are transmitted to the principal spirit ἡγεμονικόν,[6] from whom also come all impulses. This produces in the entire world that harmony, that conspiracy of forces, or, to use Stoic language, that sympathy, which forces itself, as they think, upon every observer, and which is for them the best proof of the unity of the divine spirit.[7] They had multiplied

[1] *Quæst. nat.*, II, 6. [2] See above, page 48.
[3] Plut., *De Stoic. repugn.*, 43. [4] Stob., *Ecl.*, II, 64, 18.
[5] Plut., *De Is.*, 40. [6] Cf. Stein, p. 33, n. 42; Zeller, IV, 137.
[7] Cic., *De Nat. Deor.*, II, 7, 19.

their observations to establish the truth of its existence,[1] for which they deemed the evidence to be so irresistible that ignorance alone could escape it[2]; they were, moreover, sustained in their faith by Oriental astrology which also taught this doctrine of universal 'sympathy.'[3] They made numerous converts to it; many philosophers and men of science, who did not adhere to their system as a whole, admitted, as a fact, this harmony of all beings throughout the whole world.[4]

We can understand what advantages the Stoics obtained from such a concession; by means of it they authorised their theory of omens. Everything is connected in nature; there is, then, a necessary connection between events which one predicts and the signs which announce them, as, for instance, the direction of the flight of birds, or the state of the entrails of a victim of sacrifice.[5] This connection may be observed, and divination becomes in this way an exact science.[6]

Still more precious than this magical technique and more immediately consecrated by the Stoic principles, is the faculty of knowing the future; every human soul possesses this faculty by the very fact of its unity with the universal spirit.[7] No doubt we do not always enjoy the exercise of this power, because our soul is too distracted by our body, and the thousand anxieties of material life; but the soul recovers its natural privilege of divination:

> 'when it is entirely emancipated, that is, when it has no longer any relation with the body. This is what happens in inspiration and in time of sleep . . . The soul of an inspired person, despising the body, flies away from it, and, under the action of the fire which heats and excites it, it sees the events which it predicts. . . . What happens to the inspired one when awake, happens also to us when asleep; our soul, when dreaming, is in its full strength, free of the senses and emancipated from worries, the body being motionless as a corpse.'[8]

[1] Cic., *De divin.*, II, 14, 33–4. [2] Cic., *De Nat. Deor.*, II, 46, 119.
[3] Cf. Cumont, *Les religions orientales*, 207.
[4] Cic., *De divin.*, II, 14, 33.
[5] *Ibid.*, I, 52, 118. [6] Cf. *Fr. st.*, II, 1207–13.
[7] Chalcid., *in Tim.*, 251; Cic., *De divin.*, I, 30; *ibid.*, 49, 110.
[8] Chalcid., *in Tim.*, 50–51, 113–115.

This theory, following logically from the rest of the system, does not conceive of inspiration as of an action exerted by a personal God on the soul, but as the spontaneous exercise of a natural energy, which the body usually obstructs, but which from time to time emancipates itself.

In the same passage Cicero adds: 'I also think that exhalations coming from the earth can fill the spirit of diviners and cause them to give forth oracles.'[1] This explanation also is quite consistent with the Stoic system; just as the first contact with the air by breathing perfects the spirit of the infant and transforms it into a human soul,[2] so the exhalations of the earth may unite with the spirit of the diviner or of the pythoness, thereby giving him or her more purity and clairvoyance. This explanation is developed at length by Plutarch in purely Stoic terms, in his treatise on *The Cessation of Oracles* (ch. xxxix *seq.*); there is, he thinks, in the soul a faculty of divination, the exercise of which is usually obstructed by the body; the vaporous current of divination which comes from the earth, purifies the spirit, and, like iron plunged into water, it acquires more strength and tonicity.[3] Even so, the subject must be adapted to receive this contact,[4] and the exhalation itself be in full force, for it wears out like everything else here below.[5]

This explanation is simple and consistent with the Stoic system as a whole; but it entirely destroys the religious character of inspiration. Plutarch is aware of this, and mentions it as an objection (xlvi). He replies that he merely intended to give the immediate explanation of the physical phenomenon, without forgetting that the earth has received these properties from the gods, and that demons administer them (xlviii). In another treatise, however, he proposes a more religious theory of inspiration: the soul of the pythoness is the instrument of the god, and two movements can be distinguished in her ecstasy; one which she undergoes, the other which comes from her own nature; and, indeed, her oracles, although inspired by the God, depend for their form and composition on the education of the pythoness.[6] In this theory inspiration is

[1] Chalcid., *in Tim.*, 50, 115.
[2] See above, p. 61.
[3] Plut., *op. cit.*, chaps. xl and xli.
[4] Plut., *op. cit.*, ch. li.
[5] *Ibid.*
[6] *Ibid.*, ch. xxi *seq.*

explained not by a material shock or contact, but by the influence of a superior spirit which moves the human soul. This conception, foreign to Stoicism, is widely spread at this date[1]; we shall find it again in Philo.[2]

Seneca is more faithful than Plutarch to the Stoic conception; the theory of spirit in his case remains materialist and pantheist, as certain passages from his work quoted above[3] have shown us. But often it assumes a religious aspect very similar to the theory of the Logos which we shall see later in Marcus Aurelius. The human spirit, an emanation of the universal spirit, is represented as our host, our supervisor, our guardian: 'He treats us as we ourselves treat him'[4]: 'He converses with us, but he remains united to his principle'[5]: reason is nothing else than a part of the divine spirit dwelling in our body[6]: 'You are surprised,' says he to Lucilius, 'that man approaches the gods? God approaches men, and what is still more intimate, he dwells within them: without the presence of God no soul is good. Divine seed has been sown in the bodies of men; if well cultivated it corresponds to its origin and is equal to the source from which it comes.'[7]

We know that these religious expressions have more than once given rise to an illusion as to their true significance and origin: they have furnished the proof of the Christianity of Seneca and his dependence on St. Paul.[8] It was a strange error: this *pars divini spiritus mersa in corpus humanum* has nothing in common with the Holy Spirit of Christian dogma; it is a material emanation coming from the universal spirit[9]; but, by a religious fiction in keeping with the system, Seneca, like Marcus Aurelius, establishes a distinction between us and this emanation which is, nevertheless, our soul; at times both of them describe it as a god carried in us, venerated and obeyed by us, and at other times as a deposit to be preserved, or a seed to be fructified. In these religious conceptions, unauthorised by the metaphysics of the system, we can see a deep-seated and powerful instinct at work, an instinct which materialistic pantheism could no longer satisfy.

[1] Cf. LUCAN, *Pharsale*, V, 120 *seq.* These and similar texts are in H. LIETZMANN's *Handbuch zum N. T.*, III (Tubingen, 1919), 79.

[2] See below, pp. 139, 140.

[3] *Cons. ad Helv.*, 8; *Quæst. nat.*, II, 6.

[4] *Ep.*, 41, 2.

[5] *Ibid.*

[6] *Ep.*, 66, 12; cf. 120, 15.

[7] *Ep.*, 73, 16.

[8] See LIGHTFOOT, *Philippians*, 270–333: *St. Paul and Seneca.*

[9] SENECA, *Ep.*, 57, 8; cf. EPICTET., *Diss.*, I, 14, 6.

Christianity was to find strength in this need of souls; it was to find obstacles and dangers in the different philosophic conceptions that we have discussed. It is difficult for us, two thousand years later, to see this conflict of doctrines in its true perspective. After the laborious analysis by which we reconstruct the principal religious theories which might have affected the dogma of the Trinity, we are able to see such a profound contrast between the two sets of doctrines that it is well-nigh impossible for us to admit the danger of ambiguity, still less the possibility of compromise. What relationship can there be between the Word, Son of God, and this Logos, force and law of the world, germ of life in each of us, principle of thought and moral law? How is it possible to confound the Holy Spirit, the Paraclete, with this burning air which penetrates all beings, which encloses them all, and animates them? In the second century this contrast was not so obvious; Stoic theories were familiar to cultivated minds, and Christian dogmas almost unknown; thus, hearing of a God who filled the whole universe, of an incarnate Logos, of a Spirit dwelling in each of us, they readily interpreted all that in a Stoical sense, of a material soul penetrating the world and animating man.

Even in the Church misunderstanding was not always avoided, and we shall recognise in the theology of more than one ecclesiastical writer traces of these philosophies which he had professed in his youth and still saw reigning around him. Stoicism, for instance, can be recognised in the often unfortunate attempts to Christianise the theory of the seminal word, or the theory of the double state of the Word, interior and manifested; Stoicism will also still more often be found checking the flight of Christian thought by loading it with its material imaginations. Tertullian, for instance, who thinks himself so emancipated from all philosophy, could not escape its clutches; doubtless few theologians remained so dependent as he on Stoic conceptions, but some, who are remote from the system, here and there betray its influence. It would seem that we must, at least partly, attribute to such habits of thought and language the slowness with which the theology of the Holy Spirit developed, and the too-often impersonal character of the terms used to designate the third Person of the Trinity.

Platonism, as we have already found it in Plutarch and will shortly discover it in Philo, had a still deeper and more dangerous influence. Minds formed in that school represented the divine world as a hierarchy, the supreme being disappearing in the infinite and only perceptible in ecstasy, and beneath him intermediary beings, the Logos, powers, gods, demons, united to him by mysterious bonds and condescending to men to raise them from the earth to the heavens. This schematic conception was applied to all mythologies and had transformed them without difficulty. The attempt was also made on Christianity ; it appears in the imagination of the Gnostics, interposing innumerable æons between God and matter, it is even found in several Church writers, principally Origen, dissolving the Trinity into three unequal deities, of unequal rank.

At this period of compromise, in which nothing is to be seen but eclecticism in philosophy and syncretism in religion, the Church needed a more than human strength to preserve the uncompromising transcendence of her faith, to defend the purity of her dogma against her enemies, and sometimes indeed against her own doctors. The three first centuries of our era tell us how long and cruel were these struggles ; the fourth demonstrates their fruitfulness.

Book II

THE JEWISH PREPARATION

CHAPTER I

The Old Testament

If Christian theology was developed in a Hellenic environment, Christianity itself was born in Judaism; to discover the origin of its doctrines, we must study the beliefs of Judaism. Various relations may be discovered between them: certain Christian dogmas—for instance, the dogmas of creation and of the resurrection of the body, are established in the earlier dispensation; others, on the other hand, were unknown to the Jews, although, in spite of their ignorance of the fact, they were being prepared by God for the revelation which Christ was to bring them. Among these must be placed the dogma of the Trinity.[1]

We may here transcribe the justly celebrated page in which St. Gregory Nazianzen recalls this ignorance and describes this preparation.

> 'The Old Testament clearly manifested the Father, but only obscurely the Son. The New Testament revealed the Son, and implied the divinity of the Spirit. To-day the Spirit dwells among us and makes himself more clearly known. For it would have been dangerous, when the divinity of the Father was not recognised, to preach openly the message of the Son, and, as long as the divinity of the Son was not admitted, to impose, if I may use the term, as an extra, the Holy Spirit. One might have feared that the faithful, like people who have eaten too much or have fixed their feeble eyes too closely on the sun, would lose even what they were capable of bearing; it was necessary that, increasing little by little, and, as David says, by ascensions from glory to glory, the full splendour of the Trinity should gradually shine forth.'[2]

[1] Cf. Note I, p. 415.
[2] *Orat. theol.*, V, 26 (*P.G.*, XXXVI, 161). Cf. *ibid.*, 25 (160).

This text is of capital importance and throws light on several points of the history of the dogma of the Trinity. If, when studying this subject, we think we find some obscurity in the New Testament theology of the Holy Spirit, we should recall these wise words of the Theologian of Nazianzus: 'The New Testament revealed to us the Son and implied the divinity of the Spirit.'

For the moment, our investigation is directed to the Old Testament; we do not ask of history to discover there what the most illustrious Fathers of the Church did not see; and, without looking in the books of the Jews for a revelation which God reserved to Christians, we will sketch the growth of the religious ideas by which he prepared his people for the revelation of the Trinity.

1. God

Ezechiel, to teach his nation to understand her ingratitude, reminds her (ch. xvi, 3) how God has drawn her out of the greatest misery; the child of an Amorrhite father and a mother from the land of Ceth, she lay on the ground abandoned in the defilement of her birth, and God has raised her up and made her live. Is not this a striking image of the religious abjection from which God converted her? When the Fathers speak of the revelation of the Trinity, they do not hesitate to recall the falls and idolatry of the nation, to mark the distance which has been covered by God's act, and also the providential reasons of his delay and slowness of manifestation.[1]

There can be no question here of retracing, in its entirety, the slow religious education of Israel. So vast a panorama would be too large for the scale of this study: here we propose to describe only the immediate preparation by which God led his people to the revelation of the Trinity; it is therefore only in the last phase of its development, i.e., after their return from exile, that we shall study the progress of the idea of God.

All idolatrous worship had been abolished by that time. We read in the Greek text of the book of *Judith* (viii, 18): 'There is to-day no tribe, no race, no family, no town, which adores gods made by human hands as of

[1] Chrysost., *De incomprehens.*, 5, 3 (*P.G.*, XLVIII, 740).

old.' For some time, Hellenic domination had stained the purity of this Monotheism: in the ranks of the army of Judas Machabeus, soldiers were found carrying votive objects consecrated to idols.[1] But the ensuing national reaction gave more vigour and vehemence to faith in the one only God. The sacred authors multiply their satirical attacks on idolatry; the letter of Jeremias, which is quoted in the sixth chapter of Baruch, describes with pitiless precision all the miseries of false gods; they can protect themselves neither from rust nor moth, they need dusting from time to time by their attendants; their eyes are completely blinded by dust; they hold in their hands a sword or an axe, yet they cannot defend themselves from robbers; they have to be locked up like prisoners for their own defence; they cannot rise if they fall, nor avenge themselves if they are affronted, nor punish their worshippers who fail to keep their promises. We find similar remarks in Ps. cxiii: 'The idols of the Gentiles are silver and gold, the works of the hands of men. They have mouths and speak not: they have eyes and see not. They have ears and hear not: they have noses and smell not. They have hands and feel not, they have feet and walk not: neither shall they cry out through their throat. Let them that make them become like unto them.' This nothingness of idols is frequently affirmed and described both in the book of the *Jubilees*[2] and in the book of *Henoch*.[3] It is also one of the favourite themes of the Jews of the Dispersion: it is developed at length in the book of *Wisdom*,[4] and frequently mentioned in the Sibylline Books, particularly the third.[5] It is quite intelligible that the situation of the Jews of the Dispersion forced them to a greater vigilance and made these warnings more necessary; moreover, this polemic against idolatry was more offensive than defensive; the Jews were conscious of the superiority of their religion, they were impatient to spread it, and in their attacks on idolatry they were sustained by the most enlightened Pagan opinion,[6] at the same time that,

[1] 2 *Mach.*, xii, 40.
[2] Translated by Kautsch; xii, 2, 3; xx, 7, 8; xxii, 18.
[3] Translated by Martin; xlvi, 7; xci, 9; xcix, 7.
[4] *Wisd.*, xiii, 10–xiv, 31.
[5] *Orac. Sibyll.*, III, 13, 31, 58, 279, 547 *sq.*, 586 *sq.*, 605; collected by J. Geffken in his *Oracles sibyllins*.
[6] See above, page 11.

though unconsciously, they were preparing the road for Christian apologists.[1]

Still better than literature, historical facts show us the profound aversion of the people from idolatry.[2] Herod had placed a golden eagle on the great door of the Temple, the people cast it down[3]; Pilate provoked a revolt by ordering his troops to enter Jerusalem bearing images of the Emperors[4]; to avoid a similar revolt, Vitellius, on his way from Antioch to Petra, yielding to the objections of the Jews, made a long circuit rather than cross the soil of Palestine.[5] When Caligula wished to place his statue in the Temple at Jerusalem popular emotion was such that Petronius, the governor of Syria, desisted; we should read Philo's long account[6] of this affair to perceive, beneath a somewhat rhetorical form, the sincere and profound indignation of his faith.

This faith is expressed in the verse of *Deuteronomy* (vi, 4), which the Jews recite every day at the beginning of their prayers: 'Hear, O Israel, the Lord our God is one Lord.' According to the Rabbinical tradition, the accent should be placed on the word 'one,' and it is said that, when Aqiba was put to death, he kept up his courage by the repetition of that sacred word, 'ONE.'[7]

This monotheistic faith was very inspiring and an efficacious preparation for Christianity. Similarly, when our Lord was asked which was the first Commandment, he replied: 'Hear, O Israel, the Lord thy God is one God' (*Mark* xii, 29). Unfortunately the Jews were soon to make an obstinate use of these holy words in their conflict with Christianity: in the Talmud, Trinitarian faith is refuted on the grounds of polytheism by this verse of Deuteronomy.[8]

At the date of which we are speaking, the decisive test has not yet been applied; Christ has not appeared, and the monotheism of the Jews is not yet in opposition to the dogma of the Trinity; on the contrary, that Monotheism was a preparation for belief in the Trinity by

[1] Cf. FRIEDLAENDER, *Gesch. d. jud. Apologetik*, 82 *sq.*

[2] Cf. SCHUERER, II, 68.

[3] JOSEPHUS, *Ant. Jud.*, XVII, 6, 2, 3; *Bell. Jud.*, I, 33, 2, 3.

[4] *Ant. Jud.*, XVIII, 3, 1.

[5] *Ibid.*, XVIII, 5, 3.

[6] *Legat. ad Caium*, *M.* II, 573–97.

[7] WEBER, *Judische Theologie*, 151.

[8] *Ibid.*, 152 *sq.*

widening the conception of God, and making it more universal and less national.

It is true that even before the exile, Jahve was already recognised and preached as the all-powerful God: he chases away the fly from the river of Egypt, and the bee from the land of Assur[1]; the nations are not only the instruments, but also the subjects of his justice: in his name Jeremias threatens Edom, Moab, Ammon, Tyre, and Sidon:

> 'I made the earth and the men and the beasts that are upon the face of the earth . . . and I have given it to whom it seemed good in my eyes; now I have given all these lands into the hand of Nabuchodonosor, King of Babylon, my servant.'[2]

After the exile it became customary to call Jahve God of heaven,[3] God of heaven and earth,[4] Lord of heaven,[5] King of the ages,[6] Master of the world,[7] God and Master of all,[8] King of the whole creation.[9]

These are not empty epithets, and Persian influence is not enough to explain their use; they express one of the beliefs most dear to Israel, the universal domain of the creative God. Jewish piety, already fully formed and penetrated with the spirit of the Psalms, loves to find its nourishment in this thought that the whole world created by God belongs to him, and is filled by him. 'Thine is the day and thine is the night: thou hast made the morning light and the sun. Thou hast made all the borders of the earth: the summer and the spring were formed by thee.'[10] He it is who gives grass to the flocks, bread and life to men, everything here below expects its food from him; he opens his hand and everything is enriched; if he turns his head away everything is overthrown; if he withdraws his spirit all things return to dust.[11] This action of God reaches us everywhere. 'Whither shall I flee from

[1] *Is.*, vii, 18; v, 26. Cf. KAUTSCH, Religion of Israel, in *DB*, v, 680.

[2] *Jer.*, xxvii, 5.

[3] 1 *Esdras*, v, 12, etc., 2 *Esdras*, i, 4, 5, *Jonas*, i, 9, *Daniel*, ii, 18, etc., 1 *Mach.*, iii, 18 (in the *Codex Sinaiticus*).

[4] 1 *Esdras*, v, 11; *Tobias*, x, 13 (*Sinaiticus*).

[5] *Dan.* v, 23; 2 *Mach.* xv, 23; *Tob.* i, 18 (*Sinaiticus*).

[6] *Tob.* xiii, 10.

[7] 2 *Mach.* xiii, 15.

[8] *Ecclus.* xxxvi, 1.

[9] *Judith*, ix, 12.

[10] *Ps.* lxxiii, 16.

[11] *Pss.* ciii, 13 *seq.*; lxiii, 10 *seq.*; cxliv, 15 *seq.*; cxlvi, 8 *seq.*

thy face? If I ascend into heaven thou art there; if I descend into hell thou art present; if I take my wings early in the morning and dwell in the uttermost parts of the sea, even there also shall thy hand lead me: and thy right hand shall hold me.'[1] This same belief in the universal presence of God is expressed in a more Hellenic style by the author of the *Book of Wisdom:* 'The spirit of the Lord hath filled the whole world' (i, 7), and again: 'O how good and sweet is thy spirit, O Lord, in all things' (xii, 1). He who believed in the absolute and sovereign dominion of God could not conceive his reign as exclusively national, but rather as universal. No doubt official Judaism never became cosmopolitan in the sense of Philo[2]; it never renounced the privileged hopes of Israel, nor forgot the preferences of Jahve for the people whom he had chosen, his paternal affection for his 'first-born.'[3] But the other nations also belonged to him; his reign extends over them and one day they will know this.[4]

The Dispersion, in scattering Israel among the nations and collecting groups of proselytes round her synagogues, revived these hopes and desires. Malachias hails this time when he writes (i, 11): 'From the rising of the sun even to the going down, my name is great among the Gentiles; and in every place there is sacrifice and there is offered to my name a clean oblation. For my name is great among the Gentiles, saith the Lord of Hosts.' This 'clean oblation' cannot be the idolatrous sacrifice offered by the Pagans, for which prophets and hagiographers have nothing but horror; it is rather a pure and holy worship offered by the nations after they have submitted to the reign of God.[5] At the same time that this dominion of God is more definitely recognised as universal, it is also more vividly felt to be individual, directly reaching every man. After Jeremias, and particularly after Ezechiel,[6] this thought of the providence and judgment of God ruling over each man is constantly present to Jewish piety.[7]

[1] *Ps.* cxxxviii, 7. [2] See below, page 141 *seq.*

[3] Compare the two passages of *Esther*: xiii, 9 and xiv, 3.

[4] Cf. LAGRANGE, *Le Messianisme*, 154–7.

[5] Cf. LAGRANGE, *RB* (1906), 80; and VAN HOONACKER, *op. cit. infra*, 712–4.

[6] See KITTEL, art. *Spruche*, in *RE*, XVIII, 693.

[7] *Ps.* lxi, 13; *Prov.* xxiv, 12; *Ecclus.* xvi, 12; xvi, 14; xviii, 1; xxv, 15, 24.

Belief in creation spontaneously leads in that direction, as it also leads to the conception of God's universal reign. Hence those accents of confidence contained in so many Psalms: 'Jahve is my light, my rock, my strength'; hence the assurance given by the mother of the Machabees to her martyred sons: 'I beseech thee, my son, look upon heaven and earth and all that is in them: and consider that God made them out of nothing, and mankind also: so thou shalt not fear this tormentor.'[1] Hence, finally, that unshakeable hope untroubled even by Sheol:

> 'For what have I in heaven? And besides thee what do I desire upon earth?
>
> For thee my flesh and my heart hath fainted away. Thou art the God of my heart, and the God that is my portion for ever.
>
> For behold they that go far from thee shall perish: thou hast destroyed all them that are disloyal to thee.
>
> But it is good for me to adhere to my God, to put my hope in the Lord God.'[2]

Father Lagrange writes[3]:

> 'We will not weaken by any commentary these words, the most beautiful of the Old Testament. . . . God alone is before the Psalmist, and he wants no one else. If his flesh and his heart are consumed, it is no doubt because they are associated with his hope. To be with God in heaven or on earth is enough. There is no cosmogony here. God is the abode of souls. We are at the heart of the faith of Israel.'

Are we not also on the threshold of the Christian faith? Do we not recognise its accents in these appeals to the fatherly mercy of God for man whom he has created: 'As a father hath compassion on his children, so hath the Lord compassion on them that fear him: for he knoweth our frame. He remembereth that we are dust.'[4] That God is father of the just is only suggested in this passage through a comparison; in the book of *Isaias* (lxiv, 8 *seq.*) Israel said with more assurance: 'And now, O Lord, thou art our Father, and we are clay: and thou art our maker,

[1] 2 *Mach.* vii, 27, 28. [2] *Ps.* lxxii, 25–28. [3] *RB* (1905), 195.
[4] *Ps.* cii, 13, 14; cf. 4 *Esdras*, viii, 6 *seq.*

and we all are the works of thy hands. Be not very angry, O Lord, and remember no longer our iniquity: behold, see we are all thy people.' The reason is that the two conceptions were not equally developed at the same date: at the beginning, and very often, God appears as the father of Israel; it is only quite late and very occasionally that he is represented as the father of the just.[1]

In *Exodus* (iv, 22) we read: 'Thus saith the Lord: Israel is my son, my firstborn.'[2] *Deuteronomy*[3] and the prophetic books[4] often repeat this word. God is the father of the entire people, he is also the father of the Israelites taken singly: and this is his title to filial veneration[5]; he recalls them to himself when they have sinned.[6] They, for their part, address him as sons, and appeal to his fatherly mercy.[7] In later days, the infidelity of many Israelites brings about the distinction among the people, who, as a whole, are sons of God: the impious who no longer belong to him, and the just who may still call him their Father. This conception is made most clear in the *Book of Wisdom;* the impious say, when speaking of the just man (*Wisd.* ii, 16-18): 'He glorieth that he hath God for his father; let us see then if his words be true and let us prove what shall happen to him: for if he be the true son of God, he will defend him and deliver him from the hands of his enemies.'

The test over, the impious cry out in disappointment (v, 5): 'Behold how they are numbered among the children of God, and their lot is among the Saints.'

Further on, the just man speaks and says with assurance to God (xiv, 3): 'But thy providence, O Father, governeth it.'[8] These passages already strike a Gospel note; the first indeed resembles the narration of the Passion in so startling a degree that many of the Fathers have indicated their prophetic character[9] and certain contemporary

[1] Cf. LAGRANGE, *La paternité de Dieu dans l'ancien Testament* (*RB*, 1908, 481–99); DALMAN, *Die Worte Jesu*, I, 150–9; JACKSON and LAKE, *op. cit. infra*, I, 392 *seq*.

[2] See DALMAN, *loc. cit.*, 150.

[3] *Deut.* xiv, 1; xxxii, 5, 6.

[4] *Is.* i, 4, xxx, 9, etc.; *Osee* ii, 1, xi, 1; *Jer.* iii, 4, etc.; *Mal.* ii, 10.

[5] *Mal.* ii, 10.

[6] *Jer.* iii, 14, 22.

[7] *Is.* lxiv, 7 *seq.*

[8] In this same book (xviii, 13), the people of Israel itself is called 'son of God.'

[9] DEANE, in his note on this passage (pp. 119, 120), gives many quotations, including AUGUSTINE, *De civ Dei*, xvii, 20.

critics have preferred, contrary to all probability, to regard the passage as an interpolation.[1] Several analogous texts, though less definite, are to be found in *Ecclesiasticus* (xxiii, 1, 4; li, 10)[2] and in the third book of *Machabees* (v, 7; vi, 8; vii, 6); but it is only in the Gospel that the dogma of the divine Paternity will be fully displayed, and that the spirit of Christ will make the proper filial prayer of the Christian rise to God from the heart of the just.[3]

Bibliography, Section 1:—W. Bousset, *Die Religion des Judentums* (3rd ed. by H. Gressman, Tubingen, 1926). M. J. Lagrange, *Le règne de Dieu dans l'A. T.* and *Le règne de Dieu dans le judaisme*, in *RB* (1908). A. van Hoonacker, *Les douze petits prophètes* (Paris, 1908). F. Jackson and K. Lake, *The Beginnings of Christianity* (London, 1920). E. Grafe, *Das Verhaltniss der pauln. Schriften zur Sapientia Salomonis* (*Theol. Abhandlungen C. v. Weizacker gewidmet*, 1892). F. Focke, *Die Entstehung der Weisheit Salomons* (Gottingen, 1913).

2. *The Spirit*[4]

The conceptions of the Spirit, of Wisdom, of the Word are attached to the idea of God in the Old Testament; and if these various obscure and elementary conceptions are not sufficient of themselves to constitute a doctrine of the Trinity, they at least prepare the soul for the Christian revelation.[5]

We must begin by examining the belief in the Spirit of God, which was the first conception to appear. The sacred writers represent the Spirit as a divine force, or, rather, as God himself in his action on man and the universe; and, inasmuch as the divine energy is more particularly manifested in the production and conservation of life, the Spirit is often regarded as a vivifying principle. In the first chapter of *Genesis* the Spirit appears as brooding upon the waters in order to fill them with life (*Gen.*, 1-2). Later on, God, seeing that man is but flesh, is not willing that his Spirit should dwell for ever in him, and fixes a limit to his life (*Gen.* vi, 3). If God withdraws his Spirit everything fails and falls into

[1] See Deane, p. 121. Cf. Grafe, *op. cit. infra*, 251–86; Focke, *op. cit. infra*, 113–26, opposes Grafe.

[2] At the beginning of the prayer in *Ecclus.* li, 1, the Hebrew text has 'my God, my Father,' which appears to be a gloss.

[3] For the concept of God as father of the Messias, see below, page 100; on the Divine paternity in Rabbinical Judaism, see below, page 109.

[4] For general bibliography, see below. [5] See Heinisch, *opp. cit. infra.*

dust ; if he sends out his Spirit all things are created and the face of the earth is renewed.[1] There is a tendency to oppose the flesh to the Spirit: the flesh is infirmity and nothingness, the Spirit is the life-giving force which comes from God.[2] Hence comes in *Numbers* the name given to God: ' The God of the spirits of all flesh.[3]

We find the same idea again in the vision of Ezechiel (xxxvii, 8-10). On the dry bones in the vision of the Prophet the flesh and the nerves are re-made, the skin covers them, but the bodies lie inert, for they have no spirit. At a fresh command of the Prophet the spirit rushes towards them on the four winds of heaven, and reanimates this great army.[4] In the same way, in the second book of the *Machabees* (vii, 23), the mother promises to her martyr-children that God will restore to them ' the spirit and the life.'[5]

In this last text the spirit spoken of is no longer the Spirit of God, but the vital spirit which is in man ; these two conceptions are intimately connected, but their connection is quite different from what it is in Stoic physics : here the spirit is not a divine substance identical with the universe and animating it, nor is it a particle of divinity dwelling in creatures ; in them it is a vital principle, depending indeed on the divine Spirit, but distinct from him ; in God, it is the force which gives life to everything, or, rather, it is God himself considered as acting, as creating, as vivifying.[6]

This conception of the life-giving Spirit will reappear in the New Testament, transformed, as the conception of life itself: the characteristic action of the Spirit will no longer have for its limit the natural life which we lead here below, but eternal life initiated at present in sanctity, consummated in heaven in glory. Judaism sketches only in outline this transformation of the concept of life, and in those books which mention belief in

[1] *Ps.* ciii, 29, 30 ; cf. xxxii, 6, cxlv, 4 ; *Is.* xxxii, 15 ; *Job* xii, 10, xxxiv, 14, 15 ; *Zach.* xii, 1.

[2] *Is.* xxxi, 3.

[3] *Num.* xvi, 22 ; cf. xxvii, 16.

[4] This is not the only place where the Spirit is symbolized by a wind, but one need not agree with Wendt (*Fleisch und Geist*, 18) that the Hebrews considered the wind as something immaterial.

[5] Cf. *ibid.*, xiv, 46 ; *Judith*, xvi, 14 (17).

[6] Cf. Smend, *Alttestamentl. Religionsgesch.*,[2] p. 444 ; Sokolowski, *Geist und Leben*, 202.

the resurrection of the body and the future life, it does not appear that this renewal and expansion of life is attributed especially to the Spirit of God.

Another aspect of the doctrine of the Spirit completed the aspect we have just outlined, and the two conceptions in their mutual influence and development blended in Christian theology: extraordinary gifts, or charismata, of which we must now speak, will appear as a manifestation of life in the Spirit.

In the case of the most ancient heroes of the Bible, their more clearly divine actions are attributed to the Spirit of God: if Joseph can interpret the dreams of Pharao, it is because he is 'full of the Spirit of God,' he governs the people wisely by the same Spirit.[1] The seventy ancients, chosen by Moses to assist him in the government of the people, are to receive from God a participation in the Spirit which Moses has already been given.[2] It is again to the Spirit that the physical strength of Samson is attributed when he goes down to Thamnatha with his father and mother; he meets a lion and the Spirit of Jahve comes on him and he tears the lion to pieces like a kid.[3] In another passage Gedeon, clothed with the Spirit of Jahve, leads to battle his three hundred men, and conquers Madian and Amalec[4]; Saul, who is filled with the Spirit of God, chases the Ammonites out of Jabes Galaad.[5]

We should not conclude from these texts that the Spirit was conceived at that time as an indifferent principle of physical energy unrelated to religious life. Under whatever aspect their action was manifested, in the cases of Samson and Gedeon, as in those of Joseph or Moses, it is evident that it was always directed to the development or defence of the religion of Israel. No doubt at the epoch of the prophets and, above all, under the new alliance, such action is higher and purer, because the chosen people are more capable of bearing and responding to it; but already the heroes of the age of the Judges, Debbora, Gedeon, and Samson play a truly religious rôle by liberating the people of God from the yoke of idolatry.[6]

[1] *Gen.* xli, 38. [2] *Num.* xi, 17. [3] *Judges* xiv, 6, 7. [4] *Judges* vi, 34.
[5] 1 *Kings* xi, 6.
[6] Wood (*Spirit of God*, 16–20) defends this position against Gunkel (*Wirkungen*, 10) and W. E. Addis's article *Spirit* in *EB*, col. 1752.

This characteristic is more apparent in the inspiration of the prophets, which assumes an increasingly large place in the manifestations of the Spirit of God, and which later in Judaism and Christianity is looked upon as the special action of the Holy Spirit, the Spirit of the prophets.[1] Samuel, when consecrating Saul, promises him that the Spirit will take hold of him, make him a prophet, and change him into another man.[2] This prediction was soon accomplished, and the spectators, surprised at this sudden change, are compelled to repeat: 'Is Saul also among the prophets?'[3] A little later[4] the question is raised of an evil spirit who comes from Jahve and seizes upon Saul. Certain critics think that no distinction can be drawn between two spirits, one good and the other evil, but that the Spirit of God may have an effect sometimes good, and sometimes evil.[5] The text does not permit of this interpretation and makes a definite distinction between the two spirits: 'But the Spirit of the Lord departed from Saul; and an evil spirit from the Lord troubled him' (xvi, 14).[6] The same remark applies to the spirit of lying which is sent to Achab on his march to Ramoth Galaad.[7] No doubt this evil spirit is conceived as being dependent on God, and even as being sent by him, in the same sense as was Satan in the book of Job; but certainly this spirit of lying cannot be confused with the Holy Spirit, the Spirit of Jahve.

The point is not without importance: the critics who attempt to enlarge the conception of the Spirit and take away its character of a moral and sanctifying agent, expose themselves to the misinterpretation, not only of the nature, but of the origin of this doctrine. For I. F. Wood, in his *Spirit of God,* it would be but a survival of a polytheist, or, rather, a polydemonic religion[8]; if this hypothesis were exact the spirit would have to be conceived, like the demons of Greek polytheism, as an intermediary agent between God and men, whose action may be beneficent or the reverse.

There is no difficulty in avoiding this hypothesis, if care

[1] Cf. WEBER, *Jud. Theol.*, 192; JUSTIN, *Apol.*, I, 6 and *passim*.
[2] 1 *Kings* x, 6. [3] *Ibid.*, 11. [4] 1 *Kings* xvi, 14, 16; xix, 9.
[5] WOOD, *loc. cit.*, p. 6, n. 2; GUNKEL, *loc. cit.*, 17.
[6] See SWETE, art. Holy Spirit, *DB*, 404a.
[7] 3 *Kings* xxii 22 *seq.* [8] *Loc. cit.*, 31.

is taken to dissipate the equivocations created by the various senses in which the word Spirit is used in the Scriptures. In the above-quoted passages of *Kings* the same word *rûah* designates the Spirit of Jahve and the spirit of falsehood,[1] as in the New Testament the word *pneuma* will be applied sometimes to the Holy Spirit, sometimes to the spirits of impurity; such verbal similarities are usually easy to distinguish,[2] and the Spirit of Jahve can be distinguished from the crowd of good and evil spirits, and is as definitively transcendent as Jahve himself, with whom, indeed, it is identical.[3] This conception and this formula have an origin quite analogous to that of the Word of Jahve: the divine life and action are described in terms of human analogy, and the Spirit of Jahve is represented as the primary principle of the energies and operations which God awakens and carries on in our spirit.

During the period of the prophets the characteristic of God's action in sanctification and illumination appears more manifestly. This function, already mentioned by the ancient prophets, for instance, by Micheas (ii, 7, 11, 8), and by Osee (ix, 7), is frequently described by Ezechiel; the words which the prophet hears, or the visions which he perceives, come from an operation of the Spirit of God.[4] Nevertheless, here, also, we find mentioned only the extraordinary charismata granted to certain privileged souls, to the 'men of the Spirit'[5]; we do not find that the Spirit of God extends his sanctifying action over all the Israelites[6]; and, in the case even of those whom he favours, he appears rather as a source of extraordinary gifts than as a principle of sanctity. It is another matter in the *Psalms*: the worshipper, addressing God, asks for himself his Spirit: he prays to God to 'renew his Spirit within him,' not to 'take away his holy Spirit from him.'[7] And in another Psalm he says: 'teach me to do thy will,

[1] Cf. *Judges* ix, 23; *Osee* iv, 12, v, 4; *Is.* xix, 14, xxix, 10.

[2] Cf. *Zach.* xii, 10.

[3] Wood, *loc. cit.*, 20: 'Did the Hebrews make a clear distinction between Jahweh or Elohim and the Spirit of Jahweh or the Spirit of Elohim? There is no reason to suppose that, in the times we are considering, they did. All the phenomena ascribed to the Spirit were also ascribed directly to Jahweh or Elohim.'

[4] *Ezech.* ii, 2; iii, 12, 14, 24; viii, 3; xi, 1, 5, 24, etc.

[5] *Osee* ix, 7. [6] Cf. *Num.* xi, 29. [7] *Ps.* l, 12, 13.

for thou art my God, thy good Spirit shall place me in the land of justice' (cxii, 10).

The Spirit is sometimes represented as a force acting on men from without, bearing them, raising them up, leading them on[1]; more often he penetrates them either by his transitory influence[2] or by his permanent indwelling. Thus Joseph is full of the Spirit of God.[3] Beseleel, who is to construct the Ark of God, is filled with the Spirit of God.[4] Josue was pointed out to Moses as a man in whom dwelt the Spirit.[5]

This belief in the immanence of the Spirit of God in the soul does not yet bear all its fruits, because, as has been said above, this presence of the Spirit is described more often as a privilege, accorded to heroes or prophets, than as a gift of God dispensed to all the faithful. From now on, however, this doctrine constitutes one of the most important and precious elements in the religion of Israel. God is conceived more and more as the Highest, whose inaccessible holiness places him at an infinite height above man. There would be danger that this idea might impoverish religious life, if this God of holiness did not dwell in man by his Spirit, and, as will be said below, by his Wisdom.

Moreover, this belief in the Spirit of God, still very imperfect, is directed, like all the religion of the Old Testament, towards the Messias, and expects to find its perfection in him.

It is principally in *Isaias* that the relation of the Spirit to the Messias is very explicit and accentuated. We read (xi, 1, 2): 'And there shall come forth a rod out of the root of Jesse: and a flower shall rise up out of his root. And the Spirit of the Lord shall rest upon him: the spirit of wisdom and of understanding, the spirit of counsel and of fortitude, the spirit of knowledge and of godliness.' The same promises are repeated in the poem which deals with the servant of Jahve, the chosen people and his Messias (xlii, 1 *seq.*):

> 'Behold my servant: I will uphold him. My elect: my soul delighteth in him. I have given my spirit upon

[1] Cf. *Ezech.* iii, 12, 14; viii, 3; xi, 1, 24; 4 *Kings* ii, 16.
[2] As in most cases of prophetic inspiration.
[3] *Gen.* xli, 38.
[4] *Exod.* xxxi, 3.
[5] *Num.* xxvii, 18. Cf. xi, 17; 4 *Kings* ii, 9, 15.

him: he shall bring forth judgment to the Gentiles. He shall not cry, nor have respect to person: neither shall his voice be heard abroad. The bruised reed he shall not break, and smoking flax he shall not quench: he shall bring forth judgment unto truth. He shall not be sad nor troublesome till he set judgment in the earth: and the islands shall wait for his law.'

And further on (lxi, 1):

'The Spirit of the Lord is upon me, because the Lord hath anointed me. He hath sent me to preach to the meek, to heal the contrite of heart, and to preach a release to the captives and deliverance to them that are shut up.'

The Messias is not the only one to receive these gifts of the Spirit; the time of his coming is foretold as a period in which divine graces will be poured forth: 'The Spirit from above shall be poured upon Israel and the desert shall be as an orchard, and the orchard shall be counted for a forest, and the Law shall dwell in the desert and righteousness in the orchard.'[1] And in the poem addressed to the servant of Jahve: 'And now hear, O Jacob, my servant, and Israel, whom I have chosen. Fear not, O my servant Jacob, and thou most righteous whom I have chosen. . . . I will pour out my Spirit upon thy seed and my blessing upon thy stock' (xliv, 1 *seq.*). The same promises occur in *Ezechiel*: 'I will give them one heart, and will put a new spirit in their bowels: and I will take away the stony heart out of their flesh and will give them a heart of flesh, that they may walk in my commandments and keep my judgements' (xi, 19; xxxvi, 26). And after the prophet's vision of the bones revived by the Spirit: 'Prophesy and say to them: thus saith the Lord God: Behold I will open your graves and bring you out of your sepulchres, O my people, and will bring you into the land of Israel. And you shall know that I am the Lord when . . . I shall have put my Spirit in you, and you shall live' (xxxvii, 12).

God made the same promise through Joel, in the text of

[1] *Is.* xxxii, 15.

which St. Peter reminded the Jews on the day of Pentecost:

> 'And it shall come to pass after this, that I will pour out my spirit upon all flesh: and your sons and your daughters shall prophesy: your old men shall dream dreams, and your young men shall see visions.
>
> Moreover upon my servants and handmaids in those days I will pour forth my spirit' (*Joel* ii, 28, 29).

And again in *Zacharias:* 'And I will pour out upon the house of David and upon the inhabitants of Jerusalem the Spirit of grace and of prayers' (xii, 10).

All these prophecies state clearly enough that the Spirit is, together with the Messias, the supreme Messianic gift, and that all the graces accorded to the holy men and prophets of the Old Testament were but anticipations in comparison with the effusion promised to Christ's faithful. It thus becomes intelligible how St. John could write (vii, 39), when he recalls the analogous promises of our Lord: 'As yet the Spirit was not given, because Jesus was not yet glorified.'

It also becomes intelligible why, in all the doctrine we have surveyed, the personality proper of the Spirit is so faint. More often nothing is perceptible but the action of the Spirit, who is represented as a force communicated by Jahve[1]; on other occasions, instead of describing his action upon men, he is represented as united to Jahve, without a very clear distinction between the two terms. Thus we read in the Canticle of David[2]: 'The Spirit of the Lord hath spoken by me: and his word by my tongue. The God of Israel said to me, the strong one of Israel spoke, . . .' In the sacred books of Jewry, and particularly in those of the New Testament, the Holy Spirit is often represented as speaking to men; in this text the words are the same but the meaning is different, as is clearly indicated by the end of the sentence: by the Spirit of Jahve the sacred author does not mean to indicate a person distinct from him.[3]

Isaias says the same[4]: 'Woe to the apostate children, saith the Lord, that take counsel and not of me, and make

[1] See Hackspill (*RB*, 1902, p. 68).
[2] 2 *Kings* xxiii, 2. [3] See Wood, p. 45. [4] *Is.* xxx, 1.

pacts contrary to my Spirit, so adding sin upon sin.' It is in the same acceptation of the word that the Spirit of Jahve is placed in line with the 'Face of Jahve'[1]: 'Whither shall I go from thy Spirit? Or whither shall I flee from thy face?' (*Ps*. cxxxviii, 7). This similarity is still more accentuated in the following passage which recalls the miracles of Exodus: 'It was not a messenger or an angel, but his Face that saved them. And in his goodness and his mercy, he redeemed them. And he lifted them up and carried them all the days of old. But they revolted and afflicted his holy Spirit.'[2] These last words recall the text of St. Paul: 'Grieve not the holy spirit of God.'[3] The apostolic theology, more explicit and more complete, gives to this text a more definite value; the prophetic doctrine is less clear and therefore does not permit the introduction into these verses of a personal distinction which they do not suggest themselves.

Later on, in the Sapiential books, and particularly in the Book of the *Wisdom of Solomon*, the Spirit is represented as intimately united with Wisdom, described under the same traits and sometimes even identified with it.[4] As a result of this assimilation, the conception of the Spirit develops and its personification becomes accentuated, but we shall understand this progress better if we study the doctrine of Wisdom, on which the whole development depends.

BIBLIOGRAPHY, Section 2:—H. WENDT, *Die Begriffe Fleisch und Geist im biblischen Sprachgebrauch* (Gotha, 1878). H. Gunkel, *Die Wirkungen des hl. Geistes nach der populären Anschauung der Apostolischen Zeit und der Lehre des Apostels Paulus* (Gottingen, 1899). J. F. Wood, *The Spirit of God in Biblical Literature* (London, 1904). P. Volz, *Der Geist Gottes und die verwandten Erscheinungen im Alten Testament und im anschliessenden Judentum* (Tubingen, 1910). P. Heinisch, *Personifikationen und Hypostasen im A. T. und im alten Orient* (Munster, 1921); *Griechische Philosophie und A. T.* (Munster, 1913).

[1] Concerning the 'Face of Jahve' cf. LAGRANGE, *RB*, 1903, p. 215: the 'Face of Jahve,' far from signifying an intermediary being, expressly denotes the personal presence of God, and this meaning is accurately rendered by the Greek translators, *Exod.* xxxiii, 14.

[2] *Is.* lxiii, 9, 10. This text confirms the preceding remark; it obviously excludes every intermediary between Jahve and his people.

[3] *Ephes.* iv, 30.

[4] *Wisd.* vii, 22; i, 6; see below, page 97, note 1.

3. *Wisdom*[1]

The Jewish theology of Wisdom has for the most part a practical and moral character. Like Solomon, the Sage *par excellence,* to whom they give willing homage, the wise men discuss nature and man, and love to condense in a proverb (*mashâl*) the results of their experience.

The whole of this practical aspect of Jewish speculation does not concern our study: what we wish to trace is not the moral philosophy of the Hebrews, it is their conception of God, of his Providence, of his Wisdom. To engage in this study we must first of all investigate the *Book of Job ;* whatever date we assign to this book it is certain that the theology of Wisdom is less developed in its pages than in the *Book of Proverbs.* In chapter xxviii Job first enumerates the riches hidden from men in the earth:

> 'But where is Wisdom to be found? And where is the place of understanding? Man knoweth not the price thereof: neither is it found in the land of them that live in delights. . . . God understandeth the way of it, and he knoweth the place thereof. For he beholdeth the ends of the world: and looketh on all things that are under heaven.'

Oehler[2] thinks he finds in this passage a proof of the distinction drawn between Wisdom and Jahve. Hackspill[3] is of another opinion, and one which seems to me more probable: 'No objective distinction between God and his wisdom is meant, merely a poetical personification of an abstract idea.'

We should also mention another passage of the same book. Eliphaz says to Job in refutation of what he considers to be his unjust pretensions: 'Art thou the first man that was born, or wast thou made before the hills? Hast thou heard God's counsel, and shall his wisdom be inferior to thee?'[4] It is remarkable that this pre-existence, here ironically attributed to Job, should be described in the very terms applied by the *Book of Proverbs* to

[1] See Bibliography of Section 3.
[2] *Theol. des A. T.*, II, 284.
[3] *RB*, 1901, 208.
[4] *Job* xv, 7, 8.

Wisdom,[1] which, moreover, indicates that at that time, 'Before the hills,' Wisdom already existed. We may add, however, that nothing here indicates a personal distinction.

The *Book of Baruch* (iii, iv) echoes the words of Job:

> 'Who hath found out her place? And who hath gone into her treasures? . . . It hath not been heard of in the land of Chanaan: neither hath it been seen in Theman . . . but he that knoweth all things, knoweth her and hath found her out with his understanding.'

The last verse of chapter iii is equally inspired by *Proverbs*: 'Afterwards he was seen upon earth and conversed with men,'[2] and the writer adds (iv, 1): 'Wisdom[3] is the book of the commandments of God and the law that is for ever.'

In the *Book of Proverbs* the theology of Wisdom is more developed; we find it in two poems forming chapters viii and ix, which throw light on each other; the source of these chapters is not apparently the most ancient of those which form the book[4]; the date is hard enough to determine, but it is at least earlier than *Ecclesiasticus*.

In these two chapters Wisdom is presented in its relation now with God, and now with men. The second aspect is the easier to understand and it should be the first to be described. Wisdom gives men a pressing invitation to frequent her school:

> 'Standing in the top of the highest places by the way, in the midst of the paths,
> Beside the gates of the city, in the very doors she speaketh, saying:
> O ye men, to you I call, and my voice is to the sons of men.
> O little ones, understand subtilty, and ye unwise, take notice.
> Hear, for I will speak of great things: and my lips shall be opened to preach right things' (*Prov.* viii, 2-6).

The good things that Wisdom promises are the same which God gives, and above all, life: 'He that shall find

[1] Cf. *Prov.* viii, 25. See C. H. Toy, *Proverbs*, p. xxix.
[2] Vulg.: visus est et cum hominibus conversatus est.
[3] Douai Version: 'This is.'
[4] Cf. Kittel, *RE*, xviii, 690; Toy, *Proverbs*, p. xxviii.

me shall find life, and shall have salvation from the Lord. But he that shall sin against me shall hurt his own soul. All that hate me love death' (*Prov.* viii, 35, 36).

These traits indicate the divine character of Wisdom; the personal character of Wisdom is, at first sight, definitely emphasised. These invitations and promises make us recognise Wisdom as a person and not an abstraction, as does the following setting of the scene in *Proverbs* ix (1 *seq.*):

> 'Wisdom hath built herself a house: she hath hewn her out seven pillars.
> She hath slain her victims, mingled her wine, and set forth her table.
> She hath sent her maids to invite to the tower, and to the walls of the city:
> Whosoever is a little one, let him come to me.'

This little picture recalls the gospel parables in which the Messianic king is represented as inviting all men to his table. The question may, however, still be asked whether Wisdom is here described in the proper sense of the word as a person, or as a personified abstraction. What might incline us to the second hypothesis is the parallel description in which Folly is personified, at the end of the same chapter (*Prov.* ix, 13 *seq.*):

> 'A foolish woman and clamorous, and full of allurements, and knowing nothing at all,
> Sat at the door of her house, upon a seat, in a high place of the city,
> To call them that pass by the way, and go on their journey:
> He that is a little one, let him turn to me.'

It is evident here that the sacred writer does not intend to hypostatise folly, but only to personify it. We may ask ourselves if he wished to go further than this when speaking of Wisdom.

The reply to this question is to be found at the end of the preceding poem (*Prov.* viii, 22-31), where Wisdom is assimilated to God and yet definitely distinguished from him. This very important passage must be quoted in full:

'The Lord possessed[1] me in the beginning of his ways, before he made any thing from the beginning.

I was set up[2] from eternity, and of old before the earth was made.

The depths were not as yet, and I was already conceived: neither had the fountains of waters as yet sprung out.

The mountains with their huge bulk had not as yet been established: before the hills I was brought forth.

He had not yet made the earth, nor the rivers, nor the poles of the world.

When he prepared the heavens, I was present: when with a certain law and compass he enclosed the depths:

When he established the sky above, and poised the fountains of waters:

When he compassed the sea with its bounds, and set a law to the waters that they should not pass their limits: when he balanced the foundations of the earth:

I was with him as a child[3] and was delighted every day, playing before him at all times;

Playing in the world. And my delights were to be with the children of men.'[4]

It is difficult to see in this passage only poetical personification and, in fact, the majority of commentators agree in the view that Wisdom is presented here as already distinguished from God, constituting a hypostasis or, at least, tending in that direction.[5]

No text of the Old Testament is more frequently quoted by the theologians of old in the course of their enquiries into the dogma of the Trinity. Already Jewish speculation had been occupied with it and gladly saw in

[1] Vulgate, *possedit*; Septuagint, ἔκτισε; cf. *Ps.* cxxxiii, 13.

[2] See C. F. Burney in *Journal of Theol. Studies*, XXVII (1926), 165 *seq.*

[3] It would seem that 'child' is the more correct translation, rather than 'workman'; it is a question of diacritical marks; the letters of the two Hebrew words are the same. See below, page 94, note 5.

[4] This last sentence is of doubtful authenticity.

[5] Examining this text in the light of traditional commentaries it would seem that we could go beyond this prudent conclusion and assert a distinction of person. Historically considered, the text would not seem to admit of such an interpretation. It is true that it is suggested, but, considered in itself, neither its context nor its poetic form admit such a close interpretation of the expressions used. See Lagrange, *RB*, 1908, 496.

it the affirmation of the pre-existence of the Law which was easily identified with the Wisdom of God.[1] St. Paul in his turn will apply it to the Son of God, 'The firstborn of every creature.'[2] The apologists will make use of it as a chosen weapon to prove to the Gentiles or Jews the pre-existence of the Word and his rôle in the work of creation.[3] Later on the Arians will find there a decisive argument in favour of their heresy: 'The Lord hath created me,' they read in the Septuagint. It seemed to them the authentic consecration of their doctrine on the origin of the divine Word. The Fathers produced several solutions of this objection: St. Epiphanius at length put aside the ἔκτισε of the Septuagint and used the Hebrew 'possessed me.' St. Jerome translated it as '*possedit me.*' It seems that here, as in *Ps.* cxxxviii, 13 (*possedisti renes meos*), it means rather: 'has formed me.' The precise idea of creation is set aside, but is not replaced by a more definite conception. A little further on (23) Wisdom says that she 'was set up' or 'established'[4] by God: and, in verse 25, 'brought forth' by him. These last terms are no doubt very expressive, and open up views of the divine life which the Christian faith illuminates; but, considered alone, they are not sufficient to reveal the mystery of the divine generation.

The close relation between Wisdom and the world in the whole of this quotation should be noted: Wisdom is prior to all the works of God, and plays among them.[5]

This doctrine of the pre-existence of Wisdom is resumed and developed in the twenty-fourth chapter of *Ecclesiasticus* (5-15):

> 'I came out of the mouth of the most High [the first-born before all creatures].
>
> I made that in the heavens there should rise light

[1] *Berechith Rabba*, 17; *Exod. Rabba*, 30 (89d). See below, page 120; Strack-Billerbeck, *Kommentar*, II, 353 *seq.*; A. Bugge, *Das Gesetz und Christus*, in *Zeitschr. f. N. T. W.*, IV (1903), 89–110. Cf. Philo, *De ebrietate*, 31 (M., I. 362).

[2] *Col.* i, 15; cf. Burney, *loc. cit.*, 173 *seq.*

[3] Justin, *Dial.*, 61, 3; Athenag., *Legat.*, 10.

[4] Cf. *Ps.* ii, 6.

[5] One is inclined to define this rôle by the help of verse 30, where Wisdom is described by a term that the Vulgate, Septuagint, and Syriac translate as 'workman.' Aquila and most of the modern writers (Delitzsch, Gunkel, Toy, Gesenius-Kautsch, etc.) understand the passive sense: 'child brought up or cherished by God'; the context seems to suggest this, as Wisdom is described not as working at the creation, but as 'playing.'

that never faileth, and as a cloud I covered all the earth.

I dwelt in the highest places, and my throne is in a pillar of a cloud.[1]

I alone have compassed the circuit of heaven, and have penetrated into the bottom of the deep, and have walked in the waves of the sea,

And have stood in all the earth. And in every people,

And in every nation I have had the chief rule.

And by my power I have trodden under my feet the hearts of all the high and low: and in all these I sought rest, and I shall abide in the inheritance of the Lord.

Then the creator of all things commanded and said to me: and he that made me rested in my tabernacle.

And he said to me: Let thy dwelling be in Jacob, and thy inheritance in Israel, and take root in my elect.

From the beginning, and before the world, was I created, and unto the world to come I shall not cease to be: and in the holy dwelling place I have ministered before him.

And so was I established in Sion, and in the holy city likewise I rested: and my power was in Jerusalem.'

This discourse pronounced by Wisdom in the 'Churches of the most High' (xxiv, 2) cannot, any more than the passage quoted from *Proverbs*, be interpreted as a simple prosopopœia. Here, evidently, is more than a figure of speech; this Wisdom that talks in the assembly of the angels, that declares her own creation before time, and her eternal subsistence, exercising her ministry in the temple, is no mere abstraction, although even here, Wisdom is neither clearly nor distinctly presented as a hypostasis.[2]

The origin of Wisdom is described no more explicitly than in *Proverbs*. No doubt the fifth verse ('I came out of the mouth of the most High') indicates an important advance in the meaning of the doctrine of the Word of

[1] PHILO even identifies with the 'pillar of cloud that guided the Israelites' both Wisdom and the Logos; see *Q. rerum divin. her.*, 204–5 (M., I, 501).

[2] Cf. HACKSPILL, *loc. cit.*, 211.

God: but we must not force this expression, any more, indeed, than the idea of creation, used three or four times to express the origin of Wisdom (*Ecclus.* i, 9 ; xxiv, 12, 14 ; perhaps i, 4).

The rôle of Wisdom in the Creation is fairly obscure : apart from a gloss of the Vulgate (*Ego feci in cœlis ut oriretur lumen indeficiens*), there is nothing to indicate in this whole passage an active rôle in the production and organisation of the world: on the other hand, here, as in *Proverbs,* Wisdom walks about and plays among the works of God. The entire earth is her empire, but God made her choose out of all the nations, Israel, where she dwells at Zion, in the temple. The liturgical function that she performs there suggests the symbolic interpretation which, in later days, saw in the High Priest the image of the divine Word.

Wisdom is identified with the law in this twenty-fourth chapter (23 *seq.*), and also in a verse the authenticity of which is doubted by certain critics: 'The word of God on high is the fountain of Wisdom: and her ways are everlasting commandments' (*Ecclus.* i, 5).[1]

In the Alexandrine book of the *Wisdom of Solomon,* the same doctrine appears more complete and precise. Here Wisdom is clearly distinguished from God:

> 'For she is a vapour of the power of God and a certain pure emanation of the glory of the almighty God: and therefore no defiled thing cometh into her. For she is the brightness of eternal light, and the unspotted mirror of God's majesty, and the image of his goodness' (*Wisd.* vii, 25, 26).

Several of these expressions were used again by the author of the *Epistle to the Hebrews,* and the Fathers used them insistently in the Arian controversy. In fact, they announced both the distinction which separates God and Wisdom, and the unique relations which connect them together. These terms should not be considered by themselves, and all these metaphors—breath, emanation, brightness, mirror—complete and correct each other ; they thus give the collective impression of a very intimate, very necessary, dependence, of which the purest images in

[1] Bousset, *loc. cit.*, 343, n. 3, calls this an Alexandrine gloss.

our experience here below can only suggest a fragmentary and imperfect idea.

If we ask what Wisdom is in herself, the sacred writer replies that she is a spirit. This identification is certainly affirmed in *Wisdom* i, 6 and ix, 17; it is probably expressed in chapter vii, 22.[1] At the same time, Wisdom appears more clearly as a person, a conscious agent; she can do all things (vii, 27), she ordereth all things (viii, 1), she makes her choice among the works of God (viii, 4); above all, she is the guide of men and leads the chosen people with an all-powerful and kindly solicitude (x *seq.*). In the creation she appears as the 'worker' of all that exists.[2] Looked at from this point of view, she plays the same rôle as the word or the Logos of God:

> 'God of my fathers, and Lord of mercy, who hast made all things with thy word, and by thy wisdom hast appointed man. . . . Give me wisdom that sitteth by thy throne' (*Wisd.* ix, 1, 2, 4).[3]

In this description I have not noted the suggestions of Hellenism which are both numerous and characteristic. In order to get an impression of them, we should read over the twenty-one epithets given to the spirit (vii, 22, 23): the general form of the phrase, like the detail of the expressions, recalls the Alexandrine writers and, in particular, Philo. But under the Platonist or Stoic vocabulary[4] we surely discover the Jewish doctrine, more conscious of itself and more clearly set forth.[5]

This is not to say that the whole Trinity is to be found here. Wisdom alone is distinguished from God, and even so, has not all the clearness of a living personality. The Spirit, as we have seen, is no more distinguished from God than the Logos; we need not then be surprised to find that, in the second century, St. Theophilus of Antioch and St. Irenæus see in Wisdom, not the second, but the third Person of the Holy Trinity. However, it is

[1] The variant, ἔστιν γὰρ αὐτή . . . is found in *Codex Alexandrinus* but not in *Vaticanus*, *Sinaiticus*, the Vulgate, etc.

[2] viii, 6 and vii, 21.

[3] This last verse shows what will often appear later in the theology of the Holy Spirit, i.e., Wisdom considered both as a person very close to God, and as a gift communicated by him.

[4] See Clem. Alex., *Strom.*, v, 14.

[5] See F. Focke, *Die Entstehung der Weisheit Salomons* (Göttingen, 1913), 92.

in this book that we find the clearest foreshadowing of the Christian dogma; and, later, the authentic interpretation of the author of the Epistle to the Hebrews will clearly bring out that theology of the Word which we have only been able to perceive obscurely. We shall notice, however, when describing the history of theology in the second century, that the influence of the *Book of Wisdom,* very obvious in the *Epistle to the Hebrews,* still apparent in St. Clement, is foreign to the apologists, and only reappears in the works of St. Irenæus. This limited and tardy influence may be explained by a fact of which we must not lose sight: Christianity was born in Palestine and the Palestinian influences affecting it were much earlier and deeper than those of Alexandria.

In the non-canonical books the doctrine of Wisdom is much more confused. Thus, just as the doctrine of the Spirit was in process of disappearance during the last days of Judaism,[1] so the doctrine of Wisdom was about to vanish, when Christianity appeared and revived both of them. The doctrine of the Word, on the other hand, much less rich and fruitful up to that time, lived much longer in Judaism, although not without grave distortion.

Bibliography, Section 3:—J. Gottsberger, *Die gottliche Weisheit als Personlichk it im A. T.* (Munster, 1919). A. Vaccari, *Il concetto della Sapienza nell' A. T., Gregorianum,* I (1920), 218–51.

4. The Word[2]

The sacred books often represent the creative act as a word of God: we read in *Genesis* (i, 3): 'God said: Be light made. And light was made.' As in the *Psalms* (xxxii, 9): 'He spoke, and they were made.' Sometimes indeed they seem to attribute a specific action, although not independent of Jahve, to the word. Thus *Isaias* (lv, 10, 11):

> 'And as the rain and the snow come down from heaven, and return no more thither, but soak the earth and water it and make it to spring, and give seed to the sower, and bread to the eater: so shall my word be, which shall go forth from my mouth. It shall

[1] See below, page 120.

[2] See Bibliography of this Section.

not return to me void, but it shall do whatsoever I please and shall prosper in the things for which I sent it.'

The *Psalms* speak of the word sent by God, which heals[1]: elsewhere as a rapid messenger.[2]

Similarly, the word of malediction is personified by the prophet Zacharias,[3] under the form of a flying volume, twenty cubits in length and ten in breadth, which sweeps everything out of its way; and Jahve, interpreting his vision to the prophet, says to him:

> 'This is the curse that goeth forth over the face of the earth; for every thief shall be judged, as is there written, and every one that sweareth in like manner shall be judged by it. . . . And it shall remain in the midst of his house and shall consume it, with the timber thereof and the stones thereof.'

In all this we may see nothing but bold figures of speech; the word of creation, or salvation, or reprobation is personified, it is not conceived, as a hypostasis distinct from God.

In the Sapiential books the doctrine of the word is developed on lines parallel to those of Wisdom, but it is much less developed.[4] Thus we read in *Ecclesiasticus* (xlii, 15): 'By the words of the Lord are his works'; also (xliii, 28): 'And by his word all things are regulated.' It is chiefly in the *Book of Wisdom* that the personification of the word is dwelt upon (ix, 1): 'God of my fathers, and Lord of mercy, who hast made all things with thy word, and by thy wisdom hast appointed man, that he should have dominion over the creature . . .'; and (xviii, 14): 'For while all things were in quiet silence, and the night was in the midst of her course, thy almighty word leapt down from heaven from thy royal throne, as a fierce conqueror into the midst of the land of destruction, with a sharp sword carrying thy unfeigned commandment.' This last text, if taken by itself, would hardly have more significance than those of the *Psalms* or Prophets; but when it is found in a book which indicates

[1] *Ps.* cvi, 20. [2] cxlvii, 15. [3] v, 1–4.
[4] Cf. LAGRANGE, *Évangile selon saint Jean* (Paris, 1925), 29.

so clearly the distinct personification of Wisdom, it is difficult not to give it more importance.

Shortly, indeed, with the aid of Hellenic influence, this conception of the word or of the Logos will find considerable development in the works of Philo[1]; in Palestine its rôle will be less apparent; even there, however, among the more or less personified abstractions that we find in the environment of God, we shall distinguish, more particularly in the *Targums,* the word or Memra.[2]

BIBLIOGRAPHY, Section 4:—P. Heinisch, *Das Wort im A. T. und im alten Orient. Zugleich ein Beitrag zum Verstandnis des Prologs des Johannesevangeliums* (Munster, 1922).

5. *The Messianic Hope*

Side by side with the doctrines of the Spirit, Wisdom, the Word, a belief of a totally different character, the Messianic faith, was developing. Obviously, there is no place here for a complete study of Messianism; this great religious movement only has interest for us in so far as it was able to affect the early belief in the Trinity.

We must, moreover, recognise that that influence was not very great; it is by means of the doctrine of Wisdom much more than by Messianism that the Jewish people was prepared for the revelation of the Trinity[3]; we must, however, note certain data which are not negligible. Many liberal commentators, when they meet in the gospel the name of the Son of God applied to Jesus, are disposed to consider it as a simple equivalent of the word 'Messias'[4]; it would seem from what they say that this title was frequently and traditionally used in this sense. This is a mistake[5]: very few texts are to be found in which Jahve calls the Messias his Son; but neither in the Old Testament proper nor in the apocryphal books do we find the title 'Son of God' applied by the writer to the Messias.[6]

We have seen above[7] how God, in the Old Testament, loved to call the chosen people his *son:* the same title is

[1] See below, pages 157 *sqq.*
[2] See below, pages 121 *sqq.*
[3] See TOUZARD, *loc. cit. infra*, 85, 102; WARFIELD, *loc. cit. infra*, 369–416.
[4] E.g., LOISY, *L'Evangile et l'Église*, 42, 56, 57.
[5] Cf. DALMAN, *Die Worte Jesu*, 223; LAGRANGE, *RB*, 1908, 491.
[6] See *III Sibyl.*, 776.
[7] See above, pages 80 *sq.*

given by him to David and to the heir who is promised to him.[1] The Messias, in his turn, is called by God his *son* and all nations are given to him as his heritage.

> 'The Lord hath said to me: Thou art my son ; this day have I begotten thee. Ask of me and I will give thee the Gentiles for thy inheritance, and the utmost parts of the earth for thy possession. Thou shalt rule them with a rod of iron, and shalt break them in pieces like a potter's vessel.'[2]

It would be difficult to see in this text the eternal generation of the Word ; the context suggests, on the contrary, the glorification of the Messias and the inauguration of his reign.[3] This title of *Son,* given by God to the Messias in the second *Psalm,* is also attributed to him in various texts of the Latin version of the fourth *Book of Esdras.* But the evidence of the other versions suggests rather the title of Servant than that of Son.[4]

It seems, however, that texts are not wanting in the ancient prophets which might have revealed to the Jews the more than human dignity of the Messias. In *Isaias* he is called not only Emmanuel[5]—this name, God-with-us, like several others, might have only a symbolic value[6]—but 'Wonderful, Counsellor, God the Mighty, Father of the world to come, Price of Peace'[7] ; the reality was to fulfil literally these magnificent promises, but the contemporaries of the prophet did not grasp their full meaning.[8] The writers of the Septuagint in their day, more timid than the prophet, were disconcerted by these expressions, and did not in their translation venture to reproduce their boldness.[9]

In his origin, however, as in his personal dignity, the

[1] 2 *Kings* vii, 14 ; cf. 1 *Par.* xvii, 11–14 ; *Ps.* lxxxviii, 27 *sq.*

[2] *Ps.* ii, 7 *seq.*

[3] This passage in the psalm is applied to the baptism of Christ in the western MSS. of *Luke* iii, 22 (cf. Blass, *Evang. sec. Lucam,* pp. xxxv–xxxix) and by Justin, *Dial.,* 88, 103 ; Clem. Alex., *Paed.,* I, 6, 25 ; Augustine, *De cons. evang.,* II, 14, etc.

[4] 1 *Esdras* vii, 28, 29 ; xiii, 32, 37, 52.

[5] vii, 14 ; viii, 8, 10.

[6] 'The meaning of Emmanuel ("God with us") by no means implies the attribute of Messias . . . but may merely express confidence in God's help.' (Condamin, *Le livre d'Isaïe,* 62.)

[7] ix, 6.

[8] See Condamin (*op. cit.,* 58).

[9] All the titles which were in the original text have been suppressed and replaced by 'angel of great counsel.'

predicted Messias surpassed humanity; 'His going forth is from the beginning, from the days of eternity.'[1] It would no doubt be rash to attribute a strictly metaphysical sense to this expression,[2] but it is, on the other hand, impossible to see nothing there but a mention of the antiquity of the race of David, or an ideal pre-existence, whether in the designs of God or in the hopes of the people.

At last the visions of Daniel opened out new perspectives and the Messias appeared in them on the clouds of heaven close to God:

> 'I beheld therefore in the vision of the night, and lo, one like the Son of man came with the clouds of heaven. And he came even to the Ancient of days: and they presented him before him. And he gave him power and glory and a kingdom: and all peoples, tribes, and tongues shall serve him. His power is an everlasting power that shall not be taken away: and his kingdom that shall not be destroyed.'[3]

This prophecy did not pass unnoticed; its influence on the *Book of the Parables of Henoch* is obvious[4]; even after the coming of our Lord it imposed itself on the Rabbis, however difficult they found it to explain.[5] In the gospel, above all, its trace is evident; it is enough to recall the final reply of Christ to his Judges[6]: 'Hereafter you shall see the Son of Man sitting on the right hand of the power of God, and coming in the clouds of heaven.'

The same remark applies to the above-quoted prophecies as to this text of Daniel: the gospel gives them all their value by the illumination of the light of Christ, in whom all these characteristics stand out and are united: he is the Son of God, the strong God, born from all eternity, seated at the right hand of the Father, as also the King of Israel, the Redeemer of the people, the Servant of Jahve. Thus, as the Fathers love to point out, his manifestation alone interprets prophecies, misunderstood

[1] *Micheas* v, 2.
[2] In *Deut.* xxxii, 7, the 'days of eternity' are rendered 'days of old'; Vulgate, dierum antiquorum. [3] *Dan.* vii, 13–14.
[4] *Henoch* xxxvii–lxxi. Cf. Lagrange, *Le Messianisme*, 87–98.
[5] *Ibid.*, 224–8. [6] *Matt.* xxvi, 64.

before his day.[1] No doubt this misunderstanding was not complete; traces survive of the sketch traced by a divine hand, but they are faint and scattered.[2]

What has just been said of Messianism should also be applied to the doctrines previously studied[3]: we have discovered in the Old Testament many features which we shall find again in the doctrine of the Trinity; belief in the paternity of God, in the sanctifying action of his Spirit, the conception of his Wisdom, and, secondarily, of his Word, as of a being distinct from himself and clearly enough personified, the affirmation of the transcendence of the Messias: can we say that, on the eve of Christianity, all these doctrines had already reacted on each other, and were tending to organise themselves into a coherent system? Or must we recognise that these elements remained scattered, each living its own life, and developing independently of the others? It seems to me that the second conception is much nearer the facts. I do not think that the doctrine of the Spirit developed as quickly as the doctrine of Wisdom, or that the theology of Wisdom enriched Messianism by combining with it. All these features will soon blend in the unity of one and the same belief, but only after they have appeared to us in the unity of one and the same Person.

It is towards this person, towards the Son of God, that the whole history of Israel moves. In reading over in this chapter the books of the Old Testament, we have found many characteristics, roughly sketched and scattered, to which the Christian revelation will give their definite outline and harmonious unity; but these texts may and should also be considered from another point of view, we search no more in them for the data of a still imperfect revelation, but rather for the impulse which, from the moment of their appearance, led Israel unconsciously towards the supreme revelation, towards the Christ: 'No man can come to me if my Father does not draw him.' This divine guidance determines the whole trend of sacred

[1] JUSTIN, *Apol.*, I, 32, 2. [2] See LAGRANGE, *op. cit.*, 265.

[3] I shall say nothing here about the Angel of Jahve, as I do not think that the Old Testament seems to identify that Angel either with the Son, or with Wisdom. See TOUZARD, art. *Ange de Yahweh* in the Supplement to *DB*, cols. 251-3.

history; and it is that drawing, above all, that the Church, the authentic Israel, saw when, during the first years of Christianity, she looked back over the past. When we come to expound the faith of the primitive Church, we shall see how all the New Testament writers apply to Christ the texts of the Prophets which relate directly to Jahve. It will suffice to recall here the vision of Isaias interpreted by St. John (xii, 41). This theophany is one of the most sublime in the Old Testament: Jahve appears to the prophet in the Temple seated on a lofty throne: he is surrounded by the seraphim, who cover their faces with their wings and exclaim: 'Holy, holy, holy, the Lord God of hosts, all the earth is full of his glory!' It was the glory of Christ, St. John tells us, that the Prophet saw at that moment. This interpretation, among many others, shows us in the Old Testament him who indeed fulfils it, him who was to be the 'end of the law' and its fulfilment, the Christ.[1]

Still more important than the theophanies were the promises, so often given by God to his people, to come himself to their help and to save them.[2] Was it possible that the early Christians, who had all these texts present in their memory, should not discover their mysterious meaning, when they contemplated, or still more when they remembered, the Son of God who had appeared among them? Was it not he whom the Prophets announced as the good Shepherd who should come among his people:

> 'He that scattered Israel will gather him: and he will keep him as the shepherd does his flock.'[3] 'For thus saith the Lord God: behold I myself will seek my sheep and will visit them. As the shepherd visiteth his flock in the day when he shall be in the midst of his sheep that were scattered, so will I visit my sheep and will deliver them out of all the places where they have been scattered.'[4]

Is it not the bridegroom of Israel, he who speaks to her in Osee?

[1] See below, page 165.
[2] See LAGRANGE, *RB*, 1917, 595.
[3] *Jer.* xxxi, 10.
[4] *Ezech.* xxxiv, 11–12.

'I will espouse thee to me for ever: I will espouse thee to me in justice and judgment and in mercy and in commiserations. And I will espouse thee to me in faith: and thou shalt know that I am the Lord . . . and I will say to that which was not my people: Thou art my people. And they shall say: Thou art my God.'[1]

In all these prophecies, so transparent in the light of the Gospel, Christ appeared to the first Christians; up till then the Jews had not been able to perceive him there; but at least they had been borne towards him by these divine promises: it was he whom they were expecting as their Redeemer. When the terrible days of the ruin and exile of Israel came, hope and prayer reached out more ardently than ever towards Jahve; the breaking up of the national life had made more apparent the bond, which united each believer with his God. At the same time new and wider horizons opened before the exiles; they understood better that the God whom they served was the Lord and Master of the whole world. And at the same time that the action of God appeared more intimate and more universal, his worship became dearer and more sacred to them: in contact with the lies and turpitude of idolatry, they understood better how precious was their law of justice and sanctity: and was it not precisely in order to spread that bright vision around them that God had thus dispersed them over the whole earth? Exiles, without home or temple, but richer than ever through their faith, they also became more impatient than ever to see the reign of God, so often promised, at last become a fact; the centuries which followed the exile saw new trials menacing more directly the faith and hopes of Israel: first the Greek domination, endeavouring to plant itself not merely by right of conquest, but also by the prestige of a brilliant civilisation; and then the rule of Rome, persecuting less, but more irresistible, came upon them: Rome seized the entire world and governed it with an ability and a power which intimidated the greatest of the Jews.

Struck by such terrible blows the national hope was not broken; no doubt in many hearts it became inflamed too much with human passion; narrow, jealous, fanatical,

[1] ii, 19–25.

it thought of nothing but armed rebellion ; it proceeded to exhaust itself in the supreme convulsions which were to achieve the ruin of the country ; other souls had been overcome by so many trials ; despairing of the future, forgetting the promises of the Prophets, they tried to make themselves at home with the foreign domination and to live comfortably among the ruins of their land. But there is still a faithful remnant: all have not bowed the knee to Baal, Jahve has reserved for himself seven thousand men. This remnant, predicted by Sophonias as a 'poor and needy people' (iii, 12), is indeed a people made up of the poor, of those who love to repeat the prayers and laments of the Psalmist:

> 'All my bones shall say: Lord, who is like to thee? Who deliverest the poor from the hand of them that are stronger than he: the needy and the poor from them that strip him.'[1] 'Thou knowest my reproach, and my confusion, and my shame. In thy sight are all they that afflict me . . . But I am poor and sorrowful: thy salvation, O God, hath set me up . . . For the Lord hath heard the poor: and hath not despised his prisoners.'[2]

We should re-read into these verses all those cries of suffering in the *Psalms ;* no prayer has ever been more full of anguish and distress, but also of humble confidence[3]: still more touching perhaps are the laments of the Israelite before the vine of Jahve ravaged by the Gentiles, the temple defiled, the Messias so slow to come, the prophets who have been slain.[4] And in spite of everything the assurance given of old by Jahve to his prophets is given in response:

> 'Behold I will bring them from the north country and will gather them from the ends of the earth : and among them shall be the blind and the lame, the woman with child and she that is bringing forth, together, a great company of them returning hither.

[1] *Ps.* xxxiv, 10. [2] *Ps.* lxviii, 20 *seq.*

[3] All these texts have been collected by I. Loeb, *La Littérature des pauvres dans la Bible*, in *Revue des études juives*, XX (1890), 161 *sq.* ; XXI, 1, 161 ; XXIII, 1, 161. See Causse, *op. cit. infra.*

[4] *Pss.* xliii, lxxiii, lxxxviii, etc.

They shall come with weeping: and I will bring them back in mercy. And I will bring them through the torrents of waters in a right way: and they shall not stumble in it. For I am a father to Israel, and Ephraim is my firstborn.'[1]

And again:

'The Lord thy God in the midst of thee is mighty: he will save, he will rejoice over thee with gladness, he will be silent in his love, he will be joyful over thee in praise.'[2]

This will open the era of a new alliance, an alliance of peace and justice, sealed in the depth of the heart, and the Lord himself will instruct each one as his Master.[3]

This is the Lord who is coming: this is the Master whose words we shall hear ; his kingdom is near at hand.

BIBLIOGRAPHY, Section 5 :—J. Touzard, *L'argument prophétique* (*Revue prat. d'apol.*, VII (1908) ; and his article *Juif* (peuple) in *Dict. apolog.*, II, 1614–37. B. J. Warfield, *The Divine Messiah in the Old Testament* in *Princeton Theol, Review*, XIV (1916). A. Causse, *Les Pauvres d'Israël* (*Prophètes, Psalmistes. Messianistes*) (Strasbourg, 1922).

[1] *Jer.* xxxi, 8-9.
[2] *Sophonias*, iii, 17.
[3] *Jer.* xxxi, 31–34 ; *Is.* liv, 10.

CHAPTER II

Palestinian Judaism

The books of the Old Testament had a supreme interest for us; although we could not find there the dogma of the Trinity clearly and fully revealed, at least we were able to discover at their sources many a doctrine which, in later days, was to take its place in Christian dogma. The later books of Palestinian Judaism, *Apocalypses, Targums, Talmuds, Midrashes,* cannot claim the same rôle; they are not the sources of our dogma, and they exercised only a very slight influence on the theology of the Trinity. Yet they cannot be entirely overlooked: placed in relation to the Jewish revelation from which they are derived, but which they distort, they show us more clearly its true direction; compared with the Christian books, composed at the same date, they show all the difference which distinguishes the tradition of men from the revelation of God. If my account of them is sufficiently faithful, this twofold comparison will become clear of itself, without any need for me to insist on it.

This account does not propose to retrace in all their complexities the conceptions of God, of the powers and intermediary beings who mingle confusedly in the Rabbinical writings, and still less to reduce them to unity. As L. Blau wisely observes, speaking precisely of these theses: 'We find neither in the *Targum* nor in the *Talmud* nor in the *Midrash* any absolute coherence, because so many have expressed their views in them.'[1]

We shall therefore merely note here, in the Judaism of this period, those doctrines which bear a less remote relation to the theology of the Trinity.

[1] Article *Shekinah*, in *Jewish Encyclopedia*, 259. Cf. Schechter, *Some Aspects of Rabbinic Theology*, in *JQR*, VI (1894); G. F. Moore, *Christian Writers on Judaism*, in *Harvard Theol. Review*, XIV (1921), 197–254.

1. God

If we consider nothing but the apocalypses and the *Targums,* we see chiefly, in Jewish theology, an effort to affirm the divine transcendence, at the risk of isolating God from the world. This characteristic is in fact very strongly marked, particularly in the most ancient form of Judaism, and we shall shortly need to insist upon it; but it should not make us lose sight of the conception of the paternity of God: the seers of the apocalypses more often neglect this conception,[1] the translators of the *Targums* efface it in the Biblical texts,[2] but from the end of the first century of our era[3] the Rabbis take it up and implement their doctrine with it.[4]

> 'One should not say,' taught Eleazar ben Azaria (A.D. 100), 'I have no desire to wear clothes of mingled fabrics, nor to eat pork, nor to contract a prohibited marriage; I consequently abstain from these actions. One should rather say: I should indeed like to do these things, but what is my duty since my Father in heaven has forbidden me to do them?'[5]

A century later Jehuda ben Tema said: 'Be courageous as a leopard, swift as an eagle, agile as a gazelle, and strong as a lion to do the will of thy Father in heaven.'[6] In the prayers, particularly in the *Chemone-Esre,*[7] the title of Father is often given to God, usually associated with the title of King, which gives it a more definite significance; it expresses more veneration than tenderness, and recalls the text of *Malachias:* 'If I am your Father, where is the honour that is due to me?' rather than the prayers or parables of the gospel.[8]

At other times it is Israel who is represented as the Son of God; the texts here are much more numerous, and their accent more familiar and more tender.[9] But we feel in them a wild exclusiveness and sometimes an intolerable pride; God belongs to Israel as much as Israel to

[1] In *Jubilees*, 1, 28, God is called 'the Father of all the children of Jacob.'

[2] Cf. DALMAN, *Die Worte Jesu*, 156–7.

[3] *Ibid.*, 152.

[4] See ABRAHAMS, *op. cit. infra*, 119, 139; ABELSON, *op. cit. infra*, 286; WALKER, *op. cit. infra*, 36–8.

[5] *Sifrâ*, 93d, tr. LAGRANGE (*Le Messianisme*, 152).

[6] *Aboth*, V, 20a (ed. STRACK, 46).

[7] See DALMAN, *op. cit.*, 156.

[8] *Ibid.*, 157.

[9] Cf. Rabbi JEHOUDA (*Mekilta*, on *Ex.* xiv, 19).

God. Eleazar ben Azaria interpreted in this sense *Deut.* xxvi, 17-18: (Thou hast chosen the Lord this day to be thy God . . . And the Lord hath chosen thee this day); 'As thou,' he makes God say, 'recognisest me as sole God in the world so I recognise thee as the sole people on the earth.'[1] In the same way Aqiba says in his commentary on *Exodus* xv, 2:

> 'I wish to speak of the beauties and charms of the Holy One, blessed be his name, before all the peoples of the world. For behold the peoples of the world ask the Israelites (*Cant.* v, 9): "What manner of one is thy beloved of the beloved, that thou hast so adjured us" that you should be so determined to die for him, to be beaten for him, as it is written (*ibid.* 1, 2): "Therefore young maidens have loved thee," that is to say, thou art loved even unto death [a play upon the similar Hebrew words for "young maidens" and "unto death"]; and again (*Ps.* xliii, 22): "For thy sake we are killed all the day long"? Behold, you are beautiful; behold, you are heroes; come and join yourselves to us! But the Israelites answer them: Do you know him? We will tell you of some of his charms: "My beloved is white and ruddy" (*Cant.* v, 10). When they hear these praises, they say to the Israelites: We wish to go with you, as it is written (*ibid.* v, 17): "Whither is thy beloved gone, O thou most beautiful among women? Whither is thy beloved turned aside, and we will seek him with thee?" But the Israelites answer them: You have no part at all in him, but (*ibid.* ii, 16): "My beloved to me, and I to him"; and again (*ibid.* vi, 2): "I to my beloved, and my beloved to me."' (*Mekilta,* on *Ex.* xv, 2; translation by Winter-Wuensche, 122.)

The ardour of this religious faith cannot be ignored, and the death of Aqiba says enough for its sincerity, but it is labour lost to try and conceal its exclusiveness[2]; the above-quoted page, so eloquent in spite of its subtleties, so passionate, so wild, is worthy of him who was the master and martyr of Judaism; but it is no surprise that its author was the principal support of the false Messias, of the unhappy and cruel Bar-Kokeba.

[1] BACHER, I[2], p. 226. [2] See WINTER-WUENSCHE, *loc. cit.*, 123, n. 1.

Nor is it astonishing that this jealous and narrow conception of the God of Israel should have impoverished religion: later on they reached the point of representing God as himself subject to the law, keeping the Sabbath, reciting his daily prayer,[1] having himself purified by Aaron after being defiled by contact with Egypt[2] or purifying himself by fire after he had buried Moses.[3] By making the yoke of the law applicable to God himself, the Jews thought they were making it more tolerable as well as more sacred; they did, however, but render their own servitude more inevitable by extending it to God.

In the conceptions of the divine paternity, and the relations of God with Israel hitherto examined, we find an effort on the part of pious Jews to approach nearer to God, or, rather, to bring God nearer to them. Another current of thought, less profound, no doubt, but more patent in the more ancient books, has a tendency to keep God far from the world and men.

This preoccupation shows itself in the apocalypses, particularly in the *Ascensions,* in which the imagination of the writers developed itself freely in order to describe the immense itinerary of the Seer.

> 'Henoch carried off by the winds approaches a palace built by hailstones, surrounded by flames, and inhabited by the Cherubim. This is not yet the house of God. He arrives at length before a house built of tongues of fire, and in every way so excellent in its magnificence, its splendour, and its grandeur that it cannot be described. Its floor was of fire, its higher parts were formed of the stars and light, and its roof of burning flame.'[4]

It was still relatively simple: in the Slav version of *Henoch,* in the apocalypse of Abraham the journey was much more complicated.[5] Father Lagrange, from whom I quote these lines, adds with reason: 'If the object of religion is to unite man with God, we cannot but regret the ancient God of Israel, who was always in the midst of his people.'

The speculations of the Rabbis, whose esoteric tradition will weave its fantasies round the throne of God,

[1] Cf. Abelson, 70, n. 1. [2] *Chemoth rabba,* 15 (Weber, 159).
[3] *Sanhedrin,* 30a (*ibid.*). [4] *Henoch* xiv, 7. [5] Lagrange, *Le Messianisme,* 53.

his glory, and, above all, the chariot described in the vision of Ezechiel, go still further than the imagination of the authors of the *Apocalypses.*[1]

These apocalyptic or theosophic reveries only reached fairly limited groups of initiates. But the Aramaic translations of the Bible, the *Targums,* were read by all Israelites, and led them by other ways to the same conception of a God separated from the world.

The anthropomorphic images, so frequent in the Biblical narrative, are scrupulously effaced, being replaced by the familiar style of the authors of the apocalypses. These, in order the better to indicate the transcendence of their visions, often avoid direct descriptions, replacing them with comparisons: 'The walls of this house were like a mosaic of hailstones, its roof was like the path of the stars.'[2] The Targumists willingly employ the same periphrasis; we read in *Genesis* (xviii, 8) that the angels received by Abraham ate, as well as those taken in by Lot (xix, 3). The *Targum* of Jonathan translates 'it was as if they ate.'[3]

More frequently the writer has recourse to another procedure, often employed in the apocalypses[4]: instead of saying that God does or sees something, he states that something is said or done before God: the passive turn of the phrase shows the effect, but conceals the agent, and God appears no longer as an actor in the drama, but rather as the judge or the witness in whose presence everything happens. The writer no longer ventures to say that God wishes or knows something, but that something has been agreeable or manifested to him.[5] Often these slight retouches are insufficient, and a more energetic treatment had to be applied to the text to soften it. Man is no longer created in the image of God (*Gen.* i, 26), but 'in the image of the angels'; 'Adam has become as one of us' (*Gen.* iii, 32) is translated: 'Adam has become unique in the world.' God says to Jacob: 'Thou hast been strong against God' (*Gen.* xxxii, 28), becomes in the *Targum* of Onkelos: 'Thou hast become great before Jahve and men.' We read in *Exodus* (xxxiii, 11) that

[1] See the references to the great Rabbis in BACHER, I[2], 39, 56, 70, 261, 332, etc.

[2] *Henoch* xix, 10, 11.

[3] Cf. WEBER, 155.

[4] Cf. LAGRANGE, *Le Messianisme*, 43.

[5] See GINSBURGER, *op. cit. infra*, 29–34.

Moses spoke to God 'face to face'; in the *Targum* of Jonathan: 'Moses heard the sound of his voice but did not see the splendour of his face.'

The accumulation of all these corrections of detail completely distorts the Biblical narrative; God disappears from the history of his people. His very name Jahve is no longer pronounced. Already in the Septuagint the sentence of *Leviticus* (xxiv, 16) against blasphemers is translated: 'Let him who pronounces the name of the Lord be punished with death.' Josephus also says: 'God taught Moses the pronunciation of his name which men did not yet know; I have not the right to mention it.'[1]

In order to name God epithets are used: the Most High, the Holy One, He who is Blessed, the Eternal, the All-powerful, the Merciful, the Living One (or the Living God), etc.[2]; or names that express his dominion are used: the Lord or the God of Heaven, the Lord of Spirits, the King of Kings, etc.[3] Elsewhere abstract or figurative words are preferred: the Glory, the Power, the Name, the Word, the Place, the Heaven, the Dwelling. These figures of speech are inoffensive in themselves and we may note that they are employed even in the New Testament, but when they are exclusively used they tend to impoverish religion and to paralyse prayer. These exaggerated scruples may also develop superstition, or substitute the worship of intermediary powers for the worship of a God who has become inaccessible.

Judaism has not escaped these dangers: the name of Jahve in becoming mysterious, has also become a magic formula which has only to be pronounced to work wonders. Moses kills the Egyptian by merely pronouncing the name of his God[4]; Pharao, having begged Moses to whisper the name into his ear, fell to the ground unconscious; Moses restores his consciousness; Pharao wrote the name on a tablet and sealed it up: a priest who did not respect this secret was struck by death[5]; the Red Sea was divided because it had seen on the rod of Moses the divine name.[6] For God himself his name is a weapon,

[1] *Ant. Jud.*, II, 276.
[2] On these names see Bousset and Dalman, *opp. cit.*
[3] Bousset, 311–13.
[4] R. Nekhemia, in Bacher, II, 252.
[5] Artapan, in Euseb., *Præp. evang.*, IX, 27 (*P.G.*, XXI, 733).
[6] R. Nekhemia, in Bacher, II, 273.

and the only one he needs.[1] This superstition developed later: it was by pronouncing his own name that God created the world; the high priest Pinkhas, on pronouncing it, flew through the air in pursuit of Bileam, and Abisai kept David suspended between heaven and earth in order to escape the sword of the Philistine.[2]

Around and beneath this solitary and nameless God we sometimes find intermediary beings, as in this curious passage of the *Testament of Juda* (xxv, 1, 2):

> 'I and my brothers will be leaders in Israel, Levi the first, myself the second, Joseph the third, Benjamin the fourth, Simeon the fifth, Issachar the sixth, each of us in his proper rank. And the Lord has blessed Levi; the angel of the countenance has blessed me; the powers of the glory, Simeon; the heaven, Ruben; the earth, Issachar; the sea, Zabulon; the mountains, Joseph; the tabernacle, Benjamin; the luminaries, Dan; Eden, Nephtali; the sun, Gad; the moon, Aser.'

It would be imprudent to exaggerate these personifications, so heterogeneous in comparison with the elements and the stars, the angel of the Face, the powers of the glory, and also no doubt the dwelling-place or Shekina, as it was called later in Judaism. We must recognise, however, that the distinction of these forces and their personification are no less clearly pointed out in this Palestinian text of the second century B.C. than the personification of the powers in Philo.

It is not, therefore, a matter for surprise that the Jews should have been tempted to worship the angels and the elements. The prohibition of *Exodus* (xx, 23): 'You shall not make gods of silver nor . . . of gold,' is interpreted by Rabbi Ishmael[3] as forbidding the making of statues of angels, of ophanim, or of cherubim, and in the *Targum* of Jerusalem as forbidding the adoration of representations of the sun, the moon, the stars, the planets, and angels. The history of the Judaising heresy of Colosse is enough to show that this worship of the angels was no imaginary danger.[4]

[1] R. JEHUDA, in *Mekilta*, on *Ex.* xv, 3.

[2] See HEITMUELLER, *Im Namen Jesu*, 132 *sq.*

[3] *Mekilta*, in *h.l.*

[4] Cf. A. L. WILLIAMS, *Cult of the Angels at Colossæ* (*JTS*, 1909), 413–39.

According to a curious conversation of Rabbis Ishmael and Aqiba, on the first verse of *Genesis,* we see that some Jewish doctors were tempted to deify the heaven and the earth and to interpret this verse in the manner of certain later Gnostics.[1]

But it was the very attributes of God which tended to become imperfectly distinguished from God, and to become powers, as in the teaching of Philo. We know that for the Alexandrine philosopher the two principal powers were distinguished as the two names of God: *theos,* Elohim, which is the creative or beneficent power, and *kyrios,* Jahve, which is the royal power, or justice.[2] This distinction is truly Jewish in origin[3]; an analogue, in the inverse sense, is to be found in Palestinian Judaism; wherever God is called Jahve, he is acting with mercy —when he is called Elohim, he is acting with strict justice.[4] Certain Rabbis make this distinction sharper: when interpreting the passage in *Daniel* where it is said: '. . . until the seats were placed,' Rabbi Joseph the Galilean and Rabbi Aqiba explain that one of the seats is for justice and the other for benevolence.[5] Nevertheless, the passage of the *Talmud* in which this interpretation is mentioned also refers to the lively disapproval which it encountered from another Rabbi, Eleazar, son of Azariah. By that date indeed the controversy with the *Minim,* that is to say, probably with the Christians,[6] had made all distinction of powers in God suspect.[7]

Bibliography, Section 1:—I. Abrahams, *Studies in Pharisaism and the Gospels*, I (Cambridge, 1917). J. Abelson, *The Immanence of God.* T. Walker, *Teaching of Jesus and the Jewish Teaching of His Age* (London, 1923). M. Ginsburger, *Die Anthropomorphismen in den Thargumim* (Brunswick, 1891). M. Joel, *Blicke in die Religionsgeschichte zu Aufang des zweiten christlichen Jahrhunderts* (Breslau, 1880). M. Friedlaender, *Die religiösen Bewegungen innerhalb des Judentums im Zeitalter Jesu* (Berlin, 1905). R. T. Herford, *Christianity in Talmud and Midrash.* G. Hoennicke, *Der Minaismus*, in *Das Judenchristentum im 1ten und 2ten Jahrh.* (Berlin, 1908).

1 *b. Khagiga*, 12a.
2 See below, page 153.
3 Cf. Bréhier, *Les idées philosophiques de Philon*, 147.
4 *Sifre*, 71a (on *Deut.* iii, 24).
5 *b. Sanh.*, 38b.
6 See Friedlaender, Herford, Hoennicke, *opp. cit. infra.*
7 Cf. Herford, *op. cit. infra*, 261; Friedlaender, *op. cit. infra*, 186.

2. *The Spirit*

The doctrinal development which has just been outlined deformed rather than enriched Jewish theology. It presents at all events the interest of a spontaneous and living evolution. We cannot say as much for the doctrines of the Spirit, of Wisdom, or of the Word, which must now be expounded.

At first sight it may seem that these different aspects of the theology of the Old Testament are progressively clarified in Judaism. As regards the Spirit, several historians point out as proof of progress[1] the name of 'Holy Spirit' which is given to the Spirit in the Old Testament as it will be one day in the New.[2] I do not know that we should attach so much significance to this custom: it would seem that it should be mostly attributed to the desuetude into which the name of Jahve began to fall; when the Jews could no longer say: Spirit of Jahve, they said: Spirit of holiness, or Holy Spirit.[3]

More remarkable, no doubt, is the personification of the Spirit, frequent enough in the Rabbinical writings; the authors do not hesitate to say that the 'Holy Spirit' speaks, the 'Holy Spirit' cries out.[4] These habits of style are noteworthy and very different from those that we have previously remarked in the Old Testament; nevertheless, we find in the writings of the Rabbis so many personified abstractions that it is rash to attribute to the Spirit a more defined hypostasis than to the Shekina or to the Memra.

A much more important fact than these usages of language is that the Holy Spirit is no longer represented, as in the Prophets, as an actual and active force. Neither the authors of the Apocalypses nor the Rabbis are aware of undergoing the action of the Spirit, of being inspired and moved by him, as were Isaias or Ezechiel, and in the near future the Apostles will be. We read in the *Talmud* that the ancient temple contained five treasures which Israel lost with it: the heavenly fire, the Ark of the Covenant, Urim and Thummim, the oil of consecration,

[1] See Hackspill, *RB*, 1902, 70.
[2] See *Is.* lxiii, 10, 11; *Ps.* l, 13; *Dan.* iv, 5, 6, 15; v, 11.
[3] See Abelson, *Immanence of God*, 174–277.
[4] See *Mekilta*, on *Ex.* xv, 2, 9.

and the Holy Spirit.[1] We have here no doubt one of those fantastic enumerations which pleased the Rabbis, but it is a characteristic statement of which the post-exilic books show many traces: 'There are no more prophets.'[2] Hence that impression so often expressed, of the provisional, of expectation. They refrain from settling doubtful cases; the decision of them is reserved to the Prophet who shall come. He will decide the fate of those sacerdotal families whose pedigrees have been lost[3]; he will say what is to be done with the remains of the Altar of Holocausts, profaned by the Gentiles.[4]

Simon is appointed chief, and high priest, 'till there should arise a faithful prophet,'[5] and when John the Baptist shall appear they will come and ask him 'Art thou the Prophet?'[6] We may attribute to the same cause the servility towards the written law and tradition: all light is to be found in the past, the doctors of Israel do but repeat a lesson they have learnt; we know what astonishment was provoked by Jesus, when he began to teach 'as one having authority.'

From this slavery of the letter, the Spirit delivered Christians, and one has but to read over the *Epistle to the Galatians* to feel the value of this deliverance, to appreciate the contrast of these two religions. But once this is understood we shall no longer seek a living doctrine of the Spirit among the slaves of the letter; on this point also, Christianity depends on the teaching of the prophets; from Judaism it has only received a few formulas.

Apart from this, in Judaism itself the most striking features of the doctrine of the Spirit come from the theology of the prophets. Very notable is the influence of a text of *Isaias* (xi, 2 *seq.*): 'And the spirit of the Lord shall rest upon him: the spirit of wisdom and of understanding ...' We find an echo of this in *Henoch* (xlix, 3): 'in him (the elect) dwells the spirit of wisdom and the spirit of illumination, and the spirit of science and of force, and the spirit of those who are sleeping in justice.'[7] In the

1 *b. Ioma*, 21b; *j. Taanith*, II, 1; *j. Makkoth*, II, 6.
2 *Ps.* lxxiii, 9; cf. 1 *Mach.* ix, 27.
3 1 *Esdr.* ii, 63; 2 *Esdr.* vii, 65.
4 1 *Mach.* iv, 46.
5 *Ibid.*, xiv, 41; cf. PHILO, *De spec. leg.*, I, 65 (*M.*, II, 222).
6 *John* i, 21.
7 The quotations from *Henoch* are from MARTIN's translation.

Testament of Levi (xviii, 7): 'the spirit of intelligence and holiness shall rest on him.' In the *Psalms of Solomon* (xvii, 42): 'God has made him powerful by the holy spirit, and wise by the gift of clear counsel, accompanied by force and justice,' and in other similar texts.[1]

Yet other passages mention incidentally the sanctifying action of the Spirit of God. Thus Joseph 'had the Spirit of God in him' (*Testament Sim.* iv, 4); the good man 'loves him who has the grace of the good Spirit' (*Test. Benj.* iv, 4). In some other texts the prophetic operation of the Spirit is mentioned; in the *Book of the Jubilees* (xxxi, 12) we are told how Isaac blessed the sons of Jacob: 'the Spirit of prophecy descended into his mouth, with his right hand he took Levi, and with his left hand Juda, and, turning towards Levi, he blessed him first, and said . . .' Esdras, wishing to rewrite the destroyed law, prays to God in these terms: "If I have found grace before thee, send to me thy Holy Spirit, and I will write all that has happened from the beginning" (4 *Esdras* xiv, 22).'[2]

These various texts are isolated in the midst of this literature. Evidently the belief in spirits was at that time much more living than the belief in the Spirit. The *Book of the Testaments* is the work in which these doctrines are the most developed, but the Spirit of God is rarely mentioned[3]; and several passages where the Spirit is mentioned are of doubtful authenticity. On the other hand, they constantly mention the spirits of Satan,[5] the spirits of Beliar,[6], of error,[7] of envy,[8] of anger,[9] of fornication,[10] of hatred,[11] and also the spirits who are the ministers of divine vengeance.[12] What is more surprising is that we find even in this book the Stoic conception of the seven spirits

[1] Cf. *Henoch* lxii, 2.

[2] This belief in the prophetic Spirit is most frequently found in the Rabbinical books. Although they reveal very few original ideas, one of them is worth noticing, the doctrine of the transmission of the Spirit by the imposition of hands; cf. Coppens, *L'imposition des mains* (Paris, 1925), 162–9.

[3] *Sim.* iv, 4; *Levi*, ii, 3, xviii, 7, 11; *Juda*, xx, 1, 5, xxiv, 2; *Benj.* iv, 5, viii, 2, ix, 4.

[5] *Dan*, vi, 1. [6] *Issach.* vii, 7; *Dan*, i, 7; *Jos.* vii, 4; *Benj.* iii, 3, 4, vi, 1.

[7] *Rub.* ii, 1, 2, iii, 3; *Sim.* iii, 1, vi, 6; *Levi*, iii, 3; *Juda*, xiv, 8, xx, 1, 2, xxv, 3; *Issach.* iv, 4; *Nephth.* iii, 3; *Aser*, vi, 2; cf. *Simeon*, ii, 7.

[8] *Sim.* ii, 7, iv, 7; *Juda*, xiii, 3; *Dan*, i, 6.

[9] *Dan*, i, 8, ii, 1, ii, 4, iii, 6, iv, 5.

[10] *Rub.* v, 3; *Levi*, ix, 9; *Juda*, xiii, 3, xiv, 2.

[11] *Gad*, i, 9, iii, 1, iv, 7, vi, 2. [12] *Levi*, iii, 2.

which are the principles of the seven senses.[1] This is no doubt an interpolation, but a very ancient one, since it is found in the two Greek versions[2] ; moreover, even in its earliest parts, the book indicates a materialist conception of the spirit which agrees well enough with the Stoic doctrine.[3]

After the *Book of the Testaments,* the *Book of Henoch* gives us most information on the doctrine of the spirit at this stage. Here again the Spirit of God rarely appears[4] ; everywhere good and bad spirits are to the fore, chiefly in the *Book of Parables* (xxxvii-lxxi). The very name given to God more than a hundred[5] times in these thirty-five chapters is characteristic: He is called the 'Lord of Spirits.' It is not our intention to dwell on the angelology of this book,[6] nor to recall the profound and mischievous influence which it exercised on early Christian angelology. But we may note, for this concerns the notion of spirit, the extension of the rôle of spirits. To them is attributed, as in the *Testaments,* an influence over virtues and vices, but the point is little insisted on[7] ; on the other hand, they are intimately connected with natural phenomena, 'the spirit of the sea is masculine and vigorous ; the spirit of the frost is its own angel, and the spirit of hail is a good angel ; the spirit of snow lets it fall by its own weight ; the snow has a special spirit, what mounts from it is like smoke and its name is freshness. The spirit of fog has nothing to do with snow and hail . . . the spirit of the dew dwells in the extremities of heaven . . .' (lx, 16, 20). Elsewhere the changes in temperature of medicinal springs are attributed to the presence of spirits, and to the chastisements which they are undergoing (lxvii, 11). This conception has been justly compared to Babylonian animism[8] ; it is not very far either from Stoic 'pneumatism.'[9] It is not, however, necessary to suppose direct borrowing in order to explain these coincidences ; it

[1] *Rub.* ii, 3–8. [2] See CHARLES, English translation, p. 4.

[3] According to *Ruben*, iii, 3, the seven evil spirits are located in various parts of the body (belly, liver, etc.).

[4] Cf. BEER (in KAUTSCH, *Apokryphen des A. T.*).

[5] 104 times, according to CHARLES.

[6] Cf. MARTIN, *Le livre d'Hénoch*, pp. xxvi–xxxi.

[7] xv, 8 *sq.*, 'evil spirits' ; cf. lxi, 11, 'spirit of fidelity' ; and lxii, 2, 'spirit of justice.'

[8] MARTIN, *Le livre d'Hénoch*, p. xxv.

[9] Cf. PLUT., *De cess. orac.*, 39–41 (see page 66, above).

is sufficient to refer them to popular superstition, always inclined, and at that date more than ever, to people the world with spirits.

3. Wisdom

Wisdom, so clearly personified in the books of the Old Testament, has now lost much of its outline. It is usually confused with the Law.[1]

We find once more in the *Book of Henoch*, side by side with frequent but very short mentions of Wisdom,[2] an isolated fragment, which forms to-day chapter xlii, and which draws the contrast between wisdom and folly.

> 'Wisdom has not found a place to dwell in, so her home is in the heavens. She issued thence in order to dwell with the children of men where she found nowhere to dwell, so she returned to her home and established herself among the angels. And Injustice came out of her lair and found those whom she was not seeking and dwelt amongst them, as rain in the desert and dew falling on the thirsty earth.'

This short allegory, which is very reminiscent of the passage in *Proverbs* on Wisdom and Folly, evidently cannot be taken literally any more than the analogous images that are to be found in all the literatures of the world.[3]

In the book of the *secrets of Henoch* (xxx, 8), Wisdom is more definitely personified: 'On the sixth day,' said God, 'I commanded my Wisdom to make man.' We find here an interpretation of the text of *Gen.* i, 26: 'Let us make man . . . ,' very similar to that given by the majority of the Fathers; the Rabbis, on the contrary, find here an order given by God to his angels.[4]

It is not long before the whole of this doctrine becomes effaced, and Wisdom is confused with the Law, or disappears before it. In the Testament of Levi, the Aramaic fragments which come, it is thought, from a more ancient source, give the first rôle to Wisdom; the Greek text

[1] This identification may be found already in *Ecclus.* 1, 5 and *Baruch* iv, 1.

[2] Wisdom is represented as the assessor of God (lxxxiv, 3), and as judge of the whole earth (xcii, 1); this last reference may be an interpolation.

[3] E.g. Hesiod, *Works and Days*, 197 *sq.*; Virgil, *Georgics*, II, 473. Cf. Bultmann, *op. cit. infra*, 8–11.

[4] See Note I at end of volume.

gives it, on the contrary, to the Law.[1] In the first lines of the Berechith-rabba, Rabbi Hosea the Great interprets the first verse of *Genesis* by the text of *Proverbs* (viii, 30), which describes the rôle played by Wisdom with Jahve in the creation, but he does so by substituting the Law for Wisdom: it was the Thora that was then God's instrument, and also the ideal model in accordance with which God conceived the world.[2] Elsewhere in other compilations of a more or less degraded period, the Law is represented as being created by God before other beings, and as being his counsellor and aid in his creation of the world.[3]

BIBLIOGRAPHY Section 3 :—R. Bultmann, *Der religionsgeschichtl. Hintergrund des Prologs*, in ΕΥΧΑΡΙΣΤΗΡΙΟΝ (Gottingen, 1923).

4. *The Word*

The Word does not play the same rôle: in the *Wisdom of Solomon* it was compared with Wisdom, but we no longer find this comparison in the Rabbinical writings. The Word, or *Memra,* however, is very frequently mentioned by them, at least in the *Targums,* and many historians have seen in this the remains of a dogmatic tradition, from which the Johannine conception of the Word was derived.

Assuredly all is not false in this hypothesis: St. John, like the Targumists, derives from the prophets and the Psalmists, who had so often sung the sudden and irresistible efficacy of the divine word[4]; but this religious conception became enriched in the Sapiential books, and the Christian revelation was, in its turn, to transform it. This supreme transformation, it is unnecessary to say, did not reach the *Memra* of Judaism, and does not even give indications of the dogmatic progress realised in the Sapiential books. We come constantly, in the *Targums,* on the *Memra* of Jahve, living, speaking, acting; but if we attempt to render the significance of this expression more precisely we find, for the most part, nothing but a periphrasis, substituted by the Targumist for the name of

[1] *Testaments,* ed. CHARLES, app. iii, p. 255.
[2] *Berechith Rabba,* on *Gen. i,* 1 (WUENSCHE, p. 1).
[3] The references are given by STRACK-BILLERBECK, II, 353 *sq.*
[4] See above, page 98.

Jahve. As M. Dalman has justly remarked, 'There is no idea of constituting a divine hypostasis; "the Word" is pronounced, but "God" is meant.'[1]

Similarly the text in *Numbers* (xxiii, 4): 'God met Balaam,' is translated by Onkelos: 'The *Memra*[2] of the Face of the Lord met Balaam.' Again, he makes Moses say (*Deut.* v, 3): 'I stood between the *Memra* of the Lord and you.' We find the same in the *Targum of Jonathan* (*Is.* i, 14, 16, 20): 'Your new moons and your festivals are an abomination to my *Memra* . . . remove your evil actions from the sight of my *Memra* . . . You shall be slain with the sword, for thus has the *Memra* of the Lord decided.' Jacob no longer says (*Gen.* xxviii, 21): 'Jahve shall be my God,' but according to Onkelos: 'The *Memra* of Jahve shall be my God.' One of the most touching passages of *Isaias* (lxvi, 13) reads: 'As one whom the mother caresseth, so will I comfort you.' The *Targum of Jonathan* translates the same passage: 'My *Memra* shall console you.'

Such examples could be multiplied indefinitely[3]: in the *Targum of Jonathan* in particular, as Bousset remarks, this periphrasis is so frequently employed that it is almost always substituted for the name of God. But its significance is also obvious: it does not usually indicate an intermediary agent between God and the world,[4] but it throws a veil by this circumlocution over the divine presence or action. It may also be noted that the *Memra* is as unlike the Logos of Philo as the preoccupations of the Rabbis of Palestine are unlike the speculations of Alexandria; the problem which the Logos of Philo must solve is of a purely philosophical order: between God and man, infinitely distant one from the other, relations of action and prayer have to be established; the Logos is required as the intermediary. The difficulty preoccupying the Rabbis belongs above all to the order and practice of ritual: a religious scruple did not allow them to name God as often as he was named in the Bible, nor above all, did they dare attribute to him, directly and

[1] *Die Worte Jesu*, p. 188.

[2] *Memra* is the most common form; but, in the Targums of Jonathan and Jerusalem, *Dibbura* is also found, with the same meaning.

[3] See GINSBURGER, *op. cit. infra*, 7–20.

[4] KOHLER thinks differently; also DENNEFELD, art. *Judaïsme* in *Dict. de Théol.*, col. 1620. Cf. G. F. MOORE, 53–4; and STRACK-BILLERBECK, 333.

immediately, as many actions as did the sacred books; to calm their scruples it was enough to veil the divine Majesty under an abstract periphrasis: they speak of the Word, or the Glory,[1] or the Dwelling-place.[2] Doubtless from this point of view, the path was slippery which led them to the personification of these abstractions, and perhaps the *Memra* would have been more or less treated as a hypostasis, if that conception had been freely developed. Such was not the case. This word, so familiar to the Targumists, is very rarely employed in the *Talmud* and the *Midrash*. M. Kohler attributes this rarity to the mistrust felt by the Rabbis towards everything that had any resemblance to Christian dogma, and this hypothesis is likely enough. We must nevertheless recognise that between the *Memra* of the Targumists and the Logos of St. John there was hardly anything but a verbal analogy: the one is an abstract paraphrase which gives language a more impersonal tone, but without proposing to the thinker a reality distinct from God[3]; the other is a living and active Person, capable of incarnation, and of living among us. When Onkelos makes Jacob (*Gen.* xxviii, 21) say 'The *Memra* of Jahve shall be my God,' he does not mean to express the adoration of the patriarch for a divine Person, distinct from the Father; whereas when St. John writes, at the beginning of his Gospel, 'In the beginning was the *Logos* and the *Logos* was with God and the *Logos* was God,' he wishes to show from the very first the divine Word, shortly to take flesh, at the side of the heavenly Father. No doubt when he was writing his prologue the Rabbinical terminology was present to the mind of the Evangelist, and perhaps we should see a trace of this, not only in the mention of the *Logos*, but in that of his *glory* and of his *dwelling* among us.[4] But if the vocabularies are similar the meanings are profoundly different.

Bibliography, Section 4:—G. F. Moore, *Intermediaries in Jewish Theology*, in *Harvard Theol. Review*, XV (1922). F. C. Burkitt, *Memra, Shekinah, Metatron*, in *JTS*, XXIV (1923). Strack-Billerbeck, *Exkurs uber den Memra Jahves.* M. Ginsburger, *Die Anthropomorphismen in den Thargumim* (Brunswick, 1891).

[1] Cf. Ginsburger, 20.
[2] See Section 5, below.
[3] Cf. Ginsburger, 12.
[4] Dalman, 189.

5. *The Shekina*

What has been said of the *Memra* may also be applied to the Dwelling-place or Shekina; Weber has noticed a notable difference of use between these terms: in the *Targum* the Shekina had a more impersonal and abstract significance than the *Memra;* in the *Talmud,* on the other hand, it was substituted for the *Memra,* and played the part of an intermediary between God and the world. This interpretation, reproduced by certain commentators,[1] does not seem exact and has been generally abandoned.[2] It is true that in the *Talmud* and the *Midrash* the Shekina is more frequently mentioned than in the *Targum,*[3] but the value given to the expression is the same.

Most frequently that value is an abstraction replacing the divine Name, without introducing, at the side of God, a reality distinct from him.[4] Thus we read in the *Targum* of Onkelos (*Ex.* xxxiii, 14, 15) that God says: 'My Shekina shall go and I will give you rest,' and Moses replied before the Lord: 'If thy Shekina comes not with us, it were better not to make us leave this place'; and a little lower down (20) God says: 'Thou canst not see the face of my Shekina.' These texts and many others that could be added are similar to those quoted above with reference to the *Memra.*[5] The usage is the same in the *Midrashim.* Speaking of the flight from Egypt, Aqiba says:

> 'A parable: the son of a king went to live in a town by the sea; the king accompanied him and dwelt with him: he went to another town, the king still accompanied him and dwelt with him. Thus was it with the Israelites when they went down into Egypt, the Shekina was with them, as it is written (*Gen.* xlvi, 4): "I will go down with thee into Egypt"; and when they left, the Shekina was still with them according to what is written (*Ib.* xxvi, 17): "I will lead thee"; when they went down to the sea the Shekina was with them according to what

[1] HOLTZMANN, *Lehrb. d. neutest. Theol.* (1st edit.), I, 57.

[2] DALMAN, p. 188 and n. 2.

[3] According to LANDAU (48), the term *Shekina* was probably introduced by AQIBA; it certainly does not occur before his time.

[4] See MAYBAUM, *op. cit. infra*, and LANDAU (*loc. cit.*, p. 54).

[5] Cf. GFRÖRER, 314 *sq.*

is written (*Ex.* xiv, 19): "The angel of the Lord who preceded Israel advanced"; when they proceeded into the desert, the Shekina was still with them according to what is written (*Ib.* xiii, 21): "The Lord preceded them during the day." '[1]

It is clear that God is here represented by the father in the parable, as well as in the Bible texts quoted. But we also see that for Aqiba, 'the Lord,' 'the Angel of the Lord,' and the 'Shekina,' are equivalent and interchangeable terms.

It may be noted, however, that the Shekina is mentioned in order to express the dwelling of God with his people or his faithful.[2] This denotes a certain vestige of the primitive meaning of this term. We find again such a vestige in the very frequent association of the Shekina and glory, the dwelling-place of Jahve appearing to the Israelites as shining with his splendour.[3]

It is useless to speak here of other expressions, like the 'Place'[4] or the 'Heaven,'[5] which, like the *Memra* and the Shekina, have been used to designate God[6]; for here there is no appearance of personification, nor, consequently, any ambiguity to dissipate. The same may be said of the 'Voice of God' or of the 'Finger of God'[7] of which the Rabbis celebrated the power but in which no one will be tempted to see hypostases. As regards the Metatron, the term denotes the chief of the angels and in no sense a divine person; it was only introduced fairly late into Rabbinic theology, and with the object of getting rid of the Alexandrine doctrine of divine intermediaries.[8]

BIBLIOGRAPHY, Section 5:—Maybaum, *Die Anthropomorphien und Anthropopathien bei Onkelos und den spateren Targumim* (Breslau, 1870).

[1] *Mekilta*, on *Exod.* xv, 2.
[2] Cf. also *Pirké Aboth*, III, 8, and other texts in SCHWAB, I, 240.
[3] Cf. WEBER, 185 *sq.*
[4] Cf. LANDAU, 30–45; DALMAN, 189.
[5] Cf. LANDAU, 14–30; DALMAN, 179.
[6] LANDAU (6–10) has a list of fifty-seven expressions used by Rabbis to designate 'God.'
[7] See BACHER, I, 148; WUENSCHE, 19.
[8] See HERFORD, *Christianity in Talmud*, 287.

6. *The Messias*

Of all the religious conceptions of the Old Testament there is none which acted more efficaciously on primitive Christianity than the belief in the Messias: it was by recognising in Jesus the expected Messias that the disciples began to believe in him. A peculiar interest is therefore attached to enquiry into the progress or distortion in Jewish literature of the Messianic doctrine which the Old Testament has taught us. It is impossible to describe, in a few pages, so complex a reality; so we shall refer the reader for matters of detail to the studies of Volz and of Père Lagrange,[1] we will devote our own efforts to disengaging the elements which had most influence on the faith of the first Christians.

It is enough to read the Gospels to be aware that the Jewish people in the time of Jesus Christ were awaiting a Messias, and that they represented him above all as the son of David, and the King of Israel. The writings of Josephus show the same image. This popular belief, unanimously attested by the historical writings of the Jews or Christians, is also expressed in the Sibylline Books, and the works of Philo, that is to say, generally, in Hellenic literature.

This belief, very ancient and almost universal, has nevertheless been modified in certain circles under the influence of the events which overthrew Jewish history. The long and brilliant domination of the Asmonean princes, themselves of sacerdotal stock, has sometimes caused the attribution of the privileges of Juda to the tribe of Levi: in the *Testament* of the twelve Patriarchs the Messias is a descendant of Levi[2]: so, the author of the Sadocite *Treatise* constantly presents the Messias as the descendant of 'Aaron and Israel.'[3]

This Levitical tendency has left but slight traces and has exercised no influence on the origins of Christian dogma. The same cannot be said of the universalist conceptions. We have observed above[4] how, after the exile,

[1] VOLZ, *Jüdische Eschatologie von Daniel bis Akiba* (Tubingen, 1903), 197–236; LAGRANGE, *Le Messianisme chez les Juifs* (Paris, 1909), 66–115, 210–56.

[2] CHARLES, *Testaments*, pp. xcvii–xcviii.

[3] II, 10, VIII, 2, IX, 10, 29, XV, 4, XVIII, 8 (published by SCHECHTER, 1910).

[4] Page 76 *sq.*

Judaism had enlarged its horizons: Jahve is always worshipped as the God of Israel, but at the same time, and more and more, as the God of the universe. This progress of religious thought also transforms Jewish eschatology, and with it, belief in the Messias. Instead of being totally absorbed in the destiny of Israel, by the restoration of his kingdom and the advent of the son of David, the hopes of many Jewish writers of this period extend over the whole world, and are at the same time concentrated on each individual soul: what these apocalypses describe is no longer merely the triumph of Israel; it is the arrival of a new world, and also the salvation of the just.

But many have not a sufficiently exalted idea of the Messias to attribute to him a rôle so universal and so important: they therefore turn aside from the idea and describe an eschatology from which the Messias is absent, as is the case in most of the *Book of Henoch*,[1] in the fourth of the *Sibylline Books*, and in the *Assumption of Moses*.

The conception of the Messias, as well as the hope of salvation, is elevated and enlarged in other books; this transformation may be observed in the seventeenth psalm of Solomon: the Messias is there represented as the King of Israel, but so powerful, and, above all, so holy that he dominates all humanity: 'There is a just King instructed by God, established over them (the sons of Jerusalem); and, during his days, there is no iniquity among them; for all are holy and their King is the Christ (of) the Lord.[2] . . . The Lord himself is their king and their hope, and he is powerful in his hope in God; and he will have pity on all the nations who tremble before him. For he will overcome the earth for ever by the word of his mouth and will bless the people of the Lord in joy and wisdom. And he will be pure of sin in order to govern these great peoples, to reprove their leaders and to destroy sinners by the force of his word. And, relying on his God, he will not grow weak during the days of his rule, because God has made him powerful by the holy spirit, and wise in counsel and intelligence, and force and justice . . . he is powerful in his works and strong in the fear of God.

[1] Both MARTIN and GRY, in their works on the *Book of Henoch*, deny the authenticity of the passage at the end of the fifth part where the Messias is given the title of 'son.'

[2] 'The Christ Lord' in the text; I agree with the majority of critics in rejecting it as unauthentic.

He feeds the Lord's flock in faith and justice and he will not allow disease among them in their pasturage ; he will lead them all equally, and there will not be any spirit of pride or domination among them. Such is the majesty of the King of Israel that God foresaw, raising him up over the house of Israel for its correction ' (*Ps. Sol.* xvii, 35-47).

When this song was written, Pompey had just made his entry into Jerusalem (B.C. 63) ; on the morrow of this triumph of the Pagans, followed by the massacre and captivity of so many Jews, the unknown psalmist evokes the Messianic hopes. In this psalm (xvii) he gives them their purest and highest form ; the reign that he longs for is a reign of justice and holiness established over the whole earth by the Christ of the Lord. This King of Israel will be all-powerful but with a purely spiritual power, the source of which is the divine gifts that Jahve, according to the ancient prophecy of Isaias, will impart to him.

Some years before these psalms[1] another book had been written, which traced an even more transcendent portrait of the Messias ; this book, which we can read to-day in chapters xxxvii-lxix of the *Book of Henoch,* is commonly called the *Book of Parables ;* there also the Messias appears clothed with all spiritual gifts:

> ' In him dwells the spirit of wisdom, and the spirit who enlightens, and the spirit of knowledge and of power, and the spirit of those who are sleeping in justice ' (xlix, 3).

His glory is universal and eternal (xlix, 2) ; but above all, his person is presented clothed in a mysterious majesty, transcending the whole of humanity:

> ' There I saw another who had a head of days, whose head was white as wool ; and with him another whose face resembled a man's, full of grace, like one of the holy angels. I questioned the angel who was walking with me and who taught me all secrets concerning this Son of man: " Who is he and whence does he come, why does he walk with the Head of days? "—He replied to me: " It is the Son of man, the possessor of justice, and with whom justice dwelleth, who will reveal all the

[1] MARTIN, p. xcvii, dates the *Book of Parables* 95–78 B.C. ; it may be even later, 70–64 B.C.

treasures that are hidden because the Lord of spirits has chosen him, and he has rightly conquered before the Lord of spirits for eternity. The Son of man whom thou has seen will cause kings and rulers to rise from their couches and strong men from their seats; he will burst the bonds of the strong, and break the teeth of sinners; he will overturn kings on their thrones and destroy their power because they have not exalted and glorified him and have not humbly confessed him who had given them their royalty" (xlvi, 1, 5). At this moment that name was given to the Son of man in the presence of the Lord of Spirits, and his name (was named) before the Head of days. And before the sun and the signs were created, and the stars of heaven were made, his name was given him before the Lord of spirits. He shall be a staff for the just that they may lean on him without falling; and the hope of those who suffer in their hearts and the light of the peoples. All those who dwell in the desert shall prostrate themselves before him and adore him; they shall bless and glorify and sing the praises of the Lord of Spirits. It is for this that he was chosen and dwelt secretly before him (the Lord), before the creation of the world and from all eternity. The wisdom of the Lord of spirits has revealed him to the just and holy, for he has preserved what is due to the just, because they have hated and despised this world of injustice and all its ways and works, in the name of the Lord of spirits; for by his name shall they be saved and he is the avenger of their life. In these days the kings of the earth and the mighty ones who possess the desert will be humbled through the work of their hands, for they shall not be saved in the day of their anguish and affliction . . . there shall be no one to give them a hand and lift them up, because they have denied the Lord of spirits and his Messias. Blessed be the name of the Lord of spirits! (xlviii, 2-10). Then it came to pass that his name (Henoch) was glorified, while he was yet alive, before this Son of man and before the Lord of Spirits, far from those who dwell in the desert . . . And there I saw the first fathers and the saints who dwell from all eternity in that place' (lxx, 1-4).

One has only to read these texts to recognise the transcendence attributed to the Messias; his rôle is no doubt that which is described in the *Psalms of Solomon* and by the Jewish tradition as a whole; it is he who will break all the powers raised against God and avenge the just. But this conquering king is at the same time the universal judge before whom, not only all men, saints, and sinners, but the angels themselves, have to appear. And the grandeur of his person surpasses all the holiness and grandeur which we find here below; he appears as 'one of the holy angels.' Yet he is distinct from the angels and superior to them; he is called 'the Son of man,' and we perceive him in heaven mingling and dwelling with just men glorified (xxxix, 6; lxii, 4); he exists before the creation of the world and dwells close to God, under his wings. He is his elect and his adviser, and receives with him the benedictions and the worship which men pay him. 'He represents,' says Martin,[1] 'the most ideal type conceived by Jewish Messianism before Christianity.' We see already in this outline many of the traits which will be adopted and accentuated by Christianity: they are primarily the names given here to this supernatural personage: The Messias,[2] the Just One,[3] the Elect,[4] above all, the Son of man, a title which we already found in *Daniel* and which Jesus Christ will adopt as his own name.[5] Then there are also the descriptions of the judgment in which one hears here and there,[6] as it were, an anticipated echo of the gospel. But we also see how uncertain and vague are these characteristics: this supernatural personage, this Son of man, is properly speaking neither a man nor a God: if he mixes with men, it is only in the distant paradise in which the just 'will become angels' (li, 4); nothing in him recalls the humility of the Saviour nor his sufferings, nor his mercy, nor is there anything in him that reveals the Son of God.[7] He appears as a privileged being at the side of the Lord of the spirits, elect among all and placed over their heads; but this superhuman grandeur proceeds from a free choice of God, and not from a community of nature nor a filiation. We may add that it would be rash to insist too much on

[1] Martin, p. xxxviii.

[2] xlviii, 10, lii, 4.

[3] xxxviii, 2, liii, 6.

[4] xl, 5, etc.

[5] Cf. L. Gry, *Les Parables d'Hénoch*, 50–74.

[6] lxii, 3, 5; lxix, 27.

[7] See above, page 127, note 1.

details of expression: the *Book of Henoch* comes before us as a compilation of which the original texts have been lost; the Ethiopian translations which we possess have not been made on the original texts, whether Hebrew or Aramaic, but on Greek translations; these double translations have been made in surroundings completely saturated with Christian ideas and are very probably influenced by them. These reasons impose a reserve on the part of the historian.[1] This lofty conception of the Messias, which appears in the *Book of the Parables of Henoch,* is to be found in Jewish literature, without exercising any profound influence on it: in the later Apocalypses there are some insignificant similarities with the *Book of Henoch;* it has not left any traces after the second century in Jewish literature.[2]

Towards the end of the first century of our era, after the fall of Jerusalem, the *Apocalypse of Esdras* describes once more the Messianic times and the great vindication which the Jews expect from them. This book was certainly written at Rome by a Pharisee at the end of the first century, and enjoyed a fairly large circulation among the Jewish and Christian circles of Palestine and Egypt.[3]

Here again the original texts have been lost; we only get at them through various versions, the witness of which is not always in agreement, and unfortunately these divergencies often concern the most important passages.[4]

Certain features may, however, be selected which, without having anything like the definite outline of the descriptions of Henoch, nevertheless attribute to the Messias a supernatural grandeur. He is already in existence, but is hidden with the just in a place where none can see him, whence God will suddenly cause him to appear (xiii, 26, 52): there is here no doubt a kind of pre-

[1] LAGRANGE (*Le Messianisme*, pp. 89–90) thinks that the *Book of Parables* may have undergone interpolation by a Christian writer who identified the 'Elect' of the original book with Jesus. 'What confirms this supposition,' he adds, 'is that this part of the *Book of Henoch* is the only one among all the apocalypses which presents remarkable similarities to the Gospels. Have all the evangelists been uniformly inspired by this book, or has a Christian, conversant with the Gospels, made an interpolation? . . . Very great prudence is therefore necessary when arguing from the *Book of Henoch*, especially in respect of the title of "Son of man."'

[2] Cf. CHARLES, *Pseudepigrapha*, 179–80.

[3] See VIOLET's introduction (Leipzig, 1924) and J. KEULERS, *Die eschatologische Lehre des vierten Esrabuches* (Freiburg, 1922), 41–55.

[4] See the variants in VIOLET's ed. (Leipzig, 1910).

existence, but very different from what the *Book of Henoch* described; nor is it in any case a unique privilege; together with the Messias, the just are also set apart by God.[1] It does not seem that God calls the Messias 'my son'; for several Oriental versions have the words 'my servant' where the Latin says 'my son'; it is therefore very probable that we have here merely an echo of the ancient prophecies on the Servant of Jahve[2]; but, even if the name of 'son' is retained, we should observe that the writer himself never uses the term: 'Son of God.' 'This attenuation of language,' remarks Père Lagrange (*Le Messianisme,* p. 105), 'corresponds no doubt to a real distinction in meaning; it is one thing that God should say "my son," a term which he had already employed in Scripture when speaking of Israel and of the descendants of David; it is another that the writer should definitely call the Messias the Son of God.'

After this book the Messianic hope sinks lower, where it is not entirely effaced; by a spirit of opposition to Christianity, Judaism places the Messias at an ever-increasing distance from the divine sphere. Celsus[3] makes a Jew say 'that one day the son of God will come to judge the saints and chastise the wicked.' Origen replies:

> 'A Jew will never agree that a prophet has predicted the coming of a son of God: what they say is, that one day the Christ of God will come; it is precisely the idea of this "Son of God" which they attack, denying his existence and that any prophet has ever spoken of him.'[4]

St. Hippolytus[5] and St. Justin[6] had already pointed out this position of the Jews, and we can easily still recognise it in the Rabbinical writings.[7] The Rabbis effaced *a priori* all references in the Prophets to the transcendence of the Messias, and if by chance some Rabbi should so far forget himself as to represent the Messias as God, he is accused of blasphemy.[8] The Messias himself had also been accused of blasphemy; the Jews did not understand that, in his doctrine, and still more in his Person, he revealed the mystery of God, so unfathomable to man.

[1] Cf. Abelson, *Immanence of God*, 162, 171.
[2] See Violet's translation.
[3] In *The True Word*.
[4] *C. Cels.*, I, 49 (*GCS*, I, 100–1).
[5] *Philosoph.*, IX, 30 (*P.G.*, XVI, 3416).
[6] *Dial.*, 49.
[7] Strack-Billerbeck, II, 333; *ibid.*, 334–52.
[8] Cf. Lagrange, *Messianisme*, 224 *sq.*

CHAPTER III

Alexandrine Judaism

Many contacts occurred and many attempts at fusion were undertaken between the Judaic theology, of which an outline has just been given, and the Hellenic conceptions previously studied. On the one hand Pagans were attracted towards the God of the Jews; and sometimes, without renouncing their polytheism, they honoured with a special worship the Most High (ὕψιστος), and placed themselves under his protection; others integrally adopted the Jewish beliefs, and followed the prayers of the synagogue; finally, a certain number took the last step and were aggregated to the Jewish people by circumcision. Nothing will be said here of all these Judaisers, as their conversion does not concern the history with which I am dealing.

What happened to the Jewish Hellenists is, however, of great importance; for it is in connection with the synagogues of the Dispersion that the Church will begin to spread. It is necessary therefore to determine the beliefs held at that time in these circles, and more particularly what representation was made of God, and what rôle, close to him, was assigned to those divine intermediary beings which Palestinian Judaism has introduced to our knowledge.

It would be a long and, considering our sources, an impossible task to describe the religious beliefs of Jewry in dispersion; and such a catalogue is indeed unnecessary: it will be sufficient to study the Jewish colony at Alexandria. By the number, the social rank, the culture of its members, even more than by its privileged position as the commercial centre of the Roman Empire, this colony occupies a preponderant situation, with a decisive influence over the whole Hellenic Diaspora. Its literary activity was considerable, and although most of the works produced have perished, sufficient traces remain to enable us to perceive the principal religious movements that were going on.

We may distinguish first, on the margin of Judaism, the impious, in whom Philo sees the posterity of Cain; Greek sophistry has perverted them and induced them to despise God and the Law.[1]

Others, while still adhering to Judaism, evade its laws by their system of allegorical exegesis: the Sabbath, circumcision, the ecclesiastical feasts, are for them nothing but symbols.[2] Others accept literally the books of the Bible; but they see there nothing but legends analogous to those of Greek mythology. At the beginning of his treatise on the *Confusion of Tongues,* Philo, having quoted the story in *Genesis* (xi, 1 *seq.*), proceeds: 'Those who are at variance with the laws of their fathers are always mocking and attacking them; they make use in their impiety of this and other similar stories as a weapon for their atheism. Do you still venture, they say to us, to honour the claims of the Law as the very rules of truth? Do you not see that these books which you call holy are full of myths exactly like those you meet elsewhere, and laugh over?'[3] These commentators who so readily assimilate Biblical narratives and Pagan myths, explain without difficulty the legends of Greek polytheism and see in them, following the method of Euhemerus, stories of historical facts more or less distorted.[4] Others, whose syncretism is as wide, and whose goodwill is still wider, accept the exegetical method of the Stoics and use it to interpret the whole of Greek polytheism. This method, like Euhemerism, has left traces in a letter of Aristæus, and in Philo himself[5]; which shows it penetrated into the most pious circles of Alexandrine Judaism.

It would, however, be a great error to represent the Jews of Alexandria as inclined *en masse* to this apostasy, or even to this religious syncretism; they remained for the most part much attached to their national religion, observing the Sabbath, frequenting the synagogue, sending their subscriptions to Jerusalem, and glad to be able to go there themselves. But at the same time, they are

[1] *De posteritate Caini*, 33–48.
[2] *De migrat. Abr.*, 89.
[3] *De confus. Ling.*, 2, 3.
[4] Cf. *Orac. sibyll.*, III, 97–155.
[5] Cf. F. Cumont, *Philonis, de aeternitate mundi*, prolegomena, p. x.

citizens of the world; they love to represent their patriarchs as cosmopolitans, and their law as a legislation established by nature for the whole world. They are also Greeks, or, rather, Hellenists; in love with the philosophy and the arts of Greece, they endeavour not only to assimilate them, but to derive advantage from them; with no more scruple than their contemporaries, who fabricate in large quantities supposed works of Pythagoras, of Timæus, or of Thucydides, they attribute to such glorious names as the Sibyls, Orpheus, and the great Greek poets, very mediocre productions full of their own beliefs, hopes, and hates. Their holy books are translated into Greek and their translators wear the aureole of a glorious legend. They become the 'Seventy,' prophets inspired by God, dear to king and people, whose work reveals to the Pagans a pure and spiritual religion. Not content with this glory, the Jews further consider the Bible as the source of all philosophy and all science; for that they need only apply to it the same exegetical method that the Stoics used to apply to the poems of Homer.

The best known of these exegetes is Philo;[1] but he was neither the first nor the only one. Even though the writings of his predecessors have disappeared to the last fragment, one has only to go through his works to see how numerous were those predecessors who loved to discover in the Bible the whole philosophical teaching of Greece, her physics, her psychology, and her ethics.[2]

In the story of *Genesis* they distinguish the creation of ideal man from that of man as actually known to experience.[3] The former is placed in the world of ideas; the latter in the earthly paradise.[4] In the precepts of the Law relating to the selection of victims for the Temple sacrifices, the disciples of Heraclitus, like the Stoics, recognise their whole cosmology; the first discover there that all things are one; the others that all things proceed from and return to unity.[5] The seven planets are represented by the seven branches of the candlestick[6]; the air, which is dark in

[1] Philo will be our chief study here; the *Book of Wisdom* has already been studied (p. 95 *sqq.*), and the gleanings to be obtained in the other Alexandrine books are few and far between, e.g., the letter of Aristeus and Book III of the Sibylline Oracles.

[2] See Focke, *Entstehung der Weisheit Salomons*, 95–101.

[3] *In Gen.*, I, 8 (Aucher, 6). [4] See Drummond, *Philo Judæus*, II, 187–9, 275–7.

[5] *De spec. leg.*, I, 208. [6] *In Exod.*, II, 78.

colour and placed under the sky and the ether, is represented by the under-tunic of the High Priest, which is therefore violet in colour.[1] The two precious stones worn by the High Priest symbolise either the sun and the moon or the two hemispheres,[2] which are also represented by the two cherubim of the tabernacle.[3] The fathers to whom Abraham must return (*Gen.* xv, 15) are either the stars or the four elements or again the ideas.[4]

The whole psychology is to be found in the history of Pharao and his eunuchs:

> 'The king of Egypt is our spirit, he reigns over the body and governs it as a king; if he is a friend of the body he endeavours to procure for himself three things, bread, meat, and wine; and for this purpose he makes use of three officers, a baker, a cup-bearer, and a butcher. All three are eunuchs, that is to say, that the man of pleasure is barren of the most necessary virtues; temperance, modesty, continence, justice, and the rest . . .'

The lot of the three officers concerned was interpreted by the same method.[5]

As for ethics, it was everywhere on the surface of the text, or at least they so believed. Thus the Pasch signifies the passage of the soul, leaving the body and the passions[6]; the tree of life is the most generic virtue, that is to say, goodness[7]; the alliance of Abraham and Sara represents the union of the good man and virtue[8]; the fertility promised to Sara symbolises the fecundation of the soul by divine grace, producing the virtues.[9]

Such a method was valuable for the Hellenising Jews, but dangerous for the Bible and the religion contained in it. Armed with that kind of exegesis, Philo could, in good faith, discover in the Mosaic law all systems of philosophy and religion, as his contemporary Heraclitus read, in perfectly good faith, the whole of Stoicism into the poems of Homer.[10] If he kept his footing on so dangerous a slope it was less due to the sacred text, which took any shape in his

[1] *In Exod.*, II, 117. [2] *Mos.*, II, 123. [3] *Ibid.*, 98 (150).
[4] *Quis rer. divin. her.*, 280 (M. I, 513). [5] *De Joseph.*, 151 *sq.* (M., II, 63).
[6] *De spec. leg.*, II, 147 (M. II, 292). [7] *Leg. alleg.*, I, 59 (M., I, 54).
[8] *De Abrah.*, 99 (M. II, 15). [9] *De mutat. nom.*, 141 (M., I, 599).
[10] Cf. SIEGFRIED, *Philo von Alexandria als Ausleger des A. T.*, 168–98.

hands, than to his sincere attachment to his God, to his religion, and to his national traditions.[1]

BIBLIOGRAPHY :—L. Cerfaux, *Influence des Mystères sur le Judaisme alexandrin avant Philon* (Louvain, 1924 : extract from *Muséon*, XXXVII, 29–88). J. von Arnim, *Dio von Prusa* (Berlin, 1898). W. Bousset, *Judisch-Christlicher Schulbetrieb in Alexandria und Rom* (Göttingen, 1915). B. Ritter, *Philo und die Halacha* (Leipzig, 1879).

1. God

The Judaism of Philo appears above all in his conception of God.[2] In most other philosophical questions, the beliefs of Israel gave him little more than a general direction, and a historical framework. Jewish civilisation, more particularly as reflected in the Bible, was too profoundly different from Greek civilisation for the study of the sacred books and Rabbinical traditions to furnish a precise reply to the many questions raised by Hellenic speculation. More frequently it was in the Greek philosophers,[3] and more particularly the neo-Stoics[4] and Platonists,[5] that Philo found its guiding inspiration. It is another matter in the fundamental question of the existence and nature of God. On that point Biblical theology was incomparably richer and firmer than the philosophy of Plato or of Posidonius ; the belief which it imposed was sacred for Philo, and it saved him from doubt and fixed him in the truth, a truth higher than was attainable by his contemporaries.

A primary feature, distinctive of the whole of Philo's system, but more accentuated in his theodicy, is the relation of his philosophy to his belief. The speculations of the Greek philosophers had never up till then claimed a divine revelation ; they had freely developed side by side with religion, without in most cases having any

[1] One is sometimes inclined to exaggerate Philo's tendency to allegorical exegesis ; in reality he neither denies, nor does he neglect, the literal meaning of the law.

[2] The Greek text of Philo is quoted from that of COHN-WENDLAND (Berlin, 1896 *sqq.*), but from that of MANGEY (London, 1742, 2 vol.) for the treatises not yet published in the former. Reference will be made to the paragraph in COHN-WENDLAND and, in brackets, to the volume and page in MANGEY (M.). Passages which are not extant in Greek are quoted from AUCHER (Venice, 1822–26).

[3] Cf. SIEGFRIED, *loc. cit.*, p. 39.

[4] See SCHMEKEL, *Die mittlere Stoa*, 238–90.

[5] For Philo's Platonism see HOROVITZ, *Untersuchungen uber Philons u. Platons Lehre von der Weltschöpfung*, 95–103.

contact with it, without seeking alliance or giving battle. Philo, on the contrary, is unable to separate philosophy from faith; he does not even see either the distinctness of the two domains or the difference of the two methods. In the Mosaic revelation he finds the witness of God to himself, to his nature, and to his government of the world. His philosophy therefore possesses a firmness and an assurance, and, at the same time, an imperious and authoritative accent distinguishing it from Greek philosophy, in general so reserved and so disinclined to commit itself fundamentally.

At the same time that philosophy gains more assurance from this alliance, it also speaks with a religious accent which is new to it. This transformation is particularly evident in the conception of God; that conception is enriched by moral and religious attributes which up till then had been gravely lacking. This criticism had already been made long ago by J. G. Müller, who edited the *Treatise of the Creation*.[1] Philo, starting from a classical passage of the *Timæus* of Plato, develops this idea: that God being good can create nothing but what is excellent:

> 'If we enquire into the cause why God has constructed the universe, it seems to me that we can reply with an ancient that the father and the maker of the world was good . . . He derived the inspiration of doing so from no one—no one existed but himself;—but he knew for himself that he should spread profusely the riches of his graces on nature which, without a divine gift, could not of itself have any good in it.'[2]

The goodness here described is no longer that of which Plato speaks: God appears no longer as a cause too exalted to be jealous of his work, and too good himself not to make it good; he is above all, a father full of goodness and condescension, who pours his graces on the world. The Biblical influence is here manifest; this conception of the goodness of God owes more to the *Psalms* than to the *Dialogues* of Plato. Is not this commentary on the psalm: 'I will sing thy mercy and thy justice,' more Jewish than Greek? 'If God were to judge the human

[1] MÜLLER, *op. cit. infra*, 156, quoted by DRUMMOND, *Philo Judæus*, II, 54.
[2] *De op. mundi*, 21–23 (M., I, 5).

race without pity, he would condemn it. For no man can, by his own strength, run the whole of his course without a fall, whether voluntary or involuntary; and, indeed, in order to save the race, while he permits individual falls, he mingles mercy with justice, even towards the unworthy; and it is not after having judged that he has pity, it is after having had pity that he judges; for his pity precedes the exercise of his justice.'[1] Without dwelling on this vivid sense of sin and human infirmity, so foreign to Greek thought, it is plain that this conception of the divine mercy and justice comes also from a higher and purer source.

We must recognise also, I think, a Jewish belief in the clearly personal character attributed to God. In the second *Book of Dreams*[2] Philo, speaking of Jerusalem, the name of which he translates 'The Vision of Peace,' says that God has no other city than the peaceful and contemplative soul; and suddenly interrupts his discourse to communicate a personal inspiration:

> 'The invisible spirit who comes to me, makes himself heard and says: My friend, you are ignorant of something precious and difficult which I will gladly teach you; I have already taught you so much! Learn then that God alone is true peace and that all corruptible nature is nothing but a perpetual struggle; for God is liberty, and matter is necessity; he who has been able to fly from war and necessity and reproduction and death, and to attain to that which is without beginning, incorruptible, free, and peaceful, he truly is the dwelling-place and the city of God.'

One understands that Philo, in writing thus, believed himself to be favoured by a heavenly inspiration, for he has few pages so lofty. At any rate, he appears in these words to surpass the Hellenic conception of his time. For long, no doubt, the idea of matter had been connected with the idea of necessity, and in the Platonist school these concepts are associated with those of disorder and evil; but we do not find in that school this powerfully drawn contrast between the two poles of being, matter as pure necessity, and God as liberty itself. Frequently also,

[1] *Quod Deus sit immut.*, 74–76 (M., I, 284).
[2] *De somn.*, II, 252 (M., I, 692).

and in Plato, we find exhortations to free ourselves from matter; but the reward proposed for these efforts is a less obstructed and more immediate vision; whereas here it is a greater independence, a more perfect participation in the divine freedom.

It is also easy to see how profoundly this idea differs from the Stoic conception, in spite of certain superficial resemblances. God is not the immanent law of the world, he is its Creator; his spontaneity is not the inevitable development of his being, it is the free determination of his Spirit. Also when the sage is exhorted to emancipate himself from matter and approach God, he is not asked to re-absorb himself in the immense force from which he emanates, but to make himself like to his Creator.

This personal character of the God of Philo is also very apparent in the descriptions which he frequently gives of the divine happiness:

> 'God,' he tells us, in the *Treatise of the Cherubim*,[1] 'speaks to us of *his* feasts: in truth he alone can have feasts; he alone knows happiness, joy, and pleasure; he alone can have peace unmixed. He is without sadness, without fear, without any evil, without necessities, without suffering, without fatigue, full of pure beatitude, his nature is most perfect, or, rather, he himself is perfection, the end and limit of happiness . . .'

These considerations on the divine beatitude are fairly frequent in Philo's pages; in order to find their equivalent in the Pagan authors of that period, we must seek them in what they have written about the gods rather than about God. They readily and habitually speak of the happiness of the immortal gods, much less of the happiness of the one god apprehended by their philosophy; it is because this one god has not for them the definitely personal character of the others. The relations of God with man have also, in Philo, a strictly personal character. God sees each one of us and watches over our actions. 'With an untiring eye he watches everything, and by a special grace he calls and welcomes to himself the best of what he sees.'[2]

We saw just now that happiness and joy, properly speaking, belong to God alone; but since he is good and

[1] 86 (M., I, 154). [2] *De mutat. nom.*, 40 (M., I, 585).

the friend of men, he wishes us to participate in them according to our capacity, and whoever approaches him has less fear, less grief, and more joy, more peace.[1]

To illustrate clearly this aspect of Philo's God, it would be necessary to run through the very numerous passages which speak of his goodness, his beneficence, his generosity, his mercy, his love of men, and his holiness.[2]

The preceding indications will have enabled us to envisage it sufficiently and will have given an impression of a new world. The God of Philo is not the god of Plato, nor of Cicero, nor of Plutarch ; he is a living God.

The Biblical source of this theology is easy to recognise, but we must not think that it alone has influenced Philo, and that Greek speculation has not modified, on many points, this exalted conception of God.

In the case of Philo such a distortion was almost inevitable. He was sensitive, perhaps to excess, to the attraction of systematic philosophy, and he thought to give more value to his belief by constructing a correct and symmetrical theory of it. Now it was a difficult and dangerous task to systematise the data of the Bible, and to harmonise them with the philosophic theses of Platonism and Stoicism. We must now explain how this attempt distorted the conception of God which we have just described.

On a first reading one criticism imposes itself: it is the universalist character of the God of Philo: it is no longer the God of the Jews but the God of the world. Drummond (*Philo Judæus*, II, 63) has drawn up a very curious list of all the names given by Philo to God. They all have the same character ; some of them merely describe God in himself and call him: He who is ; He who truly is ; Being ; True Being. The majority announce his relations with the world, and have all the same universalist aspect. He is the cause, the father,[3] the saviour, the master, the king of the universe ; he is the soul of the world, the spirit of the universe. These appellations and others closely resembling them clearly show not only the universal dominion of God, but also the speculative and abstract character of the Philonian philosophy. If Philo

[1] *De Abrah.*, 203 (M., II, 29). [2] Cf. Drummond, *Philo Judæus*, II, 56.

[3] Note that, for Philo, God is not the Father of Israel, but Father of the Universe.

comes across the Biblical expression: the God of Abraham, of Isaac, and of Jacob; he at once effaces its personal and concrete character by his symbolic allegorism: Abraham becomes instruction, Isaac nature, Jacob exercise or *ascesis,* and the three names no longer indicate anything except these three sources of our knowledge of God.[1]

Philo applies the same procedure to the whole Biblical history. These allegorical interpretations do not exclude all their historical and literal meaning, but Philo certainly prefers them, and they give his books their uniformly dull and monotonous tone. As for Biblical theology, they remove the best part of its distinctness and life. It is by his action on his people that God makes himself known in the Old Testament, and when all this history is reduced to symbols, the features of the divine character are effaced.

Philosophy, however, pursues its task, and in its attempt to purify the notion of God it impoverishes it. The texts quoted above give a truly positive and personal idea of God, but there are many others which appear to nullify them and reduce the conception of God to an indeterminate and unknowable abstraction. Certain historians think that these two series are mutually contradictory, others that they can be reconciled; but before attempting to solve the problem we must expound the data and briefly explain the negative philosophy of Philo.

One characteristic primarily distinguishes that philosophy from Jewish doctrine. In Judaism the divine transcendence is not inculcated with less force, but it has a distinctly moral character; it is the sanctity of Jahve which isolates him, whereas, according to Philo, it is his ideal grandeur. According to the Jewish prophets man cannot see God, because he is impure and his lips are defiled: for Philo such contemplation is impossible because it exceeds the power of human intelligence.

According to Philo, man can demonstrate, for example, by the reign of order in the world, the existence of a first cause, which he calls God; man can go no further; God can neither be known nor named by him:

> 'All that the human reason can do is to arrive at the knowledge that there is a cause of the universe; to wish

[1] *De mutat. nom.*, 12 (M., I, 580).

to go further and to know the nature and qualities of that cause is an extreme piece of folly.'[1]

And again:

> 'God does not resemble man; he is not like the heaven nor yet like the earth; for these things have determinate and material forms; God, on the contrary, is not even comprehensible by the spirit, except in so far as he exists: for what we understand of him, apart from the fact of his existence, is nothing.'[2]

And again elsewhere:

> 'Among men, some love the soul, and others the body; the former, being able to mingle with spiritual and incorporeal natures, do not compare being to any idea that can be derived from created things, but strip being of every quality—for it is one of the elements of the happiness and sovereign beatitude of being, that its existence should be conceived as one, and without any distinctive mark—and they represent it to themselves merely as being, without giving it any form.'[3]

In these and other analogous passages a double assertion can be distinguished, one relative to our knowledge of God, the other to the being of God in himself. The first is more easily explicable; we can understand that the intellectual representations that we draw from sense-objects are unable to give us a proper conception of God; whence the thesis, that has become classical with many Christian philosophers, that we can know the existence of God, but cannot comprehend his nature. It is more strange to present, as the highest religious idea, one which denies to God all determination, all specific character, all distinctive mark. But what is more disconcerting in the case of Philo is that God, considered not merely in relation to our knowledge, but in himself, has no determination or quality.

What is to be understood by this indetermination? In what sense is God without quality, ἄποιος?[4]

[1] *De poster. Caïni*, 168 (M., I, 258).

[2] *Quod Deus sit immut.*, 62 (M., I, 282). [3] *Ibid.*, 55 (M., I, 281).

[4] GUYOT, *opp. cit. infra* (*L'infinité divine*, 45–52; and *Les Réminiscences*, 5–7), sees in this an affirmation of the divine infinity. Cf. MARTIN, *op. cit. infra*, 54; and ZELLER (*Philos. der Griech.*, V[3], p. 354).

For Philo, as for the Stoics, the word quality (ποιότης) has an extremely technical meaning. All the beings that we see are made up of two principles: substance and quality, substance being conceived as passive and determinable, and quality as the active and determining element. It is then quality which constitutes each of us a member of our species, and which, in that species, distinguishes us from other individuals: our quality is the principle of our specific determination, and of our individuation.

For one who understands the word quality in this sense it is evident that God is without quality, and this for at least two reasons. God is infinitely simple, and, consequently is not susceptible of that compositeness which would be implied by distinguishing in him essence and quality. God is not contained in a genus or a species, but transcends all species and genera; there is therefore in him no specific and individualising determination, which would class him in a species, and distinguish him from other individuals making part of that species.

To say, in the language of this school, that God is without quality, is to say that he cannot, on account of his transcendence, be placed by us in any of the logical categories in which we class various beings, but that he surpasses them all; which is not to say that he is in fact undetermined.

The philosophy of Philo permits us to confirm this interpretation by a quite valid example. The Logos, as we shall see presently, is the most generic of beings, and therefore symbolised by the manna of Exodus: yet it is frequently represented as the principle of the determination of the universe, as the seal which is stamped and imprinted on the world.

How can these two aspects of one and the same concept be reconciled, except by the recognition that the transcendence that makes the Logos the most generic of beings does not efface in it all determination?

We have but to apply this remark to justify the divine transcendence. Philo, continuing his interpretation of the manna, tells us that, of all beings, God is the most generic, and after him the Logos; while as for other beings they only exist in name, and are, in fact, equal to nothing.[1] This does not mean that all attributes should be denied to

[1] *Leg. Alleg.*, II, 86 (M., I, 82).

God, but rather that he should not be classed with other beings ; because, as Philo says elsewhere,[1] nothing is equal to God, nothing is even near him, and in order to pass from God to other beings we must descend to another genus.

This God, so highly placed and so distant, is not on that account an empty abstraction ; on the contrary, he is a brimming plenitude of being: 'He is full of himself, he is self-sufficient ; the rest is deficient, empty, and void ; God surrounds it and fills it without being himself contained by anything, being himself both one and all.'[2]

And to make these metaphors more precise, God is primarily rich with the perfections proper to him, which we have recognised above: eternity, omnipotence, omniscience, and complete liberty.

But he further possesses certain properties which we also attribute to men: goodness, wisdom, justice ; how is this participation to be understood? Philo's answer is very clear: it is not merely a question of attributing even a simple logical priority to these qualities in reference to God. Justice, goodness, *is* God, or, more exactly, since we are speaking of the justice and the goodness to which our spirit can attain, God is beyond them, not as unknowable without link or relation with all these human perfections, but as the infinitely rich source from which they come forth ; as we saw just now in Philo's words:

> 'God is the summit and the term and the supreme height of happiness, not receiving his perfection from anything else, but diffusing over all things the particular goodness of that source of all beauty, which is himself : for all the beauty in the world would never have come into being if it had not been formed to the image of that archetype which is truly beautiful, without origin, happy and incorruptible.'[3]

And similarly elsewhere: 'Nothing is beautiful but what comes from God and is divine.'[4]

This doctrine is certainly very exalted, and contains nothing that a Christian philosopher must disavow. But it also contains nothing which surpasses the range of 'natural religion' ; the attraction of Hellenic specula-

[1] *De Sacrif. Abel*, 92 (M., I, 181). [2] *Leg. Alleg.*, I, 44 (M., I, 52).
[3] *De Cherub.*, 86 (M., I, 154). [4] *De Sacrif. Abel*, 63 (M., I, 174).

tions has diverted Philo from the higher and above all the more personal, more real, more intimate revelation which God had made of himself to his people.

This oversight is above all significant if we consider no longer what God is in himself, but what he is as the object of our knowledge. Philo loves to repeat that God cannot be seen by man, not because he is invisible by nature, but because man is too feeble to be able to support the vision of him. He says: 'We should have to be God to be able to understand him.'[1] This thesis, very dear to philosophers at that period, is quite correct, at least, if true regard is had to keep it within its limits. It is certain that God is incomprehensible and beyond the range of every created intelligence, from the very fact that it is created.

But Philo goes further and thinks that it is impossible, in any order of providence, whatever it may be, to know God otherwise than by his works. Thus when Scripture tells us that Abraham was the first to believe in God, it was merely saying that he was the first to recognise that the world has a supreme cause, and is ruled by a Providence.[2] By means of a similar exegesis, Abraham may be the first philosopher, but he is no longer the father of believers; the theophany of Sinai is interpreted in the same way: God permits Moses to see what is behind him, that is, according to Philo, his powers and his works, or indeed the world of ideas.[3]

In these conditions God is no longer reached as a person, but as a cause; he no longer manifests himself by a gratuitous and supernatural revelation, but lets himself be known solely by his works.

This naturalistic quality of Philo's theodicy forms a striking contrast with the early Christian notion of God. The dogma of the Trinity has exercised here a decisive influence in opening to faith perspectives wholly closed to reason, and in establishing between the soul and God personal relations which no philosophy had suspected. In the light of these perspectives, not only the Christian revelation—which Philo could not know—but the Jewish revelation itself keeps its strictly privileged character, and

[1] *Fr.*, M., II, 654, *ap.* JOAN. DAMASC. (*P.G.*, XCVI, 472a).
[2] *De virtut.*, 216 (M., II, 442).
[3] *De vita Mos.*, I, 158 (M., II, 106).

appears in the history of humanity as a unique phenomenon.

A century and a half later than Philo, St. Irenæus was to write:

> 'If we consider his grandeur, and his admirable glory, God is such that no living being can see him, for he is incomprehensible; but, in his charity, his love of men, and his omnipotence, he grants to those who love him the vision of himself, and this what the prophets declared . . . He is then seen by whom he wishes, and when he wishes, and as he wishes, for he is all-powerful. By the Spirit he made himself seen prophetically; by the Son he made himself seen adoptively; in heaven he will make himself seen paternally.'[1]

Such texts have no parallels in Philo: the knowledge of God, the vision of God is the goal proposed to every virtuous life; an effort must be made to aim at it. But we have neither the support of a special revelation, already accorded by God, nor the assurance of a promised manifestation by him in heaven. The pious Jew, whom Philo exhorts, is in the same position as the Pagan of Plutarch, and of Maximus of Tyre:

> 'It is uncertain if you will find the God whom you are seeking, for God has refused himself to many of those who sought him, and their effort has always been in vain; but search alone is sufficient to enrich the soul.'[2]

And elsewhere:

> 'When one is conquered in this search by necessity, that is to say by the loftiness of an inaccessible power, one is worthy of pity but not of hatred.'[3]

It must be admitted that this consolation is weak, and that this religious doctrine is very impoverished if we compare it not merely with Christian theology, but even with Jewish doctrine as, for instance, it is contained in the *Psalms*.

The rôle that intermediary forces (the Logos and the powers) will have to play here, as in Hellenic philosophy,

[1] *Hær.*, IV, 20, 6 (*P.G.*, VII, 1035). [2] *Leg. Alleg.*, III, 47 (M., I, 96).
[3] *De poster. C.*, 9. Cf. 21 (M., I, 227–30).

is readily conceivable. Between man so feeble and God so exalted they will have to render possible the relations of knowledge and religion ; they will have to reveal God to man, and raise man towards God.

BIBLIOGRAPHY, Section 1 :—E. Bréhier, *Les idées philosophiques et religieuses de Philon d'Alexandrie* (Paris, 1908). J. Drummond, *Philo Judæus* (2 vols., London, 1888). J. Lebreton, *Les théories du logos*, in *Études*, 20 March, 1906. J. G. Müller, *Des Juden Philo Buch von der Weltschöpfung* (Berlin, 1841). H. Guyot, *L'infinité divine depuis Philon le Juif jusqu'à Plotin* (Paris, 1906) ; *Les réminiscences de Philon le Juif chez Plotin* (Paris, 1906). J. Martin, *Philon* (Paris, 1907).

2. *The Powers*

An incontestable influence has been exerted over the Trinitarian theology of several Fathers by the Philonian theory of the powers, and above all of the Logos ; even more, it has been thought to be the principal source of Johannine theology, and J. Réville, for example, thinks that he can explain the whole of the fourth gospel by Philonism. To discuss this thesis here would be premature: the Philonian doctrines must first be studied for their own sake, and we must neglect the comparisons which they may suggest with Christian theology ; later, when the doctrine of St. John has been expounded in the same way, it will be easy to compare the two writers and enquire into their possible relations.

The first characteristic which must be recognised in the Powers, as in the Logos, is that of intermediary beings between God and the world. Thus, in the ontological order, Philo draws up the scale of beings as follows:

> 'At the head of the scale is God ; in the second place the Logos, in the third and fourth the creative and the royal powers, in the fifth, depending on the creative power, the power of beneficence ; in the sixth, deriving from the royal power, the power of punishment ; and finally, in the seventh, the world composed by the ideas.'[1]

In the logical order of knowledge or contemplation, we find the same degrees: the lowest sort of knowledge only reaches the exterior world ; it rises thence by degrees to the inferior powers, the powers of mercy and of command,

[1] *In Exod.*, II, 68 (AUCHER, p. 516).

then to the higher powers of creation and kingship, then to the Logos, then finally to God himself.[1]

If we ask what this Logos and these powers are in themselves, the answer is much more difficult.[2] To begin with the powers; sometimes they seem very clearly personifications; at other times there is only an abstract distinction between them and God. In the first category of passages we notice first the allegorical commentaries of Scripture: the angels referred to in the sacred text become, for Philo, powers. Thus he distinguishes two kinds of powers: some are united to mortal bodies, others, the purer, dwell on high in the ether. The Greek philosophers call them heroes; Moses, more justly, angels.[3] In the same sense he says elsewhere that: 'the holy place is full of incorporeal Logoi, who are immortal souls.' And again:

> 'The superior souls are called demons by other philosophers; holy Scripture calls them more justly angels (ἄγγελοι); they carry the orders of the father to the children, and the prayers of the children to the father. This is why the sacred narrative shows them to us ascending and descending: no doubt God forestalls them everywhere, has no need of their information, but it was better for us mortals that he should make use of these Logoi as intermediaries on account of the stupefaction and terror which are caused us by the supreme master and his sovereign power.'[4]

In these passages, Philo is endeavouring to translate in his own philosophic language the teaching of the Bible about the angels, and he finds no more exact equivalent than δυνάμεις, or λόγοι; but we should not conclude that his whole theory of the powers admits of interpretation in terms of Biblical angelology; this is far from being the case. There is no equivalence between the two conceptions, merely here and there a distant resemblance. Is it not evident in the first of the texts quoted that the term 'powers' is applied not only to the angels, but also to human souls? In reality the 'powers' of Philo have nothing in common with the angels but their rôle of

[1] *De confus. ling.*, 97 (M., I, 419); *De fuga*, 97 *sqq.* (560); *Leg. Alleg.*, III, 100 (107).

[2] Cf. *Revue de philosophie*, 1908, II, 432.

[3] *De plantat. Noë*, 14 (M., I, 331).

[4] *De somn.*, I, 141, 142 (M., I, 642).

intermediaries; in other ways they are completely different, on this point in particular, that while the angels are definitely represented as persons, the powers appear to be ideas or forces. It is probably this definitely personal character of the angels which diverted Philo from a conception so dear to Jewish theology: the angels seemed to him too near to us to be conceived as the supreme organs of divine causality, and, side by side with the above-quoted passages timidly affirming the identity of the angels and the powers, there are others to be found representing the angels as the servants of the powers.[1]

The Platonist conception of the ideas had more influence on Philo's thought, and enables us to see further into his theory of the powers. In his treatise of the *Laws* Philo speaks with indignation of those impious ones who dare to deny the ideas, and consequently reduce the whole world to confusion and chaos:

> 'God has drawn the world from chaos, not by touching it himself—for the Blessed One could not touch confused and indeterminate matter—but by making use of his incorporeal powers whose real name is the ideas, and by imprinting by their means on each species the form which belongs to it.'[2]

Elsewhere, on the demand of Moses to see him or at least his powers, God thus explains to him what these powers are:

> 'The powers which you desire (to see) are entirely invisible, and only intelligible just as I am intelligible and invisible. I call them intelligible, not because they are in fact perceived by the spirit, but because if they were perceived it would not be by the senses, for it would only be the purest spirit that could perceive them. Although they are unattainable by their essence, they nevertheless show forth an imprint and likeness of their action; in your world seals, when applied to wax or other similar substances, engrave a thousand imprints without themselves being in any way modified; it is in this way that you should imagine the powers which surround me giving qualities and forms to the indeterminate without changing or losing any-

[1] *De spec. leg.*, I, 66 (M., II, 222). [2] *Ibid.*, I, 329 (261).

thing of their eternal nature. Some of you wise men have called them ideas, and rightly so, because they specify all beings, placing them in order, defining, determining, informing, and, in one word, improving them.'[1]

The source of this doctrine is obvious enough, it is to be found in the *Timæus* of Plato. It is true that the ideas do not appear there in the form they have in Philo: they are independent substances, and not thoughts conceived by God, and consequently intermediaries between him and the world. For Philo, on the contrary, they are the ideal models which God has constructed in his mind before the creation of the world, just as an architect draws up beforehand the plan of the city that he wishes to build.[2] This modification of the Platonic theory is, certainly, very remarkable, but Philo is not its first exponent; Plato was thus understood in his day.[3]

It is also from Plato's *Timæus* that Philo has borrowed his theory of the powers as secondary agents of creation. We read in the *Timæus* (41c) that God, having made the secondary gods, delegated to them the task of making inferior beings, advising them to imitate his own work. Philo remembered this passage when interpreting the verse in *Genesis*, in which God says: 'Let us make man after our image.' 'The father of the world,' he says, 'is speaking to his powers, he has entrusted to them the task of making the mortal part of our soul, in imitation of the manner in which he himself has made the rational part.'[4]

This interpretation, which recurs at least three times in Philo, is remarkable, and has justly exercised the sagacity of his commentators. The powers indeed have there a more distinct and marked independence, and, further, it is the creation of man alone and not that of the other beings which is attributed to them. However subtle the reason which Philo gives us of this exclusive attribution,[5] it is easy to realise that he has been led to it by the Biblical text; he only found the plural, 'let us make,' in verse 26, and it was necessary to explain this anomaly. In

[1] *De spec. leg.*, I, 46–48 (M., II, 218–219).
[2] *De opif. mundi*, 17 *sqq.* (M., I, 4). [3] See above, page 43, note 2.
[4] *De fuga*, 69 (M., I, 556). [5] Cf. *De opif. mundi*, 73 *sqq.* (M., I, 17).

the same way, the rôle so definitely personal played by the powers, is partly due to Platonic reminiscences, noted above, and partly to the Jewish tradition which saw in this passage a dialogue between God and the angels, his assistants in the creation.

In any case, one essential feature stands out from this narrative which is thoroughly Philonian: the active rôle attributed to the powers. They are not merely exemplars or models, they are, as their name indicates, forces. They are the instruments of God in the creation of the visible world, and they even appear to play the same part in the production of the invisible universe. 'By these powers,' says Philo, 'the immaterial and intelligible world, the archetype of the world of the senses, has been constructed and is composed of invisible ideas, as the latter is of visible bodies.[1] This text is rather disconcerting in so far as it opposes ideas and powers to each other, previously so clearly identified. We shall return later to the consideration of these antinomies. We may content ourselves here by noting the new point of view already recognised in the text of *De Fuga :* Philo is no longer concerned with exemplary causes, but with efficient causes ; he has passed from Platonism to Stoicism.[2]

The Stoic doctrine of powers or forces is still more clearly expressed in the texts which represent the powers as holding the world together:

> 'Moses,' says Philo, talking like a Stoic, 'subscribed to the doctrine of the inter-communion and sympathy of the whole universe. He affirmed that the world was unique and created . . . but he surpassed (the philosophers) by his conception of God: he saw clearly enough that neither the world nor the soul of the world was the supreme God, that the stars and their revolutions were not the first causes of the destiny of men, but that this universe is maintained by the invisible powers, which the demiurge has stretched from the extremities of the earth to the limits of heaven, so that what he had bound should not become unbound ; for the powers are the unbreakable bonds of the world.'[3]

[1] *De confus. ling.*, 172 (M., I, 431). [2] Cf. Zeller, V, 362, n. 5.
[3] *De migrat. Abr.*, 180–181 (M., I, 464).

Elsewhere again he explains the divine omnipresence by this tension of the powers which are the invisible bonds with which God has chained everything together ;[1] again they are compared to columns which support like a house the whole world as well as the human race.[2]

We are now far from the angels and almost as far from the Platonic ideas. While following through so many references so wavering a system of thought, we may ask ourselves what connection holds it together in Philo's mind: there is only one, I think, and it is the notion of an intermediary. Between God and the world, angels, ideas, and forces play analogous parts, in this sense at least of uniting two extremes and creating relations between them.

But one would wish to determine more exactly this essential and characteristic rôle of the powers: in what sense are they intermediaries between God and the world ? Ought we to see in them subsisting and personal beings inferior to God, and superior to the world ?

The first passages that we studied suggest this solution. But it would seem illegitimate to press them too much, for the personal character which they attribute to the powers seems to be imposed on Philo by the Biblical text which he is interpreting, and not spontaneously affirmed by him. An even graver difficulty lies in the fact that if a more or less consistent personality is attributed to these beings, contradictions arise on all sides ; more often Philo distinguishes two powers: one, the creative power which is called in Scripture God (*theos*); the other the royal power called Lord (*kyrios*)[3] ; but elsewhere he enumerates three,[4] four,[5] five,[6] or even an infinite[7] number of powers. Many times, as we have seen, he identifies them with the angels ; at other times, he makes the angels their ministers ; often he affirms that the powers are indistinguishable from ideas ; and sometimes that the world of ideas has been made by the powers.

All these fluctuations of thought would be incomprehensible if Philo had attributed to the powers a firm and

[1] *De confus. ling.*, 136 (M., I, 425).

[2] *Fr. ex quæst. in Gen.* (M., II, 655, 662), *ap.* Jo. DAMASC. (*P.G.*, XCVI, 473a).

[3] *De sacrificant.*, 307 (*De spec. leg.*, I ; M., II, 258).

[4] *De sacrif. Ab. et C.*, 131 (M., I, 189).

[5] *In Exod.*, II, 68 (AUCHER, 516).

[6] *De fuga*, 94 *sqq.* (M., I, 560).

[7] *De confus. ling.*, 171 (M., I, 431).

consistent personality; they become more easily intelligible, if he took them merely for abstractions, to be personified on occasion for the needs of exegesis. This impersonal character is evident whenever the powers are represented as the thoughts of God, or as forces sustaining and enclosing nature.

This enquiry permits us to solve easily what, for us, is the gravest problem: that is to say, the relations existing between the powers and God. There can be no question of discovering in Philo the mystery of the Trinity, nor even any doctrine resembling it; and a recent critic (M. Martin) has made a bad mistake in saying: 'Philo is not absolutely ignorant of the Trinity.'[1] He quotes in support of this statement the interpretation given by Philo of the apparition of the three angels to Abraham:

> 'When the Sage (Abraham) begs the personages who appear to be three travellers, to accept his hospitality, he speaks to them not as to three but as to one only, and says: Lord, if I have found grace before you, do not leave your servant.'[2]

And in an earlier passage the three personages are in reality

> 'The father of all things, he whom the sacred writings name "Him who is'; and at the side of Him who is, are the most ancient and nearest of the Powers, the creative and the royal. The creative power is called God . . . the royal is called Lord.'[3]

It is enough to transcribe the immediately preceding lines in order to determine the true meaning of this text:

> 'When the soul is, as it were, at its noonday, illuminated by God, and entirely flooded with intellectual light by the splendour spread around her, and without any shadow, she receives at that moment a triple impression of a single subject, one of these appearing as being and the two others as two shadows cast by it. Something of the same sort happens under the action

[1] Martin, *Philon*, 57. [2] *De Abrah.*, 131 (M., II, 20).
[3] *Ibid.*, 121 (M., II, 19).

of ordinary light; for objects, whether motionless or in movement, often cast a double shadow. We must not think, however, that there are, properly speaking, shadows in God; the use of this similitude is but an abuse of language to make my meaning more intelligible.'[1]

And after the explanation which I have quoted, he continues:

> 'God, then, in the midst of the two powers assisting him, presents to the spirit contemplating him sometimes a single object and sometimes three objects: a single object, when the purified spirit, having transcended not only the multiplicity of numbers, but also the dyad which is nearest to the monad, moves towards the pure idea, simple and perfect in itself; three objects, when not having been initiated into the great mysteries, the contemplating spirit is still celebrating the lesser mysteries, and being unable to perceive Being in itself without some extraneous help, attains it in his works as creator or ruler.'[2]

Further on he returns again to this 'triple impression produced by a single subject.'[3] And in his interpretation of the same story in his *Questions on Genesis*, he confirms his first exegesis:

> 'Just as the bodily eye when weakened perceives in one illumination a double object, so the eye of the soul, unable to perceive the One as one, experiences a triple perception conformably to the apparition of the two principal powers, the ministers and assistants of the One.'[4]

It is no doubt difficult to state more clearly the subjective character of the distinction between God and his powers: the human spirit being too weak is dazzled by God, and its vision is doubled or trebled; it perceives God not only as existing but as creating and ruling, and this perception is the principle of the distinction introduced between God and the two supreme powers.

[1] *De Abrah.*, 119 (M., II, 18).
[2] *Ibid.*, 122 (M., II, 19).
[3] *Ibid.*, 131 (M., II, 20).
[4] *In Gen.*, IX, 8 (Aucher, p. 251).

In the light of these express declarations, we can easily discern the significance of several other passages which without them would be unintelligible. Thus Philo preaches with insistence the omnipresence of God; God penetrates and fills everything; in the treatise on the 'Confusion of Tongues,' however, he says that God himself is nowhere, but fills every place by his powers.[1] Such a statement could be contradictory of the whole Philonian philosophy, if the powers were conceived as agents distinct from God, and not as his activity and his energy. It is the same doctrine as in those texts in which the powers are represented as the attributes or perfections of God; it is by them that God is wise, good, merciful, Lord, God, etc.[2]

These statements are clear and I do not think it possible to doubt of Philo's meaning in these passages. But then an objection very difficult to solve presents itself: the whole of this theory of the powers comes from the doctrine of the divine transcendence. It is because God cannot by himself either act on the world or make himself known to it, that Philo is brought to admit the intermediary beings who are his instruments and revealers; the whole of this system falls to the ground if they are identified with God.

Before discussing this objection, we must observe that it supposes in Philonism an insoluble contradiction, the very same contradiction to which Gnosticism later was to succumb.

> 'On the one hand," says Zeller,[3] 'the intermediary beings have to be identical with God in order that by their means the finite may be able to participate in the divinity; on the other hand, they have to be distinct from God, in order that the divinity, in spite of this participation, may remain free of all contact with the world.'

Very competent critics[4] agree with Zeller in recognising this contradiction in Philo's doctrine, and, indeed, if we were to take literally the principle which seems to

[1] *De confus. ling.*, 136 (M., I, 425).

[2] *De mutat. nom.*, 19 (M., I, 581); *De somn.*, I, 163 (645); *De vita Mos.*, II, 99–100 (II, 150); and in many other texts, which are quoted by DRUMMOND, *loc. cit.*, II, 101 *sqq.*

[3] ZELLER, V, 365.

[4] See E. CAIRD, *Evolution of Theology*, II, 201.

dominate the whole of his philosophy, that is to say, the exclusive affirmation of the divine transcendence, we should necessarily find ourselves brought up against a blank wall. But Philo's philosophy is so wavering and uncertain that one always hesitates to press his principles too far, and in this particular case there are texts which seem to suggest to us a more prudent reserve. God, it would seem, can only act upon the world through his powers, and yet Philo teaches in his treatise (*De Exilio,* lxviii, p. 556) that 'all other things have been made by God alone, but that man has been made by the help of the powers'; God, it is said again, is unknowable to man and only reveals himself by his Logos and his powers; and yet, as we have seen above, the perfect man can attain to the immediate contemplation of God, while elsewhere Philo teaches, in his treatise *de Monarchia,*[1] that the powers are as unknowable as God himself.

What are we to conclude from these apparent contradictions, if not that it would be wrong to consider all these beings of which Philo speaks, as absolute realities? Perhaps we should be nearer the truth by distinguishing in God, on the one hand, the perfect Being who surpasses us, and, on the other, the action which we can feel and the glory which strikes us; it would thus be easier to understand how the divine essence is inaccessible to the world, and yet that the world, as it were, hangs on God by the relations which attach it to God: similarly, the religious soul experiences all round her and within her the divine action; she venerates that action, but she goes beyond it to the infinitely deep and peaceful source from which all flows forth.[2]

3. *The Logos*

This discussion on the theory of the powers facilitates the study of the theory of the Logos. The two conceptions are inspired by the same philosophical and religious preoccupations; and, in fact, the doctrine of the Logos is but one particular application of the theory of intermediaries, which is completely outlined in the theory of the powers.

[1] *De spec. leg.*, I, 46 (M., II, 218).
[2] Cf. CAIRD, *op. cit.*, II, 200; DRUMMOND, II, 48.

We must, however, recognise, that among all the intermediary beings, the Logos is the most important and interesting to study: it plays the first rôle in Philo's philosophy and has exercised more influence than any other element of that philosophy on Christian theology.

Long before the days of Philo, Jewish theology had developed the concept of the Word of God, and the Alexandrine *Book of Wisdom* had attributed the same rôle to the λόγος and σοφία.[1] The allegorising Hellenists who preceded Philo had loved to introduce into the sacred books their speculations on the Logos. For Ezechiel the Tragic, who wrote, it appears, in the second century B.C.,[2] it was the λόγος θεῖος who appeared to Moses in the burning bush.[3] Philo comments on this phrase of *Genesis*: 'when he was come to a certain place and would rest in it after sunset . . .' (*Gen.* xxviii, 11). 'Many,' he says, 'see in the sun the symbol of sensation and intelligence which are regarded by us as criteria of knowledge; and in the place (which Jacob had come to) the divine Logos; they explain the text thus: the ascetic met the divine Logos when the mortal and human sun of his senses had set; and truly, as long as the intelligence and the senses exalt themselves on the pedestal of a steady perception of the intelligible and the sensible, the divine Logos is far away; but when they have both recognised their weakness and are veiled in the sunset of their powers, right reason appears, salutes, and seizes the soul of the ascetic, who is waiting in desperation and obscurity for him who is to come from without.'[4]

Philo then had predecessors among the Alexandrine Jews, and also imitators. Celsus, in his work, *The True Word,* written about the year 180, attests the belief of the Jews of his period in a divine Logos[5]; and Origen, if he corrects Celsus' evidence on other points, appears in this to recognise his accuracy.

This tradition which lasted so long is hardly known to us to-day except through Philo; it is desirable therefore to study it closely.

The study which we have just made of God and the

[1] See above, pages 96–98.
[2] Cf. SCHUERER, III, 373–6.
[3] *Ap.* EUSEB., *Praep. evang.*, IX, 29 (*P.G.*, XXI, 741a).
[4] *De somn.*, I, 118 *sqq.* (M., I, 638).
[5] *Ap.* ORIGEN, *Contra Cels.*, II, 31 (*GCS*, I, 158).

powers has already suggested to us the nature of Philo's Logos; above all that of an intermediary, permitting God to act on the world, and the world to rise to God. Manifold influences coming from a Jewish or a Hellenic source have in their turn led away the mobile intelligence of Philo; the texts of the Bible suggested to him many ingenious and varying applications, and, if we would discern among all these philosophical and exegetical speculations the personal thought of Philo, it is necessary incessantly to direct our minds toward the religious problem which is his primary preoccupation: how can creatures attain to God, and how can God act on creatures?

To recall the interpretation of the theophany of Mambre,[1] the perfectly purified spirit rises to the pure and simple idea, perfect in itself; if it is less perfect it stops at the dyad nearest to the monad; if it is still weaker, if it has not been initiated into the great mysteries, it only attains to God in his works as creator and governor. Philo very often outlines this conception of knowledge rising toward God by higher or lower degrees according to the greater or lesser perfection of the soul: many can only know God through the exterior world[2]; others attain, if not actually to the Logos, at least to one of the divine powers. This is what is allegorically signified by the law concerning the cix cities of refuge[3]: the swiftest only of the fugitives reach the metropolis, the Logos; the others can only arrive at the powers, whether they be the higher creative and royal powers, or the lower, the power of mercy, and the power which commands and forbids.

Thus, beyond the very imperfect knowledge of God that can be derived from the contemplation of his works, Philo distinguishes various degrees of knowledge concerned with the different powers, and beyond these a higher degree which attains to the Logos: above that there remains nothing but the direct contemplation of God: this latter is reserved to the perfect, for example to Moses:

> 'There exists a purer and more exalted spirit, who is initiated into the greater mysteries; he does not

[1] See above, page 153 *sq.* [2] *De confus. ling.*, 97 (M., I, 419).
[3] *De fuga*, 97 *sqq.* (M., I, 560).

> know the cause by its effects, nor the eternal Being by means of his shadow, but surpassing all that is created he attains to a clear manifestation of the uncreated Being, and in so doing reaches that Being himself as well as his shadow, which is the Logos and the visible world. Such a spirit was Moses when he said: Show thyself to me that I may know thee and see thee.'[1]

For those who have no pretension to that immediate vision, the contemplation of the Logos is a most precious advantage. 'It is a great benefit for those who cannot see God, to come in contact at least with the Logos.'[2] We may conclude that, for Philo, the Logos is not only or chiefly the term of a metaphysical speculation, but the object of a religious cult, enlightening and sustaining the soul and guiding her toward God.

Moreover, this intermediary may also be conceived as an intercessor, who presents to God the homage of the world:

> 'The all-engendering Father has given to the Logos this glorious privilege of dwelling half-way between the Creator and the creature, and keeping them apart. For in the presence of the incorruptible, he is the suppliant of mortal nature, always on the verge of destruction, and he is the King's ambassador to his subjects. Then he rejoices in and exalts this privilege, saying: I stood between the Lord and you (*Deut.* v, 5). Indeed, being neither without origin like God, nor begotten like you, but intermediary between these two extremes, I am as it were a hostage for both parties ; to the Creator I give the assurance that the entire race will not disappear or destroy itself by overthrowing the order of the world ; to the creature I give hope that the merciful God will never neglect the work of his hands.'[3]

Closely connected with this religious conception is the cosmological conception which makes of the Logos God's instrument in the creation of the world: it is another aspect of the intermediary rôle of the Logos between the Creator and the universe.

> 'For the production of any being many principles have to co-operate: the cause properly so called, the

[1] *Leg. Alleg.*, III, 100 (M., I, 107). [2] *De somn.*, I, 117 (M., I, 638).
[3] *Quis rer. divin. her.*, 205–206 (M., I, 501–502).

material, the instrumental means, the purpose. If someone were to ask what was necessary for the construction of a house or a city, we should reply: a workman, stones, wood, and tools . . . and if we go on from such particular constructions to that great city, which is the world, we shall find that the cause is God, who has made it: the material is the four elements, of which it has been composed: the instrumental means is the divine Logos, by whom it has been constructed; and the end of its construction is the goodness of the Demiurge.'[1]

So these manifold functions of the Logos come back to one fundamental conception. Between God, the infinitely perfect, and this wretched world, the Logos is the intermediary making possible an exchange of thought and action. But as we already know, the problem thus solved preoccupies all Philo's contemporaries, Jews or Greeks, and the solution which he gives resembles those already proposed by many philosophers or commentators. It is not therefore surprising that the intelligence of Philo, inquisitive rather than powerful, has given to this master-thought various different aspects corresponding to the manifold influences which he underwent.

He was a Jew, and we have seen in our study of his conception of God how profoundly Judaism had penetrated his religious thought; recognising at the same time its influence on his theory of the Logos. In Alexandrine Judaism the theology of Wisdom had been developed very far; several of the traits that we have noticed in the *Wisdom of Solomon* are to be recognised in the writings of Philo. Wisdom is the maker of all that exists (vii, 22; vii, 6); the Logos plays a similar rôle in Philo; if there is any difference to be noted, it is that Wisdom is more clearly personified in the Sapiential books than the Logos in Philo. Wisdom is a 'worker'[2]; the Logos is an 'instrument.'[3] Moreover, in the Sapiential books we find the Logos brought very near to Wisdom,[4] whereas in Philo Wisdom is identified with the Logos.[5]

[1] *De cherub.*, 125–127 (M., I, 162). Cf. *Leg. Alleg.*, III, 96 (106); *Q. Deus sit immut.*, 57 (281); *De sacrif. Ab. et Cain*, 8 (165). Cf. NORDEN, *Agnostos Theos*, 240 *sqq.*

[2] Cf. *Secrets of Henoch*, xxx, 8.

[3] See above, note [1]; the same references to PHILO are applicable.

[4] *Wisd.* ix, 1, 2.

[5] *De fuga*, 137–8 (M., I, 566).

The relations of Wisdom and of God were described by means of images which corrected and completed each other:

> 'Wisdom is the breath of the power of God, a pure emanation of the glory of the Almighty; she cannot be touched by anything defiled. She is the splendour of the eternal light, the stainless mirror reflecting the activity of God, and the image of his goodness' (*Sap. Sal,* vii, 25-26).

No such description is to be found in Philo; which shows that Wisdom appears more definitely personified than the Logos in the Sapiential books. We shall, however, often find in his pages that exemplarist conception which recalls, at least in certain of its features, this theology of Wisdom: he loves to repeat that the Logos is the 'image of God'[1] or again 'the imprint of the seal of God.'[2]

More significant than these exemplarist metaphors, and giving them all their force, are the expressions which describe, in the Sapiential books, Wisdom as engendered by God; we found such expressions in *Proverbs* (viii, 25), and also the description of Wisdom playing round the feet of God like a child, while he strengthened the foundations of the earth. This traditional conception, echoed by *Ecclesiasticus* and *Wisdom,* no doubt induced Philo to represent the Logos as the eldest son of God.[3]

This expression is the more remarkable that it does not appear to have been brought about, like many others, by an artifice of exegesis; Philo uses it, not because the text on which he is commenting imposes it on him or suggests it to him, but merely because it corresponds to his thought. Moreover, in order to explain it, we must take fully into account Philo's habits of mind: he loves to personify everything and expresses every relation of origin by metaphors drawn from the idea of generation.[4] Further, and this is the most important point, the world

[1] *De fuga,* 101 (M., I, 561); *De confus. ling.,* 147 (427); *De spec. leg.,* I, 81 (II, 225).

[2] *De plant.,* 18 (I, 332); *De somn.,* II, 45 (I, 665).

[3] *De agricult.,* 51 (M., I, 308); *De confus. ling.,* 63 (414), 146 (427); *De fuga,* 109 (562); *De somn.,* I, 215 (653).

[4] Cf. *De fuga,* 109 (M., I, 562); *De ebriet.,* 30 (360); *ibid.,* 33 (362); *De mutat. nom.,* 131 (598).

is for him the younger son of God, as the Logos is the elder.[1] This conception of the divine filiation is above all cosmological, and I doubt if it can be explained by the Jewish tradition which represents Israel as the 'first-born son' of God: nor do I believe that it should be interpreted as due to the influence of the myths of Isis[2]; on the contrary, it seems to me that only the theology of Wisdom can have led Philo to this conception of the Logos and the world.

In connection with this conception of Wisdom, and sometimes identified with it, other real or purely symbolical objects made their appearance in Judaism on the fringes of the divine world, and in due course blended with the Philonian conception of the Logos. The most important of these is the 'Angel of Jahve.' In the Biblical text which Philo used, this Angel intervenes in most of the theophanies of the Old Testament: it is he who appears to men and speaks to them; while the context states clearly that it is Jahve himself who is seen and heard. This apparent contradiction, solved for us by the criticism of the texts,[3] was no embarrassment to Philo. For him it proved suggestive; this Angel who was not God yet presents himself as God, is he not the Logos whose vague personality may at the same time reveal God and veil him?[4] In this Philo finds a confirmation of the theory, to him so dear, that God only shows himself to imperfect beings through intermediaries, on account of their feeble vision; here is his explanation of the point:

> 'It is natural that he should manifest himself as he is to the disembodied souls who are his familiars, conversing with them as a friend with his friends; but for those who are still in the body he appears in the similitude of an angel, not that he changes his nature, for it is immutable, but because he infuses into their imaginations a different representation in such a way that they think that this image is no imitation but the original form itself.'

Having confirmed this theory by recalling the fact

[1] *Q. Deus sit immut.*, 31 (M., I, 277); *De ebriet.*, 30 (361).
[2] See Bréhier, 110; Lagrange, *RB* (1910), 590.
[3] Cf. Lagrange, *RB* (1903), 212–25; (1908), 497–9.
[4] *Ibid.*, (1908), 498, n. 2.

that Scripture sometimes compares God to a man, although he is not man, he proceeds:

> 'Why then should we be astonished if God takes on the appearance sometimes of angels and sometimes even of men, in order to help those who have need of him? Thus when Scripture says: I am the God who appeared to thee in the place of God[1]—we should think that he took on the appearance of an angel, but without any real change, in order to help him who could not otherwise see the true God. Just as those who cannot see the sun itself, see its reflection, and those who see the halo of the moon think they see the moon, so we perceive the image of God, his angel, the Logos, as God himself.'[2]

This principle of interpretation is applied by Philo to the divine apparitions reported in the Old Testament ; it was the Logos who appeared to Agar when driven out by Abraham,[3] and to Jacob on leaving Laban[4] ; the Logos wrestled with Jacob and changed his name to Israel[5] ; he talked with Moses in the burning bush[6] ; the Logos was in the cloud guiding the Israelites in their departure from Egypt[7] and conducting them through the desert.[8]

This exegesis is precisely similar to what we studied above when describing the Philonian theory of the powers ; it may even happen that the same manifestation is interpreted in one passage as an apparition of the powers, in another as an apparition of the Logos, simply because the sacred text speaks in one of several angels, and in the other of one only.[9] What we already know of Philo enables us to understand that he is not much concerned with this difference. The Logos and the powers play the same rôle of intermediaries, revealers, and agents of God, and, in exegesis as in philosophy, Philo treats them as interchangeable values.

This identification of the Logos and the Angel of Jahve

[1] *Gen.* xxxi, 13.
[2] *De somn.*, I, 232–239 (M., I, 655–656). See LAGRANGE, *RB* (1923), 344.
[3] *De Cherubim*, 3 (M., I, 139) ; *De fuga*, 5 (547).
[4] *De somniis*, I, 226 (655). [5] *De mutat. nom.*, 87 (591).
[6] *De vita Mosis*, I, 66 (II, 91).
[7] *Q. rer. divin. heres.*, 203–5 (I, 501) ; *De vita Mosis*, I, 166 (II, 107).
[8] *De somniis*, I, 117 (I, 638) ; *De migrat. Abrah.*, 174 (463).
[9] See *De Abrahamo*, 145 (II, 22) ; *De somniis*, I, 86 (I, 634) ; *De mutat. nom.*, 15 (I, 581).

has in Philonism a considerable importance: it tends to give to the figure of the Logos, sometimes so vague, the distinctness of a living person. It will play a still more important rôle in later tradition. The Christian apologists, wishing to prove against the Jews the divinity of the Word and his distinctness from the Father, will have recourse to the argument of the theophanies; he who appears in the Old Testament has all the attributes of divinity, and yet is distinct from the God of Israel. The exegesis of the apologists is very different to that of Philo;[1] both of them, however, are inspired by the same concern for the divine transcendence, and often find the justification of their view in the same texts. But side by side with this exegesis of philosophic inspiration, we have to recognise another of which the source is specifically Christian: several of the Fathers, St. Irenæus in particular, see in these appearances of the Word of God as it were rehearsals and preludes of the Incarnation; that is a purely Christian conception and wholly foreign to Philonism.[2]

Another allegorical interpretation equally dear to Philo leads him often to see in the Jewish High Priest a figure of the Logos or the world. This symbolism was suggested to him by his conception of the Logos placed between the world and God as a suppliant.[3] Here, no doubt, he was also affected by influences which are recognisable in the Jewish world of his time. Since the days of the Machabees, the figure of the High Priest had taken on a new majesty; there were indeed certain Jewish circles in which Levi took precedence over Juda, and the Messias was expected from the tribe of Levi.[4] In other circles, in which cosmological preoccupations were more active, the vestments of the High Priest were interpreted as representing allegorically the world and its elements; 'in the priestly robe which he wore,' we already find, in the *Wisdom of Solomon* (xviii, 24), 'was the whole world.' This allegorical interpretation was dear to Philo, who often develops it and follows it out in all its

[1] In the earlier editions of this work I had admitted (following P. Heinisch, *op. cit. infra*, 143) the direct influence of Philo's exegesis of the theophanies upon the apologists. A closer study of the text of St. Justin has led to my correcting this judgement. The question will be discussed in Vol. II.

[2] Cf. Mangey's edition, II, 169.

[3] See above, page 160.

[4] *Ibid.*, page 126.

details.[1] And for him, the ideal High Priest, of whom the Jewish High Priest is but the symbol, is the Logos who is clothed with the world, as the High Priest with his symbolic vestments. And all that the law ordains or exacts of the High Priest is interpreted allegorically of the Logos.

> 'His father and his mother must be pure: his father is God, the father of the universe; his mother is the wisdom by which all beings have come into existence . . . This most venerable Logos of being is clothed with the world as with a vestment; for he is concealed under the earth and under water, air, and fire and all that comes from them . . . he may never take off his mitre, that is, his royal diadem, the symbol of a power that is not sovereign, but subordinate, and nevertheless wonderful; he may not tear his vestments, for, as has been said, he is the bond of unity of the universe, of which he keeps together all the parts, binding them together, and preventing their dissolution and separation.'[2]

Philo often adopts such allegorical interpretation, and he always extends this symbolism, beyond the framework of Judaism, to the whole of humanity, and even to the whole of creation. In *Ecclesiasticus* we hear the musical ministry of Wisdom in the presence of Jahve in the tabernacle (xxiv, 10); this idea suggests no doubt a resemblance between the divine Wisdom and the High Priest of the law, but with a quite different character than in Philo; the immediately preceding words of Jahve: 'dwell in Jacob and have thy heritage in Israel' clearly recall the privileges of the chosen people and the divine predilections: in Philo all that is absent; the symbols are still borrowed from Judaism, but the religious ideas expressed by them are now those of a citizen of the world. If we pursue the study of the Philonian Logos, yet other traces may be found of Judaic symbolism, themselves clothing ideas which are no longer specifically Jewish, but which originate in Hellenism or in Oriental syncretism. We know that Judaism, in order to avoid mentioning the name of God, often had recourse to abstract terms like the Glory, the Name, the Place, the

[1] Especially in *De vita Mosis*, II, 117–35 (M., II, 152–5).
[2] *De fuga*, 109–118 (M., I, 562–563).

Dwelling-place[1]; it was easy to make these abstract beings into intermediaries between God and the world. We need not therefore be surprised to find Philo interpreting all these names as names of the Logos and the powers; he thus manifests in his theory of intermediaries the contact which he maintains with Jewish speculation; but while this identification is his heritage from Judaism, he more often gives it a philosophical interpretation borrowed from Hellenism.

In the *Treatise of Dreams* Philo, interpreting the story in *Genesis* (xxviii, 11), where it is said of Jacob: 'he came to the place,' explains that this word can be understood in three different ways. The place may signify, first, the space filled by a body: secondly, the divine Logos whom God has entirely filled with incorporeal powers . . . thirdly, it may signify God himself, because God contains all beings and is not contained by any.[2] And putting aside the first and the third meanings, he devotes himself to showing in the 'place' the symbol of the Logos. This interpretation assumes the whole Philonian philosophy: the Logos is here conceived as the place of the ideas, and consequently of the powers as well.[3]

Elsewhere the Logos is similarly identified with the Name,[4] the Dwelling-place,[5] and the Rock[6]—the powers with the Glory.[7] Thus all Jewish speculation on the intermediary beings is placed by Philo in these categories of the Logos and the powers and eventually loses itself in Hellenist syncretism.

If the Alexandrine philosopher welcomes all these speculations, at the price, however, of transforming them, he rejects the too-material representations given by the Rabbis surrounding him, of the voice and the word of God. When he presents the Logos as the voice of God he is careful to spiritualise it as much as he can; it is no mere vibration of the ether, like our voices; it is a pure substance which our mind's eye can see, but which our bodily ear cannot hear[8]; thus it is said in *Exodus* that all the people saw the voice (*Ex.* xx, 18) and not that they heard it. Our speech, he says again elsewhere, is a dyad,

[1] See above, page 113.
[2] *De somn.*, I, 62 (M., I, 630).
[3] See below, page 170.
[4] *De confus. ling.*, 146 (M., I, 427).
[5] *De migrat. Abrah.*, 3–7 (437).
[6] *Q. det. pot.*, 118 (213).
[7] *De spec. leg.*, I, 45 (II, 218).
[8] *De migrat. Abr.*, 52 (M., I, 444).

formed by the articulation of our organs and the compression of the air; God speaks only by monads or by unities, in which sense his word is incorporeal and one.[1]

This attempt to spiritualise the Rabbinic tradition is still more clearly evident in the case of the Decalogue: for the Rabbis the ten Commandments had been audibly articulated by God[2]; Philo corrects this tradition thus:

> 'Did God utter the Commandments vocally? It is an absurd hypothesis which should not even occur to our minds; for God is not as a man, making use of mouth, tongue, and lungs. But it seems to me in these circumstances God worked a great marvel, forming in the air an invisible voice more wonderful than any organ, formed of perfect harmonies, not inanimate, nor like an animal composed of body and soul, but itself a rational soul, wholly transparent and pure, which, shaping the air and changing it into flame, produces this articulate voice like air in a trumpet, making it equally audible to the most distant and the nearest bystanders'[3]

This 'rational soul,' which further on is called a power of God, is sufficiently like the Logos by his nature and his rôle, and this example makes us understand the way in which Philo modifies and spiritualises the Jewish conception of the Word.

There is finally a last trait of authentically Jewish origin which we may distinguish in the Philonian conception of the Logos: it is the omnipotence, the immediate efficacy of the divine Word; 'When God speaks he acts,' says Philo, 'there is no interval between his word and his action; or, to speak more exactly, his word is his action: *ὁ λόγος ἔργον ἦν αὐτοῦ.*'[4]

This statement, which he readily repeats, is obviously inspired by the sacred writings: 'He speaks and all is done; he ordains and all is created.' That is certainly an admirable conception of God, and no other can give a higher or more just idea of his power. But far from explaining the proper rôle of intermediary agents, it tends

[1] *Q. Deus sit immut.*, 83 (M., I, 285).
[2] Weber, *Jüd. Theol.*, 180.
[3] *De decalogo*, 32–33 (M., II, 185).
[4] *De sacrif. Ab. et C.*, 65 (M., I, 157).

to suppress it wholly, for it represents the will of God as reaching immediately all beings and acting directly on them.

Philo then has accepted on this point the traditional teaching of his faith, and transmits it, but without incorporating it in his system. In fact, his conception of the Logos as God's word remains secondary; it is the one proposed to him by the Bible; he accepts it no doubt, and sometimes repeats it in his works, but he nearly always transforms it. His usual conception of the Logos to which he instinctively refers, is less a word than a thought, an ideal existing between heaven and earth; the exemplar of our world and the force sustaining it; a mysterious being half way between God and the world, revealer of God and support of the world. He thinks he finds this conception on every page of the Biblical narratives; but if the sacred texts with their traditional commentary suggest it to him, it is not they, or at least it is not they alone who have formed it. A mere point of contact arouses his mind and at the same time awakes a whole world of ideas of which Judaism knew nothing.

These ideas are already familiar to us; we have analysed them when studying the contemporary Hellenic *milieu* of Philo; we have again found them in Philo's own conception of God and the powers; it remains for us to study them in the passages where they are most clearly expressed, which treat of his theory of the Logos.

The Logos is above all, for Philo, an intermediary between God and the world, enabling God to reveal himself to the world and to act on it; a light is thrown on this double rôle of the Logos by the religious philosophy inspired by Platonism and Stoicism, as commonly understood in Hellenist circles.

Platonist exemplarism has its own interpretation of the revealing rôle of the Logos. In Jewish theology the angel of Jahve makes God known because he is his messenger; for Philo the Logos reveals God because he is his image[1] and his imprint.[2] If we understand this we also grasp the distinctions of the various degrees of God's manifestation. Each power, that is to say, each idea,[3] is

[1] *De spec. leg.*, III, 83 (M., II, 313), I, 81 (II, 225). *De confus. ling.*, 97 (I, 419); etc. [2] *De plantat.*, 18 (M., I, 332).

[3] On the identification of the 'powers' with the 'ideas,' see above, page 151.

but a fragmentary and incomplete image of God, while the Logos represents God as a whole; the idea is only attached to God by the slender and fragile thread that attaches a thought to the mind which has conceived it; the Logos is the shadow of God,[1] that is to say, his natural and essential image.

The same exemplarist theory also throws light on one of the aspects of the action of the Logos on the world: 'Just as God is the exemplar of the image, so the image is the exemplar of other beings, as Moses made known when he wrote at the beginning of the law: God has made man in his own image.'[2] On this point also the theory of the Logos is exactly parallel to the theory of the powers. In the *Treatise of Creation* the powers appear as the ideas conceived by the divine architect before he made the world; in the same way, the Logos is presented as the totality of these ideas, or the intelligible world[3]:

> 'If anyone wishes,' says Philo, 'to use the simplest words, one may say that the intelligible world is no other than the Logos of God constructing the world; for the intelligible city is nothing else than the reason of the architect drawing his plans. This doctrine is not mine but that of Moses; for when relating the formation of man, he definitely says that he was made in the image of God; but if the part (man) is the image of an image, and if the entire construction, that is to say, the whole of this sensible universe . . . is the likeness of the divine image, it is evident that the archetypal imprint which we call the intelligible world must be the divine Logos.'[4]

According to this theory the Logos is considered as a book, 'in which God has written and engraved the constitution of all other created beings'[5]; or, still more frequently, as the dwelling-place of ideas; this is the meaning which Philo generally attributes to Scripture when he interprets τόπος by λόγος, when it is a question of place.[6] It follows necessarily that the Logos, in relation

[1] *Leg. Alleg.*, III, 96 (106). [2] *Ibid.*

[3] At the beginning of the *Berechith rabba*, God, creating the world, is compared to an architect building a palace, and the Thora has a rôle somewhat like that of Philo's Logos.

[4] *De op. mundi*, 24–25 (M., I, 6). [5] *Leg. Alleg.*, I, 19 (M., I, 47).

[6] *De somn.*, I, 62 (M., I, 630).

to the world of the senses, should be considered as a model or exemplar, acting on it as a seal imprinting itself on wax. The Logos is 'the seal of the universe, the archetypal idea from which beings without form or quality have received their significance and their shape.'[1] And again: 'The Logos of the demiurge is the seal imprinted on every being; thus each created thing has from its origin a perfect form, impression, and image of the perfect Logos.'[2]

The Logos, being reason and word, is in a special sense the exemplar of man, as well as of all that exists in the world. 'Nothing is more sacred than man, or more like to God, for he is the excellent imprint of an excellent image, being formed on the model of the ideal archetype'[3]; and similarly in the *Treatise of the Anathemas*: 'God has granted the human race an exceptional privilege, that is, kinship with his Logos, in the likeness of whom the human spirit has been made.'[4]

These speculations which Philo loves to consecrate by the authority of Scripture (*Gen.* i, 26, 27) lead him to represent the Logos sometimes as the ideal man; hence the words of the sons of Joseph: 'We are all the sons of one man,' mean, according to him, that we are all the sons of the Logos, the eternal image of God.[5]

All these metaphors of imitation, reflection, and imprint leave the most obscure point of the problem unaccounted for: they do not explain how the immaterial Logos or idea can imprint itself on matter like a seal and mark it with its likeness. If we interrogate Philo on this point he would no doubt reply, as Plato of old, that things are thus moulded by the ideas in an ineffable and wonderful way.[6]

Elsewhere he has recourse to a metaphor which throws a new light on his thought: he speaks of the dividing or 'cutting' Logos, and compares its action to that of a sharp blade which pierces amorphous matter, distinguishing the different properties of beings: 'and when it has differentiated all material beings as far as the atoms that we call indivisible elements, it begins again to divide these elements, which reason alone can perceive, into an infinite

[1] *De mut. nom.*, 135 (M., I, 598). [2] *De fug.*, 12 (M., I, 547).
[3] *De spec. leg.*, III, 83, 207 (M., II, 313, 333).
[4] *De execrat.*, 163 (M., II, 435).
[5] *De confus. ling.*, 147 (M., I, 427). [6] *Tim.*, 50c.

number of parts . . . it thus divides souls into rational and irrational, language into truth and falsehood . . .'[1]

This theory of the 'Cutter' has attracted the attention of the interpreters of Philo. M. Heinze[2] finds its source in the philosophy of Heraclitus ; and it is certain that some of the elements composing it are to be found there ; Philo himself has been careful to recall the memory of Heraclitus when he developed in this connection his theory of contraries.[3] But it seems to me that the dialectic of Plato has also played a great rôle in this conception ; what we find therein, above all, is the problem of unity in multiplicity that Plato so often discussed ; and that the solution given by Philo is at bottom a Platonist solution: the idea that penetrates the world, specifies its material elements, then distinguishes them and eventually opposes them one to another. Like the human spirit, so also the divine reason separates and isolates the qualities of beings[4] ; but the action of the divine reason is more profound and efficacious. We find again there, under a new metaphor, the idea expressed by the image of the seal and the imprint ; the difference between the two expressions is that the first explains better in things the absolute qualities which specify them, and the second, the relations which put them in opposition to each other.

All these comparisons and metaphors merely express in a very imperfect manner the action of the Logos in the world. It was not from Plato, but from the Stoics, that Philo demanded on this point a more exact answer, and the conceptions which he borrowed from them have left their stamp more deeply on his theory of the Logos than any others.[5]

In Philo, as in Chrysippus, the Logos is at the same time a principle of energy and a principle of determination. As the seminal Logos he is the force which fertilises everything: mind, in order to produce intellectual conceptions ; speech, to stimulate vocal energy, the senses in general, to awaken the images derived from physical

[1] *Quis rer. divin. her.*, 130–140 (M., I, 491–492).
[2] Heinze, *op. cit.*, 228.
[3] *Quis rer. divin. her*, 214 (M., I, 503). [4] *Ibid.*, 235 (M., I, 506).
[5] Cf. Zeller, *Philosophie der Griechen*[3], V, 385 ; Heinze, *Die Lehre vom Logos*, 238 ; Schuerer, *loc. cit.*, 557 ; Aall, *Gesch. d. Logosidee*, I, 223 ; Montefiore, *Florilegium Philonis*, in *JQR*, VII (1895), 482 ; Bousset-Gressman, *Religion des Judentums*, 441, n. 2.

objects; the body, to give it its characteristic shape and movements.[1] The Logos plays in the universe the same rôle as the soul in each of us[2]; the diversity of the elements is but the garment which clothes it as the body clothes the soul.[3]

The Logos is at once the support and the bond of union of the world:

> 'No material element is strong enough to carry the world: but the eternal Logos of the eternal God is the strong and solid support of the universe. He it is who, stretching from the centre to the circumference, and back again, directs the infallible course of nature, maintaining all its parts, and binding them strongly together: for the Father who has begotten him has made him the unbreakable bond of union of the whole world.'[4]

Elsewhere he says:

> 'Earth and water placed in the midst of air and fire and surrounded by the heavens have no external support, but hold together, attached to each other by the divine Logos, who himself is the most wise architect and the most perfect harmony.'[5]

And again:

> 'The Logos being the bond of union of all beings, as has been said, holds all the parts of the world closely united, preventing their separation and dissociation.'[6]

The Logos is symbolised by gold:

> 'In the same way that gold is impenetrable to arrows, and remains unbreakable when stretched out in the finest threads, the Logos extends himself, diffuses himself, and reaches everything, dwelling fully and entirely in all beings, and uniting all the rest of the universe in one and the same tissue.'[7]

By this extraordinary accumulation of metaphors Philo intends to signify two properties of the Logos which he very often unites: the one, universal expansion; the

[1] *Q. rer. divin. her.*, 118–9 (M., I, 489). [2] *Ibid.*, 230–3 (505).
[3] *De Fuga*, 110 (M., I, 562). [4] *De Plantat. Noe*, 8, 9 (M., I, 330–331).
[5] *Qu. in Exod.*, II, 90 (Aucher, p. 528).
[6] *De Fuga*, I, 112 (M., I, 562). [7] *Quis rer. divin. her.*, 217 (M., I, 503).

other, plenitude or density: he thus expresses in rather material fashion the virtue of this divine force which spreads everywhere without weakening or, so to speak, without rarefying itself. In the same way, therefore, that the Logos unites and secures the cohesion of beings, he consolidates them and causes them to subsist: 'Of themselves all things are void; if they are substantial it is because they are held together by the divine Logos, as it were by the cement and bond of union which pervades all things with its essence.'[1] Elsewhere he gives expression to an analogous idea by a grammatical metaphor, which to-day seems strange to our ears: 'The divine Logos places himself in the midst of beings as a vowel-sound between two consonants, so that the whole world may resound.'[2]

All these images cover the same concept: the Logos is the one and only principle of unity and determination in the world. Philo, it is true, like Marcus Aurelius, has made a breach in the Stoic monism; he admits, together with the Logos, a material principle distinct from it, but this principle has of itself neither determination nor quality; it is from the Logos that every being holds its nature, and by means of the Logos that all beings are mutually connected, and so constitute the world.

The concept of destiny is attached to this concept of physical law, and Philo, like the Stoics, further applies it to the Logos. After having spoken in his *Treatise of the Divine Immutability* of the revolutions of empires, he thus explains them:

> 'It is a circular process led by the divine Logos, that the majority of men call fortune; he drags after him cities, nations, and countries, giving to some what belongs to others, and to all what belongs to all, by a series of periodical changes, so that the entire universe should enjoy, like a single city, the best of governments, that of democracy.'[3]

This universal city has its laws and constitution, to which all its citizens are subject; it is the Logos:

> 'Since every well-governed city has its constitution, it is necessary that the citizen of the world should be

[1] *Quis rer. divin. her.*, 188 (M., I, 499).
[2] *De Plantat. Noe*, 10 (M., I, 331).
[3] *Quod Deus sit immut.*, 176 (M., I, 298).

governed by the constitution of the world; but this is unerring rationality of nature—the divine law which assigns to each one what is suitable and proper for him.'[1]

This identification of the Logos and the moral law occurs constantly in Philo; moreover, there is nothing in that specially Philonian, and that we have not already found in the analysis of Stoicism. It will therefore be sufficient to point out a few texts selected from many others in which this theory is clearly set forth.[2]

That we should find these Stoic ideas in Philo should not surprise us. The Logos, who for him unites the world to God, must at the same time be immanent and transcendent, and conciliate in a strange synthesis the theories of Marcus Aurelius and of Plutarch. God, on the other hand, is kept at a distance from the world with so jealous a care that one is surprised to see Philo apply to him certain Stoic expressions, which agree better with the pantheism of Chrysippus than with Alexandrine dualism. 'The entire heaven,' says he, 'and the world are, truth to tell, a fruit of God sustained as by a tree, by his eternal and always flourishing nature.'[3] Stoic influence is again to be recognised in the expression *ὁ τῶν ὅλων νοῦς*, by which Philo frequently refers to God,[4] and also in the antithesis which he loves to establish between the soul of the world, who is God, and the individual soul proper to each man.[5]

These expressions betray Stoic influence the more clearly, since Philo's doctrine as a whole is so clearly opposed to monism.[6] He readily attacks the impiety of the Chaldeans who believed that the world is God, or that God is the soul of the world, and who deify destiny or necessity[7]; but in the very passages in which he refutes them he cannot escape the influence of Stoic ideas:

'Moses has not,' he says, 'taught all these impieties, but he believed that the whole of this universe was

[1] *De opif. mundi*, 143 (M., I, 34).
[2] *Mos.*, I, 48 (M., II, 88); *Q. omn. prob. lib.*, 46, 62 (II, 452, 455); *De migrat.*, 130 (I, 456); *De Ebriet.*, 142 (I, 379); *De Praem.*, 55 (II, 417); *Jos.*, 29 (II, 46).
[3] *De mutat. nom.*, 140 (M., I, 599).
[4] *De Gigant.*, 40 (M., I, 268); *De migrat.*, 4 (437), 186 (465); 192–3 (466); *De opif. mundi*, 8 (2).
[5] *Leg. Alleg.*, III, 29 (M., I, 93).
[6] See CUMONT, *De æternitate mundi*, p. x.
[7] *De Migrat.*, 179–84 (M., I, 464–5).

sustained by invisible powers, widely scattered by the demiurge from the extremities of the earth to the limits of heaven, disposing everything in a perfect order so as to prevent the separation of the elements thus connected: for the powers are the unbreakable bonds of the world.'[1]

It is easy to recognise in this conception of the powers the Stoic theory of the powers and habits,[2] except for the point that the powers are here attached to God, and no longer conceived as the inherent properties of matter.[3] This essential distinction definitely separates the theodicy of Philo from Stoic Pantheism; but it leaves intact the characteristics which appear in our analysis of his theory of the Logos: the law which rules the world, the force which sustains it, the bond which chains its elements together, the Logos was all that for Chrysippus, and all that for Philo; and one is justified in finding in these traits of Stoicism the most definite and characteristic element of the Philonian theory.

Having thus reviewed all the various elements which are knit together in the philosophy of Philo, and particularly in his theory of the Logos, it would be interesting if we could discover the underlying unity which dominates and co-ordinates them all. This desire for consistency is too legitimate for us to decline the research involved in its discovery, but we must beware of pursuing it too rigorously. The more one studies Philo the more convinced one becomes that he lacks our standards in the matter; he, so profoundly attached to his Jewish faith, was nevertheless able in the treatises he wrote as a young man, the *De æternitate mundi* and the *De Providentia,* to speak as a worshipper of the gods[4]; he, so hostile to Stoic determinism, could borrow from his Stoic predecessors wholly fatalist tendencies.[5] The very form of his writings inclines him to these borrowings to which he commits himself so willingly: nearly all his books are allegorical commentaries of Scripture, the woof of which is not formed

[1] *De migrat.*, 181 (M. I, 464). [2] See above, page 152 *sq.*
[3] See *Leg. Alleg.*, III, 97 (M., I, 107); *De Congr. erudit. grat.*, 55 (527); *Quis rer. divin. her.*, 281 (513).
[4] Cf. *De Providentia*, III (Aucher, II, 75–6).
[5] Cf. Bousset quoting *Qu. in Exod.*, II, 69 *sqq.*

by continuity of thought, but by the sequence of the sacred text. The narratives, even the sentences which succeed each other, evoke a thousand different reflections, some due to Philo, the others taken by him from his predecessors. It is not surprising to find in so varied a whole incongruous fragments, and we should not try too hard to reduce them to a consistent whole.

These remarks being made, it will be granted that, in default of a clearly defined philosophic system, we may recognise in Philo certain ideas which are specially dear to him, and which give to most of his exegetical developments more or less convergent directions. One of his leading ideas, as we have often seen, is that of the transcendence of God, and, consequently, of the necessity of intermediary beings which facilitate an exchange of thought and action between him and the world.

Of these intermediaries the Logos is the first; it is this conception that dominates Philo's whole theory, and gives what unity they have to these many representations, so diverse in their origin and value: the wisdom and reason of God, his son, his angel, his high priest, the ideal world, image of God, and the model of the world of experience, the immanent law of the world, vital force, the bond of the elements: the Logos is all that for Philo; and if we seek among so many names and so many diverse functions for the fundamental conception which shall reconcile them all, it cannot be better expressed than in *Q. rer. div. her.*, 205. 'The Father who engendered all things has given to the Logos this singular privilege of being intermediary between the creature and the Creator.'

In order better to understand this Philonian conception of the Logos as an intermediary being between God and the world, we may compare it to the belief of Christians in the mediatory Word: the problem to be solved is the same, namely, to bring the infinitely perfect God near to his weak and guilty creatures, but the two solutions are completely different. The Incarnate Word unites in his person these two extremes, God and the flesh, being at the same time truly God and truly man; on the contrary, Philo's Logos does not unite in himself the two terms, he is half way between them; as Philo makes him say in the passage to which we have just referred: 'being neither without beginning like God, nor created like you, but intermediary between these two extremes, I am, as it were, a hostage for both parties.'

This very obvious observation permits us to solve with certainty the first question which may be put in connection with the Logos of Philo: his Logos is not God, at least if we give to the name of God the definite meaning that it had for every Jew, and particularly for Philo. To affirm that the Word is equal to and consubstantial with his Father, is for Christians a fundamental dogma implied by that very notion of mediation of which we spoke above. The union affirmed by faith between God and man would be illusory if the Son incarnated in Jesus Christ were not God, equal to, and consubstantial with, his Father. For Philo, on the contrary, such an affirmation would ruin his whole system; if the Logos is truly God, he is no longer that intermediary being of whom he dreams, half way between creature and Creator, that revealer whose diminished perfection can be attained by the imperfect ones who would be blinded by the vision of God. In a passage of the *Treatise of Dreams* Philo interprets, not without touching it up,[1] a passage of *Leviticus* speaking of the High Priest; he sees in it, as usual, an image of the Logos, which he interprets as follows:

> 'The High Priest hardly counts when he is mentioned in company with others; but when he is alone he counts for a great deal. In himself he is the whole tribunal, the whole senate, the whole people, the entire human race, or, rather, if the truth must be told, a nature midway between God and man, inferior to God, superior to man. For when the High Priest—it is said—shall enter the Holy of Holies, he will not be a man. What will he be if he is not a man? Will he then be God? I would not wish to say that—the great prophet Moses was given that name, when still in Egypt, being called the god of Pharao—yet no more will he be man, but he will attain both these terms by their limits, so to speak, the peak of one and the base of the other.'[2]

[1] *Lev.* xvi, 17: 'Let no man be in the tabernacle when the high priest goeth in to the sanctuary'; but Philo says (below) that, when the high priest enters the Holy of Holies, 'he will not be a man.'

[2] *De somn.*, II, 188–189 (M., I, 683).

Elsewhere Philo interprets in the same way the rôle of the High Priest and of the Logos which he symbolises: he is explaining why the law forbids him to take part in any ceremonial mourning, and gives this reason:

> 'The law wishes him to be of a nature more than human, and approaching more nearly the divine, or, to speak exactly, half way between the two natures, so that by such an intermediary men may be able to influence God and that God may give his graces to men, using a subordinate for that purpose.'[1]

Texts of this nature, of which the list could be prolonged, allow us clearly to understand Philo's thought: the Logos is for him an intermediary being 'between the creature and the Creator,'[2] 'between the mortal and the immortal race.'[3] We cannot oppose to this theory, which is very definite and consistent, the passages in which Philo calls the Logos God; these passages are three in number.[4] They are these: first, in the *Treatise of Dreams* Philo interprets a text of *Genesis* (xxxi, 13), which he quotes in accordance with the Septuagint:

> 'I am the God whom thou hast seen in the place of God.' 'We must not,' says he, 'pass too quickly over this saying, but carefully enquire whether indeed there are two gods: for it is said: "I am the God whom thou hast seen," not "in my place," but "in the place of God," as if that was in the place of another. What then are we to say? There is but one true God, but there are several who are wrongly thus called: also the sacred text here indicates the true God by the definite article, saying: "I am *the* God," but him who is wrongly so called, without the article, by saying "in the place," not "of *the* God," but only "of God." He calls God his most venerable Logos, paying no attention to verbal scruples, but having only one object in view, the narration of facts.'[5]

The second text is to be found in the *Book of the Allegories;* Philo there explains, while commenting on

[1] *De spec. leg.*, I, 116 (M., II, 330).
[2] *Quis rer div. her.*, 205.
[3] *De somn.*, II, 228 (M., I, 689).
[4] See AUCHER, 331.
[5] *De somn.*, I, 228–230 (M., I, 655). Note here that, for Philo, the word God, even without the article, is wrongly used of the Logos.

Genesis xxii, 16, how God can swear by himself. This difficulty embarrasses Philo.[1] He discusses it at some length, and comes to this conclusion:

> 'God alone can vouch for himself, and for his acts, and it is reasonable that he should swear by himself, a thing impossible to others. This is why we consider those who affirm that they swear by God as impious; for no one should swear by God because nothing can be decided about his nature. It is enough to be able to swear by his name, that is to say, by his interpreter, the Logos, who is the god of us imperfect ones; the primary God is the God of the wise and perfect; Moses, having admired the superiority of the unbegotten being, says: "and thou shalt swear by his name, not by him." It is sufficient to take as guarantee and witness the divine Logos; that God be for himself his guarantee and surest witness.'[2]

This text clearly maintains the intermediary character which Philo always gives to the Logos; the name of God is always given him with hesitation and in a purely relative sense: 'He may be called the God of us imperfect ones.'

The third text resembles the preceding ones (*Qu. in Gen.*, II, 62; Aucher, 146); this work has only come down to us in an Armenian translation: but the relevant fragment has been quoted in Greek by Eusebius (*Praep. Evang.*, VII, 13); here is the translation: 'Why does God say that he has made man "in the image of God," as if he were speaking of another god, and not "in his own image"? These words are a wonderful oracle of wisdom. Nothing mortal can be likened to the Supreme Being, the Father of the universe, but only to the secondary god who is his Logos. It was necessary that the imprint of reason in man should be engraved by the divine Logos; for the God who is prior to the Logos transcends rational nature; and it was impossible that anything that was created should be likened to him who is above the Logos, and whose essence is excellent and unique.'

Here again, as in the *Treatise of Dreams,* the name of God is suggested, or imposed, on Philo, by the text on

[1] See *Qu. in Gen.*, IV, 180 (AUCHER, 382).
[2] *Leg. Alleg.*, III, 207–208 (M., I, 128).

which he is commenting, and he weakens this title, which he feels to be improper, as much as he can; hence this expression of 'secondary god,' only found in this passage of his writings. What is characteristically Philonian in this commentary is the affirmation of the transcendence of God, who could never be the archetype of the rational creature; a rôle which must therefore belong to an intermediary being, who is the Logos: that is what Philo thinks he sees in the text of *Genesis* and what he frequently repeats.[1] Thus explained and modified, the appellation of God is no longer a strictly reserved title, and if Philo applies it three times to the Logos under pressure of the text on which he is commenting, he also gives it to other beings who, in his thought, deserve it even less; the world[2] and the stars.[3]

This problem of the divinity of the Logos is, then, easy to solve; but another question, raised by many texts, presents itself, and is less easy to solve: is the Logos for Philo an abstract force, or a person? We have already come across and solved an analogous problem when we were studying the Philonian theory of the powers[4]; some texts described them as abstractions, others presented them as persons. It is the same here; not to speak of the three texts which we have just been studying, in which the Logos is called God, we have previously mentioned many others, in which he appears as High Priest, suppliant, angel: these seem quite personal functions. No doubt these texts are not the only ones which should be taken into consideration in Philo, and no interpretation of his theory would be acceptable, which on the strength of these few passages would overlook the more numerous and characteristic texts studied above, in which the Logos is certainly described as an impersonal force. On this point indeed, all critics are in agreement.[5] But Philonism is so uncertain and wavering a doctrine that we may ask whether, alongside of the impersonal Logos of the Stoics, we must not admit in his philosophy a personal Logos of Jewish or Alexandrine origin. Such a contradiction

[1] *Leg. Alleg.*, III, 96 (M., I, 106).

[2] See *De æternitate mundi* (ed. Cumont), 4, 17, 21, and introduction, p. x.

[3] *De opif. mundi*, 27 (M., I, 6).

[4] See above, page 152 *sqq.*

[5] Drummond, II, 222–73; Heinze, 280; Aall, I, 217; Zeller, V, p. 378; Réville, *Logos d'après Philon*, 61; Soulier, *Doctrine du Logos chez Philon.*, 157; Bréhier, 107–11.

would be less surprising in a philosopher of that period than in a thinker of our own day: in the whole of Greek philosophy, the concept of person, and even of the individual, has remained vague.[1] It would follow from this that Philo may have unconsciously professed on this point two incompatible opinions.[2] However, before admitting this contradiction we must discuss more closely the texts in which the Logos is personified; most of these are presented under conditions that greatly diminish their demonstrative value.

This personification is often imposed on Philo by the text on which he is commenting. In the whole of his works, as we have just seen, we find only three passages in which the Logos is called god, and on these three occasions exegetical reasons have forced him into this impropriety of language, which he attenuates and excuses as much as he can. More often the Logos is identified with an angel, but there is nothing in that to show that Philo meant to attribute to the Logos a distinct personality. Nothing is more usual with him than to see in the personages of the Bible the symbols of abstract notions, in several, indeed, of the passages with which we are concerned. For instance, Agar meeting the angel, is encyclopædic education meeting the Logos.[3] Should the second part of this interpretation be taken literally when the first is manifestly nothing but a rhetorical figure?

Even when the sacred text does not give Philo the support of a historic personality, his taste for prosopopœia leads him to personify everything, and there are no concrete names of the Logos which we do not find applied to the most abstract ideas. The world is the son of God and of divine knowledge, 'for knowledge, having received the divine seed, has brought forth in fruitful pains her only and darling earthly child, this world.'[4] Elsewhere with reference to Isaac it is joy—who is named the 'indwelling son of God.'[5]

The human Logos in particular is as readily personified as God's, and yet it is certain that no personality is attributed to him by Philo. Our Logos is the High Priest

[1] Cf. Zeller, V, p. 365, n. 2; Heinze, 294.

[2] See Dorner, *Die Lehre von der Person Christi*, I, 33; Grill, *Untersuchungen über die Entstehung des vierten Evangeliums*, 140 *sqq.*

[3] *De Cherub.*, 3 *sqq.* (M., I, 139).

[4] *De Ebriet.*, 30–1 (M., I, 361–2).

[5] *De mutat. nom.*, 131 (M., I, 598).

approaching alone every year the Holy of Holies, that is to say, only attaining in silence and at rare intervals the contemplation of truth.[1] In so far as he is our conscience, he is the High Priest, holy and without spot: 'we must therefore beg this High Priest and king to live in our soul; our judge and our conscience, who, having the power of supreme judgement over our spirit, cannot be intimidated by any who are brought before his bar.'[2]

The Logos manifested, the word, is interpreter, herald, prophet, brother of reason.[3] He rejoices and is happy when, being enlightened, he sees clearly the meaning of what he is expressing . . . 'on the contrary, he groans in the presence of braggarts and chatterers, who cannot define their thought in their endless phrases.'[4] He is for us not only a defender,[5] but a friend, a familiar, a companion, a counsellor.[6] Like his model, Aaron, he should be a Levite, priest, and perfect, to express the thoughts which grow out of a perfect soul.[7] If the High Priest carries the doctrine (Urim) and the truth (Thummim),[8] it is to show the clarity and the sincerity of the Logos of the perfect man.[9] For the wicked, on the contrary, this Logos is a dangerous auxiliary, he is the bold and terrible king symbolised by the king of Egypt whom, however, Moses the prophet can check.[10]

The other human faculties are personified in the same way; when Petronius receives the order to inaugurate the statue of Caligula at Jerusalem, 'he called in council all the thoughts of his soul, took advice from each of them, and found them all unanimous.'[11] On the Sabbath day one should 'in the council of one's soul take account of all that one has said or done, the laws also being present and taking part in the examination.'[12] When the Israelites, on the day of the Messias, shall return to God,

[1] *De gigant.*, 52 (M., I, 269).

[2] In this and similar passages, the individual logos is considered as a part or an emanation of the universal Logos; cf. *De somn.*, I, 34 (M., I, 625).

[3] *Q. det. pot.*, 40 (M., I, 199); 126 (215). [4] *Ibid.*, 129–30 (M., I, 216).

[5] *De somn.*, I, 103 (M., I, 636). [6] *Ibid.*, I, 111, 113 (M., I, 637).

[7] *Q. det. pot.*, 132 (M., I, 216).

[8] The LXX translates *Urim* and *Thummim* by *delosis* and *aletheia*; see *Exod.*, xxviii, 30.

[9] *Q. rer. divin.*, 303 (M., I, 517).

[10] *De confus. ling.*, 29, 34 (M., I, 409–10).

[11] *De legat. ad Caium*, 213 (M., II, 577).

[12] *De Decal.*, 98 (M., II, 197).

they will have three advocates in his presence: the goodness of God, the holiness of their ancestors, and their own improvement.[1]

Quotations of this kind could be indefinitely multiplied[2]; these are sufficient, I think, to give us an idea of Philo's style, and to put us on our guard against too hasty conclusions. It is not because the Logos is called suppliant,[3] angel, or High Priest that we can attribute to him a personal individuality. Moreover, we should create inextricable difficulties if we wished to take Philo's metaphors literally and materialise the abstractions which he personifies and opposes one to the other. Wisdom is, for Philo, identical with the Logos[4]; nevertheless, he tells us in *Treatise of Exile* (109, p. 562) that the Logos has wisdom for his mother, although he has told us (97, p. 560) that the Logos is the source of wisdom[5]; inversely, we learn in the *Treatise of Dreams* (ii, 242, p. 690) that the Logos comes from wisdom, as a river flows from its source. The reciprocal relations of these abstractions are further complicated by a third term, the knowledge of God, which in the *Treatise of Drunkenness* (30, 31, pp. 361-2) is presented as identical with wisdom and as the mother of the world, and becomes in the *Treatise of Exile* (76) the native land of the Logos.[6] A final reflection may be drawn from the conception of the powers. The above-quoted texts of Philo declare most explicitly that between God and his powers there is but a subjective distinction, based on the feebleness of our minds. It is impossible in these conditions to attribute to the Logos a distinct personality. Not only does he bear, according to Philo, the same characteristics as the powers (angel, idea, force, etc.), but he occupies in the scale of beings an intermediary state between God and his powers; the extremes cannot be reduced to a real identity if the middle term is really distinct from both.

Must we then see in all these personifications of the

[1] *De Exsecrat.*, 160, 167 (M., II, 436).

[2] Cf. DRUMMOND, *op. cit.*, II, 124–6.

[3] The translation 'suppliant' is more exact and closer to the Greek than the generally accepted 'intercession.'

[4] See above, page 161 *sqq.*

[5] In this context, wisdom might possibly mean human wisdom.

[6] Again there is a possible alternative: *episteme Theon* could be rendered knowledge of God.'

Logos nothing but mere figures of speech? That would doubtless be too summary a judgment: rhetoric is not sufficient to explain everything. The mythology, or, if the phrase is preferred, the religious philosophy, of the time also played its part. Bréhier (107) has reminded us that 'the concept of these half-abstract, half-concrete beings was current at an epoch of allegorical interpretation of myths, and that such beings as the Zeus of the Stoics, in the *Hymn of Cleanthes,* retained in the physical or moral notion which they symbolically represented, a little of their mythical individuality.' Perhaps M. Bréhier has limited the range of this remark by trying to make it too precise, and seeking in Philo's Logos the features of the Stoic Hermes.[1] It would seem that if the Stoic religion has here exercised its influence, it was much less by loading the Philonian Logos with mythological attributes than by accustoming the minds of Philo and his readers to these vague personalities, which from forces of nature had become objects of worship, yet without destroying their fundamental unity or breaking it up into distinct personalities.

This difference, however, must be pointed out, that the gods of the Hellenic Pantheon kept, even in the Stoic school, very evident vestiges of the personal character imprinted on them in secular legend while, in Philo, the powers and the Logos remain still involved in the world of abstractions where they were born.[2]

To the human soul, too weak to gaze fixedly at the divine sun, they appear as distinct beings, and slowly, by contemplation and worship, the soul lifts itself from one to the other towards God. But this multiplicity is wholly in appearance; if the eye is holy, if the soul is strong, if she can fix her gaze on the sun without seeing double or treble, then she sees God as he is, in his unity.[3]

In concluding this study of Philonism we are unable, as yet, to compare it in detail with Christian theology, which will be expounded further on.[4] At this point, however, the two religious conceptions are sufficiently well known for comparison with each other. The Christians'

[1] Compare CORNUTUS, p. 20, l. 22 with PHILO, *De somn.*, I, 103 (M., I, 636).
[2] See BRÉHIER, 170.
[3] Cf. *De Abrah.*, 122 (M., II, 19); *Q. in Gen.*, IV, 8 (AUCHER, 251).
[4] See Notes V and VII at end of this Volume.

aim is the same as Philo's: union with God; like Philo they measure the infinite distance which keeps them far from him, and they distinguish more clearly than he the sin which separates them from him; nevertheless, they tend towards that end and they reach it: in Jesus Christ. One of those who have most profoundly understood Christianity explains the situation as follows in his *Confessions*:

> 'I searched by what road to travel in order to arrive at the power which would enable me to enjoy thee, and I did not find it until the day on which I perceived the Mediator between God and man, the man Christ Jesus, who is above all things God blessed in all ages.'[1]

This sentence of St. Augustine's—and of St. Paul's—makes clear the essential features of Christianity, in contrast to the philosophy of Philo. Philo's Logos has been conceived to play the rôle of mediator, or, rather, intermediary, between God and man; for that purpose he is imagined to be so great that he can fill the infinite distance separating these terms and can touch them both, as Philo says, 'on their extremities.' But this is only an imagination, scarcely veiling the contradiction inherent in the system: if this distance is infinite, what intermediary can fill it? If he is God, he is still inaccessible to us; if he is but a creature, God remains beyond his reach. Unable to solve the difficulty, Philo evades it by saying that the Logos is 'neither uncreated like God, nor created like us.' What is he then? No precise reply is possible; reason vainly wears itself out in pursuit of this mythical being, which the metaphysical imagination has vaguely outlined, and which the soul thinks she contemplates. Face to face with that mythical being, Christ Jesus appears in the full light of his living personality, uniting in the unity of his person both these distant and separated terms: he is this man, Christ Jesus, whose human speech still echoes in the Gospel, and he is the God blessed through all ages. Philo's Logos can only be defined by negations which equally efface in him all the traits of those beings whom he has to unite; in Jesus Christ the Christian faith confesses the features of both: he is 'uncreated' and 'created.'

[1] AUGUSTINE, *Conf.*, VII, 18.

The Messianic belief is as foreign as belief in the Incarnation to the Philonian theory of the Logos, and is equally characteristic of Christianity. As the Messias, prepared for by the whole past of Israel, awaited and predicted by the prophets, come upon earth to inaugurate the Kingdom of God and redeem the elect, and due, later on, to return to judge the whole world, Jesus fills the whole of history. The Philonian Logos is foreign to history; he may be the object of the speculation of philosophers, he has no contact with the life of man.

And these fundamental differences react immediately on the religious life: between these two conceptions there exists the whole difference between a dream and the faith. In the sentence which we recalled just now, St. Augustine said that he had only found the power he needed by laying hold of the unique Mediator, Jesus Christ; and, in saying this, he did but re-echo the words of St. Paul: 'I can do all things in him who makes me strong.' Never had Philo experienced anything of the kind when contemplating his Logos: he may have grown complacent over his ingenious speculations, and have loved to follow, through the Biblical texts, the heavenly entities which gave to the sacred narrative those new and mysterious depths. He may have savoured his symbolic interpretations as initiations into higher truths; but in reality he only found there what he brought himself: the desire of God, the sense of the immense distance that separates us from him, the need of a meeting with him, and the illusion of its achievement; a halt by the way, some 'city of refuge' where the soul can contemplate from afar him whom she cannot reach, and gather herself together for a new effort.

This irreducible opposition of the Christian faith and the Philonian philosophy appears to us now very clearly; but it was less evident in the first days of Christianity, in those Alexandrine or Hellenic *milieux* which were preoccupied by the cosmological problems discussed by Philo; would not the Jews who passed over from these *milieux* to Christianity be tempted to adorn their new faith with the prestige of that philosophy which had been theirs, to place on the forehead of Jesus of Nazareth all those crowns apparently so brilliant, with which Philo had loaded his Logos?[1] What a temptation to apply to the Christ all those lofty speculations in which Jews and Greeks would have rejoiced! Would not one thus secure for the benefit of the new faith, combining with all this the Messianic claims, the whole content of religious aspiration contained by Judaism and Hellenism? It was a most seductive temptation, but there could not be a more dangerous one for Christianity.

The introduction of Philonism into the faith would ruin it by degrading the Son of God to the rank of a subordinate agent, unworthy of our adoration and incapable of saving us. The history of Arianism will show us in later days to what lengths those who yielded themselves to it were drawn; and before reaching the great crisis we shall discover that certain Doctors, Origen, for example, were hard put to it to resist those seductions. In the apostolic writings, on the other hand, we shall find no compromise: it is from the heavenly Father, and not from flesh and blood, that the Apostles received the faith in the Son of God: the object of that faith is no mythical being, but that Master whom they saw live, die, and rise from the dead. They have not the foolish pretension of enriching so lofty a revelation by human speculations, or of illuminating so luminous an object by flashes from individual dreams.

Bibliography, Section 3:—P. Heinisch, *Der Einfluss Philos auf die àlteste Exegese* (Münster, 1908). R. Reitzenstein, *Zwei religionsgeschichtliche Fragen* (Strasburg, 1901). See also the Bibliography of Section 1 of Chapter II, Book I, in this Volume.

[1] I here reproduce the thought and, in part, the terms used by Lagrange in *Revue biblique* (1910), 590.

Book III

THE CHRISTIAN REVELATION

THE NEW TESTAMENT

Every historian who passes from the Old Testament to the writings of St. Paul and St. John receives the impression, whatever may be his religious belief, of entering into a wholly different world from the one he has left, a world in which prayer, beliefs, and the whole of life are penetrated with new ideas and given a new direction. The synoptic Gospels give us this impression less vividly, at least at a first reading: their central conceptions, of the Divine Paternity, of the kingdom of God, of the Messias, are not novelties to a student of the prophets, nor will the moral teaching of the Sermon on the Mount surprise a reader of the *Psalms*. Nevertheless, a close study will discover in these familiar doctrines new riches and a deeper meaning.

This transformation is most evident in the doctrines of the Messias and of the Son of God; it may also be seen in the conception of the heavenly Father, and, to a lesser degree, in that of the Holy Spirit; the other books of the New Testament, especially those of St. Paul and St. John, will be found to express an even more explicit theology on these points.

A historian claiming to trace the development of these doctrines must here take sides: if he considers the witness of the Evangelists acceptable, he will attribute to Jesus himself the decisive rôle in the revelation of these dogmas, and will consequently give primary attention to the part played by him, save in dealing with the further development of the doctrine in St. Paul and St. John. If he considers such an attribution illegitimate, he will be bound to make the disciples of Christ the creators of all this theology; he will no longer hope to find in the gospels an authentic echo of the teaching of Jesus, but a doctrine already elaborated by other masters, whom he will first have to study, in order to determine their belief, and, if he can, recognise the source from which they have drawn it.

The reader already knows the fruits borne by this second method[1]; no doubt those who originated it have obtained advantages from it which they consider very valuable. On the one hand, they make Christianity and, in particular, the whole of Christian doctrine, arise out of a religious disturbance having at first no definite tendency or dogma, an origin which appears to them more plausible; on the other, by distributing the initiative of Christianity among a large number of collaborators, they reduce each of them, and above all Christ himself, to more human proportions, more closely resembling our own.

But these advantages are dearly bought. All the documents of the New Testament have to be twisted, at whatever price, to this hypothesis which everything in them contradicts; on that hypothesis the historical books, the Synoptics, and the Acts, as well as the gospel of St. John, lose all their meaning, and the Epistles of St. Paul, whose authenticity it is impossible to deny, and whose evidence, in consequence, cannot be refuted, become an indecipherable enigma. For these documents attest, in the bosom of the Christian churches, less than twenty-five years after the death of Christ, an already definite and conscious faith, which the Apostle does not preach as a novelty, but which he recalls to his hearers as an already traditional doctrine; and no man can say either where this doctrine took its rise, nor what authority could impose it so rapidly and so universally on the Jews, who remained so attached to their hereditary beliefs. And we find these objections everywhere in the study of the origins of our faith; whatever effort is made to fit the documents into the system, the construction of Christian dogma remains an irreducible fact; and no one will believe that this mighty and harmonious edifice, the general design and construction of which are so different from others of the same period, could have been built with borrowed materials, without any general plan, and be but a fortuitous assemblage of successive constructions.

These considerations have been developed at greater length in the introduction to this book; we merely recall them here as a justification of the method we propose to follow in this study: for us, Jesus was, from the

[1] See above, Introduction.

very first, the revealer of Christian dogma and its real object; for this double reason we should hold that it was the Christ who made Christology, and not that a Christology, come we know not whence, out of Jesus made the Christ.

In order to interpret the documents according to these principles there is no need to do them violence, or to substitute for them gratuitous hypotheses; we have but to follow them.[1] We must, however, recognise that the road they point out is imperfectly lighted: we find sufficient light for our direction, but not sufficient to distinguish all the detail of facts and doctrines. The New Testament is not a series of systematically conceived memoirs, shedding its light equally on all periods of the Apostolic age, or on all the countries where the gospel was preached; it is a collection of writings prompted by circumstance, which project an intense light on certain phases of the development and certain actors of the drama, and leave all else in the background. And we clearly perceive that it does not contain methodically defined and classified theses such as are to be found in treatises of theology, but living and extremely complex realities. The historian's effort will not attempt to dissociate this concrete synthesis so as to disengage the different elements of the Trinitarian dogma, but rather to gather them all into the living organism of which they are a part, and so present them to the reader. The various fragments of this study will certainly thus lose something of their symmetry; each of them may lose something in precision, but this will not be too high a price to pay for a more direct and more faithful perception of the truth.

[1] There is no intention of discussing the authenticity or historicity of any of the N.T. writings; we think we have the right to use the Synoptics, the *Acts*, the Epistles of St. Paul (including the letters written in captivity) and St. John (including the *Apocalypse*), and we take it that any conclusions drawn from them are well founded.

CHAPTER I

The Synoptic Gospels

1. The Heavenly Father

The preaching of Our Lord as reported in the Synoptics has, for its principal object, faith in the heavenly Father, and the prayer which he taught his disciples is the *Pater Noster*. These facts are evident, but their interpretation not so easy. In the Old Testament the name of Father is sometimes given to God, and, in later Judaism, this formula is more frequently used; thus the just, the Israelites, and above all the people of Israel (considered as a single moral person), called God their Father, and themselves his sons.[1] The Pagan Hellenists are themselves not ignorant of the phrase, and, if they do not make use of it in their prayers, they employ it frequently on other occasions, whether to mark the divine origin which they attribute to themselves, or to express the providence of God towards them.[2] The religion of Christ goes further,[3] and we recognise a deeper meaning in this expression, which was so dear to him.

What this term of Father primarily expresses, is faith and filial confidence in God:

> 'Therefore I say to you, be not solicitous for your life, what you shall eat, nor for your body, what you shall put on. Is not the life more than the meat and the body more than the raiment?
>
> Behold the birds of the air, for they neither sow, nor do they reap nor gather into barns: and your heavenly Father[4] feedeth them. Are not you of much more value than they? . . .

[1] See above, pages 79, 109, and Strack-Billerbeck, *Kommentar*, I, 392-6.
[2] Cf. Diod. Sic., *Bibl.*, V, 72.
[3] See Jackson and Lake, *Beginnings of Christianity*, I, p. 401 *sq.*
[4] Cf. Harnack, *Sprüche und Reden Jesu*, 61.

Be not solicitous therefore, saying, What shall we eat: or, What shall we drink: or, Wherewith shall we be clothed?

For after all these things do the heathens seek. For your Father knoweth that you have need of all these things.'[1]

Above all prayer should be inspired by this confidence. The heavenly Father hears his sons almost before they speak, and grants their requests.

'And when you are praying, speak not much, as the heathens. For they think that in their much speaking they may be heard.

Be not you therefore like to them: for your Father knoweth what is needful for you, before you ask him. Thus therefore shall you pray: Our Father . . .'[2]

'Ask and it shall be given you: seek and you shall find: knock and it shall be opened to you: for every one that asketh, receiveth: and he that seeketh, findeth; and to him that knocketh, it shall be opened. Or what man is there among you of whom, if his son shall ask bread, will he reach him a stone? or if he shall ask a fish, will he reach him a serpent? If you then being evil, know how to give good gifts to your children: how much more will your Father who is in heaven give good things[3] to them that ask him?'[4]

This fatherly mercy of God appears above all in the pardon of sins; every man is evil, and has, by his faults, contracted debts towards God; but God will forgive him them all, as a father his child, if the sinner himself will forgive his brothers the debts they owe him:

'Forgive us our trespasses as we forgive them that trespass against us,' is the prayer which Christ has taught us all, and he has constantly assured us that this prayer will be heard, that we shall always obtain forgiveness if we ourselves sincerely forgive.[5]

Moreover, he has himself granted this divine pardon. To the great scandal of the Pharisees, he forgave the sins of the paralytic of Capharnaum, of the woman who had

[1] *Matt.* vi, 25–32; cf. *Luke* xii, 22–23. [2] *Matt*, vi, 7–9; cf. *Luke* xi, 2.
[3] *Luke*: 'give the good Spirit.' [4] *Matt.* vii, 7–11; *Luke* xi, 9–13.
[5] Cf. *Matt.* vi, 14–5; *Mark* xi, 25.

been a sinner, and of Zacheus: and no doctrine is more energetically preached in his parables. There is no need to recall the parable of the prodigal son. It is present to the memories of all of us, and in the whole gospel there is not one which teaches us more intimately the nature of the heavenly Father: no theological formula can reveal it to us so fully as this simple scene of the father awaiting the return of the prodigal son, seeing him in the distance, running to meet him, and embracing him.

Most of the preceding features could be compared with analogous traits drawn from the Old Testament or from Jewish literature; they are no doubt only to be found here and there, and do not form, as in the New Testament, the substance of the doctrine: they speak to us of the providence and the fatherly mercy of God for his people, for the just, for the poor, and the forsaken; I dare add, for sinners. Without any doubt the God of the Old Testament is a merciful and forgiving God; He has infinite tenderness for his guilty people, and Israel implores his mercy like a child.[1] But if we consider the individuals and not the people as a whole, we do not see the sinner addressing God as his Father; only the just man dares to speak thus and 'glorieth that he hath God for his father.'[2]

Nor do we see that mutual pardon among men is a guarantee and condition of the divine pardon. The divine paternity already appears to us in the gospel, as establishing between God and men, and also between men, closer and more universal relations: all, even publicans and harlots, have the right, if they are willing to be converted, to call God their Father; even Samaritans have a claim to our love, to our assistance, and, if necessary, to our pardon. The foundation of these relations can then no longer be a racial privilege,[3] and still less a personal merit; this sonship is offered to all men and that gratuitously.

Nevertheless, an individual participates more or less in it according to his greater or less resemblance to the Father:

> 'But I say to you: Love your enemies: do good to them that hate you: and pray for them that persecute

[1] Cf. *Isa.* lxiv, 8–9. [2] *Wisdom* ii, 16. See above, page 80
[3] Cf. *Matt.* viii, 11, 13; *Luke* xiii, 28–9.

> and calumniate you: that you may be the children of your Father who is in heaven; who maketh his sun to rise upon the good and bad, raineth upon the just and the unjust . . . Be you therefore perfect, as also your heavenly Father is perfect.'[1]

St. Luke expresses this last phrase in slightly different words: 'Be ye therefore merciful, as your Father also is merciful.' In both cases the meaning is the same, as the context shows; the perfection of the Father which the sons of God should endeavour to reproduce is, above all, his universal mercy.

Thus understood, the divine sonship gives to the whole religious life a new direction. It is the imitation of God, and also the life with and for God:

> 'And when thou dost alms let not thy left hand know what thy right hand doth. That thy alms may be in secret: and thy Father who seeth in secret will repay thee . . . but thou when thou shalt pray, enter into thy chamber and, having shut the door, pray to thy Father in secret: and thy Father who seeth in secret will repay thee . . . but thou, when thou fastest, anoint thy head and wash thy face: that thou appear not to men to fast, but to thy Father who is in secret, and thy Father who seeth in secret shall repay thee.'[2]

The whole effort of the soul, which Judaism applied principally to external observances, is referred to the interior development of the religious life, and the ideal proposed is union in holiness with God our Father.

These moral dispositions characteristic of Christians, were the most efficacious preparation for the revelation of the Trinity.[3] This will be better understood if we pause to consider the doctrine of St. Paul, who does nothing but develop this teaching of the Lord's: if Christians are the children of God it is because they have been incorporated with his only Son, and are participants of his

[1] *Matt.* v, 44–48; *Luke* vi, 27–36. [2] *Matt.* vi, 3–18.

[3] We will see in the course of this History how closely the two doctrines are bound together. In those writers, like Hermas and St. Justin, who did not develop the dogma of the Trinity, the doctrine of the Heavenly Father is also left in the background, while in those, like St. Ignatius and St. Irenæus who were very attached to the dogma of the Trinity, this doctrine is very much in evidence.

life: the divine Sonship of Jesus Christ is the source from which flows the sonship of Christians, and if this appears in the first pages of the gospel so lofty and so supernatural, it is because it is in fact derived from that infinite fulness.

At first the bond of the two doctrines is veiled, and the natural sonship of Christ remains obscure. It is, moreover, true that the Jews, as we have seen, were very badly prepared to understand that mystery, whereas they already anticipated the dogma of the divine paternity, and, by means of it, entered without difficulty into the gospel. Christ will reveal himself to them by degrees, or, rather, to speak the gospel language, the heavenly Father, whose children they have become, will reveal to them his Son.

2. *The Son*[1]

The history of the revelation of the Son of God has been studied from two points of view. Many liberal interpreters have claimed to trace the psychological development of Christ, to describe the awakening and progressive expansion of his Messianic consciousness. Other historians are content to trace the progress of the Messianic faith among the hearers of Christ. The former method, as it has been put into practice,[2] clearly contradicts the data of the dogma ; moreover, it is clear that it has not produced the advantages it promised,[3] but provokes at the present time, in different circles, satisfaction and suspicion. It is obvious that people are weary of supposed psychological studies of the 'consciousness of Jesus,' they effect nothing but a travesty of the gospel, turning it into a romantic novel.[4] Evidently the historian of the New Testament cannot do without psychology ; he must by its means throw light on the teaching of Christ, and also on certain intimate aspects of his life[5] ; but we no longer hope to discover by means of such observations all the secrets of

[1] The Bibliography of this very long Section 2 will be found on page 252.

[2] A necessary qualification, since Catholic dogma does not deny all development in Christ's knowledge and does not forbid our tracing the development. What it cannot admit, is that Christ acquired, only as time went on, consciousness of his Messianic dignity and divine Sonship.

[3] See MONNIER, *op. cit. infra*, 29.

[4] SCHWEITZER, *op. cit. infra*, 370–1 ; SANDAY, *op. cit. infra*, 94 ; WELLHAUSEN, *Einleitung in die drei ersten Evangelien*, 94 ; BURKITT *Gospel History*, 77 ; WREDE, *Das Messiasgeheimnis*, 3.

[5] Cf. SANDAY, *JTS*, V (1904), 321–9.

the consciousness of Jesus, nor, in particular, the first awakening and the progress in him of the divine revelation.

Leaving then to others this ambitious enquiry, anyhow doomed in advance to failure, we shall endeavour to ascertain, as far as the disciples were concerned, the birth and growth of faith in the Son of God. This enquiry itself is not so easy; the hearers of Christ differed profoundly from one another in their degree of preparation of soul, and in their moral worth; the Lord took their various dispositions into account, and adapted his teaching to them. He reveals himself more explicitly to those privileged disciples whom he intends to make his apostles. He is more reserved with the generality of his hearers; with the Pharisees, who have not the excuse of good faith and ignorance, he observes fewer precautions, and when their attacks provoke him to reveal himself he does not wholly decline the challenge. It must be noted, further, that the revelation of the Son of God never took the form of a systematic exposition; it followed its course in contact with the thousand occasions which chance, or, rather, Providence, produced. The evangelists respected these divine realities too much, and were also too much under their control to reduce them to a schematic form; and it is impossible to imagine a uniform progress of the revelation, and draw up here a plan of it throughout these episodes, all laden with truth and life, but yet so diverse.

Nevertheless, if we resign any pretensions to too rigorous an exactitude, we can distinguish in the teaching of Christ several successive phases which progressively initiate his disciples into the revelation of the mystery. The preaching of Jesus had at first, above all, the character of an ethical teaching: but, after this period, Christ appears as himself the centre of this religion which he preached: as their Master in this life, as their Judge on the last day, he takes hold of souls with such a power that one cannot help recognising in him an authority belonging to him personally, which is truly divine. Alongside of this moral preaching we find, especially in private conversations with his disciples or in controversies with the Pharisees, more direct declarations in which Jesus, presenting himself as the Son of man, shews them glimpses of his Messianic rôle; his communications become very frequent and explicit after the scene of Cæsarea Philippi, they clearly predict to the apostles the sufferings and the glorious return of their Master. These revelations are not the last word of the teaching of Christ; other texts make us enter more intimately into the mystery: they are those in which Jesus manifests himself as the Son, or the Son of God: when he speaks of his rôle of mediator between his Father and men, of his union with the Father, in that far-off mystery inaccessible to every other intelligence, in which they seize and wholly penetrate each other; that is the great secret of the gospel, the supreme revelation of the heavenly Father. When we have thus followed in the steps of the Synoptics, this progress of the revelation in the souls of the disciples, we shall reach the last week of the ministry of Jesus. Face to face with his still undecided hearers, face to face with his bitter enemies, Christ redoubles his efforts; he unveils himself in transparent parables like those of the vine-dressers, in urgent controversies such as those dealing with the Son of David, and above all, in the incomparably majestic pictures in which he describes his advent at the last day. He finally concludes all this revelation by the supreme testimony delivered before the High Priest, and confirmed by his death. And God the Father in his turn consecrates the witness of his Son by the resurrection, the glorious apparitions of Christ, the Ascension.

God had wished to prepare souls for this revelation of his Son by the message of the Precursor; we will briefly recall his preaching.[1] 'There cometh after me one mightier than I, the latchet of whose shoes I am not worthy to stoop down and loose.'[2] St. John the Baptist is still ignorant who this will be[3]; but while waiting for the divine sign he preaches penance.

This was the traditional theme of the preaching of the prophets, and John was a prophet[4]; it was also the exhortation often yet to be repeated by the Rabbis, to prepare souls for the kingdom of God. 'If Israel does penance he will be redeemed,' will be the message of Eliezer ben Hyrcanos,[5] and when his disciples ask Simeon ben

[1] Cf. D. Buzy, *S. Jean-Baptiste* (Paris, 1922), 164–85.
[2] *Mark* i, 7. [3] *John* i, 33. [4] *Luke* vii, 26.
[5] See *Sanhedrin*, 97b; cf. I. Lévy, *REJ*, XXXV, 282 *sqq*.

Jokhai 'What is the obstacle to our salvation?' he replies, 'Nothing is wanting but repentance.'[1]

John the Baptist also repeats: 'Do penance,' but he adds 'for the kingdom of heaven is near.' The Rabbis, whose words we have just quoted, merely perceive in this 'visit'[2] of God the glorious deliverance of Israel of which the moment must be hastened by penitence; John the Baptist sees, above all, the judgement for which men must prepare by penitence. 'The axe is laid to the root of the trees. Every tree therefore that doth not yield good fruit shall be cut down and cast into the fire.'[3] The Messias, the powerful One for whom John is preparing, will come like a reaper, whose fan is in his hand to clean up his threshing floor, and collect the grain in his barns, and cast the straw into everlasting fire.'[4]

In these traits preserved by the Evangelists, we may distinguish primarily the religious character of the Precursor's mission. 'The redemption of Israel,' which he comes to announce, is not the national restoration of which all are dreaming, it is something more intimate, more divine, of which the scribes are ignorant, but which the true Israelites desire without rightly understanding what it is.

Privileges of race are useless for its attainment: 'Think not to say within yourselves: We have Abraham for our father. For I tell you that God is able of these stones to raise up children to Abraham.'[5] What God demands is justice and almsgiving.[6]

This message is a good preparation for the message of Jesus: like him, he aims at what is deepest in the soul, and preaches what is most essential in religion; like him he is eagerly received by upright and simple hearts, even by sinners and harlots; but, like him, he is despised and rejected by the Pharisees.[7] And the person of the Precursor is received like his word: the Pharisees despise or hate him, the people recognise him as a prophet. But what prophet is he? He is not the Messias, whatever may have been thought at first[8]; he has denied it himself; but, again, similar in this to the Master whom he is announcing, he does not seek his own glory, but only lets himself be known indirectly, and little by little, by

[1] *J. Taanith*, I, 1 (SCHWAB, VI, 144). [2] See VOLZ, 189 *sq.*
[3] *Matt.* iii, 10. [4] *Matt.* iii, 12. [5] *Matt.* iii, 9. [6] *Luke* iii, 10–14.
[7] *Matt.* xxi, 23–32. [8] *Luke* iii, 15.

his preaching, and by his works. What can be clearly understood is that he is preparing the way for One greater than himself; but even there he disconcerts the imaginations and the dreams of his hearers; the Precursor for whom the nation is waiting, Elias, is so different from him![1] Many months after the death of John, when the light of Christ has already dissipated so many prejudices, and enlightened so many souls, the best among his disciples will still be asking: 'What, then, say the scribes, that Elias should come first?' And Jesus will reply to them: 'But I say to you that Elias is already come: and they knew him not but have done unto him whatsoever they had a mind. So also the Son of man shall suffer from them.'[2]

Misunderstanding and death, such indeed was to be the fate of Jesus, as it had been the fate of John; but, from these clouds of darkness, the light was to shine forth, through these conflicts and hatreds the Son of God was to reveal himself.

The point of departure of this revelation, at least, of its being made public, is the Baptism of Jesus. No doubt, many divine manifestations had already occurred: the Annunciation, the Birth of Christ, followed by the adoration of the shepherds and the Magi, the entrance of the Child Jesus into the Temple and his mysterious words to his parents: 'How is it that you sought me? Did you not know that I must be about my Father's business?' But these revelations were reserved to a few privileged souls; later, no doubt, they were to become the common property of the whole Church; but during the first years they belonged only to Mary, to Joseph, to the few witnesses of these intimate scenes. 'The beginning of the gospel of Jesus Christ, the Son of God,'[3] as it was first preached, was the mission of the Precursor and baptism; and when, in the first days of the Church, St. Peter wishes to complete the apostolic college by the election of a twelfth Apostle, to take the place of Judas, he makes the condition that this new witness of the Lord Jesus should have followed him throughout his career: 'Beginning

[1] On the Messianic rôle of Elias according to Rabbinical tradition, see LAGRANGE, *loc. cit.*, 210–3.

[2] *Matt.* xvii, 10–12.

[3] *Mark* i, 1.

with the baptism of John until the day wherein he was taken from us.'[1]

One day then, among the crowd on the banks of the Jordan, Jesus advanced in his turn to receive baptism. John did not know him yet, but on seeing him approach he had the intuition of an incomparable sanctity, before which he can but confound himself in humility; the baptism which he administers is a baptism of penance, there can be no question of such baptism for Him who presents himself thus before him: 'I ought to be baptised by thee, and comest thou to me?' Jesus answers him: 'Suffer it to be so now. For so it becometh us to fulfil all justice.'[2] This reply makes it clear enough that he who thus presents himself for baptism is conscious of what he is, but that, at the moment, he wishes to humiliate himself before John in order to 'fulfil all righteousness': he recognised the divine origin of John's baptism, and therefore he loves the humiliation of it, as he loves the heavy burden of the law.

And as Jesus came out of the water after his baptism and was in prayer, behold the heaven opened, and the Holy Spirit descended in the form of a dove, while at the same time the words were heard: 'Thou art my beloved Son; in thee I am well pleased.'[3] This scene is one of the most solemn of the whole gospel: it crowns the whole ministry of the Precursor; God gave him the decisive revelation which he had promised.[4] At the same time God gave to Jesus at the opening of his mission of evangelisation, a solemn guarantee. This appears above all in the narrative of St. Luke and still more in that of St. Matthew: the heavenly voice is addressed to the bystanders and presents Jesus to them as the only Son[5]: in St. Mark's account, on the contrary, it is to Jesus the voice is addressed, and it is he who sees the heavens opened. The two forms of the narrative are not mutually exclusive. Here, as in the scene of the Transfiguration, or, as in the heavenly revelation related by St. John,[6] as also in the appearance of Christ to St. Paul on the road to Damascus, the divine manifestation was no doubt perceived by

[1] *Acts* i, 22. [2] *Matt.* iii, 13–15.

[3] *Mark* i, 11. The meaning of the Greek here is 'only Son.' For a study of this phrase *vide* Turner, *Journal of Theol. Stud.*, XXVII (1926), 113–29.

[4] *John* i, 32–34. [5] *Matt.* iii, 16–17; *Luke* iii, 21–22. [6] xii, 28.

several witnesses, but unequally: the less prepared were moved by the miracle without clearly perceiving its significance: John the Baptist recognised in it the sign promised by God; finally, Jesus experienced the infinite sweetness of the love of His Father, and, at the same time a powerful impulse of the Spirit which urged him to the desert and inaugurated his Messianic ministry. Here, as in the two other divine manifestations recalled above, at the Transfiguration and on the eve of the Passion, the heavenly voice was heard after the prayer of Jesus in solemn reply: at the moment of announcing the reign of his Father, and procuring its advent, Jesus prays to him, and the Father assures him of the infinite satisfaction he has in him.

This is also the first solemn manifestation of the Holy Trinity. This mystery was later to be affirmed in Christian baptism by the formula which Our Lord was to teach to his disciples: 'Going therefore, teach ye all nations: baptising them in the name of the Father, and of the Son, and of the Holy Ghost.' Already revealed in this baptism of Christ, this mystery will only be understood later by Christians whom Christ himself will have instructed and whom the Holy Spirit will have interiorly enlightened; they will then recall this first day of the Lord's public life, and they will love to recognise in it the first manifestation of the Christian mystery of God, Father, Son, and Holy Spirit.[1]

Immediately after his baptism, Jesus was driven by the Spirit into the desert, there to be tempted by the devil. In the desert he passes forty days, fasting, praying, and resisting temptations. The author of the *Epistle to the Hebrews* was later to write: 'Wherefore it behoved him in all things to be made like unto his brethren, that he might become a merciful and faithful High Priest before God, that he might be a propitiation for the sins of the people. For in that wherein he himself hath suffered and been tempted he is able to succour them also that are tempted.'[2] And further on: 'For we have not a High Priest who cannot have compassion on our infirmities: but one tempted in all things like as we are, without sin.'[3]

[1] Cf. the Gospel of the Nazarenes, quoted by St. Jerome (*In Isaiam*, XI, 2); the Gospel of the Ebionites, quoted by St. Epiphanius (*Haer.*, XXX, 13); St. Justin (*Dial.*, 88).

[2] ii, 17–18. [3] iv, 15.

This mystery of the temptation of the Son of God is then for us one of the most touching features of the gospel, one of those in which our Saviour appears most near to us. It is also one of the decisive episodes of the history of Christ: Jesus is about to initiate his Messianic ministry, but in what conditions and what a programme! Later at Cæsarea Philippi, when the Lord predicts to his apostles all that he will have to suffer, Peter, who, nevertheless, has just recognised him as the Son of God, cannot endure this revelation, but takes his Master on one side and says to him: 'Lord, be it far from thee, this shall not be unto thee.' Who, turning, said to Peter: 'Go behind me, Satan! Thou art a scandal unto me because thou savourest not the things that are of God, but the things that are of men.'

What the devotion of Peter, so sincere but as yet so unenlightened, could not bear, could no more be endured by the disciples, or the mass of the Jews, and that is what gives its full meaning to the scene of the temptation. Ostentatious wonders, like a descent from the roof of the Temple, and still more, universal domination, were they not in the eyes of the crowd the due accompaniments of the Messias? No doubt Satan betrayed himself by claiming adoration, but behind the insolence of the tempter Jesus perceived the immense crowd of the Jews, who, on hearing the name of the Messias, dreamt of prodigies and power.

> 'If thou art the Christ give us a sign from heaven.'
> 'If thou art the Christ tell us plainly.'
> 'If thou art the Christ come down from the cross.'

And it will be necessary little by little to disillusion these crowds, and, without extinguishing the spark of faith which still shines in this darkness, gradually to reveal to them the suffering and the crucified Messias, who will be for the majority but a scandal and yet alone their Saviour. During the whole course of his ministry Jesus will have the feeling that the doctrine which he preaches is too lofty, the Messianic idea which he represents too divine for his hearers. In these days he sees the crowds who pressed ardently and feverishly around John. They do violence to the kingdom of God, and force themselves to enter into it; but how few will have the courage to submit to it! If Jesus lowered his standards, if he proposed to them the kingdom of which they are dreaming, what enthusiasm he would call forth, what unanimous irresistible enthusiasm! Jesus sees all that, and looks away from it: the gospel he brings will but blind the proud, but will reveal God and his Christ to the humble and simple; and Jesus rejoices in this mysterious dispensation. 'I give thanks to thee,' he will shortly say: 'O Father, Lord of heaven and of earth, I thank thee that thou hast hidden these things from the wise and the intelligent, and that thou hast revealed them to little children. Yea, Father, for such has been thy good pleasure!' Every reader will draw from this scene of the temptation the teaching which it implies; recollecting that Christ has before him a blind and materially minded people, whom the name of the Messias inflames and deceives, whom the name of the Son of God can but scandalise, we shall easily understand the precautions, the slowness, the reserve of the teaching of Christ; before showing the people the light, he must open their eyes; before teaching them he must convert them. This lesson is explicitly given by the evangelists in reference to the parables of the kingdom, but we must always have it present to our minds; if we forget it, we seek in the gospel peremptory declarations which for us perhaps would be precious, but which for the hearers of Christ in those days could have been nothing but enigmas, and occasions for misunderstanding. There is also another lesson to be drawn; this Messianism so sublime for faith, so disconcerting for human ambition, could only be understood by 'little children'; 'the wise,' and 'the intelligent' were blinded by it. The gospel is always the same, and human nature has not changed; if we approach the gospel with ambitious and lofty views, we are blinded; the simple docility of children is the necessary condition of entering that kingdom. As we shall see, the preaching of Christ begins by moral teaching; he does not put forth at first the mysteries of Christian dogma, his own Divinity, his substantial unity with the Father; but he preaches the ideal of the Christian life: humility, poverty, gentleness, the pardon of injuries, that interior religion which prays and acts in secret; then he urges his disciples to put all that in practice, so as not to build upon the sand and see their building fall to pieces. In a word, we must act the truth in order to come to the light. That is the first word of Christ's method of teaching; those who find the gospel obscure and cannot see there the divine features of the Lord, should first read again the Sermon on the Mount; if that teaching penetrates their mind and their life, little by little all will grow clear.

The commencement of the ministry of Christ is similar to that of John the Baptist: its object is to prepare the Jews for the imminent arrival of the kingdom. 'The time is accomplished and the kingdom of God is at hand; repent, and believe the Gospel.'[1] A few disciples joined themselves to the Master; he does not draw up for their benefit the whole programme in advance, he does not declare to them his nature, nor his mission, but shows them a glimpse of great things: 'Come after me,' he says to Simon and Andrew, 'and I will make you to become fishers of men.'[2]

And the work of evangelisation begins. The narrative of St. Mark, in which one still feels all the lively emotion of St. Peter, permits us to follow closely the beginning of this apostolate at Capharnaum. On the Sabbath day Jesus goes to the synagogue and preaches there: 'and they were astonished at his doctrine. For he was teaching them as one having power, and not as the scribes.'[3] Already the word of Jesus produces that supreme impression which all the witnesses note,[4] and which, from the first moment of contact, arouses the soul and begins to reveal to her her Master. And also on this first day adversaries arise. One possessed by the devil gets up shouting: 'What have we to do with thee, Jesus of Nazareth? Art thou come to destroy us? We know who thou art, the Holy One of God!' and Jesus commanded him: 'Speak no more, and go out of the man.' Already the battle has begun, the strong man who held the house feels the approach of one stronger than he, and gives a cry of hatred, of terror, and of servility. At once Christ closes his mouth; he always acts thus with Satan; not only through anxiety for the Messianic secret, but above all through horror of the contact: he has but one word for him, 'Depart!'[5] The rest of the day was passed by Jesus in the house of Simon, whose mother-in-law he healed. In the evening the

[1] *Mark* i, 15. [2] *Ibid.*, i, 17. [3] *Ibid.*, 22.
[4] *Luke* iv, 32; Cf. *Matt.* vii, 29.
[5] Cf. Joh. Smit, *De Daemoniacis in historia evangelica* (Rome, 1913), 320.

neighbours came and crowded round him: 'They brought to him all that were ill and that were possessed with devils . . . that were troubled with divers diseases. And he cast out many devils: and he suffered them not to speak because they knew him.'[1] On this first day of Jesus' ministry the whole of his history becomes clear; St. Matthew recognised it as Isaias had described it: 'he took our infirmities, and bore our diseases'[2]; and it is thus also that tradition makes Jesus speak himself in this *logion* reported by Origen[3]: 'For the sake of the infirm I have been infirm; for the sake of the hungry I have hungered; for the sake of the thirsty I have thirsted.'

Jesus, with great difficulty, disengages himself from this crowd and retires apart, in order to pray; Simon runs to look for him and rejoins him, and Jesus says to him: 'Let us go into the neighbouring towns and cities, that I may preach there also; for to this purpose am I come. And he was preaching in their synagogues and in all Galilee and casting out devils.'[4] This brief sketch of Christ's first mission in Galilee enables us to see what his whole ministry will be: 'He went about doing good, and healing all that were oppressed by the devil.'[5]

Thus he teaches, he heals, and he delivers, and it is by doing so that he gradually reveals himself; when healing bodies he also purifies and enlightens souls; and the jealousy of his enemies on the lookout to provoke him, sometimes forces him to unveil himself more completely. The healing of the paralytic of Capharnaum is one of the episodes in which we may best see this progressive revelation of the Son of God, manifesting himself in these works of mercy.

> 'And again he entered into Capharnaum after some days.
>
> And it was heard that he was in the house. And many came together, so that there was no room: no, not even at the door. And he spoke to them the word.
>
> And they came to him, bringing one sick of the palsy, who was carried by four.
>
> And when they could not offer him unto him for the multitude, they uncovered the roof where he was: and

[1] *Mark* i, 32–34. [2] *Matt.* viii, 17. [3] *In Matt.*, xiii.
[4] *Mark* i, 37–39. [5] *Acts* x, 38.

opening it, they let down the bed wherein the man sick of the palsy lay.

And when Jesus had seen their faith, he saith to the sick of the palsy: Son, thy sins are forgiven thee.

And there were some of the scribes sitting there and thinking in their hearts:

Why doth this man speak thus? He blasphemeth. Who can forgive sins, but God only?

Which Jesus presently knowing in his spirit that they so thought within themselves, saith to them: Why think you these things in your hearts?

Which is easier, to say to the sick of the palsy: Thy sins are forgiven thee; or to say: Arise, take up thy bed, and walk?

But that you may know that the Son of man hath power on earth to forgive sins (he saith to the sick of the palsy):

I say to thee: Arise. Take up thy bed and go into thy house.

And immediately he arose and, taking up his bed, went his way in the sight of all; so that all wondered and glorified God, saying: We never saw the like.'[1]

Several months have already passed, filled by many miracles and sermons, since that first sermon at Capharnaum; the crowds surround him as on the first day of his preaching, eager to see and to hear him, but intimidated by the jealous and menacing scribes, who have come from all parts. These masters in Israel who guard the law and who believe that they can bind and deliver souls at their will, are disquieted and irritated at the sight of this new Master, who had not sat at their feet, who disdained the ancient tradition which he had not received from them, and who spoke to souls as their supreme master. And the people were in doubt as in the days of Achab they doubted between Elias and the prophets of Baal, hesitating between Jesus and the scribes; and it was his miracles that decided the question.

But even in this conflict forced upon him by the bad faith of his adversaries, Jesus does not depart from a prudent reserve: 'No one can forgive sins but God alone,' think the Pharisees. As to that, Jesus neither directly

[1] *Mark* ii, 1–12; cf. *Matt.* xi, 1–8; *Luke* v, 17–26.

affirms it nor denies it; he limits himself to saying and to proving by a miracle, that 'the Son of man hath power on earth to forgive sin.' They quite understand that he does not merely notify this pardon, as of old Nathan had declared God's forgiveness to David: that was appropriate to the ministry of a prophet, and no one would have been scandalised. It is Jesus himself who delivers this sentence in virtue of his own authority; but by what title does this authority belong to him? He explains himself no further. No doubt the most attentive and perceptive of his audience must have been struck by the sovereign accent of these words: Elias had implored the grace of the miracle of Carmel; Jesus healed the paralytic of Capharnaum by his own authority, without recourse to one more powerful than himself; without saying that this right which he claims of forgiving sins is delegated to him, he exercises it by his own sovereign power as a personal right. All this is deeply significant but only for those who are willing and able to see; the others will not be blinded by this discreet revelation. And in point of fact, the narrative of the Evangelist makes it clear enough that the spectators wondered and glorified God, without entirely understanding what they had just seen.[1]

St. Mark has collected in this narrative various incidents in which the growing hostility of the Pharisees appears, and in which Jesus, provoked by them, reveals himself little by little. First we have the vocation of Levi the publican, and the meal taken by Christ with his new apostle in the midst of publicans and sinners. The Scribes are scandalised and ask his disciples: 'Why does he eat with publicans and sinners?' And Jesus answers: 'They that are well have no need of a physician, but they that are sick'; and he adds: 'I came not to call the just but sinners.'[2] This *logion*, reported by the three Synoptics, clearly manifests the mercy of the Saviour: but it also partially discloses a great mystery: what is this 'coming' of which Jesus speaks? He had already alluded to it on the second day of his ministry at Capharnaum when urging St. Peter to evangelise Galilee: 'Let us go into the neighbouring towns and cities that I may preach there also;

[1] See John Chrysost. (*P.G.*, LVII, 361).
[2] *Mark* ii, 17; *Matt.* ix, 13; *Luke* v, 32.

for that is why I have come out,'[1] or, in St. Luke's words, 'therefore am I sent'[2]: these words, so significant to us, were, no doubt, for the first apostles too discreetly indicated to be fully understood[3]; in this new situation the Lord repeats and accentuates them: the 'coming out' of which he spoke before could, strictly speaking, be understood of his departure from Capharnaum; but the 'coming' of which he now speaks has evidently a wider and deeper meaning.

On the occasion of this meal,[4] the enemies of Christ try to pick a new quarrel with him: 'Why do the disciples of John and of the Pharisees fast; and thy disciples do not fast? And Jesus saith to them: Can the children of the marriage fast, as long as the bridegroom is with them? As long as they have the bridegroom with them they cannot fast, but the days will come when the bridegroom shall be taken away from them: and then they shall fast in those days.'[5] John the Baptist, according to the evangelist John, had compared Jesus to the bridegroom, and himself to the friend of the bridegroom;[6] Christ, making use here of the same image, recalls it to the disciples of the Precursor who were embittered by misfortune and jealousy; but there is more in the words than an *argumentum ad hominem*; this title of bridegroom, so often given to Jahve by the prophets, was glorious and sacred to all; by taking it Jesus claims both the attachment and the love it expresses. In the same phrase Christ dimly discloses the violent death which will snatch him from his friends; it is indeed but a passing indication, which, at the moment, they did not understand; but in later days fresh light would be thrown on it and other indications, whether revelations or prophecies, and would show the disciples of the Lord that their Master from the first days of his ministry was already fully conscious of his nature, as well as of his mission, and the bloody death that was to crown it.

[1] Douai Version: 'for to this purpose am I come;' *Mark* i, 38.

[2] *Luke* iv, 43.

[3] Cf. SWETE on *Mark* i, 38: '*exelthon* does not refer to His departure from Capernaum, but to His mission from the Father; whether it was so understood at the time by the disciples, is of course another question.' See also PLUMMER on *Luke* iv, 43.

[4] The bringing together of these incidents is at least indicated by *Matt.* ix, 14 and *Luke* v, 33.

[5] *Mark* ii, 18–20.

[6] *John* iii, 29.

St. Mark and St. Luke proceed to relate the discussions entered into by the Pharisees with Christ about the Sabbath: first we have the episode of the ears of corn plucked by the apostles on the Sabbath day,[1] then the story of the man with the withered hand whom Jesus heals with a word, in a synagogue, on the Sabbath. On both these occasions, the conflict which grows bitter throws a fuller light on the person of the Lord, who little by little and, in spite of himself, so to say, reveals himself. After having affirmed the principle of emancipation, 'the Sabbath was made for man and not man for the Sabbath,' Jesus adds: 'The Son of man is the Lord of the Sabbath.' It follows therefore that the whole positive law, instituted for the good of man, depends on the authority of the Son of man; he can dispense with it or abrogate it; the principle is laid down from that day forward; soon the conclusion will follow.[2]

All these episodes which St. Mark has collected together, complete and throw light on each other: we may see in them not only the growing hostility of the Pharisees, but also the progressive revelation of the Son of God: from the first moment of his ministry, Jesus manifests the clear consciousness that he has of his nature and his mission; he does so prudently, discreetly, in unprovocative words, but without weakness. God alone, they say to him, has power to forgive sins; the Son of man has this power on earth, he replies, and he proves it. Similarly at dinner with the publican, he says: 'I came not to call the just but sinners'; when asked about the fast, 'Can the children of the marriage fast as long as the bridegroom is with them?' Apropos of the plucked ears of corn, 'the Son of man is Lord even of the Sabbath.' These are but indications, yet startling to the soul, which open the way to the questions: who is this Son of man? and how comes he to have these superhuman powers? What is this 'coming' of which he speaks? Whence does he come? How is he the bridegroom, and what does this title mean given him by John, and which he claims? All these questions present themselves inevitably to souls of good-will: they have heard the affirmations of Jesus, they have seen the miracles which support them; what a perspective opens before them! The hearers of Christ needed a

[1] *Mark* ii, 23–28. [2] St. Matthew adds another argument (xii, 5–6).

great loyalty and a great courage to commit themselves to the road which would lead them so far and so high; but his mysterious words urged them on, and the attraction of the Father drew them on by revealing to them his Son.

These brief declarations, with which Jesus underlined the significance of his miracles, and opposed his own authority to the envious attacks of the Pharisees, were then, as it were, so many flashes of light, which began to illuminate the souls of his hearers, but the *ensemble* of his moral teaching was still more instructive: he opened their hearts to the truth and made them ascertain and love it. The Sermon on the Mount, we may say, is the résumé of his moral teaching, and there his revelation is most apparent. From the moment of Christ's first discourses, his hearers were struck by the authority with which he spoke, but never could this impression have been so vivid as when they heard him promulgating this wonderful charter of the kingdom of heaven.[1]

Recalling one after another the greatest commandments of the law, on murder, adultery, divorce, the nature of the oath, patience, the love of the neighbour, Christ makes them more pressing and more intimate, and every time by the use of the same formula of supreme authority: 'You have heard that it hath been said . . . but I say to you . . .' He disposes of all this as a sovereign, and when he addresses the conscience of men he speaks to them as their Master.

We may already note in the Beatitudes the form in which Jesus announces the beatific nature of persecution: 'Blessed are ye when they shall revile you and persecute you and speak all that is evil against you, untruly, for my sake.' It is then eternal happiness to sacrifice our life for Christ. Not less striking is the scene of judgement at the end of the sermon: 'Many will say to me in that day: Lord, Lord, have we not prophesied in thy name, and cast out devils in thy name, and done many miracles in thy name? And then will I profess unto them: I never knew you; depart from me, you that work iniquity.'[2] Thus at the last day, the only hope of men will be in him: to be known by him will mean eternal life; not to be known by him, damnation.

[1] Cf. St. Matthew's commentary after this discourse, vii, 28–29.
[2] *Matt.* vii, 22–23.

The entire gospel confirms these remarks suggested by the reading of the Sermon on the Mount. To-day every reader feels that authority of Christ which filled his hearers with astonishment; particularly striking is the supreme authority which Jesus exercises over souls; 'His home is in the hearts of others,'[1] he claims all for himself, knowing that everything is his due, and that he can pay everything back:

> 'He that loveth father or mother more than me is not worthy of me: and he that loveth son or daughter more than me is not worthy of me. And he that taketh not up his cross and followeth me is not worthy of me. He that findeth his life shall lose it: and he that shall lose his life for me shall find it.'[2]

At the same time that he exacts a devotion that no man can demand, Christ makes promises that no man but himself can keep: 'Come to me, all you that labour and are burdened: and I will refresh you. Take up my yoke upon you and learn of me, because I am meek and humble of heart: and you shall find rest to your souls. For my yoke is sweet and my burden light.'[3] And here again the experience of all Christians has confirmed this promise for the last twenty centuries; they have laden themselves with the yoke of Christ, and in bearing it, they have loved it; they were disquieted, and they have found peace; they were heavy laden and they have found rest. Who but a God can exercise such sovereignty over souls, and give them so profound a peace?

This donation of self to Christ, which he demands in so sovereign a manner, sums up for him all our duties and can efface all our faults. The reader will recollect the pardon granted to the sinful woman as St. Luke relates it;[4] the narrative is too long, and also too familiar in our memories for it to be integrally quoted here: Jesus is eating at the table of a Pharisee; a woman, who was a sinner, enters, washes his feet, kisses them, and anoints them with perfume; the Pharisee is shocked, and Jesus replies to him by the parable of the creditor and the two debtors; he contrasts the coldness of his host with the love of the sinner and concludes with these words: 'Many

[1] ROUSSELOT-HUBY, *La religion chrétienne* (*Christus*[2], p. 989).
[2] *Matt.* x, 37–39. [3] *Ib.*, xi, 28–30. [4] vii, 36–50.

sins have been forgiven her, because she has loved much.' What is more remarkable here than the sentence itself, is the parable and its application; this sinner, because she has sinned, is in the position of a debtor to Jesus, and her love for him is at once the motive and the effect of her forgiveness. This conception is still more striking if we recollect that, according to the teaching of Christ as reported in the Synoptics, sin is essentially a debt owed to God; the Lord teaches us to implore pardon of sin under that form in the *Pater*: 'Forgive us our debts as we forgive our debtors'; for him, sinners are 'debtors,'[1] and all men are, in relation to God, insolvent debtors who can only obtain the remission of their debts by themselves renouncing what is owed them by their brothers.[2]

Such words and such thought show more clearly the rôle here taken by Christ; it is indeed that which all through the Gospel he attributes to God: by sinning we have become his debtors; but, by loving him, we bring upon ourselves his pardon. In this last trait a fundamental conception of the gospel, and one which throws a powerful light on the problem of Christ, may be recognised: it is on his relations with Christ that the religious value of every man depends: by them the sinful woman was saved; it is by them, as we shall see later, that all men will be judged at the last day: 'Come, ye blessed of my Father, possess you the kingdom prepared for you from the foundation of the world. For I was hungry and you gave me to eat . . .'[3] The conditions of the sentence of damnation are precisely parallel; from both points of view one question only is asked: What has the man done for Christ? Like the sinful woman, he was his debtor: Has he loved him as she did?[4]

Other texts propose to us under another aspect, but with equal force, these essential relations between Christ and the human soul. Those who have not performed here below the will of the heavenly Father will come and say to him on the last day: 'Lord, Lord, have we not prophesied in thy name, and cast out devils in thy name, and done many miracles in thy name? And then will I profess unto them: I never knew you; depart from me, you

[1] See *Luke* xiii, 4.

[2] *Matt.* xviii, 23–35. Cf. CHASE, *The Lord's Prayer in the early Church. Texts and Studies*, I, 3, p. 54–7.

[3] *Matt.* xxv, 35–46. [4] See HOLTZMANN, *N.T. Theol.* (2nd edit.), I, 394.

that work iniquity.'[1] And both prayer and sentence express the same thought: to be attached to Jesus is salvation, to be unknown by him is death.[2]

These passages also show forth one of the most characteristic prerogatives of Christ: that of Judge of the world. According to the conception commonly received in Judaism, judgement belongs to God.[3] The Messias never appears as judge except in the *Book of the Parables of Henoch,* when he is not alone in exercising universal judgement[4]; everywhere else God is the Judge, and he reserves this right jealously: just as he alone has created and not by means of another, so he alone will judge, and not by means of anyone else.[5]

The rôle of Christ is quite different: already in the Sermon on the Mount, Jesus presents himself as the judge of men on the last day[6]; this teaching is found throughout the gospel and particularly in the Parables of the Kingdom of God, chiefly in the explanations of these parables which Jesus gives to his disciples. Just as it is the Son of man who sows the good grain, so also it is he who on the last day will preside at the harvest: he will send forth his angels and they will collect out of his kingdom all scandals and all those who work iniquity, and will cast them into the fiery furnace.[7] The same teaching is given in the parable of the sower according to the version given by St. Mark.[8] Christ has cast the seed upon the earth, he leaves it to germinate and grow; he will return later to reap it.[9]

Jesus multiplies his warnings in the last part of his ministry. He himself, the Son of man, will return; he will take his servants by surprise and fix their lot for eternity. It will be like the coming of a robber, like the unexpected return of the master of the house, like the cast of a net thrown over the world[10]; and he who will come so suddenly will also be the Judge who will preside over the assizes of the whole world: 'The Son of man shall come in the glory of his Father, with his angels: and

[1] *Matt.* vii, 21–23; cf. *Luke* xiii, 26–7.
[2] Cf. *Mark* viii, 38; *Matt.* x, 32–33; *Luke* xii, 8–9.
[3] Cf. Volz, *Jüdische Eschatalogie*, 259 *sq.*
[4] Volz, *op. cit.*, 260.
[5] 4 *Esdr.*, v, 56; vi, 6.
[6] *Matt.* vii, 21–23.
[7] *Matt.* xiii, 37–42.
[8] iv, 26–29.
[9] See Lagrange, *Commentaire sur Saint Marc*, 114.
[10] *Mark* xiii, 34–37; *Luke* xii, 36–38; *Matt.* xxiv, 48–51; cf. *Luke* xii, 45–8; xxi, 34–6, etc.

then will he render to every man according to his works.'[1] All the races of the earth shall see the Son of man arriving on the clouds of heaven with power and great glory. And he shall send forth his angels with a loud trumpet and they shall gather together his elect from the four winds, from one end of heaven to the other.[2] His rôle is specially described in the scene of the judgement given in the twenty-fifth chapter of *St. Matthew,* and we shall have occasion to refer to it later.

From these affirmations and parables was born the belief in the Parousia of Christ; it clearly appears in the Synoptics and penetrates all the apostolic writings; there is no historical belief better attested in the whole of the New Testament: now the Parousia and Judgement are two inseparable conceptions; he who is to come and for whom we are waiting is the Judge of the world.[3] Judaism conceives this Parousia as the coming of God himself[4]; it is the day of the Lord,[5] the day of his visitation.[6] In the New Testament we find all these expressions, but in the Synoptics they are applied to Christ and not to God, his Father[7]: thus Jesus announces on various occasions, 'the coming of the Son of man'[8]; he speaks of the supreme day no longer as the day of Jahve but as his own day,[9] 'The day when the Son of man shall be revealed.'[10] In the other writings of the New Testament, and above all, in the Epistles of St. Paul, these expressions will be used much more frequently.[11]

Thus, in the doctrine of the Last End, or to speak more exactly, in the whole doctrine of salvation, Christ has transformed everything by claiming the rôle hitherto reserved to God: sin, penance, charity, pardon, judgement

[1] *Matt.* xvi, 27. [2] *Ibid.*, xxiv, 30–31.

[3] So closely are the two ideas united that in 1 *Cor.* iv, 3, St. Paul uses 'day' in the sense of 'judgement.'

[4] See above, page 216, note 4; Volz, 188–90; *Assumption of Moses*, x, 7 (tr. Lagrange, *Messianisme*, 86).

[5] The 'day of God,' *Bar. syr.*, xlviii, 47; 'day of the Almighty,' *ibid.*, lv, 6.

[6] *Testam. Aser.*, vii, 3.

[7] Cf. *Apoc.* vi, 17, xvi, 14; 1 *Pet.* ii, 12; 2 *Pet.* iii, 12; *Rom.* ii, 5.

[8] *Matt.* xxiv, 27, 37, 39. *Vide* Plummer, *Luke*, p. 487–488 on the historical value of these texts.

[9] *Luke* xvii, 24. [10] *Ibid.*, 30.

[11] 1 *Thess.* v, 2; 2 *Thess.* ii, 2; 1 *Cor.* i, 8, v, 5; 2 *Cor.* i, 14; *Phil.* i, 6, 10; 2 *Pet.* iii, 10; *James* v, 7; etc.

—these moral relations, the most profound that can exist between God and man—appear now as established between man and Christ Jesus. One feels no surprise at hearing him assure his disciples even before his resurrection, of his perpetual presence among them; 'Where there are two or three gathered together in my name, there am I in the midst of them.'[1]

II

In the preceding analysis, we have considered the person of Christ as it is involved in the whole religion of the Gospel. It is thus that it was first manifested to the disciples, and it is thus that we can most surely approach it even to-day. If we become imbued with the religion which Jesus preached, we become capable of understanding his personality: and, more, it is relatively easy for an upright and sincere conscience to discern the origin and scope of this religion, of this whole network of obligations and promises, and to recognise in Christ the divine authority which imposes those obligations and guarantees those promises.

Nevertheless, more explicit and more direct declarations are not wanting in the Gospel, and we must now turn to their consideration. The first remark we are forced to make on this subject is the humble and prudent reserve of Christ: all around him people are acclaiming him with passionate enthusiasm, seeking in him a leader or distrusting him, combating him, hunting him down; he keeps at an equal distance from both parties: 'he knows what is in man.' When he approaches the possessed in order to deliver them, the devils recognise him: 'Thou art the Son of God': but he forbids them to speak.[2] He acts in the same way with the sick whom he heals; it seems as if his compassion leads him further than he wishes to go, but at least he endeavours to dim the glory of his works; in the first days of his ministry, having healed a leper, he says to him: 'See thou tell no one.'[3] Thus, in all his actions, we notice this same characteristic of manifestation and of reserve.[4] The motives of this reserve are already known to the reader: when Jesus begins

[1] *Matt.* xviii, 20. [2] See *Mark* i, 34; iii, 12; *Luke* iv, 41. [3] *Mark* i, 44.
[4] Cf. SANDAY, *Injunctions of Silence in the Gospels*, in *JTS*, V, 321–9.

to preach he finds, in the people to whom he is addressing himself, so false and violent a conception of the rôle of the Messias that it is necessary for him at first to reform the belief of his hearers before appealing to it. Nevertheless, there is also in Jesus himself a deeper reason for this attitude: he is the humble and gentle Messias, the servant of Jahve, who 'shall not contend nor cry out: neither shall any man hear his voice in the streets. The bruised reed he shall not break: and smoking flax he shall not extinguish.'[1]

Thus in his sermons to the people he aims first at the moral reformation of his hearers. In the parables at the lake he will begin to expound the mystery of the kingdom of God; but he will do so under that parabolic form, which in its very exposition veils the truth so as not to dazzle feeble eyes, and at the same time to provoke, by the mystery proposed, the curiosity of those who heard them. And in his exposition of the Messianic mystery, it is rather the kingdom than the king that he reveals; his own person remains in the background of his work. When he speaks of himself he does so most frequently under the humble and mysterious title of 'the Son of man.'

On opening the Gospel we are struck with this formula: it is to be met with in the four Gospels[2] and scarcely anywhere else; it is only found three times in all the rest of the New Testament: once in the *Book of Acts* (vii, 56), the narrative of the martyrdom of St. Stephen; and twice in the *Apocalypse* (i, 13; xiv, 14). We may also observe that in the Gospels it is Jesus who thus designates himself; neither the crowd[3] nor the disciples call him by this name; on the other hand it never appears that this title shocked anyone listening to him.

From the textual evidence we may draw a first conclusion that the title of 'Son of man' was employed by Jesus in speaking of himself. Until recent years this fact was more or less uncontested; the denials of it which have appeared, principally during the last fifteen or twenty years,[4] have not made it less certain. Bousset thought he saw in this

[1] *Matt.* xii, 19–20.

[2] Cf. TILLMANN, *op. cit. infra*, 107; DRIVER, art. *Son of Man* in *DB*; SANDAY, *op. cit. infra*, 124.

[3] In *John* xii, 34, the crowd merely take up the words of Jesus and asks for an explanation.

[4] See BOUSSET, *Kyrios Christos*, 5–22; JACKSON and LAKE, *Beginnings* I, 382.

designation of Jesus as the 'Son of man,' the first stage of his progressive apotheosis: according to him it was the early Christian community that, inspired by apocalyptic Messianism, transformed the 'Son of David' into the 'Son of man.' To arrive at this conclusion he has to efface from the Gospel narrative all the texts in which Jesus presents himself as the Son of man,[1] and these successive eliminations cannot be made without doing violence to the whole text. But, it is not sufficient to deny the authenticity of the words of Christ; it is, further, necessary to explain their presence in the Gospel, and their confinement to the New Testament. We are assured that this conception of the Son of man was predominant in the primitive Christian circles of Jerusalem, and that, influenced by this, the first editors of the Gospels attributed this term to Christ himself; why then did they not make use of it in their own narratives? And, apart from the gospels, how does it happen that no one ventured to make use of this term, so frequently placed on the lips of the Lord, in the first Christian books, with the exception of the three above-mentioned texts?

In reality this mutilation of the gospel texts is motivated by nothing but the exigencies of a thesis which runs as follows: Jesus never considers himself as a suffering and glorious Messias; the prevision of his death was quite foreign to him, and equally so, any eschatological perspective; it was only in the early Christian community that the whole of this theology was elaborated.[2] The mere reading of the Gospel is sufficient to prove the weakness of this thesis; and even among those who maintain the comparative method of study, there are several who agree on this point[3]; the texts relating to the Son of man are the best proofs of the fact, and the efforts made to tear these texts out of the Gospel have made these proofs even clearer.[4]

We came across this formula in Messianism, first in *Daniel*,[5] and then in the *Book of the Parables of Henoch*.[6] It constitutes a still further connection between the

[1] *Kyrios Christos*, 5–12.
[2] *Ibid.*, 14–15; cf. KLOSTERMANN, *op. cit. infra*, 93.
[3] REITZENSTEIN, *Das iranische Erlösungsmysterium*, 130.
[4] On this controversy see the works given below in the Bibliography by FEINE, HOLTZMANN, CLEMEN, and WEINEL.
[5] See above, page 102. [6] See above, page 128 *sqq.*

Gospel and Jewish tradition, and Our Lord appealed to it in the most solemn circumstances, when, before his judges, he applied to himself the text of the prophet Daniel: 'Hereafter you shall see the Son of man, sitting on the right hand of the power of God, and coming in the clouds of Heaven.'[1] But we may ask, up to what point were these memories present to the spirit of the Jews who were listening to Jesus, and what precise meaning was suggested to them by this expression? To this question the Gospel texts give the answer, which seems clear: in certain literary *milieux* where the apocalyptic literature was more familiar, this title of Son of man may have had a fairly definite Messianic significance; but for the majority of the Jews its meaning was vague, to be made more precise by the teaching of Christ; it is possible therefore for Jesus to claim it in the early days of his ministry without making himself clearly recognised as the Messias; he can ask Peter: 'Whom do men say that the Son of man is?' and in his last days, the Jews will ask him: 'Who then is this Son of man?'[2]

The first months of the ministry of Christ are only related by St. John, and it is in his Gospel that we come across the first occasions on which Jesus made use of this expression; we shall therefore collect them here so as not to return to them later. At his first interview with his disciples, when Jesus says to Nathaniel: 'Greater things than these shalt thou see,' he thus develops his thought: 'You shall see the heaven opened, and the angels of God ascending and descending upon the Son of man.'[3] Nathanael has just said to him: 'Rabbi, thou art the Son of God, thou art the king of Israel.' He has recognised him as the Messias, and it is the Messias who answers and presents himself as the Son of man; as a heavenly Messias, appearing in the opened heavens, in the company of angels; in this way he connects himself with the prophecy of Daniel.[4]

We find again, and more distinctly, the same memories and the same images in the conversation with Nicodemus:

> 'If I have spoken to you earthly things, and you believe not: how will you believe if I shall speak to

[1] *Matt.* xxvi, 64. [2] Cf. Lagrange, *S. Jean*, p. cliii. [3] *John* i, 51. [4] Cf. Tillmann, 119.

you heavenly things? And no man hath ascended into heaven, but he that descended from heaven, the Son of man, who is in heaven. And as Moses lifted up the serpent in the desert, so must the Son of man be lifted up: that whosoever believeth in him may not perish, but may have life everlasting.'[1]

Nicodemus, the master in Israel, can recognise under this description the heavenly personage predicted by Daniel, the Son of man who dwells in heaven with the Ancient of Days.[2]

These narratives describing the first days of the ministry of Jesus only relate private conversations; his title of Son of man is only claimed by the Lord in the company of those who are prepared to listen to him.

The reading of the Synoptics suggests similar remarks.

The two primary texts refer to the discussions of Jesus with the Pharisees, the first *apropos* of the paralytic of Capharnaum: 'But that you may know that the Son of man hath power on earth to forgive sins.'[3] The second *apropos* of the Sabbath day: 'The Son of man is Lord of the Sabbath also.'[4]

To a slightly later date, but during the same period of Christ's ministry, before the scene of Cæsarea Philippi, belong certain other texts.[5] Considering them in general one may say that their Messianic meaning is fairly apparent; the difficulty is rather to know, with reference to this or that passage, whether we should read 'the Son of man' or 'me'; it is also not easy to determine the precise period of the Gospel ministry to which the episode related belongs: this question presents itself, for instance, in the cases of the texts where the Lord speaks of the sign of Jonas, or of the promise which he makes of acknowledging before his Father whoever shall have confessed before men.

Without entering into a detailed discussion, we may say that, during this first period of his ministry, Jesus

[1] *John* iii, 12–15.

[2] It is the heavenly Messias who figures in John's other texts on the Son of man: vi, 27, 53, 61–62; viii, 28; ix, 35; xii, 23, 34; xiii, 31.

[3] *Mark* ii, 10; *Matt.* ix, 6; *Luke* v, 24. See LAGRANGE, 35.

[4] *Mark* ii, 28; *Matt.* xii, 8; *Luke* vi, 5.

[5] *Matt.* viii, 20; *Luke* ix, 58. *Matt.* xii, 32; *Luke* xii, 10; *Mark* iii, 28–29. *Matt.* xi, 18–19; *Luke* vii, 33–34. *Luke* vi, 22; *Matt.* v, 11. *Luke* xii, 8; *Matt.* x, 32. *Matt.* xii, 40; *Luke* xi, 30. *Matt.* xiii, 37, 41.

made a comparatively infrequent use of the formula, 'Son of man,' particularly if we compare that use with the way in which he employed the phrase later, after Cæsarea Philippi. This reserve is accentuated by the fact that, always or nearly always, this phrase is not used by Jesus in his discourses to the multitude, but in his private conversations with his disciples, or in his discussions with the Pharisees. Moreover, the meaning of the words is not yet as definite or as full as it will later become; in particular, the perspective of the Passion is not yet apparent; but it is already the Messias who can be dimly discerned in the Son of man and the heavenly Messias as Daniel had seen him.

It was at Cæsarea Philippi that the Son of man began to show himself clearly:

> 'And Jesus came into the quarters of Cæsarea Philippi: and asked his disciples, saying: Whom do men say that the Son of man is?[1] But they said: Some John the Baptist, and other some Elias, and others Jeremias or one of the prophets. Jesus saith to them: But whom do you say that I am? Simon Peter answered and said: Thou art Christ, the Son of the Living God.[2] And Jesus answering, said to him: Blessed are thou, Simon Bar-Jona: because flesh and blood hath not revealed it to thee, but my Father, who is in heaven. And I say to thee: That thou art Peter . . . Then he commanded his disciples that they should tell no one that he was Jesus the Christ. From that time Jesus began to show to his disciples that he must go to Jerusalem, and suffer many things from the ancients and the scribes and chief priests: and be put to death, and the third day rise again. And Peter, taking him, began to rebuke him, saying: Lord, be it far from thee, this shall not be unto thee. Who, turning, said to Peter: Get behind me, Satan: thou art a scandal unto me, because thou savourest not the things that are of God, but the things that are of men.'[3]

[1] *Mark* viii, 27: 'Whom do men say that I am?' *Luke* ix, 18: 'Whom do the people say that I am?'

[2] *Mark* viii, 29: 'Thou art the Christ.' *Luke* ix, 20: 'The Christ of God.'

[3] *Matt.* xvi, 13–18, 20–23.

When Jesus put this decisive question to his disciples, he had already been a long time with them. He had taught them often and had performed many miracles; they had also seen the first enthusiasm of the crowd, then its hesitation, and the bitter opposition of the Pharisees; they had sufficient light to take the decision which it was their duty to take. Peter replied in the name of all; and Christ consecrates his reply by recognising it as the revelation of his Father, which he rewards by the new vocation to the apostle. We shall shortly return to this reply of Peter's in order to determine more exactly its significance. Its general meaning is manifest at first sight. Recognition of the Messianic character in Jesus is directly affirmed in it. We get this from the accounts of St. Mark and St. Luke, and in the words of St. Matthew significance is given to the Lord's command: 'He commanded his disciples that they should tell no one that he was Jesus the Christ.' That, then, was what they had just recognised and proclaimed.

And he whom they had thus recognised as the Messias is the Son of man. It is evident, by the question that Jesus asks[1] and the replies that he receives, that this identity was far from being recognised by all; the Son of man was already for the disciples as well as for the Jews a familiar title and belonging to Jesus, but its meaning was still uncertain; on this day that uncertainty was removed: the Son of man is the Messias.

Immediately after this solemn declaration, at once the foundation and the expression of the faith of the Church, Jesus begins to announce the hostility and the death which are awaiting him to his disciples; St. Matthew and St. Mark carefully note that this is the date of the first predictions by Jesus of his Passion. Up till then the faith of his apostles had been too weak to support these revelations, but the time has now come to make them: 'the Son of man must suffer many things and be rejected by the ancients and by the High Priests and by the scribes: and be killed and after three days rise again.'[2] Henceforward all the prophecies of his sufferings, which Jesus multiplies, are connected by him with the title of Son of

[1] 'Son of man' is not in the question posed by Our Lord in *Mark* and *Luke*, but it comes in the prophecies which follow: *Mark* viii, 31; *Luke* ix, 22.
[2] *Mark* viii, 31.

man.[1] Still more often, that title is associated in his predictions, as had been the case in the visions of Daniel, with the glorious prospects of the Parousia.[2]

Not without a definite purpose did Christ bring together these two series of predictions, preserving in this way his disciples both from the discouragement that the prospect of his Passion might provoke, and from the exaltation which the glorious scenes of the Parousia might awaken in their minds; there was, moreover, another reason besides these instructional requirements for this constant association; in reality the ignominious death was to be the price of the glory, and thus these two aspects of the Lord's destiny were intimately united as merit and reward, 'it was necessary that the Christ should suffer and thus enter into his glory.'

The preceding analysis, in which we have followed text by text the progressive development of the revelation of the Son of man, has permitted us to understand more clearly why Jesus chose this expression for his own designation. Used once or twice to represent the Messias, the formula was able to awaken in the mind of the Jews the memory of the ancient prophecies. Those reminiscences were, however, very weak and no doubt half effaced by popular usage, which tended to make the expression 'Son of man' the simple equivalent of 'man.' The phrase consequently lent itself to the cautious and leisurely development of the revelation of his nature and task which Jesus wished to make. Finally we should note that it did not awaken, like the title of 'Son of David,' national aspiration to independence and political domination; it detached Messianism from the narrow frame of Judaism, and assured it the wide universally human significance that it had in the words of Daniel. It could also

[1] *Matt.* xvii, 12; *Mark* ix, 12. *Matt.* xvii, 21–22; *Mark* ix, 31; *Luke* ix, 44. *Matt.* xx, 18–19; *Mark* x, 33; *Luke* xviii, 31. *Matt.* xx, 28; *Mark* x, 45; *Luke* xxii, 27. *Matt.* xxvi, 2; *Mark* xiv, 1; *Luke* xxii, 22. *Matt.* xxvi, 45; *Mark* xiv, 41; *Luke* xxii, 48; cf. *Matt.* xxvi, 49; *Mark* xiv, 45. *Luke* xxiv, 7; cf. *Matt.* xxviii, 6; *Mark* xvi, 6.

[2] *Matt.* xvi, 27. *Mark* viii, 38. *Matt.* xvi, 28. *Matt.* xvii, 9; *Mark* ix, 9. *Matt.* xix, 28; cf. *Mark* x, 29, *Luke* xviii, 29. *Matt.* xxiv, 27; *Luke* xvii, 24. *Matt.* xxiv, 30; cf. *Mark* xiii, 26; *Luke* xxi, 27. *Matt.* xxiv, 30; *Mark* xiii, 26; *Luke* xxi, 27. *Luke* xxi, 36. *Matt.* xxiv, 37; *Luke* xvii, 26. *Matt.* xxiv, 39; cf. *Luke* xvii, 27. *Luke* xvii, 29–30. *Luke* xviii, 8. *Matt.* xxiv, 44; *Luke* xii, 40; cf. *Mark* xiii, 33. *Matt.* xxv, 31. *Matt.* xxvi, 63–64; *Mark* xiv, 62; *Luke* xxii, 69. Against these numerous texts there are only one or two which do not contain the idea of suffering or of glory: *Luke* xvii, 22; xix, 10.

recall to the mind the memory of other Biblical texts, which, without any direct reference to the Messias, described the humility and greatness of man, of the Son of man, e.g., *Psalm* viii, which Jesus himself loved to quote: 'What is man that thou art mindful of him? or the son of man that thou visitest him?' We may then conclude with Sanday[1]:

> 'This title of so wide and deep a meaning awakened on the one hand the Messianic and eschatological expectations on account of the use to which it had been put in certain Jewish circles (*Book of Henoch*). At the opposite extreme of thought, it awakened the idea of the suffering Saviour; but, in the centre, so to speak, it was principally supported by an infinite sense of fraternity with labouring and suffering humanity, and no one could better appeal to this sentiment than he who had so fully accepted these conditions of life. As Son of God, Jesus looked upward towards his Father; as Son of man he looked round him on his brothers, the sheep who have no shepherd.'

We must not, however, press too far the opposition indicated by these last words: no doubt, it is not unfounded; the two expressions, Son of God and Son of man, in themselves suggest two different ideas; but when applied, as they do, to the same Lord Jesus, they may be applicable to the same descriptions and clothed with the same attributes, and, in point of fact, we may sometimes notice, side by side with the more definite perspective of the Passion and the Parousia, another perspective which the text partly conceals and partly reveals, indeed, sometimes expressly reveals: that of the pre-existence of the Son of man in heaven. This perspective is very clearly indicated by St. John. 'No man hath ascended into heaven, but he that descended from heaven, the Son of man . . .' 'If then you shall see the Son of man ascend up where he was before?'[2]

It may no doubt be also recognised in certain texts of the Synoptics: 'The Son of man is not come to be ministered unto, but to minister, and to give his life a redemption for many,'[3] and 'For the Son of man is come to seek

[1] *DB*, II, 623. [2] *John* iii, 13; vi, 63. [3] *Matt.* xx, 28.

and to save that which was lost.'[1] We have already quoted above[2] several of these judicious revealing texts, in which Jesus speaks of his coming; doubtless, in itself, the formula 'is come' does not necessarily indicate a supernatural origin; indeed, Christ applied it to John the Baptist[3]; but as used here, applied to the Son of man in his Messianic rôle, it seems more significant; Jesus indicates by it his mission, the point of departure of which was his pre-existence in heaven at the side of his Father, just as its conclusion will be his glorious apparition at the right hand of God.

III

This Messianic title of the Son of man, chosen by Jesus, manifests at the same time his humility and his transcendence; nevertheless, his pre-existence and his unity with the Father are more explicitly expressed by the name of the Son of God, or the Son, which Jesus also took, and which became his proper and personal title to the first Christian generation. The comparative absence of preparation for this choice in the earlier tradition makes it the more significant. There is no doubt that the Jews liked to use the image of filiation as the expression of the special bonds that united to God either his chosen people, or their magistrates, their king, or their Messias[4]; but no metaphysical relation was here involved; it was but a special protection, a particular benevolence granted by God to his people or to the men whom he loved as his 'first-born.'[5] This Semitic phrascology gave to Christ a starting point from which to explain his thought, and, if necessary, justify it[6]; but it is not sufficient to explain the strictly theological value which the title of the 'Son of God' bears in the New Testament,[7] and, in point of fact, at the moment of the appearance of Christianity the Jews firmly rejected the conception of a Messias who should be the Son of God, protesting that the prophets had never spoken of him.[8]

[1] *Luke* xix, 10. [2] See above, page 211. [3] *Matt.* xi, 18; *Mark* ix, 13.

[4] See above, pages 79 *sqq.*, 100, 109 *sqq.*, 131, and STRACK-BILLERBECK, III, 15–22.

[5] Cf. DALMAN, *Die Worte Jesu*, 223.

[6] This has been very clearly put by LAGRANGE, *S. Jean*, p. clxxvi.

[7] Cf. DALMAN, *Die Worte Jesu*, 219–24; BOUSSET, *Kyrios Christos*, 52–7.

[8] Cf. JUSTIN, *Dial.*, 49, 137.

To-day, therefore, the attempt has been given up to explain by Jewish theology and, in particular, by the belief in the Messias, the origin of Christian faith in the Son of God. But among those who maintain the comparative method of enquiry, many still think that Hellenism is the source from which the evangelists drew their doctrine. We have discussed this thesis in the first book of this work,[1] and have recognised that Hellenism is, like Judaism, quite unable to solve the problem which these historians propound, that is, the origin of Christian dogma, and in particular of the faith in the Son of God, without admitting the historical teaching of Jesus as the evangelists put it before us ; Wetter has found in certain passages of Celsus, or of the ancient Gnostics, traces of a belief in a Son of God,[2] outside Christian, or at least orthodox, environments ; but these instances, in any case rare, are all taken from writers who underwent the influence of Christian dogma whether as partisans or as opponents ; as to the Mandean texts quoted by several writers, Wetter wisely leaves them alone as probably due to Christian influence.[3]

The title of Son of God appears on the first page of the Gospel, 'The beginning of the gospel of Jesus Christ, the Son of God'[4]: these latter words of St. Mark signify the divine filiation in the strict sense, and express the faith of the evangelist and of the Christians for whom he is writing. In the gospel narrative itself the title of Son of God is given to Jesus by the angel from the day of Mary's annunciation: 'The Holy Ghost shall come upon thee, and the power of the most High shall overshadow thee. And therefore also the Holy which shall be born of thee shall be called the Son of God.'[5] Twelve years later the Child Jesus comes to the Temple with his parents ; he remains there three days after their departure ; and when his Mother, on finding him, asks him : 'Son, why hast thou done so to us? Behold thy father and I have sought thee sorrowing,' he replies: 'How is it that you sought me? Did you not know that I must be about my Father's business?'[6] This prudent manifestation

[1] Especially on pages 13 *sqq.*, 22 *sqq.*, and 29 *sqq.*

[2] WETTER, *Der Sohn Gottes*, 4–10. [3] *Ibid.*, 9, note 1.

[4] *Vide* LAGRANGE on the authenticity and meaning of these words.

[5] *Luke* i, 35 ; cf. the *Revised Version*, and H. M. SCOTT in *DB*, V, 309 ; also DURAND, *op. cit. infra*, 156.

[6] *Luke* ii, 48.

raises for an instant the veil which covers the childhood of Christ; then he follows his parents to Nazareth, and resumes his life of silence, obedience, and mystery.

At the beginning of the public life, after the baptism, the Father gives to his 'only Son' the solemn attestation on which we have already commented.[1] It is the consecration of the mission of Christ, and, at the same time, at least for certain privileged witnesses, a first revelation of his personal dignity. The temptations of the devil in the wilderness open with those heavenly words: 'If thou be the Son of God, command that these stones be made bread.' 'If thou be the Son of God, cast thyself down.' Many commentators have seen in these suggestions not merely temptations to presumption, but also the efforts of Satan to provoke more precise declarations on this decisive point of the divine filiation. Ought we to see the same purpose in the protestations of the possessed,[2] or must we recognise in them the cry of terror of a power which feels itself conquered, of the strong man armed who meets an adversary more powerful than himself, who will drive him out from his home and from his people? Whatever the case may be, it is certain that Jesus never would make use of such testimony, but imposed silence on the possessed; we, too, may ignore it; there are witnesses with a more serious right to be heard.

These witnesses are, above all, the disciples of Jesus; but before gathering their testimony, we must understand how Jesus has gradually led them to understand a term so foreign to their natural conceptions. Here, too, we must start from the Sermon on the Mount. The ideal of Christian life there proposed by Jesus to his disciples is chiefly characterised by the filial spirit with which they ought to regard God their Father; this spirit will also introduce them to the knowledge of the Son, for only the children of God can recognise the Son of God. 'I must be about my Father's business,' said the Child Jesus, in those early days, to his parents; later he will say, as St. John tells us: 'I do always what pleases him.' 'My food is to do the will of him that sent me.' This is the characteristic by which he recognises his own: 'Whosoever shall do the will of my Father that is in heaven, he is my brother, and sister, and mother.'[3] If we read in the

[1] See above, page 203. [2] *Mark* v, 7. [3] *Matt.* xii, 50.

Sermon on the Mount, and particularly in the sixth chapter of St. Matthew, the programme of the religious life that Jesus puts before his disciples, we see that his whole effort is directed towards the initiation of the Christian into a constant intimacy with his Father in heaven; whatever good action he performs, almsdeed, fasting, or prayer, he must put aside all wish to please men, and preoccupy himself solely 'with his Father who sees in secret'; the end to which Christians should tend is to 'become sons of their heavenly Father,' is to 'be perfect as their heavenly Father is perfect.' The sentiment of the divine paternity is to be so vivid in their hearts that they will no longer be able to give to anyone upon earth the name of father; they have but one Father, their heavenly Father[1]; and all this finds its expression in the prayer that Christ teaches them, which will become their own prayer: 'Our Father.'

But what is still more remarkable is that, while he endeavours to initiate his disciples into these filial relations with their heavenly Father, Jesus never identifies his own position with theirs. He teaches them to say: 'Our Father'; but he himself does not speak thus; he says: 'Your Father' and: 'My Father.'[2] Even when addressing them he observes this distinction: 'And I dispose to you, as my Father hath disposed to me, a kingdom.'[3] 'And I send the promise of my Father upon you,'[4] and, on the other hand: 'How much more will your Father who is in heaven give good things to them that ask him,'[5] and 'Your Father knoweth that you have need of all these things.'[6]

There is here evidently more than a manner of speech. In the case of a Master so humble, and so anxious to preach by example, this constant care to distinguish his prayer from that of his disciples, and his filiation from theirs, cannot but be imperatively dictated by his consciousness of what he is, and of what they are: they have to endeavour to become the children of their Father who is in heaven.[7] In his own case there is no trace of his effort or progress: he *is* the Son.

[1] *Matt.* xxiii, 9.

[2] Cf. AUGUST., *In Joan. tract.* xxi, 3 (*P.L.*, XXXV, 1565–6); and DALMAN, *Die Worte Jesu*, 156–8.

[3] *Luke* xxii, 29. [4] *Luke* xxiv, 49. [5] *Matt.* vii, 11. [6] *Matt.* vi, 32.

[7] *Matt.* v, 45.

This insuperable distance which separates Christ from his disciples in their relations with the heavenly Father appears very definitely in the mediatorial character which Jesus Christ claims as his own between his Father and men. Himself sent by the Father, he also sends his disciples, and he loves to compare the two missions in order to make clearer his rôle and theirs, and, above all, to unite in himself Christians with their Father: 'He who receives you receives me, and he who receives me receives him who sent me.'[1] 'He that despiseth you despiseth me, and he that despiseth me despiseth him that sent me.'[2] Again, in one of the texts, quoted above, 'And I dispose to you, as my Father hath disposed to me, a kingdom.' In *St. John* also the thought of Christ is developed in parallel phrases, and with regard to deeper realities, not merely the mission of the Son of God and that of the apostles, but their intimate life, their love, their union with God: 'As the living Father hath sent me, and I live by the Father: so he that eateth me, the same also shall live by me.'[3] 'I know mine and mine know me. As the Father knoweth me, and I know the Father.'[4] 'As the Father hath loved me, I also have loved you. . . . If you keep my commandments, you shall abide in my love: as I also have kept my Father's commandments, and do abide in his love.'[5] 'That they may all be one even as thou, Father, art in me and I in thee, that they also may be one in us.'[6] 'Peace be to you. As the Father hath sent me, I also send you.'[7]

In these two series of texts we obviously find the same trend of thought[8]; the only difference between them is the difference of Christ's teaching as found in the Synoptics and in *St. John*.

From a reading of these texts we may learn how this mediation of the Son of God should be understood. Should we interpret it in the Arian sense and see in the Son an inferior divinity half way between heaven and earth? Or must we admit with the Catholic Church that Christ is the Mediator, not because he is at an equal distance from both terms, man and God, but because he unites them both in his own person, being true man and

[1] *Matt.* x, 40. [2] *Luke* x, 16. [3] *John* vi, 58. [4] *Ibid.*, x, 14, 15.
[5] *John* xv, 9–10. [6] *Ibid.*, xvii, 21. [7] *Ibid.*, xx, 21.
[8] And it is also found in St. Paul; cf. 1 *Cor.* iii, 22–3, xi, 3.

true God? The debate is easily decided if we continue reading the Gospel, but even without doing so we should be able to observe in Jesus Christ a superhuman grandeur which raises him above humanity and assimilates him to the Father. This is also confirmed in the famous text in which Jesus, speaking of the Day of Judgement, says: 'But of that day or hour no man knoweth, neither the angels in heaven, nor the Son, but the Father.'[1] The authenticity of this *logion* is guaranteed by its content: no later editor would have dared to attribute ignorance of the day of judgement to the Son. Its significance is both evident and considerable, for in the gradation established by it Jesus is placed at an elevation above humanity and even above the angels; he is the Son in the proper and unique sense of the term, as God is the Father.[2]

The nature of the special relation uniting the Son and the Father is determined by another utterance of the Lord's preserved for us by St. Matthew (xi, 25) and St. Luke (x, 21).

> 'At that time, Jesus answered and said: I confess to thee, O Father, Lord of heaven and earth, because thou hast hid these things from the wise and prudent and hast revealed them to little ones.
>
> Yea, Father: for so hath it seemed good in thy sight.
>
> All things are delivered to me by my Father. And no one knoweth the Son, but the Father: neither doth any one know the Father, but the Son and he to whom it shall please the Son to reveal him.
>
> Come to me, all you that labour and are burdened: and I will refresh you.
>
> Take my yoke upon you and learn of me, because I am meek, and humble of heart; and you shall find rest to your souls.
>
> For my yoke is sweet and my burden light.'[3]

This *logion*, spoken, as St. Luke tells us, under the action of the Holy Spirit, full of emotion and joy, reveals to us the most intimate secret in Jesus Christ, that of his divine filiation.

[1] *Mark* xiii, 32.
[2] See below, page 236; and Note II at end of this Volume.
[3] *Matt.* xi, 25–30. See Note III at end of this Volume.

'This title makes him the depository of all his Father's secrets, and master of all his Father's power; it makes him our indispensable initiator into the mystery of the divine life, the model and the consoler of all those who are willing to go to school to him. There is no human misery that he cannot help, no wound for which he has no healing balm, no weariness that he cannot comfort. What this beloved Son is, in the depths of his nature, the Father knows well and he only; nothing less than the piercing vision of the divine gaze can appreciate those riches—just as it is only the gaze of the Son which can scrutinise and understand the immense Being of his Father.'[1]

Several of our Lord's sayings, referred to above, might have suggested to the Jews the pre-existence of the Son of man with his Father; others, more explicit, caused him to appear in that heavenly glory at the end of time; but in the transparent simplicity of this sentence the whole of eternity is revealed, and the mystery of the divine life, in which the Father and the Son mutually and wholly penetrate each other in a manner incomprehensible to every creature. The whole gospel is illuminated by these words: on other occasions Christ has presented himself in hidden language as the end to which the whole of Israel was tending: 'Many prophets and just men have desired to see the things that you see, and have not seen them.'[2] In that very circumstance he has just shown his disciples how the law and the prophets were but the preparation for the ministry of John the Baptist, and John himself less than the least in the kingdom of heaven.[3] We now understand what makes the incomparable grandeur of the new order: it is the revelation of the mystery of God, hitherto inaccessible, a revelation made by him who alone could communicate it to us, by the Son: as St. John says at the beginning of his gospel: 'No man hath seen God at any time: the only begotten Son who is in the bosom of the Father, he hath declared him.'[4]

These words alone would be sufficient to determine the

[1] L. de Grandmaison, art. *Jésus Christ*, in *Dictionnaire apologétique de la foi catholique*, II, 1351.
[2] *Matt.* xiii, 17. [3] *Matt.* xi, 11–15. [4] *John* i, 18.

Christian dogma, to make us recognise in the Son of God no intermediary being such as had been conceived by Philo, but the Son equal to and consubstantial with his Father[1]; St. Paul and St. John may add complementary details to this revelation of Christ; they will not surpass it.[2]

But these revelations of perfect reciprocity, of community of nature, are not the only ones which the Gospel shows us between the Son and the Father. Other texts, and in greater number, show in Jesus a supreme respect and a total dependence with regard to God his Father. The text from *Deuteronomy* of which he made use to repel temptation: 'Thou shalt adore the Lord thy God, and him only thou shalt serve,' governs all his conduct; he finds the first commandment in this other text of *Deuteronomy* repeated daily by the Jews in their prayer: 'Hear, O Israel: the Lord thy God is one God. And thou shalt love the Lord thy God with thy whole heart and with thy whole soul and with thy whole mind and with thy whole strength.'[3] He loves to spend the night in prayer,[4] and it was by prayer that he prepared himself for the supreme conflict of his Passion; we know how he prayed then, making his supplication with filial confidence, but also resigning himself with infinite respect: 'Abba, Father, all things are possible to thee: remove this chalice from me; but not what I will, but what thou wilt.'[5] On the Cross, feeling himself abandoned by God, he repeats the words of the Psalm: 'My God, my God, why hast thou forsaken me?'[6] There is nothing more profound in the Gospel than these prayers and cries from the heart of Christ, and every interpretation which disregards these relations between the Son and Father, of dependence and adoration, is condemned out of its own mouth.

This sentiment of humble adoration with which the religious life of Christ is penetrated, also inspires his actions and his words: he effaces himself as far as possible so that his Father may appear to turn towards him the devotion, love, and prayer of his disciples.

[1] Cf. John Chrysost., (*P.G.*, LVII, 430).

[2] Cf. Feine, *Jesus Christus und Paulus*, 263–7.

[3] *Mark* xii, 29; cf. *Matt.* xxii, 37; *Luke* x, 27.

[4] *Luke* vi, 12.

[5] *Mark* xiv, 36; cf. *Matt.* xxvi, 39; *Luke* xxii, 42.

[6] *Mark* xv, 34; cf. *Matt.* xxvii, 46.

'And as he was gone forth into the way, a certain man, running up and kneeling before him, asked him: Good Master, what shall I do that I may receive life everlasting? And Jesus said to him: Why callest thou me good? None is good save one, that is God. Thou knowest the commandments . . .'[1]

The radical commentators see in this reply Jesus' consciousness of personal faults; the whole Gospel contradicts this interpretation: from the day of his baptism on the banks of the Jordan to the day of Calvary, Our Lord appears as one certain of his perfect righteousness before God and before men; he bids others beg the pardon of their faults; he himself, although so humble and so sincere, never makes such a prayer; moreover, the 'goodness' referred to here is not virtue or moral excellence: and if Jesus attributes it exclusively to God it is not in order to make clear that God only is morally perfect, but rather that he alone is goodness itself, infinitely beneficent and kind.[2] Jesus turns aside this homage from himself to refer it to God alone, because he wishes to avoid all suspicion of flattery, and to direct towards his Father this new disciple who approached him with such veneration and who knows him as yet so imperfectly.[3] By replying thus to this disciple who sees in him only a man, one master among many others, Jesus does not intend to deny all goodness in himself or in other men, but he wishes to teach his hearer that all human goodness is nothing compared to the goodness of God. He expresses a similar sentiment elsewhere: 'Call none your father upon earth: for one is your Father, who is in heaven. Neither be ye called masters, for one is your master, Christ.'[4] Another day the two sons of Zebedee approached Christ and asked him for the two first places in his kingdom, on his right hand and on his left:

'Jesus, answering, said: You know not what you ask. Can you drink the chalice that I shall drink? They say to him: We can. He saith to them: My chalice indeed you shall drink: but to sit on my right or left

[1] *Mark* x, 17–19. [2] DALMAN, *Die Worte Jesu*, 277.
[3] See VICTOR in his Commentary on St. Mark, *ap.* CRAMER, 376.
[4] *Matt.* xxiii, 9–10.

hand is not mine to give to you, but to them for whom it is prepared by my Father.'[1]

By this reply Christ did not seek to elude an importunate request. Still less did he mean by those words to deny what he elsewhere affirms, that he has the right over the disposal of the kingdom, and that he makes that disposal in favour of his own ;[2] he wished to remind his presumptuous disciples that all these graces come from the Father as from their first source, and that they should primarily be humbly begged from him. A similar lesson may be gathered from the text referring to the day of judgement: 'No man knoweth, neither the angels in heaven, nor the Son, but the Father.'[3] Here again we should not interpret this merely in the sense that Christ wished to put aside an indiscreet question ; it would have sufficed in that case to reply as on a later occasion: 'It is not for you to know the times or moments, which the Father hath put in his own power.'[4] Nor should we say that he presents himself as ignorant of the divine secrets as other men ; the Father, as we read just now, has confided all his secrets to him ; he alone knows the Father, as he is known by him alone ; in fact, he manifests an even complete and constant knowledge of the divinity, of which we can discover neither the beginning nor the development ; he has also the gift of reading hearts ; he appears in the narrative of the Synoptics,[5] as well as those of St. John,[6] as the Κύριος καρδιογνώστης.[7] He reveals a prophetic knowledge of the future: he predicts the behaviour of his disciples and the fate reserved to them, the fall of Jerusalem, and the end of the world. Is it, in these conditions, to do violence to the Gospel to refuse to attribute to Christ ignorance of the Last Day ? As Messias, living and preaching upon earth, the places of the kingdom are not at his disposal, and it is in that sense, as we have just seen, that he reserves that right to his Father. In the same way, as Master and Revealer, teaching here below, it is not for him to communicate to men the secret of days and times ; he reserves that likewise to his Father.[8]

[1] *Matt.* xx, 22, 23. [2] *Luke* xxii, 29. [3] *Mark* xiii, 32. [4] *Acts* i, 7.
[5] *Mark* ii, 8 ; cf. *Matt.* ix, 4 ; *Luke* v, 22 ; vi, 8 ; ix, 47 ; xi, 17 ; cf. *Matt.* xii, 25. [6] *John* ii, 24–5 ; vi, 10. [7] *Acts* i, 24.
[8] Cf. St. Augustine, *in Psalm.* xxxvi, 1 (*P.L.*, XXXVI, 355).

Those stubborn dialecticians, the Arians, were later to seize on all these texts and use them against the Catholic dogma of the consubstantiality of the Father and the Son; their attacks have often been repulsed, but this is not enough. The words of the Lord are not, for us, objections to be answered; they are the light which guides us, and these particular ones are among the most precious, for they introduce us to the very heart of the Christian mystery in the humility of the incarnate Son of God. One is at once struck on opening the Gospel by these sentiments of humility so new to Judaism, and so powerful among all those who have approached Christ, and been led by his Spirit. If we ask the Precursor about himself, he replies that he is nothing: neither a prophet nor Elias, nothing but a voice. If we run through the domestic memories of the Virgin Mary, handed on to us by the Evangelist, we find almost everywhere silence, self-effacement, often the humble astonishment which wonders and does not understand. But if we contemplate Christ himself we perceive a dependence on his Father, a self-annihilation, which no human analogy can represent to us: neither his doctrine, his life, nor his works belong to himself; the Father shews him what he is to say and to do, and with his eyes on this supreme and dearly loved standard, Jesus Christ speaks, acts, and dies. This natural dependence of the Son of God is accompanied by an infinite willingness; just as the Father empties himself into the Son with unutterable love, so the joy of the Son is to receive that gift and depend on his Father. Herein we discern the intimate life of Our Lord; and the more we penetrate the secret of this life, the better we understand his words of humble dependence inviting the disciples to mount to the source of life, of goodness and of knowledge, God the Father. Most of the traits referred to here are taken from the gospel of St. John, and we shall have later on the opportunity of studying them more closely; it was useful to compare them to the Synoptic texts: this spiritual gospel was written with the intention of making known the Son of God (xx, 31); the teachings and miracles it relates have been selected from that point of view; is it not, then, highly significant that it should be precisely this book that makes us understand most completely the fathomless dependence of the

Son on his Father? This trait, far from compromising the doctrine of the Divine Filiation, is an essential element of it; it should not veil it from our eyes, but, on the contrary, reveal it.

Thus, little by little, Jesus manifests himself to his apostles, and, at the same time, the intimate action of grace touched them; the Father revealed to them his Son and drew them to him. The Gospel has preserved but few instances of this mysterious influence, but at least it permits us a glimpse of that revelation.

After the scenes on the banks of the Jordan and their first contact with Christ comes their call on the shore of the lake, and, for Peter, the miraculous draught of fish[1]: the apostle and his companions had already seen very notable examples of Christ's power, but this new miracle impressed them more vividly; they were fishermen themselves and knew the patient efforts demanded by their craft, and for them to fill two boats with a single catch at that hour was the effect of a manifestly superhuman power. 'Which, when Simon Peter saw, he fell down at Jesus' knees, saying: Depart from me, for I am a sinful man, O Lord.' As Moses at the burning bush, as Isaias when he had the vision of Jahve, as Zacharias before the angel, Peter felt his guilt and was afraid; he, too, has recognised the holiness of the Being before him; who can he be? He does not as yet see clearly; little by little, God is to reveal him to him.

Later on, after the multiplication of the loaves, the apostles are crossing the lake in their boat: the wind rises and suddenly Jesus appears to them walking upon the water. Peter, the most impetuous of them all, cries out: 'Lord, if it be thou, bid me come to thee upon the waters'; Jesus answers him: 'Come!' Peter advances, but, overcome by fear, begins to sink; Jesus raises him up and enters the boat with him, and when they are seated the storm dies down; and those who were in the boat prostrated themselves before Jesus saying: 'Indeed thou art the Son of God.'[2]

Shortly afterwards the still more solemn confession which Peter made in the name of all at Cæsarea Philippi, marked a new progress of the apostles' faith, and Jesus

[1] *Luke* v, 4–11. [2] *Matt.* xiv, 22–33. Cf. *John* vi, 67–9.

by his reply consecrated his divine origin: 'Whom do men say that the Son of man is?' And the disciples replied: 'Some John the Baptist, and other some Elias, and others Jeremias or one of the prophets.' And Jesus said to them: 'But whom do you say that I am?' Simon Peter answered him: 'Thou art Christ, the Son of the Living God.' And Jesus replied: 'Blessed art thou, Simon Bar-Jona: because flesh and blood hath not revealed it to thee, but my Father who is in heaven.'[1]

As has been remarked above, the precise object of this confession was the Messianic dignity of Jesus: the two other Synoptics report it in a less explicit form: in *St. Mark* we only read: 'Thou art the Christ'; and in *St. Luke*: 'Thou art the Christ of God'; and St. Matthew himself goes on to say immediately afterwards[2] that Jesus forbade his disciples to say that he was the Christ. The text of *St. Matthew* differs from the other two, not only because it gives a more explicit form to the confession of St. Peter (verse 16), but because it is followed by the declaration of Jesus, recognising in Peter's reply a revelation of the Father, and giving to Peter, in exchange for his confession, the promise to make of him the unshakeable rock on which the Church should be built, and to give him the keys of the kingdom of heaven.[3] This longer account describes best the scene and its unique character[4]. It is certain that the three evangelists agree in presenting the confession of Peter as something peculiarly decisive, and Jesus does not hesitate to attribute it to a revelation from his Father in Heaven. There is then here something more than the acclamations of the crowd hailing the Son of David; Christ felt that he was understood. It follows that the Messianism, recognised and confessed by St. Peter, was the true Messianism, the religious and divine Messianism; and if, from the first days, we see Christ recognised by his faithful, not only as the Messianic King,

[1] *Matt.* xvi, 13–17. [2] xvi, 20.

[3] The countless controversies over vv. 17–19 do not directly concern v. 16; nevertheless, if their historical value and their authenticity are firmly established, as indeed they are, we have a good argument in favour of 16*b*: the text in *Matt.* has a perfect sequence, the explicit confession of St. Peter calling forth the reply from Jesus. For the controversies, see: attack; HARNACK, *Sitzungsberichte der k. preuss. Akad. d. Wissenschaft*, 1918, 637–54; defence; FONCK, *Biblica*, 1920, 240–63; SCHEPENS, *Rech. d. Sc. Rel.*, 1920, 269–302; LAGRANGE, *S. Matthieu*, 319 *sqq.*

[4] Cf. DURAND, *S. Matthieu*, 277; LAGRANGE, *S. Marc*, 218.

but as the Son of God, this belief, novel for Judaism, is much more easily explained if it rests upon a confession of faith of the apostles explicitly approved by Jesus.[1]

This solemn scene of Cæsarea Philippi is connected by the three Synoptics with the still more solemn scene of the Transfiguration: all three carefully note the shortness of the interval of time separating these two revelations of Christ.[2] Such chronological data are rare enough in the Synoptics; if the three evangelists introduce this precision, it was because they wished to underline the connection of the two events; and this impression, already suggested by the date, is confirmed by the narrative.

> 'And after six days, Jesus taketh unto him Peter and James, and John his brother, and bringeth them up into a high mountain apart.
>
> And he was transfigured before them. And his face did shine as the sun: and his garments became white as snow.
>
> And behold there appeared to them Moses and Elias talking with him.
>
> And Peter, answering, said to Jesus: Lord, it is good for us to be here: if thou wilt, let us make here three tabernacles, one for thee, and one for Moses, and one for Elias.
>
> And as he was yet speaking, behold a bright cloud overshadowed them. And lo, a voice out of the cloud, saying: This is my beloved Son[3] in whom I am well pleased. Hear ye him.
>
> And the disciples hearing, fell upon their face and were very much afraid.
>
> And Jesus came and touched them and said to them: Arise, and fear not.
>
> And they lifting up their eyes saw no one, but only Jesus.'[4]

The accounts of the two other Synoptics are identical; St. Luke, however, adds a remarkable feature: 'Two men were talking with him. And they were Moses and Elias, appearing in majesty. And they spoke of his decease

[1] Cf. SANDAY, art. *Son of God*, in *DB*, IV, 572, 574; BATIFFOL, *L'Église naissante et le catholicisme*, 99–113.
[2] *Matt.* xvii, 1; *Mark* ix, 2; *Luke* ix, 28.
[3] See above, page 203, n. 3.
[4] *Matt.* xvii, 1–8.

which he should accomplish in Jerusalem.'[1] St. Matthew and St. Mark, not mentioning this conversation on the Passion, relate, however, Christ's prediction of it on his descent from the mountain.[2] The Son of man must suffer.

These two scenes, so decisive for the Gospel revelation and so closely connected with each other by the three Synoptics, are, then, two revelations of the same mysteries: Christ, the glorious Son of God, and Christ suffering.[3] This explains the significance attributed by the evangelists to the witness of the Father, reported by all three[4]; six days earlier at Cæsarea, Peter, replying to Jesus, in the name of all, said to him: 'Thou art Christ, the Son of the Living God'; and Jesus had replied: 'Blessed art thou, Simon Bar-Jona: because flesh and blood hath not revealed it to thee, but my Father who is in Heaven.' The voice from heaven at the Transfiguration echoes this intimate and silent revelation: 'This is my only Son, in whom I am well pleased.'[5] In the future Peter will write:

> 'For we have not by following artificial fables made known to you the power and presence of our Lord Jesus Christ: but we were eye-witnesses of his greatness.
>
> For he received from God the Father honour and glory, this voice coming down to him from the excellent glory: *This is my beloved Son, in whom I am well pleased. Hear ye him.*
>
> And this voice, we heard brought from heaven, when we were with him in the holy mount.
>
> And we have the more firm prophetical word: whereunto you do well to attend . . .'[6]

This vision contained other teachings, which the Church would later on collect and treasure: the presence of Elias and Moses beside Jesus signified the continuity of the two Testaments; it was the most manifest confirmation to the apostles of the teaching of their Master: 'I have not come to destroy the law, but to fulfil it.'[7]

Nevertheless, this revelation which, at a later date, was

[1] *Luke* ix, 30–31. [2] *Matt.* xvii, 12; *Mark* ix, 12.

[3] Cf. Holmes, *Purpose of the Transfiguration*, in *JTS*, IV (1903), 545; Ed. Meyer, *Ursprung und Anfänge des Christentums*, I, 111–20, 152–7.

[4] See above, page 203. [5] Douai: beloved Son.

[6] 2 *Peter* i, 16–19. See Mayor, *Second Epistle of St. Peter*, 195; Plummer, *St. Matthew*, 238.

[7] See Tertullian, *Adv. Marc.*, IV, 22.

to illuminate the whole Church, was kept secret during the life of Christ: 'Tell the vision to no man,' said Jesus to his three companions, 'till the Son of man be risen from the dead.'[1] In the passage which was quoted just now from the second *Epistle of St. Peter* the vision was represented as the initiation into the great mysteries: the three apostles are the eye-witnesses (ἐπόπται). For a certain time, indeed, this glorious manifestation, this divine attestation, was to remain their secret; but a day would shortly come on which they would summon the whole world to that blessed initiation.

We here recognise the providential plan of the Gospel preaching, as Christ formulated it on the shore of the lake, when he taught the crowd in parables and reserved their interpretation to his disciples: 'To you it is given to know the mystery of the kingdom of God: but to them that are without, all things are done in parables.'[2] He thus made them feel the joy of their privileged vision: 'Blessed are your eyes because they see, and your ears because they hear. For, amen, I say to you, many prophets and just men have desired to see the things that you see, and have not seen them, and to hear the things that you hear and have not heard them.'[3] But immediately afterwards he made them understand that this vision would not always be for them only, and that their joy was also a responsibility: 'There is nothing hid which shall not be made manifest: neither was it made secret but that it may come abroad.'[4] And he made them understand their function of faithful stewards, who would find in the treasure-house of their memories all these things, new and old, which they would teach to all.[5]

This teaching of Christ had to be recalled here because it throws light on the whole of this history; if we lose sight of it we can no longer understand why the manifestations of the Son of God are more jealously reserved to a few in proportion as they are decisive: the scene at Cæsarea Philippi has but twelve witnesses: the Transfiguration only three. More than one reader of the Gospel has been disconcerted by this prudent reserve, and would

[1] *Matt.* xvii, 9. [2] *Mark* iv, 11. [3] *Matt.* xiii, 16. [4] *Mark* iv, 22. [5] *Matt.* xiii, 51.

willingly say with the brethren of the Lord: 'For there is no man that doth anything in secret, and he himself seeketh to be known openly. If thou do these things manifest thyself to the world.'[1] But if we read the Gospel carefully we shall soon notice that these are but particular applications of the plan which Christ had put before himself; his work of evangelisation became daily less extended, but deeper: at first it covered the whole of Palestine, Jerusalem, Judæa, Samaria: then it became confined to Galilee and, finally, almost entirely concentrated on the group of the twelve, among whom the three privileged ones formed an inner circle. External events, the growing opposition of his enemies, seem to have imposed this line of action on Jesus, but in reality he was master of the events, and made them serve his own ends: wishing to entrust his Church with the honourable charge of preaching the Gospel, of converting Israel and the world, he prepared her for this rôle by concentrating on her and her leaders his most decisive efforts, and his most precious graces, contenting himself with spreading around among the people of God the seed of the kingdom, which, later, under the action of the Holy Spirit, was to germinate and give the apostles their earliest harvests.

IV

Thus, driven from Jerusalem by the proceedings of the Pharisees, forced to leave Galilee, where the Herodians threatened him, Jesus took refuge with his little band of apostles in the territory of Philip, revealing himself to them, and continuing their training. The future being thus assured, he walks to his death; he goes up to Jerusalem. During his last week there, he made a supreme effort to gain the people and the Pharisees; they repulsed him, but in this conflict a new light shone forth; for the blinding, alas, of the Jews, but for the illumination in the near future of the Church.

This great week was opened by the triumphant entry of Jesus into Jerusalem. The preparations made by Christ for this event were humble enough, but they clearly

[1] *John* vii, 4.

reveal his intention. All Jews were familiar with the prophecy of Zacharias (ix, 9):

> 'Rejoice greatly, O daughter of Sion, shout for joy, O daughter of Jerusalem: BEHOLD THY KING will come to thee, the just and saviour. He is poor and riding upon an ass and upon a colt, the foal of an ass.'[1]

Jesus literally accomplished this prophecy; he sent two of his disciples to find the foal of an ass: they brought it and covered it with their garments, and helped their Master to mount it. The crowd whom the approaching solemnities of the Passover were drawing to Jerusalem received this humble procession with enthusiastic cries: 'Hosanna! Blessed is he that cometh in the name of the Lord! Blessed be the kingdom of our father David that cometh! Hosanna in the highest!'[2] These cries of the children follow him into the Temple; the Pharisees are indignant, and, not venturing to reprove the people directly, they say to Jesus: 'Hearest thou what these say?' and he replies: 'Yea, have you never read: "Out of the mouths of infants and of sucklings, thou hast perfected praise." And leaving them he went out of the city into Bethania.'[3]

According to the testimony of St. Luke, it was on this day of triumph, when he saw the city, that Jesus wept over it, saying:

> 'If thou also hadst known, and that in this thy day, the things that are to thy peace: but now they are hidden from thy eyes.'[4]

The mere bringing together of these texts throws light upon them, and gives all its meaning to the scene: Jesus wished to make a supreme effort, to present to the people of God their Messias, but in doing so he wished to give the humblest character to this manifestation; he chose out of all the prophetic descriptions of his arrival the most modest, the very one that astounded the pride of the Jews; they recognised him, they acclaimed the Messias, but alas, the Messias in *their* sense of the word; despising all that Jesus had taught, and that this humble ceremony brought before them that day, they would only see in

[1] See LAGRANGE, *Messianisme*, 227.
[2] *Mark* xi, 9–10. [3] *Matt.* xxi, 15–17. [4] *Luke* xix, 41–42.

the Messias whom they acclaimed the national King of their dreams, and in the Kingdom of God, which he came to establish, only 'the Kingdom of David their father.' Thenceforward the whole movement was condemned in advance; to-day it was but a feverish excitement, and to-morrow a mortal depression and, in many, hatred was born of the bitterness of the deception; what happened was the death of the Messias, and the ruin of the holy city.[1]

At least, during the short week that remained to him of life, Christ multiplied his efforts to make himself known to the Jews in so far as it was possible for them to tolerate him; and the violent opposition of the Pharisees, who, from the earliest days of his ministry, had called forth some of his first declarations, induced him again to manifest himself more clearly; and when this conflict, growing daily more violent, at length came to a head, a brighter light than ever shone forth from it: the adjuration of Jesus by the High Priest in the name of God, and the reply of Christ, affirming the divine Sonship.

It would take too long to repeat here all the incidents of these last six days of the life of Christ. Among many pressing warnings, the object of which was to remind the Jews of their immense responsibility, the Son of God revealed himself more insistently than he had done before. The parable of the banquet, which is related elsewhere in *St. Luke*,[2] appears here[3] with new features. The invitation is sent by a king on the occasion of his son's wedding; the crime of the guests seems to be greater, for not only do they fail to accept it, but they put to death the messengers of the king.[4] These features are repeated with even more insistence, and a more evident significance, in the parable of the vine-dressers:

> 'And he began to speak to them in parables: A certain man planted a vineyard and made a hedge about it and dug a place for the winefat and built a tower and let it to husbandmen: and went into a far country.
>
> And at the season he sent to the husbandmen a

[1] Cf. VICTOR, in his Commentary on St. Mark (CRAMER, 389).
[2] xiv, 16–24. [3] *Matt.* xxii, 1–14.
[4] Cf. PLUMMER, *St. Matthew*, 300–1.

servant to receive of the husbandmen of the fruit of the vineyard.

Who, having laid hands on him, beat him and sent him away empty.

And again he sent to them another servant: and him they wounded in the head and used him reproachfully.

And again he sent another, and him they killed: and many others, of whom some they beat, and others they killed.

Therefore, having yet one son, most dear to him, he also sent him unto them last of all, saying: They will reverence my son.

But the husbandmen said one to another: This is the heir. Come let us kill him and the inheritance shall be ours.

And laying hold on him, they killed him and cast him out of the vineyard.

What therefore will the lord of the vineyard do? He will come and destroy those husbandmen and will give the vineyard to others.'[1]

This discourse is certainly authentic[2] and its meaning is evident. It teaches not only the death of Christ and the punishment of the Jews, but the whole history of the people of God is sent forth in it under the traditional likeness of a vineyard: the prophets, sent in the first place by God, are the servants, and the Messias whom God sends is his only Son.[3]

A little later Jesus, teaching in the Temple, endeavours to correct the too-narrowly national idea which the Jews had formed of the Messias:

'How do the scribes say that Christ is the son of David? For David himself saith by the Holy Ghost: "The Lord said to my Lord: Sit on my right hand, until I make thy enemies thy footstool." David therefore himself calleth him Lord; and whence is he then his son?'[4]

[1] *Mark* xii, 1–9; cf. *Matt.* xxi, 33–41; *Luke* xx, 9–16.

[2] Cf. Burkitt, *op. cit. infra*, II, 321; van Crombrughe, *op. cit. infra*, 32–42.

[3] *Mark* xii, 6.—The reader may wish to consult the lengthy and very erudite footnote no. 2, page 324, in the French original of the present work, i.e., Lebreton, *Histoire du dogme de la Trinité* (8th edition, vol. I, Paris, 1927). See also above, page 203, note 3, Cf. Abelson, *Immanence of God*, 164, n. 27.

[4] *Mark* xii, 35–37; cf. *Matt.* xxii, 41–6; *Luke* xx, 41–4.

In speaking thus, Jesus did not mean to reject the descent from David, which all recognised in him, but wished to make them see at the same time the greater majesty of him whom David called his Lord.

It was during these last days, on the eve of his death, that Jesus predicted in the strongest terms the final catastrophe which should consummate the ruin of Jerusalem, and of the whole world; on this occasion he once more described the triumphant return of the Son of man, but never before had he given to the figure of the returning Messias a character of a so manifestly superhuman transcendence. We should above all read the scene of the Judgement as described in *St. Matthew* (xxv, 31-46):

'And when the Son of man shall come in his majesty, and all the angels with him, then shall he sit upon the seat of his majesty.

And all nations shall be gathered together before him: and he shall separate them one from another, as the shepherd separateth the sheep from the goats:

And he shall set the sheep on his right hand, but the goats on his left.

Then shall the king say to them that shall be on his right hand: Come, ye blessed of my Father, possess you the kingdom prepared for you from the foundation of the world.

For I was hungry, and you gave me to eat . . .

And the king answering shall say to them: Amen I say to you, as long as you did it to one of these my least brethren, you did it to me.

Then he shall say to them also that shall be on his left hand: Depart from me, you cursed, into everlasting fire, which was prepared for the devil and his angels.

For I was hungry and you gave me not to eat . . .

Then he shall answer them, saying: Amen I say to you, as long as you did it not to one of these least, neither did you do it to me.

And these shall go into everlasting punishment: but the just into life everlasting.'[1]

[1] Cf. SANDAY, *Life of Christ in Recent Research*, 128, n. 1.

The most characteristic features of this solemn theme are found elsewhere in the Gospel, more frequently in *St. Matthew,* but often in the other Synoptics: in the other discourses Jesus represents the angels as his assessors on the last day,[1] and all the nations of the earth as subject to his justice[2]: once more he here claims in all its majesty the rôle of universal and supreme Judge; while at the same time he more than ever appears as the centre of the moral life of the whole human race; all that men can do, whether good or evil, it is to Christ they do it, and it is solely in accordance with their attitude towards him that they will be judged. We have already noticed[3] this teaching of the Lord; we have seen how Christ's attitude here below towards sinners suggests the anticipation of the sentence of the Judge. But there is more: the Son of man appears here not only as the Judge, but as the Head of humanity, who is wounded by all the sufferings of his members, and comforted by all the help that is given them; do we not see here the germ of the teaching of St. Paul? Many historians have connected the apostle's Christology with his vision at Damascus; on that occasion he understood that in attacking the Church he was persecuting Jesus himself: but was this revelation anything more than a foreshadowing of the final sentence: 'As long as you did it to one of these my least brethren, you did it to me'?[4]

By putting before the Jews during the last days of his ministry this picture of the last judgement, Christ gave them, not only the gravest possible warning, but in addition the clearest revelation that they could bear; he had now only to seal his witness with his blood.

In order to condemn Jesus, the High Priests suborned false witnesses; these wretches gave their evidence one after another before Caiphas; Christ did not deign to answer them, he left their lies to contradict each other:

> 'And the high priest rising up, said to him: Answerest thou nothing to the things which these witness against thee?

[1] *Matt.* xiii, 39, 41, 49; *Matt.* xvi, 27, cf. *Mark* viii, 38; *Luke* ix, 26; xii, 8, 9; *Matt.* xxiv, 31, cf. *Mark* xiii, 27.

[2] *Matt.* xxiv, 30.

[3] See above, page 215.

[4] Cf. TERTULLIAN, *De Orat.*, 26; CLEM. ALEX., *Strom.*, I, 19, 94; II, 15, 70.

But Jesus held his peace. And the high priest said to him: I adjure thee by the living God, that thou tell us if thou be the Christ, the Son of God.

Jesus saith to him: Thou hast said it. Nevertheless I say to you, hereafter you shall see the Son of man sitting on the right hand of the power of God and coming in the clouds of heaven.

Then the high priest rent his garments, saying: He hath blasphemed. What further need have we of witnesses? Behold, now you have heard the blasphemy.

What think you? But they answering, said: He is guilty of death.'[1]

This was how the Son of God wished to give his supreme testimony—adjured in the name of God, before the highest religious authorities of his nation at the price of his blood. He wished that his death, which was to be the foundation of our hope, should, at the same time, be the assurance of our faith; that the sacrifice by which he redeemed us should also be the martyr's death by which he attested that he was truly the Christ, the Son of God, the Judge of the world. Strengthened by this 'good confession' of their Master,[2] as St. Paul calls it, all Christians have in their turn pledged thereto their faith and if need be their lives.

In order to grasp the precise meaning of this testimony, it is not necessary to think that Caiphas saw the full significance of the formula which he employed; yet, even in his mouth, that formula was not simply equivalent to the title of Messias: we have already pointed out several times that the Jewish tradition did not admit the equivalence of the terms Messias and the Son of God. If therefore Caiphas made the title of Christ more precise by adding the words 'Son of God' it was because he wished to attack the Messianic pretensions of Jesus as they had been put forward by him and maintained by his adherents. In addition, as all the context indicates, he chose a formula that Jesus could not reject without denying the work of his life, nor accept without being condemned for blasphemy, as in fact he was. But, as is freely admitted,[3]

[1] *Matt.* xxvi, 62–66. [2] 1 *Tim.* vi, 13.
[3] Cf. Loisy, *Synoptiques*, II, 604.

there was no blasphemy in the simple claim to the title of Messias, or in calling himself the Son of God, if he meant by that merely a moral and religious filiation.

It would seem therefore that both these titles must have been given extra significance by Jesus in the version of his teaching known to Caiphas, that is, as the populace had understood it, and as the disciples had received it. It must be admitted, without analysing further, that, in the thought of Caiphas, this title of the Son of God, which he did not borrow from the Jewish tradition, but from the teaching of Jesus, must have expressed so intimate and transcendent a relation with the divinity, that no man could claim it without blasphemy.

To the question put so clearly and authoritatively: Art thou the Christ, the Son of God ? ' Jesus replied unequivocally: 'I am.' He thus pronounced his own sentence of death, and, at the same time, gave his own supreme testimony.

During his agony on the Cross, his enemies derisively recalled his pretensions to be the Son of God,[1] and after his death the centurion said, 'Indeed, this man was the Son of God.'[2]

The Lord's resurrection and the apparitions which followed it confirmed and strengthened the shaken faith of the disciples. From this point of view these last narratives of the Gospels have a decisive importance for the historian of the dogma of the Trinity: they alone explain the attachment of the Apostles to a doctrine so novel, so mysterious, and so disputed.

But if Jesus, more than ever during the last few days, is the Friend who consoles and the God who reveals himself, he is, less than during the days of his life, the Master who instructs. The initiation of the Apostles into the Christian mysteries was still very imperfect, but it was to be the task of the Holy Spirit to complete it. Only a few sentences of Our Lord's teaching at this time are concerned with the development of the doctrine of the Trinity; but, on the other hand, there are none more significant in the whole of the Gospel.

[1] *Matt.* xxvii, 40, 43. [2] *Mark* xv, 39.

'And the eleven disciples went into Galilee, unto the mountain where Jesus had appointed them.

And seeing him they adored: but some doubted.

And Jesus coming, spoke to them, saying: All power is given to me in heaven and in earth.

Going therefore, teach ye all nations: baptizing them in the name of the Father and of the Son and of the Holy Ghost.

Teaching them to observe all things whatsoever I have commanded you. And behold I am with you all days, even to the consummation of the world.'[1]

Before speaking of the Trinitarian formula, it is very important to note the part that concerns Christ himself. The first words of the text recall the phrase previously studied: 'All has been entrusted to me by my Father'; but, in that case, the words referred rather to secrets confided and doctrine transmitted; here it is all power which is given to the Son; in *Matthew* xi, 27, he represented himself as the sole revealer of the Father; here, as the universal Sovereign, who sends his apostles everywhere. Moreover, he will follow them, he will be everywhere and always with them; this phrase was familiar to the Apostles and had a perfectly definite meaning for them: it was the very promise made by Jahve to Moses and the prophets; the parallelism was significant and revealed their rôle and their Master.

As to the baptismal formula expressed in these words, it is the most explicit of all the Trinitarian texts of the New Testament: no other has played a more decisive rôle in the controversies of later ages; in the fourth century the Fathers used it as a favourite weapon. St. Hilary, for instance, thus commences his argument:

> 'The word of God was sufficient for the faithful, which word itself has been transmitted to us with the power of its truth through the testimony of the evangelist, on the occasion when the Lord said: Go ye and teach all nations: for what is there concerning the sacrament of human salvation that is not contained in these words? . . .' (*De Trinitate*, ii, 1).

No doubt can be cast on the meaning of this text, and

[1] *Matt.* xxviii, 16–20.

we shall return to it later when we have studied the doctrine of the Holy Spirit in the Synoptics; its authenticity is very certain, in spite of being much disputed to-day.[1]

BIBLIOGRAPHY, Section 2:—H. Monnier, *La mission historique de Jésus* (Paris, 1906). A. Schweitzer, *Gesch. d. Leben-Jesu-Forschung*² (Tubingen, 1913). W. Sanday, *The Life of Christ in recent Research* (Oxford, 1907). F. Tillmann, *Der Menschensohn, Jesu Selbstzeugnis für seine Messianische Würde* (Freiburg im Breisgau, 1907). Klostermann, *Marcusevangelium* (Tübingen, 1926). P. Feine, *Theol. des N.T.* (Leipzig, 1919). H. J. Holtzmann, *N.T. Theol.* (Tübingen, 1911). C. Clemen, *Religionsgeschichtl. Erklärung des N.T.* (Giessen, 1924). Weinel, *Theol. des N.T.* (Tübingen, 1921). A. Durand, *L'enfance de Jésus-Christ* (Paris, 1908). F. C. Burkitt, *Parable of the Wicked Husbandmen*, in *Transactions of the Third International Congress of the History of Religions* (Oxford, 1908), II. C. van Crombrughe, *De soteriologiæ christianæ primis fontibus* (Louvain, 1905).

3. *The Holy Spirit*

In his above-quoted theological discourse on the Holy Spirit St. Gregory Nazianzen said that 'the New Testament manifested the Son and implied (ὑπέδειξε) the divinity of the Spirit.' By these words the holy doctor did not intend to say that the dogma of the divinity of the Holy Spirit was contained in the New Testament in a merely uncertain and doubtful way. He himself has shown better than anyone that decisive arguments can be drawn from it. He merely meant that the person of the Holy Spirit was not manifested with such clarity as was that of the Son.

The Son, by his Incarnation, appeared to us in person; but the Holy Spirit only revealed himself by his gifts; we do not know his person by a direct and immediate manifestation, but only by the teaching of Christ and his apostles. This teaching, moreover, was given progressively, as was the case with the whole of the Christian revelation in the Apostolic age. Light is thrown on the data of the Synoptic gospels, in themselves mostly obscure, by St. Paul and more fully by St. John. If the initial obscurity is here greater and but slowly dissipated, no Christian can be surprised; he recalls Our Lord's promises: he knows that it was only after his death and glorious resurrection that he poured forth in abundance the Holy Spirit on his disciples.

[1] See Note IV at end of this Volume.

The first effect attributed to the Holy Spirit by the Gospel was the Virginal Conception. This divine work has always been attacked by rationalist exegetists. During the last thirty years the comparative history of religions has been the principal armoury of the attackers, and the attempt has been made to interpret St. Luke's narrative in terms of Chinese, Buddhist, Persian, Assyrian, Babylonian, Arab, Egyptian, and Hellenic legends[1]; Hellenism has indeed been most frequently represented as the source of the belief[2]; yet everything in the Gospel text is opposed to this explanation: first of all, the whole character of these two chapters, so clearly Semitic in composition and style, and then the very idea of a virginal conception, wholly foreign to Hellenic mythology, and incompatible with the legends with which they try to connect it.[3] Recently E. Norden, whose competence in the matter of Hellenic philology no one can deny and who will not be suspected of theological prejudices, resumed the study of this question and came to the conclusion that neither those two chapters nor any part of the Gospel contained any Hellenic elements[4]; his own view is that all can be explained by Egyptian theosophical speculations, attested on the one hand by Plutarch, on the other by Philo[5]; this ancient hypothesis has often been refuted, even by scholars of the comparative school.[6]

When we have thus criticised these imaginary assimilations we see more clearly the distance between these impure fables and St. Luke's narrative, so reserved, so chaste, and in its simplicity, so divine. The fact that the evangelist narrates then appears in its true proportions, transcendent and unique in human history as the Incarnation itself, but heralded, like the Incarnation, by a long series of miracles; a special intervention of God occurs in the conception of many of the great men in the Old Testament, such as Isaac and Samuel; we recognise it also in the maternity of Elizabeth; from the moment of

[1] These systems are described in CLEMEN, *Religionsgeschichtl. Erklarung des N.T.*, 117–21.

[2] Cf. LOISY, *Évangiles synoptiques*, I, 291 *sq.*; CLEMEN, *op. cit.*, 120–1, LEISEGANG, *op. cit. infra*, 22 *sqq.*; ED. MEYER, *Ursprung*, I, 54 *sqq.*

[3] Cf. LAGRANGE, *R.B*, XI (1914), 60–71, 188–208; MÉDEBIELLE, art. *Annonciation* in *Suppl. DB*, col. 273 *sq.*

[4] NORDEN, *op. cit. infra*, 82; 79, n. 3.

[5] Cf. PLUTARCH, *Isis et Osiris*, 36.

[6] CLEMEN, 120.

his conception, St. John the Baptist appears as the Precursor, and this great miracle is presented by Gabriel to Mary as the sign of God's power, and the presage of her own maternity.

'The Holy Ghost shall come upon thee,' said the angel to Mary, 'and the power of the most High shall overshadow thee.'[1]

Many of the more ancient Fathers, influenced by the vagueness of the terminology, have understood here by the Holy Spirit the Son, and by his coming his Incarnation: thus St. Justin, St. Callixtus, St. Hippolytus, Tertullian, St. Cyprian, Lactantius, St. Athanasius, St. Hilary[2]; others, finding in the 'power of God' one of the names given to the Son by St. Paul, have distinguished in this text of Luke two divine persons and two actions.[3] Both these interpretations have rightly been set on one side, but they give us an idea, on the threshold of this history, of the incertitudes of terminology and sometimes of thought, of which we shall find other examples.

If we consider *St. Luke's* text by itself there is no doubt that the two expressions, Holy Spirit, Power of the Most High, are equivalent. Neither one nor the other has the article[4]; while the second is neither in the language of St. Luke nor in that of the other sacred writers a personal name of the Holy Spirit. The passage, therefore, indicates one action, one divine force; but it does not permit us to accept with certitude the existence of a divine Person, distinct from the Father and the Son.[5]

Around the cradle of Jesus the Spirit is poured forth abundantly, John the Baptist was filled with it,[6] also Elizabeth[7] and Zacharias[8]; Simeon had for long received the promise of the Spirit,[9] and it is the Spirit that leads him to the Temple.[10] In all this we recognise the dawn of Messianic times, the first-fruits of that great effusion of

[1] *Luke* i, 35.

[2] JUSTIN, *Apol.*, I, 33, 6; CALLIST., in *Philosoph.*, IX, 12; TERTULL., *Prax.*, XXVI; CYPRIAN, *Q. idola dii non sint*, XI; LACT., IV, 12; ATHANAS., *De Incarn.*, XVIII; HILARY, *De Trinit.*, II, 26.

[3] RUFIN., *In symbol.*, IX.

[4] See ATHAN. *Ad Serap.*, I, 4 (*P.G.*, XXVI, 536–7).

[5] Furthermore, the virginal conception, being an act of God *ad extra*, has the Divine essence as principle, and the Divine essence is one, not one person to the exclusion of the other two. The virginal conception is attributed to the Holy Spirit as are all works of love.

[6] *Luke* i, 15. [7] i, 41. [8] i, 67. [9] ii, 26; cf. 25. [10] ii, 27.

the Spirit predicted by the prophets, but we do not see any more clearly than in the Old Testament the nature of this Spirit which is promised and given.

John the Baptist recalls and confirms the promises of the past: 'There cometh after me one mightier than I . . . I have baptised you with water; but he shall baptise you with the Holy Ghost.'[1]

Shortly afterwards Christ was baptised and the Spirit was manifested:

> 'It came to pass, in those days Jesus came from Nazareth of Galilee; and was baptised by John in the Jordan. And forthwith coming up out of the water he saw the heavens opened, and the Spirit as a dove[2] descending, and remaining on him. And there came a voice from heaven: "Thou art my beloved Son, in thee I am well pleased."'[3]

We have already studied the testimony here given by the Father to his Son; the Spirit also manifests himself, it is no longer a question of a Holy Spirit, as above, but of the Spirit (*Mark*), the Spirit of God (*Matthew*), of the Holy Spirit (*Luke*).

The definite form of the expression and, still more, the distinct manifestation of the Spirit and his association with the Father and the Son, enable us to understand the meaning of the evangelists; in this baptism of Christ the presence of the Trinity is perceived, as it is attested in the baptism of the Christian. Was the occurrence itself fully understood by the witnesses? We can hardly think so; it would seem doubtful whether the crowds thronging the banks of the Jordan either saw or heard all that passed; they were, in any case, ill-prepared to understand such a mystery. The Baptist, at least, recognised the sign given him by God, and according to *St. John* (i, 33, 34), he gave his witness thenceforward that Jesus was the Son of God.

In the narrative of the public life of Our Lord and in his discourses, as we read them in the Synoptics, we find

[1] *Mark* i, 8.

[2] It is not necessary to go to Hellenic myths to explain the appearance of the dove. *Gen.* i, 2 already provides us with a similar image; cf. H. B. Swete, *The Holy Spirit in the N.T.* (London, 1909), 365–366, note A.

[3] *Mark* i, 9–11.

a few references to the Holy Spirit similar to those contained in the books of the Prophets: Jesus is impelled by the Holy Spirit into the desert[1]; he turns under the influence of the Spirit towards Galilee,[2] he rejoices in the Holy Spirit[3]; David speaks, inspired by the Holy Spirit.[4]

Two sentences of Christ must be looked at more closely. The Pharisees blasphemed against the actions of Jesus, and, in particular, against his exorcisms, and accused him of being possessed by an impure spirit. Our Lord replied:

> 'Every sin and blasphemy shall be forgiven men, but the blasphemy of the Spirit shall not be forgiven. And whosoever shall speak a word against the Son of man, it shall be forgiven him: but he that shall speak against the Holy Ghost, it shall not be forgiven him, neither in this world nor in the world to come.'[5]

In the theological discussions of the fourth century, when the divinity of the Holy Spirit had to be defended against the Macedonians, a decisive argument was furnished by this text; his divinity raised no doubt in the hearers of Christ; as to the distinct personality of the Holy Spirit, which was unknown to them, it is unlikely that this parable revealed it to them. What they must, at least, have understood was that the works of Christ, like the works of the prophets and even more so, than which they were greater, were holy and divine works, works proceeding consequently from the Spirit of God,[6] which could not without blasphemy be attributed to demons.

The most explicit words of Jesus on the subject are not those addressed to the Jewish crowds, in which he presents the Son of God as already in action among them; they are, rather, the promises made to his disciples, when he speaks to them of the Spirit as a gift, which they have not yet received, but which the Father reserves and assures to them. Thus, when they are led before the judges they will not have to premeditate their defence: 'for it shall be given you in that hour what to speak. For it is not you that speak, but the Spirit of your Father

[1] *Mark* i, 12. [2] *Luke* iv, 14. [3] *Luke* x, 21.
[4] *Mark* xii, 36. [5] *Matt.* xii, 31–32. [6] Cf. *Matt.* xii, 28.

that speaketh in you.'[1] And St. Luke, reporting these words, insists even more strongly on the personal assistance of the Holy Spirit. 'The Holy Ghost shall teach you what you must say.'[2] The phrase is similar to those used in the discourse after the Last Supper, as reported by St. John. We hear here an echo of the promises which have only been explicitly reported by the fourth evangelist, and of which there are, elsewhere, but rare and passing mentions. On the day of the Ascension, Jesus said to his disciples: 'And I send the promise of my Father upon you: but stay you in the city, till you be endued with power from on high.'[3] 'You shall receive the power of the Holy Spirit coming upon you, and you shall be witnesses unto me.'[4]

The *Book of Acts,* which has been justly called 'the gospel of the Holy Spirit,' tells us plainly what was the effect of these promises: the Synoptics, and even the Gospel of St. John, merely announce it more or less explicitly. Also the revelation of the Spirit contained there is wholly directed to the future; it is a prophecy. The Trinitarian text (*Matt.* xxviii, 19) also presents itself under this form: the precept given in it will only have its accomplishment in the future. The Lord having recalled his universal dominion, commands his disciples to teach all nations and to baptise them, in the name of the Father and of the Son and of the Holy Spirit. If we see in this before all the prescription of a liturgical formula, we may find it difficult to explain baptism in the name of Jesus, as mentioned in the Acts.[5] The context seems to invite a wider interpretation. Christ has just invoked the supreme power, which has been given to him in heaven and on earth:

> 'It is this supreme authority of the risen Christ, which authorises his Church to act in the name of the Supreme God, who is now, or shortly will be, fully manifested as the Father, the Son, and the Holy Spirit; and behind the Apostles, in the exercise of their delegated authority, in their use of the supreme name, there will be the promised presence of the Lord himself.'[6]

[1] *Matt.* x, 20. [2] *Luke* xii, 12. [3] xxiv, 49. [4] *Acts* i, 8. [5] ii, 38.
[6] J. A. Robinson, in *J.T.S.*, Jan., 1906, p. 195.

Thus, this decisive act, by which man will be incorporated into Christ, and consecrated to God, will be performed in the name and by the authority of God, Father, Son, and Holy Spirit.[1]

Understood in this sense, this Trinitarian formula, standing out in such bold relief, is not an anachronism; it is, at the most, an anticipation: and, like the precept itself in which it is contained, it is directed towards the future, and will shortly be interpreted to the Apostles by the Holy Spirit, together with so many other sayings of Jesus that they have imperfectly understood.

Moreover, the surprise or the difficulty experienced in these days by certain historians on reading this verse, comes chiefly from a false impression; reducing the whole real teaching of Jesus, about himself and the Holy Spirit, to a few texts reported by the Synoptics, they see too great a disproportion between that elementary doctrine and this completed formula; and, even if they admit that the relations of Father and Son are as explicitly indicated in other words of Christ, they are nevertheless disconcerted by the attribution to the Holy Spirit of a rôle and personality which the other texts, according to them, do not imply.

It would seem that this objection, in so far as it has any value, is less fatal to the text which it attacks than to the method of criticism on which it is based. For if it is true that this formula is more explicit than those met with elsewhere in the Synoptics, we must admit, on the other hand, that the later development of Trinitarian doctrine supposes, in the teaching of Jesus himself, a richness and a precision which the other texts do not reveal.[2] The discourses reported by St. John will help us to fill this gap, so far confirming their historical value; but even after we have studied them we shall not claim to reduce the whole reality to the measure of our texts, or to deny, in the name of a superficial science, facts which the evangelists relate, and the teachings of the apostles suppose.

Bibliography, Section 3:—Leisegang, *Pneuma Hagion* (Leipzig, 1922). E. Norden, *Die Geburt des Kindes* (Leipzig, 1924).

[1] Cf. Strack-Billerbeck, I, 1055.
[2] Cf. Sanday, *DB*, II, 214a; H. M. Scott, *ibid.*, V, 313b.

CHAPTER II

The Birth of the Church

1. The Lord Jesus

If the Christian faith were a metaphysic, and the religion of Christ a philosophical system like those of Plato and Aristotle, it would be necessary, after the exposition of the Master's teaching, to pass almost immediately to that of the two great disciples, St. Paul and St. John, with but a brief mention of the preaching of St. Peter and the other apostles. But in order to trace the history of a religion, we must adopt another method, and endeavour to reach the intimate faith of the believers, which is manifested as much by worship and prayer as by theology.

This enquiry is the more necessary in this case, because without it the narrative of the life of Christ would be incomplete: in spite of all the misunderstandings and all the disappointments that balked the enthusiasm of the crowds, the faith of the disciples grew gradually nobler and stronger; although, even after the resurrection, that faith had still a very imperfect perception of Christ, and remained embarrassed by its earlier dreams, the departure of Jesus purified it and the coming of the Holy Spirit enlightened it. After Pentecost, when the faith affirms itself more definitely, it will better manifest the revelation from which it proceeds, and its goal. We will endeavour to collect the evidence on these points, whether in the narrative of the *Acts* or in the discourses or the Epistles of the Apostles, leaving on one side the teaching of St. Paul and St. John.

A double aspect of the Christian faith may be discovered in all these documents: one, external and apologetic, shown in the discourses of St. Peter, St. Stephen, or St. Paul; the other and more intimate aspect, to be distinguished here and there in those same discourses by certain more revealing expressions, but chiefly to be discovered in prayer, worship, way of living and language, and which, eventually, reveals itself explicitly in the Epistles addressed to the Christian communities. There is nothing surprising about the necessity of this distinction: it was already necessary for the understanding of Christ's teaching as reported by the Synoptics,[1] and its necessity will be no less evident in the case of many other Christian documents; it is, moreover, very natural; every preacher, anxious to convert his hearers, leads souls gradually to the truth; he does not throw them at once into the midst of the unknown, but only reveals mysteries accessible to their mentality.[2]

The apologetic teaching reported in the *Acts* presents Jesus as a just and holy man[3]: 'God anointed him with the Holy Ghost and with power, who went about doing good, and healing all that were oppressed by the devil, for God was with him'[4]; God gave witness to him by working through his means, wonders, miracles, and signs[5]; he raised him from the dead[6] and made him Lord and Christ.[7]

This affirmation of Jesus as the Messias is the purpose of the whole of this apologetic; its demonstration is taken from the prophecies, from the miracles and, above all, from the resurrection of Christ; but we should be careful to note that the Messianic faith thus preached surpasses greatly the Messianic doctrine of the Jews. Not only is Christ greater than David,[8] but he is the Judge of the living and the dead,[9] he is the Prince of Life,[10] he is the Corner Stone,[11] he is the indispensable Mediator and the universal Saviour,[12] he is the Lord of All[13]: this last expression is very strong, and M. Dalman[14] justly assimilates it to the formula of the Apocalypse, 'The King of Kings and Lord of Lords,'[15] and to the passage in the *Epistle to the Philippians* where it is said that, 'in the Name of Jesus, every knee should bow of those that are in heaven, on earth, and under the earth.'[16]

[1] This is clear from the care taken by Jesus to prevent the revelation of his Messianic dignity, and also to interpret his parables only to his disciples.
[2] Harnack, *Apostelgeschichte*, 108–10.
[3] iii, 14 (St. Peter's discourse); vii, 52 (St. Stephen's); xxii, 14 (St. Paul's). [4] x, 38. [5] ii, 22.
[6] iii, 15, 26; iv, 10; v, 30; x, 40 (St. Peter); xiii, 30 *sqq.* (St. Paul).
[7] ii, 36. [8] ii, 29, 34. [9] x, 42; xvii, 31. [10] iii, 15. [11] iv, 11.
[12] iv, 12. [13] x, 36. [14] *Der Gottesname Adonaj*, 83. [15] xix, 16.
[16] ii, 10.

This universal lordship is certainly a Divine attribute, as is also the mission of the Holy Spirit[1] or the possession of a name so sublime as to be the only one that will save,[2] and whose mere invocation will heal the sick.[3] Yet, if we consider the relations of Christ with God that appear in these discourses, we see above all a relation of dependence: if he worked miracles it was because God was with him[4] and himself worked them by his means[5]; it was God who raised him from the dead,[6] who appointed him Judge of the living and the dead,[7] who made him Lord and Christ,[8] who raised him to his right hand,[9] who glorified him.[10] All these traits form a perfectly consistent whole, and impose themselves on the attention of the historian and the faith of the Christian: for one who accepts the authority of the Apostles and Holy Scripture, it is equally impossible to reject this witness as the errors of an archaic theology or the compromises of a complaisant apologetic.

It is then certain that Christ depends in every way on God, and holds of him all that he has and is. Many critics, such as Reuss[11] and Loisy,[12] find here their starting-point for the interpretation of the whole of this Christology in an Adoptionist sense: they consider that, in the minds of St. Peter and St. Paul,[13] if not for the author of the *Acts*,[14] Jesus would have only been made Christ and Lord by his resurrection. This exegesis fails to recognise what is most certain in the faith of both St. Peter and St. Paul: already in the days of his earthly life, Jesus was the Christ, but his resurrection was at once the decisive proof and the supreme manifestation of his Messianic dignity,[15] and, at the same time, of his Divine Sonship: the

[1] ii, 3. [2] iv, 12. [3] iii, 16. [4] x, 38. [5] ii, 28.

[6] This expression occurs very often in the whole New Testament: *Rom.* iv, 24; viii, 11; x, 9; 1 *Cor.* vi, 14; xv, 15; 2 *Cor.*, iv, 14; *Gal.* i, 1; *Eph.* i, 20; *Col.* ii, 12; 1 *Thess.* i, 10; 1 *Pet.* i, 21.

[7] x, 42. [8] ii, 36. [9] ii, 33. [10] iii, 13.

[11] *Théol. chrét.*, I, 454 *sq.* [12] *L'Evangile et l'Église*, 69.

[13] *Acts* xiii, 33. Cf. *Rom.* i, 4. See SANDAY-HEADLAM, *in h. l.*: 'It is certain that St. Paul did not hold that the son of God *became* Son by the Resurrection. The undoubted Epistles are clear on this point (esp. 2 *Cor.* iv, 4; viii, 9; cf. *Col.* i, 15–19). At the same time he *did* regard the Resurrection as making a difference—if not in the transcendental relations of the Father to the Son (which lie beyond our cognizance), yet in the visible manifestation of Sonship as addressed to the understanding of men (cf. esp. *Phil.* iv, 9).'

[14] Cf. LOISY, *Rev. d'hist. et de littér. relig.*, XI (1906), 69.

[15] Cf. E. MANGENOT, *Jésus, Messie et Fils de Dieu d'après les Actes des Apôtres*, in *Rev. de l'Instit. cath. de Paris*, XII (1907), 405–8.

prophetic words, 'Thou art my Son, this day have I begotten thee,' were applied by St. Paul to the mystery of the Resurrection (xiii, 33); an echo of them had already been heard at the Transfiguration and the Baptism: those great dates do not indicate the origin of the Divine Filiation, but stages in its progressive manifestation.[1]

As for the precise meaning to be attributed here to the Divine Filiation, the text itself is insufficient to determine it; we may note, however, that the title of Son (υἱὸς)[2] of God only occurs certainly in two passages of the *Acts* (ix, 20; xiii, 33), and that, in both cases, the historian is reproducing the preaching of St. Paul; it will therefore be better to reserve its discussion for the consideration that will shortly be made of the Apostle's theology. St. Peter, in his discourses, calls Jesus, not υἱὸς θεοῦ but παῖς θεοῦ[3]; this expression has an uncertain value: it suggests at once a reminiscence of the prophecy relating to the 'servant of Jahve,'[4] and, consequently, the translation of παῖς by 'servant'; on the other hand, the *Book of Wisdom* gives to the words παῖς θεοῦ the meaning of 'son of God,'[5] and the phrase has certainly that meaning in the most ancient Christian literature,[6] such as the works of Clement of Alexandria and Athenagoras. It is, then, safer to leave the term in the natural ambiguity which it probably had even for the author of *Acts*,[7] and which it must always have for us, except when the context determines its value.

To sum up, when we consider as a whole the apologetic discourses reported in the book of *Acts*, we find in the foreground faith in Jesus the Messias; but the Messianism thus affirmed is at once more universal and more profound than that of the Jews: what Christ brings is salvation, he alone can give it and he offers it to all. This transcendent rôle of universal Lord and Saviour rests upon his unique relations with God: it is from God that

[1] SANDAY-HEADLAM, *Romans*, 9.

[2] In viii, 37, the words: 'I believe that Jesus Christ is the Son of God,' seem a gloss of the Western text. See MANGENOT, *loc. cit.*, 413.

[3] *Acts* iii, 13, 26; iv, 27, 30.

[4] *Isa.* xlii, 1 *sqq.* Cf. *Matt.* xii, 18.

[5] *Wisd.* ii, 13; cf. ii, 18. DALMAN (*Die Worte Jesu*, 228) notes the significance of this since the *Book of Wisdom* is certainly referring to Isaias' prophecy.

[6] CLEM., LIX, 2, 3; ATHENAG., *Leg.*, 10; CLEM. AL., *Strom.*, VII, 1, 4.

[7] In the same passage, iv, 25–27, the word παῖς is applied to David and then to Jesus, but there is also a quotation from *Ps.* ii, where God calls the Messias his Son.

Jesus has received everything, and he is united to him as no man has ever been, he is his Child, his Son.

This elementary catechesis proposed to non-believers appears with greater richness and brilliancy in the lives of believers. Already before Pentecost, on the day of the election of St. Matthias, the disciples pray to the Lord 'who knows all hearts' and beg him to choose himself an apostle.[1] Here we begin to feel the presence of Jesus in his Church, promised by him to his apostles on the day of farewell[2]; we are in touch with the same mystery in the revelations of Christ to Ananias,[3] to St. Peter,[4] and to St. Paul[5]; these apparitions are not, as those which preceded the Ascension, proofs given to the Apostles of the Resurrection of the Lord. They are interventions of Christ, expressing at decisive moments his instructions to his Church, triumphing over the fears of Ananias, the scruples of Peter, the last hesitations of Paul; he appears as what in fact he is, according to St. Peter's strong expression, 'The Author of Life.'

And, on their side, his believers turn towards him as to their chief always present in their midst, and capable of sustaining them: the long discourse of St. Stephen in the Sanhedrin expresses but a very summary Christology: Jesus is the just man, whose coming was predicted by the prophets; and yet he has scarcely finished speaking when, ravished in spirit, he cries out: 'Behold I see the heavens opened and the Son of man standing on the right hand of God'; he is dragged away and stoned, and at the point of death he prays: 'Lord Jesus, receive my spirit,' and, falling on his knees, cries with a loud voice: 'Lord, lay not this sin to their charge,' and with these words he dies.[6] These prayers are a faithful echo of the last words of Jesus on the cross; St. Stephen implores Christ in the same terms in which Jesus prayed to God; later on, other martyrs will repeat his prayers.[7]

If, at the supreme moment of martyrdom, the Christian instinctively invokes Jesus, it is because this invocation

[1] *Acts* i, 24.

[2] *Matt.* xxviii, 20. [3] *Acts* ix, 10 *sqq.* [4] *Acts* x, 9 *sqq.*; xi, 5 *sqq.*

[5] *Acts* xxii, 18 *sqq.* No mention is made here of Christ's apparition to St. Paul on the road to Damascus (ix, 3 *sqq.*); it has an entirely different character and is much more closely related to the apparitions during the forty days.

[6] *Acts* vii, 55–60. Cf. KLAWEK, *op. cit. infra*, 45–7.

[7] Cf. VON DER GOLTZ, *op. cit. infra*, 131.

has become for him a profound religious habit. We find it also in this short formula, 'Come, Lord,' by which the first Christians implored the return of Christ; this prayer was so familiar to them that we find it in St. Paul, in St. John, and in the *Teaching of the Apostles*, both in the Greek and the Aramaic versions.[1]

By the side of these prayers we find, here and there, fragments of hymns to the honour of Christ; we must no doubt recognise one in these verses of the first *Epistle to Timothy*; 'which was manifested in the flesh, was justified in the spirit, appeared unto angels, hath been preached unto the Gentiles, is believed in the world, is taken up in glory.'[2]

Here again is the echo of a Christian hymn in the *Epistle to the Ephesians*: 'Rise, thou that sleepest, and arise from the dead: and Christ shall enlighten thee.'[3] In the canticles of the Apocalypse we may probably discern certain fragments of liturgical hymns[4]; in any case, we recognise in these songs of heaven the echo of Christian prayers; the four animals and the twenty-four ancients sing to Christ:[5]

> 'Thou art worthy, O Lord, to take the book, and open the seals thereof: because thou wast slain, and hast redeemed us to God, in thy blood, out of every tribe, and tongue, and people, and nation, and hast made us to our God a kingdom and priests, and we shall reign on the earth.'

And the angels reply:

> 'The Lamb that was slain is worthy to receive power, and divinity, and wisdom, and strength, and honour, and glory, and benediction,
>
> 'And every creature which is in heaven, and on the earth, and under the earth, and such as are in the sea, and all that are in them: I heard all saying: To him that sitteth on the throne, and to the Lamb, benediction, and honour, and glory, and power for ever and ever. And the four living creatures said: Amen. And the four-and-twenty ancients fell down on their faces and adored.'

[1] *Apoc.* xxii, 20. [2] 1 *Tim.* iii, 16. [3] *Eph.* v, 14.
[4] Cf. Swete, *Apocalypse*, 80. [5] *Apoc.* v, 9–13.

The reader will surely have noticed, after the two hymns of the ancients and the angels, the doxology which glorifies at the same time 'him who is seated on the throne and the Lamb.' We shall have to come back to this formula, when we are studying the Johannine theology; but it should be pointed out at once that the apostolic epoch has many instances of it; it is, in fact, one of the most interesting features of Christian piety.

The Jews looked upon the doxology as one of the consecrated forms of worship[1]; it consisted in the recognition of the proper attributes of God[2]: 'to him belongs (or; to him be) glory in eternity.'[3] This formula, which was susceptible of much variation or development, was exclusively reserved for the worship of God; we never find in the Old Testament or the apocryphal writings a doxology in honour of Moses, of the Angels, or even of the Messias.

In the New Testament the doxology is more often referred to God the Father[4]; occasionally, however, Christ is mentioned, whether as the Mediator in whom the Father is glorified,[5] or even as he who is glorified,[6] or finally as united in glory with his Father as being with him the object of the same act of worship.[7] These invocations, these hymns, these doxologies are spontaneous and self-revealing evidences of a new faith. The historians who assert that Jesus did but draw to himself the homage up till then lavished on angels and other intermediary beings, cannot show any such cultus equivalent to this, or any such formulas of worship as full of prayer and adoration. In the words of the author of the *Epistle to the Hebrews*: 'To which of the angels hath he said at any time: "Thou art my Son, to-day have I begotten thee?"' We may repeat the same argument and ask those historians[8] who endeavour to explain faith in Christ by

[1] Cf. F. H. Chase, *The Lord's Prayer in the Early Church*, in *TS*, I, 3, pp. 168–76, whence most of these details are taken.

[2] Cf. Chase, 168.

[3] *Pss.* xxvii, 1; xciv, 7; cii, 31; 1 *Par.* xvi, 27; xxix, 11.

[4] *Gal.* i, 4–5; *Rom.* xi, 36; *Phil.* iv, 20; 1 *Tim.* i, 17; vi, 16; 1 *Peter* v, ii; *Apoc.* vii, 12.

[5] *Jude* 25; *Eph.* iii, 21.

[6] 2 *Tim.* iv, 18; 2 *Peter* iii, 18; *Apoc.* i, 6; and possibly *Heb.* xii, 20, 21; 1 *Peter* iv, 11.

[7] *Apoc.* v, 13; cf. vii, 10.

[8] Lueken, *Michael*, 133–66; Cheyne, *Bible Problems*, 213–35.

angelology, where is to be found the devotee of St. Michael, who, when dying for his sake, has said to him: 'Lord, receive my spirit,' or has repeated the doxology: 'Praise, honour, glory, and power to God and Michael for ever and ever'?

An apology would be necessary for insisting on such an obvious transcendence, were it not for the gravity and too-often forgotten nature of the consequences involved. When, in the *Epistle to the Colossians,* or in that to the Hebrews, the Apostle shews how far above the angels Christ is raised, certain critics see in the statement nothing but a theological effort stimulated and provoked by rival speculations.[1] This interpretation is wholly incorrect, as the Trinitarian theology of St. Paul will force us to recognise; but no statement will be more effective than the simple fact emerging from what has been said and forcing itself on our judgement; that, if theology reached so high a point, it was not through a rivalry of the school, but because it could not fail to do so without betraying its faith. It was not the religious genius of St. Paul which led his unconscious disciples to a dogmatic novelty; it was Christ and his Spirit who revealed this mystery to the humblest of Christians as well as to the greatest of Apostles.

It should be noted that this new faith does not corrupt but consummates the ancient faith; Jesus does not separate the Christian from God, he unites them. The Colossian heretics opposed by St. Paul parade their humility and turn the worship of their disciples away from God to the angels. Palestinian and Alexandrian Judaism of this period present many examples of this perverse humility, and its tendency to withdraw attention from the divine transcendence. There is nothing like this in the religion of the infant Church, never has prayer been more confiding and filial, or union with God closer; Christ is not an intermediary who intervenes between and separates the terms of his mediation; through him they grow nearer to each other.

Nor is there anything in early Christian devotion to suggest the dualism of Marcion or the Monarchianism of Praxeas: Jesus does not oppose the God of the Old Testament or take his place; no one can question the mono-

[1] Lueken, *loc. cit.*, 133 *sq.*, esp. 136.

theism of the first Christians, and yet they feel no scruple in using the same terms and formulas of prayer in imploring and glorifying God the Father and Jesus Christ.

We should not, however, conclude from this that the Father and the Son have an identical title as the object of Christian worship. It has been noted above that doxologies in honour of the Father occur most frequently; it is the same with hymns[1] and more particularly prayers, which are more often addressed to the Father than to the Son.[2] And, which is much more important, the entire religion supposes relations of dependence of the Son or the Father, which are never transposed; it is by the Son and in the Son that the early Church prays to the Father, praises and glorifies him.

If with these formularies of prayer or doxology we compare the formulas of greeting with which St. Paul begins his *Epistles,* we shall find that the Father and the Son are most frequently united as a single source of grace[3]; the other Apostles, when they do not omit any greeting, usually content themselves with a word to their correspondents wishing them grace or peace. Even so, their Epistles are usually opened by a mention or an invocation of God and Christ: 'James, servant of God and of our Lord Jesus Christ . . .'[4] 'Grace to you and peace be accomplished in the knowledge of God, and of Christ Jesus our Lord.'[5] 'Our fellowship may be with the Father and with his Son Jesus Christ.'[6] 'Grace be with you, mercy, and peace from God the Father, and from Christ Jesus the Son of the Father.'[7] 'Jude the servant of Jesus Christ, and brother of James: to them that are beloved in God the Father, and preserved in Jesus Christ.'[8] In one instance even, the Spirit is joined with God the Father and Jesus Christ: 'Peter, an apostle of Jesus Christ, to the strangers . . . according to the foreknowledge of God the Father, unto the sanctification of the Spirit, unto obedience and sprinkling of the blood of Jesus Christ.'[9]

This union of God and of Christ, met with, as it is, in

[1] E.g., in *Apoc.*: iv, 8, 11; xi, 17, 18; xv, 3, 4; xix, 1, 2; 6, 8.
[2] Cf. VON DER GOLTZ, *Das Gebet*, 89–93, 124–7; KLAWEK, 51 *sq.*
[3] See below, page 291 *sq.* [4] *James* i, 1. [5] 2 *Peter* i, 2.
[6] 1 *John* i, 3. [7] 2 *John* 3. [8] *Jude* i, 1. [9] 1 *Peter* i, 2.

writings so different in other ways, does not appear as the personal conception of an individual theologian, but as the spontaneous and natural expression of the common faith. Sanday, speaking of the similar formula at the beginning of the first *Epistle to the Thessalonians,* wrote : 'What is most remarkable in these words is that the glorified Jesus is thus united to "God the Father." Let us consider what signification this had for a strictly monotheistic Jew ; and yet St. Paul evidently presents this association, not as a tentative suggestion, but as a fundamental axiom of the faith' (art. 'Jesus Christ,' *D.B.*, ii, 648b). The case is the same with the other apostles ; not one of them in speaking thus of God the Father and Jesus Christ, as of the unique centre of the Christian religion, gives us the impression of introducing a theological novelty, or even of a growth in doctrine ; the formula is quite simple, I would almost say commonplace, as if merely expressing a faith received by all, and this is what makes it so valuable to us.

This common faith is also expressed in the titles habitually given to Jesus, and, above all, in the title of Lord, which has become, as it were, his own name. The use of the title of Κύριος, *Lord,* in speaking of Jesus is one of the most revealing elements of the Christian faith, but also one of those which call for most careful study, and the most obscured by controversy.

We need not here go through the history of these discussions ; it will, however, be useful to outline the thesis of Bousset.[1] A whole system has been elaborated, transitory no doubt, but specious, in order to explain the origin of faith in the Lord Jesus. This system has been widely adopted, and its sphere of influence is far wider than the circle of the immediate disciples and readers of Bousset.

'It is a marvellous spectacle, and a strangely rapid evolution,' writes Bousset (p. 77), speaking of primitive Christology ; 'the veils and garments with which Jesus was first covered have been quickly removed, and new ones are woven for him.' The community of Jerusalem had exalted him as the Son of man, whose triumphal return it was awaiting. When Christianity reached a Hellenic environment this eschatological hope found no

[1] *Kyrios Christos* ; see Bibliography of this Section.

echo there, and the title of Son of man was not understood. We note its disappearance from Christian language at the very time that the title of *Kyrios* becomes predominant: it is rarely used by St. Matthew, St. Mark, or St. John; it is more frequent in the third Gospel and in certain parts of *Acts*[1]; St. Paul makes constant use of it. Whence came this usage? It has been sought in vain, says Bousset, to explain it by the habit, which the first disciples would have had in saluting Jesus as 'Master' (Maran or Rabbi).

The origin of the term has also vainly been sought in the religious language of the Jews; the name of 'Lord' was given to God by the Hellenic, but not by the Palestinian Jews. These solutions being set aside, only one remains; it was not in Palestine, in Galilee, or Jerusalem that this title of Lord was first given to Jesus, but in the Hellenistic communities; probably at Antioch or perhaps at Damascus or Tarsus. St. Paul did not invent it; he received it from the spontaneous faith of the Hellenists amongst whom he was initiated into Christianity. And if we ask whence these Christians had derived this usage, the reply is simple; it comes from the Pagan cults of Syria and Egypt. The title of Kyrios or Kyria was given by Orientals to their gods, particularly during the celebration of the mysteries; the Egyptians apply this title to Isis, Osiris, and Serapis; the Syrians to the Syrian goddess; the Gnostics shortly adopted this usage; the Simonians called Simon *Kyrios*, and Helen *Kyria*. In a word, the title of Lord was given to the god who was the principal object of worship, and to him alone. Now Christianity, we are told, grew up in such an atmosphere at Antioch; all the worship was concentrated on Jesus, he was spontaneously called Lord; but this growth of Christian faith had incalculable consequences. In the language of the Septuagint, the Lord was Jahve; the divine title brought with it and referred to Jesus all the oracles of the prophets, in fact the whole religion of Israel; while at the same time it concentrated the whole faith of the new Christians on him as the unique source of salvation.[2]

This brief sketch gives a sufficiently clear idea of the

[1] See Bousset, *Der Gebrauch des Kyriostitels . . .*, in Bibliography below.
[2] Cf. *Kyrios Christos*, 75–104.

way in which Bousset imagines the faith in the 'Lord' Jesus to have developed in primitive times, and, without going further, objections arise on all sides, and they are decisive.[1] The first that occurs is the formula *Maranatha* : it is certainly not of Hellenistic origin, and as certainly primitive: it is to be found in St. Paul, in the Apocalypse, in the *Didache Apostolorum* ; and it proves that from the very first the Palestinian community also gave Jesus the title of Lord.[2] It would indeed be a strange piece of irony to maintain, in the face of this formula expressing in Aramaic the desire of the Church for the coming of the Lord, that faith in the 'Lord' Jesus was foreign to Palestine and incompatible with eschatological hopes. A still graver difficulty, if we adopt Bousset's hypothesis, is to explain the part played by St. Paul and Christian Hellenism in the primitive Church: how is it conceivable that such a religious transformation should have escaped the notice of the Jerusalem community, so watchful, and, in the case of many of its members, so suspicious: or how can we suppose that this new faith, so suspect in its origin and tending to supplant the Christianity of the first Apostles, should have encountered no opposition from them or their disciples? How could the people who journeyed from Jerusalem to Antioch to spy on Paul and his Church, have accepted without protest so radical a revolution? And, then, where is this supposed Hellenistic Christianity to be found, anterior to St. Paul and exercising so decisive an influence on him?[3] And when we have made up our minds to accept all these impossibilities, we come up against the collective testimony rendered to her Lord by the Church in all the books of the New Testament. We shall collect this accumulated witness and note the application to Christ of numerous Biblical texts in which, as in the 'Lord' of the *Psalms* or the Prophetical books, the Church recognises Jesus. This recognition is not peculiar to St. Paul, we can trace it in the whole New Testament from the Synoptics to the Apocalypse. We will put aside this improbable and sterile hypothesis which can neither stand up under a study of the texts, nor explain the facts, as it claims to do.

[1] See Huby, *Rech. de Sc. Relig.*, 1914, 554–80.
[2] See Bousset, *Jesus der Herr*, 22.
[3] Cf. E. Meyer, *Ursprung des Christentums*, III, 218, n. 1.

The controversy will, at least, have had the advantage of obliging us to study more closely the theological language of the first Christians and the Pagan or Jewish environment in which Christianity first appeared.[1]

Two questions must be considered in succession: the meaning of the word 'Lord'; and how it came to be used by Christians.

The word 'Lord' and its Greek, Latin, and Aramaic equivalents, Kyrios, Dominus, and Mari,[2] is often used merely as a formula of politeness: a man of the people greets an educated person as 'Mari,' the ordinary greeting of the educated classes[3]; sometimes in these formulas of politeness 'Rabbi' is joined to 'Mari': 'Master and Lord.'[4] Latins salute each other in the same sense of the word, saying: 'Domine,'[5] and Greeks by saying 'Kyrie.'[6] Determined by a genitive limiting its scope, the word may mean the master of a slave, the possessor of a piece of land or a beast of burden; the word is frequently used in this connection in the Gospel,[7] as in the current language of the period.

This title of 'Lord' is also given by subjects to their King; examples of this abound; L. Cerfaux has collected a large number in Biblical texts and in literary and epigraphical documents of Palestine and Syria.[8] And just as in Aramaic, the King is called Marana, 'our Lord,' the Herods are called in Greek κύριοι.[9] The same usage obtains in Egypt and, later, in Rome. The title does not necessarily connote a religious meaning; in itself it merely expresses the domination of the King over his subjects, like that of the master over his slaves.[10] But at this time when the royal power was exalted to divinity, the title which gave it its supreme consecration was equivalent to apotheosis. This is clearly stated by Tertullian:

> 'Augustus, the maker of the Empire, would not permit himself to be called Lord, for this is the name of

[1] See Dalman, *Gottesname Adonaj*, 81–4; *Worte Jesu*, 266–72.
[2] See Dalman, *Worte Jesu*, 268.
[3] Cf. Dalman, *ibid.*, 267.
[4] Dalman, *ibid.*; Strack-Billerbeck, I, 526.
[5] Cf. L. Friedlaender, *op. cit. infra*, 442–50.
[6] Cf. Moulton-Milligan, 365a.
[7] *Matt.* x, 24; *Luke* xii, 46; xix, 33; *Matt.* xx, 8, etc.
[8] Cerfaux, art. *Le titre Kyrios* (see Bibliography below), p. 44 *sqq.*
[9] Cerfaux, 59.
[10] Cf. Pollack, art. *Dominus*, in Pauly-Wissowa, *Real-Encyclopädie.*

a god. I will willingly call the Emperor Lord, as the term is used in daily language, but without being forced, as if I should call him Lord in the place of God. I am free of his dominion, for one only is my Lord, the Almighty and eternal God, who is also his Lord.'[1]

This text gives clearly the different meanings of the word 'Dominus': one belongs to the common speech of every day and has no particular significance; no Christian need scruple to give the Emperor the title in that sense; the other is an official and sacred name, which it is proposed to impose by coercion, giving it a strictly divine meaning; in this sense 'the Lord' is the name of God. And from this comes the conflict, to which we shall shortly refer, between the cultus of the Emperor and that of the Lord Jesus. A further confirmation of Tertullian's view is to be found in the claims of the Emperors themselves: after Augustus and Tiberius, who had rejected the title of Dominus, came Caius and Domitian, who exacted it, at the same time claiming divine honours.[2]

Moreover, this title of Lord was always given, not only to kings, but also to gods, at least in the East, where the relations of the god and his believers were conceived as the relations of master and servant. The god is represented as the sovereign master of a territory, and of the nation inhabiting it[3]; he may be the Baal of Tyre or of Sidon, or of Tarsus, or of Hermon, or of Libanus[4]; sometimes the horizon is wider, and his domain will be no longer a province but the entire heaven; he is then the Baal of the heavens, Baal Chamem.[5] The Egyptian divinities are also conceived as ruling the elements.[6] When these gods of Syria or Egypt invade the Hellenic world they keep their own character; they are Lords. The god of Gaza has no other name; he is called Marnas 'Our Lord.'[7] Most of them add to their name this title: thus we find the Lord Serapis,[8] the Lord Osiris, the Lady Isis,

[1] *Apol.*, 34.
[2] Cf. POLLACK, *loc. cit.*, col. 1307; IDRIS BELL, *op. cit. infra.*
[3] Cf. LAGRANGE, *Religions semitiques*, 83–4.
[4] Cf. MEYER, art. *Baal*, in *Lexikon* of ROSCHER, I, col. 2867 *sqq.*
[5] Cf. LAGRANGE, 93.
[6] See APULEIUS, *Metam.*, XI, 1.
[7] Cf. SCHIRMER, art. *Marnas*, in ROSCHER, II, 2378 *sqq.*; BAETHGEN, *Beitrage zur semit. Religionsgesch.*, 65 *sq.*
[8] See the *Oxyrhynchus Papyrus*, I, 110, 2.

etc.[1] When Isis appears to Lucius in Apuleius' novel, she tells him that the peoples of the earth honour her everywhere under a thousand different names, but that her true name is 'Queen Isis.'[2]

With this religious terminology, a novelty for the Græco-Roman world, these Oriental cults introduced into Hellenist Paganism new sentiments of complete devotion to the god: body and soul are consecrated to his worship blindly, frantically, and madly, as in the case of the Galli, who sacrificed their virility to the Great Mother, or to the Syrian Goddess. The lamentable folly made the Pagans themselves ashamed, but it would not have been so widespread, or have made so many victims, had it not presented souls with the allurement of a form of divine worship involving the complete sacrifice of self. The Fathers of the Church were disposed to see in the Pagan mysteries diabolical travesties of Christian worship; this religious aspiration, this need of self-donation to and adoption by God, is a most noble instinct, which God himself has placed in the depths of our hearts. The devil has abused it shamefully, but at last Christ has come and called souls, they have given themselves to him, and he has taken hold of them.

This sovereign dominion of Christ is what is meant by his title of Lord. Jesus himself hints at this with prudence and reserve in the evangelical texts, in the parables where he presents his return as that of the Master whose servants await him[3]; and do we not hear an echo of this teaching in the invocation so dear to the Apostolic Church 'Maranatha'? He also expresses this in those more explicit words in which he claims, in relation to his disciples, the rôle and the rights of a Master. Indeed, during his life Jesus was usually called Master[4] and Lord[5] by his disciples, and he himself consecrated by his approval the employment of these terms.[6] In the Gospel narratives, as

[1] Drexler, art. *Kyrios*, in Roscher, II, 1756–69. See Dumont, *op. cit. infra*, 181.

[2] *Metamorph.*, XI, 1.

[3] *Matt.* xxii, 42–51, xxv, 14–30; *Mark* xiii, 33–7; *Luke* xii, 35–46, xiii, 25–28.

[4] *Mark* ix, 5; xi, 21; xiv, 45.

[5] Cf. 1 *Cor.* xvi, 22; *Didache*, x, 6; Dalman, *Adonaj*, 81. Our Saviour was also called 'Rabboni': *Mark* x, 51; *John*, xx, 16; on this name see Dalman, *Worte Jesu*, 267.

[6] *Matt.* x, 24–26, cf. *Luke* vi, 40; *Mark* xi, 3, cf. *Matt.* xxi, 3, *Luke* xix, 31; *Matt.* xxvi, 18, cf. *Luke* xxii, 11.

they are to be read in *St. Mark* and *St. Matthew,* Jesus is very rarely called ' the Lord '[1]; in *St. Luke,* on the contrary, and *St. John* this title is often given him; the angel announces his birth to the shepherds: ' This day is born to you a Saviour, who is Christ the Lord,'[2] and the evangelist himself reporting the actions or the words of Christ, often says: ' The Lord saw . . .' ' The Lord chose . . .,' ' The Lord said . . .'[3]; in *St. John* it is principally after Jesus' Resurrection that the title is given him.[4] Is not this what he had himself predicted: ' And I, if I be lifted up from the earth, will draw all things to myself ' ?[5] And was it not the subject of Peter's earliest discourse in the *Acts* on the day of Pentecost: ' Let all the house of Israel know most certainly that God hath made both Lord, and Christ, this same Jesus, whom you have crucified ' ?[6] And to quote St. Paul: ' He humbled himself, becoming obedient unto death: even to the death of the cross. For which cause God also hath exalted him, and hath given him a name which is above all names: that in the name of Jesus every knee should bow of those that are in heaven, on earth, and under the earth: and every tongue should confess that the Lord Jesus Christ is in the glory of God the Father.'[7]

In these texts the title of Lord no longer expresses merely respect or even veneration; it is used as a definitely theological term, reserved to Christ, as to God his Father.[8] We should note also in the above-quoted passage of the *Epistle to the Philippians* how St. Paul, in order to describe the glory of Jesus, repeats and applies to him what Isaias said of Jahve: ' Every knee shall bow before him, and every tongue shall confess him.'[9] Similar applications occur all through the entire New Testament, and nothing reveals more clearly to us the faith of the first Christians in the Lord Jesus. Thus St. Mark had already

[1] It is probable that, in the prophecy *Isaias,* xl, 3, quoted in *Mark* i, 3 (cf. *Matt.* iii, 3, *Luke* iii, 4, *John* i, 23), the word *Kyrios* refers to Christ. In *Matt.* xxviii, 6, the words ' the Lord ' are considered by the editors to be a Western gloss. In the final verses of *Mark* (xvi, 19, 20), these words occur twice.

[2] *Luke* ii, 11; cf. *Lamentations* iv, 20; Dalman, *Adonaj,* 82.

[3] *Luke* vii, 13; x, 1, 39, 41; xi, 39; xii, 42; xiii, 15; xvii, 5, 6; xviii, 6; xix, 8, 34; xxii, 61; xxiv, 3, 34.

[4] xx, 2, 13, 18, 20, 25; xxi, 7, 12. Before the Resurrection: iv, 1; vi. 23; xi, 2.

[5] *John* xii, 32.

[6] *Acts* ii, 36.

[7] *Phil.* ii, 8–11.

[8] Cf. Dalman, *Adonaj,* 73.

[9] *Isa.* xlv, 24.

interpreted Isaias: 'A voice of one crying in the desert: prepare ye the way of the Lord.'[1] St. Peter understands in the same way the words in the thirty-third *Psalm*: 'O taste and see that the Lord is sweet,'[2] and the text of *Isaias* (viii, 12, 13): 'Do not fear (those who persecute us), but honour the Lord, the Christ.'[3] St. Paul still more frequently applies the term in this way: 'Whosoever shall call upon the name of the Lord shall be saved,'[4] he writes to the Romans, applying to Christ the classical text of *Joel* (iii, 5); equally in the first *Epistle to the Corinthians* (ii, 16), he says: 'Who hath known the mind of the Lord, that he may instruct him?[5] But we have the mind of Christ.' And further on (x, 9), recalling the infidelity of the Jews in the desert, mentioned in the *Psalm* (xciv, 8): 'Neither let us tempt Christ, as some of them tempted,' and (x, 21), repeating a text of Malachias (i, 7, 12): 'You cannot drink the chalice of the Lord and the chalice of devils.' It is again to Christ that the *Epistle to the Hebrews* (i, 10) applies *Psalm* ci, 26-27: 'In the beginning, O Lord, thou foundedst the earth: and the heavens are the works of thy hands; they shall perish, but thou remainest . . .'

These quotations and other similar ones which could be added to them[6] are, for the most part, merely allusions, and not definite interpretations; it would therefore be to force their meaning to seek to determine by them the significance of the prophetical texts. But what we should not fail to see in them is the meaning which the title of Lord, when given to Christ, had for the Christians of that day. It certainly had the value of a divine name, inasmuch as, when it occurs, employed in that sense by the prophets, it could be understood indifferently of God the Father or of Jesus Christ.

The same value appears as manifestly in the characteristic and traditional phrases, which in the New Testament are applied sometimes to God the Father, sometimes to Christ, as in the case of the 'invocation of the name of the Lord.'[7] In the Old Testament and in the

[1] *Mark* i, 2–3 unites the texts *Mal.* iii, 1 and *Isai.* xl, 3.

[2] 1 *Pet.* ii, 3. [3] *Ibid.*. iii, 14–15. [4] x, 13. [5] *Isai.* xl, 13.

[6] Cf. Lightfoot, *op. cit. infra*, 102.

[7] Cf. Zahn, *Skizzen*, 276; Seeberg, *op. cit. infra*, 41; von der Goltz, *Das Gebet*, 100, 128; esp. Klawek, *Das Gebet*, 39 *sqq.* (see Bibliography at end of this Section).

apocryphal books, this expression is constantly used to signify the worship of Jahve; those who invoke the name of the Lord are those who belong to him, who fear and adore him.[1] Christians have preserved the use of this formula; they apply it sometimes to the Father,[2] and much more often to Jesus Christ; when St. Paul comes to Damascus his task is to imprison those who invoke the name of Jesus[3]; Ananias, sent him by Christ, heals him and says to him: 'Why dost thou delay? Arise, receive baptism, and be purified of thy sins, invoking the name of Jesus.' At the beginning of his first *Epistle to the Corinthians* (i, 2-3) St. Paul greets 'the Church of God that is at Corinth, to them that are sanctified in Christ Jesus, called to be saints, with all that invoke the name of our Lord Jesus Christ.' Writing later to Timothy, he recommends him to keep peace with 'all those who with a pure heart invoke the Lord.'[4]

It would no doubt be extreme to attribute everywhere to this formula the technical sense of adoration of Christ[5]; it may signify confession, prayer, or various forms of worship; but it cannot be doubted that it has preserved in the New Testament all the religious value that it possessed in the Old, and has the same significance when applied to God the Father or to Jesus. The phrase of *Joel*: 'Whoever shall invoke the name of the Lord shall be saved,' has lost nothing of its force either in the book of the *Acts*,[6] where St. Peter applies it to God, or in the *Epistle to the Romans*,[7] where St. Paul applies it to Christ.

The same remarks should be made about the 'fear of the Lord,'[8] 'the grace of the Lord,'[9] 'faith in the Lord,'[10] 'conversion to the Lord,'[11] 'the service of the Lord,'[12] 'the preaching,' or 'the word of the Lord,'[13] the 'way of the Lord,'[14] 'the will of the Lord.'[15] All those expressions can be referred sometimes to the Father, sometimes to the Son; sometimes it will be impossible to discern which

[1] Cf. *Gen.* xiii, 4; xxi, 33, xxvi, 25; *Deut.* xxxii, 3; 3 *Kings* xviii, 24; *Pss.* lxxviii, 6; lxxix, 18; civ, 1; *Is.* lxiv, 6; *Jer.* x, 25; *Lam.* iii, 55; *Soph.* iii, 9; *Zach.* xiii, 9; *Joel* ii, 32; etc.

[2] *Acts* ii, 21. [3] *Acts* ix, 14, 21. [4] 2 *Tim.* ii, 22.

[5] A point which VON DER GOLTZ has confirmed, as against ZAHN and SEEBERG.

[6] ii, 21. [7] x, 13. [8] *Acts* ix, 31. [9] *Acts* xiv, 3. [10] *Acts* iv, 14.

[11] *Acts* ix, 35. [12] *Acts* xiii, 2. [13] *Acts* viii, 25; xiii, 12.

[14] *Acts* xiii, 10. [15] *Acts* xxi, 14.

interpretation is more probable, the sacred writer having left the question open.

These habits of language are very significant; they show us very clearly that, in all the theses presented by the Christian religion from the very first days, there was something new and something traditional; the belief in Christ, the worship of Christ appear in the foreground, and yet the ancient faith in Jahve is not supplanted by this new belief, nor is it transformed into it, nor placed side by side with it; Christian worship is not addressed to two Gods or to two Lords, and yet it is offered, with the same confidence and the same love to Jesus and his Father. The words of Christ, reported by St. John, will help us to interpret this attitude, and, inversely, this Christian life, the better it is known, will the better frame the words of St. John and confirm their historic value. 'You believe in God, believe also in me'; 'he who sees me, sees my Father'; 'eternal life is to know thee, who art the one true God, and him who thou hast sent, Jesus Christ.' Are not these words the whole programme of the Christian religion, as manifested in the *Acts* and in the *Epistles*?

All these manifestations are certain proofs of the faith of the Church in the divinity of Christ; but, if they are to be rightly understood, it should be noted that that divinity never appears as independent or even as distinct from that of the Father; this is so much the case that certain historians fail to recognise in these words a Trinitarian faith; 'Jesus and the Apostles,' they say, 'are just as rigorously monotheistic as Moses and the Prophets'[1]; nothing is more true, but, far from menacing the Monotheistic faith, belief in the Trinity guarantees it; the great theologians of the fourth century love to develop this truth, and show it in its full light; from the apostolic days facts demonstrate it; it will be enough to recall the divinity of Christ to the Judaizing Christians of Laodicea and Colossae, tempted by the worship of angels and intermediary beings, in order to restore their monotheism to its vigour and firmness; similarly, in order to put the Corinthians on their guard against idolatry and polytheism, St. Paul will repeat to them that 'to us there is but one God, the Father, of whom are all things, and

[1] E. Ménégoz, *Étude sur le dogme de la Trinité* (Paris, 1898), 12.

we unto him: and one Lord Jesus Christ, by whom are all things, and we by him.'[1]

More clearly than any other, this text tells us of St. Paul's way of speaking; the two terms of θεός and κύριος are to him equally divine names, which cannot, without blasphemy, be given to men; they have, moreover, become personal names, indicating respectively the Father and the Son. This will remain the usage of the Church, who will repeat in her creeds: 'I believe in one God, the Father Almighty . . . and in one Lord, Jesus Christ . . .'[2] This definite attribution was not the work of a single day or of a single man; it had already been prepared in Jewish circles by the disuse into which the name of Jahve had fallen,[3] and by the differentiation of the two divine names Elohim and Adonai, θεός and κύριος.[4] This usage, however, was never so exclusive that the name of Lord was not sometimes given to the Father, and the name of God to the Son.[5] In St. Paul, the Father is very rarely the Lord,[6] just as the Christ is very rarely called God. Nevertheless, in his discourse at Miletus, St. Paul exhorts the presbyters to 'rule the Church of God which he hath purchased with his own blood'[7]; writing to the Romans, he reminds them that from the Jews issued, according to the flesh, Christ 'who is over all things, God blessed for ever'[8]; to Titus he represents Christians as 'looking for the blessed hope and coming of the glory of the great God and our Saviour Jesus Christ.'[9] Similarly St. Peter exalts the justice 'of our God and Saviour Jesus Christ,'[10] and, as we know, the Gospel of *St. John* opens and closes on a profession of faith in the divinity of Jesus, 'the Word was God' (i, 1); 'my Lord and my God' (xx, 28).

These texts have certainly great value,[11] they confirm what the study of the Christian faith has already shewn us; but I do not think they add anything to it. It should also be noted, that they only yield all their significance and become definitely fixed in their strictly theological sense by the documents in which they occur, and, more

[1] 1 *Cor.* viii, 6.
[2] Cf. Kattenbusch, *Das Apostol. Symbol*, 515–22, 596–616.
[3] See Dalman, *Adonaj*, 36.
[4] See above, pages 115, 153.
[5] Cf. Foerster, *Herr ist Jesus*, 79.
[6] 1 *Cor.* iii, 5; cf. vii, 17.
[7] *Acts* xx, 28.
[8] *Rom.* ix, 5.
[9] *Titus* ii, 13.
[10] 2 *Peter* i, 1.
[11] Cf. C. Guignebert, *Modernisme et tradition catholique en France* (Paris, 1908), 118.

generally speaking, by the Christian faith expressed by them, which is known from other sources. Many historians are inclined to recall the apotheoses then so constantly occurring,[1] the names of God and Saviour applied to living and dead emperors; they remark the similarity of these titles with those given to Christ, principally in the pastoral epistles and in the second *Epistle of Peter*.[2] No one, no doubt, suggests that the worship of Christ was inspired by the same sentiments of flattery and adulation as the worship of the emperors; but it is thought that the attachment and enthusiasm of the disciples made a God of Jesus more easily in this environment, in which divine honours and titles so freely circulated.

In criticism of this theory we should note the Christians, like the Jews from whom they came, have always felt horror for these apotheoses. Already in the *Apocalypse* the worship of Augustus appears as the great enemy; the temple of Rome and of Augustus at Pergamum is the throne of Satan, and Antipas, in the same town, preferred martyrdom to blasphemy[3] while, for the next three centuries, it was the worship of Cæsar which was to be the greatest obstacle to the Christian faith and was to make most of the martyrs.[4] This bigotry, as they thought it, was always unintelligible to the Pagans. The irenarch Herod will say one day to Polycarp, 'What harm is there in saying Cæsar is Lord?'[5] He did not understand the Christian faith, nor the significance of the simple phrase, in which St. Paul summarised it, 'Jesus is the Lord.'

Kurios Kaisar, Kurios Iesous, are two formulas apparently identical, to which superficial historians may give the same value; in reality they have nothing in common but the words; those who say: *Kurios Kaisar,* open wide their pantheon; they are ready to place in their family chapel, Christ by the side of Orpheus, Abraham and Apollonius of Tyana,[6] and to offer to all these deities their incense and careless adoration. The Christian has given his faith to Christ and cannot share it with other objects. 'Hear,

[1] See above, pages 16–23.

[2] Cf. WENDLAND, *loc. cit.*, 349; H. LIETZMANN, *Der Weltheiland*, 56–9; E. MEYER, *Ursprung des Christentums*, III, 390–7.

[3] *Apoc.* ii, 13. Cf. M. GOGUEL, *Les chrétiens et l'empire romain à l'époque du N.T.* (Paris, 1908), 30.

[4] Cf. BEURLIER, *Le culte impérial*, 271–81.

[5] *Martyr. Polyc.*, 8.

[6] Alexander Severus did this (LAMPRIDIUS, 29).

O Israel, the Lord thy God is one Lord'; this text is for him, as for Moses, as for Jesus, the first of the commandments; and he binds himself more strictly to it by repeating St. Paul's words: 'For us there is but one God, the Father; and but one Lord Jesus Christ.'

BIBLIOGRAPHY, Section 1:—A. Klawek, *Das Gebet zu Jesus* (Munster, 1921). E. von der Goltz, *Das Gebet in der ältesten Christenheit* (Leipzig, 1901). W. Bousset, *Kyrios Christos* (Gottingen, 1st ed., 1913; 2nd ed., 1921); *Jesus der Herr* (Gottingen, 1916); *Der Gebrauch des Kyriostitels . . .* (etc.), in *Zeitschr. f. N.T.W.*, 1914, 141–62. W. Heitmueller, *Zum Problem Paulus und Jesus*, in *Zeitschrift f. N.T.W.*, 1913, 320–37. Boehlig. *Die Geisteskultur von Tarsus* (Göttingen, 1913); *Zum Begriff Kyrios bei Paulus*, in *Zeitschrift f. N.T.W.*, 1913, 23–37. W. Foerster, *Herr ist Jesus* (Gutersloh, 1924). S. Herner, *Die Anwendung des Wortes Κύριος im N.T.* (Lund, 1903). A. Seeberg, *Die Anbetung des 'Herrn' bei Paulus* (Dorpat, 1891). W. Drexler, art. *Kyrios* in the *Lexicon* of Roscher. L. Cerfaux, *Le titre Kyrios et la dignité royale de Jésus*, in *Revue des Sc. Phil. et Théol.*, XI (1922), 40–71. L. Friedlaender, *Ueber den Gebrauch der Anrede Domine im gemeinen Leben*, in *Darstellungen aus der Sittengeschichte Roms in der Zeit von August bis zum Ausgang der Antonine* (Leipzig, 1886). H. Idris Bell, *Jews and Christians in Egypt* (London, 1924). Dumont, *Inscriptions et monuments figurés de la Thrace*, in *Archives des missions scientif. et littér.*, 1st series t. III (1876). J. B. Lightfoot, *Notes on the Epistles of St. Paul* (London, 1904)

2. *The Holy Spirit*

The study which we have just made of Christianity at its birth, and of its worship, has shewn us the intimate union of God the Father and Jesus Christ in prayers, doxologies, hymns, and, generally, in the various expressions of the Christian faith and religion. The Holy Spirit is very rarely associated with them[1]; nowhere do we find prayers addressed to him, or hymns composed in his honour. And yet in this history of our religious origins, the belief in the Holy Spirit appears as one of the most characteristic and profound features of the Christian faith; all the narratives in *Acts*[2] are full of it, and this book has been called the Gospel of the Holy Spirit. For as the four Gospels relate to us the life of Christ and his mission here below, so this fifth Gospel tells us of the life and action of the Holy Spirit in the Church and by the Church. It opens with the promises of Our Lord, assuring the apostles that they will receive

[1] Twice in salutation: 2 *Cor.* xiii, 13; 1 *Peter* i, 2.

[2] The Catholic Epistles do not come under discussion here, as the doctrine of the Holy Spirit is very slightly developed there, and apart from 1 *Peter* i, 2 there are only brief references; cf. 1 *Peter* i, 11; i, 12; iv, 14; 2 *Peter* i, 21; *Jude* 20.

the power of the Spirit, which will descend on them; from the second chapter we see these promises being realised on the day of Pentecost, and, from that day forward, the manifestations of the Spirit are multiplied, transforming souls and enlivening the Church. This is truly the outpouring promised in Messianic days; St. Peter, indeed, recalls to the Jews the prophecy of Joel: 'In the last days (saith the Lord) I will pour out of my Spirit upon all flesh' (*Acts* ii, 17).

The doctrine which appears in the light of these facts is, in many points, the doctrine already expressed in the Prophetic or Sapiential books[1]; the Spirit[2] is poured forth on men,[3] it enters them,[4] it falls on them,[5] it seizes and transports them.[6] More often it is recorded as a gift[7] accorded by God, and received by men[8]; it is a principle of sanctification, it fills those who possess it[9]; sometimes, in order to express the virtues it produces in the soul, it is said that the soul is full of the Holy Spirit and of wisdom (vi, 3, 10), faith (vi, 5; xi, 24), and joy (xiii, 52).

Side by side with all these texts, in which the Spirit is represented as an impersonal force, are others which manifest it as a person; we found this double aspect in the doctrine of the *Book of Wisdom*[10]; it reappears here, but more clearly, and the person of the Holy Spirit is more living in the Book of the *Acts* than in that of *Wisdom,* the Alexandrine book. Behind the prophets of old we perceive the Holy Spirit predicting 'by the mouth of David . . . ,'[11] 'speaking by Isaias . . .'[12] In the book of *Acts* the Holy Spirit above all speaks, acts, leads the Church; he is the hidden but principal actor of the whole drama. When Ananias and Saphira tried to deceive the apostles, they are tempting the Spirit,[13] it is to him that they lie (v, 3). On the road to Gaza the Holy Spirit says to Philip: 'approach and enter this chariot'[14]; it is he who, at Joppa, says to Peter: 'Behold, three men seek thee; arise, therefore, get thee down and go with them.'[15] A little later the apostles and ancients at

[1] Cf. BÜCHSEL, *Der Geist Gottes im Neuen Testament* (Gütersloh, 1926).

[2] In *Acts*, the Holy Spirit is usually so called, or merely 'the Spirit'; in v, 9 and viii, 39, 'the Spirit of the Lord'; in xvi, 7, 'the Spirit of Jesus.'

[3] *Acts* ii, 17–18 (*Joel* iii, 1), 33; x, 45. [4] i, 8; xix, 6. [5] x, 44; xi, 15.
[6] viii, 39. [7] ii, 38. [8] xv, 8; viii, 15, 17, 19; x, 47; xix, 6.
[9] ii, 4; iv, 8, 31; ix, 17; xiii, 9, 52. [10] ix, 2. [11] *Acts* i, 16.
[12] xxviii, 25. [13] v, 9. [14] viii, 29. [15] x, 19.

Jerusalem formulate their decree in these words: 'It hath seemed good to the Holy Ghost and to us . . .'[1]

In the narrative of the mission of St. Paul, the rôle of the Holy Spirit is no less personal; 'as [the faithful of Antioch] were fasting, the Holy Ghost said to them: "Separate me Saul and Barnabas for the work whereunto I have taken them"; then they, fasting and praying, and imposing their hands upon them sent them away. So they being sent by the Holy Ghost went to Seleucia . . .'[2] Later, as Paul and Silas 'passed through Phrygia and the country of Galatia, they were forbidden by the Holy Ghost to preach the word in Asia. And when they were come into Mysia they attempted to go into Bithynia, and the Spirit of Jesus suffered them not.'[3]

Still later, when St. Paul returns to Jerusalem, in spite of the warnings and supplications of his brethren, he says to them at Miletus; 'I go to Jerusalem: not knowing the things which shall befall me there: save that the Holy Ghost in every city witnesseth to me, saying: That bands and afflictions wait for me at Jerusalem,'[4] and in the rest of his discourse he exhorts those whom the Holy Ghost has established as bishops.[5] At Cæsarea he was to receive a last warning, the most solemn of all; the prophet Agabus comes to him, takes the girdle of Paul, binds his own hands and feet, and says: 'Thus saith the Holy Ghost: The man whose girdle this is the Jews shall bind in this manner in Jerusalem.'[6] In this scene, the symbolism of which recalls so faithfully that of the ancient prophets, of Jeremias for instance, we find the same solemn formula which they employed, but instead of saying 'thus saith Jahve,' Agabus says: 'thus saith the Holy Ghost.'

This parallel expresses clearly enough the prophet's faith in the divinity of the Spirit; in any case, there cannot be any doubt of that divinity,[7] the whole Jewish tradition affirms it and, in this very book, the works attributed to the Spirit, the inspiration of the prophets, and the sanctification of the faithful, are purely divine works. All the difficulties which in later days will be raised against this dogma will come from the philosophic or Gnostic conception of intermediary beings, but will have no root in the Jewish or Christian tradition.[8]

[1] *Acts* xv, 28. [2] xiii, 2–4. [3] xvi, 6–7. [4] xx, 22–23. [5] xx, 28. [6] xxi, 11. [7] Cf. v, 34. [8] Cf. Swete, *The Holy Spirit in the N.T.*, p. 288.

The point which above all calls for study is the personal character of the Holy Spirit; the Jewish doctrine had left it obscure; this book elucidates it clearly. Unless we refuse all credence to the author of the *Acts* and attribute to him all the characteristics mentioned above, we must agree that the first Christian community lived, so to speak, in the intimacy of the Holy Spirit; he it is who inspires the final decisions of St. Peter, who dictates the decrees of the Apostles, who chooses his own missionaries and shows them their way.

In all this his action closely resembles that of the risen Christ; just as the Lord sent Ananias to Saul,[1] the Holy Spirit sends St. Peter to the centurion Cornelius[2]; just as Jesus does not permit St. Paul to remain in Jerusalem, but sends him to the nations,[3] so the Spirit of Jesus does not allow him to cross into Bithynia, but leads him to Troas.[4]

We may also compare on certain points the action of the Holy Spirit with that of the angel of the Lord,[5] but these similarities should not authorise us to identify these different agents; just as the angel is neither the Spirit nor Christ, so we should distinguish between the Holy Spirit and Jesus Christ. The very narratives of these divine manifestations indicate sufficiently this distinction: when Christ appears to his believers, it is as a Master well known to them, with whom they converse; Ananias, afraid of the mission confided to him, objects that Saul is a persecutor; Paul, trusting in the authority given him by his past and his conversion, insists on preaching in Jerusalem. Nowhere do we find a similar conversation with the Holy Spirit: his inspirations and commandments are received, and obeyed.

This difference of attitude proceeds no doubt from the memory of the life of Christ here below, and from his familiar relations with his disciples; but it is not thus entirely explained: with the heavenly Father also, Christians show a confidence, a filial attitude, differing from their relations with the Holy Spirit. These remarks should be compared with those at the beginning of this chapter: we do not find in the apostolic writings prayers addressed to the Holy Spirit, as to the Father and the Son.

[1] *Acts* ix, 10. [2] x, 19. [3] xxii, 17. [4] xvi, 7.

[5] This resemblance especially appears in reference to St. Philip; cf. viii, 26, 29.

These facts will not surprise us, if we remember that the Holy Spirit, so long recognised by the Jews as a divine force, only appears gradually as a person. No doubt Jesus promised the gift of him as a person to his disciples, and it was as a person that the Holy Spirit directed and supported them in the first days of the Church, and as such he was thenceforth known to the Apostles; the texts quoted assure us of this. But much time must pass for this belief to react fully on the lives of Christians; little by little they will grow accustomed to glorifying the Father by the Son through the Spirit,[1] then the Father, the Son, and the Spirit,[2] and it will only be near the end of the fourth century that St. Gregory Nazianzen will rejoice in the full expansion that God gives in his day to faith in the Holy Spirit and the worship paid to him.[3]

[1] The earliest Trinitarian doxologies are to be found in *Martyr. Polyc.*, XIV, 3 and XXII, 3.

[2] This formula was widespread in the fourth century and defended by St. Basil in his treatise on the *Holy Spirit*. Cf. CAVALLERA, *Le Schisme d'Antioche* (Paris, 1905), 52.

[3] *Orat. theol.*, v, 26. Ante-Nicæan doxological formulas will be studied in vol. II of this History.

CHAPTER III

St. Paul

In the course of the preceding study several texts of St. Paul have been quoted to the reader; it is indeed impossible to isolate him from the infant Church; he is no solitary theologian, who creates a new doctrine and imposes it on the churches he founds; he is above all an apostle of Christ, who hands on the message which he had received, the deposit of faith which has been entrusted to him.[1] Beyond doubt, his conceptions have a distinctive note, and one has a right to speak of a Pauline theology; it is no less certain that God, who made him doctor of the Gentiles, prepared him for and guided him in that rôle, by special revelations which have enriched the deposit of the Christian faith. But it is also certain that in his conception of the nature and rôle of Christ and of his relations with God the Father and the Holy Spirit, he felt himself in full communion of ideas with all the Christians of his time; but, although he gave to the common faith an individual form proper to himself, although he enriched and developed it, he did not create it, and he was assured that his teaching was echoed throughout the Church.

These remarks will have their value when we are studying Pauline theology, and when we are seeking its source. But, before entering into the details of this study, we must briefly discuss the character of the documents at our disposal. It will be in this chapter perhaps, more than in any part of this history, that we shall feel at the same time the gaps and the riches of early Christian literature.

The *Epistles of St. Paul* are but occasional writings, and a systematic exposition of his thought would be sought there in vain; the most significant texts emerge,

[1] Cf. A. Sabatier, *L'Apôtre Paul*[3], 286.

as if by chance, from the most unlikely contexts: the supreme action of Christ, who, from being rich, became poor,[1] is recalled in a word, to stimulate the Corinthians to almsgiving; likewise, it is in the midst of an exhortation to fraternal charity that that admirable text appears on the pre-existence of Christ 'in the form of God.'[2] All the Apostle's various teachings are so laden with truth and uplifted by so intense a passion that one does not know how to grasp all their riches or reproduce their accent; his doctrine is like his language, it discourages translators by its exuberance and zest. Finally, the problem of salvation has, more than all others, captivated the attention of St. Paul; it is the true centre-point of his theology, and he has thrown a powerful but only a partial light on other dogmas; hence, certain obscurities in Trinitarian theology, and particularly in the doctrine of the Holy Spirit, which will have to be pointed out.

The difficulties arising out of these obscurities, particularly in connection with the doctrine of the Holy Spirit, are considerable; but they are a light price to pay for the security and the strength which these documents give us. If the faith of St. Paul is shewn less by methodical expressions than by unexpected allusions or sudden exclamations, it is all to the good of the historian, who grasps in such words a belief more deeply founded in the Apostle's mind, and more familiar to his disciples. If the dogma of salvation involves all others, we may rejoice because we feel ourselves there at the centre of Christian faith, a life-giving doctrine, rather than a matter of pure contemplation; in later days, thanks no doubt above all to St. John, the area of light will spread, but, in the teachings of St. Paul, we love to see the intense light which flashes on God and on Christ from the dogma of the redemption.

1. The Source of St. Paul's Teaching. The Father and the Son

The source of St. Paul's doctrine has been looked for in many quarters; during these last twenty years attempts have been made to find it in that religious syncretism which, at the beginning of our era, invaded the Oriental world; and, in order to interpret his language and his

[1] 2 *Cor.* viii, 9. [2] *Phil.* ii, 5 *sqq.*

thought, we have constant recourse to Alexandrine theosophy, to the Hermetic philosophy, to the religious philosophy of Stoicism, and the secret initiations of the mysteries.[1] Those who have pursued these researches with most ardour have brought out some curious texts wherewith to decorate their commentaries, which sometimes give us a lively impression of certain details of the Apostle's teaching, long forgotten by modern commentators, but appreciated in all their strength by the disciples of St. Paul.[2] These comparisons are valuable, as everything is which gives us a more exact appreciation of the Apostle's thought; but the light that they throw does not reach beyond the surface. It is not by the study of Philo or of Plutarch, of the *Poemander,* of Aelius Aristides, or of Epictetus that we can penetrate the thought of St. Paul, and still less by the reading of Apuleius, or of the other adepts of the mysteries of Isis or of Attis.[3] It is true that St. Paul was born at Tarsus, but he came from a good Jewish stock, 'circumcised the eighth day . . . an Hebrew of the Hebrews; according to the law, a Pharisee: according to zeal, persecuting the Church of God according to the justice that is in the law, conversing without blame.'[4] Educated at Jerusalem, the assiduous and enthusiastic disciple of the Pharisees, it was not from them that he had learnt to venerate what every real Jew rightly held for an abomination. On the other hand he had received from them, and retained all his life, with the cult of the divine revelation contained in the Old Testament, many characteristic habits of interpretation and reasoning.[5] In the very passages where he is most directly attacking the Rabbinical doctrine he willingly uses against his adversaries their own familiar forms of argument.[6]

But if, in order to demonstrate the superiority of Christ

[1] See *opp. cit. infra* of REITZENSTEIN (*Hellenisten Mysterienreligionen*), NORDEN, and BOUSSET.

[2] See *opp. cit. infra* of DEISSMANN, BAUER, and MOUTLON and MILLIGAN.

[3] See *opp. cit. infra* of JACQUIER, PRAT, MACHEN (esp. 211–51 and 293–317),, KNOX (pp. 126–50), SCHWEITZER (ch. vi, esp. 170 *sqq.*), and REITZENSTEIN (*Religionsgeschichte und Eschatologie*).

[4] *Phil.* iii, 5–6; cf. 2 *Cor.* vi, 22.

[5] Cf. PRAT, *Théol. de S. Paul*, I, 22.

[6] Cf. STRACK-BILLERBECK, III, 204–6, on 2 *Cor.* iii, 7–18 and *Rom.* iv, 9–13; x, 6–9.

over Moses, of the Spirit over the Law, or, it may be, the gratuitous justification of Abraham, St. Paul uses the Biblical texts in the manner of the Rabbis, it is in order to establish against them an entirely new truth, which he had not learnt from his Jewish teachers, which he had for a long time misunderstood and hated. St. Paul affirms to us that he had received this truth, which was the very essence of his teaching, by a revelation from Christ: 'I give you to understand, brethren, that the Gospel which was preached by me is not according to man. For neither did I receive it of man, nor did I learn it, but by the revelation of Jesus Christ.'[1]

Neither St. Paul's personal declarations nor the narratives of the *Acts* permit us to follow in every detail the progress of these divine revelations, nor even to determine certainly the subject on which they threw immediate light[2]; what at least is certain, is that St. Paul was conscious of having been made 'an Apostle not . . . by man, but by Jesus Christ and God the Father, who raised him from the dead'[3]; and this does not merely mean that he has been chosen and set apart by God,[4] but also, and above all, that he has seen the Lord, that he has been directly instructed by him, and has received from him his Gospel.

This revelation, which immediately connects the Apostle with Christ, does not detach him from the apostolic group, or create a new gospel over against the traditional gospel. This unity of the Gospel is expounded with particular force in this very *Epistle to the Galatians:* urged by a revelation of God, he goes from Antioch to Jerusalem, and consults there the leaders of the Church, expounding to them his gospel, in order to assure himself that he has not run, and does not run, in vain.[5]

Moreover, on this occasion it was not properly speaking the theology of the Apostle that was the subject of discussion, his conception of God the Father, of Christ Our Lord, and their essential relations; it was the problem of the access of the Gentiles to salvation, and of the conditions which had to be imposed upon them. The same problems will be posed in that later conflict which is the

[1] *Gal.* i, 11–12.
[2] Cf. PRAT, I, p. 34–39 for a detailed study of these revelations.
[3] *Gal.* i, 1. [4] *Rom.* i, 1; cf. *Acts* ix, 15; xiii, 2. [5] *Gal.* ii, 2.

motive of the *Epistle to the Galatians*,[1] in the attitude of those who disturb, at about the same time, the peace of the Church at Corinth,[2] or, at least, it will be around those same problems that controversy will arise; what are the conditions of salvation, is circumcision indispensable, does the Law still bind converted Jews, and should it be imposed on converts from paganism?[3] Nowhere do we find the smallest indication of an opposition to the Christology and theology of the Apostle; there is no difference in the appreciation of the rôle of Christ, in the confession of his titles of Lord and of Son of God. St. Paul, addressing himself in the *Epistle to the Romans* to a community which he has neither founded nor visited, and which consequently has been initiated into Christian doctrine by other masters, nevertheless speaks to them of Christ in the same terms as those which he uses to the Corinthians and Galatians, and we clearly see that, in doing so, he has no intention of preaching a new doctrine, but that he supposes them to possess the faith which he himself professes.

This supremely important fact confirms what we have already seen[4]: it is useless to seek outside the Church of Jerusalem, for instance at Antioch, a Christian centre in which Paul could have been trained and initiated into a Christology which the first Apostles did not profess. It must also be recognised that Paul is attached to the first disciples of Jesus, not only by the theology which he preaches, but also by the Gospel tradition which he hands on. When we come to study the *Gospel of St. John* we shall recognise not only a theological teaching, but also a historical testimony which supports and throws light upon it. This double aspect appears equally in the preaching of St. Paul, with this essential difference—that the Apostle is a personal witness only of the glorified life which he has seen, and, as for the humble and suffering life of Jesus in the flesh, he cannot give, like St. John, his

[1] See LAGRANGE, *Galates*, pp. xxix–lviii.

[2] Although PRAT (I, 183–6) and WEISS (*Urchristentum*, 256 *sq.*) see only a personal opposition and not a doctrinal one in the trouble at Corinth, I am inclined to agree with the majority of exegetes that the texts suggest the adversaries were Judaisers. Cf. *opp. cit. infra* of PLUMMER (pp. xxxvii–xl), LIETZMANN (6 *sq.*), WINDISCH (325 *sqq.*, note on xi, 4), and KNOX (309–28).

[3] SCHWEITZER, *Gesch. der Paulinischen Forschung*, 179.

[4] See above, page 270.

immediate testimony, but merely the faithful echo of the tradition which he has received and which he repeats. It should further be noted that St. Paul did not write a gospel, but a series of letters; supposing we had nothing of St. John's but his epistles, we should have no idea of his evangelical catechesis, any more than we can learn from the *Epistles of St. Peter* the details given us in the *Gospel of St. Mark.* If we compare St. Paul's letters with the other epistles of the New Testament, they are certainly richer in Gospel memories, but, in spite of that, these memories are scattered and fragmentary; they would be insufficient to teach us the earthly life of Our Lord; they are enough to show us that it was authoritatively present to the thought of Paul, as the gospels have revealed it to us.[1] What, as I think, should specially retain our attention is not only the details of the life of Jesus referred to by St. Paul, but, still more, the impression as a whole, made upon the Apostle by the historic Christ, the Christ of the Gospel: it is surely the contemplation of the humble and gentle Christ,[2] who came to save sinners,[3] who pleased not himself,[4] who gave himself up,[5] who became obedient unto death,[6] which produced in the Apostle that strong and tender love which ruled his life.[7]

The teaching of Jesus, as reported by the Synoptics, represented all the relations of men to God as depending necessarily on their relations to Christ. This is our point of departure for the consideration of St. Paul's theology; he who is separated from Christ, by that very fact is without God.

> 'At that time,' writes the Apostle to the converted Pagans, 'you were without Christ, being aliens from the conversation of Israel, and strangers to the testament, having no hope of the promise, and without God in this world. But now, in Christ Jesus, you, who some time were afar off, are made nigh by the blood of

[1] Cf. Prat, *Paul et le paulinisme*, in *Dict. Apol.*, III, col. 1629–38; de Grandmaison, *Le Christ de l'histoire dans saint Paul*, in *Rech. de Sc. Relig.*, 1923, 481–91; J. Weiss, *Urchristentum*, 346–8: E. Meyer, *Ursprung des Christentums*, III, 354, n. 2.

[2] 2 *Cor.* x, 1. [3] 1 *Tim.* i, 15. [4] *Rom.* xv, 3. [5] *Gal.* ii, 20.

[6] *Phil.* ii, 8.

[7] Cf. Robertson-Plummer, 1 *Cor.* (Edinburgh, 1914), 286.

Christ. For he is our peace, who hath made both [Jews and Gentiles] one . . . For by him we have access both in one Spirit to the Father.'[1]

He had said the same in the *Epistle to the Romans*:

'All have sinned; and do need the glory of God. Being justified freely by his grace, through the redemption that is in Christ Jesus.'[2]

Thus, so long as man has not been united to Christ, he is separated from God—he is the enemy of God[3]; it is only by Christ that he can be reconciled. It is only in Christ that he can have access to God, but this access is so close that he, who once was the enemy of God, becomes his son, as soon as he has been incorporated with Christ.[4] God, indeed, has predestined us to conformity with 'the image of his Son: that he might be the first-born amongst many brethren'[5]; we are his heirs and co-heirs with Christ.[6]

Thus is reconstituted a new Israel, 'the Israel of God.' The divine sonship that was claimed by the ancient Israel is also the exclusive privilege of the new; and, in a certain sense, we may say that St. Paul repeats and ratifies, even more rigorously, the ancient social and collective conception of the sons of God; but the unity, which he thus reconstitutes, is much more comprehensive than the other while, at the same time, more intimate; it is no longer the intimacy of a single race, it is the body of Christ, or, in the words of the *Epistle to the Hebrews*, it is the Church of the first-born ones.

This doctrine of the divine adoption is no mere speculation; it is a religious truth on which St. Paul nourishes his soul, and which he constantly recalls. We have noted, in the writings of the other apostles, the formulas of greeting or of prayer in which God and Christ are united; the use of these formulas is even more constant with St. Paul; he begins almost all his letters with this salutation: 'Grace to you and peace, from God our Father and from the Lord Jesus Christ.'[7] He usually finishes them

[1] *Eph.* ii, 12–18. [2] iii, 23–24. [3] *Rom.* v, 10.
[4] *Gal.* iii, 26–7; cf. 1 *Cor.* i, 9.
[5] *Rom.* viii, 29. [6] *Ibid.*, 17; cf. *Col.* i, 18–22.
[7] *Rom.* i, 7; 1 *Cor.* i, 3; 2 *Cor.* i, 2; *Gal.* i, 3; *Eph.* i, 2; *Phil.* i, 2; *Philemon*, 3.

by invoking the grace of Christ.[1] Even in the body of his letters he loves to associate God the Father and Jesus Christ, praying to them both at the same time or appealing to their witness.[2]

What is much more characteristic of St. Paul is the formula we find at the head of his two earliest epistles: 'Paul, Sylvanus, and Timothy to the Church of the Thessalonians, in God the Father and the Lord Jesus Christ.'[3] Here again the Father and Christ are closely united, no longer as the source of grace or the object of prayer, but as the spiritual *milieu* in which the Church lives. At Athens the Apostle had said: 'In God we live and move and have our being': it is the same conception which is expressed here, though in more religious and more spiritual terms, and which we find so often in these formulas so dear to St. Paul: 'In God,' 'In the Holy Spirit,' and, above all, 'In Christ Jesus.'[4]

To understand these conceptions better, we must study more closely what he means by the union of the soul with Christ and with God. In the first letter to the Thessalonians the prospect which he shows to the faithful of future glory, after the Parousia of Christ, reveals his profoundest aspirations; 'We shall be always with the Lord'[5]; and a little further on in the same letter: 'God hath . . . appointed us . . . unto the purchasing of salvation by Our Lord Jesus Christ . . . that whether we watch or sleep we may live together with him.'[6] He writes in the same way to the Corinthians: 'Knowing that, while we are in the body, we are absent from the Lord. For we walk by faith and not by sight. But we are confident, and have a good will to be absent rather from the body, and to be present with the Lord.'[7] And later on during his first period of captivity: 'But I am straitened between two; having a desire to be dissolved and to be with Christ, a thing by far the better; but to abide still in the flesh is needful for you.'[8]

[1] *Rom.* xvi, 20; 1 *Cor.* xvi, 23; *Gal.* vi, 18; *Phil.* vi, 23; 1 *Thess.* v, 28; 2 *Thess.* iii, 18.

[2] 1 *Thess.* iii, 11; 2 *Thess.* ii, 16; 1 *Tim.* vi, 13; 2 *Tim.* iv, 1.

[3] 1 *Thess.* i, 1; 2 *Thess.* i. 1.

[4] Cf. Deissmann, *Die neutestamentliche Formel 'in Christo Iesu'* (Marburg, 1892).

[5] 1 *Thess.* iv, 16. [6] 1 *Thess.* v, 9, 10. [7] 2 *Cor.* v, 6–8.

[8] *Phil.* i, 23.

It is easy to recognise in all these desires a supreme love: it is evident that Christ has become the centre of the life of St. Paul, and is drawing him to himself, to Heaven. Here below, and from this present time, Christ has entered his life; 'for I, through the law, am dead to the law, that I may live to God; with Christ I am nailed to the cross. And I live, now not I: but Christ liveth in me. And that I live now in the flesh: I live in the faith of the Son of God, who loved me, and delivered himself for me.'[1]

It would be a very imperfect understanding of these texts to see in them nothing but a memory, however passionate and full of desire; we must recognise in them the affirmation of a very profound though still imperfect reality[2]; 'All we who are baptised in Christ Jesus are baptised into death; for we are buried together with him by baptism into death: that as Christ is risen from the dead by the glory of the Father, so we also may walk in newness of life . . . if we be dead with Christ, we believe that we shall live also together with Christ; knowing that Christ rising again from the dead, dieth now no more; death shall no more have dominion over him. For in that he died to sin, he died once; but in that he liveth, he liveth unto God. So do you also reckon that you are dead to sin, and alive unto God in Christ Jesus.'[3]

Around this supremely important text many others may be grouped, which throw light upon it, and confirm it[4]: all these strong expressions are by no means mere metaphors, it is certain that, for St. Paul, man dies to himself in baptism, in order to rise in Christ[5]; the whole of the past is wiped out; 'there is neither Jew nor Greek: there is neither bond nor free: there is neither male nor female. For you are all one in Christ Jesus.'[6] And elsewhere: 'Stripping yourselves of the old man with his deeds, and putting on the new, him who is renewed unto knowledge, according to the image of him that created him; where there is neither Gentile nor Jew, circumcision nor uncircumcision, Barbarian nor Scythian, bond nor free. But Christ is all and in all.'[7] Paul himself has renounced all the earthly advantages which he might have

[1] *Gal.* ii, 19–20. [2] Cf. J. Weiss, *Urchristentum*, 363 *sq.*
[3] *Rom.* vi, 3–11. [4] *Col.* ii, 12; iii, 4; cf. 2 *Cor.* v, 14–17; *Eph.* i, 5–8.
[5] Cf. Tobac, *op. cit. infra*, 225–56. [6] *Gal.* iii, 28. [7] *Col.* iii, 9–11.

derived from his race, from his circumcision, from his Jewish education; all that he has thrown away like dung, in order to gain Christ.[1] Man, then, has nothing in himself in which he can take glory, but 'of him are you in Christ Jesus, who of God is made unto us wisdom, and justice, and sanctification, and redemption: that, as it is written: He that glorieth may glory in the Lord.'[2]

This conception finds its most complete expression in the doctrine of the Body of the Church, of which the faithful are the members and Christ the Head; this doctrine is developed chiefly in the *Epistle to the Ephesians,* but it is already strongly insisted upon in the earlier epistles as a primordial truth of Christianity and familiar to all Christians: 'We being many, are one body in Christ, and every one members one of another'[3]; and with reference to the Eucharist and to baptism: 'For we, being many, are one bread, one body.'[4] 'For in one Spirit were we all baptised into one body, whether Jews or Gentiles, whether bond or free.'[5] The single principle of the life of this body is the Head, that is Christ: 'The head, from which the whole body, by joints and bands being supplied with nourishment and compacted, groweth unto the increase of God.'[6] From the head proceed the various graces by means of which the members of the body complete each other[7] and contribute to the life and glory of the body:

> 'And he gave some apostles, and some prophets, and other some evangelists—and other some pastors and doctors, for the perfecting of the saints, for the work of the ministry, for the edifying of the body of Christ: until we all meet into the unity of faith, and of the knowledge of the Son of God, unto a perfect man, unto the measure of the age of the fulness of Christ . . . but, doing the truth in charity, we may in all things grow up in him who is the head, even Christ. From whom the whole body, being compacted and fitly joined together, by what every joint supplieth, according to the operation in the measure of every part, maketh increase of the body unto the edifying of itself in charity.'[8]

[1] *Phil.* iii, 4–8. [2] 1 *Cor.* i, 30. [3] *Rom.* xii, 5. [4] 1 *Cor.* x, 17.
[5] 1 *Cor.* xii, 13; cf. 1 *Cor.* vi, 15; xii, 27. [6] *Col.* ii, 19.
[7] Cf. 1 *Cor.* xii, 12–31. [8] *Eph.* iv, 11–16.

It is not hard to recognise here, in a much stronger relief and a clearer light, the doctrine already preached by St. Peter on the morrow of the death of Christ. 'There is no other name given to men under heaven for their salvation'; and it is also the same teaching which we shall find in St. John on Our Lord's own lips: 'I am the life'; 'I am the vine and you are the branches.'

We now understand the meaning of St. Paul's words: 'For me, to live is Jesus Christ'; and also: 'Here below we are exiled from the Lord.' Jesus is not, only or principally, for him the ideal man, whom he endeavours to imitate, or the friend whom he is impatient to rejoin. He is the source of his own life, the head of the body of which he is a member. But, on the other hand, it must be noticed that the historic person of Jesus does not disappear in this doctrine, in spite of being the 'Life-giving Spirit' and the principle of all life; Christ is not stripped of his concrete reality, or reduced to a mystical symbol. The texts just quoted are clear enough: it is unto the death of Jesus that the Christian has been baptised, and it is through his Resurrection that he is raised from the dead.[1] The *Epistle to the Romans* insists still more on this truth, and makes clearer the continuity of the life of Christ on earth, and in his faithful: the whole human race appears as concentrated in two men, Adam and Jesus Christ,[2] not two symbols but real men; this world does not only contain two abstract forces, flesh and spirit, death and life, but there are two men,[3] two heads of humanity; from one of whom comes death and from the other grace and justice: and the origin of this mortal and life-giving influence is the obedience of the one and the disobedience of the other.[4]

Before making a closer study of the person of Christ, from which that action proceeds, we must stop a few

[1] Cf. *Rom.* xiv, 7–9; 2 *Cor.* v, 14–15; cf. TOBAC, *op. cit. infra*, 139–73.

[2] AUGUST., *Op. imperf. c. Julian.*, II, 163 (*P.L.*, XIV, 1211).

[3] In St. Paul's conception of the heavenly man as opposed to the terrestrial man (1 *Cor.* xv, 45 *sqq.*), many critics have tried to find the Philonian idea of generic man (PHILO, *De opif. mundi*, 134 *sqq.*; M., I, 32), the Rabbinic legend of the Primitive Man, or else, the conception of the pre-existing Messias as it is found in *Henoch*, or in 4 *Esdras*. In reality, these notions are foreign to St. Paul for whom Christ was the heavenly man because he pre-existed in Heaven as God. A good bibliography of this question is in HOLTZMANN, *N. T. Theol.*, II, 59 *sqq.* Cf. PRAT, *Théol. de St-Paul*, II, 169–171.

[4] *Rom.* v, 12–21.

moments to consider that action itself, in so far as it reveals to us the relations of God and Christ.

God is the supreme Father, he is, as the Apostle loves to repeat, 'The God and the Father of Our Lord Jesus Christ'[1]; and it is from him as source and supreme ideal that every filial and paternal relation proceeds[2]; yet Jesus Christ alone is 'his own Son,'[3] and others can only be his sons through incorporation with his first-born Son.

Thus, in that intimate union which makes Christians members of the family of God,[4] two subordinate and analogous relations must be distinguished, attaching Christians to Christ and Christ to God; 'For all things are yours . . . and you are Christ's; and Christ is God's.'[5] And a little further on in the same Epistle: 'The head of every man is Christ: and the head of the woman is the man: and the head of Christ is God.'[6] It would be forcing St. Paul's thought to press these analogies too closely; it is certain that for him the union of man and woman is but a very imperfect image of the union of Christ and man, and that the union of Christ and man is infinitely less close than the union of Christ and God: the occasion of insisting on that supreme unity, which has already been sufficiently suggested by the preceding analysis, will shortly occur. But what is very forcibly expressed by these formulas is the complete dependence of men on Christ, as of Christ himself on God.

This dependence will be consummated on the Last Day:

> 'Afterwards the end, when he shall have delivered up the kingdom to God and the Father, when he shall have brought to nought all principality and power and virtue. For he must reign, until he hath put all his enemies under his feet . . . and when all things shall be subdued unto him, then the Son also himself shall be subject unto him that put all things under him, that God may be all in all.'[7]

This supreme unity is the purpose of the whole redemption: if, even here below, Christ is 'all in all,'[8] it is in order that God should be 'all in all' for all eternity.

[1] *Rom.* xv, 6; 2 *Cor.* i, 3; xi, 31; *Eph.* i, 3; *Col.* i, 3. Cf. 1 *Cor.* xv, 24.
[2] *Eph.* iii, 14–15. [3] *Rom.* viii, 32. [4] *Eph.* ii, 19. [5] 1 *Cor.* iii, 22–23.
[6] 1 *Cor.* xi, 3. [7] 1 *Cor.* xv, 24–27. [8] *Col.* iii, 11.

This unity will not be consummated by the absorption of men or of Christ in God: they will be subject to him, but not identified with him. Nor will Christ abdicate, laying down his royalty and lordship[1]: the necessity of nature makes him the end of men and the world[2]; but, having recapitulated, in himself, the whole of humanity together with himself, he will make it subject to his Father. Thus is developed up to God, as the ultimate term, the conception of organic unity so dear to St. Paul.

Moreover, it is not only the Church which is conceived by the Apostle as directed towards Christ and concentrated in him; it is the whole world. We read in the first *Epistle to the Corinthians*: 'Yet to us there is but one God, the Father, of whom are all things, and we unto him: and one Lord Jesus Christ, by whom are all things and we by him.'[3] It would be impossible to limit the significance of this text to the redemption of men: the parallelism of the phrases indicates clearly enough that everything that comes from God owes its existence to Christ.

A few years later, the appearance of doctrinal errors at Laodicea and Colosse induced St. Paul to expound this doctrine in greater detail, and affirm it more energetically. The Christians of these two cities had allowed themselves to be seduced by the dualist conceptions which reigned around them: matter was essentially evil, and God could not be immediately reached by religious knowledge and worship. On pretence of humility, they renounced so high an aim, and paid to the angels the worship they no longer dared to offer to God.[4]

St. Paul opposes to these speculations, which perverted the whole idea of Christianity, the dogma of the transcendence and universal mediation of Christ:

> 'God . . . hath delivered us from the power of darkness, and hath translated us into the kingdom of the Son of his love: in whom we have redemption through his blood, the remission of sins: who is the image of the invisible God, the first-born of every creature: for in

[1] And not as SABATIER writes in *L'Apôtre Paul*, 363 *sqq.* [2] *Col.* i, 16.

[3] viii, 6. Cf. NORDEN, *Agnostos Theos* (Leipzig, 1913), 240 *sqq.*

[4] Cf. LIGHTFOOT, *St. Paul's Epistle to the Colossians*, 71–111; A. L. WILLIAMS, *The Cult of the Angels at Colossae*, in *JTS* (April, 1909), 413–38.

him were all things created in heaven, and on earth, visible and invisible, whether thrones, or dominations, or principalities, or powers: all things were created by him and in him. And he is before all, and by him all things consist. And he is the head of the body, the Church: who is the beginning, the first-born from the dead: that in all things he may hold the primacy: because in him, it hath well pleased the Father that all fulness should dwell: and through him to reconcile all things unto himself, making peace through the blood of his cross, both as to the things that are on earth, and the things that are in heaven.'[1]

There is no need to insist on the supreme importance of this text; it is obvious enough at a first glance. We may moreover note that the Christological dogma is here expounded for its own sake, and not, as most frequently, merely glanced at by a rapid allusion; it is, therefore, necessary to study it closely.[2] One aspect of the doctrine here put forward is already familiar to us and need detain us but little: the rôle of Christ as Redeemer and Head of the Church; it is at once the thought from which the Apostle starts his teaching[3] and the conclusion to which it eventually and finally returns.[4] Between these two developments he opens a wider perspective on the creative activity of Christ and his relations with God.

He is, he tells us, 'the image of the invisible God.' When writing to the Corinthians, St. Paul had already represented Christ as 'the image of God'[5]; the same idea recurs in the *Epistle to the Hebrews:* the Son of God is 'the brightness of his glory and the figure of his substance.'[6] These metaphors and conceptions in St. Paul's contributions to the New Testament were of frequent occurrence in Alexandrine theology; Philo furnishes many examples[7] and they may already be noted in the *Book of the Wisdom of Solomon*[8]; the influence of the latter book may very plausibly be recognised in these

[1] *Col.* i, 12–20.

[2] Lightfoot has made an excellent study of the question, *op. cit.*, pp. 139–158; also Prat, *op. cit.*, I, pp. 398–403; II, 185–6.

[3] *Col.* i, 13, 14. [4] *Ibid.*. 18–20. [5] 2 *Cor.* iv, 5. [6] *Heb.* i, 3.

[7] See above, page 169 *sqq.* For a comparison of *Colossians* with Philo, see Aall, *Gesch. der Logosidee*, II, 28 *sqq.*

[8] vii, 26.

texts from the *Epistle to the Colossians,* and more particularly in that to the *Hebrews.*[1] In Christian theology this conception of the Son as the image of God derives a new significance from the fact of the Incarnation; for, by taking flesh and manifesting himself to men, the Son reveals to them the Father; this doctrine, the trace of which can be found in St. Paul,[2] will become more explicit in the writings of St. John and in patristic theology.

The Father, whose image[3] is the Son, is called the invisible God: similarly St. Paul, writing to Timothy,[4] speaks of the blessed God, who 'inhabiteth light inaccessible, whom no man hath seen nor can see'; in these texts invisibility is presented as the proper attribute of the Father[5]; the Son, who is his splendour and his image, manifests him to men.

The Son is called the 'son of the love' of God (*τοῦ υἱοῦ τῆς ἀγάπης αὐτοῦ*), and, a few lines further on, the 'first-born.' In the first of these titles we may very probably[6] recognise that of 'well-beloved' (*ἀγαπητός, ἠγαπημένος*) with the Messianic use of which we are already familiar as well as its meaning, equivalent to that of *μονογενής*. We may say the same of 'first-born' (*πρωτότοκος*). This was a Messianic title attributed at first, like many others, to the people of God, and then to the king as representing them.[7] Thus we read in *Exodus*[8]: 'Israel, my first-born'; in *Jeremias,*[9] 'Ephraim is my first-born; and in the *Psalms*[10]: 'I will make him my first-born, high above the kings of the earth.' By using these words the sacred writer does not mean to say that the other peoples or kings of the earth are also sons of God; for him the first-born is the beloved Son and the only Son. The equivalence of the two terms is so complete that we read in the *Psalms of Solomon*[11]: 'Thou takest care to

[1] Cf. Rendel Harris, *op. cit. infra*, 13. [2] Cf. *Titus*, ii, 11; iii, 4.

[3] On this concept of the Son, see August., *Quæst.*, LXXXIII, 74 (*P.L.*, XL, 85–6); Greg. Naz., *Orat. theol.*, IV, 20 (*P.G.*, XXXVI, 129); Basil, *Epist.* XXXVIII, 8 (*P.G.*, XXXII, 340).

[4] 1 *Tim.* vi, 16.

[5] It does not follow that the nature of the Father is different from that of the Son, but the Father manifests himself only through the Son. Cf. Iren. II, 30, 9.

[6] Lightfoot (140) does not agree and interprets it as St. Aug., *De Trinit.*, XV, 19.

[7] Cf. A. Durand, *Le Christ 'premier-né,'* in *Rech. de Science Rel.*, I (1910), 56–66; Prat, *Théol. de S. Paul*, II, 196–7.

[8] iv, 22. [9] xxxi, 9. [10] lxxxviii, 28. [11] xviii, 4.

nurture us like a first-born, an only son,' and in the fourth book of *Esdras*[1]: 'We are thy people, whom thou callest thy first-born, thy only son.'

These two last texts, the first of which is slightly anterior to Our Lord, and the second roughly contemporary with the *Epistle to the Colossians,* are particularly interesting, by the equivalence that they establish in this figurative vocabulary between 'first-born' and the 'only son'; they suggest the identification of the πρωτότοκος of St. Paul with the μονογενής of St. John.[2]

The qualification which is added, 'first-born of every creature,'[3] in no way qualifies the value of the expression[4]; the context certainly excludes an interpretation which should reduce Christ to be the first of a created series, in the sense in which, for example, he is, a little further on,[5] called the 'first-born from the dead,' and, in the *Epistle to the Romans* (viii, 29), 'the first-born amongst many brethren': indeed, St. Paul's words may be taken to mean: 'He is the first-born of every creature because, in him, everything in heaven and on earth has been created.' He does not say 'of all the rest of creation,' but 'of every creature,' thus expressing the opposition between Christ and every creature as such. The expression and the thought are precisely paralleled in *John* i, 3: πάντα δι' αὐτοῦ ἐγένετο, apart from the shade of meaning distinguishing δι' αὐτοῦ from ἐν αὐτῷ.[6]

St. Paul, however, insists on the point. Enumerating all the angelic hierarchies distinguished by the Colossians: thrones, dominations, principalities, powers; all these, he says, have been created in Christ and it is, therefore, to him and not to these creatures that worship should be paid. Then, passing from the creative act to the actual state of creation, he adds: 'All things were created by him and in him.'

The first of these two expressions, 'by him' and 'in

[1] vi, 58.

[2] PHILO often calls the Logos the first-born of God; *De agricult.*, 51 (M., I, 308); *De confus. ling.*, 63 (414); 146 (427); *De somn.*, I, 215 (653). Cf. DRUMMOND, *Philo Judæus*, II, 185.

[3] Cf. *Judith*, ix, 12 (LIGHTFOOT, *ad h.l.*).

[4] Cf. DURAND, *loc. cit. supra*, 61 *sq.*; HAUPT, and ABBOTT, *in h. l.*; PRAT, *loc. cit.*, 401, n. 1; MOULTON, *Grammar of N.T. Greek*[2], 79, 245; LIGHTFOOT, 146–8.

[5] i, 18; cf. *Apoc.* i, 5.

[6] Cf. J. WEISS, *Urchristentum*, 372.

him,' we have already met in the *Epistle to the Corinthians;* and it expresses the rôle played by Christ in the work of God; St. John will repeat it in the same sense.[1] The second, εἰς αὐτόν, is rarely applied to Christ; the equivalent of it is, however, to be found in other passages of St. Paul and St. John, in which the whole creation is represented, as here, as directed towards the Son as its end. If we permit ourselves here to recall the Stoic conception of the Logos, does not the contrast of the two doctrines make evident the transcendence of the Christian revelation? For Chrysippus everything comes from the Logos by physical dissociation and degeneration, everything returns to the Logos by the progressive absorption of individual beings in the total being. Here, on the other hand, everything comes from Christ by a free act of creation which in no way diminishes his greatness; everything tends towards Christ, not to be absorbed and lost in him, but to be united to him and to live in him. And, further, the Christ of St. Paul is no impersonal Logos; he is identified with the crucified One on Calvary, who through the blood of his cross has reconciled all things.

'And he is before all.' The author of the *Fourth Book Against Eunomius*[2] (which is attributed to St. Basil) remarks on this point: 'The Apostle having said "everything has been created by him and for him," might have added: "and he came to be before all things." But by saying the contrary, "he *is* before all," he shews that he *is* always and that the creation comes to be.' The best parallel to this emphatic expression is that of Christ in *St. John*: 'Before Abraham was made, I am' (viii, 58).

'And by him all things consist[3]: and he is the head of the body, the Church . . .' The unity of St. Paul's thought is peculiarly notable in this verse; he does not separate the rôle of Christ in the Church from his rôle in the world: everywhere Christ is the first, everywhere

[1] 1 *Cor.* viii, 6; cf. *Heb.* i, 2; *John* i, 3; 10; *Rom.* xi, 36; *Heb.* ii, 10, Cf. Chrysost., *In Hebr. hom.*, IV, 3 (*P.G.*, LXIII, 40); Philo, *De cherub.*, 125–7 (M., I, 161–2); *Leg. alleg.*, III, 96 (I, 106).

[2] *Advers. Eunom.*, IV (*P.G.*, XXIX, 701).

[3] This expression belongs more to philosphic than Biblical language; see Plato, *Tim.*, 29d; 41d; 48a; etc.; *De re publ.*, 530a. Pseudo-Aristotle, *Eth. Eud.*, VII, 9; *De mundo*, 6. Philo, *Q. rer. divin. her.*, 280 (M., I, 513); *ibid.*, 58 (481). Diels, *Doxogr. gr.*, 289. There is only one N.T. text at all like it: 2 *Pet.* iii, 5.

he is the centre, everywhere he is the principle of life. In that he is to be clearly distinguished from all contemporary philosophers who discussed the origin of things: they asked themselves whence comes the world, and how does it subsist, and, because they considered it unworthy of the blessed God to have any immediate contact with matter, many of them imagined intermediary beings, like the Logos and the powers.[1] St. Paul is not interested in that: the problem which he solves is not cosmological but religious; he does not ask whence comes the world, but what is the Christ. If he insists on his rôle in the creation and government of the world, it is not to solve by his means a philosophic antinomy, it is to restore to him, in the religion of the Colossians, the place which is his own.

Moreover, this preoccupation does not make him lose sight of what for him is of supreme importance in the work of Christ, that is to say, the redemption; it is by that mystery that he opens and concludes his argument: it is interesting to note, on this point, the emphasis in this text, the first in the whole of Christian literature in which the creative rôle of the Son of God appears in full clarity: more than once, later on, we shall have to note that a too exclusive preoccupation with this rôle has been a great danger for the Trinitarian dogma; it led Christian philosophers on to their adversaries' ground, and sometimes induced them to interpret Christ according to purely human conceptions, unworthy of him; in the case of St. Paul there is nothing of the kind: 'The Jews require signs, and the Greeks seek after wisdom; but we preach Christ crucified.'[2]

Everything. moreover, is seen by St. Paul in this perspective of salvation; man is not the only one whom sin has attacked and whom Christ restores; the whole creation groans, enslaved to vanity, but the creation will pass from the servitude of corruption, set free to the liberty of glory[3]; in this text also we read that God has wished to reconcile all things to himself by Christ, and make peace through the blood of his cross on earth and in heaven.[4] These conceptions were familiar to the Jews; the Messianism of the prophets, still more that of the apocalypses,

[1] See above, pages 147 *sqq.*, 158 *sqq.*
[2] 1 *Cor.* i, 22–23. [3] *Rom.* viii, 20–22. [4] *Col.* i, 20.

associated the deliverance of nature with that of Israel[1]; more than once, no doubt, in Judaic apocalypses, imagination got the start of religion, and millenarism perverted Messianism; but it would be a serious error if these excesses were to make us suspicious of the profound truth preached by the Apostle: the world and man are not two juxtaposed beings, independent of each other; if it is true that the world has been created for the sake of man, it is not difficult to conceive that, as a result of man's fall, it has been pulled out of its course and subjected to vanity, and only the restoration of man can set the world free.[2]

This intimate union of man and the world helps us to understand the facility with which St. Paul passes from the conception of Christ as Head of the Church to that of Christ as Creator and support of the world: no doubt these two relations are by no means equivalent; Christians are 'created in Christ Jesus'[3] in a very different way from that in which the world has been 'created in him'[4]; Christians are of the family of God, his children; this is a singular privilege, which they derive from their 'fellowship' with the Son of God, Jesus Christ[5]; far from being lost in the crowd of creatures, they can say that everything is theirs, they are Christ's, and Christ is God's.[6] But this organic hierarchy is only itself intelligible if the action of Christ extends to all these creatures over whom Christians reign; it is in him that they subsist and live, and that is why Christians, who are his members, share in his lordship over them.

It does not follow from all this that one may not most legitimately, according to St. Paul's own thought, distinguish between the relations belonging to Christ, as Creator, in his pre-existence, and, as Saviour, in his human life, earthly or glorified.[7] But it should be noted that all these relations are co-ordinated and directed towards one and the same end: the work of the incarnate Christ is at once the restoration (of man) and the consummation of the work of the pre-existing Christ; and the formula which expresses this work as a whole is: 'All things were

[1] Cf. SANDAY-HEADLAM, *Romans*, 210–2; STRACK-BILLERBECK, III, 247–55.
[2] Cf. *Col.*, i, 20. [3] *Eph.* ii, 10. [4] *Col.* i, 16. [5] 1 *Cor.* i, 9.
[6] 1 *Cor.* iii, 22–23. [7] Cf. LIGHTFOOT, 147; DURAND, *loc. cit. supra*, 57 *sq*.

created by him and in him.' And that is summed up for St. Paul in the fundamental dogma of the Christian faith, in that confession so efficacious that it suffices for salvation, so divine that the Spirit alone could have inspired it: Κύριος Ἰησοῦς, Jesus is the Lord.[1]

We have already come across this profession of faith when analysing the beliefs of the Church at her birth.[2] In the case of St. Paul, as in that of the other apostles, it is inspired by memories of the Old Testament, and recognises in the 'Lord Jesus' the majesty of Jahve the Lord.[3]

But St. Paul affirms with peculiar energy certain divine features, of which this name of Lord reminded his Jewish or Pagan hearers; the Lord is the Judge; he it is who 'will bring to light the hidden things of darkness, and will make manifest the counsels of the hearts'[4]; it is as the Judge that the Apostle represents him when he speaks of 'the day of the Lord,'[5] 'the coming of the Lord,'[6] 'the Epiphany of the Lord' (τῆς ἐπιφανείας τοῦ κυρίου).

From this moment the Lord is the master to whom all belongs:

> 'For none of us liveth to himself; and no man dieth to himself. For whether we live, we live unto the Lord; or whether we die, we die unto the Lord. Therefore, whether we live or whether we die, we are the Lord's. For to this end Christ died and rose again; that he might be Lord both of the dead and of the living.'[7]

Thus the confession of the Lordship of Jesus is primarily a recognition of the absolute dominion which he has over his own, over his 'slaves' as St. Paul loves to say.[8] Those who are not his own have, for their lord, sin,[9] death,[10] and the law[11]; Christ has redeemed us from that servitude,[12] but by this redemption has made us his own: 'You are not your own. For you are bought with a great price.'[13]

[1] *Rom.* x, 9, cf. *Acts* xvi, 29; I *Cor.* xii, 3. Cf. Kattenbusch, *op. cit. infra*, II, 608–10.
[2] See above, page 268 *sqq.*
[3] Cf. Prat, *Théol. de S. Paul*, II, 216–7.
[4] I *Cor.* iv, 5.
[5] I *Cor.* iv, 5; v, 5; 2 *Cor.* i, 14; I *Thess.* v, 2; 2 *Thess.* ii, 2.
[6] I *Thess.* iv, 19; iii, 13; v, 23; 2 *Thess.* ii, I.
[7] *Rom.* xiv, 7–9.
[8] *Rom.* i, I; I *Cor.* vii, 22; *Gal.* i, 10; *Eph.* vi, 6; *Phil.* i, I; *Col.* iv, 12.
[9] *Rom.* vi, 14, 17, 20.
[10] *Rom.* v, 14; cf. 17; vi, 9.
[11] *Rom.* vi, I; cf. *Gal.* iv, 5; iii, 23.
[12] *Gal.* iv, 4, 5; cf. iii, 13.
[13] I *Cor.* vi, 19–20.

To make himself more clearly understood St. Paul uses the very terms that were customary in the solemn emancipation of slaves among Pagans[1]: the slave who wished to place his recovered liberty under the protection of a god handed over to the temple the price of his ransom: then his master handed him over to the god by a fictitious sale in exchange for his purchase-money; and the slave was bought 'for liberty,'[2] and no one could enslave him after that. The Christian also has been emancipated 'for liberty'; in vain do certain false brethren 'spy our liberty which we have in Christ Jesus, that they might bring us into servitude.'[3] Whether he be free man or slave, the Christian belongs only to Christ:

> 'For he that is called in the Lord, being a bondman, is the freeman of the Lord. Likewise he that is called, being free, is the bondman of Christ. You are bought with a price: be not made the bondslaves of men.'[4]

We know the moral consequences that St. Paul draws from this doctrine. All Christians have the same Master,[5] and to him alone do they owe obedience.[6] And just as this new servitude has redeemed them from every other, this responsibility to their Lord places them beyond every other jurisdiction.[7]

But we also see the immense difference between this real redemption and the fictitious purchases to which the Apostle refers: the God who has redeemed the Christian has himself paid the ransom, and paid it with his blood[8]; and the liberty which the Christian has thus acquired is not that given by Apollo to his freedmen, 'to go where they will, or to do what they will,'[9] it is the liberty of the children of God. Also, the dominion of the Lord over Christians is both intimate and universal; because they owe to him all they are, they belong wholly to him;

[1] See DITTENBERGER, *Sylloge*, 845. P. FOUCART, *Mémoire sur l'affranchissement des esclaves par forme de vent à une divinité*, in *Archives des mission scientifiques*, part II, vol. III (Paris, 1866), 375–424; *Bulletin de corespondance hellénique*, VIII (1884), 53–75; XVII (1893), 343–409. DEISSMANN, *Licht vom Osten*[4], 274 *sqq.*

[2] *Gal.* v, 19; cf. v, 1. [3] *Gal.* ii, 4. [4] 1 *Cor.* vii, 22–24.

[5] *Rom.* x, 12; 1 *Cor.* iv, 3, 4; cf. 2 *Cor.* x, 18.

[6] *Eph.* v, 22; vi, 7–8; *Col.* iii, 23–4. [7] *Rom.* xiv, 4; cf. 2 *Cor.* x, 18.

[8] *Eph.* i, 7; cf. WESTCOTT, *Hebrews*, 298.

[9] See DEISSMANN *loc. cit.*, 276.

Pagans may require several gods and lords; a Christian cannot split up his allegiance: for him there is but 'one Lord Jesus Christ.'[1]

It is easy to see that so profound and exclusive a faith can only come from the Holy Spirit: 'No man can say the Lord Jesus, but by the Holy Ghost.'[2]

But this lordship has not in itself its *raison d'être*; this unity constituted and maintained by the life-giving action of Christ in the world, is derived from another source and is referred to another head: 'The head of every man is Christ . . . the head of Christ is God.'[3] We must now consider what is involved in this supreme relation.

The very passage with which we were just dealing enables us to penetrate the meaning of this doctrine: 'In him, it hath well pleased the Father that all fulness should dwell'[4] and, again, 'In him dwelleth all the fulness of the Godhead corporeally, and you are filled in him, who is the head of all principality and power.'[5] We recognise here almost the identical terms of the teaching of St. John: 'and of his fulness we all have received.'[6] Moreover, there is nothing in these passages that does not imply the teaching of the earlier Epistles: to say that we are in Christ Jesus, who of God is made unto us wisdom, and justice, sanctification, and redemption,[7] is to say that he has caused to dwell in him that plenitude in which we all participate. Equally, the doctrine of our adoptive filiation, as preached by St. Paul, is necessarily based on the doctrine of the unique filiation of Christ, the 'own Son' of God.[8]

Most of these texts are immediately related only to the glorified Christ. It is as such that he is the Head of the Church and the principle of her life; for it is by his resurrection that he has become 'a quickening Spirit.'[9] By his incarnation and his passion he humbled himself and was obedient unto death (2 *Cor.* viii, 9; *Phil.* ii, 7-8):

> 'For which cause God also hath exalted him, and hath given him a name which is above all names: that in the name of Jesus every knee should bow of those

[1] 1 *Cor.* viii, 6. [2] 1 *Cor.* xii, 3. [3] 1 *Cor.* xi, 3.
[4] *Col.* i, 19. Cf. Lightfoot, *Colossians*, 255–71. [5] *Col.* ii, 9–10.
[6] *John* i, 16. [7] 1 *Cor.* i, 30. [8] *Rom.* viii, 29–32. [9] 1 *Cor.* xv, 45.

that are in heaven, on earth, and under the earth: and that every tongue should confess that the Lord Jesus Christ is in the glory of God the Father.'[1]

This very doctrine is to be found less developed in the first verses of the *Epistle to the Romans* (i, 1-4):

> 'Paul, a servant of Jesus Christ, called to be an apostle, separated unto the gospel of God, which he had promised before, by his prophets in the holy scriptures, concerning his Son, who was made to him of the seed of David, according to the flesh, who was predestinated the Son of God in power, according to the spirit of sanctification, by the resurrection of our Lord Jesus Christ from the dead . . .'

This strange accumulation of phrases renders but very imperfectly the spontaneity and the power of the Apostle's thought; one hesitates to analyse them after so many commentators, for fear of breaking up the image they reflect, which is a little confused, but wonderfully ardent; we must, however, consider them more closely, throwing light upon them by means of the other teachings of the Apostle, particularly those of the *Epistle to the Romans*, from which this passage is taken. At first sight we see the contrast of the two elements in Christ, the flesh and the spirit of holiness; according to the first, he is born of the race of David; according to the second, he has been enthroned as the Son of God by his resurrection. This contrast has a certain analogy with the duality that St. Paul sees in other men: they also are flesh and spirit, but the differences are profound; in their case the flesh is enslaved to sin, a sinful flesh which strives against the spirit[2]; Christ, on the contrary, has not taken a sinful flesh, but the likeness of sinful flesh (*Rom.* viii, 3); the flesh was not in him a principle of concupiscence, but merely a principle of infirmity: 'He was crucified through weakness, yet he liveth by the power of God.'[3] We find the same thought in St. Peter: 'Christ was put to death indeed in the flesh, but enlivened in the spirit.'[4]

If we consider the spirit of holiness, we find here again an imperfect resemblance between Christ and Christians;

[1] *Phil.* ii, 9–11. [2] *Rom.* vii, 14, 25; viii, 6–14; *Gal.* v, 17. [3] 2 *Cor.* xiii, 4. [4] 1 *Peter* iii, 18.

in Jesus, if the flesh is the principle of infirmity, the spirit is the principle of life; if the flesh is the principle of his Davidic filiation, the spirit is the principle of his divine filiation. The dwelling of the Spirit in Christians has the same two effects: 'If the Spirit of him that raised up Jesus from the dead dwell in you; he that raised up Jesus Christ from the dead shall quicken also your mortal bodies, because of his Spirit that dwelleth in you.[1] . . . For whosoever are led by the Spirit of God, they are the sons of God. For you have not received the spirit of bondage again in fear: but you have received the spirit of adoption of sons, whereby we cry: Abba (Father).'[2] It should be further noted that in the days of this mortal life we have the Spirit of God in us; and yet that 'we ourselves groan within ourselves, waiting for the adoption of the sons of God, the redemption of our body'[3]; so that it is not on the day of the resurrection that the Spirit will be given us, but that then he will be fully manifested at the moment of the revelation of the sons of God.[4] Must we not conceive in some such way of this manifestation, the enthronement of Christ as Son of God on the Day of his Resurrection? It was not on that day that he received the Spirit, but on that day that the power of the Spirit was manifested in him by his own works. At his resurrection, which is the model of ours, all that was mortal in him was absorbed by life; his body became a spiritual body, and he himself, the second Adam, became 'a quickening spirit,'[5] not only in the sense that he gave life to his own body, but because in him we shall all be made alive.[6]

Yet these profound analogies should not make us lose sight of the infinite distance on this point between Christ and Christians: I have just referred to it; Christians are quickened by Christ, Christ himself is the quickening Spirit; they receive the spirit of adoption, as co-heirs of Christ, he is the 'own Son' of God; in a word, they receive the spirit of Christ by participation and as a grace; Christ possesses that Spirit in its plenitude and as his very own nature; 'the Lord is a Spirit.'[7] It is also in Christ, as in their source, that the authentic riches of the Spirit,

[1] Cf. E. Sokolowski, *Geist und Leben*, 61 *sqq.* [2] *Rom.* viii, 11–15. [3] *Ib.*, 23. [4] *Ib.*, 19. [5] 1 *Cor.* xv, 45. [6] *Ib.*, 22. [7] 2 *Cor.* iii, 17.

glory, power, and life, are to be found; he is the 'Lord of glory'[1]; the faithful, contemplating that glory face to face, are transformed into the same image and made glorious in his glory[2]; the faithless, on the contrary, blinded by the prince of this world, cannot fix their gaze on the light of the gospel of the glory of Christ, who is the image of God.[3] This last detail recalls and completes what has been said above[4] concerning the relations of Christ with his Father; if by his glory he sheds light on his faithful, he does so because he himself is the image of God, and, as St. Paul adds a little further on,[5] 'The glory of God, in the face of Christ Jesus.'[6] As he is the image of God, so is he the strength and wisdom of God[7]; it is he who strengthens his faithful; his is the strength which works so powerfully within them[8]; they can do everything in him who strengthens them.[9]

To sum up, he is their life,[10] now hidden, which will be manifested in glory, when Christ, our life, shall appear.[11]

Thus on earth was Christ's own life hidden, his own body was not yet a body of glory,[12] a spiritual body; all that could be seen in him was the infirmity of his flesh, and the princes of this world crucified him, not recognising in him the Lord of glory,[13] although he was so already, not merely by his vocation, but in reality.[14] The first verses of the *Epistle to the Romans* have shewn us that, already during his mortal life, Christ possessed that spirit of holiness which was to manifest itself on the day of his resurrection in glory, power, and life, and that, at that time, the Son of David was to be distinguished from the Son of God in him.

We find this distinction in the ninth chapter of this same Epistle, in the famous text in which St. Paul, when celebrating all the privileges of the Israelites, finally reminds them that 'Of whom (the fathers) is Christ, according to the flesh, who is over all things, God blessed for

[1] 1 *Cor.* ii, 8. Cf. GRILL, *Untersuchungen*, 275; DALMAN, *Worte Jesu*, 139; J. WEISS, *I Kor.* (1925), 126.
[2] 2 *Cor.* iii, 18. [3] 2 *Cor.* iv, 4. [4] See above, page 298.
[5] iv, 6. [6] Cf. *Phil.* iii, 21; 1 *Tim.* iii, 16; *Titus* ii, 13.
[7] 1 *Cor.* i, 24. [8] *Col.* i, 29. [9] *Phil.* iv, 13.
[10] *Gal.* ii, 20; *Phil.* i, 21. [11] *Col.* iii, 4. [12] *Phil.* iii, 21.
[13] 1 *Cor.* ii, 8. [14] Cf. J. WEISS, *I Kor.*, *in h. loc.*

ever.'[1] Many other passages teach more or less explicitly this doctrine and confirm our interpretation.[2]

We have first the very clear text of the *Epistle to Titus*, referred to above[3]: 'Looking for the blessed hope and coming of the glory of the great God and our Saviour, Jesus Christ.'[4] Then we have the texts referring to the death of Christ: they represent his death as reconciling the world to God,[5] redeeming men,[6] satisfying for sin,[7] abolishing death.[8] This supreme efficacy of the Passion has always been rightly regarded as the most certain proof of the Saviour's divinity; St. Paul himself has sufficiently noted in his *Epistle to the Colossians* the connection between the two doctrines.[9]

Yet the transcendent relation which unites the Father and the Son is more explicitly evident in those texts in which the death of Christ is represented as the supreme test of the love of God: 'God commendeth his charity towards us: because when as yet we were sinners, Christ died for us.'[10] 'He that spared not even his own Son: but delivered him up for us all, how hath he not also with him given us all things?'[11] The whole value of this argument depends on the relation uniting Christ and God; if this proof of love is decisive it is because God has given his own Son for us.[12]

But if we wish to grasp this relation fully, we must go back further in thought with the apostle; just as his point of departure is not the resurrection of Christ or his passion, neither is it his baptism nor his nativity; on two occasions St. Paul speaks of the mission of the Incarnation, and in both these passages he who is sent by God is presented as already his Son: 'When the fulness of the time was come, God sent his Son, made of a woman, made under the law: that he might redeem them who were

[1] *Rom.* ix, 5; cf. SANDAY-HEADLAM, *Romans*, 233–8; A. DURAND, *La divinité de Jésus-Christ dans Saint Paul, Rom.* ix, 5 (*RB*, 1903, 550–70); PRAT, *Théol. de S. Paul*, II, 181–4; B. H. KENNEDY, *Examination of Rom.* ix, 5 (Cambridge, 1883), 68.

[2] This Christology allows us to safely interpret *Acts* xiii, 33 in the sense of a manifestation of the filiation of Christ (see above, page 261).

[3] Page 278. [4] *Titus* ii, 13.

[5] 2 *Cor.* v, 18–20; cf. *Rom.* iv, 10, 11; *Eph.* ii, 14–16; *Col.* i, 20–2.

[6] 1 *Cor.* vi, 20; vii, 23; *Gal.* iii, 13; iv, 5; *Rom.* iii, 24; *Eph.* i, 7; 1 *Tim.* ii, 6.

[7] *Gal.* i, 4; *Rom.* iii, 25; iv, 25; viii, 3; 1 *Cor.* xv, 3; *Eph.* v, 2.

[8] 1 *Cor.* xv, 54. [9] *Col.* i, 19–20. [10] *Rom.* v, 8. [11] *Rom.* viii, 32.

[12] Cf. SANDAY-HEADLAM, on *Rom.* v, 8.

under the law.'[1] 'God sent his own Son in the likeness of sinful flesh.'[2]

This course was for the Lord a humiliation and an impoverishment. 'You know the grace of our Lord Jesus Christ, that being rich he became poor, for your sakes: that through his poverty you might become rich.'[3]

This conception is more fully developed in the classic text of the *Epistle of the Philippians* (ii, 5-11):

> 'For let this mind be in you, which was also in Christ Jesus[4]:
>
> Who being in the form of God, thought it not robbery to be equal with God:
>
> But emptied himself, taking the form of a servant, being made in the likeness of men, and in habit found as a man.
>
> He humbled himself, becoming obedient unto death: even to the death of the cross.
>
> For which cause God also hath exalted him, and hath given him a name which is above all names:
>
> That in the name of Jesus every knee should bow, of those that are in heaven, on earth, and under the earth:
>
> And that every tongue should confess that the Lord Jesus Christ is in the glory of God the Father.'[5]

This passage, the dogmatic value of which is incalculable, has, from the first, been interpreted in so many different senses that it is impossible to comment on it or translate a single word of it without taking sides; I may perhaps be permitted to leave this controversy on one side, in order to express the thought of the Apostle as I see it, giving the reasons for my views in footnotes.[6]

[1] *Gal.* iv, 4. [2] *Rom.* viii, 3. [3] 2 *Cor.* viii, 9.

[4] Cf. Deissman, *In Christo Jesu*, 113. [5] *Phil*, ii, 5-11.

[6] [Translator's Note :—At this point in the French original, there are a number of very lengthy and erudite footnotes, which do not lend themselves to condensation; the reader may wish to consult them in the original, i.e., J. Lebreton, *Histoire du dogme de la Trinité*, vol. I (8th edit., Paris, 1927), pp. 416-420.]

Among the Fathers, the most useful to consult here is Chrysostom, *In Phil. hom.*, VI, VII (*P.G.*, LXII, 217-38). Among modern exegetes: Lightfoot, *Philippians*, 110-15, 127-38; Gifford, *The Incarnation, a study of Phil.* ii, 9, 11, in *Expositor* (London, 1896-97). J. Labourt, *Notes d'exégèse* on *Phil.* ii, 5-11 (*RB*, 1898), 402-15, 553-63; Prat, *Théologie de Saint Paul*, I, 373-8, 533-43; II, 154-5. H. Schuhmacher, *Christus in seiner Präexistenz und Kenose nach Phil., ii*, 5-8. T. *Historische Untersuchung*. (Rome, 1914.)

The chapter in which this passage occurs has not as a whole a dogmatic character; it consists of an exhortation to peace, charity, and Christian humility; the example of Christ is incidentally invoked in order to lead the faithful to the practice of these virtues, just as, in the parallel passage to the *Corinthians,* the impoverishment of Christ at the Incarnation was only recalled in order to stimulate them to almsgiving; we shall not therefore find here a theological thesis expressed in technical language, but only the mention of a very familiar truth.[1]

This truth consists in the spontaneous humiliation of Christ: while he was in the likeness of God, *in forma Dei,* he did not attach himself to this equality of his rights with God, as a jealously defended prize, but stripped himself, by assuming the form of a slave, becoming like unto men. The comparison of these two conditions, of God and of the slave, permitted the Philippians to appreciate the voluntary humiliation of Christ; we shall note above all the affirmation and the description of the divine pre-existence; when Christ took that decisive step, when he stripped himself in order to become a man, he was already 'in the form of God.' The contrast is very clearly marked between this permanent existence and the new mode of existence on which Christ is about to enter. Chrysostom has underlined the antithesis of the two terms of his action, ὑπάρχων, γενόμενος,[2] and the contrast of them is neither fortuitous nor isolated in the works of St. Paul[3]; moreover, the new condition of Christ does not supplant his previous state, which remains permanently.[4]

The two conditions are described by two parallel expressions: the form of God, and the form of a servant. The parallelism of these two phrases determines much more surely than the word 'form'[5] the meaning of the expression. It is impossible to doubt that, for St. Paul, Christ became truly man, and that he expressed that conviction in the words 'taking the form of a servant.' We must therefore recognise that he was already truly God, 'being in the form of God.'

[1] Cf. Prat, *loc. cit.*, 373.
[2] *Hom.*, VI, 4 (*P.G.*, LXII, 223).
[3] Cf. *Col.* i, 17; *Rom.* i, 3; *Gal.* iv, 4.
[4] See French original, p. 418, note 2.
[5] Cf. Lightfoot, *Philippians*, 127–33.

From this, his natural state, came the equality of his rights with God, 'to be equal with God.'[1] But, far from attaching himself to his prerogatives as something to be prized,[2] he stripped himself of them. This stripping is not an abdication of the Divine nature, nor of his essential attributes of life, of holiness, of knowledge, and power,[3] but the renunciation of the enjoyments of his rights and divine honours[4]; the Incarnate Christ kept for himself merely the form of a slave, and the death of the Cross.[5]

'For which cause God also hath exalted him, and hath given him a name which is above all names . . .' Thus, after having recalled the divine pre-existence of Christ, and his life of humiliation here below, St. Paul returns to the glorified Christ, the habitual object of his contemplation and of his preaching; he it is who, lately crucified and now exalted, the entire universe should adore and recognise as its Lord 'in the glory of God the Father.'

In the preceding analyses, we have attempted only to follow the Apostle along his own road of penetration into the mystery of the Lord; it is indeed the action of Christ in his faithful, in the Church, in the world, which has guided our steps into the very heart of the dogma. Perhaps it will not be useless now to consider these same truths from another point of view, and briefly sketch the theology of the Father and the Son, as contained in the texts which we have been studying.

'There is but one God, the Father, the principle of all, and our last end, and there is but one Lord Jesus Christ, by whom everything and ourselves exist.' The Lord himself comes from the Father, not as his creature, but as his own Son, as his image, his power, his wisdom. 'Before every creature, he is'; but his earthly existence has a beginning. 'He became' man, but his pre-existence cannot be so dated, 'he is.' All creatures come from the Father as from their principle; all have been created by the Son, and only subsist by and in him; their end is the Father and also the Son.

[1] See French original, p. 418, note 4.

[2] See French original, p. 418, note 5 (continued to p. 420); SCHUMACHER, *loc. cit.*, 17–129.

[3] For the various theories on the Kenosis put forth by Protestant theologians, cf. GORE, *Dissertations*, 184–207.

[4] See French original, p. 420, note 2; GIFFORD, 54.

[5] Cf. *Rom.* xv, 3.

From all eternity God had chosen in his Son, his elect; when the fulness of the time came, he sent him: and he, who was in the form of God, took the form of a slave, he was born of a woman, of the race of Abraham, an Israelite according to the flesh, he who was God blessed from all eternity. He humbled himself even to the death of the Cross, was crucified in the infirmity of his flesh, but rose again in the power of the Spirit; and God has infinitely exalted him, and given him the name which every creature adores.

Whoever confesses him and believes in him, and incorporates himself into him by baptism, dies to sin and lives to God, becomes his brother and co-heir, and adopted heir and Son of God. The Lord is the quickening spirit, the head of the Church, and gradually, according to the divine plan, he recapitulates all things in himself, in order to offer them all to his Father, so that finally God shall be all in all.

BIBLIOGRAPHY, Section 1:—R. Reitzenstein, *Die hellenistischen Mysterienreligionen*[2] (Leipzig, 1921); *Religionsgeschichte und Eschatologie*, in *Zeitschrift f. N.T.W.* (1912), 1–28. E. Norden, *Agnostos Theos* (Leipzig, 1913). W. Bousset, *Kyrios Christos*[2] (Göttingen, 1921). A. Deissmann, *Licht vom Osten*[4] (Tubingen, 1923). Bauer's *Lexicon*, 1925 *sqq.* Moulton and Milligan, *Vocabulary of the Greek Testament* (London, 1914 *sq.*). E. Jacquier, *Les Mystères païens et saint Paul*, in *Dict. Apol.*, III, 964–1014. F. Prat, *Le Paulinisme et les religions orientales hellénisées*, in *Dict. Apol.*, 1647–51. J. G. Machen, *Origin of Paul's Religion* (New York), 1921). W. L. Knox, *St. Paul and the Church of Jerusalem* (Cambridge, 1925). A. Schweitzer, *Geschichte der Paulinischen Forschung* (Tubingen, 1911). A. Plummer, *II Corinthians* (Edinburgh, 1915). H. Lietzmann, *Kor. I, II* (Tubingen, 1923). H. Windisch, *II Kor.* (Gottingen, 1924). E. Tobac, *Le problème de la justification dans saint Paul* (Louvain, 1908). J. Rendel Harris, *Origin of the Prologue to St. John* (Cambridge, 1917). F. Kattenbusch, *Das apostolische Symbol* (Leipzig, 1900).

2. *The Holy Spirit*

In the preceding exposition we have been obliged to leave on one side everything referring to the Holy Spirit. I fully recognise that this unfortunate omission mutilates St. Paul's thought: in his view, the Spirit is so inseparable from the Father and the Son that we can only be united to them through and by him. The omission, however, was inevitable: St. Paul's conception of the Spirit is so complex, and consequently so difficult to grasp and express, that it was necessary to consider it by itself.

After this analysis we shall be able to fill in the picture with a more certain hand.[1]

If the study of the theology of the Spirit in St. Paul's writings is difficult, it is certainly not on account of the lack of texts, for they abound[2]; nor is it because this doctrine of the Spirit is not in the foreground of his thought; but it is because the Apostle uses the word Spirit to express very diverse conceptions; it is also and chiefly because he reaches, in one synthetic glance, various very distinct realities which have for long been dissociated by theological analysis. Analogous difficulties are often to be found in the very concrete theology of the New Testament, and are greater in proportion to the richness of the conception studied, whether it be, for instance, that of the Kingdom of God in the Synoptics, of 'justice' in St. Paul, or of 'life' in St. John. But it seems that no conception is more complex than the one on the exposition of which we are now entering[3]; we must not therefore be surprised if, on occasion, our analysis is inclined to hesitate, and is unable to classify certain texts in categories too narrow to hold them.

Moreover, I shall attempt here less to analyse into logical categories the texts and ideas of St. Paul, than to penetrate his thought, to grasp his intimate belief, the profound life from which all his teaching proceeds. We are no longer dealing with an impersonal and literary doctrine, like that of the Rabbis; we feel ourselves in contact with a soul full of the Spirit of God, and who speaks of it out of his own experience. More than any of his believers he has himself received the gifts of the Spirit, gifts of tongues, visions, revelations; these are his sacred and private treasures, which he reveals but unwillingly, and one feels the value he attaches to these divine secrets,[4] in the very constraint which he puts upon himself. The advice which he gives to his disciples reveals the same point of view[5]; in spite of the fact that the Corinthians

[1] See H. BERTRAMS, *Das Wesen des Geistes nach der Anschauung des Apostels Paulus* (Munster, 1913).

[2] According to WINSTANLEY (*The Spirit in the N.T.*), 122, the word 'Spirit' occurs 379 times in *N.T.*, of which 146 are in St. Paul's writings, apart from *Hebrews*.

[3] Cf. *Rom.* viii, 9, 10.

[4] 2 *Cor.* xii, 1–10; *Gal.* ii, 2; 1 *Cor.* ii, 6–16. Cf. GUNKEL, 59; WEIZSAECKER, 313.

[5] Cf. 1 *Thess.* v, 19–20.

abuse the *charismata,* in spite of the illusions into which they fall, the Apostle is careful not to depreciate these gifts; he establishes a hierarchy among them; above them all, he exalts charity, but he recognises that they are all good and desirable.

All of them, as a matter of fact, proceed from the Spirit, which gives life to the body of Christ, and which gives to each member the mode of operation which is proper to him and which serves the whole body: the word of wisdom, the word of knowledge, faith, the gifts of healing and of working miracles, prophecy, the discernment of spirits, the gift of speaking in various tongues, and the gift of interpretation.

> 'But all these things, one and the same Spirit worketh, dividing to every one according as he will. For as the body is one and hath many members; and all the members of the body, whereas they are many, yet are one body: so also is Christ: for in one Spirit were we all baptised into one body.'[1]

We grasp here the profound conception which, in St. Paul's teaching, transforms the whole doctrine of the Spirit. Moses said of old: 'O that all the people might prophesy, and that the Lord would give them his spirit!'[2] What to Moses was but a hyperbole had become a reality to St. Paul; the 'man of the spirit' is no longer a solitary among the people of God: 'in one Spirit we have all been made to drink.'[3] This gift (of the Spirit) is so essential to the Christian that, without it, there is no union with Christ. 'If any man have not the Spirit of Christ, he is none of his.'[4] Indeed, if the union of carnal men is made in the flesh, the union of the Christian with Christ, who is spirit, is only effected in the spirit. 'He who is joined to a harlot is made one body . . . but he who is joined to the Lord is one spirit.'[5]

From this it follows that life in Christ and life in the Spirit are for St. Paul but one and the same reality; it will be the same thing to him to say that the Christian is justified in Christ,[6] and justified in the Spirit[7]; sanctified in Christ Jesus,[8] and sanctified in the Holy Spirit[9]; signed

[1] 1 *Cor.* xii, 8–13. [2] *Num.* xi, 29. [3] 1 *Cor.* xii, 13.
[4] *Rom.* viii, 9. [5] 1 *Cor.* vi, 16–17. [6] *Gal.* ii, 17.
[7] 1 *Cor.* vi, 11. [8] 1 *Cor.* i, 2. [9] *Rom.* xv, 16.

in Christ,[1] and in the Holy Spirit[2]; circumcised in Christ,[3] and circumcised in the Spirit[4]; he will exhort his faithful to stand fast in the Lord[5] and in one Spirit[6]; he will speak in the same way of joy, of justice, of faith, of love, in Christ and in the Spirit.[7] Similarly Christians are called unto the fellowship of the Son,[8] as they are to the communion of the Holy Spirit,[9] and the dwelling of Christ in them is not distinguished from that of the Holy Spirit.[10]

It would be quite unjustifiable to argue from these texts to the personal identity of Christ and the Holy Spirit, the more so that, by pushing the argument further, we should arrive at the identification of the Spirit and the Father.[11] We have, however, a perfect right to draw the conclusion that the action of Christ and the action of the Spirit are inseparable, or, to speak more precisely, Christ only acts in and unites himself to the soul by the Holy Spirit. This doctrine makes us understand better what has been said above about the rôle of Christ in humanity: Jesus, as we have noted, is not merely, for St. Paul, the friend he longs to rejoin or the ideal he wishes to imitate; he is, for St. Paul as for all Christians, the principle of his life, the head of whom he is a member; but this union, this influence, is purely metaphorical, unless we take account of the Spirit imparted to Christians by Christ. In the *Epistle to the Ephesians* (iv, 11, 16) St. Paul describes these numerous contacts which unite the head to the members, and, in consequence of which, life is diffused through the whole body, according to the special activity of each member; the doctrine is the same as that quoted in the passage above from the *Epistle to the Corinthians* (1 *Cor.* xii, 8-13), but, in this instance, the rôle of the Spirit is more explicitly indicated; it is he, the one Spirit received in baptism, who works these many graces in the body of Christ, all of them ordained for the edification of the whole.

We are thus able better to understand the distinction between the first Adam, a living soul, and the second Adam, a quickening spirit; the natural men who can

[1] *Eph.* i, 13. [2] *Eph.* iv, 30. [3] *Col.* ii, 11. [4] *Rom.* ii, 29.
[5] *Phil.* iv, 1. [6] *Phil.* i, 27.
[7] *Phil.* iii, 1; *Rom.* xiv, 17; *Gal.* iii, 26; 1 *Cor.* xii, 9; *Rom.* viii, 39; *Col.* i, 8. See Deissmann, *Die Formel in Christo Jesu*, 86 *sq.*
[8] 1 *Cor.* i, 9. [9] 2 *Cor.* xiii, 13; *Phil.* ii, 1.
[10] This identity is very evident in *Rom.* viii, 9–11. [11] Cf. 1 *Cor.* xii, 6.

understand nothing of the Spirit of God are the descendants of the first (1 *Cor.* ii, 14); but spiritual men, that is to say, those who are of the Spirit, who walk according to the Spirit, who are moved by the Spirit, who are one Spirit with Christ,[1] belong to the second.

This does not mean that St. Paul opposes to one another, as the Gnostics were to do later, spiritual men and carnal men,[2] as if they were two races, fatally predestined to the life of the spirit and the life of the flesh[3]: his Christians, like himself, are converts; from carnal they have become spiritual, or, rather, most of them are slowly in process of becoming spiritual. St. Paul writes to the Galatians (vi, 1): 'If a man be overtaken in any fault, you, who are spiritual, instruct such a one in the spirit of meekness'; but he says to the Corinthians (1 *Cor.* iii, 1 *seq.*):

> 'I could not speak to you as unto spiritual, but as unto carnal. As unto little ones in Christ. I gave you milk to drink, not meat: for you were not able as yet. But neither indeed are you now able: for you are yet carnal. For, whereas there is among you envying and contention, are you not carnal and walk you not according to man?'

It is then neither by a fatality of birth, nor by a sudden transformation that man becomes spiritual; we know that at baptism he has been given to drink of the Holy Spirit, but it is slowly that that new life develops in him, and shows itself by its proper fruits, 'charity, joy, peace, patience, benignity, goodness, longanimity, mildness, faith, modesty, continency, chastity.'[4] This is truly a new life, a 'new creature,'[5] and St. Paul may declare himself the father, the one and only father, of his disciples.[6]

St. Paul was the first to show, in its full light, this aspect of the doctrine of the Spirit; in doing so he has made evident the most intimate springs of the action of the Holy Spirit; we have not here the energy shown by the ancient heroes of the *Book of Judges,* nor have we the

[1] *Rom.* vii, 6; viii, 4 *sqq.*; 1 *Cor.* vii, 17; 2 *Cor.* xii, 18; *Gal.* v, 16, 18, 25.
[2] Cf. 1 *Cor.* xv, 44 sq.; *James,* iii, 15; *Jude,* 19.
[3] Cf. Clemen, *Religionsgeschichtl. Erklarung des N.T.*, 134; Pfleiderer, *Urchristentum,* I, 31 *sq.*; Sabatier, *L'Apôtre Paul,* 308; Stevens, *Theology of the N.T.*, 343 *sq.*; Tobac, *Le problème de la justification chez saint Paul,* 160–2.
[4] *Gal.* v, 22–23. [5] 2 *Cor.* v, 17; *Gal.* vi, 15. [6] 1 *Cor.* iv, 15.

visions or ecstasies of Ezechiel, nor even the *charismata* granted to the first Christians; but it is this new life, freed from the tyranny of the flesh, freed from the slavery of the letter, a life lived by Christ and in Christ, and as its end, God all in all.

These profound realities can be only fully perceived by faith; they, at least, make themselves manifested by certain signs, by the testimony of the Spirit: the Pagans themselves are aware of them in the presence of Christian virtues[1]; above all, Christians can perceive them, and St. Paul wishes for no other proof of his apostolic mission to the Corinthians:

> 'Do we begin again to commend ourselves? Or do we need (as some do) epistles of commendation to you, or from you?
>
> You are our epistle, written in our hearts, which is known and read by all men:
>
> Being manifested, that you are the epistle of Christ, ministered by us, and written: not with ink but with the Spirit of the living God: not in tables of stone, but in the fleshly tables of the heart.'[2]

In order to make this action of the Holy Spirit more evident to them, the Apostle often incites his correspondents to compare what they have been with what they are[3]; he, himself, loves to recall his past, and thus take cognisance of the power of God in which he can do everything.[4]

Looking further afield, he points out to the Romans the moral degradation of the Pagans, the inability of the Jews to observe the law, and, in all men, the sad and fruitless fight between the conscience which sees the good and the will which fails to accomplish it. This epitome of suffering ends with a cry of sorrow: 'Unhappy man that I am, who shall deliver me from the body of this death?' The Apostle immediately contrasts with this description of the law of sin and death the law of the Spirit and of life:

> 'For they that are according to the flesh mind the things that are of the flesh: but they that are according to the spirit mind the things that are of the spirit.

[1] 1 *Thess.* i, 7 *sqq.*; cf. 2 *Thess.* i, 4.
[2] 2 *Cor.* iii, 1–3.
[3] 1 *Cor.* vi, 9 *sqq.*: *Titus* iii, 3, *sqq.*
[4] 1 *Cor.* xv, 9 *sqq.*; *Gal.* i, 13–16; 1 *Tim.* i, 12–16; cf. *Phil.* iv, 13.

For the wisdom of the flesh is death: but the wisdom of the spirit is life and peace.

Because the wisdom of the flesh is an enemy to God. For it is not subject to the law of God: neither can it be.

And they who are in the flesh cannot please God.

But you are not in the flesh, but in the spirit, if so be that the Spirit of God dwell in you. Now if any man have not the Spirit of Christ, he is none of his.

And if Christ be in you, the body indeed is dead, because of sin: but the spirit liveth, because of justification.

And if the Spirit of him that raised up Jesus from the dead dwell in you; he that raised up Jesus Christ from the dead shall quicken also your mortal bodies, because of his Spirit that dwelleth in you.'[1]

This supremely important passage, on which many others throw light, makes us understand well enough what, for St. Paul, is the Spirit and his action in us: the flesh is infirmity, the Spirit is power; the flesh is the seat of sin and of death, the Spirit is the principle of justice and life; those who live according to the flesh can only do the works of the flesh, 'fornication, uncleanness, immodesty, luxury, idolatry . . .' Those who live according to the Spirit bear the fruits of the Spirit, 'charity, joy, peace . . . ; against such there is no law.'[2]

This does not mean that there is no law of the Spirit, and we have seen above how St. Paul describes it, but this law of the Spirit is quite different from the ancient law; which without doubt was good, spiritual, given to men by the ministry of angels, to be their schoolmaster and prepare them for Christ; but it could give neither life nor strength; it pointed out man's duty, but left him incapable of accomplishing it. The law of the Spirit, on the contrary, is not given from without, but is in the depths of the heart; it is no mere notification, it is light and strength.

The man who is deprived of that light has but the wisdom of the flesh, but from it he receives the wisdom of the Spirit,[3] that is to say, that he begins to learn the

[1] *Rom.* viii, 5–11. [2] *Gal.* v, 19–23.
[3] *Rom.* viii, 6; cf. *Phil.* iii, 19; *Col.* iii, 2; *Mark* viii, 33; *Matt.* xvi, 23.

secrets of God, to discern his ways, to judge everything by that light:

> 'For the Spirit searcheth all things, yea, the deep things of God.
>
> For what man knoweth the things of a man, but the spirit of a man that is in him? So the things also that are of God, no man knoweth, but the Spirit of God.
>
> Now, we have received not the spirit of this world, but the Spirit that is of God: that we may know the things that are given us from God.
>
> Which things also we speak: not in the learned words of human wisdom, but in the doctrine of the Spirit, comparing spiritual things with spiritual.
>
> But the sensual man perceiveth not these things that are of the Spirit of God. For it is foolishness to him: and he cannot understand, because it is spiritually examined.
>
> But the spiritual man judgeth all things; and he himself is judged of no man.
>
> For who hath known the mind of the Lord, that he may instruct him? But we have the mind of Christ.'[1]

Elsewhere, again, the Apostle recalls this illumination of man by the Holy Spirit[2]; the characteristic of it is, not the making known of mysteries or of the hidden designs of God—were not the Jews the depositaries of the promises? —it is the intimate revelation of them, through the union of the Spirit of God with the spirit of man; it is also, and necessarily, a new orientation of the thoughts and judgements of man, which re-form themselves in accordance with the thoughts of God, and acquire little by little the 'mind of Christ,' and thus tend to conformity with the absolute standard which judges everything, and is judged by no one.

That is to say, in another way, that, for the spiritual man there is no law, no rule imposed on him from without; he is to himself his own law, but in a totally different sense to that of the Pagan; the latter sees in his conscience the elementary rules of morality, but his vision gives him no strength, and, while he sees the good, he does evil. The Christian is not only illuminated, but moved by the Spirit; he is in communion with the secrets of God,

[1] 1 *Cor.* ii, 10–16. [2] *Eph.* i, 17 *sqq.*

and he is raised by the Spirit of adoption which cries in him to the Father:

> 'For whosoever are led by the Spirit of God, they are the sons of God.
>
> For you have not received the spirit of bondage again in fear: but you have received the spirit of adoption of sons, whereby we cry: Abba (Father).
>
> For the Spirit himself giveth testimony to our spirit that we are the sons of God . . .
>
> We also, who have the firstfruits of the Spirit: even we ourselves groan within ourselves, waiting for the adoption of the sons of God, the redemption of our body . . .
>
> Likewise, the Spirit also helpeth our infirmity. For, we know not what we should pray for as we ought: but the Spirit himself asketh for us with unspeakable groanings.
>
> And he that searcheth the hearts knoweth what the Spirit desireth: because he asketh for the saints according to God.'[1]

The Christian receives from this an assurance that nothing can shake, neither sin, nor death, nor hell:

> 'For I am sure that neither death, nor life, nor angels, nor principalities, nor powers, nor things present, nor things to come, nor might, nor height, nor depth, nor any other creature, shall be able to separate us from the love of God which is in Christ Jesus our Lord.'[2]

He, no doubt, owes this certitude to the infinite love of God, to the death and resurrection of Christ, but the actual witness that he has to prove it is the witness of the Spirit which guarantees his sonship of God.

From the Spirit also comes to him that strength in which he can do everything.[3] The intimate alliance of the two concepts of spirit and power has been rightly pointed out[4] as one of the characteristic features of Pauline

[1] *Rom.* viii, 14–27. [2] *Ib.*, 38–39.
[3] *Phil.* iv, 13; cf. 1 *Tim.* i, 12; 2 *Tim.* iv, 17; 1 *Cor.* xiii, 7.
[4] WENDT, *Fleisch und Geist* 146; GUNKEL, 72.

theology; it is quite true that this conception is particularly dear to St. Paul, and to his disciple St. Luke.[1] Wendt has remarked in this connection that, in the Old Testament as well, the Spirit was represented as a force; this observation is accurate, but it should be added that every notion of force or power is much more profound in St. Paul than in the Old Testament; what the Apostle is thinking of primarily is the divine power which triumphs over sin and confounds the wisdom of men.

The same observation is inevitable with regard to the concept of life[2]; already, in the Old Testament, the Spirit was considered as the principle of life; in St. Paul we find the same relation between the terms, but they have both been profoundly modified. The glorified life of the risen Christ is to St. Paul the type of all life, and the whole of his doctrine is transformed by this fundamental fact of Christianity: 'For we are buried together with him by baptism into death: that, as Christ is risen from the dead by the glory of the Father, so we also may walk in newness of life.'[3] This truth is incessantly present to the Apostle's thought, and when he speaks of the life of the Spirit, this is what he has in view.

Also, the Spirit is, for him, the unique principle of life: Pagans are alienated from the life of God[4]; the law itself cannot give life[5] any more than it can give the Spirit[6]; so Paul dies to the law, so that he may live to God; he has been crucified with Christ, and Christ lives in him.[7]

This life is already present in the Christian, but imperfectly: the body is dead by sin, the Spirit is alive by justification,[8] so that the Christian is, at once, dead and living,[9] and life, which is often described as a good which he already possesses,[10] is also often proposed as the future good to which he is tending[11]; both aspects are true; the Christian is indeed saved, but in a state of hope, and he has yet to wait for the redemption of his body[12];

[1] *Rom.* i, 4; xv, 13, 19; 1 *Cor.* ii, 4; *Gal.* iii, 5; 1 *Thess.* i, 5; *Eph.* iii, 16. Cf. 2 *Tim.* i, 7; *Luke* i, 17; iv, 14; *Acts* i, 8; x, 38; also *Mark* xiv, 38; *Matt.* xxvi, 41.

[2] See above, page 81 *sqq.* STRACK-BILLERBECK, III, 240.

[3] *Rom.* vi, 4.

[4] *Eph.* iv, 18; cf. *Rom.* iii, 23.

[5] *Gal.* iii, 21.

[6] *Gal.* iii, 2. See French original, p. 432, note 2.

[7] *Gal.* ii, 19–20.

[8] *Rom.* viii, 10. Cf. SOKOLOWSKI, *Geist und Leben.* 48 *sq.*

[9] *Rom.* vi, 11; *Gal.* v, 24, 25; 2 *Cor.* iv, 10, 11; *Col.* iii, 4.

[10] *Gal.* ii, 20; *Rom.* viii, 6; *Phil.* i, 21.

[11] *Rom.* vi, 8, 22; viii, 11; *Gal.* vi, 8.

[12] *Rom.* viii, 23, 24.

he possesses the Spirit, but only as a first-fruit, an earnest[1]; he lives, but he aspires, with groanings, to see the mortal part of him at length absorbed by his new life[2]; from now on he bears his fruit, holiness, but he tends to his end, eternal life.[3]

The Spirit, to consummate his work, will then raise his body and give it life: 'If the Spirit of him that raised up Jesus from the dead dwell in you; he that raised up Jesus Christ from the dead shall quicken also your mortal bodies, because of his Spirit that dwelleth in you.'[4] This transformation of the body by the Spirit is compared to the transformation of the seed: '(The body) is sown in weakness: it shall rise in power. It is sown a natural body: it shall rise a spiritual body.'[5] But to arrive at this it is necessary that a man should live here below by the Spirit: 'God is not mocked. For what things a man shall sow, those also shall he reap. For he that soweth in his flesh, of the flesh also shall reap corruption. But he that soweth in the spirit, of the spirit shall reap life everlasting.'[6]

This rapid description of the action of the Spirit, according to St. Paul, shows us clearly enough the origin of his doctrine; it is certainly in continuity with the theology of the Old Testament, and the greater part of the Pauline conceptions can be found in the prophetical books and the *Psalms;* there, also, the Spirit is represented as light, strength, and life, and the source of extraordinary gifts, and, occasionally, though more rarely, as a principle of holiness.

But in St. Paul all these doctrines are transformed. They are expressed much more profoundly and, in consequence, they manifest a unity, up till then unsuspected. The light of the Spirit no longer flashes through human life like lightning in the night, it lights it up from end to end with the brightness of Christ; 'For you were heretofore darkness, but now light in the Lord.'[7] The Spirit fortifies man not by giving a miraculous vigour to his body, but by communicating to his spirit the strength of Christ: 'I can do all things in him who strengtheneth me'; the Spirit gives him life by filling him with the very life of Christ; he multiplies *charismata*

[1] *Rom.* viii, 23; 2 *Cor.* i, 22. [2] 2 *Cor.* v, 4, 5. [3] *Rom.* vi, 22.
[4] *Rom.* viii, 11. [5] 1 *Cor.* xv, 43–44. [6] *Gal.* vi, 7–8. [7] *Eph.* v, 8.

in the Church for the edification of the body of Christ; he sanctifies her members so that she may be the worthy spouse of Christ, holy and unspotted. In a word, all these transformations of the theology of the Spirit have their principle in the conception of Christ; in him God has revealed to St. Paul wisdom, strength, life, and holiness; and since Christ is the first-born of many brethren, since these divine gifts, which he possesses in their plenitude, are communicated by the Spirit to other men, we must recognise that, in all Christians, the Spirit is the principle of a truly divine life. It is also easy to see that, apart from the Spirit, there is in man nothing but infirmity and sin, but that, on the other hand, man, taken hold of by the Spirit, adheres to the Lord so as to be one spirit with him.

As for the Spirit himself and his nature, it is evident, if we judge by his effects and action, that he is purely a divine principle. From one point of view of the doctrine of St. Paul, it might seem that he is no more than an impersonal force; it is often said that God gives him to us, and diffuses him in our hearts[1]; we are already familiar with these expressions, which fit without difficulty into a very personal conception of the Spirit, as of Wisdom.[2] We should interpret also, and for stronger reasons, this other formula 'in the Holy Spirit,' strictly parallel to 'in Christ'; the Spirit and Christ are represented as the vital element of the Christian, no one will dream, on that account, of denying the personality of Christ; the same applies to the personality of the Spirit.

And, on the other hand, we must consider the definitely personal rôle attributed to the Spirit by St. Paul: 'He dwells in us'[3] just as Christ dwells there (*Romans* viii, 10); we are the temple of the Spirit[4] in the same way that we are the temple of God[5]; he groans in us,[6] he intercedes for us[7]; God sends him into our hearts[8] in the same way as he sent his Son through the mystery of the Incarnation.[9] In the following passage is described the distribution of divine graces at the good pleasure of the Spirit of God.

[1] *Rom.* v, 5; 1 *Cor.* vi, 19; *Gal.* iii, 5; *Eph.* i, 7; *Phil.* i, 19; 1 *Thess.* iv, 8; *Titus* iii, 6.

[2] See above, page 97, note 3.

[3] *Rom.* viii, 9–12; 1 *Cor.* iii, 16. [4] 1 *Cor.* vi, 19. [5] 1 *Cor.* iii, 16.

[6] *Rom.* viii, 26. [7] *Rom.* viii, 27. [8] *Gal.* iv, 6. [9] *Gal.* iv. 4.

'Now there are diversities of graces, but the same Spirit.

And there are diversities of ministries, but the same Lord.

And there are diversities of operations, but the same God, who worketh all in all.

And the manifestation of the Spirit is given to every man unto profit.

To one indeed, by the Spirit, is given the word of wisdom: and to another, the word of knowledge, according to the same Spirit:

To another, faith in the same spirit: to another, the grace of healing in one Spirit:

To another, the working of miracles: to another, prophecy: to another, the discerning of spirits: to another, diverse kinds of tongues: to another, interpretation of speeches.

But all these things, one and the same Spirit worketh, dividing to every one according as he will.'[1]

In this text St. Paul insists, particularly, upon the unity from which everything proceeds; all these diverse gifts, which create such jealousy in the community at Corinth, come all, as St. John Chrysostom says, 'from the same root, the same source, the same treasure.' But this 'source' is not a blind force of destiny, but a supreme Master, having consciousness and will, who distributes his gifts as he chooses, to make of all these members, with their various endowments, the living body of the Church. All of which implies the personality of the Spirit,[2] and, at the same time, his divinity, for a God only can be supreme Master of these divine gifts.[3]

And, if we glance again at the first verses of this passage, we see how the parallelism of the style underlines the distinction and the equality of the three divine Persons.[4] The same reflection inevitably results when we read the salutation, at the end of the second letter to the Corinthians: 'The grace of our Lord Jesus Christ and the

[1] 1 *Cor.* xii, 4–11.

[2] Cf. ROBERTSON-PLUMMER, 268, quoting ST. BASIL, *De Spir.*, XVI, 37; XXVI, 61, and *Epist.*, XXXVIII, 4.

[3] Cf. PRAT, II, 15 *sqq.*

[4] Cf. BERTRAMS, 164–6; J. WEISS (p. 297), whom LIETZMANN quotes and follows (*I Kor.*, p. 62).

charity of God and the communication of the Holy Ghost be with you all.'[1]

This parallelism is peculiarly interesting, as showing us how the apostolic theology has reached a distinct conception of the personality of the Holy Spirit; it has not done so under the influence of Jewish or Hellenic ideas of intermediary beings, but in the light of Christ. Just as Jesus Christ, by revealing the divine life in himself, has made intelligible the action of the Spirit in man, so, by revealing himself as a divine Person distinct from the Father, he has given us a clearer conception, as such, of the distinct divine Person of the Holy Spirit. In the case of St. John, whose doctrine on this point is more explicit, the influence of Christology will be still more manifest; the Holy Spirit will be 'another Paraclete'; but, in St. Paul, the influence of Christology is already certain.

The personal distinction, which has just been drawn between Christ and the Holy Spirit, should not make us conceive of the divine Persons as merely in juxtaposition to one another; we must remember that the Father and the Son are united, according to St. Paul, by an infinitely close relation of dependence, of which we find a certain image in the dependence of man on Christ, and of woman on man. The Spirit also depends on God the Father: we have seen that he is sent, given, diffused by him; the frequent expression, 'the Spirit of God,'[2] makes known this relation of origin. It is replaced once by an even more precise qualification: 'the Spirit who comes from God' (1 *Cor.* ii, 12).

Not infrequently St. Paul also says: 'the Spirit of the Lord,'[3] 'the Spirit of the Son,'[4] 'the Spirit of Jesus Christ.'[5] We hesitate to see in these expressions the sending of the Spirit by the Son; while St. John attributes to Christ the sending of the Holy Spirit, St. Paul does not explicitly do so. In these very formulas, the genitive seems less to mark origin than possession and ownership; thus in *Gal.* (iv, 6),

[1] 2 *Cor.* xiii, 13; cf. Prat, II, p. 158; Lietzmann, *II Kor.*. 159; R. Seeberg, *Zum dogmatischen Verstandnis der Trinitatslehre*, in *Theol. Studien Theod. Zahn . . . dargebracht*, Leipzig, 1908, 345. The Trinitarian texts have been collected by Prat, *Théol. de S. Paul*, II, 518–21.

[2] *Rom.* viii, 9, 14; 1 *Cor.* ii, 14; iii, 16; vi, 11; vii, 40; xii, 3; 2 *Cor.* iii, 3; *Eph.* iii, 16; *Phil.* iii, 3. See also 1 *Cor.* ii, 11; *Rom.* viii, 9; 1 *Cor.* xii, 3.

[3] 2 *Cor.* iii, 17, 18. [4] *Gal.* iv, 6. [5] *Phil.* i, 19.

'because you are sons, God hath sent the Spirit of his Son into your hearts, crying: Abba, Father. Therefore, now he is not a servant but a son. And if a son, an heir also through God.' This passage is exactly parallel to *Romans* (viii, 15): 'you have received the spirit of adoption of sons, whereby we cry: Abba (Father). For the Spirit himself giveth testimony to our spirit that we are the sons of God. And if sons heirs also.' In both these texts the Spirit, sent by the Father, is called the Spirit of the Son, or the Spirit of filial adoption, because it is he (the Spirit) who associates us with the filiation of the 'Son of God by nature' and makes us his co-heirs.

In the texts at our disposition, these relations of the Son and the Spirit are only made plain to us in the sanctification of Christians, but there they are clear enough: Christ *is* the Spirit[1]: Christians can only be united to him and transformed in and through the Spirit. All the privileges of Christ, his glory, his power, his life, his holiness, and, above all, his divine filiation, the foundation of all his other privileges, belong to him in accordance with his divine nature, or, to use St. Paul's words, according to the Spirit, in so far as he is Spirit; if Christians are to participate in all these privileges, if they are to be glorified, fortified, animated, sanctified, and above all, adopted by God, they must participate in the Spirit. And, like the individual Christian, the whole Church is animated by the Holy Spirit: she constitutes only one body, the body of Christ, she has but one soul, the Spirit of Christ.

The second *Epistle of St. Peter* merely translates into other terms this very doctrine, when it speaks of our participation in 'the divine nature,'[2] and in later days, when the Fathers of the fourth century wish to prove the divinity of the Holy Spirit, they will have merely to refer to these teachings of St. Paul, and draw the conclusion that only a God can deify us.

It must be recognised, on the other hand, that, in consequence of the point of view adopted by the Apostle, the action of the Spirit appears much more definitely than his Person; the distinct personality of the Son is manifested very clearly in both his mortal and glorious life, and, even his pre-existence has been more than once described

[1] See above, page 308. [2] i, 4.

by St. Paul, above all, when provoked by the birth of heresies. The personality of the Holy Spirit, on the contrary, though certainly taught by the Apostle, remains in the background; that personality did not appear to us in an incarnation, and the mysteries of his procession and his eternal life are, as yet, only indirectly manifested by the reflections of his action here below. We understand sufficiently his dependence on the Father, because the Father sent him to us, but without being able to determine precisely the intimate relations which unite the two Persons. Between the Son and the Spirit we perceive a very close union, and beyond the sanctifying action in which we directly perceive the Spirit, we divine mysteries of an infinite intimacy, but they are, as yet, the secrets of God: St. John will shortly reveal them; the words of Christ, which he will report, will thus help us better to understand the words of St. Paul.[1]

If St. Paul has partially veiled the secrets of the divine life itself, at least he has thrown a bright light on the mysteries of the divine life in man and in the Church, and, in that light, we can understand more clearly his Trinitarian doctrine as a whole. It may be summed up in this text: 'By him we have access both in one Spirit to the Father.'[2] As long as he has not been saved by Christ, man is 'without God,' 'deprived of the glory of God,' 'separated from the life of God'; when the action of redemption has been completed 'God will be all in all.' But man can only be drawn thus into the divine life if he is taken hold of by Christ; crucified with Christ, he rises with him; he becomes his brother, his co-heir, member of the body of which Christ is the head, 'Christ is all in all.' But this union is impossible unless man is transformed by the Spirit; Christ is spirit, and one cannot adhere to Christ without being of one spirit with him; no sooner is man baptised than he receives the Holy Spirit, and he mortifies his flesh through the spirit in order to live, so that one day 'all that is mortal of him will be absorbed by life.' It is always the same condition that is given to us; God, all in all. The highest religious ideal proposed in the Old Testament was expressed in

[1] Cf. T. DE REGNON, *Études de théol. positive sur la Sainte Trinité*, IV, 136–52.
[2] *Eph.* ii, 18.

the words of the Psalm, 'It is good for me to cling to God.' The grace of Christ carries the Christian higher; God is wholly within him, and the condition of the consummation of this unhoped-for union between two terms infinitely distant is the transformation of man, through the Holy Spirit, by Christ, who has filled him with his own life and drawn him, in the Spirit, up to the Father. Man is only united to God by participation in the reciprocal union of the Divine Persons.

A simple consideration of this doctrine makes us recognise its transcendence. All that is attractive in human systems is to be found here, in a state of great purity and of greater perfection, and in a synthesis in which their negations are effaced; the unity achieved is more intimate than in Stoic Monism, because more personal and more living; the divine transcendence is better safeguarded than in Platonism, because the holiness of God is conceived more profoundly; all the intermediary beings imagined by Alexandrianism are put on one side, while man is united to God by a mediator, weak as ourselves in his flesh, but holy as God in his Spirit. And all this is no mere speculation, but a reality which appeared in Christ, which was consummated by his death and resurrection, and which is daily perpetuated in Christians by his Spirit. Thus, in this religion, the facts and ideas are intimately related, like the flesh and the spirit, like man and God, and the believer is wholly absorbed by it; he adheres to no system, but he is incorporated with Christ.

It is not easy to trace the progress of this doctrine in the mind of St. Paul; his Epistles only throw light on the last third of his Christian life; the first twenty years of it remain obscure, and, further, if the Epistles written in captivity are more explicit than their forerunners, this must be attributed rather to the spiritual progress of his correspondents than to that of the Apostle; do not his great Epistles contain in a few short phrases the whole substance of his later developments?[1]

What at least is quite clear is St. Paul's consciousness of the divine revelation. I noted this at the beginning of this study,[2] when recalling the declarations made in the

[1] Compare 1 *Cor.* viii, 6 with *Col.* i, 15–20; 2 *Cor.* viii, 9 with *Phil.* ii, 5–11. See PRAT, I. 50–62.

[2] See above, page 288.

Epistle to the Galatians. We also read in the *Epistle to the Ephesians :*

> 'If yet you have heard of the dispensation of the grace of God which is given me towards you:
>
> How that, according to revelation, the mystery[1] has been made known to me, as I have written above in a few words ;
>
> As you reading, may understand my knowledge in the mystery of Christ,
>
> Which in other generations was not known to the sons of men, as it is now revealed to his holy apostles and prophets in the Spirit.'[2]

The interpreters of St. Paul cannot do better to-day than repeat his invitation, feeling certain that whosoever has the Spirit of God will recognise in this doctrine the word of the Lord.[3]

[1] Cf. J. ARMITAGE ROBINSON, *Ephesians*, 234–40 ; MILLIGAN, art. *Μυστήριον*, in *Vocabulary of the Greek Testament*, 1924, col. 420.

[2] *Eph.* iii, 2–5.

[3] 1 *Cor.* xiv, 37.

CHAPTER IV

THE EPISTLE TO THE HEBREWS

THE place occupied by the *Epistle to the Hebrews* in our Bibles explains very clearly the rôle played by it in the development of the Christian revelation ; it is attached to the letters of St. Paul, and, in point of fact, is a faithful expression of his doctrine. On the other hand, it is not organically connected with the other epistles, but seems to be added to them as an appendix. In early days, indeed, its distinguishing qualities of style and manner impressed its readers ; Origen, having pointed them out,[1] concluded: 'If I gave my opinion I should say:

> 'that the thoughts are the thoughts of the Apostle, but that the phraseology and the composition belong to someone who reported his teachings, as might a scholar writing down the words of his master. Any Church, then, that considers this epistle as coming from Paul is to be congratulated ; for it is not by chance that the ancients have handed it down to us as his. But who wrote the Epistle? God knows the truth.'[2]

In a study of the historical development of the dogma, this Epistle must be considered by itself: it presents the doctrine of St. Paul in an aspect peculiar to itself, under a less mystical and more speculative form than we usually associate with his writings. To speak here only of Trinitarian theology, we do not find in the *Epistle to the Hebrews* the conception, so dear to St. Paul, of our incorporation with and our life in Christ ; indeed, the formula, 'in Christ Jesus,' does not appear in it. By a consequence that could easily have been foreseen, the theology of the Holy Spirit is left in the background: several passages attribute to the Holy Spirit the oracles of the Old Testament[3] ; his action in the faithful[4] is briefly

[1] *Ap*. EUS., *Hist. Eccl.*, VI, 25, 11–12 ; transl. by GRAPIN.
[2] *Ibid.*, 13–14. This distinction between the author and the scribe was approved in a reply of the 24th June, 1914, by the Biblical Commission.
[3] *Heb.* iii, 7 ; ix, 8 ; x, 15. [4] *Ibid.* ii, 4 ; vi, 4 ; x, 29.

mentioned two or three times, but nowhere is it described with that intensity of life and emotion which characterises the *Epistle to the Galatians* and the *Epistle to the Romans.*

On the other hand, the sacred writer takes pleasure in the contemplation of the nature and prerogatives of the Son; the most revealing texts of St. Paul appeared to be concerned with moral exhortation; in the *Epistle to the Hebrews,* on the contrary, as in the *Gospel of St. John,* the prologue throws full light on the Christological dogma and expounds it clearly for its own sake. This makes the task of the commentator easier; the lucidity of the style further facilitates it: the writer who edited the *Epistle to the Hebrews* had not St. Paul's impetuosity, but he had a perfect command of language, a rich vocabulary, and a supple phrase; he does not take hold of the reader in the way that his master does, but he is none the less engrossing, and does not confuse.

> 'God, who, at sundry times and in divers manners, spoke in times past to the fathers by the prophets, last of all,
>
> In these days, hath spoken to us by his Son, whom he hath appointed heir of all things, by whom also he made the world.
>
> Who being the brightness of his glory and the figure of his substance and upholding all things by the word of his power, making purgation of sins, sitteth on the right hand of the majesty on high:
>
> Being made so much better than the angels as he hath inherited a more excellent name than they.
>
> For to which of the angels hath he said at any time: *Thou art my Son, to-day have I begotten thee?*' (i, 1, 5).

These last words, accentuated still more by the verses which follow them, recall the teaching of the *Epistle to the Colossians* on the pre-eminence of the Son over the angels. The first words of the Epistle describe the interval separating him from the prophets; until his day men had heard nothing but fragmentary revelations of God, veiled under divers forms; the Son brought the supreme revelation to the world. This comparison between the prophets and the Son, whom God has made the heir of all, is but a development of the teaching of the parable of the vine-dressers.

Between these two comparisons with the prophets and the angels, the nature and prerogatives of the Son are celebrated for their own sake, in such splendid and magnificent terms that the prologue of *St. John's Gospel* will not surpass them. There again we find conceptions with which the *Epistle to the Colossians* has made us familiar: Christ is there called 'the image of the invisible God' (i, 15); here he is called 'the brightness of his glory, and the figure of his substance.' 'All things were created by him and in him' (i, 16); similarly in *Hebrews*: '[God] hath appointed (him) heir of all things by whom also he made the world.' 'By him all things consist,' is the precise equivalent of 'upholding all things by the word of his power.' Finally the expression, 'first-born' (15, 18), found twice in this passage of the *Epistle to the Colossians,* occurs in the sixth verse of this chapter to the *Hebrews,* and is used in an absolute sense as the special attribute of the Son. 'And again, when he bringeth in the first begotten into the world, he saith . . .'

It was necessary to begin by noting the similarities in the writings of the evangelists and St. Paul: we shall soon have occasion to observe in the vocabulary of the *Epistle to the Hebrews* many features of Alexandrine origin which, consequently, suggest the influence of the writings of Philo.

In order to avoid misunderstanding, it was well to remark the Christian origin and character of the doctrines to be found there.[1] This will become more evident when we study them more closely.

The very prologue which we have just read suggests our taking as our point of departure for this study, no longer, as in the case of the other Epistles of St. Paul, the life of the glorified Christ in the Christian, but rather the life of the pre-existing Christ in God.

One of the characteristic features of the Epistle is the employment of the title of 'Son' without an article, to designate our Lord; as, in the writings of St. Paul, 'Χριστός' had become as it were his proper name, and was consequently employed most frequently without an article, so, here, the word 'υἱός' is always, except on one

[1] See Westcott, *Hebrews*, 429.

occasion,[1] used in the same absolute[2] manner; and this is a new[3] and significant fact.

The relations of origin attaching the Son to the Father[4] are described by means of two metaphors; he is the 'brightness of his glory,' and 'the figure of his substance.' This description resembles closely what we read in the *Book of Wisdom* (vii, 26); Wisdom is 'the brightness of eternal light, and the unspotted mirror of God's majesty, and the image of his goodness.'[5] The two writers, in order to convey some notion of a mysterious reality, describe it by several symbols, of which the one completes and corrects the other; the image of splendour or of radiance[6] gives a good idea of the unity and inseparability of the Father and the Son, as well as of the original relations attaching them to each other; and it is furthermore as little material as a concrete image can be, thus helping the human intelligence to free itself from grosser imaginations. This Scriptural comparison will be employed by the Fathers and the Councils; and we shall find it in the Creed of Nicæa: 'Light of light'; the controversialists of the fourth century, and, in particular, St. Athanasius will make use of it in the defence of the consubstantiality of the Son, the eternity and the necessity of his generation.[7]

On the other hand we must recognise that the metaphor was not without danger; it was possible to interpret it in a modalist sense, making us think of the Son as an aspect of the Father,[8] rather than as a distinct Person. The author of the Epistle cuts these equivocations short by using the comparison of the 'figure.' This image,

[1] *Heb.* i, 8. Also, we must note that the article is always used in the formula 'the Son of God'; iv, 14; vi, 6; vii, 3; x, 29.

[2] *Heb.* i, 2; vii, 28; cf. iii, 6; v, 8.

[3] Only once and then attributively is it used without the article in St. Paul; *Rom.* i, 4.

[4] It is remarkable that the name 'Father', so frequently given to God by St. Paul elsewhere, only occurs twice in *Hebrews*: i, 5 and xii, 9; and the former is only a quotation from 2 *Kings* vii, 14.

[5] Cf. Rendel Harris, *Origin of Prologue to St. John's Gospel* (Cambridge, 1917), 13.

[6] The Greek word is ἀπαύγασμα. See French original, I, 447, note 2; and Westcott, *loc. cit.*, 10 *sq.*

[7] Athanasius, *Or. c. Arian.*, I, 20 (*P.G.*, XXVI, 23b). Cf. 14 (41b); 24 (61b); 25 (64b); 27 (68b); 29 (73a); II, 32 (216b), etc.; Greg. Naz., *Or.*, XXIX, 17 (*P.G.*, XXXVI, 92a); Cyril Alex., *Thes.*, IV (*P.G.*, LXXV, 40a); Augustine, *Epist.* 238, 24 (*P.L.*, XXXIII, 1047); etc.

[8] Cf. Justin, *Dial.*, 128.

like the first, of Alexandrine origin,[1] does not lead us in the same way to the notion of consubstantiality, but indicates much more clearly a subsistent reality.[2]

Applied to Wisdom, these metaphors suggested their divine origin, and it is the same here; in other contexts, as for example in Philo, these images, more brilliant than precise, may receive much wider interpretations; man, as well as the Logos, could be called the 'brightness'[3] or the 'figure'[4] of God. But the very explicit doctrine of the *Epistle to the Hebrews* here determines the value of all these symbols: this radiance, this imprint of God, is not of any other nature than God himself; all others, prophets or angels, however great they may be, are servants,[5] Christ is the Son, he is God: to the Son he says: 'thy throne, O God, is for ever and ever: a sceptre of justice is the sceptre of thy kingdom. Thou hast loved justice and hated iniquity: therefore God, thy God, hath anointed thee with the oil of gladness above thy fellows.' And again:

> 'Thou, in the beginning, O Lord, didst found the earth: and the works of thy hands are the heavens. They shall perish: but thou shalt continue. And they shall all grow old as a garment. And as a vesture shalt thou change them: and they shall be changed. But thou art the selfsame: and thy years shall not fail . . .' (i, 8-12).

What should be looked at in these quotations is not this or that textual detail, which the writer of the Epistle has transcribed without attaching any particular value to it,[6] but the general significance of these passages as it spontaneously appears, more particularly in the writer's own interpretation. There is no doubt about this significance; all the texts accumulated in this long series, according to the favourite Jewish method of *ḥaraz,* tend to prove that Jesus is the Son of God (5), that the very angels must adore him (6, 7), that he is God (8, 9), that he is the

[1] Cf. PHILO, *De Plantat.*, 18 (M., I, 332); *Q. det. pot.*, 83 (207).
[2] WESTCOTT, *loc. cit.*, 427. Cf. PETAU, *De Trinitate*, VI, 6; RÉGNON, *Études*, III, 351 *sqq.*; BETHUNE-BAKER, *TS*, VII, 1, p. 74 *sqq.*; MÉNÉGOZ, *Théol. de l'Ep. aux Héb.*, 79; SCHWARTZS' edition of TATIAN, *Orat.*, vi, xv (pp. 24, 4, 9).
[3] *De opif. mundi*, 146. (M., I, 35); *De spec. leg.*, IV, 123 (II, 356).
[4] *Q. det. pot.*, 83 (M, I, 207).
[5] i, 5-14; iii, 5.
[6] Cf. MÉNÉGOZ, 84 *sq.*

immutable Creator (10, 12)), that he is at the right hand of God (13). One wonders what more the author could have added to express the community of nature and privileges between the Father and the Son.

The eternity of the Son, clearly affirmed in these texts (10, 12), is recalled again by the writer; 'Christ, by the Holy Ghost[1] offered himself unspotted unto God' (ix, 14); we recognise here St. Paul's vocabulary[2]; this eternal Spirit is the Spirit of sanctity, of which the *Epistle to the Romans* spoke, that is to say, the divine nature of Christ. These affirmations determine the meaning to be given to the text of the Psalm quoted here: 'Thou art my Son, to-day have I begotten thee'; this refers to the 'to-day' of eternity.[3] We find the same idea again in the description given of the divine attributes of the Son being 'the brightness of the glory'; there is no question here of time, or of any 'becoming,' but of a permanent being.[4] Further on it is said of Melchisedec that, in so far as he resembles the Son of God, 'he has neither beginning of days nor end of life, but continueth a priest for ever' (vii, 3)[5]; and in the final exhortation of the Epistle the whole of this doctrine is summed up in the formula, 'Jesus Christ, yesterday and to-day: and the same for ever' (xiii, 8).

After the study we have just made of the nature of the Son, and of his relations with the Father, it is easy to understand the position he occupies in the world; we must, however, describe it more closely, as does the sacred writer. We have already seen the essential difference distinguishing the Son from all creatures; he has been begotten, they have been made[6]; but a relation of dependence exists between these two infinitely distant terms; God has appointed his Son 'heir of all things, by

[1] Some of the ancient Codices support the R.V. in reading 'eternal Spirit,' instead of 'Holy Ghost'; see French original, p. 450, note 1.

[2] See above, page 306 *sqq*.

[3] See Philo, *De fuga*, 56–7 (M., I, 554); Grill, 82.

[4] Westcott, 427: 'The use of the absolute, timeless, term "being" guards against the thought that the Lord's Sonship was by adoption and not by nature.'

[5] Cf. *Heb*. vii, 8, 16, 28.

[6] Cf. Ménégoz, 98, n. 1; Westcott, *in h. l.*, says: 'The Lord, both as Son of God and as Son of Man, can be spoken of as ἐκ Πατρός, and so men also both in their creation and in their re-creation. At the same time, the language used naturally fixes attention on Christ and Christians in relation to the work of redemption and sanctification wrought out on earth.'

whom also he made the world'; again it is the Son who 'upholds all things by the word of his power.'

The first of these expressions recalls the parable of the husbandmen: 'This is the heir,' these wretches whisper to one another, 'come, let us kill him, and we shall have his inheritance.'[1] If we confine ourselves to the data of the parable, the inheritance of which it speaks is the vineyard, that is to say the people of God, so often represented in the Old Testament as the 'inheritance of God'; in the *Epistle to the Hebrews* this inheritance is the whole universe. In both cases the words 'heir' and 'inheritance' must retain their Biblical sense, if the metaphor is to be understood[2]: the inheritance, or, as we should rather say, the portion, is what belongs to a person, not by right of purchase or conquest, but in virtue of a divine or human gift; it is a privilege; thus the Promised Land is the inheritance of Israel, Jahve is the inheritance of the Levites, and Israel the inheritance of Jahve; in the same way in the New Testament, eternal life, the kingdom of God, is the inheritance of the righteous.[3] Hence to say that 'the Son is the heir of all' is to say in Biblical language that the entire universe is his portion, his possession.[4] It is what St. Paul said in other terms to the Colossians (i, 16): 'All things were created by him and *in him* (εἰς αὐτὸν).'

The following sentence echoes the first words of this very text of St. Paul's: 'By whom also he made the world' (αἰῶνας: *æons*); but if the idea is the same, the expression here again is different: the *æons* (αἰῶνας, the 'world' of *Hebrews* xi, 3) are not the Gnostic *æons*[5]; they are either the successive periods or ages of the world containing all material beings in existence,[6] or rather the co-existing material worlds which together constitute the universe.[7] This conception, analogous to that of the 'heavens,' of which traces are found in St. Paul (2 *Cor.* xii, 2), is foreign

[1] *Matt.* xxi, 38.

[2] Cf. WESTCOTT, 169–71, 'the Biblical idea of inheritance.'

[3] *Titus* iii, 7; *James* ii, 5; *Heb.* vi, 17. Cf. *Matt*, v, 5; xix, 29; xxv, 34; etc.

[4] Cf. *Gal.* iv, 7; *Rom.* viii, 17.

[5] See *Constitutions apostoliques* (VIII, 12), quoted here by WESTCOTT.

[6] WESTCOTT: 'the sum of the periods of time including all that is manifested in and through them.'

[7] CHEYNE (*EB*, 1147): 'The phrase [' the æons'] means, not the ages of human history (as in *Heb.* ix, 26, cf. 1 *Cor.* x, 11), but the material worlds which make up the universe.'

to Philo but familiar to Palestinian Judaism[1]; moreover, it is not directly concerned with Trinitarian theology: what we should note is that the worlds have been made by the Son. In the third verse of the eleventh chapter it is said that God, by his word, has constituted the worlds[2]: these two statements are not contradictory; in this Epistle, as elsewhere in St. Paul, the action of the Father and that of the Son are not mutually exclusive, on the contrary, they are one and the same action; the Father does everything by the Son.

In the following verse (i, 3) the Son is represented as 'upholding all things by the word of his power.' Once more the thought coincides with that of the *Epistle to the Colossians*, 'by him all things consist' (i, 17), but it is differently expressed, and bears a more definitely Jewish mark.[3]

It is then no surprise to see the supreme authority conferred on the Son by the Father: 'He hath appointed him heir of all things'[4]; the place of Moses in God's house is that of a faithful servant, Christ is put in authority like a Son[5]: he is also appointed a high priest.[6] The future world, like the present, is subject to the Son of God, for everything has been subjected to him and nothing has been left outside his dominion.[7] However, we do not yet see the effects of this universal domination,[8] it will be made manifest when God has given his Son victory over all his enemies.[9] Here we may recognise the Pauline conception of the reign of Christ: it is as yet imperfect, but it tends infallibly to its completion.[10]

In the whole of this exposition the sacred writer, faithful in this to the habits of thought of his master St. Paul, does not separate the different phases of the existence of Christ. He is careful, on the contrary, to enchain the series of them in a short phrase in which the unity of the Person of Christ is made manifest:

> 'Who, being the brightness of his glory and the figure of his substance, and upholding all things by the word of

[1] Cf. *Ecclus*. xxxvi, 22 (19); *Tob*. xiii, 6, 10; 1 *Tim*. i, 17. See French original, 452, n. 6.
[2] Cf. iii, 4; PRAT, *Théol. de S. Paul*, I, 523.
[3] WESTCOTT compares *Chem. R.*, section 36. PHILO often uses a very similar expression in a very different sense: *Q. rer. divin. her.*, 36 (M., I, 478); *De mutat. nomin.*, 256 (617). Cf. MÉNÉGOZ, 205; PRAT, I, 504, n. 3.
[4] *Heb*. i, 2.
[5] iii, 5.
[6] x, 21.
[7] ii, 5–8.
[8] ii, 8.
[9] i, 13; x, 13.
[10] Cf. 1 *Cor*. xv, 27–8.

his power, making purgation of sins, sitteth on the right hand of the majesty on high: being made so much better than the angels, as he hath inherited a more excellent name than they' (*Heb.* i, 3-4).

The two first phrases of this text show the relations of the Son with the Father, and the Son's action in the world; the two participles (being and upholding) are in the present tense; they express the perpetuity and the energy of this life, which even the Incarnation does not interrupt. Then the writer recalls the two facts dominating the human life of Christ; the redemption that he has accomplished, and his exaltation to the right hand of God; two features finally characterise this glorified life of the Lord: his superiority over the angels,[1] and the supreme name which is given him.[2]

The events of the human life of Jesus are recalled and described at much greater length in the rest of the Epistle.[3] As Trinitarian doctrine is not directly concerned with them, it is unnecessary to reproduce them here in detail. We must, however, study closely the idea of the completion or perfecting of Christ as expounded by the author.[4] This idea is dear to him, and we must recognise in it one of the most characteristic and also profound conceptions of his Christology. It has been thought that decisive objections against the Trinitarian dogma may be drawn from his exposition; but the study of the texts in which it is expressed will show us that, far from shaking that dogma, it confirms it.

'But we see Jesus, who was made a little lower than the angels, for the suffering of death, crowned with glory and honour: that, through the grace of God he might taste death for all.

For it became him for whom are all things and by whom are all things, who had brought many children into glory, to perfect the author of their salvation, by his passion.'[5]

'Wherefore, it behoved him in all things to be made like unto his brethren, that he might become a merci-

[1] Not the superiority consequent upon his nature as Son of God, but which he acquired, as man, at his resurrection. Cf. CHRYSOSTOM, *in h. l.*
[2] *Phil.* ii, 9. [3] See WESTCOTT, 33–5. [4] *Ibid.*, 64–8.
[5] *Heb.* ii, 9, 10.

ful and faithful high priest before God, that he might be a propitiation for the sins of the people.

For in that wherein he himself hath suffered and been tempted he is able to succour them also that are tempted.'[1]

'Who in the days of his flesh, with a strong cry and tears, offering up prayers and supplications to him that was able to save him from death, was heard for his reverence.

And whereas indeed he was the Son of God, he learned obedience by the things which he suffered.

And being consummated, he became, to all that obey him, the cause of eternal salvation:

Called by God a high priest, according to the order of Melchisedech.'[2]

Must we conclude from these texts that Christ became the Son of God on the path of his renunciation and sacrifice?[3] No, indeed; when he submitted to this sorrowful process, he was already the Son, and he did not cease, even in these hours of blood and tears, to sustain the world in being by the word of his power, and to be the brightness of the glory of the Father. All these texts most certainly describe a development, a progress; but the goal of that progress is not his divine Sonship, but the sacerdotal mediation of Christ. Jesus did not acquire by his sufferings a new title to his divinity, but rather the experimental knowledge of our miseries, and, thereby, a new claim on our trust.

Nor should we conclude that his knowledge was limited if he did not know our troubles by experience, and his nature imperfect if it needed to be perfected by a trial.[4] No doubt divine knowledge reached all our miseries with a certainty and precision which no human knowledge can equal, but it sees them in the eternal serenity of the contemplation which no personal suffering can disturb; but, for the Priest and Saviour of men, another kind of knowledge of our woes was necessary, humbler but more emotional, less perfect but penetrated through and through by human compassion. It also behoved him who was to lead the sons of God to glory to enter like them

[1] *Heb.* ii, 17–18. [2] v, 7–10. [3] Bovon, *Théol. du N.T.*, II, 375. [4] Ménégoz, 92, 93.

through the gate of suffering[1] and that, in order to save those who should be obedient to him, he should submit himself to trial, and, in prayers and tears learn to obey.[2]

Thus from the first moment, all is consummated in him: his knowledge, his sanctity, his glory; he is the imprint of the substance of the Father, eternally perfect and ineffaceable. But what he had not, and what his life in the flesh gave him from day to day, was the common experience of our miseries, of our temptations, of our tears. He was God and he was Lord; from the day that he became man he willingly became a scholar in the hard school of humanity, in order to become our Saviour and our Priest.

Far from obscuring the dogma of the Trinity, all this divine doctrine throws light upon it. Already in his pre-existing life the Son is clearly distinguished from the Father; he is the brightness of his glory and the figure of his substance; God, who by him had created the worlds, made him heir of the universe, he depends in all things, regarding his nature or his action, on God[3]; in a word God is the Father, and he is the Son. But the infirmity of his flesh becomes the basis of a new relation; for Christ, the Father becomes he who can save him from death, he to whom he prays with lamentations and tears.

This double relation cannot be reduced to a simple duality of aspect in God[4]; but the second series of texts, even more than the first, resists any unitarian interpretation. One may use the terms of radiance and imprint[5]—as we see in the case of Philo—without affirming in so doing a personal distinction; we may even endeavour to reduce the terms of Father and Son to symbolic expressions which do not necessarily imply a real relation. But there is no possibility of interpreting in that way the prayers of Jesus and his cries to his Father.

On the other hand, it is impossible not to recognise in the *Epistle to the Hebrews* the unity of the Person of the Son, impossible to break the chain uniting his divinity,

[1] *Heb.* ii, 10. [2] v, 7–9.

[3] It would be imprudent to insist on i, 9 and x, 7 where the Father is called the God of the Son, since the author is only quoting from the O.T.

[4] Cf. R. C. Moberly, *Atonement and Personality* (5th edit., London, 1907), 86.

[5] The Douai Version employs the words 'brightness' and 'figure' throughout in this connection, and the terms 'radiance' and 'imprint' are synonymous with these.

his sufferings, and his glory. It is truly one and the same Person who is the radiance of God and who is like unto us, who sustains the world and who prays; that Person is no transitory emanation of the Father, leaving him at the Incarnation to appear on our earth; but the Son, the whole of whose career, if one may use the term, is revealed to us, as much in his immutable and divine life before the creation as in his humble life of trial here below, or in his glorified life in heaven at the right hand of the Divine Majesty.[1]

[1] See Note V, at end of Volume.

CHAPTER V

The Apocalypse of St. John

1. God

It would be useless to speak of the theology of the *Apocalypse* as a compilation of a Christian editor, made up of elements of the Jewish apocalypses welded together and lightly glossed; one might perhaps collect various scattered indications here and there of such editorship, but it would be impossible to find any substantial body of doctrine. Providentially, the brilliant fortune of Vischer's theories[1] has been very short-lived, and, even in non-Catholic circles, the attempt to make the author of the *Apocalypse* a mere editor has been given up.[2] We note that both language and style everywhere indicate the same hand[3]; that the use made of the Old Testament, so constant and, at the same time so free, makes it very improbable that the book merely consists of the mechanical transcription of documents otherwise unknown.[4] Finally, and above all, the powerful personality of the writer, affirmed from the very beginning in the letters to the seven churches, is evidently that of a prophet and not that of a compiler[5]; the entire book reechoes with the same accents. The period was about that at which the fourth *Book of Esdras* was written; the unknown author of that Jewish apocalypse entirely effaces himself behind his hero, as other apocalyptic authors behind Henoch, Baruch, and Adam. The Christian prophet has no need to disguise himself in this way under the

[1] E. Vischer, *Die Offenbarung Ioh. eine judische Schrift in christl. Bearbeitung*, in *TU*, II, 3 (1886). See also W. Bousset, art. *Apocalypse*, in *EB*, 202 *sqq.*; Swete, *Apocalypse*, p. xlix *sqq.*

[2] See Bousset, *loc. cit.*, 205; Swete, *Apocalypse* (1907), pp. xlvi–lv.

[3] Swete, xlvi, *sq.*

[4] *Ibid.*, liii.

[5] Bousset, 242. Cf. J. Wellhausen, *Analyse der Offenbarung Johannis*, in *Abhandlungen der Konigl. Gesellschaft der Wissensch. zu Gottingen*, neue Folge, IX, 4.

names of ancient heroes, nor to antedate his prophecy to make it more venerable; he calls himself: 'John, your brother and your partner in tribulation and in the kingdom and patience in Christ Jesus, was in the island which is called Patmos, for the word of God and for the testimony of Jesus.'[1] And, under this tribulation, the weight of which he is bearing himself, he is not overcome like the author of *Esdras;* the bloody duel raging round him between the Empire and the Church, between the worshippers of the beast and the servants of the Lamb, can have but one issue, and he is so sure of victory, and describes it with such enthusiasm, that his prophecy becomes henceforth the consolation of the martyrs.[2]

It is useless to seek in these visions an exposition of Christian doctrine like the one we read in the *Epistle to the Hebrews,* with its majestic prologue, its harmonious and flexible periods, its learned and simple theology; nothing of the kind is to be found here; the writer is the Son of Thunder; he whose message he bears is the Lion of Juda, his voice is like the roaring of great waters, and his eyes are of burning flame. We can, however, grasp in these prophecies the faith affirmed with such enthusiasm, and if we cannot make a complete exposition of it, we can glean, here and there in the book, the leading doctrinal features so emphatically stated.

It is at the first glance that these features are to be distinguished from those which we note in the other books of the New Testament. The God of the *Apocalypse* is much more like the God of the prophecies and the *Psalms* than the God of the Gospels and the Epistles. He is the omnipotent God,[3] the holy God,[4] truthful[5] and just,[6] the strong God,[7] the living God.[8] He is Alpha and Omega,[9] the beginning and the end,[10] he has been, he is, and he is to come[11]; he is the King,[12] the Master,[13] the Creator of

[1] *Apoc.* i, 9. On the authenticity of the Apocalypse, see JACQUIER, IV 321–30; SWETE, clxxiv–clxxxv; and especially ALLO, clxxi–ccxxv.

[2] See the letter of the Martyrs of Lyons, in EUSEBIUS, *Hist. Eccl.*, v, 1, 10, 58; 2, 3.

[3] *Apoc.* i, 8; iv, 8; xi, 17; xv, 3; xvi, 7, 14; xix, 6, 15; xxi, 22.

[4] iv, 8; vi, 10; xv, 4; xvi, 5.

[5] vi, 10.

[6] xv, 3. Cf. xvi, 7; xix, 1, 2.

[7] xviii, 8.

[8] i, 18; iv, 9, 10; vii, 2; x, 6; xv, 7.

[9] i, 8; xxi, 6.

[10] xxi, 6; xxii, 13.

[11] iv, 8; i, 4, 8.

[12] xv, 3. Cf. *Matt.* v, 35; 1 *Tim.* i, 17; vi, 15.

[13] vi, 10. Cf. *Luke* ii, 29; *Acts* iv, 24.

heaven and earth and all that they contain,[1] he is the Judge and the Avenger[2]; all must fear him and adore him.[3] We search in vain for any mention of the heavenly Father to set off these stern pictures; there is only one reference with regard to the paternity of God to men, and that is a quotation from the Old Testament: 'He that shall overcome shall possess these things. And I will be his God; and he shall be my son.'[4]

We no doubt recognise in these accents, him whom Christ himself called 'the son of thunder'; but it should be added that nearly all the expressions are borrowed from the Old Testament, and indicate an influence affecting the author rather than his personal tendencies; his doctrine, like his visions, often recalls point by point the books of the prophets, of Isaias, of Ezechiel, of Zacharias, and, above all, of Daniel.[5] It is not surprising that this influence should be more prominent here than in the rest of the New Testament; for, by its purpose as well as by its literary character, the *Apocalypse* is much more associated with the past than the Gospels and the Epistles. The duel of the Empire and the Church is the dominant idea of the whole book; the visions reflected by its pages are the scourges which will ravage the world, and the final triumph of God. We cannot expect to find in these scenes of terror and glory the accents of the Sermon on the Mount, or of the discourse after the Last Supper. Beside God we see only the martyrs whom he is avenging, or the rebels whom he is overthrowing; we no longer see, as in St. Paul's pages, Christians gradually approaching to the Father through union with Christ and life in the Spirit, or, as in St. John's Gospel, receiving in themselves the Father and the Son who come to take up their habitation in their souls. We do, indeed, find here and there traits of infinite tenderness, as for instance, God wiping all tears from the eyes of his servants.[6] But such traits are rare, and, in any case, are descriptive of the happiness of heaven, rather than of Christian life here below.

We see that, by its general orientation, the *Apocalypse* resembles the prophecies of Judaism; the triumph of

[1] *Apoc.* x, 6; iv, 11; xiv, 7. [2] vi, 10; xix, 2; xx, 11–15.
[3] xiv, 7; xv, 4. See Swete, clviii, clix.
[4] *Apoc.* xxi, 7. Cf. 2 *Kings* vii, 14.
[5] Cf. Swete, xxii–xxxii; Bousset, 1–19, 272–4; Swete, clvii.
[6] vii, 17.

God over the enemies of his people is, in both cases, the great hope it describes. But, side by side with God, Christ or the Lamb plays, in the *Apocalypse,* a rôle which could only be understood by Christians, and that fact distinguishes this book of John from those of Ezechiel and Daniel.

2. *Christ*

It is true that there are many traces of Jewish origin in its description of the Messias. St. John loves to represent Christ and even the individual Christian as 'ruling the peoples with a rod of iron'[1]; the image is borrowed from *Psalm* ii, and is also found in the *Psalms of Solomon,*[2] applied to the Messias. The two-edged sword which issues from the mouth of Christ[3] recalls various passages of *Isaias* and of the *Book of Wisdom.*[4] The description of the Son of man[5] is above all inspired by Daniel (vii, 13; x, 5),[6] but it is very remarkable that St. John represents Christ under the appearance given by Daniel to the Ancient of Days, that is, as God.[7]

These similitudes of detail should not deceive us: it is above all in his Christology that St. John shows that he is no Jewish scholiast[8] but a Christian prophet. His Messias is truly the same Jesus of whom the Gospels and the Epistles teach us, but, in the visions of the *Apocalypse* he is revealed otherwise than in the narratives of the evangelists, or in the letters of St. Paul; he is no longer the Master who humbly walks about the countryside of Galilee, who is crucified at Jerusalem; nor is he considered any more as the mystical Head of the Church, the spiritual Christ, in whom all Christians live; he is the Conqueror:

> 'And being turned, I saw seven golden candlesticks; and in the midst of the seven golden candlesticks, one like to the Son of man, clothed with a garment down to the feet, and girt about the paps with a golden girdle. And his head and his hairs were white, as white wool and as snow. And his eyes were as a flame of fire; and

[1] *Apoc.* ii, 27; xii, 5; xix, 15. [2] xvii, 24.
[3] *Apoc.* i, 16; ii, 12, 16; xix, 15. [4] *Is.* xi, 4; xlix, 2; *Wisdom* xviii, 15.
[5] *Apoc.* i, 13 *seq.*
[6] There are also borrowings from *Ezechiel* xliii, 2, and from *Zacharias* xii, 10.
[7] *Dan.* vii, 9. [8] See WERNLE, *Die Anfange*, 260, 257.

his feet like unto fine brass, as in a burning furnace. And his voice as the sound of many waters. And he had in his right hand seven stars. And from his mouth came out a sharp two-edged sword. And his face was as the sun shineth in his power.'[1] 'And I saw: and behold a white cloud, and upon the cloud one sitting like unto the Son of man, having on his head a crown of gold and in his hand a sharp sickle.'[2]

'And I saw heaven opened: and behold a white horse. And he that sat upon him was called faithful and true: and with justice doth he judge and fight.

And his eyes were as a flame of fire: and on his head were many diadems. And he had a name written, which no man knoweth but himself.

And he was clothed with a garment sprinkled with blood. And his name is called: THE WORD OF GOD.

And the armies that are in heaven followed him on white horses, clothed in fine linen, white and clean.

And out of his mouth proceedeth a sharp two-edged sword, that with it he may strike the nations. And he shall rule them with a rod of iron: and he treadeth the winepress of the fierceness of the wrath of God the Almighty.

And he hath on his garment and on his thigh written: KING OF KINGS AND LORD OF LORDS.'[3]

It was useful to read over these triumphal passages so as to remind ourselves of the point of view of the prophet of the *Apocalypse*; we do not find in his teaching the theology or the mysticism of the Pauline Epistles or of the fourth Gospel, but rather an ardent faith in the triumph of Christ. His sufferings and his bloody death are often recalled, but always as a claim to glory:

'The Lamb that was slain is worthy to receive power and divinity and wisdom and strength and honour and glory and benediction.'[4]

Similarly, his relations with the faithful are more often represented, not in the progressive training of the Christian upon earth, but in the coronation in heaven of all these kings, redeemed by Christ and triumphing with him.[5]

This glory of Christ, on which the *Apocalypse* fixes our

[1] *Apoc.* i, 12–16. [2] xiv, 14. [3] xix, 11–16. [4] v, 12. [5] v, 10.

gaze, appears under two differing aspects, which seem to many critics incompatible. Sometimes it is represented as the price of the sufferings of Christ, sometimes as the privilege of his nature.

> 'To him that shall overcome, I will give to sit with me in my throne: as I also have overcome and am set down with my Father in his throne.'[1]

Some critics have seen in these words the Adoptionist heresy[2]; in order to do so it is necessary to give to this conception of the glory of Jesus an exclusive signification, as if, according to St. John, it only belonged to Christ in virtue of his sufferings and his death. This is to create gratuitous contradictions. There is indeed no difficulty in recognising that this affirmation of the merits of Jesus and their recompense in heaven is perhaps dearer to the author of the *Apocalypse* than to any other New Testament writer. He sees in that recompense the guarantee of Christian hope, the first-fruits of the triumph of the Church.[3] And he loves to recall by the very names which he gives to the Lord his humanity and his sufferings. Most often he calls him Jesus[4] or the Lamb; the names of Christ,[5] of the Son,[6] of Lord,[7] are much more rarely employed than by St. Paul, or in the fourth Gospel, and then usually as titles rather than proper names; the same idea may be found in the symbolic appellations of 'Lion of Juda,'[8] or of the 'root of David.'[9] Nor is one surprised to see Jesus, on several occasions, call God *his* God.[10]

On the other hand, the description given of his glory surpasses all human proportions: he is 'the prince of the kings of the earth[11]; he is 'the King of kings and the Lord of lords'[12]; he holds the keys of death and hell[13]; he alone can open the seals of the divine book.[14] This glory itself is but the radiance of a truly divine and eternal majesty; he is the beginning of the creation[15];

[1] *Apoc.* iii, 21. [2] WERNLE, 271.

[3] It is in this sense that Our Lord is called 'first-begotten of the dead' in *Apoc.* i, 5 and *Col.* i, 18.

[4] *Apoc.* i, 9; xii, 17; xiv, 12; xvii, 6; xix, 10; xx, 4; xxii, 16.

[5] xi, 15; xii, 10; xx, 4, 6. [6] ii, 18. [7] xiv, 13; xxii, 20, 21.

[8] v, 5. [9] xxii, 16. [10] iii, 2, 12. [11] i, 5. [12] xvii, 14; xix, 16.

[13] i, 18. [14] v, 5 *sqq.*

[15] iii, 14; cf. *Prov.* viii, 22. *Col.* i, 15, 18. SWETE says: 'He (Christ) is not, as the Arians inferred, ἓν τῶν κτισμάτων, but the ἀρχὴ τῆς κτίσεως, the uncreated principle of creation, from whom it took its origin.' Cf. CHARLES, cxi–cxii.

he is, like God, the beginning and the end, the first and the last, Alpha and Omega[1]; like God, he is the living One[2]; like God, he is the holy One and the true One[3]; like God he searches the reins and the hearts of men,[4] he causes them to die, and snatches them from hell.[5] In order to explain this community of functions and titles between God and Christ, several critics suggest 'the naïvety of a lay theologian,' who identifies God and Jesus, while preserving, in spite of doing so, the elements of an older Christology.[6] Such opinions merely show that, to those who express them, the faith of the Apostles has become so foreign that they can no longer understand it. In reality there is nothing in all this doctrine to disconcert a Christian, neither its supposed archaism, nor the union and equality between God and Jesus Christ implied by it. John unhesitatingly confesses that the glory of Jesus is the incommunicable privilege of his divinity, and also the recompense of his sufferings and the first-fruits of our own glory, and both these statements are so familiar to him, and at the same time, so fundamental, that he feels no need to reconcile them, and leaves to the theologians of the future the task of shewing their agreement.[7]

This faith expresses itself spontaneously in worship; the same impetus carries the religion of the Christian towards Jesus and towards God; the saints 'keep the commandments of God and the faith of Jesus'[8]; they are the servants of Jesus[9] as they are the servants of God[10]; the martyrs are the witnesses of Jesus.[11] Those who will take part in the first resurrection will 'be priests of God and of Christ.'[12] In heaven the hymns which are sometimes addressed to God alone[13] are also, on occasion, addressed to the Lamb, and in the same high-sounding terms; while the adoration of the heavenly court is as much addressed to the Lamb[14] as to God. These traits are the more significant on account of the strictness of the monotheism of the *Apocalypse*; on two occasions[15] John attempts to prostrate himself at the feet of the revealing Angel, but he is at

[1] *Apoc.* i, 17; ii, 8; xxii, 13. [2] i, 18. [3] iii, 7; cf. CHARLES, I, 85.
[4] i, 18; ii, 23. [5] ii, 23
[6] BOUSSET, *Offenbarung*, 239; cf. WERNLE, *Anfänge*, 268–74.
[7] Cf. SWETE, *Apoc.*, p. clxii. [8] *Apoc.* xiv, 12. [9] i, 1; ii, 20.
[10] vii, 3; x, 7, etc. [11] ii, 13. [12] xx, 6. [13] vii, 12; xix, 1, 5, 6.
[14] v, 8, 12–14. [15] xix, 10; xxii, 9.

once forbidden: 'See thou do it not. I am thy fellow-servant and of thy brethren who have the testimony of Jesus. Adore God.' As to suspecting here any influence of the polytheistic environment, and in particular of the cultus of the emperors—no one can dream of it; that is a pure abomination, the worship of the Beast.

We must then recognise in this adoration of Jesus the spontaneous expression of Christian faith; it did not owe its origin to the cultus of angels or to Pagan superstitions: it appears in the bosom of the strictest and most jealous monotheism, and neither the prophet who preaches it nor the faithful who practise it perceive the slightest discord between their traditional belief and their new faith; innumerable texts of the Old Testament are to be found in the *Apocalypse*, singing with the same accent the glory of Jahve and that of Jesus: that glory is one and unique; the new revelation has not made men forget the old one, and it is in the ever-incommunicable glory of the Father that the Son appears.

The prophet is wholly absorbed in the contemplation of this glory; he believes in the eternal reign of the Lamb, and looks forward to his swiftly-coming triumph. By the side of these glowing visions the gleams of theology are very pale, and the seer of Patmos does not make them any clearer. As to the relations of the Father and the Son, we do not find, in the *Apocalypse*, so explicit a doctrine as in the *Epistle to the Colossians*, or in the *Epistle to the Hebrews*, or in the *Gospel of St. John*.[1] We are the more surprised to read in the midst of the description of the triumph of Christ; 'his name is called: the Word of God.'[2] This is the first time that this term appears in the New Testament; we shall shortly find it again in the prologue of the fourth Gospel, where we shall not be so surprised to meet it; the theological context in which it appears seems to call for it. Here, on the contrary, it appears suddenly in the midst of an apocalyptic vision. It is possible, with reference to the text of the fourth Gospel, to recall memories of Philo, and, with more or less plausibility, to suppose it is a case of his

[1] Only once, ii, 18, is Jesus called the Son of God. God is called his Father several times (i, 6; ii, 28; iii, 5; iii, 21; xiv, 1), but they are only brief references to the relationship, which do not throw any light upon it.

[2] *Apoc.* xix, 13.

influence. In the passage before us there is nothing to suggest this supposition; there is no question of the origin of the world, or of the rôle played in it by the Word, but we see the armies of heaven, mounted on white horses and, at their head, an awe-inspiring Warrior, with flaming eyes, his head crowned with a thousand diadems and a sharp sword coming out of his mouth: he is the Word of God. In vain would one seek in Philo[1] for a similar text; but we find one in the *Book of Wisdom*[2]: 'Thy almighty word leapt down from heaven from thy royal throne, as a fierce conqueror into the midst of the land of destruction, with a sharp sword carrying thy unfeigned commandment . . .' This very text of the Alexandrine book depends less on Hellenic speculation than on Jewish theology, as expressed in the *Psalms* or the *Prophets;* it accentuates the personification of the word, but depicts it in the traditional manner.[3] It would no doubt be rash to insist too much on these similarities, and to draw a conclusion from this single text of the *Apocalypse* to the full Johannine theology of the Word; it will be in the fourth Gospel only that this theology, explicitly developed, can be grasped exactly. But it was interesting to note that, as far as Christian literature goes, the Logos appears for the first time in a book of purely Jewish inspiration, and in an apocalyptic vision.

3. *The Spirit*

The theology of the Spirit[4] is but slightly developed in the *Apocalypse,* and we can easily see why; the principal subject of the book is not the spiritual life of the Christian but the final triumph of Christ; we find there but few mentions of the Spirit,[5] and particularly of the Spirit of prophecy. These texts, like those of the *Acts* and of the Pauline Epistles, represent the Spirit sometimes as a force animating the prophet,[6] sometimes as a person who speaks, gives orders, and reveals.[7] They increase, however, the

[1] Cf. PHILO, *De præm. et poen.*, 95 (M., II, 423); CHARLES, II, 131.

[2] xviii, 15.

[3] Cf. CHARLES, II, 134, and ALLO, 280, for the authenticity and meaning of this text.

[4] In *Apoc.*, never called 'the Holy Spirit,' but always 'the Spirit.'

[5] xi, 11; cf. xiii, 15.

[6] i, 10. Cf. iv, 2; xvii, 3; xxi, 10.

[7] ii, 7; cf. ii, 11, 17, 29; iii, 6, 13, 22; xiv, 13; xxii, 17; cf. ALLO, p. xi.

precision of earlier teachings, in that they teach more expressly the relations of Christ and the Spirit. One might have hesitated to interpret in the pages of St. Paul the expression, 'Spirit of Christ,' in the sense of 'the Spirit given or communicated by Christ'; this relation of origin becomes very clear in the *Apocalypse;* it is already perceptible in the letters to the churches. In them Jesus is speaking, yet every message is concluded by the formula, 'He that hath an ear, let him hear what the Spirit saith to the churches.' The theology of the *Apocalypse* excludes the personal identification of Christ and the Spirit; but it is the Spirit who makes the Church hear the voice of Christ. Further on the angel says to St. John: 'I am thy fellow servant, and of thy brethren who have the testimony of Jesus . . . For the testimony of Jesus is the spirit of prophecy.'[1] If we understand, according to the most probable interpretation, by the 'testimony of Jesus,' 'the testimony given by Jesus,'[2] we find here the same idea; the Spirit of prophecy echoes the witness given by Jesus; the prophets bear the witness of Jesus, because they have the Spirit of prophecy. In this text we not only find the necessary relation affirmed by St. Paul between possession of the Spirit and partnership with Christ,[3] but we see in addition how the action of Jesus is propagated by that of the Spirit.

Similarly, as in St. Paul, the Spirit of the Father cries to him out of the heart of the Christian, calling on him with ineffable groanings, as we read in the *Apocalypse*[5]: 'The spirit and the bride say: Come. . . . He that giveth testimony of these things, saith: Surely, I come quickly.' Jesus the faithful witness once more makes himself heard in reply to the appeal of the Spirit, who is praying to him in the Church.

These few details are completed by the symbolism of the *Apocalypse*: in this book, as in his Gospel,[6] St. John represents the Spirit under the symbol of living water[7]; it is Christ who gives this water[8]; it proceeds from his throne and the throne of God: 'He shewed me a river of water of life, clear as crystal, proceeding from

[1] xix, 10. [2] Cf. Bousset, 429. [3] 1 *Cor.* xii, 3; *Rom.* viii, 9.
[5] xxii, 17–20. [6] *John* vii, 38.
[7] Cf. Swete, *The Holy Spirit in the N.T.*, 144, note 2.
[8] *Apoc.* xxi, 6; cf. vii, 17; xxii, 17.

the throne of God and of the Lamb'[1]; it is impossible to avoid the comparison of this text with the passage of the *Gospel of St. John* where it says that the Spirit proceeds from the Father and receives of the Son.[2]

The same evidence of origin is once more expressed by the texts where Jesus is represented as 'holding the seven Spirits of God,'[3] or again as 'having seven eyes which are the seven Spirits of God sent forth into all the earth.'[4] We recognise here the seven spirits who are mentioned in the opening formula of salvation[5]; 'Grace be unto you and peace, from him that is and that was and that is to come: and from the seven Spirits which are before his throne: and from Jesus Christ, who is the faithful witness.' It is less easy to determine who are these seven spirits: the *Septiformis Spiritus,* the Holy Spirit with his seven gifts; or the seven angels of the presence. If the first interpretation is adopted we shall, in chapters iii, 1 and v, 6, see new proofs of the relations of origin and dependence attaching the Holy Spirit to Christ.

[1] *Apoc.* xxii, 1. [2] *John* xv, 26; xvi, 15. [3] *Apoc.* iii, 1. [4] v, 6. [5] i, 4.

CHAPTER VI

The Gospel of St. John

The preceding chapters have traced the progressive development of the revelation of the Trinitarian dogma throughout the Apostolic age. In the first documents analysed, the Synoptic Gospels, we received a vivid and naïve impression of the life of Christ, producing a deep feeling of mystery not as yet fully cleared up. The facts and discourses reported in *Acts* describe the progress of the faith in the first Christian community. In these four books, and particularly in the three first, the individuality of the authors is effaced, all their endeavour is to give a faithful rendering of the apostolic catechesis. Assuredly, each evangelist has his own preferences, and is interested in a particular aspect of his subject, but what he tells us of Christ is always derived from a collective testimony of which it bears the mark.

The other books, epistles or *Apocalypse*, have an altogether different character; they are no doubt produced in the Church, they reflect the common faith of believers, but, at the same time, they are individual works as well as works adapted to circumstances, due to the inspiration of a particular man, destined to a particular community, and written in answer to special needs. Furthermore, they are not narratives but teachings, exhortations, prophecies. These books are therefore less intimately connected with the past, as also less occupied with the collective life of the Church. Also, in spite of the fact that several of these epistles are earlier than the Gospels, they represent a more explicit stage of the development of dogma. While the Gospels and the *Acts* enable us to reach the very origins of the apostolic catechesis, the epistles allow us to follow, day by day, the progress of Christianity, not only in the sense of the conquest of souls, but also in that of the more intimate and more conscious penetration of the divine mystery.

It is not by metaphysical speculation that the faith makes this progress, nor yet by historical research ; Christ, the central object of the faith, is neither a concept to be analysed nor a dead man whose memory we recall. He is the living and life-giving Head of the Church ; that is the mystery revealed by God to St. Paul, and in the light of that mystery the whole Trinity is seen: by Christ and in the Spirit the soul of the believer tends towards the Father. The epistles of the captivity throw more light on the unique mediation of Christ, the *Apocalypse* on his divine glory.

Having reached this point, had not Christian dogma achieved completion, at least in so far as completion was possible here below ? One might think so, and, in point of fact, no further revelation could more exalt Christ Jesus. And yet God still had new lights in reserve which were going to transform the whole faith.

It is in the *Gospel of St. John* that this new light appears, in the whole Gospel, and not solely in the prologue of the evangelist, or in this or that sentence pronounced by the Lord. It is no isolated word—others can be found as lofty—that is here further revealed ; it is the union, or, rather, the intimate co-penetration of the doctrine and the life of Christ. Of the two groups of documents, which we can distinguish up till then, in the New Testament, some describe the human life of Jesus, others the mystery of his pre-existence and his glory. In the fourth Gospel all these features are blended in the unity of the one same Figure, which shines with a superhuman clarity ; only when veiled could this clarity be unrecognisable: the torturers of the Passion veiled his face and yet we feel that it is truly human and living, that it does not owe its form to theological speculation, but is the impression left by a man like ourselves on the heart of a man.

This unity, so complete and so living, cannot be explained by a combination of the evangelical tradition and the Pauline doctrine. No doubt the traditional narratives were illuminated by the growing clarity of the revelation, and the very witnesses themselves of the Lord's ministry must have understood more clearly what must have been his life on earth, in proportion as they learnt better what was now his life in them. But, in the book, the study of which we are commencing, there is more than such influences; there are personal memories and intimate revelations; St. John might have said, with as much truth as St. Paul: 'The Gospel which was preached by me is not according to man, for neither did I receive it of man nor did I learn it, but by the revelation of Jesus Christ.'[1]

This originality appears clearly enough in the narratives—their historicity is open to discussion and will be studied further on—but they cannot all be explained by the influence of the Synoptics; realities or fictions, they evidently demand another origin. It is no less impossible to reduce all the Johannine doctrine to Paulinism; 'The significance of John,' says Wernle,[2] 'was that he connected Jesus with Paul, that he translated the Pauline Gospel into the discourses and life of Jesus; it was owing to him that Paulinism dominated the Church.' This thesis is historically indefensible; St. John and St. Paul have no doubt in common a fund of identical doctrine, which has become the common doctrine of the whole Church; but each has certain doctrinal points of view which are truly personal, and distinguish them one from the other; it will be sufficient to mention, as examples of this, their theology of the Redemption or of the Eucharist. And it is fairly easy to discern in the later development of dogma the influence of both, perpetuating itself in two distinct theological schools.

It is unnecessary to insist any longer here on similarities or differences which will be more clearly seen when we analyse the doctrines themselves; but from the commencement of this study a strong light had to be thrown on the originality of the work of St. John. Moreover, no one who has read it can fail to retain the impression of an altogether intimate and spontaneous piece of work; many traits in it recall the Synoptics; others St. Paul; others again Alexandrine Hellenism; but all are profoundly Johannine.

This personal touch is powerfully imprinted on the whole work, and the attentive reader must perceive it; but it is still more remarkable that this master, whose influence on humanity has been so profound and lasting, was but a disciple, and did not wish to be anything else, 'the disciple whom Jesus loved.' His thought has been

[1] *Gal.* i, 11–12. [2] *Anfange*, 446.

dominated through and through by the thought of his one and only Master; critics have attempted to make of the Son of God who appears in the fourth Gospel a creation of John's; on the contrary, it is John who is the living handiwork of Jesus, who has stamped with his own personal and ineffaceable imprint his affections, his thoughts, and his religious aspirations. It is only necessary to re-read the boo kto feel this action of Jesus. If, in the discourse after the Last Supper, and, particularly, in the prayer which closes it (xvii) we cannot recognise real memories, intense in life and emotion, if we can see nothing but Alexandrine speculations in these deep vibrations of the soul, all criticism must be given up in despair.

Moreover, this Gospel is the fruit of a long teaching[1]; while at Ephesus John, the last survivor of the Apostolic College, constantly related and explained to his disciples the miracles and discourses of Christ; it was the very essence of his catechesis, by which he taught converts to know him, who was to be for them—as he was for John himself—the Way, the Truth, and the Life. It was through this initiation that his neophytes made contact with Jesus, and that the Apostle could say to them what St. Peter said to his disciples: You have not seen him and you love him.[2]

This daily teaching, repeated throughout so many years, engraved on the memory of the Apostle not only the thought of Christ, but the very turns of expression he used, and we are not surprised to find that the discourses of Our Lord, whether reported by St. John or the Synoptics, not only reveal to us the same soul, but often report his words with the same accent and rhythm.[3] In order to assure oneself that this is not a chance coincidence, one should compare, from the point of view of form and rhythm, the discourses of Christ with other New Testament texts, for instance, with the *Epistles of St. Paul*; the difference will at once appear.

These coincidences are no doubt but partial; if we compare the discourses of Christ in St. John with those

[1] Cf. Stanton, III, 50 *sqq.*; *Rech. de Sc. Rel.*, XI (1921), 235–44.

[2] Cf. 1 *Peter* i, 8.

[3] Cf. Burney, *The Poetry of Our Lord* (London, 1925), and *Rech. de Sc. Rel.*, 1926, 342, for a detailed study of such parallelisms.

in the Synoptics, we shall note in both cases unique fragments; St. John's Gospel does not contain the Sermon on the Mount, nor do the Synoptics mention the discourse after the Last Supper or the Sacerdotal Prayer. In the moral teaching addressed to the multitudes, during the early months of the Galilean ministry, we feel a confident and spontaneous freshness which we shall not find later on. Inversely, the Synoptics tell us nothing of those touching and sorrowful effusions of soul which moved the little group of intimate companions, and which the beloved disciple conveys to us.

And what we say about the accent and words of Jesus applies equally to the teaching which they contain. The moral catechesis reproduced by St. Matthew, the parables of mercy reported by St. Luke, have no equivalent in St. John; but we shall equally seek in vain in the Synoptics for the theology of the Holy Spirit, revealed in the discourse after the Last Supper. And yet it is indeed the same Master who teaches in the Synoptics and St. John.

If we examine the principal themes of the teaching of Jesus from all sides, we note that the discourses reported, though placed in very different *milieux* and addressed to very different audiences, contain the doctrine of the same Master and reveal the same profound aspirations. This identity is particularly evident in the theology of the Son of man; the Synoptics had faithfully preserved, in his discourses, that Messianic title, so mysterious and humble, that Jesus had claimed for himself; the other books of the New Testament only use it on occasion; it reappears in the teaching of Jesus as reported by St. John, with the distinguishing characteristics of the Synoptics—suffering, glory, the sovereign power of judgement.[1] 'John has preserved in the clearest fashion the dogma of the Son of man, as it was believed by the first Christian community'; this judgement of one of the most hostile critics of the historicity and of the apostolic origin of the fourth Gospel[2] was forced upon him, as it is upon every reader of it.

The Messianic claims, which this title of Son of man both proclaims and veils at the same time, are presented by St. John with the same essential features as by the

[1] Texts quoted above, pages 221–225; cf. LAGRANGE, *Saint Jean*, p. clii *sq.*
[2] BOUSSET, *Kyrios Christos*, p. 19.

Synoptics; Jesus manifests himself to a few privileged disciples, and is explicitly recognised by them[1]; by his teaching and miracles he prepares the multitudes for this belief, without giving them the precise declarations they demand[2]; this reserve is still greater with regard to the heads of the nation, who only listen to spy upon him, and only ask him questions to entrap him[3]; Jesus will only give the decisive declaration when his hour is come on the day of his Passion.[4]

He adopts the same attitude in his claim to the sublimest title of all,' Son of God; the revelation of this mystery develops gradually throughout the whole gospel, prudently and firmly, as Jesus wished; the anger of the Jews can neither impose on him a timid silence, nor snatch from him a premature declaration. The light is spread, sufficiently veiled not to dazzle feeble eyes, yet so clear that no one can avoid it without sin. We ought to read here all the discussions in the Temple, particularly in chapters v, viii, and x; they show, in his method of claiming the most sublime privileges, alternations of revelation and reserve,[5] in which we recognise the truly divine pedagogy which the Synoptics have already shewn us in the discussions of Jesus in the Temple with the Pharisees and Sadducees[6]; it is he himself—so fearless that no violence can silence him, so completely master of his thought that no cleverness can take advantage of him, and, what is still more admirable, so persevering in the task of enlightening these blind ones that he never takes refuge behind an equivocation; the replies or the questions by which he refutes their objections ought, if they were sincere, to lead them to the truth.[7]

The Evangelist's fidelity in the reproduction of these features is a guarantee of the truthfulness of his testimony; but we see its significance still better if we remember the purpose of his book; he is writing to establish and enlighten men's faith in the Son of God[8]; it is enough to read his First Epistle, or the Prologue of his Gospel, to see how he teaches this dogma, when he is

[1] *John* i, 41, 49; ix, 37; xi, 27.
[2] vi, 14 *sqq.*; vii, 26 *sqq.*, 41 *sqq.*; viii, 25 *sqq.*, 53 *sqq.*
[3] x, 24 *sqq.*; xii, 34 *sqq.*
[4] xviii, 37.
[5] v, 17 *sqq.*; viii, 12–19, 25–29, 51–59; x, 29–38.
[6] See above, page 245 *sqq.*
[7] Cf. LAGRANGE, p. clxxvi.
[8] Cf. STREETER, *The Four Gospels* (London, 1924), 365.

preaching in the name of Christ to his Christians. If the discourses he attributes to Jesus were fictitious, would he not have painted them as more imperious, more categorical? Would he have presented his claims under so reserved a form if they had been, as our adversaries say to-day, but the echo of an enthusiastic liturgy?

Let us note finally that the special character of St. John's Gospel guarantees the historicity of the facts which he relates, and of the discourses which he repeats. This book, like the other Gospels, is the fruit of a catechesis; we hear in it an echo of the daily teaching, by which the Apostle made Christians of his hearers. It was not on dreams or legends that he based the faith of his catechumens, but on the marvellous works which Jesus wrought, and of which John was the witness. 'But these,' he writes at the end of his Gospel, 'are written that you may believe that Jesus is the Christ, the Son of God: and that believing, you may have life in his name.'[1] It was by the contemplation of these marvels that the first disciples of Jesus were brought to the faith[2]; it was by hearing, or reading the account of them, that the new Christians attained to it. The rôle of the evangelist was, above all, that of a witness, attesting what he had seen, heard, and touched, thus, by his testimony, putting his catechumens in contact with Christ. If the facts that he relates are not real, his witness is false, and the faith of his Christian disciples vain.[3] Hence the insistence with which St. John affirms the reality of what he reports: 'That which was from the beginning, which we have heard, which we have seen with our eyes, which we have looked upon and our hands have handled, of the word of life.'[4] And also when he tells us of the spear-thrust given to Jesus: 'One of the soldiers with a spear opened his side: and immediately there came out blood and water. And he that saw it, hath given testimony: and his testimony is true. And he knoweth that he saith true[5]: that you also may believe.'[6]

Quite as much as his apologetic, St. John's theology implies and demands this historical realism. In his first

[1] *John* xx, 31. [2] *Ibid.*, ii, 11. [3] Cf. 1 *Cor.* xv, 14–15.

[4] 1 *John* i, 1 *sqq.* We are supposing the same author for both Epistle and Gospel; cf. STANTON, III, 83–103.

[5] Cf. BURNEY, *Aramaic Origin of the Fourth Gospel* (Oxford, 1922), 82.

[6] *John* xix, 34–35.

Epistle the Apostle has the same purpose as in his Gospel —to ground the faith of his disciples on Christ the Son of God—so that, by that faith, Christians may have eternal life,[1] and he shows by the insistence of his affirmations and condemnations that that faith is in danger: 'Who is a liar, but he who denieth that Jesus is the Christ?[2] 'By this is the spirit of God known: every spirit which confesseth that Jesus Christ is come in the flesh is of God: and every spirit that dissolveth Jesus is not of God.'[3] 'We have seen and do testify that the Father hath sent his Son to be the Saviour of the world. Whosoever shall confess that Jesus is the Son of God, God abideth in him and he in God.'[4] 'Whosoever believeth that Jesus is the Christ is born of God.'[5] 'This is the victory which overcometh the world: Our faith. Who is he that overcometh the world but he that believeth that Jesus is the Son of God . . . ?'[6] 'He that believeth in the Son of God hath the testimony of God in himself.'[7] 'He that hath the Son hath life.'[8] And, finally, the Epistle terminates with this supreme attestation: 'And we know that the Son of God is come. And he hath given us understanding that we may know the true God and may be in his true Son. This is the true God and life eternal.'[9]

The exact knowledge of the heresies aimed at by this letter would make us understand more clearly the dogma which St. John opposes to them. Without any intention of precisely defining errors so ancient and so short-lived, they can, I think, be reduced to those two theses: Jesus is not the Christ; the Son of God has not come in the flesh.[10] With all his energy St. John opposes to these heresies two dogmas: Jesus is the Messias; the Son of God has truly become incarnate. The Gospel is not a controversial work like the Epistle, but, above all, a testimony and a teaching; but this testimony bears chiefly on the points contested by the heretics, this teaching throws a special light on the dogmas which they make obscure[11]: the Messianic rank of Jesus; and the reality of his Incarnation. And this

[1] 1 *John* v, 13. [2] *Ib.*, ii, 22. [3] *Ib.*, iv, 2–3.
[4] *Ib.*, iv, 14–15. [5] *Ib.*, v, 1. [6] *Ib.*, v, 4 *seq.*
[7] *Ib.*, v, 10. [8] *Ib.*, v, 12. [9] *Ib.*, v, 20.

[10] A. Wurm, *Die Irrlehrer im ersten Johannesbrief* (Freib., 1903); cf. Lagrange, *Saint Jean*, p. lxxi *sq.*

[11] Wurm (pp. 24–52) agrees that both the gospel andthe epistle are directed against the same opponents.

conclusion, to which the study of the Epistle and the Gospel leads us, is confirmed by a tradition handed down to us by Irenæus that the fourth Gospel was written to refute the heresy of Cerinthus.[1] This heretic, says Irenæus, taught that Christ did not take flesh, or suffer, for a spirit cannot suffer; but, at the baptism, taking the form of a dove, he descended upon Jesus, and Jesus alone suffered and rose from the dead.[2]

Twenty years later the churches of Asia were still disturbed by the Gnosticism of the Docetists, so closely connected with that of Cerinthus; St. Ignatius and St. Polycarp opposed it with the same energy as St. John did Cerinthus, and sometimes by using the same expressions as the Apostle: 'Whoso does not confess that Jesus Christ has come in the flesh, is an anti-Christ; and whoso does not confess the witness of the Cross is a devil.'[3] For them, as for John, the visible and tangible reality of the flesh of Christ is one of the essential dogmas of the Christian faith: 'It is very truth that he was born, that he ate and drank, that he was persecuted under Pontius Pilate, that he suffered and died . . . and that he rose from the dead.'[4]

These controversies which continued to disturb Asia so short a time after the death of St. John, help us to understand the *milieu* in which he lived and taught and fought, and the theses, so strongly maintained by his most faithful disciples, are mirrors which throw light on his own doctrine: 'The Word was made flesh.' This affirmation, written at the beginning of his Gospel, dominates it entirely; after that, it was impossible, without violence, to reduce that real body to a mere phantom, or his works, his sufferings, his death to mere allegories.

Thus, from whatever aspect we consider St. John, as catechist, or apologist, or controversialist, we are always brought back to this fundamental fact: the beloved disciple is also the faithful witness. But we cannot forget that he is also the Theologian; by this title, which in later days will become as it were his name, we are not affirming the sublimity of his speculations, but rather that he,

[1] *Hær.*, III, xi, 1.

[2] Cf. C. Schmidt, *Gespräche Jesu mit seinen Jüngern*, 403–52.

[3] Polyc., *ad Philipp.*, VII.

[4] Ignat., *ad Trall.*, IX, X.

among all the sacred writers, has most clearly recognised and revealed the divinity of Christ.[1]

This is evident from the words of the prologue: 'We saw his glory.' This flesh, real, visible, and tangible, which John has seen and touched, is the flesh of the Word of life; this man, whose words, acts, and gestures have impressed themselves so deeply on his soul, is the Word, the only Son of the Father, the Son of man, who came down from heaven, and he alone re-ascended to heaven, the Living Bread come down from heaven. The contemplation of this mystery which illuminates the prologue permeates the entire Gospel.[2] Indissolubly bound up with the affirmation of the real humanity of Christ, it is one of the characters of the theological teaching attached to the name of St. John; we shall find it in the pages of St. Ignatius of Antioch,[3] St. Irenæus,[4] and in the whole of their tradition,[5] which is the school in which Docetism will find its firmest adversaries, and the divinity of Christ its most vigorous defenders.

In order to show forth this glory of Christ it was enough for the beloved disciple to make him live under the eyes of his Christians, as he himself had contemplated him, without imagining more striking miracles or more explicit discourses. By his works Jesus had proved clearly enough that he was in the Father and the Father in him[6]; moreover, for truly faithful disciples enlightened by the Holy Spirit, miracles were not needed[7]; those whom the Father has given to the Son and drawn to him,[8] recognise the voice of their Master, as sheep recognise the voice of their shepherd[9]; his word takes hold of them,[10] they feel that he, and only he, has the words of eternal life,[11] and, little by little, they discover and contemplate in him his glory.

It is true, and St. John recalls it, the Apostles themselves were slow to understand; at the Last Supper Philip naïvely says to Jesus: 'Lord, shew us the Father, and it

[1] Cf. Euseb., *Hist. Eccl.*, v, 28, 5; Deissmann, *Licht vom Osten*, 297.
[2] ii, 11; xi, 4. Cf. Cornely, *Introductio in N. T.*, 253 *sqq.*
[3] Cf. *Rech. de Sc. Relig.*, 1925, 114 *sqq.*
[4] Cf. *Analecta Tarraconensia*, II, 137–9.
[5] Cf. C. Schmidt, *Gespräche Jesu, Excurs* III, 577–725, esp. pp. 597–611; Baumstark, *Théol. Revue*, 1921, 264 *sqq.*
[6] *John* x, 38; xiv, 11. [7] iv, 48; cf. xx, 29. [8] xvii, 6; vi, 44.
[9] x, 14–16. [10] Cf. viii, 37. [11] vi, 68.

is enough for us'; and Jesus answers him: 'Have I been so long a time with you, and have you not known me? Philip, he that seeth me seeth the Father also.'[1] On many other occasions John is aware of not having understood at once the full meaning of the words of Christ[2]; thus, after having mentioned the prophecy of Jesus: 'Destroy this temple; and in three days I will raise it up'; St. John writes[3]: 'When therefore he was risen again from the dead, his disciples remembered that he had said this: and they believed the scripture and the word that Jesus had said.' Further on, speaking of the entry of our Lord into Jerusalem, he recalls the prophecies which had announced that event and adds: 'These things his disciples did not know at the first: but when Jesus was glorified, then they remembered that these things were written of him and that they had done these things to him.'[4] After the Last Supper, Our Lord addresses his disciples as follows: 'But these things I have told you, that when the hour shall come, you may remember that I told you of them' (*John* xvi, 4); this same discourse of Jesus contains a most explicit remark, the promise of the Holy Spirit: 'He will teach you all things and bring all things to your mind, whatsoever I shall have said to you' (xiv, 26).

These repeated indications[5] mark clearly enough the character of St. John's narratives.[6] They indicate a deeper interpretation of the facts originally imperfectly understood; all these events date, no doubt, from sixty years before; but time, instead of effacing these distant memories, has, little by little, revealed their significance. Is not this the way that the decisive events of life engrave themselves on the soul who contemplates them? Certain details out of a cumbrous multiplicity of facts are retained, but the essential fact, systematised and, as it were, whittled down, is more intimately grasped by the mind and, in its turn, more profoundly impregnated with its life. Here, moreover, there is something more and better than this slow reflexion of the soul, which ripens and revives its memories; there is the action of the Spirit, which throws light upon them, and reveals their most intimate aspect. It is St. John, as was mentioned just

[1] *John* xiv, 8, 9. [2] Cf. SANDAY, *Criticism of the Fourth Gospel*, 93 *sqq*.
[3] ii, 22. [4] xii, 16. [5] Cf. xiii, 7.
[6] Cf. BATIFFOL, *Orpheus et l'Évangile*, 196–201.

now, who has preserved that promise of Jesus: 'The Spirit will bring to your minds all that I have said to you': he had doubtless experienced this in himself. The Church was not mistaken; from the beginning she saw in the *Gospel of St. John* the gospel of the Spirit. Clement of Alexandria, repeating a tradition of the ancient presbyters, writes that John, 'the latest to write, noting that the physical facts had been related by the other evangelists, at the request of the other disciples, and with the inspiration of the Spirit, composed the Spiritual Gospel.'[1]

In order the better to realise the significance of the facts or discourses which he is reporting, John often presents them framed in illuminating theological interpretations; thus the whole Gospel is interpreted by the prologue, and, again, the narrative of the Last Supper and the Passion is preceded by these words: 'Jesus, knowing that his hour was come, that he should pass out of this world to the Father: having loved his own who were in the world, he loved them unto the end.'[2] We shall collect the indications he gives us, and before developing the doctrine of Christ, set forth by the Gospel, study the theology of the evangelist, as the prologue presents it to us.

But before beginning this investigation, let us again pause for a moment on the double character of the whole book. It is a work of history, and a work of theology, placing before us the Word made flesh, making us, so to speak, see and touch him, and at the same time contemplate his glory.[3] If anyone misunderstands the intimate union of these two elements—fact and mystery—he destroys the unity of the book, and, consequently, finds in it nothing but antinomies, all the more disconcerting that each of the terms is affirmed with so much energy. The union of Christ and the believer appears sometimes as a moral union of two friends, sometimes as a mystical fusion of two lives. Between the Son and the Father we sometimes see merely that union of wills, which shows itself throughout the life of Jesus; sometimes, on the other hand, the declarations of Christ proclaim between both an infinitely close physical unity. To explain this perpetual dualism, of which examples could be multiplied,

[1] CLEM. AL., *Hypot.*, VI. [2] *John* xiii, 1. [3] Cf. STANTON, III, p. 15.

certain critics distinguish in St. John's Gospel a wholly spontaneous religious experience, and a philosophical interpretation ; in their view these two elements, brought together in an artificial synthesis, clash and contradict each other throughout the whole book.[1] The reply to these objections will be found in the study of these complexities or apparent contradictions. But before going into details we must consider once more the point of departure of the whole Gospel ; 'The Word was made flesh' ; here, on the threshold of the book, is that mysterious duality, which pursues its course throughout the chapters. For one who rejects, *a priori,* that affirmation, who sees nothing but a contradiction in that mystery, the entire Gospel can be nothing but a long incoherency. He, on the contrary, who does not fear to face the mystery of the Incarnation, and has been prepared by the other books of the New Testament for this supreme revelation, will not be surprised to find in the Gospel the mark of the mystery there set forth, and to learn that the life of the Word made flesh bears the double imprint of glory and of weakness. And, if the contemplation of this Evangelist causes him to discover the mysteries of the divine life as seen through human facts, he will respect that unity which God himself has created, without seeking to deny the reality of the events, any more than the truth of the mysteries.[2]

1. *The Prologue*

In order to study the theology of St. John in its true light the best plan is to follow the path he has himself traced and enter his Gospel through the door of his prologue.[3] According to Harnack, these first verses were merely written by the evangelist to serve as a transition for his readers from the concept of the Logos to that of the only-begotten God[4]: most exegetes, however, see in the prologue the expression of St. John's most intimate thought. The study which we are now about to make of

[1] Cf. E. F. Scott, *The Fourth Gospel*, p. 174.

[2] Cf. J. Huby, *Rech. de Sc. Relig.*, 1927, 155–61 ; R. Bultmann, *Die Bedeutung der mandäischen und manichaischen Quellen fur das Verständnis des Johannesevangeliums*, in *Zeitschr. f. N.T.W.*, 1925, 100–46.

[3] Cf. E. Krebs, *Der Logos als Heiland*, 98 *sqq.*

[4] Harnack, *Ueber das Verhaltnis des Prologs des vierten Evangeliums zum ganzen Werk*, in *Zeitschr. fur Theol. und Kirche*, II (1892), 189–231.

the prologue and of the Gospel will suffice, we hope, to show how closely the two are bound together[1] and to decide the question here raised. Whatever else pertains to the discussion, it is clear that whether the prologue is looked upon as a simple introduction to the Gospel, or as the quintessence of the Johannine doctrine, it is through the prologue that we must enter upon the study of the Gospel.

> 'In the beginning was the Word: and the Word was with God: and the Word was God.
>
> The same was in the beginning with God.
>
> All things were made by him: and without him was made nothing that was made.
>
> In him was life: and the life was the light of men.
>
> And the light shineth in darkness: and the darkness did not comprehend it.'

This prologue resembles in its solemnity the prologue to the *Epistle to the Hebrews;* but one reading of it is enough to show the differences; the periods of the Epistle are full and supple; the phrases of the Gospel are concise and brief, and recall by their rhythm the parallelism of Hebrew poetry. The theology is, in both cases, more similar than the style; both writers throw light on the human ministry of Christ by the description of his divine glory with the Father: here, again, however, the treatment is obviously different; the author of the *Epistle to the Hebrews* contemplates, above all, the mediation of Jesus, and it is in order to show the unique transcendence of that mediation that he rapidly sketches into the picture all the glories of the Mediator. St. John, on the contrary, fixes his gaze on the Son of God himself; and he describes his life-giving and illuminating action so as to make us better understand who he is.[2]

The first words recall quite intentionally the beginning of *Genesis:* 'In the beginning God created heaven and earth'; 'in the beginning was the Word.' This simple parallel is sufficient to mark the whole distance of the creature from the Word, of that which has a beginning, from Him who is; it also shows forth the superiority of the new revelation, which unveils to man the secrets of God,

[1] Harnack, 194–7.

[2] Cf. Baldensperger, *Der Prolog des vierten Evangeliums* (Freiburg, 1898).

while the ancient dispensation merely showed him his dealings here below.

Should we also seek in the narrative of *Genesis* the explanation of this title of Word, given to the Son of God? One hesitates to do so: it is true that this narrative represents God as creating everything by his word, it can be completely summed up in the phrase of the Psalmist: 'He spoke, and all was made.' This conception was no doubt present to the mind of St. John, when, after having, like the author of *Genesis*, recalled the origins (i, 1), he recalled, likewise, the creation (i, 3). This recollection of St. John's, however, does not seem sufficient to explain the use of this personal name of the Word, which has no equivalent in the narrative of *Genesis*. Nor does the personification of the word of God in the prophets and Psalmists provide an adequate explanation. No doubt this conception was not without influence on the theology of the Sapiential Books and, later, on Christian theology; but this influence was only possible through the transformation of the conception.[1] Recourse has often been had to the *Memra* of the *Targums* in order to explain the doctrine of the Word in St. John; if the reader will refer to what has been said (p. 121 *sq.*) about this Judaic conception, it will be seen that this hypothesis is even weaker than the preceding ones: it is by no means easy to establish with any certainty the priority of the doctrine of the *Memra* in relation to the Christian theology of the Word: it will be still harder to prove that this doctrine is independent of the Alexandrine conception of the Logos; but if both these theses were demonstrated, it would still be necessary to show a doctrinal analogy between the *Memra* of the *Targums* and the Word of St. John, which would allow of the supposition of the one having influenced the other. But the analogy is purely verbal. The *Memra* is not a person, not even an intermediary force between God and the world; it merely has the value of a circumlocution, which allows the Rabbis to avoid mentioning the divine name and to veil the anthropomorphisms of the Bible.

Obviously the Johannine doctrine of the Logos is quite different in character as in origin: it does not owe its existence to a ritual scruple, nor is it the expedient of

[1] See above, page 98 *sqq.*

the translator; it is the expression of a living faith in a divine and human Person, whose pre-existence is described, and his life on earth related. And if we wish to explain why the Christian faith took this form in St. John, it is no doubt safest to refer to the Christian documents which preceded and prepared the way for the fourth Gospel.

In the first *Epistle to the Corinthians*[1] the Son is called incidentally the power and wisdom of God[2]; in the second[3] he is shown as the image of God; the *Epistle to the Colossians*[4] develops this doctrine, while insisting on the creative and conserving activity of Christ, which the first *Epistle to the Corinthians*[5] has already mentioned. In the *Epistle to the Hebrews* this theology is fully developed; and the Alexandrine influence, traces of which could be found in the two preceding letters, particularly in the *Epistle to the Colossians,* is now perfectly obvious; the influence of the *Book of Wisdom* is particularly recognisable, not only in the general tenour of style and thought, but still more in certain details of expression which are surely reminiscences.[6]

This penetration of Pauline theology by Alexandrine doctrine is readily attributed to the influence of Apollo, and the hypothesis is plausible; we know by the *Book of Acts*[7] that Apollo was an Alexandrian and a clever exegete. He had profoundly influenced Christian communities, so as to create unintentionally a distinct group of disciples in the Church at Corinth, in opposition to the others. Finally we may note that these Alexandrine conceptions appear precisely in the letters addressed to the churches of Asia and of Corinth, that is, the churches in

[1] i, 24.

[2] Although incidental, the mention is not without significance. Cf. LIGHTFOOT, *Notes on Epistles of St. Paul*, p. 164.

[3] iv, 4. [4] i, 15. [5] viii, 6.

[6] RENDEL HARRIS has made a close study of the relationship between the Prologue and the Sapiential Books in *The Origin of the Prologue to St. John's Gospel* and *The Origin of the Doctrine of the Trinity* (Cambridge, 1917 and 1919). Despite the exaggeration in his thesis that the Prologue is a hymn to Wisdom and in many of the arguments he uses to support it, many of the Biblical and patristic relationships which he establishes are exact. His hypothesis that the identification of Jesus and Wisdom was affirmed by Jesus himself is to be rejected. Cf. BETHUNE-BAKER, *Journ. Theol. Stud.*, XXI, p. 87. Cf. also BULTMANN, *Der religionsgeschichtl. Hintergrund des Prologs zum Joh.-Evangel.* in ΕΥΧΑΡΙΣΤΗΡΙΟΝ, *H. Gunkel dargebracht*, Gottingen, 1923, II, 1–26.

[7] xviii, 24.

which the influence of Apollo had been exercised; there may be more here than a chance coincidence.

On the other hand, it is well to remind ourselves that we have but a very incomplete knowledge of this work of evangelisation, of its progress, and of its apostles; it would be rash to refer to the few names that are known to us an influence which may very likely have been more widespread. At Jerusalem itself the Alexandrines had a synagogue, and at the very beginning of Christian propaganda we find them discussing with St. Stephen[1]; in the Jewish communities of the Dispersion their influence was still more considerable, and often predominant. Christian doctrine and Alexandrine theology were bound to clash: that encounter should not be entirely attributed to the initiative of one man, even of Apollo, but rather to the necessities of the situation, or, better, to the direction of Providence, which thus orientated towards Christianity all the vital and intellectual resources which divine revelation had accumulated in Judaism.

In these various documents, particularly in the *Epistle to the Hebrews,* we find all the essential elements of the Christian doctrine of the Word; the name alone is wanting. The name appears at length in the *Apocalypse,* occurring incidentally in the midst of a triumphal vision, in a context that has nothing Philonian about it, but rather recalls the *Wisdom of Solomon.*[2] We find it now again in the first verses of the Gospel; it appears without any explanation, as a term already familiar to the reader; St. John repeats it again towards the end of the prologue,[3] and then does not mention it again in the whole Gospel.[4] Must we conclude that this mention of the Word is but a passing allusion, an *argumentum ad hominem?* Did St. John borrow this conception from the philosophical discussions of his time and *milieu,* in order to make of it, not indeed the foundation, but the point of departure of his teaching, in order to raise his readers, from the philosophic category with which they were familiar, to the, properly speaking, Christian doctrine of the only-begotten Son of God, announced at the end of the prologue? This

[1] *Acts* vi, 9. [2] See above, page 351. [3] i, 14.

[4] The Greek word *logos* is often used in the gospel, but never in the technical sense it has in the Prologue. Cf. STANTON, III, 167 *sqq.*; GRILL, 31 *sqq.*

conclusion, maintained by Harnack,[1] does not seem probable; one does not understand why St. John should have insisted so strongly on a conception with which he had nothing further to do: 'In the beginning was the Word, and the Word was with God, and the Word was God.' But one is not surprised that a technical term like this should only be used in the prologue, where the evangelist is giving the interpretation of the mystery, and that it should not reappear in narratives of which it would alter the character. It is still more intelligible if we admit that the prologue was composed after the rest of the book.[2] As we have argued above, the fourth Gospel is nothing but a literary arrangement of the daily teaching given by St. John to his disciples. It seems plausible that the prologue was only written at the moment of publication, and we can understand that the author may have used in this introduction alone a philosophic expression which he had not employed in his catechesis. We may add also that the whole Gospel is dominated by the conceptions of life and light, which, according to the prologue, were the essential and characteristic attributes of the Word.

These indications of the origin of the term Logos and its employment by St. John are no doubt insufficient to determine its exact significance: in the Alexandrine world, to which they direct our researches, the Logos had a thousand different values: which of these has it preserved in passing to the Christian *milieux* of Asia? For Philo the Logos was sometimes, as for the Stoics, the immanent force which connects and vitalises all beings; sometimes, according to the doctrine of Platonic exemplarism, the ideal type, model of the world, the image and thought of God. The first of these two conceptions is certainly foreign to Johannine theology, as to all the Christian thought of this period; the second is not so far from the teaching of the *Epistle to the Colossians,* and above all, of the *Epistle to the Hebrews;* but it hardly appears in St. John, though St. Augustine found it in the fourth verse: 'In him was life'; but we may doubt the probability of his interpretation. Much more rarely, giving way to the influence of Biblical theology, Philo understands by the Logos the 'word' of God; this is the only meaning which it bears in the *Book of*

[1] See above, page 367. [2] Cf. STANTON, III, 178–9.

Wisdom, and also in the *Apocalypse,* and we must recognise this in the *Gospel of St. John ;* everything suggests it, not only the text of the *Apocalypse,* but also the tenor of the prologue, which, by its allusions to the narrative of *Genesis,* represents the world as created by the word of God. The comparison of the Johannine and of the Philonian conceptions[1] permits us to appreciate more exactly their distinguishing differences, the definitely Biblical character of the former, and the Hellenising character of the latter.[2] We now begin to perceive it in the contrast between the Word which is the word of God, and the Logos which is the law of the world. We shall understand it still better in the description given by St. John of the relations of the Word with God, and consequently of his activity in the world.

The first sentence of the evangelist revealed the existence of the Word from the beginning ; but what was he in this immutable eternity ? He was with God, he was God. The first affirmation, 'He was with God,' must not be understood as local proximity, nor as the subordination of the Word to God[3] ; it expresses simply the community of life lived together by two persons ; the meaning is the same as when our Lord, according to *St. Mark,*[4] said to his disciples: 'How long shall I be with you ?' and in a precisely parallel passage in an *Epistle of St. John*[5]: 'The life eternal which was with the Father, and hath appeared to us.'[6]

'And the Word was God.' In the preceding phrase we read πρὸς τὸν Θεόν with the article ; here, Θεὸς without it. Origen thought he saw there a distinction between him who is the source of divinity and him who possesses it only derivatively.[7] This idea of subordination is very far from the meaning of the text. The omission of the article, necessary indeed to prevent ambiguity, is explained by the simple fact that ὁ Θεὸς has the value of a personal name, and indicates God the Father ; while Θεὸς without the article has the value of a natural name, and indicates

[1] See Note VII at end of Volume.

[2] Cf. P. LASSERRE, *La Jeunesse d'Ernest Renan,* II. *Le drame de la metaphysique chrétienne* (Paris, 1925), and the very long footnote in the French original of the present work : p. 497, note 3 (continues to p. 499).

[3] Contrary to GRILL, 85.

[4] ix, 18.

[5] 1 *John* i, 2.

[6] WESTCOTT compares *Matt.* xiii, 56 ; *Mark* vi, 3 ; xiv, 49 ; *Luke* ix, 41.

[7] *In Jo.,* II, 2 (*GCS,* 54).

that the Word is divine in nature.[1] Nor is there any need to recall here the 'god' or 'secondary god' of Philo. The reader may remember that, in the works of Philo, this expression, in which certain historians try to sum up his whole doctrine of the Logos, only occurs three times; it does not at all follow on the spontaneous development of the thought, but is occasioned or rather imposed artificially by the text to be interpreted. Here, nothing of the kind; the dogmatic affirmation is energetically made at the opening of the book, in order to indicate its whole tendency; the exclamation of St. Thomas, 'My Lord and my God,' in chapter xx, echoes it.

'The same was in the beginning with God. All things were made by him: and without him was made nothing that was made.' After having reaffirmed the eternity of the Word and his relations with God, the evangelist describes his activity in the world; we find again here the dogma already so strongly insisted upon in the *Epistle to the Colossians* and to the Hebrews. To give more force to his statement St. John, adopting a well-known Hebrew turn of phrase, confirms the statement which he has just made by a negation.[2]

'In him was life, and the life was the light of men.' This verse, perhaps more than any other in the Gospel, has stimulated critical and exegetical discussions[3]; the following interpretation seems to be the most probable. We read[4]: 'God hath given to us eternal life. And this life is in his Son. He that hath the Son hath life; he that hath not the Son hath not life.' We understand the verse of the prologue in the same sense: 'In him (the Word) was life': evidently life was not there as a precarious deposit, as a gift received from without, as it is in man,[5] but as it was in God himself[6] by plenary and natural possession; life was there also as in its source, since it was from thence that it was to pour itself into men. This is more clearly marked at the end of the verse: 'And the life was the light of men.' The identity thus established between these two conceptions helps us to understand their exact significance; the Gospel will enable us to be even more precise on the subject: but in future we may

[1] See WESTCOTT's edition of St. John's Epistles, 165–7.
[2] See MALDONATUS on *Is.* xxxix, 4. [3] See Note VI at end of this Volume.
[4] 1 *John* v, 11. [5] Cf. vi, 53; 1 *John* iii, 15. [6] v, 26.

observe that, for St. John, life and light are above all a power of expansion and radiance; these two terms are much more representative of the action of the Word on men than of the inner life of God.

'And the light shineth in darkness and the darkness did not comprehend it.'[1] This antagonism of light and darkness will appear throughout the Gospel, as also the blindness of the wicked: the children of light believe in the light, the others prefer the darkness to the light, and cannot understand it.

After these introductory verses, in which the nature and action of the Word have been described, St. John recalls the witness of St. John the Baptist and the Incarnation of the Word:

> 'There was a man sent from God, whose name was John.
>
> This man came for a witness, to give testimony of the light, that all men might believe through him.
>
> He was not the light, but was to give testimony of the light.
>
> That was the true light, which enlighteneth every man that cometh into this world.
>
> He was in the world: and the world was made by him: and the world knew him not.
>
> He came unto his own: and his own received him not.
>
> But as many as received him, he gave them power to be made the sons of God, to them that believe in his name.
>
> Who are born, not of blood, nor of the will of the flesh, nor of the will of man, but of God.
>
> And the Word was made flesh and dwelt among us (and we saw his glory, the glory as it were of the only begotten of the Father), full of grace and truth' (i, 6-14).

This second section of the prologue completes the first and makes its meaning more precise: what was said above of the Word—it was life and light—and of the antagonism of light and darkness, is here developed in the progressive manifestations of the Word, and in the reception with which they meet. While John the Baptist

[1] See Westcott, and B. Weiss, *in h. l.*

was but a witness,[1] the Word was the true light, which enlighteneth every man coming into the world.[2]

The evangelist goes on to describe the presence of the Word in the world, which was made by him and yet did not know him ; there is no reference here as yet to the Incarnation, nor even of any particular manifestation, but merely to the presence of the Creator in his creation ; St. Paul, following in the steps of the author of *Wisdom*, had reproached the Pagans with their failure to know God[3] ; the same idea is here applied to the Word.

'He came unto his own: and his own received him not' ; St. John is no longer speaking here of the immanence of the Word (ἦν), but of his arrival (ἦλθεν) ; it is no longer only in the world that he makes himself known and is unrecognised, but amongst his own (οἱ ἴδιοι). There is certainly a development in the thought here ; this domain of his own, to which the Word came, and where he was not received, is the Jewish people. In the Gospel[4] the theophanies of the Old Testament are recalled as manifestations of the Word ; we may find the same idea here, provided that we recognise that St. John is referring here, above all, to the supreme manifestation—the Incarnation.[5] This is clearly indicated by the following verses, which describe the divine adoption conferred by the Word on all those who believe in his name.

'And the Word was made flesh and dwelt among us, and we saw his glory, the glory as it were of the only begotten of the Father, full of grace and truth.'

This verse sums up the whole of the prologue, just as the prologue interprets the whole of the Gospel. The first point is the infinite humiliation of the Word, 'He was made flesh.' The thought is the same as that in the *Epistle to the Philippians*, the expression still stronger : in the language of St. John, as of the rest of the Bible, the flesh is weakness ; and that is what the Word has become. Yet he has remained what he was: the entire Gospel is devoted to the task of showing the presence of God among mankind, and this very verse of the prologue states

[1] Cf. Baldensperger, *Der Prolog*, 6.

[2] Cf. Augustine, *De peccatorum meritis*, I, 25, 38 (*P.L.*, XLIV, 130) ; Cyril Alex. (*in h. l.* ; *P.G.*, LXXIII, 129) ; Burney, *Aramaic Origin*, 33 ; Strack-Billerbeck, II, 358.

[3] *Acts* xiv, 15–17 ; xvii, 30 ; *Rom.* i, 18–22 ; *Wisd.* xiii, 1 *sqq.*

[4] *John* xii, 41 ; viii, 56.

[5] Cf. *Matt.* xxiii, 37.

it quite clearly: 'The Word dwelt amongst us, and we saw his glory.' The expression 'dwelt' is dear to St. John[1]; it recalls the greatest religious memories of the Old Testament; the dwelling of Jahve in the tent in the midst of Israel,[2] and his promises to return to live again among his people[3]; it recalls still more expressly the hymn of Wisdom[4]: 'I dwelt in the highest places . . . he that made me rested in my tabernacle. And he said to me: Let thy dwelling be in Jacob, and thy inheritance in Israel . . .'[5] These prophecies have already been echoed in the *Apocalypse*, in the scene of the renewal of the world, when the new Jerusalem came down from heaven. 'And I heard a great voice from the throne, saying: Behold the tabernacle of God with men: and he will dwell with them.'[6] Here the construction of the picture is quite different, but the reality is the same; it is already the dwelling of God among us. In this passage, as in so many others, St. John applies to Christ the Biblical oracles relating to Jahve. We may also recognise there the application to the Word of what the Jewish doctors said of the Shekina: it is Jesus who is truly the Presence of God among men, and those who approach him contemplate his glory.[7]

'He was full of grace and truth . . . and of his fulness we all have received: and grace for grace; for the law was given by Moses: grace and truth came by Jesus Christ.' The gifts of the new alliance are here compared with those granted by God through Moses. Grace, mentioned here so insistently, will not be referred to again in the Gospel. In the whole of the rest of the Johannine literature it is only to be found three times, in formulas of greeting.[8] 'Truth,' on the other hand, is a characteristic concept of Johannine theology, one of those which, with 'light' and 'life,' make his doctrine of God and of Christ penetrate our souls most profoundly; we shall shortly study it. All these gifts come to us from Christ, not that he dispenses them as a minister, like

[1] It is only found, in N.T., here, and in *Apoc.* vii, 15; xii, 12; xiii, 6; xxi, 3.

[2] 2 *Kings* vii, 6.

[3] *Ezech.* xxxvii, 27; *Zach.* ii, 10; viii, 3, 8.

[4] *Ecclus.* xxiv, 7 *sq.*

[5] Cf. Rendel Harris, 32–34.

[6] *Apoc.* xxi, 3.

[7] On the Shekina, see above, pages 124–126. Cf. Dalman, *Worte Jesu*, 189; Burney, 35–6.

[8] *Apoc.* i, 4; xxii, 21; 2 *John*, 3.

Moses, but because they are the overflow of his plenitude, as St. Paul taught the Colossians (*supra*, p. 305 *sq*.).

Verse 18 is the crown of the prologue: 'No man hath seen God at any time: the only begotten Son who is in the bosom of the Father, he hath declared him.' The first phrase has seemed sometimes an affirmation of the invisibility proper to the Father as such, who can only manifest himself through the Son[1]; this conception is very widespread among the ante-Nicene Fathers, but it does not appear that we should recognise it here. In this text, and the parallel one of the first Epistle,[2] the word Θεὸς is employed without an article[3]: it is rather a natural description than the name of a person; the two phrases do not express a property of the Father as such, but an essential attribute of the Divinity: it is invisible to man.[4] But the only Son, or, as St. John says here, the only begotten God[5] who is in the bosom of the Father,[6] has himself brought it to our knowledge. This revelation is presented here as a teaching; elsewhere it will be presented rather as a manifestation[7]; nor are these two meanings mutually exclusive. Christ is at once the Master who teaches us God, and the Son who shews him in shewing us himself.[8]

In the interpretation of the prologue we have not touched on several verses,[9] which are not directly concerned with the doctrine of the Trinity, but which recall the testimony given by St. John the Baptist to Jesus Christ. Their presence in this doctrinal exposition contributes to its characterisation; in the whole of the New Testament there is no more theological page than this one, but here also the theology is not pure speculation, but rests entirely and inseparably on the life of Christ. The mystery of the divine life, the creation of the world by the Word are merely recalled in the opening verses, in order to prepare the way for what will shortly be said of the appearance of the Word among men, and the

[1] Cf. LOISY, *Quatriéme evangile*², 194 *sqq*. [2] iv, 12.

[3] *John* i, 18; I *John* iv, 12.

[4] On God's invisibility, cf. *John* v, 37; vi, 46; I *John* iv, 20; *Rom*. i, 20; *Col*. i, 15; I *Tim*. i, 17; vi, 16; IGNATIUS, *Polyc*. III, 2; BAUER, *in h.l.*

[5] HORT has devoted the first of his *Two Dissertations* (pp. 1–72) to defending this reading. Cf. LAGRANGE's note on this text.

[6] See MOULTON, *Grammar of N.T. Greek*, 62 *sq*., 234 *sq*. [7] *John* xiv, 9.

[8] Cf. IREN., *Hær*., iv, 6, 4. [9] 6–8; 15.

revelation brought by him. This Word is Jesus Christ; he is only called by this name towards the end of the prologue, but from the beginning it is he alone of whom the evangelist is thinking, and towards him that he is leading us.

By this close fusion of the theology of the Word and the history of Christ, the prologue makes us think of two other pages that have frequently been recalled in the course of this exposition: *Colossians* (i, 15-20) and *Hebrews* (i, 1-4). It is to be distinguished from them, however, not only by the more explicit doctrine which it gives to the Word of God, but also by the aspect under which it presents the rôle of Christ. He does not appear here as Priest making reconciliation, but as Revealer; he is light, life, and truth, who will say, at the end of his mission: 'Eternal life is to know thee, the only true God, and Jesus Christ, whom thou hast sent' (xvii, 3).

Here, as in the teaching of St. Paul, the personal identity, so strongly affirmed between the pre-existing Word and Christ, does not admit any doubt of the personality of the Word before the Incarnation[1]; indeed, the evangelist expressly indicates this: the Word *comes* to his own (11), he *gives* to his own the power to become the sons of God (12), he *dwells* among us (14); the use of the masculine *him* (11-12) compared with the neuter word *light,* shows clearly that, under these abstract terms, the author speaks of a *Person*. The same may be said of the filiation: the Word does not become Son by his incarnation; from all eternity he is 'The only begotten Son,[2] in the bosom of the Father.'

We should, however, note that these terms, Father and Son, only occur once or twice (18, cf. 14) in the prologue; St. John only employs them when he begins to speak of the revelation made by Jesus Christ; thenceforward that revelation will fill the whole Gospel, and we shall find these two terms constantly repeated. What Jesus Christ has come to reveal to us above all is not the creative action of the Word, but the mutual relations of the Father and the Son, in which Christians are called to participate.

[1] Cf. Holtzmann, *N.T. Theol.*², II, 449 *sqq*.

[2] Douai (*John* i, 14); our French original has 'Dieu' instead of 'Son,' with an erudite footnote, to which the reader is referred (p. 507, note 3).

2. *The Gospel. The Only Son*

Christ appeared in the prologue, eternally pre-existing before his arrival here below; for this doctrine penetrates the whole Gospel, and, starting from that point of view, we perceive the unity of the whole work, and the intimate union of its two parts.

From the beginning St. John the Baptist indicates Christ as one who 'was before him.' Further on it is said that Isaias saw the glory of Jesus,[1] that Abraham saw his day and rejoiced[2]; and, as the Jews grew angry, Jesus insisted: 'Before Abraham was made, I am.'[3] On his last day Jesus prays thus: 'Glorify thou me, O Father, with thyself, with the glory which I had, before the world was, with thee.'[4]

All these texts declare clearly enough the eternal pre-existence of Christ; but it is even more interesting to note those which show the revelation of Jesus, proceeding from his eternal knowledge; after having reported a new testimony of St. John the Baptist, the evangelist proceeds in these words: 'He that cometh from heaven is above all. And what he hath seen and heard, that he testifieth: and no man receiveth his testimony.'[5] To Nicodemus Jesus said almost in the same terms: 'Amen, amen, I say to thee that we speak what we know and we testify what we have seen: and you receive not our testimony. If I have spoken to you earthly things, and you believe not: how will you believe, if I shall speak to you heavenly things? And no man hath ascended into heaven, but he that descended from heaven, the Son of man.'[6] Many other passages of the Gospel reiterate the same assurance: 'Not that any man hath seen the Father: but he who is of God, he hath seen the Father.'[7] 'You are from beneath: I am from above . . . I speak that which I have seen with my Father: and you do the things that you have seen with your father.'[8] The same idea is to be found in the many texts where reference is made 'to the testimony of Jesus'[9]; in the Gospel, as in the *Apocalypse*, Jesus is the 'faithful witness,' and his revelation is nothing else than the 'testimony' which he bears to the divine

[1] *John* xii, 41. [2] viii, 56. [3] viii, 58. [4] xvii, 5.
[5] iii, 31–32. [6] iii, 11–13. [7] vi, 46. [8] viii, 23, 38.
[9] iii, 11, 32, 33; v, 31–36; viii, 13–19; xviii, 37; cf. vii, 7.

mysteries, to his Father, to himself. On the last day of his life he said to Pilate: 'For this came I into the world: that I should give testimony to the truth.'[1]

This character of his teaching is more explicitly affirmed in the attestations which have just been recalled, but it is to be found everywhere: each of these sentences had the authority of an irrefragable witness and the serene assurance of eternal knowledge. This, for the unbeliever, is one of the most disconcerting traits of the Johannine Christ, and, for the Christian, one of his most revealing traits: it is surely in such words that a God made man would speak of the mysteries of God.[2]

Jesus is conscious that he has come not only as Master,[3] but also as Saviour: 'God sent not his Son into the world, to judge the world: but that the world may be saved by him.'[4] This salvation is generally presented as a communication of life: 'The bread of God is that which cometh down from heaven and giveth life to the world.' The Jews said to him: 'Lord, give us always this bread.' Jesus said to them: 'I am the bread of life . . .'[5] The whole chapter is full of this idea; we find it also in the teaching given by Jesus to the Samaritan woman on the living water,[6] in the parable of the Good Shepherd,[7] and throughout the Gospel.

No doubt this doctrine was not new: Christ promised life to his own in the preaching reported by the Synoptics.[8] St. Peter at Cæsarea Philippi recognised him as the 'Son of the living God,'[9] and in one of his first sermons at Jerusalem, as the 'Author of Life.'[10] St. Paul above all showed Christ as the unique source of life for men: he is the 'quickening Spirit.'[11] All these data, already so rich, are completed by the Johannine doctrine, in which Christ is revealed as the principle of life, no longer, primarily, in the glory of his resurrection, but in the eternity of his pre-existence: from heaven he descended as the Bread of Life, in order to give life to men. This is the teaching of the prologue: 'In him was life'; it was the solemn teaching of Jesus himself: 'I am the

[1] *John* xviii, 37.

[2] Cf. Bossuet, *Disc. sur l'hist. univ.*, II, 19; Pascal, *Pensées*, ed. Brunschvicg, 799.

[3] *John* iii, 2. [4] iii, 17. [5] vi, 33 *seq.* [6] iv, 10 *seq.* [7] x, 10.

[8] *Mark* x, 30, etc. [9] *Matt.* xvi, 16. [10] *Acts* iii, 15. [11] 1 *Cor.* xv, 45.

resurrection and the life '[1] ; 'I am the way, and the truth, and the life.'[2]

This conception of life is central in the Gospel of St. John.[3] It would be useless to seek its origin in the Alexandrine philosophy ; Philo never thought of the Logos as life, and the Biblical doctrine of life had no influence on his speculations.[4] In Palestine, however, it was very active: under its eschatological aspect it was concerned with the resurrection and eternal life ; under its moral aspect it included the 'living works,' by means of which we prepared ourselves here below for that destiny ; it tended, moreover, to materialise itself increasingly under the influence of Rabbinic legalism.[5] These two aspects of the conception of life are both to be found in St. John, but blended in the unity of Christ's activity. 'I am the resurrection and the life: he that believeth in me, although he be dead, shall live: and every one that liveth and believeth in me shall not die for ever.'[6] Jesus claims here the life-giving power of God, as he had put it forward himself in the Synoptics, when, in order to prove the resurrection to the Sadducees, he said to them: 'He is not the God of the dead, but of the living: for all live to him.'[7] Elsewhere indeed he compares his activity with that of his Father, on the same level: 'For as the Father raiseth up the dead and giveth life: so the Son also giveth life to whom he will.'[8] In the other books of the New Testament, and particularly in St. Paul's Epistles, the resurrection of the dead is always attributed to God the Father ; Christians will, no doubt, be raised *in* Christ, on account of his Spirit who dwells in them, yet they will be quickened by the Father.[9] In the writings of St. John, on the other hand, Jesus promises to his faithful on several occasions that he will raise them to life on the last day.[10] There is the same difference in the description of Christ's own Resurrection: elsewhere it is to be considered as a work of the Father ; St. John represents it as the effect of

[1] *John* xi, 25. [2] xiv, 6.

[3] Cf. J. B. Frey, *Le concept de vie dans l'évangile de saint Jean*, in *Biblica*, I (1920), 37–58, 211–39.

[4] See Note VII at end of this Volume.

[5] Cf. Lagrange, *Messianisme*, 158 *sqq.* ; Weber, 24.

[6] *John* xi, 25, 26. [7] *Luke* xx, 38. [8] *John* v, 21.

[9] *Rom.* viii, 11 ; 2 *Cor.* i, 9 ; iv, 14 ; cf. *Heb.* xi, 19.

[10] *John* vi, 39, 40, 44, 54.

the power of Jesus.[1] These two conceptions are evidently not contradictory: shortly after the Gospel of St. John we find them brought together in the letter of St. Ignatius to the Smyrnians[2]: we must recognise, however, that they represent two different aspects of the doctrine—Christological and Trinitarian. St. John sees in the Son the fulness of life, in which we all participate: the other apostles refer it to the Father, as the sole source from which everything proceeds.

We do not find the same difference between the doctrine of St. Paul and that of St. John, if we consider the life-giving action of Christ, no longer under its eschatological aspect, but in its present reality: the allegory of the vine, as reported in chapter xv, has the same significance as the Pauline image of the human body: the vine and the branches are united like the head and the members: 'Abide in me: and I in you. As the branch cannot bear fruit of itself, unless it abide in the vine, so neither can you, unless you abide in me. I am the vine: you the branches. He that abideth in me, and I in him, the same beareth much fruit: for without me you can do nothing' (xv, 4-5).

The people of God were also the vine of Jahve, but, too often, a barren vine. The Church is the true Israel and the true vine, fecundated by the trunk that bears it, Jesus Christ, and through him, loaded with fruit. This is the whole theology of the *Epistle to the Ephesians*, presented under a Biblical image, and rendered more touching and persuasive, because it was taught by Jesus himself on his way to his Passion; on his lips, and at that hour, these last recommendations have a poignancy which no other master could give them; in St. Paul we feel an assurance and an enthusiasm which seizes the soul: he is in Christ, and he is sure that neither death nor life will be able to separate him from the love of God, which is in Christ. Now the note becomes more restrained, but still more intimate and penetrating: 'Abide in me'; the hour of death and separation has come, but Jesus knows that he is the life, the inseparable life[3] of his disciples: 'Abide in me.'[4]

[1] *John* ii, 19. Cf. AUGUSTINE, *In Jo.*, *Tract.* xlvii, 7 (*P.L.*, XXXV, 1736).
[2] ii; cf. vii, 1.
[3] ST. IGNATIUS, *Eph.* iii, 2. [4] See DEISSMANN, *In Christo Jesu*, p. 130.

The doctrine of the Church is less developed in this passage than in 1 *Corinthians* xii or in *Ephesians* iv; we do not distinguish in the mystical vine the diversities of gifts and ministries so easily as in the body of Christ; but the union of the Christian with Jesus is perhaps more strongly accentuated; it is Christ himself, living with his own, who speaks thus to them, and he re-enforces his words in order to make them understand his union with them: 'Abide in me, and I in you'; this formula is characteristic of the Johannine writings, we meet with it elsewhere, both in the Gospel and the first Epistle.[1]

The Eucharistic discourse of chapter vi suggests naturally this discourse after the Supper. The doctrine of Christ as our life which fills the whole of this chapter is directed towards and completed in the Eucharistic doctrine, developed in the last verses (54-58):

> 'Amen, amen, I say unto you: except you eat the flesh of the Son of man and drink his blood, you shall not have life in you. He that eateth my flesh and drinketh my blood hath everlasting life: and I will raise him up in the last day. For my flesh is meat indeed: and my blood is drink indeed. He that eateth my flesh and drinketh my blood abideth in me: and I in him. As the living Father hath sent me and I live by the Father: so he that eateth me, the same also shall live by me.'

It would be out of place here to insist on the Eucharistic significance of this doctrine, and all the riches which a later tradition, in particular the Greek tradition, has drawn from it. We are here considering only what refers directly to the divine nature and the life-giving action of Christ. The teaching contained in the parable of the vine is hardly distinguished from the theology of St. Paul; but here we find a new doctrinal perspective. In the Eucharist the union of Christ and the believer is consummated, and the life-giving transformation which is the fruit of that union is produced; it is no longer a matter of adhesion to Christ by faith, or of incorporation into the body of Christ by baptism; it is a new form of union, at once most real and most spiritual: by it he who adheres to the Lord is not only one spirit with him,

[1] vi, 56; xiv, 20; xv, 4; xv, 5; 1 *John* iii, 24;

but also one flesh. This union is so intimate that Jesus does not hesitate to say: 'As I live by the Father, so he that eateth me shall live by me.'

Doubtless we have here only an analogy: yet, in order to respect it, we must understand not merely a moral union founded on a community of sentiments,[1] but a true physical union, implying the blending of two lives, or rather the participation of the Christian in the very life of Christ.[2]

From this standpoint we easily see the unity of the life-giving action of Jesus: he appeared in the first series of texts as the Resurrection, as the one who is to raise his believers from the dead at the last day; in his discourse after the Supper he revealed himself as the unique and eternal principle of their Christian life. Both these partial aspects are here blended in one same perspective. 'He that eateth my flesh and drinketh my blood hath everlasting life: and I will raise him up in the last day.' The whole man, flesh and spirit, is united to Christ and vitalised by him[3]; from the moment of regeneration he possesses eternal life; and on the last day he will rise from the dead, not only 'on account of the Spirit of Christ who dwells in him,' but because his very flesh has been united to the life-giving flesh of Christ. It is easier to understand in the light of this, 'sown in corruption, it shall rise in incorruption,' and 'this mortal must put on immortality'; the body of Christ is not only the first-fruits of the resurrection and its model, but it is Christ who has sown the seed of incorruptibility and who will clothe it with that robe of glory.[4]

We grasp here, better perhaps than anywhere else, the two most striking features of Johannine Christology; both its unflinching realism: 'Except you eat the flesh of the Son of man and drink his blood, you shall not have life in you,'[5] and on the other hand, the contempt for the flesh and the exclusive esteem for the Spirit: 'It is the spirit that uickeneth, the flesh profiteth nothing' (64).

[1] According to St. Paul also, the mystical union of Christ and the Christian is more than a moral union (see above, pages 292 *sqq.*), although the physical character is less accentuated than in St. John.

[2] Cf. HILARY, *De Trinit.*, VIII, 13 *sqq.*

[3] See CYRIL ALEX., *In Jo.*, VI, 50 (*P.G.*, LXXIII, 577–80).

[4] Cf. ST. THOMAS, *Summa*, III, Qu. 73, a. 3.

[5] ST. IGNATIUS, *Smyrn.*, VII, 1.

Thus the Apostle pursues a course between Cerinthus and the Docetists, confessing with all his soul the real and integral humanity of Christ, but also recognising that that humanity is wholly penetrated by the Spirit and therefore life-giving; this double aspect of his doctrine may be recognised in these two first verses of his first Epistle: 'That which was from the beginning, which we have heard, which we have seen with our eyes, which we have looked upon and our hands have handled, of the word of life. For the life was manifested: and we have seen and do bear witness and declare unto you the life eternal, which was with the Father, and hath appeared to us. That which we have seen and have heard, we declare unto you.' In the first verse nothing appears but the visible and tangible reality; in the second, nothing but eternal life; and these two objects are identical, which is what the Apostle has seen and announces.

The concept of light is closely connected with that of life[1]: 'The life was the light of men,' is said in the prologue (i, 4); in the Gospel we read, 'he that followeth me shall have the light of life.'[2] Here again we find ourselves in the central current of Biblical tradition[3]: the light is life[4] just as darkness is death. As God is living and the source of life, he is also light[5]; he appears on Sinai in the midst of lightnings[6]; he leads his people during the night by a pillar of fire[7]; light is the symbol of all his government of Israel: the prophets and the psalmists love to sing of him as the light of Israel,[8] and to recognise in his law the light which leads them.[9] The servant of Jahve is foretold as the 'light of nations,'[10] and Wisdom is celebrated as the 'brightness of eternal light.'[11]

All these conceptions are as living in the New Testament as in the Old: when the Child Jesus is presented in the Temple, Simeon, recalling the prophecy of Isaias, hails in him 'the light to the revelation of the Gentiles.'[12] At the Transfiguration the face of Christ 'did shine as the sun'[13]; thus St. John will see it in the *Apocalypse*: 'his

[1] Cf. FREY, 232 *sqq.* [2] *John* viii, 12.
[3] Cf. GRILL, *Untersuchungen*, 259 *sqq.*; LAGRANGE, p. clxi *sq.*
[4] *Job* xxxiii, 30; *Ps.* lv, 13.
[5] *Ps.* xxxv, 10. [6] *Exod.* xix, 16. [7] *Exod.* xiii, 21.
[8] *Is.* x, 17; lx, 19, 20; *Mich.* vii, 8; *Ps.* iv, 7; xxvii, 1, etc.
[9] *Ps.* cxviii, 105. [10] *Isaias* xlix, 6. [11] *Wisd.* vii, 26.
[12] *Luke* ii, 32. [13] *Matt.* xvii, 2.

face was as the sun shineth in its power'[1]: the heavenly Jerusalem has no need of sun or of moon, for 'the glory thereof.'[2] When St. Paul had the vision of Christ which of God hath enlightened it: and the Lamb is the lamp converted him on the road to Damascus, 'a light from heaven shined round about him'[3]; and he loves in his letters to represent the action of Christ on his faithful as illumination: 'You were heretofore darkness, but now light in the Lord. Walk then as children of the light'[4]; and he says to the Thessalonians, 'you are not the children of the light and children of the day; we are not of the night or darkness.'[5] In the *Epistle to the Ephesians*[6] we find this fragment of a hymn: 'Rise, thou that sleepest, and arise from the dead: and Christ shall enlighten thee.' And, at the last day, when Christ shall come, he shall 'bring to light the hidden things of darkness and will make manifest the counsels of the hearts.'[7]

St. John has the same conception of light, and we should not seek in his writings the traces of other influences, Oriental, Alexandrine, or Gnostic. But we may note that neither the Gospel nor the Epistles contain any description of the glorified Christ, recalling the Transfiguration, or the apparition to St. Paul, or the visions of the *Apocalypse*: the glory and the light of Christ shine everywhere, but the glory is super-sensible,[8] the light is invisible to the eyes. It is, above all, St. Paul's Epistles which may be fruitfully compared to the Johannine writings; in both these groups of documents we find the children of light and the children of darkness, the illumination of souls by Christ, the revelation of the secrets of hearts. But the doctrine is more striking in St. John's writings, because it is manifested in the very life of Jesus, and it is taught by himself: 'I am the light of the world,' he affirms on several occasions[9]; or again, expressing more definitely his pre-existence and his mission, 'I am come, a light into the world.'[10] During his life on earth he shines on men, good and evil: those who believe in the light become children of light[11]; they are no longer

[1] *Apoc.* i, 16. [2] *Apoc.* xxi, 23. [3] *Acts* ix, 3. [4] *Eph.* v, 8.
[5] 1 *Thess.* v, 5. [6] v, 14.
[7] Cf. *Rom.* xii, 12; 2 *Cor.* iv, 6; vi, 14, 15; *Eph.* i, 18; iii, 9; v, 13; *Col.* i, 12; 2 *Tim.* i, 10; 1 *Pet.* ii, 9.
[8] Cf. 1 *Pet.* ii, 16–18; *John* i, 14.
[9] *John* viii, 12; ix, 5. [10] xii, 46. [11] xii, 36.

in darkness, they walk with complete confidence, without fearing a fall by the way.[1] The Israelite of old said to Jahve: 'Thy word is a light to my paths'[2]; Christ is still more for Christians; he is an intimate light which surrounds and penetrates them; they walk in that light, and that light is in them (xii, 35; 1 *John* i, 7; ii, 10).

The wicked also are reached by that light; it reveals and judges them: 'And this is the judgement: Because the light is come into the world and men loved darkness rather than light. For their works were evil . . .'[3] Jesus says the same thing later on in these words: 'For judgement am I come into this world; that they who see not may see; and they who see may become blind.'[4] According to St. Paul, it is, above all, at the last day[5] that the light of Christ will make this discernment. According to St. John, it is already accomplished by Jesus in his human life: 'He that doth not believe is already judged.'[6]

Pursuing his teaching, St. John adds: 'He that doth truth cometh to the light, that his works may be made manifest: because they are done in God'[7]: in the first Epistle we find several times an analogous connection between the truth and the light: true disciples have the truth in them,[8] just as they are in the light,[9] and this doctrine of salvation depends entirely on St. John's Christology; as Jesus is light, so also he is truth.

By this word, which is so dear to him,[10] St. John signifies the veracity of a teaching or of a testimony[11]; but above all he means the divine reality. To say that Jesus is the truth, is not only to say that he is the authentic Master and the faithful witness, but also that before he came all was in shadow, and that, in him, reality appeared. It is in this sense that the Word is called 'the true light,'[12] and that he, himself, calls himself 'the true bread,'[13] 'the true vine,'[14] and his flesh and blood true food and drink[15]; his disciples are 'true worshippers,' adoring the Father 'in spirit and in truth'[16]; 'they shall know the truth and the truth shall make them free'[17]; they do the truth,[18] they are 'of the truth.'[19] In a word, truth is

[1] *John* xii, 46; xi, 9; viii, 12. [2] *Ps.* cxviii, 105. [3] *John* iii, 19. [4] ix, 39. [5] 1 *Cor.* iv, 5; cf. *Eph.* v, 11–13. [6] iii, 18. [7] iii, 21. [8] i, 8; ii, 4. [9] i, 7; ii, 10. [10] Cf. Grill, 201. [11] xvi, 7; xvii, 17. [12] i, 9. [13] vi, 32. [14] xv, 1. [15] vi, 56. [16] iv, 23. [17] viii, 32. [18] iii, 21. [19] xviii, 37.

the divine world in which they live, the only real world; God is 'the only true God,'[1] Jesus Christ is the truth,[2] the Holy Spirit is 'the Spirit of Truth,'[3] or, again, simply the truth.[4]

This use of the word truth and its derivatives was not entirely original; we meet it in other writers of the New Testament[5]; but it is specially characteristic of St. John. It denotes in his works that vivid sense of the reality of the divine world, and, if one may say so, of its exclusive reality; besides, he does not contemplate it from the point of view of an idealist, for it would be a complete misunderstanding of the Johannine 'truth' to endeavour to reduce it to the Platonists or Alexandrine 'idea.'[6] It is not a philosophical conception, it is a religious faith; it is not attained by speculation, but by the whole effort of the Christian life: Christ, the Spirit, the Father—these are the personal living realities with which the Christian is united. Opposed to them, the flesh, the world, and the devil are not, as in Alexandrine dualism, the world of our experience as opposed to the ideal world, but 'lies' as opposed to 'truth.'

We may note, moreover, that the evangelist, who loves to represent Christ as the Truth, is also led to conceive salvation as knowledge: 'This is eternal life: That they may know thee, the only true God, and Jesus Christ, whom thou hast sent.'[7] It would be a strange distortion of the word to see in this 'knowledge' a purely abstract and speculative conclusion; we must understand here a complete possession of God by the soul, and at the same time a complete penetration of the soul by God. It is thus that St. John himself explains his meaning in his first Epistle: 'We know that the Son of God is come. And he hath given us understanding that we may know the true God and may be in his true Son.'[8] This tells us better than all the commentaries the nature of the God who is the Truth, and of the 'knowledge' by which he is to be apprehended.

[1] *John* xvii, 3. [2] xiv, 6. [3] xiv, 17. [4] 1 *John* v, 6.
[5] 1 *Thess.* i, 9; *Heb.* viii, 2; ix, 24. [6] Aall, II, 80; Grill, 205.
[7] *John* xvii, 3. [8] 1 *John* v, 20.

3. The Gospel. The Father and the Son

The relations between Jesus Christ and men were the principal subject of the preceding studies: he appeared in them as the witness of heavenly things, as the life, the light, and the truth, and under these different attributes manifested his divine nature. For a closer penetration of that nature, we must consider the relations of the Son and the Father; and our study of the texts will have to be very careful, because of the varying conclusions reached by critics: no one doubts the divinity of Christ on the pages of St. John, but many recognise merely a divinity subordinated to that of the Father: for them, as for the Arians, all the theology of the fourth Gospel is dominated by the phrase: 'The Father is greater than I '[1]; if they recognise that other texts yield a different impression, the most that they will admit is that the Gospel contains two currents of doctrine, one tending towards the subordination of the Son to the Father, and the other towards their equality.[2] Such a dualism would be surprising in a work of such profound unity; if its theological elements appear to be so disparate, I hope that careful study will enable us to reconstruct a synthesis of them.

In order to determine the relations of the Father and the Son, we ought to be able to establish the precise relations of origin connecting them. This is a vain hope. The Gospel does not furnish any additional data to those contained in the prologue. Several of the Fathers, St. Hilary in particular, think they see the eternal generation of the Word referred to when Christ declares: 'from God I proceeded and came '[3]: it seems more probable that the reference is to the mystery of the Incarnation: the Son who was in the 'bosom of the Father,' came forth thence, so to speak, to fulfil his mission here below; many of such passages, moreover, indicate this interpretation by the parallelism of their phrasing: 'Knowing that he came from God and goeth to God.'[4] 'I came forth from the Father and am come into the world: again I leave the world and I go to the Father.'[5] What is in any case per-

[1] Harnack, art. quoted, 194–7.
[2] Reuss, *Théol. chrét.*, II, 440–4; Holtzmann, *N.T. Theol*²., II, 490 *sqq*.
[3] *John* viii, 42. [4] xiii, 3. [5] xvi, 28.

fectly clear in these passages is the mission of the Son by the Father, and the Son's dependence on the Father.

This dependence is shewn as stricter and more complete in the writings of St. John than in any other book of the New Testament. Occasionally it seems to refer immediately to the humanity of Christ, manifested in the loving subjection of Jesus to God his Father: 'My meat is to do the will of him that sent me, that I may perfect his work.'[1] 'He hath not left me alone. For I do always the things that please him.'[2] 'I do know him and do keep his word.'[3] 'I have not spoken of myself: but the Father who sent me, he gave me commandment what I should say and what I should speak. And I know that his commandment is life everlasting. The things therefore that I speak, even as the Father said unto me, so do I speak.'[4] 'That the world may know that I love the Father: and as the Father hath given me commandment, so do I.'[5] 'If you keep my commandments, you shall abide in my love: as I also have kept my Father's commandments and do abide in his love.'[6] 'Father, glorify thy Son, that thy Son may glorify thee. As thou hast given him power over all flesh, that he may give eternal life to all whom thou hast given him.'[7]

If we consider these texts together, leaving on one side certain details which suggest other perspectives, all that we find in them is the dependence of a man on God; a dependence full of love, confidence, intimacy, but, at the same time, strict and total. Jesus presents this dependence to his disciples as a model,[8] and rightly, not only because it is perfect, but because it is truly a human model; a fact of which the *Epistle to the Hebrews* reminds us when it shews us Christ in the days of his flesh sending up supplications to him who could save him from death, and learning obedience through his sufferings.[9] We find again this dependence in those words so full of desire and humility which Jesus, impatient to return to his Father, addressed to his disciples: 'If you loved me, you would indeed be glad, because I go to the Father: for the Father is greater than I.'[10]

Certain details of these texts, however, do, as I have

[1] *John* iv, 34. [2] viii, 29. [3] viii, 55. [4] xii, 49–50. [5] xiv, 31. [6] xv, 10. [7] xvii, 1–2. [8] xv, 10. [9] *Heb.* v, 7–8. [10] *John* xiv, 28.

remarked, transcend the narrow limits of human life. Thus the mission mentioned in xii, 49, refers to the Son as pre-existing, and the words which immediately follow those quoted above do so even more clearly: 'And now glorify thou me, O Father, with thyself, with the glory which I had, before the world was, with thee.'[1] The fact is, to St. John perhaps in a higher degree than to St. Paul, the chief object of contemplation is the unity of the person of Christ; St. John is well aware of the distinction of natures in that unity—he knows that the 'Word has become flesh'; he remembers the diversity of relations which they set up—he would never say of the pre-existing Son that 'the Father was greater than he'; but above all he is anxious not to 'divide Christ.' Nothing then is more natural than for him to recognise in the same sentence the human subjection of Jesus and the eternal dependence of the Son. We must, however, clearly distinguish these two relations and study them consecutively.

'Amen, amen, I say unto you, the Son cannot do anything of himself, but what he seeth the Father doing: for what things soever he doth, these the Son also doth in like manner . . .'[2] Evidently there is no question here of the human actions of Christ, but of his eternal and divine activity. It is the same throughout this discourse; the divinity of the Son is its principal topic, although, here and there, his humanity is mentioned. 'As the Father hath life in himself, so hath he given to the Son also to have life in himself.'[3] 'As the living Father hath sent me and I live by the Father: so he that eateth me the same also shall live by me.'[4] We see by these texts that, if Christ is the life, he is so only by communication from and by dependence on the Father.

On the other hand, the knowledge of the Son is perfect, universal, and, in the strict sense of the word, divine. 'We know that thou knowest all things and thou needest not that any man should ask thee. By this we believe that thou camest forth from God.'[5] The action of the Father and that of the Son have an identical continuity, efficacy, and power: 'My Father worketh until now,' replies Jesus to those who accuse him of violation of the

[1] *John* xvii, 5; cf. viii, 28. [2] v, 19–23. [3] v, 26. [4] vi, 58. [5] xvi, 30.

Sabbath, 'and I work'; and the evangelist adds: 'Hereupon therefore the Jews sought the more to kill him, because he did not only break the Sabbath, but also said God was his Father, making himself equal to God.'[1] Continuing the discussion, Jesus adds: 'As the Father raised up the dead and giveth life: so the Son also giveth life to whom he will.'[2] And later: 'I give them life everlasting: and they shall not perish for ever. And no man shall pluck them out of my hand. That which my Father hath given me is greater than all: and no one can snatch them out of the hand of my Father. I and my Father are one.'[3]

It is evident that for St. John the power of the Son is identical with that of the Father; he never represents the Son as a mere instrument of the Father; he even refrains—and the fact is remarkable—from the phrases occurring so frequently in the other books of the New Testament which indicate in the divine action the hierarchy of the divine Persons. Thus, for instance, St. Peter reminded the Jews of the miracles that God had worked through Jesus,[4] and afterwards said to Cornelius that God had announced peace through Jesus Christ.[5] Similarly, St. Paul speaks of the day on which 'God will judge the secrets of men by Jesus Christ'[6]; he thanks God, 'who hath given us the victory through our Lord Jesus Christ,'[7] and the writer of the *Epistle to the Hebrews* also teaches that, by his Son, God made the world.[8] All these documents, so different in purpose and character, re-echo the formula of St. Paul: 'One God, the Father, of whom are all things . . . and one Lord Jesus Christ, by whom are all things.'[9]

Assuredly, the doctrine expressed in these words is familiar to St. John: that the Father is the sole source from which everything proceeds, and the Son he through whom all good comes to us, is the very essence of the Christian faith, and no one preached that faith more energetically than St. John; but he does not express that doctrine under that form. We do not read in his pages that God has created the world through his Word, nor that the Father works miracles through his Son. To convey this idea he makes use of two mutually complementary

[1] *John* v, 17. [2] v, 21. [3] x, 28–30.
[4] *Acts* ii, 22. [5] *Ib.*, x, 36. [6] *Rom.* ii, 16.
[7] 1 *Cor.* xv, 57. [8] *Heb.* i, 2. [9] 1 *Cor.* viii, 6.

series of expressions which help us to understand his Trinitarian theology.

All that the Son has and does has been given him by the Father. Thus the Father has given him the works he performs,[1] he has given him the possession of his own life,[2] he has given him the privilege of judgement,[3] and power over all flesh,[4] in a word, as Jesus loves to repeat, he has given him everything, he has placed everything in his hands.[5] So, when Jesus thanked God for the resurrection of Lazarus, it was for the sake of the crowd which surrounded him ; as for himself, he was certain that his prayers were always heard and granted.[6] He can say to his disciples: 'All things whatsoever the Father hath are mine,'[7] and to his Father: 'All my things are thine, and thine are mine.'[8] This gift made by the Father to the Son is universal, as well as eternal and irrevocable ; by which St. John gives us to understand, as far as human language can, this double truth, that all comes from the Father, and the Son himself also possesses the plenitude of everything.

This expression, however, if isolated, leaves in the background another no less essential feature of Trinitarian theology: the continuous union of the divine Persons, and the eternal dependence of the Son on the Father ; one might represent their relations in the likeness of a human filiation, and suppose that originally a sort of investiture of universal power had been conferred on the Son by the Father, which established him from that moment in an independent sovereignty. St. John forestalls this error and makes his doctrine more precise by teaching the reciprocal immanence of the Father and the Son: 'I am in the Father,' says Jesus, 'and the Father is in me,'[9] and the Father is there as the origin of the words and deeds of the Son: 'The words that I speak to you, I speak not of myself. But the Father who abideth in me, he doeth the works. Believe you not that I am in the Father and the Father in me ? Otherwise believe for the very works' sake.'[10] The argument presented here by Jesus to his disciples had

[1] *John* v, 36. [2] v, 26. [3] v, 22, 27. [4] xvii, 2. [5] iii, 35 ; xiii, 3.

[6] xi, 41–42. Martha had said: 'I know that whatsoever thou wilt ask of God, God will give it thee': this profession of faith was not sufficient and Our Lord urges Martha to greater heights: 'I am the resurrection and the life. . . .'

[7] xvi, 15. [8] xvii, 10. [9] xiv, 10 ; xvii, 21. [10] xiv, 10, 11.

already been offered to the Jews: 'If I do not the works of my Father, believe me not. But if I do, though you will not believe me, believe the works: that you may know and believe that the Father is in me and I in the Father,'[1] and previously in the same discourse: 'Many good works I have shewed you from my Father.'[2] Thus the works of the Son are the works of the Father, not only because the Father has bestowed on the Son the power of doing them, but because he dwells in the Son, producing them continuously. This is no doubt the idea expressed by St. Peter in his discourse in the *Acts:* God has worked miracles and wonders through Jesus,[3] but the expression is more precise in the words: 'the Father, who is in me, does his works'; St. John shews in a clear light the unity of the Father and Son in action as in being.

This unity also manifests itself in glory, the natural fruit of the divine works: the Father is glorified *in* the Son rather than *by* the Son: 'When he (the traitor) was gone out, Jesus said: Now is the Son of man glorified; and God is glorified in him. If God be glorified in him, God also will glorify him in himself; and immediately will he glorify him,'[4] and further on in the same discourse: 'Whatsoever you shall ask the Father in my name, that will I do: that the Father may be glorified in the Son.'[5]

In the same way Christian worship will reach the Father *in* the Son rather than *by* the Son. It is true that in the discourse after the Supper, speaking of his own departure to his Father, Jesus presents himself as the way that leads to him: 'I am the way, and the truth, and the life. No man cometh to the Father but by me'[6]; but he immediately adds: 'If you had known me, you would without doubt have known my Father also,' and, developing his thought, continues: 'He that seeth me seeth the Father also. How sayest thou: Shew us the Father? Do you not believe that I am in the Father, and the Father in me?'[7] St. John's doctrine is clearly revealed in this passage: he has never conceived the Son, as Philo conceived the Logos, as an intermediary being, attainable by imperfect contemplation, but left behind in a perfect vision; the Son is not a stepping-stone to the

[1] *John* x, 37, 38. [2] x, 32. [3] *Acts* ii, 22. [4] *John* xiii, 31, 32. [5] xiv, 13. [6] xiv, 6. [7] xiv, 7–10.

Father; it is not possible to know him without at the same time knowing the Father who is in him.[1] 'This is eternal life: That they may know thee the only true God, and Jesus Christ, whom thou hast sent.'[2] There are not two distinct and unequal sources of beatitude; eternal life is one, and its object is one. It is therefore useless to try and separate, either in worship or creed, the Father and the Son: one cannot possess the one without the other, or dwell in the one without dwelling in the other: 'Whosoever denieth the Son, the same hath not the Father. He that confesseth the Son, hath the Father also. . . . If that abide in you which you have heard from the beginning, you also shall abide in the Son and in the Father.'[3]

It is difficult, I think, not to recognise the strict cohesion of all these theses; it is no doubt possible to make two parallel series of Johannine texts, establishing on the one hand the dependence of the Son, and on the other his unity with the Father, and conclude that they are incoherent; one may go on further and distinguish two influences, one of religious experience, and another, of metaphysical speculation. All such hypothetical interpretations merely glance to and fro on the surface of the Johannine doctrine without touching, so to speak, its soul: let us, on the contrary, make an effort to enter with the evangelist into the deep central current of Christianity, to unite ourselves with Christ, to contemplate his life and to become penetrated by his thought; we shall feel the unity and the truth of St. John's doctrine. In later days, particularly from the fourth century onwards, theologians will shew that these relations of origin and dependence alone enable us to distinguish between Persons whose nature is possessed in common, and that consequently this dependence of the Son on the Father, which seems at first sight to threaten the unity and even the equality of the two Persons, is, on the contrary, the consecration of that unity and the condition that enables us to conceive it. It was not such reasons as these that guided the pen of St. John, but rather that divine teaching controlled his memory and his actual religion. In the Hellenic world, where it was thought that the divinity could only be reached through the multiplication of intermediaries, and both the worship of pious Pagans and the contemplation of phil-

[1] Cf. Irenæus, *Haer.*, IV, 6, 3 (987). [2] *John* xvii, 3. [3] 1 *John* ii, 23–24.

osophers was wasted on imaginary and unworthy beings, the author of the fourth Gospel could only find in the words of Jesus and the revelation of the Spirit this conception, at once so disconcerting and so divine, of an incarnate Word, and there contemplate, through a humanity that had become for him wholly transparent, a Son of God enriched with all the knowledge, the power, and the holiness of the Father, while, at the same time his whole being consists of nothing but dependence; for, of himself, that Incarnate Word performs no action and speaks no word. If he is the life, the light and the truth, he receives it all from the Father. But the more we penetrate that dependence, the more deeply and clearly we perceive the indissoluble unity which it consecrates. If the Son says and does nothing of himself, if he *has* nothing but what he has received from the Father, it is because everything, action, life, being, is in common between the Father and the Son; it is because the Son is *in* the Father and the Father is *in* the Son.

And so both this dependence and this unity, contemplated in the Son and the Father, become the ideal of the Christian life. We have seen this in the sketch already made of St. John's view of the union of Christians with Christ: that sketch can now easily be completed: 'In that day you shall know that I am in my Father: and you in me, and I in you'[1]: and, praying to his Father, Jesus says once more: 'That they all may be one, as thou, Father, in me, and I in thee; that they also may be one in us: that the world may believe that thou hast sent me. And the glory which thou hast given me, I have given to them: that they may be one as we also are one. I in them, and thou in me: that they may be made perfect in one.'[2] St. Paul said in his *Epistle to the Ephesians*[3]: 'By him we have access both in one Spirit to the Father,' which formula admirably sums up his habitual thought, so eager for the divine union, but so sensitively aware of all that, as yet, separates us from God; it is rarely and in a distant future that he contemplates the ultimate term of all these efforts: 'God, all in all.' It is, on the contrary, to this ultimate term that the thought of St. John is most frequently directed: Christians are in Christ as Christ is in God, and thus all are consummated in unity. But in

[1] *John* xiv, 20. [2] xvii, 21–23. [3] ii, 18.

order better to understand that unity, we must study the Johannine doctrine of the Holy Spirit; it is much less developed than the evangelist's doctrine of the Father and the Son, but is nevertheless its necessary complement.

4. *The Spirit*

We may distinguish, with reference to the doctrine of the Spirit in the Johannine writings, leaving the *Apocalypse* on one side, three fairly dissimilar groups of texts; the narrative of Christ's ministry,[1] of his Passion and glorified life,[2] and the first Epistle. Of the first period the evangelist himself says: 'As yet the Spirit was not given, because Jesus was not yet glorified'[3]; in the first section therefore we shall only find a few features here and there pointing to the coming of the Spirit, and throwing an anticipatory light on that event; on the other hand, the discourses of Christ after the Supper contain the whole Johannine doctrine. They prepare the way for the new era which is about to open, the life of the Spirit in the Church, explaining it wholly and fully; which era is inaugurated by Jesus after his Resurrection in giving the Holy Spirit to his disciples. The Epistle, finally, testifies to the fact of that life, but without explicitly describing it; it shows forth the accomplishment of Christ's promises, yet throws but little light on their significance.

The first part presents, on the subject of the Spirit, or, to speak more generally, of spiritual being, teaching that is reminiscent of Pauline theology: 'God is a spirit: and they that adore him must adore him in spirit and in truth.'[4] 'It is the Spirit that quickeneth: the flesh profiteth nothing. The words that I have spoken to you are spirit and life.'[5] We see here how closely all these terms of spirit, life, and truth are connected; they are the characteristics proper to the nature and action of God; St. John, like St. Paul, is the pupil of the Bible and not of Greek philosophy, and in order to indicate or to describe the Divine nature, these Biblical terms, particularly that of spirit, are sufficient for them both. St. John, as well as St. Paul, uses them to shew the infinite distance separating God from man, the spirit from the flesh; it is

[1] *John* i–xiii. [2] xiv–xxi. [3] vii, 39. [4] iv, 24. [5] vi, 64.

only in and by the spirit that man can approach to God, and since man is flesh, he must be born in order to do so. Jesus answered (Nicodemus): 'Amen, amen, I say to thee, unless a man be born again of water and the Holy Ghost he cannot enter into the kingdom of God. That which is born of the flesh is flesh: and that which is born of the Spirit is spirit.'[1] Christian baptism, the necessity and power of which are so explicitly described by Jesus, had been from the beginning predicted by John the Baptist: 'John gave testimony, saying: I saw the Spirit coming down, as a dove from heaven; and he remained upon him. And I knew him not; but he who sent me to baptise with water said to me: He upon whom thou shalt see the Spirit descending and remaining upon him, he it is that baptiseth with the Holy Ghost.'[2] The whole of this narrative supposes those of the Synoptics; but, as Maldonatus rightly observes, St. John retains nothing of the baptismal scene but the manifestation of the glory of Christ. Moreover, the descent of the Holy Spirit has the same significance in his account as in those of the Synoptics,[3] with this distinction that the relation of Christ's baptism to Christian baptism is more especially indicated: he on whom the Spirit shall remain, he shall baptise with the Holy Spirit.

Perhaps we should attribute to this scene the words added by the evangelist to the last testimony of St. John the Baptist: 'He whom God hath sent speaketh the words of God: for God doth not give the Spirit by measure'[4]; if so, they will be understood, with almost all modern exegetists, to mean: 'It is not by measure that (God) giveth the Spirit (to his Son).' This interpretation agrees well with Johannine theology as a whole: the Father who has given the Son all he has, has given him the plenitude of the Spirit. We may, perhaps, think better to refer these words to Christ: 'He speaketh the words of God, for he does not give the Spirit by measure'; in this case the text is a reaffirmation under another form of the statement in chapter vi, 63: 'The words that I have spoken to you are spirit and life,' meaning that if the Son can thus give the

[1] *John* iii, 5–6. [2] i, 32–33.

[3] Cf. Goguel, *La Doctr. johann. de l'Esprit*, 99; Holtzmann, II, 509; Burkitt, *Expository Times*, 1927, 199.

[4] *John* iii, 34.

Spirit, he does so not 'by measure,' but, as St. Cyril[1] explains it, 'from his own plenitude.'

The most remarkable of the brief references made to the Holy Spirit is Christ's promise on the last day of the Feast of Tabernacles: 'If any man thirst, let him come to me and drink. He that believeth in me, as the Scripture saith: Out of his belly shall flow rivers of living water.'[2] We recognise here an allusion to the rock of the desert, from which, in the days of old, living water had flowed, the memory of which was recalled by the Feast of Tabernacles: Jesus applies to himself this Biblical figure[3] as well as those of the Brazen Serpent and the Manna. He had previously promised the living water to the Samaritan woman[4]; in the *Apocalypse* he leads his elect to the springs of living water,[5] and from his throne, as from the throne of God, flows a stream of living water.[6]

All these symbols have the same meaning, which the evangelist himself carefully explains to us in this passage: 'This he said of the Spirit which they should receive who believed in him; for as yet the Spirit was not given, because Jesus was not yet glorified.'[7] These words clearly shew not only the meaning of the symbol, but also when the Spirit would be sent: his mission was to take the place of Christ with Christians and continue his work; he could not, therefore, be sent before Christ had been glorified.

This teaching is given more completely by Jesus himself in various passages of his discourse after the Supper, and these texts must be here reproduced. There are no others in the whole of the New Testament which contain such explicit teaching on the Holy Spirit and his personality.[8]

> 'If you love me, keep my commandments.
>
> And I will ask the Father: and he shall give you another Paraclete, that he may abide with you for ever:
>
> The spirit of truth, whom the world cannot receive, because it seeth him not, nor knoweth him. But you shall know him; because he shall abide with you and shall be in you.

[1] *In h. l.* (*P.G.*, LXXIII, 280). [2] *John* vii, 37–38. [3] Cf. *Ecclus.* xv, 3. [4] *John* iv, 10. [5] *Apoc.* vii, 17. [6] xxii, 1. [7] *John* vii, 39. [8] Cf. Coppens, *L'imposition des mains* (Louvain, 1925), 210.

I will not leave you orphans: I will come to you.

Yet a little while and the world seeth me no more. But you see me: because I live, and you shall live.'[1]

'These things have I spoken to you, abiding with you.

But the Paraclete, the Holy Ghost, whom the Father will send in my name, he will teach you all things and bring all things to your mind, whatsoever I shall have said to you.'[2]

'When the Paraclete cometh, whom I will send you from the Father, the Spirit of truth, who proceedeth from the Father, he shall give testimony of me.'[3]

'But I tell you the truth: it is expedient to you that I go. For if I go not, the Paraclete will not come to you: but if I go, I will send him to you.

And when he is come, he will convince the world of sin and of justice and of judgement.

Of sin: because they believed not in me.

And of justice: because I go to the Father: and you shall see me no longer.

And of judgement: because the prince of this world is already judged.

I have yet many things to say to you: but you cannot bear them now.

But when he, the Spirit of truth, is come, he will teach you all truth. For he shall not speak of himself: but what things soever he shall hear, he shall speak. And the things that are to come, he shall shew you.

He shall glorify me: because he shall receive of mine and shall shew it to you.

All things whatsoever the Father hath are mine. Therefore I said that he shall receive of mine and shew it to you.'[4]

From these texts taken together a definite and irresistible impression results: the Holy Spirit promised by Jesus is not merely a gift, a force, but as much a living Person as he is himself, and one whose action is so divine that his presence will for the disciples advantageously replace the visible presence of Jesus himself: 'It is expedient to you that I go.'

This impression is strengthened by an attentive ex-

[1] *John* xiv, 15–19. [2] xiv, 25–26. [3] xv, 26. [4] xvi, 7–15.

amination of the texts in detail: we observe at once that St. John, in spite of the proximity of the neuter word τὸ πνεῦμα (the spirit), always uses the masculine pronoun ἐκεῖνος (he) to designate the Holy Spirit.[1] The prologue has already suggested[2] an analogous remark with reference to the use of the neuter substantive τὸ φῶς (light), to indicate the Word, and of the pronoun ἐκεῖνος which refers to it: in both these cases St. John loses sight of the grammatical term that he has selected, and only sees the Person whom he is describing.

For it is evidently a Person whose acts he is describing: it is a Paraclete, an advocate[3]; he will teach everything to the Apostles, he will remind them of all that Christ has said to them; he will give testimony of Christ; he will convince the world; he will repeat to the Apostles all that he has heard. One cannot imagine a more personal rôle; but what is even more decisive is the analogy between the Spirit and himself presented by Jesus: 'I will ask the Father, and he shall give you another Paraclete that he may abide with you for ever'; the whole of the rest of the discourse does but accentuate this parallelism. All the attempts made to reduce the significance of this discourse to a 'metaphorical personification'[4] fail on this point: the personality of Jesus is the measure of the personality of the Holy Spirit; they must both be denied or both accepted.

That the Spirit is neither the Father nor the Son is still more evident; it is scarcely necessary to prove it. On the prayer of the Son, the Father will send another Paraclete[5]: sent by the Father in the name of the Son, this Paraclete will remind the Apostles of all that the Son has said to them (26); he proceeds from the Father, he will be sent by the Son on behalf of the Father, he will give testimony of the Son[6]; the Son will send him to us when he has departed[7]: the Spirit will glorify the Son for he will take of his and declare it to us (14).

[1] *John* xiv, 26; xv, 26; xvi, 13, 14; cf. SWETE, *Holy Spirit*, 292, n. 1.

[2] See above, page 379.

[3] Cf. WESTCOTT, *St. John*, 211–3; SWETE, *Holy Spirit*, 149, 372–3; LAGRANGE, n. on xiv.

[4] This is the expression of W. BEYSCHLAG (*Neutestamentl. Theol.*, I, Halle, 1891, 274). Cf. J. RÉVILLE, *Le quatrième Evangile*, 257; GOGUEL, *loc. cit.*, 111–2; HOLTZMANN, *N.T. Theol.*,[2] II, 516; LOISY (1st ed., p. 106); SWETE, *Holy Spirit*, 292 *sqq.*; J. B. STEVENS, *Theol. of the N.T.*, 217.

[5] *John* xiv, 16. [6] xv, 26. [7] xvi, 7.

Nevertheless, certain critics oppose to these clear and decisive texts another passage of the same discourse, in which the return of Christ appears to coincide with the advent of the Spirit. After promising his apostles that the Holy Spirit should come upon them, that the world would not be able to receive him, but that they would recognise him, Jesus continues: 'I will not leave you orphans: I will come to you. Yet a little while, and the world seeth me no more. But you see me: because I live, and you shall live.'[1] From which these critics draw the conclusion that the presence of the Spirit is nothing but the spiritual presence of Christ[2]; the utmost that they will admit is the presence here of two irreconcilable series of texts, one distinguishing Christ from the Spirit, and the other identifying the Spirit with the glorified Christ.[3]

According to our views, it must be recognised that Christ, in predicting, in these words, his coming, is not referring to his glorified apparitions or to his Parousia at the last day[4]; what he promises to his disciples, is his presence in them, a life-giving presence unknown to the world. It must be added that this latter cannot be distinguished from the promise already made to them: when the disciples receive the Spirit they will also receive the Son. Does it follow that the Spirit is identical with the Son? Surely not, any more than that the Son is identical with the Father. Yet the coming of the Father is bound up in the same way with that of the Son: 'If any one love me, he will keep my word. And my Father will love him: and we will come to him and will make our abode with him.'[5] Here once more is that indissoluble unity so often affirmed by St. John: it is impossible to possess the Son without the Father, or the Spirit without the Son, and this infinitely close unity is the model and the bond of the unity of Christians: 'that they may be one as we are one.'

The similarity of relations noted here goes much further; it may be said that, according to the doctrine of St. John, the relations of the Son and the Spirit are those of the Father and the Son. The Son is the witness of the Father,[6] so also the Spirit gives testimony of the Son[7]; he

[1] *John* xiv, 18, 19. [2] Pfleiderer, *Urchristentum*, II, 377.
[3] Holtzmann, *loc. cit.*, II, 514. Cf. Reuss, *Théol. chrét.*, II, 430–42.
[4] Loisy (p. 411); Swete, *Holy Spirit*, 300. [5] *John* xiv, 23.
[6] See above, page 380. [7] *John* xv, 26.

glorifies the Son[1] as the Son glorifies the Father.[2] The Son says nothing of himself, but only what the Father wishes him to say[3]; and the Spirit 'shall not speak of himself, but what things soever he shall hear, he shall speak . . . he shall receive of mine and shall shew it to you,' adds Jesus.[4] Finally, as the Son is sent by the Father, so the Spirit is sent by the Son.[5]

This parallelism is very close; and when St. Athanasius undertakes, in his letters to Serapion, to defend and develop the traditional doctrine of the Holy Spirit, this is the point of departure of his argument.

The analogy, moreover, is not so close as not to admit essential differences. Sonship characterises the relations of the Son and the Father; it does not appear in the theology of the Spirit. The Father is the sole origin of the Son; this is not the case in the relation between the Son and the Spirit: the Son sends the Spirit, but 'from the Father'[6]; he says 'the Spirit shall receive of mine,' but adds 'All things whatsoever the Father hath are mine. Therefore I said that he shall receive of mine.'[7] Thus, even in his relations with the Spirit, the Son is dependent on the Father; it is from the Father that he has received all that he gives to the Spirit. The Father is here, as everywhere, the fundamental and sovereignly independent first principle. 'From him proceeds the Spirit'[8]; it is he who gives the Spirit to men at the prayer of the Son[9] and sends him forth in his Son's name.[10]

All this doctrine is completely summed up in the symbolic vision of the *Apocalypse*: 'A river of water of life, clear as crystal, proceeding from the throne of God and of the Lamb'[11]; such for St. John is the nature and origin of the Spirit who proceeds from one only source, which is the throne of God and of the Lamb; but neither the prophet of the *Apocalypse* nor the evangelist forget that that throne does not belong by the same title to the Father and the Son. The Father possesses divinity as being the sole original principle of it, the Son as receiving it in its plenitude from the Father.

The gift of the Spirit made on the occasion of one of

[1] *John* xvi, 14. [2] xvii, 4. [3] xii, 49; vii, 16. [4] xvi, 13, 14. [5] xv, 26; xvi, 7. [6] xv, 26. [7] xvi, 14, 15. [8] xv, 26. [9] xiv, 16. [10] xiv, 26. [11] *Apoc.* xxii, 1.

his apparitions is attached to these promises of Christ. Having entered (the doors being closed) the room in which the disciples were, he said to them:

> 'Peace be to you. As the Father hath sent me, I also send you. When he had said this, he breathed on them; and he said to them: Receive ye the Holy Ghost. Whose sins you shall forgive, they are forgiven them: and whose sins you shall retain, they are retained.'[1]

By using the very words of *Genesis,* St. John expressly recalls the creation of the first man, and the breath of life which Jahve breathed upon him[2]; it is indeed a new world which Jesus is here creating and a new life that he is giving: the Church has been founded, and she possesses in herself the Spirit who shall make her live.

The occasional references in the first Epistle represent the Spirit above all as a witness: a witness of the Incarnation of the Son of God, and of the presence of God in Christians.

> 'Who is he that overcometh the world, but he that believeth that Jesus is the Son of God?
>
> This is he that came by water and blood, Jesus Christ: not by water only but by water and blood. And it is the Spirit which testifieth that Christ is the truth.
>
> And there are Three who give testimony in heaven, the Father, the Word, and the Holy Ghost. And these three are one.
>
> And there are three that give testimony on earth: the spirit and the water and the blood. And these three are one, εἰς τὸ ἕν εἰσιν.'[3]

The water and the blood seem to signify in the sixth verse the baptism of Christ and his Passion, and, at the same time, the effusion of water and of blood from the side of Jesus on the Cross; in the eighth verse, the Christian sacraments of baptism and the Eucharist are in the foreground. Their witness agrees with that of the Spirit and all three lead to the same end—to bear witness to the Incarnation of the Son of God. The rôle of

[1] *John* xx, 21–23. [2] *Gen.* ii, 7. [3] 1 *John* v, 5–8,

the Spirit here is that announced by Christ in his discourse after the Supper: he is to render testimony to the Son of God: and as Jesus, the witness of the Father, is the Truth, so also the Spirit, the witness of the Son, is the Truth.

> 'He that keepeth his commandments abideth in him, and he in him. And in this we know that he abideth in us by the Spirit which he hath given us.'[1] 'We know that we abide in him and he in us: because he hath given us of his spirit.'[2]

In these two texts the Spirit is described less as a person than as the gift of God in which we participate: and this gift guarantees to us the presence of God within us. This teaching of the testimony of the Spirit is entirely similar to that of St. Paul, but the slight difference of point of view which has already been indicated several times between the conceptions of the two Apostles should be noted. St. Paul feels much more keenly the imperfect and provisional elements in the Christian life; and consequently shews us the Spirit as the first-fruits or as an earnest of the happiness to come; St. John sees the Spirit above all as the guarantee of our present possession of that happiness: since we have received the Spirit of God, we know that we are in God and that God is in us; he insists above all on the actuality of this union.

This last feature of the Trinitarian theology of St. John completes and fulfils all those already mentioned; for him the mystery of the divine Trinity is above all a mystery of union: the union of the divine Persons among themselves, the union of Christians in and by Them. This mystery appeared to him in the Person of Jesus Christ; that is where he discovered by the light of the Spirit this ineffable union of the Father and the Son. The human life of Jesus makes us already foresee it: this complete disinterestedness, this sole anxiety to do the will of the Father, this love so deep and so absorbing, are but the human, and therefore imperfect, manifestation of those more intimate relations that his words reveal to those whom they truly penetrate. He is full of grace and truth, and yet he has nothing of his own, all that is in

[1] 1 *John* iii, 24. [2] iv, 13.

him is the gift of his Father; the more we contemplate this divine Person of Jesus Christ, the more we feel that he does not live in or of himself, but is wholly directed toward Another, from whom he has received everything, and who is 'well pleased' in him. And when the end of the life of Christ draws near, a third term, a third Person, is revealed; neither the Father nor the Son, for he is sent by them; and yet his coming will involve the return of the Son and the presence of the Father; and Christians who possess him will know that they are in God and that the desire of Christ is realised: 'I in them, and thou in me: that they may be made perfect in one.'

CONCLUSION

The Christian Dogma of the Trinity and its Distinctive Character according to the New Testament

A German critic who was an enthusiastic adept of eschatologist theology (Schweitzer, in *Von Reimarus zu Wrede*)[1] presented in recent years the teaching of St. John the Baptist, of Jesus himself, and of St. Paul as the links of a chain of doctrine connecting Daniel with Aqiba. Many historians give the same explanation of the origins of the Trinitarian dogma; the primitive Christian faith appears to them as one stage in the general evolution of ideas in the movement of thought from Philo to the second-century Gnostics; more solid than the speculation of Philo, more sober than the dreams of the Gnostics, but having the same origin and the same essential character.

The history related in these pages enables us to pass judgement on this hypothesis. We have seen how the Christian faith was born not of a speculation, but of a fact; how the greatest theologians of Christianity, St. Paul and St. John, far from having initiated this doctrinal movement, had been dominated by Someone greater than they, who had imposed himself on their faith as well as on the general faith of his disciples; and it must be added that Jesus Christ, the Author and Object of this faith, had given it a direction contrary to all the doctrinal currents of the period.

This last point is of supreme importance in the history of this epoch; it is sufficient to have grasped it to be able to judge of the origins of the Trinitarian dogma and to be prepared to follow its later developments.

The exposition which has been made of the theologies of St. John and of Philo has made clear the irreconcilability of the two doctrines.[2] That irreconcilability is no

[1] Page 364. [2] See Note VII at end of this Volume.

fortuitous contrast, opposing two isolated writers to each other: it is the manifestation of a profound opposition, appearing in the other New Testament writings, and continuing throughout the whole of Patristic theology.

In the very *milieux* in which Christian doctrine spread, it came into contact with a Jewish or Greek gnosis superficially very favourable to it, but whose deeper tendency was irreducibly hostile. Between an inaccessible God and an evil world religious speculation had multiplied intermediary beings: the Logos, powers, angels, or demons. This theosophy constituted for the early Christians a dangerous temptation: did it not seem open-minded and awaiting their faith, and quite ready to make room for their Christ? The *Epistle to the Colossians* is for the most part devoted to dissuading the faithful from the superstitious worship of Angels; the *Epistle to the Hebrews* reminds them, with a similar insistence, of the infinite distance separating Christ, who is the Son, from the angels, who are but servants; the pastoral Epistles continue to denounce the superstitions, fables, and interminable genealogies current in the religious world around them.

There is no exegete who does not understand the point against which these attacks are directed: what is aimed at is the gnosis, the 'so-called gnosis'; but it is important to note that the conflict is not between two theologies derived from Christianity, but between the Christian revelation and the contemporary system of Judaic-Hellenistic speculation, and between these two religious conceptions no reconciliation is possible.

To Philo, as later to Gnostics of every shade, the existence of evil and matter is the primary problem. It is not possible for the perfect and blessed divinity to have any contact with formless and disorderly matter; it is, therefore, through his intermediary powers that he makes contact with it and ordains its laws.[1] The creation of man is explained in the same way: what is evil in him cannot come from God; it must be the work of the intermediary powers.[2]

In the Gnostic system, intermediary beings—the Logos, the powers, the æons—are interposed between God and the world. They only create and are in contact with what

[1] *De spec. leg.*, I, 329 (M., II, 261). [2] *De opif. mundi*, 73 (M., I, 17).

it would soil the divine purity to touch; it follows from this that they are conceived as being less pure than God and therefore capable of such contacts without degeneracy.

We come across certain traits in the New Testament which seem to imply a similar conception: everything has been made by the Word, in him everything subsists, he supports everything by the power of his word: do not all such texts imply the doctrine of intermediary beings?

On looking more closely into the matter, we see that such a resemblance between Christian and Gnostic doctrine is but superficial and betrays very grave divergences. A primary difference which strikes the least attentive critic is the very obscure rôle played by cosmogony in Christian theology. Apart from the three passages just recalled,[1] we can only find in the whole New Testament very brief and occasional references to it. Clearly the origin of matter is no central problem for the Christian; that is not the preoccupation which leads to the doctrine of the Word; it is rather the human reality of the appearance of Christ, the memory of which fills his soul and stimulates his thought.

Again, the rôle of the Word in the world is not conceived as supplying the deficiencies of divine action; his action is not that of an inferior and subordinate agent engaged in a task unworthy of the supreme majesty. St. John's Gospel, which is the most explicit on the cosmological rôle of Christ, also indicates most clearly the nature of his action, which is united with that of the Father, or, rather, makes but one action with his; is not this the meaning of such texts as: 'My Father worketh until now; and I work'; 'I do all that my Father does'? Thus the supreme God is not isolated from the world, with which he makes contact in and by his Son. For this reason St. Paul will be able to say of the Son: 'Everything subsists in him'; and of the Father: 'In him we have being, movement, and life.' According to this doctrine, Father and Son no longer stand over against each other as a principal and a secondary God respectively, the former remaining apart from the world which the latter creates, organises and sustains; but relate them-

[1] *Col.* i, 15–18; *Heb.* i, 1–4; *John* i, 1–10.

selves to this great work in terms of one identical power and one unique source of action.[1]

An analogous opposition, though still more marked, separates the two doctrines on the question of religious knowledge. For Philo, intermediary beings are so many stages on the road by which the soul gradually rises in her ascent to God; the powers, and the Logos are, so to speak, cities of refuge which the soul attains according to the relative rapidity of her course. It is the same religious conception that we find in the gnosis from Apostolic days onwards: the Laodicean and Colossian heretics, whom St. Paul combats, look upon the Angels as superior beings, the only objects that their worship can attain, while God remains inaccessible and unknowable.

Here again, at first sight, the teaching of the New Testament may seem to coincide with such speculations. Do we not read in the Synoptics: 'No man knoweth the Father, save only the Son, and he to whom the Son will reveal him'; in St. John's words: 'No man hath seen God at any time: the only begotten Son who is in the bosom of the Father, he hath declared him.' And St. Paul says the same, when speaking of the Holy Spirit: 'The Spirit searcheth all things, yea, the deep things of God. For what man knoweth the things of a man, but the spirit of a man that is in him? So the things also that are of God, no man knoweth, but the Spirit of God.' Must we interpret these texts as later on the Gnostics were to do, as in fact Origen did, and distinguish two stages of religious knowledge: one alone being accessible to all men, who reach God only in his secondary and imperfect manifestations, in the Son and in the Spirit; the other, reserved to a few privileged souls, who have direct access to God himself?

The Christian mind condemns such an interpretation, and historical exegesis returns the same verdict. St. John relates that at the Last Supper St. Philip, encouraged by the Lord's revelations, which had never been so explicit or so lofty, said to him with naïve confidence and audacity: 'Lord, shew us the Father, and it is enough for us.' Jesus replies to him: 'Have I been so long a time with you and have you not known me? Philip, he that

[1] Irenæus, *Haer.*, II, 30, 9. 822.

seeth me seeth the Father also. How sayest thou: Shew us the Father? Do you not believe that I am in the Father, and the Father in me?'

This doctrine is very dear to the evangelist, and is, indeed, of capital importance: as we saw above that the creative action of the Father is by identity that of the Son, so we see here that, in the words of St. Irenæus, the revelation of the Father is the manifestation of the Son: '*Agnitio enim Patris est Filii manifestatio*.'[1] Consequently, two unequal terms specifying two kinds of religious knowledge cannot be distinguished: the Father and the Son are known at the same time and in the same act of knowledge, and this is essentially eternal life: 'This is eternal life: That they may know thee, the only true God, and Jesus Christ, whom thou hast sent.'

It may seem difficult at first sight to reconcile these two series of texts, in which the Son is alternatively presented as the interpreter who explains the Father, and as the appearance that reveals him. If the sight of the Son is the manifestation of the Father, what part is played by the Son's words and teaching?

This difficulty is easily solved, if we carefully distinguish the different degrees of the progressive revelation of the Son. Most of his hearers know his teaching, but not his person; they have listened to him, but have not penetrated his meaning. They may indeed be faithfully attached to him, and yet, like Philip, hear Jesus say to them on the last day of his life: 'Have I been so long a time with you, and have you not known me?'

In a word, to repeat an expression of St. Paul's, those only see the Father in the Son, who know Christ not according to the flesh, but according to the Spirit. One sees how this conception of progress in religious knowledge differs from the Gnostic conception. Christ is not at all the object of an inferior contemplation, of which one tires, and passes on; he is inexhaustible and supreme; in him there dwells corporeally the plenitude of the divinity, he is the beginning and the end; but one can penetrate him more or less imperfectly, to discern in him only his miraculous power, the purity of his teaching, and the holiness of his life, or to attain the divine source whence all these gifts flow.

[1] *Haer.*, IV, 6, 3 (*P.G.*, VII, 988).

The double opposition that has been pointed out between Gnostic speculation and Christian dogma leads to a more radical one, which may be looked upon either as consequence or premiss, according to whether we are considering the movement of thought that constructs the system, or the logical connection of its theses.

These divine beings interposed between God and the world, whether in order to explain creation, or to sustain and progressively guide our religious knowledge, must, in order to be adequate to the data of the problem they are called in to solve, possess but a diminished divinity. Whatever way we consider them, whether as necessarily emanating from God, or as freely created by him, we have to think of them as, so to speak, located *outside* the divine nature; they cannot be equal with God, nor, above all, one with him; they can only have received a defective participation in his nature which, by successive degradations, will take them further from him and nearer to our state of misery. This is how the Gnostics came to imagine their interminable genealogies of æons; this is how, in later days, the Arians conceived of the Son and the Holy Spirit: both, according to them, were freely created by God, the Son as the most perfect of creatures, the Holy Spirit inferior to the Son, though superior to the rest.

While the Arians scatter over a crowd of degenerate hypostases a diminished divinity, Christian doctors affirm a Trinity of Persons equal among themselves and subsisting in a nature one and unique. The Father is doubtless the sole source of this divinity, but he communicates it eternally, necessarily, and integrally, to the Son and the Holy Spirit.

And at the same time as the conflict of the two doctrines grew keener, their respective origins came more clearly into the light of day. It was hardly among the flock of simple Christians that the Arian or semi-Arian heresies found their defenders and made their conquests; it was rather among learned theologians, to whom Hellenic speculation was dearer than the Gospel, and who were more in the habit of composing dissertations on the Word of God, than thinking of Jesus Christ. Those, on the other hand, for whom the life of Christ had remained the centre of Christianity, continued to walk in its light; whether they were learned like Athanasius, or ignorant as the humblest of the faithful, they knew well that their Saviour was no half-God, and that by uniting themselves to him they united themselves with God himself.

The lesson to be derived from these dogmatic controversies emerges from the history of their origins: human speculation flattered itself in vain that it could sound the depths of the life of God, its proud efforts resulted in nothing but barren and deceptive dreams; it is in the humility of the Incarnation that the mystery of God has been revealed: for the Jews a scandal, a folly to the Greeks, the strength and wisdom of God for the elect.

NOTE I

(Note B, in French edition)

THE MYSTERY OF THE TRINITY AND THE OLD TESTAMENT

THERE can be no questioning the fact that the development of dogma in the Old Testament was subject to different laws from those which have governed it since the Christian revelation. The supreme and definitive revelation made to us by God through his Son, and preserved by the Church, may be more fully understood as time goes on, but can receive no addition whatsoever. On the other hand, under the Old Law successive revelations made to the patriarchs, to Moses, and to the prophets, continually added to the first deposit entrusted to man by God. Thus, revelation was not complete with Adam, nor with Moses, nor yet with the prophets; it closed with the Apostles.

In other words, we must admit that certain truths of faith, revealed to Christians, were unknown to the Jews. Is the Trinity one of these?

At first sight, tradition would seem to contradict itself. On the one hand, we find the Fathers stating clearly that Christ was the sole revealer of the Trinity; and, on the other hand, they find repeated evidence of the Trinity in the Old Testament.

The plural verb in *Genesis* i, 26 and xi, 7, and the plural pronoun in iii, 22, indicate for them a dialogue between the divine Persons. They are even more ready to recognise the plurality of persons in the various theophanies and especially in the apparition at Mambre, where three persons appeared at the same time. The triple *Sanctus* in *Isaias* vi, 3, the thrice-repeated *Deus* in *Ps.* lxvi, 7-8, and *Deut.* vi, 4 (*Dominus Deus noster Dominus unus est*), provide further argument for some, above all for the scholastic theologians.

It will be admitted that none of these passages, considered in itself, can be held to be a revelation of the Trinity; and, to my knowledge, there is no tradition which would impose a strictly Trinitarian interpretation of them on the Catholic exegete.

It is true that the Council of Sirmium in 351[1] condemned

[1] *Can.* XIV–XVIII, *ap.* ATHAN.

those who denied the distinction between the Father and Son in the account of the Creation and in the theophanies; but the council was semi-Arian and betrayed only too clearly in its canons the subordinationist heresy.

Again, the references which appear to us to be so obvious did not always seem so clear to the Fathers. We like to translate St. Ambrose's words, '*tres vidit et unum adoravit,*' as 'he saw three persons and adored one God,' failing to notice that St. Hilary originated the phrase and meant something quite different: Abraham saw three men, but only adored one of them, knowing the other two were angels.[1] Besides the Trinitarian interpretation, St. Ambrose gives St. Hilary's in another place.[2]

This does not mean that the passages that seemed so full of meaning for the Fathers must now be considered as meaningless as far as the plurality of persons is concerned. We only wish to point out that they could not provide a sufficient revelation for the Jews, and that we ourselves, who believe the doctrine of the Trinity, cannot find there a certain proof of the mystery. On the other hand, the mystery of the Trinity provides the best explanation of these texts of the Old Testament.

This interpretation seems to conform best with the thought of the Fathers; and although several of them quoted the Old Testament against the Jews to prove the distinction between the Father and Son, their thesis is not in itself a complete statement of the doctrine of the Trinity. St. Epiphanius, famed for his unwavering doctrine, says: 'The divine unity was first and foremost proclaimed by Moses, the duality (the distinction between Father and Son) was heavily stressed by the prophets, and the Trinity was clearly shown forth in the Gospel.'

Having thus examined the teaching of the Fathers who seek to find evidence of the Trinity in the Old Testament, we will find it easy to reconcile their teaching with that of the others mentioned above. As early as Tertullian we read: 'What is the fruit of the Gospel, the substance of the New Testament, unless, in the Father, Son, and Holy Ghost, we acknowledge three distinct persons and only one God?'[3]

Many of the Fathers shared Tertullian's opinion. And so did St. Thomas Aquinas.[4]

[1] HIL., *De Trinitate*, IV, 25.

[2] *De fide*, I, 13, 80.

[3] *Advers. Prax.*, 31 (*P.L.*, II, 196).

[4] *Sum. Th.*, 2^a–2^{ae}, 174, 6.

NOTE II

(Note C in French edition)

Mark xiii, 32—IGNORANCE CONCERNING THE DAY OF JUDGEMENT

Mark xiii, 32: περὶ δὲ τῆς ἡμέρας ἐκείνης ἢ τῆς ὥρας οὐδεὶς οἶδεν, οὐδὲ οἱ ἄγγελοι ἐν οὐρανῷ, οὐδὲ ὁ υἱός, εἰ μὴ ὁ πατήρ.

Matt. xxiv, 36: περὶ δὲ τῆς ἡμέρας ἐκείνης καὶ ὥρας οὐδεὶς οἶδεν, οὐδὲ οἱ ἄγγελοι τῶν οὐρανῶν οὐδὲ ὁ υἱός εἰ μὴ ὁ πατὴρ μόνος.

IN the text of Matthew the words 'οὐδὲ ὁ υἱός' are found in א B D 13, 124, 346, 28, 86, the Ethiopic, Armenian, Syriac (Jerusalem), and Latin (some MSS.) versions. They are commented on by Origen (*P.G.*, XIII, 1086), Hilary (*P.L.*, IX, 1057), Chrysostom (*P.G.*, LVIII, 702). They are lacking in the majority of Greek MSS., in the Syriac (except the Jerusalem text), Coptic, and some Latin MSS. (Cf. Westcott-Hort, *On Select Readings*, p. 17.) They are also not found in the standard text, but are restored by the majority of modern editors.

If the text of Matthew be regarded uncertain, that of Mark is, on the other hand, well established. The only important MS. which omits this clause, is the MS. X of the Vulgate. Nevertheless certain critics have rejected its authenticity on the ground that Jesus is never called 'the Son' in an unqualified sense. So Dalman, *Die Worte Jesu*, p. 159; Loisy, *Les Synoptiques*, II, p. 438. M. Goguel (*L'évangile de Marc*, p. 242) also sets it aside as being in contradiction to the declaration of Christ mentioned in v. 30. These hypotheses are unlikely. A text which thus limits, at least apparently, the knowledge of Christ, could occupy a rightful place in the Gospel, but it is not clear what influence could have motivated a later insertion. It is therefore indeed a surprise to find A. Réville using this text to prove the ignorance of Christ, and rejecting it as giving a metaphysical value to the title of 'Son'—all this *on the same page* of his *Histoire du dogme de la divinité de Jésus Christ* (ed. 3, 1904, p. 8 and n. 4, 7).

It would be outside the scope of this work to retrace, in detail, the history of the different views held by the Fathers or theologians concerning the human knowledge of Christ.[1] But, owing to the difficulty of the question and the fact that it has been obscured by much controversy, a precise account of its theological bearing seems indispensable in so far as it concerns the exegesis of the texts with which we are dealing.

§1. *The Arian and Apollinarist Controversy*

In the period preceding the Arian controversies, this text had been variously interpreted by the Fathers. St. Irenæus understood it literally and drew from it a twofold moral: Christ wished us to learn humility and to recognise the transcendence of God.[2] Origen puts forward two interpretations. According to the first, the knowledge of Christ on this point was imperfect until his resurrection, and he considers that this view is confirmed by the difference between the two replies of *Mark* xiii, 32, and *Acts* i, 7. According to the second, which he calls '*famosior,*' Christ speaks in the name of the Church.[3]

From the fourth century onward, Trinitarian and Christological controversies gave great importance to the interpretation of this text. On the one hand, the Fathers had to refute the Arians, who endeavoured to attribute ignorance to the Word of God. On the other, in the Apollinarist struggle, they use this text to prove the reality of the human knowledge and, consequently, of the human soul of Christ.

The immediate interests of this twofold controversy seemed to favour a literal interpretation of the Gospel text. To admit real human ignorance in Christ—was this not to confront the Apollinarists with a decisive argument? Against the Arians, was it not the establishment yet once more of a distinction which had become traditional in Catholic exegesis?

St. Athanasius applied to the humanity of the Word the text of *Proverbs,* which in the LXX reads 'the Lord made me' (Κύριος ἔκτισέ με), and, in this, was followed by many Fathers. Was it not natural to apply the same rule of interpretation to

[1] Cf. Petau, *Dogm. theol.*, *de Incarnat.*, Bk. XI, c. 1–4; Stentrup, *Christologia* (Innsbruck, 1882), th. 68–73; A. Vacant, art. *Agnoètes* in the *Dict. de Théol.*; Ch. Gore, *The consciousness of Our Lord in His mortal life*, in *Dissertations on subjects connected with the Incarnation* (ed. 3, London, 1897), p. 71–201; E. Schulte, *Die Entwicklung der Lehre vom menschlichen Wissen Christi bis zum Beginne der Scholastik* (Paderborn, 1914); J. Marič, *De Agnoetarum doctrina. Argumentum patristicum pro omniscienta Christi hominis relativa* (Zagreb, 1914).

[2] *Advers. haer.*, II, 28, 6–8 (*P.G.*, VII, 808–811), R., 204.

[Translator's Note.—Wherever possible, reference will be made, for patristic texts, to the *Enchiridion Patristicum* of Ronèt de Journel, S.J., ed. 5 Herder, 1922, and will be prefaced by the letter 'R,' followed by the number under which the appropriate extract is to be found.]

[3] *In Matth.*, Commentar. series, 55 (*P.G.*, XIII, 1686–1688).

the text of St. Mark, 'But of that day . . . no man knoweth . . . nor the Son'? In fact, this exegesis is fairly frequent during the fourth century. It is not, however, that most universally accepted, as may be seen by successively studying the writings of the principal exponents of Catholic dogma.[1] An analysis of the writings of St. Athanasius will show a desire to establish the fact that the Divine Word is in no way ignorant. In comparison with this capital truth, other matters are of minor importance, and he suggests several different interpretations of the text. Ignorance, removed from the divinity of Christ and attributed to his humanity, is represented sometimes as apparent, sometimes as real. In this respect he formulates the famous soteriological principle which was so often afterwards quoted in different senses, 'Christ willed to assume all our infirmities in order to heal them all.'

St. Basil, in his eighth letter to the people of Cesarea, interprets *seriatim* the scripture texts brought forward by the Arians. In the ignorance of the day of judgement he sees a providential disposition of God. He regards this latter interpretation, nevertheless, as not sufficiently thorough, and adds an allegorical one to the effect that the Apostles desired to attain the highest degree of contemplation and that the Saviour gave them to understand that this is inaccessible even to the angels themselves.[2] In his two hundred and thirty-sixth letter (to Amphilochius) St. Basil studies the text afresh and purports to give the interpretation which he himself received from the Fathers and which he had examined carefully. In two places he understands it in the sense that the Father alone is the source of this knowledge (xxxii, 877a and 880a, b; R. 236). He even affirms very explicitly (880a) that the Son cannot be ranked with his servants, among those who are ignorant. On the other hand, he considers that he can, without prejudice to true doctrine, explain the ignorance by a principle of 'economy' governing the work of the Incarnation (877c).

St. Gregory of Nazianzus, after showing that Christ must have known the hour of judgement since he described the signs which were to precede it (cf. Athan., *Or.*, III, 42), concludes that he was ignorant only as man, but knew it as God. (Cf. Athan., *Or.*, III, 43; R. 774; Ambrose, *De fide*, V, 18, 221; Cyril of Alexandria, *Thes.*, 22; *P.G.*, LXXV, 372; R. 2072.)

[1] S. Eustathius of Antioch, *Pro defens. trium capit.*, XI, 1 (*P.L.*, LXVII, 795); S. Athanasius, *Adv. Arianos orat.*, III, 42–49 (*P.G.*, XXVI, 412–428); *Epist. II ad Serapionem*, 9 (621–624); *De Incarnatione et contra Arianos*, 7 (993); cf. *Or.*, III, 38 (404c) on the questions asked by Christ; 51–53 (429–436) on his progress.

[2] *Ep.* viii, 6–7; xxxii, 256–7 (R., 913).

This explanation (*Or. Theol.*, IV, 15; *P.G.*, XXXVI, 124) became classic in Greek theology. Eulogius of Alexandria and St. John Damascene understand it in the sense that ignorance belongs to the humanity of Christ only if, by an abstraction, it is isolated from the divinity, and this interpretation seems a very legitimate one.[1] For those whom his solution fails to satisfy, St. Gregory puts forward another, viz., Christ wished to signify that the Father was the unique source of this knowledge (*ibid.*, 16, 124c).

Incidentally, in the panegyric on St. Basil (43, *P.G.*, XXXVI, 548) St. Gregory says that the progress of Christ consisted only in the exercise and progressive manifestation of his knowledge.

St. Gregory of Nyssa, in contrast to the other two Cappadocian Fathers, clearly states that the humanity of Christ was ignorant, and relies on this statement to prove its reality against the Apollinarists. He recalls the fact that Christ suffered hunger, thirst, and ignorance. Consequently there was another element besides the divinity to be taken into consideration.[2]

The other Greek writers of this epoch generally reject the hypothesis of real ignorance in Christ, and the majority produce one of the interpretations already given.

In the Arian and Apollinarist controversy, the Latin Fathers depend to a great extent on the Greeks, and this dependence is most noticeable with regard to the text in question. Nevertheless, it must be noted that the majority of them are on the side of those exegetes who deny all real ignorance in Christ.[3]

§2. *The Christological Controversy of the Fifth Century: St. Cyril of Alexandria*

In Antiochean circles, whence Nestorianism arose, the human knowledge of Christ is generally considered to be limited and subject to ignorance (cf. Schulte, p. 72ff.).

St. Cyril of Alexandria is, of all the Fathers, the one who has most frequently discussed the question of the apparent or real ignorance of Christ, and, since his authority is of special weight in Christological matters, his testimony deserves close attention.

In the first stages of his career, until the year 428, he is

[1] Cf. Gore, p. 126 and n. 2; Schulte, p. 53.

[2] *Contra Apollinar.*, 24; *P.G.*, XLV, 1173–1176.

[3] St. Hilary, *De Trinit.*, X, 71–3 (*P.L.*, X, 337–40); St. Ambrose, *De Fide*, V, 18, 221; cf. Schulte, p. 68; St. Jerome, IV *in Matth.*, xxiv, 36 (*P.L.*, XXVI, 181; R., 1389); *In Marc.*, XIII; *Anecd. Mareds.*, III, 2, p. 365 *sq.* (R., 1410).

preoccupied with the Arians. He confronts them with the arguments of his predecessors and principally of the great Alexandrian doctor, St. Athanasius. His conception and exposition of these arguments is, however, of a very personal nature. After the year 428, Nestorius is the main object of attention. This new adversary gives him fresh preoccupations, but the conception of Christ's knowledge remains the same.[1]

It is in one of his first works, the *Thesaurus de sancta et consubstantiali Trinitate,* that St. Cyril discusses the gospel text at greatest length, and it is here that his thought is best seen in its variant aspects. In the whole of the *Thesaurus*[2] St. Cyril echoes anterior tradition and particularly the thought of St. Athanasius. Nevertheless his contribution to the discussion is very personal, as is clear from evidence of reflective thought in the choice and turn given to the arguments used. They may be summarised under the following main points:

(*a*) Christ knows all, since he is the Word and the Wisdom of God. This divine knowledge has not been veiled by the Incarnation, and there is no trace here of a kenotic theory. On the contrary, St. Cyril often starts from some saying or action of the Incarnate Word during his mortal life, as a premiss from which to prove the perfection of his knowledge (*Thesaurus,* n. 1, 3, 6, 7, 9, 10, 11, 13-15, 17, 20).

(*b*) Nevertheless, Christ has said: 'the Son knoweth not,' and in thus speaking has not lied (1, 15, 17).

(*c*) These two statements, in appearance contradictory, are harmonised primarily by the fact of the Incarnation. Other explanations had been given by the Fathers, and traces of them are to be found in St. Cyril. But when these are mentioned, he always supports them by the consideration, dear to him, of Christ's Incarnation and the human limitations which he willed to undergo. Most frequently the Incarnational aspect is the only one proposed by St. Cyril. He notes that ignorance is the lot of mankind, and Christ wished to be subject to it along with our other sufferings, such as hunger and thirst (1, 3, 5, 10, 12, 15, 17).

(*d*) Nevertheless, from this time onward, St. Cyril is anxious to safeguard the unity of Christ. He never concedes absolutely, therefore, that Christ was ignorant, but maintains that it is a humiliation consequent on the Incarnation (3); a voluntary

[1] Fr. Schulte, p. 87 and 95–6, believes that these two periods mark a profound difference in St. Cyril's thought. Before the year 428, he admitted a real human ignorance in Christ, whereas after this time he held that it was only apparent. The texts do not seem to warrant this distinction. Already, in the 'Thesaurus' the alien character of all ignorance in Christ is as forcefully stated as in the later writings.

[2] Cf. especially XXII (*P.G.*, LXXV, 363–380; R., 2072).

disposition (1, 13, 14, 16, 18, 20); a resemblance to ignorant men (10); an appearance (10, 14); not a veritable ignorance (18).[1] From the year 428 the controversy shifts, and has Nestorius, not Arius, for its protagonist. St. Cyril's thought remains unaltered save that he more emphatically rejects all interpretations which tend to divide Christ. He does not favour saying that, in Jesus Christ, the Godhead knew, but the humanity was ignorant, and he expresses himself to this effect from the year 429 onwards, as may be seen in his seventeenth paschal homily (*P.G.*, LXXVII, 780-781).

In the following year, in the *Defence of the Anathemas*, written against Theodoret, St. Cyril reproaches the latter for having said that 'ignorance does not belong to the Word of God, but to the form of a servant.' This, he maintains, is to divide Christ.

Texts relative to the ignorance of Christ may be compared to those devoted to explaining his progress in wisdom and grace (*Luke* ii, 52).

The same principle of solution recurs, viz., the divine nature of the Word cannot be susceptible to progress, but the human nature can and, in fact, did admit of this (*Thes.*, XXVIII; *P.G.*, LXXV, 424b). Christ willed this human progress in order to be like us and to save us (*ibid.*). In the same way as ignorance, progress is also merely a surface phenomenon in the life of Christ. From the very beginning Christ knows all things, being the Word of God, but he progressively manifests his knowledge and grace (*ibid.*, 428 a, b). St. Cyril does not mean by this that, from the beginning, the *human* knowledge of Christ was perfect and was afterwards progressively manifested. He means that the *divine* knowledge appeared progressively in the humanity.

All relevant quotations from St. Cyril make up a coherent body of teaching which is easy enough to interpret, and may be reduced to the following salient ideas. The divine knowledge of the Word is infinitely perfect, and Christ was able to manifest it from the beginning, and on any and every occasion, through his humanity. But since he was made like unto us, he wished to share our deficiencies and desired, consequently, that his intellectual development should appear progressive in a manner analogous to his physical development. Therefore he willed on certain occasions to show himself as one ignorant, just as he willed to suffer hunger and thirst.

In this exposition, in order that St. Cyril's thought may be

[1] Cf. *Dial. de S. Trinitate*, VI; *In Zachar.*, 105 (*P.G.*, LXXII, 252).

followed more closely, we have represented ignorance as apparent, as exterior, thus keeping to the saint's most frequent usage. But we do not think that, in such usage, he desires to put forward a make-believe or false pretence. On this hypothesis we would be unable to understand the merciful design of Christ on which so much stress is placed ('He wished to assume all our infirmities in order to heal them all'), nor, further, to explain the comparison of physical bodily growth with progressive intellectual development. A more exact interpretation of this doctrine would be to conceive, with St. Cyril, the human ignorance as real, but as being, so to speak, on the surface of Christ's life. Deeper penetration would reveal the divinity and its infinite knowledge. This ignorance is only an exterior trait (σχῆμα), but the humanity of Christ is likewise called by St. Cyril, and in these same passages, 'a human form' σχῆμα ἀνθρώπινον (*Thes.*, 28 ; *P.G.*, LXXV, 429b). In adopting this expression which St. Paul had consecrated, St. Cyril certainly does not intend to question the reality of our Lord's human nature, but to show that there is in him, underneath the human nature, another more intimate and profound. In this sense he writes, 'Christ attributes ignorance to his humanity, and not to *his proper nature*' (τῇ ἀνθρωπότητι καὶ οὐ τῇ οἰκείᾳ φύσει τὸ ἀγνοεῖν περιτίθησιν. *Thes.*, *P.G.*, LXXV, 373a). The humanity of Christ is, primarily for him, the instrument used by the Word, and by which he reveals his divinity (*Thes.*, LXXV, 429c, 428b). At will, he manifests in it that ignorance which is a property of mankind, or makes the knowledge of one who is indeed God shine through it.

This conception is unquestionably very attractive, but the progress of Christian theology will necessitate considerable revision. On the one hand, it will be better understood, especially after St. Augustine, that ignorance is not comparable to physical infirmities, but that it is intimately bound up with sin as its consequence as well as its origin. On the other, the Christological controversies of the fifth century against the Monophysites and Monothelites led theologians to a closer consideration of Christ's human nature and a more attentive study of the human qualities which adorned it both in the intellectual order and in that of grace.

§3. *St. Augustine*

St. Augustine frequently expounded the text of St. Mark referring to the day of judgement. He devotes a special inquiry to it (*De div. quæst.*, LXXXIII, Q. 60 ; *P.L.*, XL, 48 ; R. 1555) ; develops it in a sermon (*Serm.* 97 ; *P.L.*, XXXVIII, 589) ;

often discusses it in his controversial works or doctrinal expositions (*De Trin.*, I, 12, 23, *P.L.*, XLII, 837; *de Genesi contra Manich.*, I, 22, 34, *P.L.*, XXXIV, 190; *in Psalm* xxxvi, 1, *P.L.*, XXVI, 355; *in Psalm* vi, 1, *P.L.*, XXXVI, 90). His interpretation never alters. Christ, like the Father, knew the day of judgement, and if he says that he is ignorant of it, this is because he neither could nor would reveal it to us.[1] In the texts which have been mentioned, St. Augustine repeats this same interpretation, clarifying it by other examples. In his commentary on *Psalm* xxxvi he adds a useful observation as to the rôle of Christ while on earth, 'Because Our Lord Jesus Christ was sent to us as a teacher, He said that even the Son of Man knew not that day, because it was not within the scope of his teaching office that this should be known by us through him.'

But the influence of St. Augustine in the matter is exercised most of all through his theological doctrine with regard to ignorance and sin. St. Athanasius and, even more so, St. Cyril of Alexandria, see a merciful dispensation in the ignorance of Our Lord. It is for them an application of the general plan of the Incarnation by which the Son of God took upon himself all our infirmities in order to heal them all. St. Augustine, on the contrary, distinguishes ignorance from all other infirmities. Hunger, thirst, even death—all these things the Son of God has borne, but not ignorance, for ignorance is not only the consequence but also the source of sin. This point is specially brought out in the Pelagian controversy.[2] Already, in the *City of God*, St. Augustine had portrayed human ignorance in the same light.[3] If Christ delivers us from the abyss of ignorance, it is not by throwing himself into it. 'He is our knowledge, he is our wisdom; it is he who makes us believe in things which are temporal; it is he who reveals to us the things that are eternal' (*De Trinit.*, XIII, 19, 24; *P.L.*, XLII, 1034).

Elsewhere, in an allegorical interpretation of the history of Lazarus, St. Augustine brings ignorance into contrast with the knowledge of Christ. 'Who has committed no sin and who has not been ignorant of anything.'[4] This conception of original sin, of the injury resulting from it, and of the salva-

[1] This exegesis is accepted by St. Thomas, III, Q. 10, a. 2, ad 1: 'He is said, therefore, not to know the day and the hour of the judgment, for that he does not make it known, since, on being asked by the apostles (*Acts* i, 7), he was unwilling to reveal it; just as, on the contrary, we read (*Gen.* xxii, 12): Now I know that thou fearest God—i.e., Now I have made thee know.'

[2] Cf. *De peccat. meritis et remiss.*, II, 29, 48.

[3] Cf. *De civit. Dei*, XXI, 22, 1 (*P.L.*, XLI, 784).

[4] *De div. quaest.*, 83, qu. 65 (*P.L.*, XL, 60).

tion which heals us, marks an incontestable and definite step forward in Catholic theology.[1]

The influence of this doctrine was already apparent in the Retractation of Leporius. This monk had spread heretical tenets, both Pelagian and Nestorian, in Gaul. On arrival in Africa he drew up, about the year 418, and under St. Augustine's influence, a retractation addressed to the bishops of Gaul. Augustine and three other African prelates put their names to this document in order to recommend it to these bishops and attest that it was indeed from the hand of Leporius.

Two passages in this profession of faith are concerned with the question of Christ's knowledge. In the first, Leporius, commenting on the text of St. Luke, affirms a progressive knowledge in Christ and attributes the reality of this progress to his redemptive design in wishing to bear all our infirmities.[2] Further on, Leporius reproves and condemns what he had written about the ignorance of Christ.[3] *'Ut autem et hinc nihil cuiquam in suspicione dereliquam, tunc dixi, immo ad objecta respondi, Dominum nostrum Jesum Christum secundum hominem ignorare. Sed nunc non solum dicere non praesumo, verum etiam priorem anathematizo prolatam in hac parte sententiam : quia dici non licet etiam secundum hominem ignorasse Dominum prophetarum.'*

This document had, certainly, no official character, and its Christology is not beyond reproach. Nevertheless, the recommendation of St. Augustine gave it great authority, which, however, was not recognised in any definitive manner, even in Africa. Towards the end of the fifth century Vigilius of Thapsus, in order to prove the reality of Christ's human soul again Eutyches, revived the argument used by St. Ambrose against the Apollinarists.[4]

[1] St. Augustine did not deny all progress in Christ's knowledge : *De diversis quaest.*, 83, qu. 75 (*P.L.*, XL, 87) ; *de Genesi ad litteram*, X, 18, 32 (XXXIV, 422) ; *contra Maximum Ar. episc.*, II, 23, 7 (XLII, 802). In the first of these texts he admits progress even in the vision of God by Christ ; but he adds : 'Si autem pietas hoc non admittit, ut primo ex parte videret homo dominicus, deinde ex toto, quamquam in sapientia proficere dictus sit ; in corpore suo intelligatur heres, id est Ecclesia, cujus coheredes sumus.'

[2] *Libellus emendationis*, 6 (*P.L.*, XXXI, 1225) : 'Et quia omnes infirmitates nostras, id est naturæ nostræ, portavit, et vere secundum carnem suscipiens in se affectus nostros, ad probationem veri hominis, currente in eodem nihilominus cursu nostræ mortalitatis, potestate scilicet, non necessitate, ætate et sapientia, Evangelista testante, profecit, esurivit, sitivit, fatigatus est, flagellatus est, crucifixus est, mortuus est, resurrexit.'

[3] *Ibid.* 10 (1229).

[4] 'Dicit de eo Isaias : Priusquam sciat puer respuere malum et eligere bonum ; antequam cognoscat puer vocare patrem aut matrem. Num quid naturam Verbi tantæ audemus ignorantiæ subicere, cui nec praeterita, nec futura habentur occulta ?' *Contra Eutychetem*, V, 13 (*P.L.*, LXII, 143) ; cf. *ibid.*, 7 (139) ; 12 (143).

At the beginning of the sixth century, St. Fulgentius, in his writings to Thrasimund, King of the Vandals, again attacks the Arians with the like arguments.[1]

This question of Christ's knowledge is treated of at greater length by St. Fulgentius in a letter to Ferrandus (*Epist.* XIV, *qu.* III, 25-34; *P.L.*, LXV, 415-424), and, in this reply, the influence of his master, St. Augustine, is more fully recognised. Ferrandus had asked St. Fulgentius whether the soul of Christ had full knowledge of the Godhead which assumed it.[2] This is the question which St. Fulgentius here answers. He does not treat of Christ's knowledge as a whole, but considers it only in relation to this object, the divinity. The reply is very definite. We others, as adoptive sons, know the divinity partially only. On the contrary, the soul of Christ possessed full knowledge of it. Nevertheless he observes that this soul did not know the divinity in the same way as the divinity comprehends itself.[3] The Augustinian doctrine concerning truth and grace which is developed in the course of this correspondence is noteworthy: 'I know not how we may interpret the words, "the only-begotten of the Father, full of grace and truth," if we say that anything of the fulness of grace is lacking to the plenitude of truth, or that the totality of truth is lacking to the fulness of grace . . . Fulness of truth is not, however, possessed, if any truth is unknown. May we never think this latter in any way of Christ' (32-33, 421).

This dissertation of St. Fulgentius had a great influence on the thought of the later Middle Ages, on Alcuin in particular, and on Hugh of St. Victor.[4]

§4. *The Agnoëtæ and the Christological Controversies of the Sixth and Seventh Centuries*

The Agnoëtæ are Monophysites who, under the leadership of the deacon Themistius, separated themselves, about the year 540, from the Monophysite patriarch of Alexandria, Timothy II.

[1] Basing himself on the same text of Isaias, he comments on it as follows: 'Si anima vel intellectus naturæ in Christo defuisse credatur humanæ, quid in infante bonum malumque dictur ignorasse? An illam divinam Filii Dei naturam ignorantiæ boni malique subicimus, ut humanam in Christo animam denegemus? . . . Anima igitur humana, quæ rationis capax naturaliter facta est, bonum malumque in infante Christo nescisse dicitur, quæ secundum evangelicam veritatem in puero Jesu sapientia et gratia profecisse narratur' (I, 8, *P.L.*, LXV, 231).

[2] 'Utrum anima Christi susceptricis deitatis plenam habeat omnino notitiam.'

[3] 'Novit quantum illa, sed non sicut illa.'

[4] Cf. P. Schulte, *op. cit.*, p. 120.

The majority of texts relative to the doctrinal position of this sect are conveniently gathered together by J. Marič at the end of his dissertation, '*De Agnoëtarum doctrina, argumentum patristicum pro omniscientia Christi hominis relativa*' (Zagreb, 1914, pp. 113-120).

Among the many Monophysite sects which arose in the course of the sixth century, the Severians were the nearest to Catholic belief. Whereas the Julianists denied the reality of human infirmities in Christ, hunger, thirst, and so on, the disciples of Severus of Antioch strongly upheld it. One of them, Themistius, deacon of Alexandria, pushed the same principle further, and affirmed the reality of human ignorance. The Monophysite patriarch of Alexandria, Timothy, rejected this conclusion and condemned Themistius.

Towards the end of the same century, some monks of the Palestinian desert, near Jerusalem, took up the same theses and consulted Anatolius, papal nuncio at Constantinople, on the subject. The latter referred the issue to Pope St. Gregory and to Eulogius, patriarch of Alexandria.

Eulogius replied by a letter, whose original is lost, but of which Photius has handed down a long résumé (*P.G.*, CIII, 1080-84).

Eulogius denied all ignorance in Christ and considered that his humanity knew all the present and future. Christ's questions are only figures of speech, like those imputed to God himself (e.g. to Adam: Where art thou?; to Cain: Where is Abel?); likewise the phrase concerning the day of judgement. This latter may also, with St. Cyril and St. Gregory of Nazianzus, be understood in the sense that ignorance is conceived as a natural property of the humanity of Christ, if, by a mental abstraction, the humanity is considered separately as such.[1] If certain of the Fathers have attributed ignorance to the humanity of Christ, they have not laid it down as a dogma, but have done so merely in order to set aside an Arian objection. Their language may also be understood figuratively.

This letter contains two interesting opinions. Eulogius considers that ignorance cannot be attributed to the divinity or to the humanity of Christ without 'considerable temerity.' At the same time he recognises that in the anti-Arian controversy certain of the Fathers thought differently.

He considers, no doubt with good reason, that he can depend on St. Gregory of Nazianzus, and also quotes the authority of

[1] A little later the same viewpoint and interpretation of St. Gregory is met with in St. John Damascene, *De fide orthodoxa*, III, 21 (XCIV, 1084).

St. Cyril of Alexandria, but nevertheless corrects the basis of his doctrine, viz., Christ took upon himself all our infirmities. Eulogius does not understand this in the strict sense save with regard to bodily infirmities such as hunger and thirst (1081b).

In the year 600, St. Gregory the Great, to whom Eulogius had sent his letter, adheres to his teaching without reservation, claiming to recognise in it the Latin tradition (*Ep.* 39 ; *P.L.*, LXXVII, 1096-1099). This document, like the preceding one, directly condemns the Agnoëtæ as heretical and confronts them with the Augustinian doctrine as to the human knowledge of Christ.

St. Sophronius, patriarch of Jerusalem (634-8), in a letter to Sergius of Constantinople, written on the occasion of taking possession of his see, condemns, among other heretics, Themistius, the chief of the Agnoëtæ (*P.G.*, LXXXVII, 3192-3). The doctrine envisaged is the heresy of the Agnoëtæ, who admitted in Christ only a 'composite nature,' and, consequently, supposing Christ to be ignorant, considered him to be merely a man.

About the same time (between 579 and 607), an anonymous but very orthodox writer, wrote a work entitled *De Sectis,* which was for a long time attributed to Leontius of Byzantium. After calling attention to the Monophysite discussions concerning Christ's knowledge, this writer mentions that the Council (of Chalcedon) refused to deal with the matter, that 'the majority of Fathers, in fact all of them, seemed to hold ignorance in Christ, and that the reality of his human nature and the tenour of the gospel lead us to the same conclusion (*De Sectis,* X, 3 ; LXXXVI, 1264a).

This text is the last in Greek patristic literature where an affirmation of human ignorance in Christ is to be found. Henceforth the distinction which has been brought forward among the Monophysites (Timothy) as well as among Catholics (Eulogius) is accepted by all. Christ took upon himself all our physical infirmities but not our ignorance.

This distinction has been enunciated with great vigour and clarity by St. Maximus (*Opusc. theol.* ; *P.G.*, XCI, 221b), who wrote towards the middle of the seventh century. Fifty years later St. Anastasius Sinaita[1] disallows all real human ignorance in Christ. He interprets in this sense the patristic texts where it is said that Christ was humanly ignorant of the last day. 'They meant by this that the human nature had not, of itself, of its own substance, knowledge of the future.' St. John

[1] Cf. *Doctrina Patrum de Incarnatione*, ed. Diekamp, p. 104.

Damascene, during the course of the eighth century, expounds the same doctrine, and confirms it by the classical text of St. Gregory of Nazianzus (*De fide orthod.*, III, 21 ; *P.G.*, XCIV, 1084). He emphatically states that Christ took upon himself all our infirmities except sin ; but understands by this only 'all physical and unblameable infirmities' such as 'hunger, thirst, weariness, grief, tears . . .' (*ibid.*, 20, 1081). Ignorance does not come within this category, and Christ had only the semblance of it (*ibid.*, IV, 18, 1185).

The precision thus brought to the question of the human knowledge of our Lord is therefore due to the Christological controversies. In raising the problem of the human infirmities which our Lord, according to them, did not take upon himself, Julian of Halicarnassus and his disciples, the Aphthartodocetæ, forced their adversaries to define their position on the subject of the human ignorance. In the light of these discussions the meaning to be assigned to the principle, 'Christ has assumed all our infirmities save sin,' is better understood. Henceforth there is a sharp distinction between those infirmities which are only a punishment for sin and those which involve disgrace, between those that characterise our nature and those which deface it. The former are recognised to be really in Christ and the latter in appearance only.

The struggle against the Monothelites leads to the same conclusion. Theodore of Byzantium, to whom St. Maximus replied, reasoned as follows. The Fathers undoubtedly recognise a human will in Christ, but also a human ignorance. If we do not wish to admit, under penalty of joining the Agnoëtæ, a real human ignorance, neither must we admit a real human will (*P.G.*, CXI, 216). St. Maximus, in reply, was forced to determine the bearing of patristic texts relative to the ignorance of Christ, and define Catholic teaching on the subject.

It will be noticed that these preoccupations are entirely different from those which occasioned the works of St. Augustine. The agreement of their respective conclusions is therefore all the more remarkable.

§5. *The Mediæval Tradition*

From the epoch at which we have arrived there is hardly a trace of the opinion which admits real ignorance in the human soul of Christ. In the East a vestige is found in the writings of Euthymius Zigabenus ; in the Latin Church some theologians are found in the later Middle Ages who attribute ignorance of the judgement, not to the divinity of Christ, but to his humanity.[1] There are to be found a greater number who, adopting the argumentation of St. Ambrose, prove the reality of Christ's Incarnation by adducing the real progress of his human knowledge.[2] But a bird's-eye view of the theological literature in the later Middle Ages shows that the opinion of St. Jerome, St. Augustine, and St. Gregory dominates almost everywhere. It is found in the Venerable Bede,[3] Alcuin,[4] Rabanus Maurus,[5] in the ordinary gloss of Walafrid Strabo,[6] Paschasius Radbertus,[7] St. Anselm,[8] and Hugh of St. Victor. The last-named even compares Christ's knowledge with that of God.[9]

Peter Lombard considers that the soul of Christ knows all that God knows, but not as clearly as God knows it.[10]

Later scholastics endeavour to distinguish different modes of knowledge in Christ.[11] It is not our intention to examine their systems in detail at this stage, but merely to indicate what is most generally accepted, namely, the definitive doctrine of St. Thomas.

In the *Summa Theologica,* III, Q. 9-12, St. Thomas expounds as follows the doctrine as to the human knowledge of Christ. Christ had the beatific vision (9, a. 2), infused knowledge (a. 3), and experimental knowledge (a. 4).

By the beatific vision the soul of Christ sees God (9, a. 2), although it does not comprehend God as God comprehends

[1] HETERII et S. BEATI, *Ad Elipandum epistula,* I, 112–116 (*P.L.*, XCVI, 964–967) : ABELARD, *Sic et non,* 76 (CLXXVIII, 1451), citing in support of the ignorance of Christ (*ps.*), HIERON., *In minori breviario,* ps. cxxxviii, and CASSIOD., *In Ps.* cxxxix, 16 ; ST. BERNARD, *De gradibus humilitatis,* III, 11–12 (CLXXXII, 947–948), explains the ignorance of the day of judgment in the sense that the human experimental knowledge of Christ did not reach as far as this object.

[2] BEDE, *In Luc.*, I, 2 ; (XCII, 350) ; AMBROS. AUTPERT., *In Apoc.*, V, 12, ed. Cologne, 1536, p. 129–30 ; AELREDI ABB. RIEVALLIS (contemporary of St. Bernard), *Tract. de Jesu duodenni,* 10 (CLXXXIV, 855).

[3] *In Marc.*, IV, 13 (*P.L.*, XCII, 265) ; cf. *In Luc. hom.* XII (XCIV, 67) : the progress of Christ was merely a progressive manifestation.

[4] *De fide Trinit.*, II, 12 (CI, 13) : 'Nescire dictur Filius, quia nescientes facit.'

[5] *In Matth.*, XXIV, 36 (CVII, 1077) he reproduces St. Jerome and St. Augustine.

[6] *In Matth.*, XXIV, 36 (CXIV, 162) ; *In Marc.*, XIII, 32 (228) ; *In Luc.*, II, 52 (252).

[7] *In Matth.*, XXIV, 36 (CXX, 826–7).

[8] *Cur Deus homo ?*, II, 13.

[9] *De Sacrament.*, II, 6 (CLXXVI, 383 *sqq.*) ; *De sapient. animæ Christi* (853 *sqq.*), cf. *Summa Sent.*, I, 16 (73–74).

[10] *Sent.*, III, d. 14, 2 ; *P.L.*, CXCII, 783.

[11] Alexander of Hales (*In Sent.*, III, d. 13, memb. 2) distinguishes six such modes, including the divine knowledge. The majority of scholastics distinguish only three, the intuitive vision, infused knowledge, and purely human or acquired knowledge. ALBERT THE GREAT, *In Sent.*, III, d. 13, a. 10, 12 ; d. 14, a. 1, 3, 4 ; ST. BONAVENTURE, *In Sent.*, III, d. 14, a. 3, q. 1.

himself (10, a. 1); it sees all things in God 'which in any way are, or will be, or were done, said, or thought, by whomsoever and at any time,' also all that creatures can do, but not all that God can do, for this would be to comprehend the Divine Essence (10, a. 2); this knowledge 'was not habitual, but actual with respect to everything he knew in this way' (11, a. 5, ad 1).

By infused knowledge, 'the soul of Christ knew whatever can be known by force of a man's active intellect—e.g. whatever pertains to human sciences; secondly, by this knowledge Christ knew all things made known to man by Divine revelation' (11, a. 1). This knowledge was not perpetually in act like the preceding. It was habitual, and Christ used it when he pleased (11, a. 5).

By his acquired or experimental knowledge Christ knew 'whatever can be known by the action of the active intellect' (12, a. 1); this knowledge developed by real progress: 'But because it seems unfitting that any natural intelligible action should be wanting to Christ, and because to extract intelligible species from phantasms is a natural action of man's active intellect, it seems becoming to place even this action in Christ. And it follows from this that in the soul of Christ there was a habit of knowledge which could increase by this abstraction of species' (12, a. 2).

This doctrine commands the respect even of those who do not take into account the personal authority of St. Thomas, or the even greater authority given to his teaching on this matter by the approbation of the Church.[1] Not only is it a perfectly coherent and harmonious theology of the Incarnation, but it has the additional merit of being a theology based on a very authentic tradition whose witness, at least since the seventh century, is morally unanimous on all essential points.

It remains for us to explain the Gospel text itself and we must recognise the difficulty as considerable, though not, however, insuperable. In his commentary on St. Mark, Fr. Lagrange explains it as follows:

'The Son knows, but he has no mission to communicate such knowledge and, in this sense, is ignorant. This exegesis may appear subtle, and something like a subterfuge. It is, nevertheless, well grounded if one carefully bears in mind that the term "Father" indicates God as inaccessible and as hidden (*John* i, 18). He communicates himself to mankind by the Son and communicates with them by the ministry of angels.

[1] *Acta Sanctæ Sedis*, July 1, 1918, p. 282; cf. *Recherches de Science religieuse*, Oct., 1918, p. 281–289.

That which must be kept absolutely secret does not, then, constitute part of the Son's mission nor of that of the angels. Inasmuch as the Son is distinguished from the Father as being sent by him to mankind, this secret is not part of his commission' (p. 327).

We here recognise one of the explanations put forward by St. Augustine and mentioned above: 'Because our Lord Jesus Christ was sent to us as a teacher, he said that even the Son of Man knew not that day, because it was not within the scope of his teaching office that this should be known by us through him.'

There is just one remark to be added to this interpretation which, indeed, seems to be the one most warranted. The text is not isolated in the Gospel. It belongs to the entire series of statements made by our Lord in which the Son effaces himself before the Father. We have already commented on these words (*supra*, pp. 234-238) and do not intend to return to them here. Let us merely recall that in all these sayings Jesus does not end in a negative fashion. When he says to the apostles that to sit on his right hand or on his left in the kingdom is not for him to give, he adds straightway that these places belong to those for whom his Father has prepared them. When he asks the young man, 'Why callest thou me good?' he adds at once, 'None is good but one, that is God.' Here, also, when declaring 'But of that day or hour no man knoweth, neither the angels in heaven nor the Son,' he continues, 'but the Father.' In all these instances when Jesus effaces himself, it is in order to disclose the Father, and his knowledge, his goodness, his sovereign power. If we are to understand this saying, it must not be isolated from the rest of the Gospel, nor must the Son be separated from the Father.

NOTE III
(Note D in French edition)

Matt. xi, 25-27. *Luke* x, 21-22

No passages have provoked more discussion than these two and we cannot therefore invoke their testimony without establishing the text.

Mt. XI, 25–27 : Ἐν ἐκείνῳ τῷ καιρῷ ἀποκριθεὶς ὁ Ἰησοῦς εἶπεν· ἐξομολογοῦμαί σοι, πάτερ, κύριε τοῦ οὐρανοῦ καὶ τῆς γῆς, ὅτι ἔκρυψας ταῦτα ἀπὸ σοφῶν καὶ συνετῶν, καὶ ἀπεκάλυψας αὐτὰ νηπίοις. Ναί, ὁ πατήρ, ὅτι οὕτως εὐδοκία ἐγένετο ἔμπροσθέν σου. Πάντα μοι παρεδόθη ὑπὸ τοῦ πατρός, καὶ οὐδεὶς ἐπιγινώσκει τὸν υἱὸν εἰ μὴ ὁ πατήρ, οὐδὲ τὸν πατέρα τις ἐπιγινώσκει εἰ μὴ ὁ υἱὸς καὶ ᾧ ἐὰν βούληται ὁ υἱὸς ἀποκαλύψαι.

Ἐγένετο εὐδοκία CDE al.—Μου *om.* ℵ*.

Lc., X, 21–22 : Ἐν αὐτῇ τῃ ὥρᾳ ἠγαλλιάσατο τῷ πνεύματι τῷ ἁγίῳ καὶ εἶπεν· ἐξομολογοῦμαί σοι, πάτερ, κύριε τοῦ οὐρανοῦ καὶ τῆς γῆς, ὅτι ἀπέκρυψας ταῦτα ἀπὸ σοφῶν καὶ συνετῶν, καὶ ἀπεκάλυψας αὐτὰ νηπίοις. Ναί, ὁ πατήρ, ὅτι οὕτως ἐγένετο εὐδοκία ἔμπροσθέν σου. Πάντα μοι παρεδόθη ὑπὸ τοῦ πατρός μου, καὶ οὐδεὶς γινώσκει τίς ἐστιν ὁ υἱὸς εἰ μὴ ὁ πατήρ, καὶ τίς ἐστιν ὁ πατὴρ εἰ μὴ ὁ υἱὸς καὶ ᾧ ἂν βούληται ὁ υἱὸς ἀποκαλύψαι.

Πνεύματι τῷ ἁγίῳ ℵBCD al. (*in sancto sp.* e).—Πάτερ *om.* F[w].—*Post* κύριε *habet* ceff[2]i.—Ἀπὸ συνετῶν καὶ σοφῶν D.—Καὶ συνετῶν *om.* e.—Ἀπό *pro* ὑπό D.—Μου *om.* Dacls[1].—Ἐπιγινώσκει CF[w]HΔ al.—Τίς ἐστιν ὁ πατήρ... τίς ἐστιν ὁ υἱός. U et minusc. un.

The critical notes, taken mostly from the two editions of Blass, show the substantial agreement of the manuscripts. The question becomes complicated when we take into consideration the quotations made by the Fathers. These quotations have been gathered together very carefully by Bousset,[1] Resch,[2] Harnack,[3] and Chapman,[4] and I content myself with drawing the conclusions which follow from their tabulations.

[1] *Die Evangeliencitate Justins des Märtyrers* (pp. 100–103).
[2] *Aussercanonische Paralleltexte zu den Evangelien,* III (pp. 196–206).
[3] *Sprüche und Reden Jesu,* Exkurs I, pp. 189–216.
[4] *Journal Theol. Stud.,* X (1909), pp. 552–566.

Two variants stand out: one which substitutes the aorist (ἔγνω) for the present (γινώσκει), the other which inverts the order of the two terms (τὸν υἱόν ... τὸν πατέρα).

The third variation, the frequent abbreviation of the last six words of St. Luke, is not of great importance here and need not be discussed.

Already St. Irenæus accused the Marcosians of introducing ἔγνω into the Gospel account in order to give people to understand that before Christ's coming the Father was not known, but only the demiurge. Harnack says the opposite. He holds that the primitive aorist has been replaced by the present, and sees in it a tendencious alteration, which substitutes an eternal relation for a historical fact.

After a careful examination of the many quotations of this text made by the Fathers, two conclusions follow.

Considering the insufficient guarantee of the manuscript tradition for many of the Fathers, we cannot prudently rely upon patristic evidence for either form. Even admitting the faithfulness of the texts as we have them, we must remember that they quote from memory without minute attention to verbal exactitude; a good example of which can be found in the use of all three forms γινώσκει, οἶδε, ἔγνω by Alexander of Alexandria, Adamantius, and Eusebius.

Even were we to place full confidence in patristic quotations, we must admit that γινώσκει in *Luke* has an almost unanimous support, and that, however widespread the reading ἔγνω in *Matthew*, it cannot be held to be the primitive reading, against the unanimous authority of the Greek manuscripts, but, at most, can only be looked upon as an interesting 'western' reading, arising, perhaps, from the other aorists in the passage.

Upon examination of the texts in which the second variation occurs (the inversion of the two terms, τὸν υἱον . . . τὸν πατέρα), it is even more noticeable than in the former list how both renderings are given, not only by the same Father, but in the same work, and even in the same sentence.[1] It is hardly surprising if one considers the ease with which the terms can be inverted when quoting from memory. It would indeed be arbitrary to rely on such an unstable tradition in order to correct all the Greek texts. At the most, we can only venture the opinion that the Biblical manuscripts that the Fathers used were less unanimous on this text than ours.

Whatever the value of this opinion, the order of sequence of the two terms remains fixed, not only by the manuscript tradition, but by the immediate context. The final clause

[1] IREN., *Haer.*, iv, 6; I, 3, 7.

(ᾧ ἂν βούληται ὁ υἱὸς ἀποκαλύψαι) obviously refers to the knowledge of the Father which the Son possesses, and which he can impart. Therefore it is certain that the term which immediately precedes it is the one which *de facto* we have. By retaining this order of sequence, we preserve the marked parallelism of the passage.

The conclusion to be drawn from these observations is that the texts of *Matthew* and of *Luke* as we have them are authentic. The identity of the two accounts points unerringly to a common source, and the manner of expression to an Aramaic one.

Thus we must agree that this discourse of Our Lord comes to us with the soundest guarantees of its authenticity.

NOTE IV

(Note E in French edition)

Matt. xxviii, 19

Πορευθέντες οὖν μαθητεύσατε πάντα τὰ ἔθνη, βαπτίζοντες αὐτοὺς εἰς τὸ ὄνομα τοῦ πατρὸς καὶ τοῦ υἱοῦ καὶ τοῦ ἁγίου πνεύματος, διδάσκοντες αὐτοὺς τηρεῖν πάντα ὅσα ἐνετειλάμην ὑμῖν.

By using what he terms 'the Eusebian form' of this text, F. C. Conybeare has considerably strengthened the objection of those critics who have long suspected this text with its clear-cut Trinitarian formula. He tried to prove that Eusebius knew this text, at least up to the Council of Nicæa, only under the form: *πορευθέντες μαθητεύσατε πάντα τὰ ἔθνη ἐν τῷ ὀνόματί μου.* This fact would be of considerable weight if we consider Eusebius's great learning and the resources of the library of Cæsarea. Conybeare has tried to carry the argument further by pointing out 'the Eusebian form' in St. Justin (*Dial.* XXIX and LIII) and in the *Pastor of Hermas* (*Simil.*, IX, 17, 4). He concludes by questioning whether the *textus receptus* was not created towards 130-140 if the readings found in Eusebius and Justin are authentic; whether it is not the result of liturgical formulæ, especially that of baptism, reacting upon the text of *Matthew;* and, finally, whether, like the text of the three witnesses, it did not come into being in the old Latin texts of Africa, whence it was introduced into the Greek texts of Rome so as to establish itself in the East at the time of the Council of Nicæa, early enough to figure in all the surviving Greek texts.

Despite the decisive refutation of these conclusions by E. Riggenbach and F. H. Chase, it would seem necessary to go back over the ground covered by the discussion in order to place the authenticity of this text, which has always been of the highest importance, above suspicion.

1. THE EVIDENCE OF MANUSCRIPTS AND VERSIONS

The fact that the *textus receptus* of *Matthew* xxviii, 19, is found in all manuscripts and versions which contain the passage is a decisive refutation of Conybeare's hypothesis.

That a reading which appeared in all manuscripts of Cæsarea at the beginning of the fourth century was the only one known to Eusebius, and disappeared without a single trace in any manuscript or version, is an impossible suggestion.

2. THE USE OF MATT. XXVIII, 19, IN THE TRINITARIAN CONTROVERSIES OF THE IV CENTURY

During the whole of the fourth century this text was the favourite weapon of the Fathers. They constantly assert that these are the very words of our Lord. If, as Conybeare would have it, the Trinitarian formula were unknown to Eusebius before 325, and if all the manuscripts of Cæsarea contained the Christological form (ἐν τῷ ὀνόματί μου), how was it possible to attach such importance to so doubtful a reading without a single objection coming from East or West or even from Palestine? St. Basil devotes three chapters to establishing the value of this text. He discusses and disposes of the objection drawn from the texts of St. Paul where Christ is alone named in connection with baptism (*Gal.* iii, 7; *Rom.* vi, 3). How could he have passed over the serious difficulty that could not but be drawn from the 'Eusebian form' of *Mt.* xxviii, 19, if this form had actually existed?

To add to the improbability of the hypothesis, Eusebius hmself uses no other text when, after the Council of Nicæa, he writes to the Church of Cæsarea to explain and justify his Trinitarian faith.

3. QUOTATIONS OF MATT. XXVIII, 19, IN EUSEBIUS[1]

One can distinguish three principal forms of this quotation:

(*a*) πορευθέντες μαθητεύσατε πάντα τὰ ἔθνη.
(*b*) πορευθέντες μαθητεύσατε πάντα τὰ ἔθνη ἐν τῷ ὀνόματί μου.
(*c*) πορευθέντες μαθητεύσατε πάντα τὰ ἔθνη βαπτίζοντες αὐτοὺς εἰς τὸ ὄνομα τοῦ πατρὸς καὶ τοῦ υἱοῦ καὶ τοῦ ἁγίου πνεύματος.

These three forms suggest the following observations:

1. It cannot be held that Eusebius dropped the Christological form after the Council of Nicæa, as although the Trinitarian form does not appear before 325 in any of the extant writings of Eusebius, yet most of the examples of the Christological forms are post-Nicæan and the *Theophania* contains both forms. The chronology, then, does not explain the difference between the quotations.

[1] Cf. Conybeare, pp. 275–282; Riggenbach, pp. 11–24.

2. Eusebius chooses between the forms according to the conclusion he wishes to draw from the text. When he uses the (*a*) form, as a rule, he is illustrating the rapid growth of Christianity and merely uses the first part of Our Lord's command: 'teach all nations.' Elsewhere, when he wishes to show whence comes the force behind this rapid expansion, he adds: 'in my name.' Lastly, when he wishes to draw attention to the Trinity or to baptism, it is form (*c*) that he uses.

3. The quotations of form (*a*) are easy to explain. Nothing is more frequent than partial quotations, which retain only the pertinent words. The quotations under (*c*) require no explanation.

The (*b*) form is not so easily explained. We must first of all take into account that although Eusebius comments on the words, 'in my name,' as words of our Lord, nowhere does he explicitly state them to be from St. Matthew.

Thus we may suppose that the form (*b*) is a variant either anterior to Eusebius or, more probably, due to Eusebius himself. In all probability it arises from a contamination of the text of *Matthew* by the other Synoptics, particularly by *Luke* xxiv, 47. This hypothesis is confirmed by Eusebius' frequent practice of using variants obtained, either by combining two texts,[1] or by introducing a gloss and presenting it as a received text.[2]

4. QUOTATIONS OF MATT. XXVIII, 19, BEFORE EUSEBIUS

Origen and St. Cyprian both quote this text several times, and Tertullian, Hippolytus, Irenæus, and Theodotus all quote it once in the form that we now possess, and to this series of quotations it is not possible to oppose a single text containing the Christological form. Conybeare quotes two passages from *St. Justin* (*Dial.* 39, and 53) and one from *Hermas* (*Simil.*, IX, 17, 4), but neither of them can be considered as a quotation from *St. Matthew*.

Thus, Conybeare's conclusions cannot stand. The form that he terms 'Eusebian,' [series (*b*) *supra*], is not found in any manuscript or version and is totally unknown to the controversial writers of the fourth century. Further, it does not exclude the use of the Trinitarian form by Eusebius himself and would seem to be the result of a contamination. Lastly, it is not found in a single text of the first three centuries while the Trinitarian form is frequently found.

[1] *John* iv, 14 and vii, 38. In *Ps.* xxx, 10; *Matt.* xix, 29 and *Luke* xviii, 30. In *Ps.* lx, 6.

[2] *John* xix, 30. In *Ps.* lxviii, 3; *Matt.* xi, 27. *Demonstr. evang.*, IV, 3, 13.

APPENDIX ON LITURGICAL FORMULAS

An entirely different question from the above may arise in connection with *Matthew* xxviii, 19.

We know that the New Testament and the early Christian writings speak alternatively of baptism 'in the name of the Father, of the Son, and of the Holy Ghost,' and of baptism 'in the name of Jesus' (or 'of the Lord'). (Cf. the *Didache*, vii, 1, 3; ix, 5.)[1]

From these texts efforts have been made to disprove the authenticity of *Matthew* xxviii, 19. Some, basing their thesis on the Trinitarian formula, argue that the liturgical usage reacted on the text of the Gospel; others, starting from the Christological formula, assert that it could not have been in use from the time of St. Paul, if Christ had imposed the Trinitarian formula on the Apostles.

Neither reasoning seems correct. The former supposes that the liturgical usage is independent of the Gospel and thus renders its origin inexplicable. The latter makes the words of our Lord, as recorded in *Matthew* xxviii, 19, a peremptory liturgical precept which, in our opinion, strains its meaning.

It seems to us that only by admitting the authenticity of the text of the Gospel can these facts be reconciled. Against the 'baptism in the name of Jesus,' which seems to be authenticated by the early Christian writings, it would be impossible to understand the origin and diffusion of the Trinitarian formula, if this latter had not the weight of an utterance of Our Lord recorded in the Gospel. On the other hand, there is no obligation to see here a liturgical precept binding the Apostles to a set formula, and excluding baptism 'in the name of Jesus.'

[1] A list of these liturgical formulas may be found in RIGGENBACH, *Der Trinit. Taufbefehl*, pp. 32–93.

NOTE V

(Note G in French edition)

PHILO'S DOCTRINE OF THE LOGOS, AND THE DOCTRINE OF THE SON IN THE EPISTLE TO THE HEBREWS

HERE we are going to discuss the question of 'Philonism' in the *Epistle to the Hebrews* only in so far as it bears on the doctrine of the Trinity. If there is any evidence of Philonism in the epistle, it is most marked in the theory of the Logos; and it is this aspect alone that we intend to discuss in the hope of arriving at a definite conclusion.

It will be readily agreed that the dogma of the Incarnation has nothing in common with Philonism. The question we have to examine is whether the Philonian, once converted to Christianity, could and did apply the attributes of the Logos to Jesus Christ.

Has this ever been done? A strong motive for doubting it is the fact that Jesus Christ was never given the name 'logos' itself by the author of the epistle. So significant is this that it has led M. Ménégoz to doubt, not indeed the Philonism of the author, but his immediate and personal affinities with Philo. Nevertheless, if Jesus Christ is not called 'logos,' he is called 'Son', and this at least denotes Alexandrine influence: "The idea of a birth of the divinity is not Jewish . . . we must seek its foundation in Platonist philosophy." (MÉNÉGOZ, *L'epître aux Hebreux*, p. 201.) This comparison is irrelevant. It must be borne in mind that the doctrine of a divine Sonship is found not only in St. Paul, but also in the Synoptics, and we should have to suppose that the idea, once introduced into Jerusalem in the Alexandrine synagogues, had exercised an influence on the thought of Jesus himself (p. 202). So gratuitous and unlikely is this hypothesis that it does not merit further discussion.

By a series of comparisons critics have nevertheless tried to render more probable the hypothesis of Philonian influence.

1. Philo called the Logos the first-born son of God, and the author of the Epistle did likewise.

When we compare the texts,[1] the resemblance is very faint

[1] *De agricult.*, 51; *De confus. ling.*, 63, etc., and *Heb.* i, 6.

and suffers badly when we notice the different terms used (πρωτόγονος in Philo; πρωτότοκος in *Heb.*). Furthermore, the title of first-born was given long before this to the Messias in the Old Testament. Finally, the two conceptions differ fundamentally. For Philo, God is the Father of the world; the Logos is his eldest son only in so far as he is a cosmological principle; whereas in the Messianic conception God is the Father of his people, and the Messias his first-born Son, in so far as he is King and representative of Israel. Christian theology goes beyond both conceptions, and unites them in a loftier synthesis, where the Messias of the Jews counts for more than the cosmological principle of the Alexandrians.

2. Philo and the author of *Hebrews* both call the Logos the chief of the Angels.

After comparing the texts,[1] the most we can recognise is a mere verbal coincidence. In *Hebrews* Christ is never called angel, he is the Son, above them and to be adored by them. The Logos in Philo is an angel, head of the angels, who, in any case, are not a hierarchy of living and personal beings as in *Hebrews*, but are merely a system of metaphysical beings.

3. The exemplarism which is found equally in both authors is a much more striking point of similarity.

It is true that Philo's exemplarism is much more significant, although the analogies found in Philo's writings[2] are less striking than those in *Hebrews* (e.g., i, 3). Furthermore, Philo extends this exemplarism to the human soul,[3] to the world,[4] and even to numbers, especially the number 'seven'.[5]

Admitting that this exemplarism points at least to an Alexandrian influence in *Hebrews* and *Colossians*, must we go further and admit a terminology and doctrine specifically Philonian? That would be a gratuitous conclusion, if we consider the partial and, in all probability, fortuitous character of the coincidences, together with the fundamental difference of doctrine. Philo's speculation floats in a world of semi-personified abstractions, where his exemplarist symbols may be applied to a number just as easily as to the Logos. In the *Epistle to the Hebrews*, on the contrary, we have a living reality, a Person who is born, who prays, and who suffers.

4. God created the world by the Son and also by the Logos.

The pertinent texts which have a surface resemblance are *Heb.* i, 2; *Col.* i, 16; *John* i, 3; *De cherub.*, 125-127; *De*

[1] *De confus. ling.*, 146; *Leg. alleg.*, III, 177; *De fuga*, 5, etc., and *Heb.* i, 4–14.

[2] e.g. *De plantat.*, 18; *De somn.*, II, 45.

[3] *De opif. mundi*, 146.

[4] *De somn.*, II, 45.

[5] *De Decal.*, 105, ii, 198.

spec. leg., I, 81. Examining the texts, we find that there is a fundamental difference. Philo considers the Logos as an *instrument* in the true sense of the word, and uses the instrumental dative to describe his action.[1] It is impossible to find such a construction in the New Testament. The reason is not far to seek: an ideal conception and a real person cannot be given the same rôle in the creation of the world. It would be much more profitable to go back to the *Book of Wisdom* to find the origin of the doctrine of the rôle of the Son in the creation, than to look for it in the teaching of Philo.

5. The doctrine of the priesthood of Christ resembles Philo's theology in many respects.

Once the principal texts[2] are examined, it becomes evident that the resulting doctrine is very different from that of *Hebrews*. Philo understands the priesthood of the Logos as something cosmological or psychological, and in both cases it is purely symbolic. The divine Logos and human reason play, in the world and in man, a rôle similar to that of the High Priest in the temple. It must be noted that this analogy is only extended to the priestly accessories, vestments, and ceremonies, and never attains the essential function, the offering of sacrifice.

Allegorical again is the interpretation of the story of Melchisedech, who symbolises the Logos, not by his sacrifice, nor by his eternal priesthood, but because of justice (signified by his name) and the intoxication he causes in souls by the wine he gives them.

In contrast, we have the soteriological function of Christ in the *Epistle to the Hebrews*, a function which he exercises as man and saviour; and a priesthood far removed from allegory, as real as the sacrifice of the cross. If Melchisedech is compared with Christ, it is not only because of his name, but because of his independence, his eternal priesthood, and because of his superiority over Abraham and, consequently, over the levitical priesthood.

It is an easy step from the idea of priesthood to that of intercessor, which is definitely applied to Christ in *Hebrews* (vii, 25), and which some critics have tried to establish as applied to Philo's Logos. Never is the Logos called an intercessor. He is sometimes called a suppliant (ἱκέτης), but nowhere with the idea of mediation. It is always a question of a cosmological function between God and the world, never of a mediator reconciling God and man.

1 *Leg. alleg.*, III, 96.

2 *De fuga*, 106–118; *De migrat. Abrahami*, 102; *De somn.*, I, 215; *De gigant.*, 52; *De cherub.*, 14–17; *Leg. Alleg.*, III, 79–82.

The following conclusions seem to follow:

The Christology in *Colossians* and *Hebrews* resembles Philonian philosophy in two main features: in the exemplarism applied to the analysis of the relations uniting the Father and the Son; and in seeing in the Son him by whom God has created and upholds the world.

This resemblance cannot be explained by a direct dependence, because of the different vocabularies. It is hardly possible to attribute it to the influence of Philonism on St. Paul or the writer of *Hebrews,* on account of the radical and constant opposition of the two conceptions: the one a metaphysical or mythological being, and the other the Son made man to redeem us by the sacrifice of the cross.

These objections are decisive only if Philonism is considered in its entirety and as a system of thought. Once the conceptions and tendencies which arose from that system are isolated, it is easy to admit the widespread diffusion of several of these elements, such as exemplarism, throughout Hellenic Judaism, and their consequent reaction on Pauline theology.

NOTE VI

(Note I in French edition)

John i, 3, 4

FOUR punctuations are assigned to these verses:

1. Χωρὶς αὐτοῦ ἐγένετο οὐδὲ ἓν ὃ γέγονεν. Ἐν αὐτῷ ζωὴ ἦν.
2. Χωρὶς αὐτοῦ ἐγένετο οὐδὲ ἓν ὃ γέγονεν ἐν αὐτῷ. Ζωὴ ἦν.
3. Χωρὶς αὐτοῦ ἐγένετο οὐδὲ ἕν. Ὃ γέγονεν, ἐν αὐτῷ ζωὴ ἦν.
4. Χωρὶς αὐτοῦ ἐγένετο οὐδὲ ἕν. Ὃ γέγονεν ἐν αὐτῷ, ζωὴ ἦν.

Of these, the last is that most anciently attested, and is found in use among the Gnostics Ptolemy and Theodotus. Later it was accepted by the Manicheans and is also found in certain ecclesiastical writers, perhaps in Clement, certainly in Origen.

The third—which is often hard to distinguish from the fourth—is found in Tatian, St. Theophilus, St. Irenæus, Tertullian, St. Athanasius, St. Cyril of Alexandria, St. Ambrose, and St. Augustine.

The first appears originally in St. Alexander of Alexandria, afterwards in Didymus, St. Epiphanius, St. Chrysostom, and St. Jerome. St. Ambrose (*In ps.* xxxvi, 35) attributes this reading to "the Alexandrines and Egyptians". In another place (*De fide,* III, 6) he refers to 'many learned persons and faithful.'

The second is found only in one or two texts of St. Epiphanius (*Ancor.*, 75).

It may be gathered from the foregoing that, until the fourth century, the punctuation which places a full-stop after οὐδὲ ἕν is that most generally accepted, and the first Gnostic commentators may have had some influence in this preference. From the fourth century onwards, the use which the Arians made of this reading caused it to be suspect and the majority of Greek Fathers connect ὃ γέγονεν to οὐδὲ ἕν. The Latins maintained the old reading for a longer period.[1] It is preferred to-day by Westcott-Hort, Loisy, van Hoonacker, Calmes and Vogels.

Nevertheless the majority of critics and contemporary

[1] At the time of Maldonatus this was still the usual reading, but nevertheless he does not adopt it.

exegetes have abandoned it, e.g., Tischendorf, Nestle, Knabenbauer, J. H. Holtzman, Grill, Zahn, Harnack, and Lagrange.

If the question were to be decided solely on paleographical arguments, the ancient reading would certainly have our preference, for the most ancient witnesses, writers, manuscripts and versions favour it. Unfortunately it has a somewhat suspect origin, agrees badly with the context, and I am unaware that anyone up to the present has given it a really satisfactory interpretation.

Fr. Calmes interprets it in this way (p. 26): "After saying that all has been made by the Logos, the evangelist teaches us that even before its creation, the world existed in a certain way in the Logos. It 'was life in Him,' i.e., it was eternally present to the divine intelligence. This interpretation, authorised by St. Augustine (*In Jo.,* i, 16) and St. Thomas (*Summa,* I, Q. 18, a. 4) is open to serious difficulties if we endeavour to see in it the unique literal sense of this passage in St. John. It is necessary, in fact, to credit the evangelist with an exemplarist conception of which we find in him no certain trace. It is necessary to understand the Word here not as the utterance of God, but as the ideal model which God has conceived, and, lastly, to interpret the word 'life' in a sense not to be found elsewhere throughout the whole Gospel.

In place of understanding the ideal and eternal existence of things in the Word, we may understand their real and actual existence. The sense would then be cognate to that of *Acts* xvii, 28, 'For in him we live.' This interpretation is more likely than the preceding one, nevertheless it also is open to decisive objections. One may say that creatures *live* in God or in the Word; *have life* in God, but it is more difficult to understand how they *are life* in God, and still more how this life is the light of men. Further, in such a hypothesis, the imperfect, 'ἦν,' should be corrected and replaced by the present, ἐστίν, as has been in fact done in many manuscripts.

Other exegetes, in place of referring 'ἐν αὐτῷ' to the Word, refer it to ὃ γέγονεν, and translate "What was made, *in that* was life."[1] From the grammatical point of view this reading is very defensible. Similar constructions are found in St. John and even in the prologue (i, 12; cf. xv, 2; xvii, 2, 24). But the sense thus obtained gives little satisfaction. Either one understands "there was life in the things created by the Word," and this is a truism which is out of place in the context and cannot be connected with what follows ("and the life was the

[1] Loisy, p. 159; cf. *id.*, n. 1. The same interpretation has since been defended by Van Hoonacker and Jannaris.

light of men "), or else one translates with Loisy: " In that which was made, in the world, there was life, that is to say, the manifestation of the Word, who is for men the source of eternal life." This exegesis is very forced and nothing in these first verses is seen to be related to the Incarnation. Besides life is not here described as appearing suddenly, but as permanent, " In him was life."

The other reading gives a much more satisfactory meaning. With its aid, v. 4 links up its predecessors and continues the description of the Logos: 2. οὗτος ἦν ἐν ἀρχῇ . . . . 3. πάντα δι' αὐτοῦ ἐγένετο . . . 4. ἐν αὐτῷ ζωὴ ἦν . . . The two portions of the verse are bound close to one another and make transparent in the Word, that life and light which the whole Gospel describes. Lastly, the construction is exactly parallel to that which we find 1 *John* v, 11. The only difference is that in this latter passage, the life is specified (αὕτη ἡ ζωή) by its occurrence in the preceding phrase, whereas here it appears for the first time in all its generality.[1]

[1] It cannot be said : ' It is entirely unconformable to the Johannine thought and style for there to be life in the Word ; for the Word has not life as a gift superadded to its being ; the Word is the life, as it is the light ' (LOISY, 159). We agree that life cannot be found in the Word as ' a superadded gift ' (cf. CHRYS., *In Jo. hom.* V, 4 ; *P.G.*, LIX, 57), but it can be found there as in its source ; and, while remaining faithful to the thought and style of St. John, we can say : ' The Word is the life,' or ' in him is life,' ' in him is eternal life.'

NOTE VII

(Note J in French edition)

The Doctrine of the Logos in Philo and in St. John

The relationship between Johannine theology and Philo's doctrine has been the subject of much discussion. Réville, on the one hand, sees nothing but Alexandrinism in the Fourth Gospel; while Harnack, at the other extreme, avers that the Logos of St. John and the Logos of Philo have only their name in common. The majority of the critics take up an intermediary position and, while admitting the essential transformation which the conception of the Logos has undergone through inclusion in the Johannine theology, they conclude that the author of the Fourth Gospel was influenced at least by Alexandrian philosophy. Although of late the Philonian interpretation of *St. John* has lost ground considerably, it would not be unprofitable to discuss the problem again.

We do not claim that there are no points of contact between the two doctrines. We wish merely to determine the exact relationship between them by examining their similarities and their differences.

1. The Logos.

Already we have seen that the various hypotheses put forward in favour of Jewish or Palestinian influences to explain the use of this term are insufficient (p. 368 *sqq*.). Evidence was found in *Corinthians, Colossians,* and in *Hebrews* of numerous similarities to Alexandrian literature, especially to *Wisdom,* and, in a lesser degree, to Philo.

These observations are confirmed by the fact that the doctrine of the Logos is absent from those early Christian writings which show a decided Jewish influence, such as the letter of St. Clement and the *Pastor of Hermas,* and that it is only found in those writings which come from Hellenic Christianity. Furthermore, taking into account that the term Logos is used without being interpreted and that it only appears in the prologue, we may conclude that it was already familiar to the readers of the Gospel, although it belonged to the technical language of the theologian rather than to the popular vocabulary of Christians.

As for the exact meaning of the word Logos as used by

either author, it is clear that Philo is strongly influenced by Hellenic speculation, whereas John is in the Biblical tradition; for Philo, it connotes the thought of God rather than his word, and for John it means the Word of God.

2. The Logos Son of God.

After examination of the texts already quoted which refer to Philo's use of this expression (p. 440, note [1]), it is clear that it is merely a question of a verbal coincidence. For Philo, God is the father of the Logos in a purely cosmological sense, just as he is father of the universe. In *St. John* God is not the Father because of the creation, nor is the world his son; he has only one Son, 'the Only-begotten who is in the bosom of the Father.'

3. The Logos as revealer.

For Philo, the Logos is an imperfect representation, the shadow, the image, the impress of God. Although 'it is a great blessing for those who are incapable of seeing God to know the Logos,' the perfect are able to reach beyond the Logos by contemplation and, like Moses, 'attain a clear manifestation of the uncaused being.'[1] In other words, the Logos is not the final goal of religious contemplation.

For St. John also, the Word is a revealer, but He reveals God perfectly and sovereignly: 'Who sees me sees my Father' and 'Now this is eternal life, that they may know thee, the only true God, and JESUS CHRIST, whom thou has sent.'

4. The rôle of the Logos in creation.

For Philo, as we have seen, God is the principal cause of the creation; the four elements are the material cause, the Logos the instrumental cause, and the final cause is the goodness of God (*supra*, p. 161). Many texts could be quoted to show that, for Philo, the Logos is an instrument of God in the true sense of the word.

St. John is far removed from this conception. The Father and the Son, being one, have the same infinite power, and both operate in the one action, the Father giving all to the Son, and the Son receiving all from the Father, each being in the other.

5. The mediation of the Logos.

Philo portrays this mediation as the action of an intermediary being, one mid-way between God and the world, uniting one to the other.[2]

The Word in St. John is not an intermediary. He is a true mediator, reuniting God and man, not because of any intermediary position, but because he is God and man.

Efforts have been made to show a similarity between those

[1] *Leg. Alleg.*, III, 100.
[2] *Q. rer. divin. her.*, 205–206; *Num.* xvi, 48.

passages in *St. John* where Christ prays that men may be one as he and the Father are one, and that he may be in us as the Father is in him, with certain texts where Philo calls the Logos the 'glue' or the 'bond,' which unites all beings.[1] The difference between the two conceptions stands out clearly. The Logos binds together or links up beings who remain separated amongst themselves, and the incarnate Word unites them to himself in one body. It is the difference between juxtaposition and compenetration.

It is the difference between these two conceptions which shows so clearly the incompatibility of the two theologies. The one conceives the divinity as dispersed throughout a thousand unequal beings, and must perforce place the mediator half-way between God and the world; the other sees the divine persons united in one and the same nature, and consequently unites the two extremes in the identity of one person. For the former conception, unity is assured extrinsically as by a cord; while for the latter, men are united one to another by their unity with God and their participation in the unity of the divine persons.

6. The divinity of the Logos.

Only three times does Philo call the Logos God,[2] and in each case it is the text on which he comments that leads him to use this expression, an expression which he himself considers a misuse of words,[3] and which he attenuates as much as possible by stressing the great distance separating God from the Logos. If, indeed, the Logos were as perfect as God, there would be no reason for his existence, as he would not suffice to explain the creation of the world, a work unworthy of a sovereign God, nor would he be within the reach of man's feeble contemplation.

For St. John the Word is God, and this is no incidental statement but the theme of the entire gospel. It was, indeed, to show this that the gospel was written. The divinity here in question is equal to, or rather identical with, that of the Father. Between the two Persons there is identity of knowledge, holiness, power, activity—in fine, of nature. Such identity is no less essential to the Johannine theology than the inequality of God and the Logos was to the doctrine of Philo. It is by means of it, in fact, that this perfect unity is found between Father and Son which is at once the origin and pattern of the unity of Christians among themselves and with God: "that they all may be one, as thou, Father, in me, and I in thee: that they also may be one in us." If the unity between Father and

[1] *Q. rer. divin. her.*, 188; *De vit. Mos.*, II, 133.
[2] *Leg. Alleg.*, III, 207; *De somn.*, I, 229; *In Genes.*, II, 62.
[3] *De somn.*, l. c.

Son is broken, then unity among Christians is no more than an empty name and the Gospel of St. John loses all meaning.

7. The personality of the Logos.

The opposition of the two conceptions is more marked than ever in this question. Philo's Logos is not a person, but a force, an idea, a metaphysical or mythological being. For St. John, the Word is Jesus Christ, the man whose sayings he sets down and whose life and death he describes.

Historians to-day are unanimous in recognising this difference. For a fuller appreciation of it we must bear in mind that the memory of personal contact with Christ has dictated the nature of the doctrine. If the Logos-theology appears to have undergone so great a transformation in the writings of St. John, it is because the Person of Jesus, to whom it has been applied, has necessitated it. It is in order not to falsify the reality, of which this theology tells, that the Word is conceived, not as an instrument, but as a Creator; not as an imperfect image of the Father, but as a plenary revelation of him; not as an intermediary being, but as God.

Once we have established not only the essential differences which separate the two doctrines, but above all their historical origin, we can allow only a secondary importance to the question of Alexandrine influences on St. John's doctrine. The fact will always remain that the doctrine of the evangelist was not moulded by philosophical speculation, but was determined by his personal memories of Jesus Christ, enlightened by the revelation of the Holy Ghost.

END OF VOLUME I

INDEX

The Mayflower Press, Plymouth. William Brendon & Son, Ltd.

www.ingramcontent.com/pod-product-compliance
Lightning Source LLC
LaVergne TN
LVHW020517100826
845148LV00010B/1263

* 9 7 9 8 3 8 5 2 6 6 1 0 4 *